W9-BJD-456

AVID

READER

PRESS

Also by Garrett M. Graff

The Only Plane in the Sky: An Oral History of 9/11

*Raven Rock: The Story of the U.S. Government's
Secret Plan to Save Itself—While the Rest of Us Die*

The Threat Matrix: The FBI at War

*The First Campaign: Globalization,
the Web, and the Race for the White House*

*Dawn of the Code War: America's Battle Against Russia, China,
and the Rising Global Cyber Threat* (with John P. Carlin)

Watergate

A New History

Garrett M. Graff

Avid Reader Press New York London Toronto Sydney New Delhi

AVID READER PRESS
An Imprint of Simon & Schuster, Inc.
1230 Avenue of the Americas
New York, NY 10020

Copyright © 2022 by Garrett M. Graff

All rights reserved, including the right to reproduce this book
or portions thereof in any form whatsoever. For information, address
Avid Reader Press Subsidiary Rights Department,
1230 Avenue of the Americas, New York, NY 10020.

First Avid Reader Press hardcover edition February 2022

AVID READER PRESS and colophon are trademarks of Simon & Schuster, Inc.

For information about special discounts for bulk purchases,
please contact Simon & Schuster Special Sales at
1-866-506-1949 or business@simonandschuster.com.

The Simon & Schuster Speakers Bureau can bring authors to
your live event. For more information or to book an event contact the
Simon & Schuster Speakers Bureau at 1-866-248-3049
or visit our website at www.simonspeakers.com.

Interior design by Kyle Kabel

Manufactured in the United States of America

1   3   5   7   9   10   8   6   4   2

Library of Congress Cataloging-in-Publication Data has been applied for.

ISBN 978-1-9821-3916-2
ISBN 978-1-9821-3918-6 (ebook)

To my editor Jack Limpert,
who was right about Watergate
and who later opened
Washington, D.C., up to me

and

to Jack Shafer,
who taught me the lore and mythology
of the D.C. press corps

Honesty is always the best policy in the end.

—Gerald R. Ford,
    remarks upon taking the oath of office,
    August 9, 1974

Contents

PART III **Brushfire** January–June 1973

PART IV **Firestorm** July–December 1973

PART V Inferno 1974

Introduction

Tears welled up in Mark Felt's eyes as he worked his way through the crowd alongside his wife, Audrey. More than seven hundred current and former FBI agents spread across the plaza outside the federal courthouse in Washington, D.C., some from as far away as field offices in Florida, Virginia, Maryland, Massachusetts, and Connecticut. Three buses of agents had left Manhattan at 3 a.m. to arrive in time for the court hearing. Now, as Felt arrived, they all applauded.

It was an unprecedented gathering for an unprecedented day: the April 20, 1978, arraignment of Felt, the bureau's former number two official, alongside former FBI acting director L. Patrick Gray III and a third bureau leader, Edward S. Miller, on felony charges that they "did unlawfully, willfully and knowingly combine, conspire, confederate and agree together to injure and oppress citizens of the United States" by authorizing FBI agents to conduct illegal break-ins and surveillance. Seventy other FBI agents now also faced disciplinary proceedings.

Felt, Gray, and Miller all planned to issue not guilty pleas—they believed their actions had been in keeping with the best interests of the national security of the United States. They hadn't hurt the country, they'd protected it. The agents who now surrounded Felt agreed. "When these men acted, they were doing exactly what Attorney General [Richard] Kleindienst, the White House, the Congress, and the American public wanted and needed to have done at that time," the head of the Society of Former Special Agents of the FBI said after the indictment.

At the courthouse entrance, Felt and his wife paused to hear two agents, one current, one former, read out statements of support. Felt looked out at the men who embodied the bureau to which he'd dedicated his life, the men he'd once hoped to lead himself as Hoover's handpicked successor as director, an opportunity he had been robbed of.

In the moment there on the courthouse steps, overcome by the support and the spectacle, all Felt could find the energy to say was a simple "God bless you all." Then he and Audrey turned and entered the courthouse.

The scene marked a final and dramatic exclamation point on six years in the life of the FBI and the nation—a period that had seen the death of Hoover and scandal inside the FBI, the Pentagon Papers and a national loss of faith in its government and its leader, the landslide reelection and then stunning downfall of Richard Nixon, and dozens upon dozens of sprawling court cases that spun out of the related political scandals summed up simply as "Watergate"—and unbeknownst to everyone on the plaza that day, Felt had played a far larger role than anyone imagined. It was a secret that he would hold long after his court case would conclude and he was eventually pardoned by President Ronald Reagan, well into the next century and his tenth decade.

He, William Mark Felt, Sr., of Twin Falls, Idaho, son of a carpenter, also went by one of the most famous names in American politics.

He was Deep Throat.

*   *   *

Richard Nixon was one of the most consequential political figures of the twentieth century. Judged on paper and résumé alone, Nixon should stand among the giants who occupied the White House through the American Century.

As a young congressman, he helped fuel the Red Scare and give life to McCarthyism, turning "Communist" into a career-ending slur. From 1952 to 1972, he was on the Republican Party's national ticket five times; when he finally ascended to the presidency, he shaped, escalated, prolonged, and eventually wound down the Vietnam War as it roiled the nation; he signed the Clean Air Act and created the Environmental Protection Agency, signed the Occupation Safety and Health Act, transformed the Post Office into a quasi-private government enterprise, hiked Social Security payments, declared war on cancer, signed Title IX to give women opportunities in academia and on athletic playing fields, transformed the military by ending the draft and creating an all-volunteer force, and helped push forward civil rights. He tried to position his government at the forefront of equal opportunity—hiring a presidential staff assistant focused solely on bringing more qualified women into government, tripling the number of women in policy-making roles, recruiting one thousand women into previously male middle-management roles, and bringing the first-ever female military aides into the White House. He even wrestled momentarily with the idea of providing a conservative-style universal basic income to lift Americans from poverty. He averted a larger war in the Middle East amid the conflagration of the Yom Kippur War; he calmed the Cold War and signed arms control treaties with the Soviet Union; and he reopened diplomatic relations with China. He was the first president to visit a Communist country, the first to visit Peking, the first to stand in Moscow.

"The Nixon presidency was an intense one—hardworking, determined, wide-ranging, organized, and creative," concluded his close advisor and onetime cabinet secretary Maurice Stans. "I don't believe any man could have been more determined to do the best possible job as president."

In an era when the newsweeklies dominated American life, Nixon filled the cover of *TIME* a total of fifty-five times—more than a year's worth of magazines over the course of his political career, more than any other figure in history. He was, as would become clear, the hinge upon which the entire American Century turned, the figure who ushered out the expansive liberal consensus of the New Deal and the Great Society and brought to the mainstream a darker, racialized, nativist, fearmongering strain of the Republican Party and American politics that would a half century later find its natural conclusion in Donald Trump.

Yet all of that would be overshadowed by a one-word scandal that would ultimately lead to the first congressional impeachment hearings in a century and would force him ignominiously from office. In the fifty years since the June night five burglars entered a then new and trendy hotel and office complex on the banks of the Potomac River, "Watergate" has become the scandal that has defined all other scandals, "gate" the suffix of choice to denote a scandal of epic proportions.* It fundamentally upended Americans' relationship with their government and revealed a cynical abuse of power that fueled a decade-long epic loss of trust and faith in the institutions that had long led American life. "To view Watergate in perspective it is essential to remember that it occurred when presidential power was great—the weakening from Vietnam was still incipient. John F. Kennedy and Lyndon B. Johnson had been very powerful, dynamic executives. Richard M. Nixon's first term in office vastly consolidated power in the White House," recalls Donald Sanders, a Watergate senate investigator. "There was a very different aura about the infallibility and inaccessibility of the White House. The balloon had yet to be punctured."

It is also, in many ways, the dividing line between "old" Washington and "new," capturing a sea change in power, institutional dynamics, and politics. Watergate stands simultaneously as the last event of an old era—when segregationists ruled Capitol Hill and World War I veterans walked its halls, and the city's rhythms were driven by print newspaper deadlines—and the introduction of a new generation of political action, sweeping up some of the biggest names in our twenty-first-century culture, from future actor and senator Fred Thompson to journalist Diane Sawyer to a young, bespectacled Hillary Rodham to a young Roger Stone, who got his first taste of dirty tricks on the national scale amid Nixon's Watergate. It ushered into Washington in 1974 the more than fifty new Democratic lawmakers, the class of "Watergate Babies," who would shape public policy well into this next century; set in motion a world-shaping shift in the Republican Party that elevated Ronald Reagan and the Bush family and a particular breed of cynical partisanship that would continue well into the twenty-first century; and inspired a generation of investigative journalists longing to emulate Woodward and Bernstein.

---

* A brief—and hardly comprehensive—survey would start with the original follow-on, 1976's Koreagate, about South Korean influence in Congress (a scandal that actually hit some of the same players as Watergate itself), as well as Bill Clinton's Travel-Gate and Monica-Gate, the New England Patriots' Deflate-Gate, Ariana Grande's Donut-Gate, Dan Rather's own Rather-Gate, and even the false conspiracy theory Pizza-Gate.

*   *   *

At its simplest, Watergate is the story of two separate criminal conspiracies: the Nixon world's "dirty tricks" that led to the burglary on June 17, 1972, and then the subsequent wider cover-up. The first conspiracy was deliberate, a sloppy and shambolic but nonetheless developed plan to subvert the 1972 election; the second was reactive, almost instinctive—it seems to have happened simply because no one said no. The popular-history version we now tell about Watergate—*the DNC break-in, Woodward, Bernstein, Deep Throat, the Ervin Committee hearings, yada, yada, yada, Nixon resigns*—represents just a sliver of the full story, which is not only bigger but oh ever so much weirder. The drama encompassed in those two conspiracies is in fact much darker than the rosy Technicolor version produced by Robert Redford—there's the alcoholism of Martha Mitchell and Nixon's own spiral of depression during the Yom Kippur War, as well as criminality of an unprecedented and sad breadth—and also tells a more human story, one filled not with giants, villains, and heroes, but with flawed everyday people worried about their families, their careers, and their legacies.

Watergate represents much more than an individual moment, decision, event, or target. It has so many parts that there is no single motive or story to tell, no single thread that makes all the pieces come together—even the break-in that triggered the whole public unraveling seems possibly to have been committed by burglars with two or even three distinct and separate motives. "Watergate" was less an event than a way of life for the Nixon administration—a mindset that evolved into a multiyear, multifaceted corruption and erosion of ethics within the office of the president.

"Watergate," wrote Tad Szulc, one of the *New York Times* reporters who covered it, "was not born in a vacuum. The men who planned, ordered, and executed the Watergate crimes were neither the product of nor a sudden aberration in American history. Both Watergate and those associated with it were, instead, the result of a strange American historical process with roots in the early years of the Cold War." What would be later summarized as "dirty tricks" really was the story of how Nixon's team, ironically blinded by the desire for law and order and national security, violated the constitutional rights of politicians, journalists, and American citizens.

Understanding the story as a whole involves not just the bugging operation and burglary at the Democratic campaign offices but a broader umbrella of nearly a dozen other distinct but related scandals: the Chennault Affair, the Huston Plan, the Kissinger wiretaps and the illegal bombing of Cambodia, the Pentagon Papers, ITT and the Dita Beard memo, the Vesco donation, milk price fixing, campaign "rat-fucking," Spiro Agnew's bribery case, and the FBI's COINTELPRO operations, plus a little bit of presidential tax fraud. (In fact, Nixon's most famous line in history, "I am not a crook," came not because of the Watergate scandal but because of an associated and concurrent tax investigation.)* Some of these other associated scandals would be monumental in their own right; the still-opaque Chennault Affair represents one of the only instances of credible treason allegations in U.S. history, and the first-ever resignation of a vice president, Spiro Agnew, came amid a scandal that under normal circumstances would have been more serious than almost any that has touched the White House in 240 years—yet they are largely forgotten or overlooked. Each event, though—unfolding before, during, and after the bugging operation—influenced the mindset of the Nixon world and shaped public opinion and Washington's atmosphere as the post-burglary investigations unfolded.

As time would make clear, the actions around the Watergate scandal were certainly criminal, and there was without a doubt a conspiracy, but labeling it all a "criminal conspiracy" implies a level of forethought, planning, and precise execution that isn't actually evident at any stage of the debacle. Instead, the key players slipped, fumbled, and stumbled their way from the White House to prison, often without ever seeming to make a conscious decision to join the cover-up. Ultimately, multiple cabinet officials would face criminal charges, an FBI director would resign and face prosecution, a congressman would commit suicide, and a CIA director would plead guilty to misleading Congress. There were secret hush money payoffs, threats of blackmail, layer upon layer of betrayal, an

---

* The second most famous line of Watergate, Deep Throat's incantation "Follow the money," actually was never said at all—it was a screenwriter's flourish in *All the President's Men*.

alleged kidnapping, and even a suspicious plane crash. There were rumors of high-priced call girls, allegations of the CIA and the Pentagon spying on the Nixon White House itself, and accusations of illegal donations from the Greek military junta. All told, sixty-nine people would be indicted on charges stemming from the related investigations—including New York Yankees owner George Steinbrenner—and companies from Goodyear Tire and Gulf Oil to American Airlines and 3M found themselves pleading guilty to illegally financing Nixon's reelection. Nixon's attorney general and commerce secretary were put on trial together, a case then dubbed the "trial of the century," despite the fact that it would be all but forgotten in the future. The careers of three consecutive attorneys general were upended.

We have come to understand many facets of this larger story only with time, and subsequent revelations make clear how little of it many understood as it unfolded. Thanks to the pop heroism of that iconic movie and book *All the President's Men*, we've long seen the *Washington Post* as a—perhaps *the*—central figure of Watergate, crediting the paper's Bob Woodward, Carl Bernstein, Ben Bradlee, and Katharine Graham with courageously cracking open the case. In fact, there were a half-dozen reporters who played key roles—including columnist Jack Anderson and a team from the *Los Angeles Times*—who rightly deserve pride of place in the Watergate story alongside Woodward and Bernstein. And with the added insight of Deep Throat's identity (Mark Felt came forward only in 2005) the story shifts to include a pitched battle for control of the Justice Department and a fight over the legacy of J. Edgar Hoover, played out inside the FBI itself and within the executive branch more broadly.

*   *   *

Answering the questions—*How could they!? What were they thinking?!*—lies in the mystique of power unique to the presidency and the capital, and the arrogance and blindness that accompany those who serve the nation's chief executive. While we often think of Watergate as a "Nixon" story, it's better understood as a "Washington" story. Jack Limpert, my former editor and predecessor at *Washingtonian* magazine, was the first person to zero in on Mark Felt as Deep Throat, back in June 1974, and to him the Watergate story was always about more than just the players. "It tells you an awful lot more about how things happen in Washington," he wrote then. It is the greatest story ever told about power—the need and hunger for it, the drive to protect it, how it is challenged, and how it flows month to month in a city governed by both well-calibrated checks and balances and all manner of official and unofficial traditions. "Power is Washington's main marketable product," wrote Jack Anderson in 1973 in the midst of Watergate. "Power is the driving force that brings together people of different philosophies and varying interests in the constantly evolving battle for control."

Watergate also explains the deeper functions and purpose of government and the interplays of the Constitution—how the checks and balances of Articles I, II, and III combine and interlock with the Bill of Rights and other constitutional amendments to enable a smooth, functioning nation—a success story of how government worked in a moment of grave crisis when America was at the peak of its power in the twentieth century. "I had thrown down a gauntlet to Congress, the bureaucracy, the media, and the Washington establishment and challenged them to engage in epic battle," Nixon wrote in his memoirs. Watergate didn't just rewrite the rules, it set new ones.

At the same time, the fall of Richard Nixon was less inevitable than we usually remember. Handled differently, the scandal might have just been a blip on the political radar, an almost forgotten headline on his triumphant march to a second term and a successful next four years in the White House. Perhaps Watergate would have ended up in history only a fun bar-trivia answer, akin to the 1974 scandal where stripper Fanne Foxe jumped into D.C.'s Tidal Basin after being caught with the powerful chair of the House Ways and Means Committee Wilbur Mills. Instead, the White House's own bad instincts and the most classic characteristic of Washington—ambition—are what ultimately caused the unraveling of Nixon's world.

* * *

An irony of Watergate is that the once secret plot to subvert American democracy now stands as one of the most documented and covered stories in American history; anyone seeking to understand the story of Richard Nixon's secrecy and subterfuge drowns in information. There are more than thirty memoirs by key participants alone—two of which, Nixon's and Kissinger's, top 1,100 and 2,800 pages, respectively—plus scores more journalistic and scholarly books, thousands of pages of oral histories, tens of thousands of news articles, and hundreds of thousands of pages of investigation and documentation in government archives around the country.* The transcripts of relevant Nixon tapes stretch to 650 pages in one volume and 740 pages in another; the Senate's Ervin Committee investigation encompasses thirty volumes, totaling 16,091 pages. Two major libel lawsuits in the 1990s added thousands more pages of documentation, testimony, and evidence. More files have been made accessible only in recent years; many recently declassified FBI documents, like those pertaining to George Steinbrenner, have only become available after the subjects' deaths.

Despite the myriad contemporaneous records, many are less than perfect accounts of history. The era's tell-all memoirs show the haste with which they were rushed into print to capitalize on the nation's fascination. In a pre-internet era when fact-checking news reports, memoirs, and oral histories was more difficult, period accounts are often littered with obvious errors, from restaurant names to calendars. Woodward and Bernstein's classic *All the President's Men* has an innocent mistake on the very first page, where the two reporters accidentally shrink the *Washington Post*'s newsroom to just "150 square feet." Sam Dash, the chief counsel of the Senate Watergate Committee, consistently gets the last name of his House Judiciary Committee colleague wrong, calling Jerry Zeifman, Jerry Zeiffert; and in profiling the security guard who busted the burglars, *JET* magazine apparently conflates James McCord and George Gordon Liddy, naming the burglar caught "George McCord." H. R. Haldeman mis-assigns *Washington Post* star political reporter David Broder to the crosstown rival *Star*.

---

* Watergate literature is so plentiful that there's even an entire subgenre that amounts to fan fiction—a half-dozen novelizations of the events, of widely varying quality and accuracy, some written by the key players themselves. That total doesn't even count the forty or so espionage potboilers written by burglary plotter E. Howard Hunt, some of which he wrote even as he awaited trial.

More than any little typos or inadvertent mistakes, it's hard to know whom to trust when you're telling a story where nearly every major player ended up being charged with lying, perjury, or obstruction of justice. Many of the participants in Watergate's swirl tend to minimize their own role or culpability in particular events. The memories of Jeb Magruder and G. Gordon Liddy, for instance, often agree generally on events, but differ in obviously self-beneficial ways on the level of criminality or nastiness implied by certain conversations. Alexander Haig's memoir, which largely covers a period when there were no corresponding tapes of White House meetings, differs significantly from available evidence in key moments. To avoid confusion and for ease of readability, I've lightly edited some direct quotes that, because of the vagaries of memory, clearly misremember known dates, names, or events, excising the incorrect information.* Through cross-referencing accounts, double-checking primary source diaries, schedules, calendars, and underlying documents, I've worked to assemble a more true version of the events than any one participant has ever been able to tell before.

The raw Nixon tapes pose a greater challenge. The tapes themselves are a verbal disaster—an almost impenetrable morass of words, overloaded and overstuffed with the filler, interruptions, asides, false starts, confusing antecedents, and digressions that populate colloquial, informal speech. The president loved to talk and talk, what John Ehrlichman would later call "chewing the cud," rehashing, circling back, and revisiting the same topic time and again. "He would turn the same rock over a dozen times and then leave it and then come back to it two weeks later and turn it

---

* D.C. prosecutor Earl Silbert, for example, spoke in one oral history of the known events of Saturday, April 15, 1973, when that particular Saturday was actually the 14th, and in written testimony to Congress he said an event happened on Friday, July 29, 1972, when the Friday was actually the 28th. Indeed, nearly every Watergate memoir is littered with mixed-up dates. Senator Ervin's own written account of his meeting with Richard Nixon amid the week of the Saturday Night Massacre accidentally dates the event to October 1975, fourteen months into Gerald Ford's presidency. Egil Krogh, in his memoir, correctly lists a meeting in one paragraph as happening July 17, while in the paragraph before he misstated it as July 16. Howard Hunt incorrectly dates an early meeting of the Plumbers to Saturday, July 10, that was actually held two weeks later, on Saturday, July 24. The memoir of CIA deputy director Vernon Walters misquotes his own memos, placing a key meeting on June 22 rather than June 23.

over another dozen times," Ehrlichman explained.* The original recordings were primitive by modern standards, and multiple investigators and scholars have struggled for decades to make sense of their scratchy nuances; famously, in the midst of the House impeachment inquiry, investigators released a transcript that repeatedly quoted Nixon referencing someone named "Earl Nash," only to determine subsequently that there was no such person and that Nixon instead had kept starting to say "national security" and then stopped short. Conversations and topics often stretch over extended periods of time—encompassing thousands of words, reels of tape, and pages of transcripts—and completely capturing them here would result in a multivolume work that would be of zero reader interest.

Even after a half century of study, there remain fights—sometimes meaningful ones—over the accuracy of the tapes. The National Archives and the Richard M. Nixon Presidential Library have declined to author "master" transcripts, so I've relied on the expert work of the Watergate investigators and three published volumes of tape transcripts, by Stanley Kutler, Douglas Brinkley, and Luke Nichter, as well as—in very limited instances—my own deciphering of certain passages not included in their works. In some cases, resolving the ambiguity still left in these remarks is critical to understanding their context and interpreting the outlines of the president's paranoid mind and an unfolding criminal conspiracy. More often than not, though, the unclear remarks are simply confusing. I've tried to lightly edit many of the Oval Office conversations for readability and concision where doing so doesn't falsely change their meaning or context, and left the full verbal soup where it's important.

This narrative is meant to distill everything we've learned in the nearly fifty years since (as well as some new insights gleaned along the

---

* Even his own staff came to realize that their role in most of their conversations with Nixon was simply to absorb him and let him process out loud. Their presence was almost extraneous. "Probably you'd grunt at the right times," Ehrlichman said. "Our minds were probably drifting off to other things." Kissinger too came to see as central to his role the strange experience of soaking up the president's "nervous tension. One would sit for hours listening to Nixon's musings, throwing an occasional log on the fire, praying for some crisis to bring relief, alert to the opportunity to pass the torch to some unwary aide who wandered in more or less by accident," he recalled.

way) into a single, readable volume that captures as much of the historical legacy—and utter bizarreness—of the world that we shorthand as "Watergate" as possible. It has taken a half century to be able to write the truest history of Watergate, which—at least until the current times—stands as the strangest chapter of the entire American presidency. It is a story, though, we're probably not finished with. As White House reporter Helen Thomas wrote, "I don't think the dust will ever entirely settle on the Watergate scandal."

Prologue

The Pentagon Papers

Even though it would continue for another 1,153 days, Saturday, June 13, 1971, was arguably the last happy and good day of Richard Nixon's presidency. There were still happy days ahead (many spent enjoying milkshakes or Ballantine's Scotches on the back deck of the presidential yacht *Sequoia*) and good days to come (a historic opening to China and the largest presidential landslide election in U.S. history), but perhaps never again would there be a day both happy and good, at least for the moody, brooding, conspiratorial, thin-skinned, self-destructive occupant of the Oval Office.

On that spring Saturday—even as unbeknownst to him the *New York Times* finalized a scoop for the next day that would begin to upend all that was happy and good about his presidency—Richard Nixon's daughter was getting married. The fact that their granddaughter was getting married at the White House would have astounded his parents, Hannah Milhous Nixon and Francis A. Nixon.

The doctor who had delivered Richard Milhous Nixon a year before the start of World War I had traveled by horse and buggy to the Irish Quaker family's house in Yorba Linda, California, on what then represented the outskirts of the continental United States. The town was so new to the map that he was the first baby born there. There had been no government social safety net, the New Deal and the Great Society still years away, and Jim Crow laws and segregation reigned almost unquestioned across the South. Now, as commander in chief, Francis and Hannah's son traveled the world in a heavily modified Boeing 707 jet, presided over a life-ending arsenal of thermonuclear missiles, and had watched from the Oval Office in 1969 as his nation became the first to walk on the moon.

Today, he would escort his daughter down the aisle at the most famous address in the world.

*   *   *

Yet, for a man who had seemed to have much to celebrate—after the conclusion of his navy service in World War II, he had risen in just six years from a newly elected congressman to the U.S. Senate to the vice presidency, served eight years alongside Dwight Eisenhower in a time of great prosperity and peace, and then returned to a triumphal victory for the nation's highest office in 1968 himself—happiness had often escaped him.

Elective office had been on Nixon's radar from the start; in eighth grade, he'd listed his life goals and included "I would like to study law and enter politics for an occupation so that I might be of some good to the people." In his presidential inaugural address, he would phrase the drive thusly: "Until he has been part of a cause larger than himself, no man is truly whole." Aide Pat Buchanan said it simply: "He wanted to be a great man."

However, years later, in his memoirs, he would look back and recall just how much stress and grief his entire political career had wrought. He recalled fondly the night his first congressional campaign ended in California, way back in 1946, circulating among rowdy victory parties. He was not even thirty-four years old. "Pat and I were happier," he wrote, "than we were ever to be again in my political career."

Nixon often struggled to connect with others. A man who spent most of thirty years at the peak of American power when American power was at its peak, he seemed to have only two meaningful, deep personal friendships—both men with strange names, and both of whom could not have existed further from high-society circles: Charles "Bebe" Rebozo, a Florida laundromat magnate, banker, and real estate speculator, and Robert Abplanalp, a man who had made his fortune inventing the mass-produced, cheap, and reliable aerosol valve that transformed consumer goods and enabled everything from spray paint to canned whipped cream. He struggled to make small talk. The first time Rebozo invited Nixon sport fishing, Nixon showed up with a briefcase of work to do on the boat and barely spoke; Abplanalp, meanwhile, provided the president the use of his private 125-acre island in the Bahamas where Nixon could exist in total solitude.* He never learned to spell his top aide John Ehrlichman's name, preferring to instead address notes to him with a simple "E," and continued to misspell it years after the presidency. Nixon's chief of staff, H. R. "Bob" Haldeman—his closest professional associate—would remark years later, "To this day, he doesn't know how many children I have." And aides would mock the president behind his back for the awkward way he would shove White House trinkets—golf balls, pens, or cuff links—at Oval Office guests without looking at them, his arm shooting out from his back as he rummaged through drawers, unsure and uncomfortable greeting people visiting him, the occupant of the most famous office in the world.

Throughout his presidency, he went to ever-greater lengths in search of solitude; he retreated from the Oval Office to work from a hideaway in the Executive Office Building and fled Washington for ever-longer stretches, to his western getaway in San Clemente, California, or his southern getaway in Key Biscayne, Florida. By his second term, he would retreat to Camp David for weeks on end. "Richard Nixon went up the walls of life with his claws," his longtime friend White House aide Bryce Harlow would say years later. "I suspect that my gifted friend somewhere in his youth, maybe when he was very young or in his teens, got badly hurt by someone he cared for very deeply or totally trusted—a parent, a dear friend, a lover, a confidante. Somewhere I figure someone hurt him badly." His comfort was assured through a strict adherence to routine. He ate the same lunch almost every day: a ring of canned pineapple, cottage cheese, crackers, and a glass of milk. (The cottage cheese was flown in weekly from his favorite dairy back home, Knudsen's.) He liked

* "To be with Bebe Rebozo is to be with a genial, discreet sponge," Ehrlichman later wrote. "Bebe makes no requests or demands."

bowling alone and walking on the beach alone. Nixon drank too much and couldn't hold his alcohol—particularly when he was exhausted, even just a drink or two could make him loopy—and fought his depression by self-medicating with Dilantin and sleeping pills.

And yet, as his biographer Jay Farrell would write, "there existed, within the angry man, a resolute optimist." He devoured movies at nights and weekends as president—more than five hundred of them—watching religiously at Camp David, the White House theater, and on vacation, and his family remembers how enthusiastically he plowed ever onward. "No matter how terrible the first reel is, he always thinks it will get better," his daughter Julie said later. "Daddy would stick with it. 'Wait,' he'd say, 'wait—it'll get better.'"

He could, in moments, radiate a warmth and exuberance for life that surprised; he loved the beauty of the White House gardens and in the evenings would bound off the elevator into the family residence to report that the crocuses had bloomed or another flower had arrived in season. While running for vice president in 1952, he'd once traded places with a lanky reporter and allowed the journalist to wave at adoring crowds alongside Pat as Nixon, watching from the press bus, laughed and laughed. During his 1968 campaign, he'd stumbled upon a young aide in the hallway, whisking a woman back to his room, and cracked, "Mike, we don't have to get those votes one at a time, you know," and one day, while talking to aide Chuck Colson in the Oval Office, Nixon saw his national security advisor Henry Kissinger approach out of the corner of his eye and quickly deadpanned, "I don't know, Chuck, about that idea you had about dropping a nuclear weapon on Hanoi. I'm not sure the time is quite ready, but if we try to do it, let's not tell Henry."

Nixon, confoundingly, considered himself a man of his word.* At the end of 1970, he sat down and sketched his goals and the qualities he hoped to project, a list that began with "compassionate, humane, fatherly, warmth, confidence in future, optimistic, upbeat" and continued, line

---

* In the closing days of the 1960 presidential election, Nixon believed it important to meet his promise to campaign in all fifty states and, rather than fight in person in the close battleground states and high-population areas, led a swing through some of the nation's most politically irrelevant states, like Alaska and South Dakota. His commitment to fulfill that pledge might well have cost him the election.

after line, through more than fifty such traits, including "moral leader, nation's conscience." And as mercurial as he was, Nixon hated arguing, confrontation, or firing people, and possessed an odd reservoir of tenderness, even gentleness, for those who served him. "Some of his most devious methods were mechanisms to avoid hurting people face-to-face," Kissinger later recalled.

It was that mixing of idealistic light and morose dark that had propelled him and allowed him to bounce back from professional humiliation, time after time, manipulating and Machiavellian-ing his way through Washington—building himself up on the back of McCarthyism in the 1950s and Vietnam in the 1960s, remaining personally ever hopeful even as he roared about how much the nation needed him precisely because it had so much to fear.

"His rise to the presidency was an amazing triumph of will and intelligence," biographer Richard Reeves concluded. "He was too suspicious, his judgments were too harsh, too negative. He clung to the word and the idea of being 'tough.' He thought that was what had brought him to the edge of greatness. But that was what betrayed him. He could not open himself to other men and he could not open himself to greatness."

Or, as his aide Bryce Harlow said, simply, "He liked rolling in the dust."

*　　*　　*

The wedding was spectacular, attended by four hundred guests, including Billy Graham, Ralph Nader, Rev. Dr. Norman Vincent Peale, Art Linkletter, and even FBI Director J. Edgar Hoover and Chief Justice Warren Burger (not a single member of Congress, however, was to be found). Martha Mitchell, the flamboyant and fiery wife of Nixon's attorney general, arrived under a yellow organza parasol and wide-brim hat, wearing a pale-apricot couture dress and high-heel slingbacks—the same outfit she'd worn earlier in the year to meet Queen Elizabeth at Buckingham Palace. The eighty-seven-year-old Alice Roosevelt Longworth, who herself had been married at the White House in 1906, fumbled through her purse for her invitation when asked for it by the guards at the gate. The male attendants wore ascots, the women mint-green organdy dresses. Three different champagnes—all American, of course—flowed through the night, and the newlyweds cut into a 355-pound, seven-tier wedding cake. Tricia called Edward "my first and last love." The music-loving president, worried earlier in the day about his first dance, nailed the tradition, then proceeded to dance on with his other daughter, his wife, and even Lynda Bird Johnson, the daughter of the man who had preceded him in the White House. "It was a day that all of us will always remember because all of us were beautifully and simply, happy," he said later in his memoirs.

The next morning, the photo of the president, arm in arm with his daughter, dominated the front page in the *New York Times*, filling the top two columns on the left. The *Times'* Nan Robertson reported how the president had escorted his twenty-five-year-old "diminutive, ethereal, blond daughter" down the curved staircase of the White House's South Portico to meet her twenty-four-year-old groom, "tall, fine-boned and handsome" and "the scion of Easterners whose ancestors go back to the leaders of the American Revolution." (The whole thing, Nixon felt, should have been shown as a prime-time special on the networks. "If it were the Kennedys, it would be rerun every night for three weeks, you know," he groused to Haldeman.)

Nearby atop the *Times* were three other columns displaying a story by investigative reporter Neil Sheehan: "Vietnam Archive: Pentagon Study Traces 3 Decades of Growing Involvement," the first installment of what would come to be known as the "Pentagon Papers," the leak of a classified yearlong seven-thousand-page study commissioned by Kennedy's defense secretary, Robert McNamara, that traced how the U.S. had become embroiled in the Vietnam War. The papers documented, richly and at great length, the official lies that had led so many young American men to die in the jungles of southeast Asia.

At first glance, Nixon was not particularly concerned; the backward-looking story about the Kennedy and Johnson years didn't seem to be his problem. His focus, instead, was on the less charitable coverage of the grand wedding by the *Washington Post*: "I just don't like that paper," he barked to his press secretary, Ron Ziegler. The *Post*, Nixon decreed, should be banned from covering all future White House social events.

It was an unsurprising response: Nixon felt the press had never been on his side. "Let's go face the enemy," he would say en route to the National Press Club. The media had fallen in love with his 1960 opponent, the young and glamorous Jack Kennedy, and sought to write his political obituary so many times that after he'd lost the California gubernatorial race in 1962, he'd promised, "As I leave you I want you to know—just think how much you're going to be missing: You won't have Nixon to kick around anymore."* He and Pat knew they lived under an unforgiving microscope; on election night in 1952, after he was elected vice president alongside Dwight Eisenhower, Pat stayed up late washing all the glasses in their hotel suite so the maids couldn't publicly lament how much alcohol the party had consumed in celebration. "Was Nixon paranoid? Yes," his aide Dwight Chapin said later. "But he also had the right to be." Haldeman separately echoed Chapin's impression: "He had strong opinions, but opinions were based on reality: That he had a battle to fight with his opponent; with a good segment of the press; with a lot of the Washington and Eastern Establishment."

Once in office, in an exercise almost akin to self-flagellation, he had pioneered a White House morning news summary, prepared by 7 a.m. each day by a young aide named Pat Buchanan, that became the first thing he read each day. It all but guaranteed he'd be in a grumpy mood by lunch; the news summary would be returned to his aides, its margins filled with scribbled notes, follow-ups, and diatribes. "It was eating at him," Buchanan observed. One of the news summary team, Mort Allin, said later, "I just don't understand how the hell he can sit there and take this shit day after day."

Those morning news summaries caught an institution in transition, as a media that for decades had been little more than stenographers of the powerful tiptoed into something more oppositional, with a sharper edge, amid the broader societal reckoning and questioning in the 1960s of powerful institutions. Washington, which had been a newspaper town since its founding, was gradually giving way to new, even more powerful forms of media. On the nation's airwaves, television anchors were becoming powerful arbiters of the nation's attention; in its magazines a

---

* Days later, ABC News had run a special documentary actually entitled, *The Political Obituary of Richard M. Nixon*, that had even featured an interview with Alger Hiss, the former Russian spy whom Nixon had made famous through his crusade on the House Un-American Activities Committee in 1948.

"New Journalism" was emerging that prized a subjective voice, personal witnessing, and narrative detail, a style characterized by writers like Gay Talese, Joan Didion, and Hunter S. Thompson. The press was becoming not just a scribe and observer of world events, but a participant too.

The Pentagon Papers contained all the right ingredients for an explosion: They played to Nixon's conspiratorial, paranoid nature, to his antipathy for the press in general and the *Washington Post* and the *New York Times* in specific; moreover, they focused on a government cover-up, catnip to reporters, that stemmed from the thing Nixon hated most next to perhaps antiwar protesters—leakers—and focused on the administration's most volatile personality: Henry Kissinger. It was the beginning of a scandal that would unfurl for most of the next decade, consume Nixon's presidency, and change American government forever.

PART I

The Kindling

1971

Chapter 1

All the President's Men

As the thirty-seventh occupant of his office, Richard Nixon had settled into the White House under a new reality: Washington, D.C., had changed dramatically since World War II, as what had once been a relatively sleepy southern town conducting part-time business had morphed into the all-consuming locus of federal power, directing the world's largest economy and driving foreign affairs the world over. With that shift—and the massive and ever-swelling bureaucracy that came with it—the presidency had changed too; what for much of America's first two centuries had been the office tasked with executing policy and spending money decided and set by Congress had seen that power dynamic reverse and instead now piloted the national agenda itself. It was a job now far too big for one man, even as the White House absorbed, stole, and agglomerated still more power and personnel. To Nixon, figuring out how to staff the oversized presidency—whom to trust, how to inspire them and manage them—consumed far too much energy. "It would be god damn easy to run this office if you didn't have to deal with people," he lamented.

He also knew he had big shoes to fill and equally big problems to address. His predecessor, Lyndon Johnson, had built one of the most ambitious domestic agendas of all time, overseeing the implementation of sweeping civil rights legislation and the Great Society, but Vietnam had so quickly and thoroughly crushed his presidency and broken his soul that he chose not to even run for reelection. The promise of prosperity

3

for white Americans at home—of suburban houses, two-car garages, and new shiny appliances like televisions—seemed to retreat among growing economic unease in the U.S. and military pessimism abroad. "The confidence of the early sixties, the belief in an inevitable destiny, the redress of old injustice and the attainment of new heights, was being displaced by insecurity; apprehension about the future; fragmenting, often angry, sometimes violent division," wrote historian Richard Goodwin.

In fact, Nixon's rise had been enabled by that very sense that the country was losing its way. The campaign year began with the seizing of the USS *Pueblo* by North Korea, the disastrous Tet Offensive in Vietnam, and Johnson's resulting announcement that he wouldn't seek or accept another term as president, a political earthquake overshadowed just days later by the assassination of Martin Luther King, Jr., in Memphis. On the campaign trail that night in Indiana, Bobby Kennedy calmed a volatile crowd, but violent riots broke out in a hundred American cities elsewhere. The National Guard and the U.S. Army patrolled the streets of Washington, D.C., to bring the looting and arson under control, and the scars and hulks from those fires would persist in the capital until the 2000s. Then, a little more than two months after that night, Kennedy himself was assassinated after winning the California presidential primary. That summer, as the Democrats gathered in Chicago to nominate LBJ's vice president, Hubert Humphrey, Mayor Richard Daley's police rampaged through the streets, beating antiwar protesters on live TV in what a later investigation would famously dub a "police riot."

As the upheaval rippled through politics, voters—or at least many southern voters—turned against the liberal dreams of the New Deal and the Great Society. The peace, love, and understanding of the "Age of Aquarius" that had begun to characterize sixties culture turned into something darker and more selfish by the end of the decade. Lyndon Johnson's dreams of a "war on poverty" became instead Nixon's "welfare mess"; the celebration of *Brown v. Board of Education* became northern fights over "school busing"; white fears of drugs, Black militants, and the New Left became enshrined in calls for "law and order." An economy that had soared since the generation educated under the GI Bill, bringing millions of white families into suburban, middle-class, Cleaver family bliss, sputtered with unemployment and inflation. America had dominated the postwar world stage for two decades, but now the great democratic superpower reckoned with its own internal dissension and weakness alone.

Befitting the political moment they inherited, the Nixon crew exuded a certain disdain and dourness. "The enemy was liberalism in both senses, political and moral," journalists Dan Rather and Gary Paul Gates observed. "They looked upon Washington as a hostile and alien city in part because, in their judgment, it reflected the moral permissiveness that had been allowed to flourish during the Kennedy-Johnson years; and beyond that because it was situated in the hated East, the region that, again in their view, was the haven for all the forces that were tearing down America: hippies on drugs, pushy Blacks, left-wing radicals as well as the Establishment groups that encouraged them, like the Kennedys and the national media."

Despite a job larger and more powerful than ever and despite the uphill struggle he'd face with Congress—he was the first president since 1849 to arrive in the White House with control of neither congressional body—Nixon had settled into the habit of an inner circle encompassing only the smallest number of staff and a minimalist approach to governing. On one visit to the Oval Office to meet with his successor, Lyndon Johnson couldn't believe how neat and functionally lacking Nixon's desk was; he had always prided himself on a massive desktop telephone apparatus that allowed him to instantly connect with people at all levels of the government and was confounded to see Nixon's tiny telephone with just three direct-connect buttons: "Just one dinky little phone to keep in touch with his people," he related in wonder to guests at dinner afterward. "That's all—just three buttons and they all go to Germans!"

Nixon had always planned for a lean staff to assist him at the White House, while in his mind most of the serious work and decision-making took place out in the cabinet departments. Inside the White House, he had planned to have five senior staff of equal rank and importance. Those hopes lasted only a few months, and as the administration advanced, he centralized ever more power and decision-making inside an ever-smaller White House team, neutralizing one cabinet post after another. Efficiency was the key to all the Oval Office operations—all the better to maximize Nixon's solitude and thinking time, a goal so all-encompassing that

Nixon stopped signing his middle initial on official documents: Dropping the "M" saved a full second, and given the volume of required presidential signatures over a full term, Nixon declared, "That's a real time-saver!"

The three Germans LBJ referred to were chief of staff H. R. Haldeman, domestic policy chief John Ehrlichman, and, of course, Henry Kissinger. Reporters who covered the administration came to know the triumvirate by a variety of ethnic-slanted monikers: the German Shepherds, the Berlin Wall, the Fourth Reich, the Teutonic Trio, and All the King's Krauts.* "Never before had so much authority with so little accountability been delegated to so few," Rather and Gates observed.

As the White House team assembled, it looked less like the flower-child hippies of American culture and more like the offices of J. Walter Thompson, the advertising powerhouse that had employed Nixon's chief of staff and which the revolution of the sixties had largely passed by. Short hair and crisp suits prevailed; the clones of brush-cut H. R. "Bob" Haldeman multiplied, including Appointments Secretary Dwight Chapin, Press Secretary Ron Ziegler, and Haldeman's chief aide, Larry Higby, who would become known as "Haldeman's Haldeman," the latter of which so defined the eager and officious staffer archetype that other White House aides-de-camp were simply known as "Higbys." By the end, even Higby had an assistant, known, of course, as "Higby's Higby."

Haldeman had long idolized Nixon, arranging to meet the rising politician in Nixon's D.C. office in 1951, just three years after he graduated from UCLA. "What appealed to me first about Nixon was that he was a fighter," Haldeman later recalled. "Nixon refused to be cowed." He had watched with enthusiasm as Nixon built a national profile amid the Red Scare; whereas many Americans—and history—would remember the Communist witch hunts as a dark chapter of politics, it long stood as Nixon's proudest episode. In his first campaign for Congress in 1946, he'd accused the incumbent, New Dealer Democrat Jerry Voorhis, of "vot[ing] straight down the line of the SOCIALIZATION OF OUR COUNTRY" and called for the Republican Party to "take a stand for freedom."

---

* Victor Gold, Spiro Agnew's press secretary, stole from the musical *Man of La Mancha* to label them the "Knights of the Woeful Countenance."

In Congress, then, he had a career-making moment targeting Alger Hiss, a State Department official accused of spying for the Soviets—hammering Hiss while railing about the hidden influence of Communism in the U.S. government and helping to launch the era of McCarthyism before even Joe McCarthy rallied to the cause. ("How he loved that case!" Haldeman recalled. "He was able, somehow, to compare every tough situation we ever encountered, even Watergate, to his handling of the Hiss case.") Nixon then used the same Hiss and Voorhis playbook to accuse his opponent in the 1950 California Senate race, Helen Gahagan Douglas, of being a "Pink Lady" and "insufficiently concerned about the Soviet menace." One biographer later called it the "most notorious, controversial campaign in American political history" (even Nixon would later express regret, saying in 1957, "I'm sorry about that episode"), but it paid off and by 1952, Dwight Eisenhower had added "the party's poster boy for anticommunism" to his ticket. As dirty and unforgivable as his strategy had been—the Communist threat in the U.S. was never as real or as grand as alarmists like Nixon, Joseph McCarthy, and J. Edgar Hoover feared—it's hard to imagine any other path that could have led him in just six years from being an obscure freshman congressman to vice president of the United States.

A Californian like Nixon, Haldeman had proudly supported him in that '52 vice presidential campaign—and even stood outside the television studio as Nixon delivered his famous "Checkers" speech when a financial scandal looked like it might sink his bid—but Haldeman's offer to volunteer for the campaign was never accepted. Instead, he signed on four years later as an advanceman on the '56 reelection effort and eventually became Nixon's head of advance for the unsuccessful presidential bid in 1960 against John F. Kennedy.

Haldeman stayed loyal through Nixon's wilderness years as he rose in his own advertising career at J. Walter Thompson, working for Disneyland, 7UP, Aerowax, and more, polishing his own selling and messaging skills that he would later deploy on Nixon's behalf. He discovered he had a knack for figuring out what would sell, what wouldn't, and how to convince people they absolutely needed things they hadn't even considered—one of his greatest product launches was of snail-killing pellets named "Snarol," positioning the common gastropod as a scourge of modern California life.

Aboard the '68 campaign, Haldeman led the way with a new tactic, using television, rather than an endless series of stump speeches, as the centerpiece of a national campaign. The new approach was not just technologically savvy, and tactically and strategically revolutionary, but it helped preserve Nixon's privacy and solitude, lessening the demand on his energy to be always on, always backslapping and glad-handing.

By election night, Nixon had proved Haldeman right: Despite being rewritten off by the political establishment following the '60 loss and even after effectively writing himself off following his '62 loss of the California gubernatorial race, Nixon had battled back to become the thirty-seventh President of the United States—the first losing presidential candidate of the twentieth century to later win.

Once in the White House, Haldeman quickly emerged as first among equals. The chief of staff, one of just a handful of aides with nearly unfettered access to the boss, was rarely more than a few feet away from the president during the workday—his office just one hundred gold-carpeted feet away from the Oval—and he saw every piece of paper before it reached the president's desk.* Whereas Nixon often demurred from direct confrontation, Haldeman was the man who said no, dispatching unwanted proposals, out-of-favor staff, and unnecessary commitments with an executioner's cold-eyed precision. In profiling him, *TIME* magazine wrote, "Spiky and glaring, he . . . personifies the Nixon Administration: the Prussian guard who keeps Mr. Nixon's door, the 'zero-defects' man who bosses the White House staff, the all-knowing assistant president of legendary arrogance, efficiency and power," while *Newsweek* was even crisper: "Harry Robbins Haldeman is, as he once put it, Richard Nixon's son-of-a-bitch."†

Haldeman's most important role was simply listening and absorbing the hopes, fears, obsessions, insecurities, victories, and losses of Richard Nixon. As Nixon's mind churned, he listened for hours, translating the

---

* The idea and role of a "White House chief of staff"—an evolution of what previous generations had called a private secretary—had only emerged in the years after World War II. As a response to the growing demands of the presidency and the complexity of operating the White House staff, postwar presidents had taken to appointing one staffer in a post that was known by various titles, including "assistant to the president," before public nomenclature settled on "chief of staff."

† Haldeman's brutal efficiency wowed and worried even the boss: Nixon once dispatched his friend Bebe Rebozo to lecture Haldeman on being more diplomatic. The lesson didn't take.

president's thoughts—both good and bad—into page after page of notes and diaries on yellow legal pads. Nixon's desire to interact with as few people as possible was a uniquely odd trait in a politician, and it's part of what gave Haldeman such historically unparalleled power. As gatekeeper, he decided which of the president's many orders, interests, and instincts were then translated into action by the White House and government beyond.

He always saw his mission as not just serving the country, or just serving the president, but serving the unique combination of man, cause, and moment. He said he doubted he would have ever served another president. "I have been accused of blind loyalty to President Nixon," Haldeman later wrote. "I plead guilty to the loyalty, but not to the blindness. My loyalty was, and is, based on a clear recognition of both great virtues and great faults in the man I served. On balance, there has never been any question in my mind as to the validity of that loyalty."

Overall, few staff met with the ongoing approval of Haldeman and the man in the Oval Office; those who did had both indulged the president's fancies and moved quickly to do so. "Nixon was an aggressive campaigner; his theme was always attack, attack, and attack again," Haldeman recalled. "He wasn't averse to using all possible means to try to defeat his opponents." Haldeman's assignments emerged from his office with such ferocity that answers seemed overdue even before they arrived on a staffer's desk; his "tickler" file, with assigned tasks and deadlines tracked religiously down to the hour, never forgot or forgave. "He dealt with most people by memo because memos were quick and impersonal," aide Jeb Stuart Magruder recalled later. Saying no by memo was as quick as checking the "Disapprove" line, no conversation, gilding, or comforting necessary. Chuck Colson would lament that while he might spend ten or fifteen minutes gabbing with the president—in theory the most tightly scheduled man in the building—he never received such attention from Haldeman. Haldeman's default message to the White House staff was simple: "There were to be results, not alibis."

*　　*　　*

Haldeman had also brought into Nixon's orbit a UCLA friend, John Ehrlichman. They had worked in campus politics together, and Ehrlichman had gone on to a career as Seattle's top zoning lawyer. He had started as Nixon's White House counsel on the first day of the new administration, a post far removed from the Oval Office, and steadily gained power by delivering the president seemingly helpful, detailed critiques of how others were mishandling issues Nixon was supposed to care about—and then proposing, almost as an afterthought, that he, Ehrlichman, should take over the issue.

One of those issues was domestic policy, a portfolio that had frustrated Nixon since he'd taken office. He had twice tried to establish a powerful domestic policy operation that could rival in authority, scope, and prestige the one assembled by Kissinger in foreign affairs. It was an odd blind spot for the president: Despite understanding innately the nation's mood and the mechanics of politics, he never seemed to care an iota for domestic policy—he saw geopolitics as the only stage worthy of a president's focus.* He had been elected with a campaign trail reprise of "the time has come to get people off the welfare rolls and onto payrolls" but had little sense of how to translate that into policy or what his own New Deal or Great Society could be. Neither, to be fair, did Ehrlichman, who was all but policy agnostic and seemed to care little about societal change. Instead, he won over Nixon with his unquestionable loyalty, executing the president's explicit orders without trying to clog them up with his own pet causes. That approach, though, led to its own paralysis, since Nixon's domestic agenda was always better at articulating what he was against rather than what he supported. As Rather and Gates observed, "Domestic policy under Ehrlichman's reign was essentially negative, both in tone and substance."

---

* First, he turned to Arthur Burns, a ponderous longtime advisor who struggled to translate his unceasing graduate school seminar–style lectures—heard, willingly or not, by the president, cabinet, and officials beyond—into action. The next candidate was Pat Moynihan, who led the president right to the edge of a radical and ahead-of-its-time plan for "income maintenance," what later generations would know as universal basic income, to guarantee Americans enough money to live their lives. The most radical piece of social legislation since the New Deal actually appeared headed for reality—the House passed Nixon's welfare reform in April 1970—until Moynihan, a rare liberal in a circle that distrusted such men instinctually, was sunk by leaks of controversial memos proposing, among other things, the "benign neglect" of race relations. Ultimately, both Burns and Moynihan were escorted out in the way that Haldeman liked to banish people: with a promotion to a seemingly big role that only with time proved meaningless and irrelevant.

Few outside of the White House campus's eighteen acres had any understanding of the power wielded by Haldeman and Ehrlichman. Some plugged-in Washingtonians even struggled to keep them straight; which was the Seattle zoning attorney and which the Los Angeles advertising executive? They appeared on the scene almost inseparable from the start and were nearly identical in their résumés: Eagle Scouts, UCLA, Christian Scientists, loyal to Nixon above all others. They differed, really, only in their appearance: Haldeman's style would have looked stern even on a Marine, whereas Ehrlichman exuded a slightly rumpled appearance even under the most formal circumstances. But their roles individually and as a unit would make themselves apparent when coming to the defense of their commander in chief.

The third German in Nixon's troika was Henry Kissinger, who became a rare public figure beyond the Nixon White House. Washington was used to presidential aides serving as ephemeral celebrities during their tenure—advisors in recent administrations like Harry Hopkins, Sherman Adams, Ted Sorensen, and Kenny O'Donnell had paraded through the city—but Nixon's men kept to themselves. Kissinger embraced the fame of his role, loving the Georgetown dinner parties and charity gala dinners, becoming "a figure of real distinction and glamour," Rather and Gates noted. In conversations around town within those more liberal social circles, conversations where it was hard to discern truth from performative outrage, Kissinger regularly decried Nixon as a "madman" and noted how he had little patience for his White House colleagues— he complained at one point in 1970 to the British ambassador: "I have never met such a gang of self-seeking bastards in my life. I used to find the Kennedy group unattractively narcissistic, but they were idealists. These people are real heels." He told his journalist friend Marvin Kalb, "I can't explain how difficult it is to work around here. I am surrounded by maniacs in a madhouse."

Nixon, for his part, distrusted Kissinger's sincerity in all matters— rightly, in many instances—and felt, again often rightly, that Kissinger talked down to him. Nixon called him "Jew boy" both behind his back and to his face. Despite such disdain and distrust, their shared ambition and insecurities melded together into one of the most fascinating (and powerful and, depending on one's definition, successful) president-advisor relations in all of U.S. history. "Kissinger and Nixon both had degrees of paranoia," future secretary of state Lawrence Eagleburger said. "It led them to worry about each other, but it also led them to make common cause on perceived mutual enemies."

Coming into Richard Nixon's presidency, he and Henry Kissinger both believed that ending the Vietnam War would cement their legacies as great men. Nixon had brought Kissinger into his White House as part of a broader effort to reshape and remake the apparatus of American foreign policy. "I've always thought that this country could run itself domestically without a president. All you need is a competent Cabinet to run the country at home," he said in 1967. "You need a president for foreign policy."

Nixon had combined the presidential national security advisor and the White House's internal National Security Council into a single entity under Kissinger—to guide foreign policy directly from the president's desk. Kissinger enlisted a generation of up-and-coming aides, like army colonel Al Haig and a fellow Harvard faculty member turned Pentagon advisor, Morton Halperin, to assemble the bureaucracy necessary to feed Nixon's agenda.

The National Security Council, established as part of the post–World War II reorganization in 1947, had until then existed as a cautious, consensus-focused planning mechanism that had little to offer presidents during a crisis and little connection to a president's own foreign policy objectives.* Nixon knew, though, that he wanted nothing to do with the State Department—purposefully choosing an uninspiring secretary of state in William P. Rogers—and even less to do with the effete Ivy Leaguers of the CIA. Under Kissinger's leadership, Nixon wanted the NSC transformed into the main instrument of American power and vision.

Kissinger aggressively vacuumed up the administration's foreign policy, running roughshod over the beleaguered and disrespected Rogers and Defense Secretary Melvin Laird, making it clear he and the president

---

* When JFK faced the Cuban Missile Crisis, he created something called the "ExComm," an executive committee of both National Security Council members and other advisors he thought would be valuable, to help lead the crisis planning and response efforts.

stood alone atop the hill. "[Nixon and Kissinger] both had a penchant for secrecy, a distaste for sharing credit with others, and a romantic view of themselves as loners," Kissinger's biographer Walter Isaacson wrote. Roger Morris says that "the brutal truth was that, at heart, neither man had a steadfast faith in the democratic process, least of all as applied to the conduct of foreign policy." The pace was grueling—one-third of the twenty-eight staff members Kissinger hired didn't last the first nine months of the administration—but "a listing of the Kissinger staff read like a *Who's Who* of some of the brightest, most innovative geopolitical thinkers in the country," according to journalists Rowland Evans and Robert Novak. (Many, as Kissinger would later regret, were Democrats— veterans of JFK's or LBJ's administrations, men in Nixon's eyes who could never be trusted.)

*   *   *

Despite the hard work and smart minds, peace in Vietnam proved elusive. Early in his presidency, Nixon tried a strategy to raise the war's stakes and force the North Vietnamese back to the bargaining table, ordering the air force's massive, lumbering B-52 bombers—the brontosauruses of the sky—to begin secretly targeting North Vietnamese and Viet Cong supply chains and bases in Cambodia. He had lied about the move to the American people, the U.S. soldiers on the ground in Vietnam, and even to the planes' own crews—only the pilots and navigators under-stood the secret that they were dropping bombs on another country. It was an escalation he hoped would send a signal to the North Vietnamese without provoking further ire from U.S. antiwar protesters. Word of the bombing, though, leaked, and *New York Times* reporter William Beecher wrote about the raids on May 9, 1969.

Kissinger flew into a rage as he read the newspapers that morning with other White House staff, in his customary sun-drenched, poolside perch in Key Biscayne, Florida, where they waited while President Nixon lounged on his friend Bebe Rebozo's houseboat *Coco-Lobo*. All through that first spring of the administration, Nixon felt his position negotiating a peace was constantly being compromised by press leaks—according to a careful tally during his first five months, they had already faced twenty-one serious leaks—and here was one of the most secret moves of the nascent administration splashed all over the front page. Nixon, when he saw the story, raged too: "What is this cock-sucking story? Find out who leaked it, and fire him," he told Kissinger.

Kissinger called J. Edgar Hoover. As the longtime FBI director wrote to his deputies after, recounting the conversation, "Dr. Kissinger said they wondered whether I could make a major effort to find out where that came from. I said I would." Hoover added that the national security advisor wanted the FBI "to put whatever resources I need to find who did this" and then "they will destroy whoever did this if we can find him, no matter where he is."

By day's end, Hoover had moved forward with a series of wiretaps to bust the leaker. (Kissinger had already settled on a likely culprit: his NSC aide Morton Halperin, a Johnson administration holdover and assumed liberal.)* Starting with the four most likely suspects, the target group swelled eventually to eighteen administration staff, including seven on the National Security Council and three at the White House—names personally delivered to the FBI's assistant director, William Sullivan, by Kissinger's deputy Al Haig.† Haig said he was operating on "the highest authority" and asked that the operation be conducted in total secrecy, with no written record of the wiretaps, but Sullivan explained that it could never be kept entirely secret inside the bureau since each wiretap would require the work of at least eight agents, technicians, and typists. Later, paperwork appeared with John Mitchell's signature at the bottom of the forms authorizing the wiretaps on presidential staff. (Mitchell always denied signing such authorizations.)

Haldeman was baffled by the theatrics of the whole wiretapping endeavor. "The FBI would place the summaries in envelopes for delivery," he recalled. "Every now and then on my way into my office or in a hotel

---

* One of the oddities of this entire episode was that Halperin hadn't worked on the Cambodia raids; he told Kissinger after he didn't even know if Beecher's story in the *New York Times* was accurate.

† The total number of so-called "Kissinger wiretaps" is usually listed as seventeen, because the FBI, which struggled to re-create who had been tapped and when, had initially failed to include NSC staffer Richard Sneider on the list. "Simply . . . no one remembered it," Mark Felt wrote later.

corridor on a trip, a man would suddenly jump out of a dark doorway, thrust an envelope in my hand, then disappear into the night." For his part, Haig visited the FBI's Sullivan to read over some of the wiretap summaries personally, and Sullivan sent some thirty-seven regular updates to Kissinger's office from May 1969 to May 1970. Even more, fifty-two, went to Haldeman. The documents and wiretap transcripts inside were all but useless. "A dry hole. Just globs and globs of crap," Nixon himself would conclude.

Frustrated by the lack of progress, Nixon himself ordered the list expanded further: The FBI had, for some reason, told the White House that syndicated columnist Joseph Kraft's phone was "untappable," so Nixon had Ehrlichman do it himself. Ehrlichman outsourced the project to a former NYPD detective, Jack Caulfield, who had joined the White House team to help out on various investigative tasks, and Caulfield then also enlisted a former FBI agent named John "Jack" Ragan. Ragan had been one of the bureau's top wiretap experts, targeting Soviet spies at its UN mission in New York, and had worked with Caulfield to secure the '68 campaign's hotel rooms from electronic surveillance. Now he was working security for the Republican National Committee and began a much more homegrown covert operation: He and another man surreptitiously tapped one of the phones in Kraft's home by climbing a ladder alongside the building, only to discover that Kraft was in Paris, attending the peace talks. Finally, the frustrated order came down for the FBI's Sullivan to travel to France and have authorities wiretap Kraft there. As weeks passed, journalists were added to the FBI target list too—the *New York Times* correspondents Hedrick Smith and Tad Szulc, as well as CBS reporter Marvin Kalb. Week by week, month by month, the wiretaps continued—never quite delivering the intelligence the White House hoped for.

The operation, as unsuccessful as it was, had laid the groundwork for the response to the Pentagon Papers, seeding the administration's taste for spying on its enemies—real or imagined. Now, just months after the end of those Kissinger wiretaps—begun too as a reaction to the damaging leaks about Vietnam—the Pentagon Papers represented another major leak about the war and one that Kissinger feared for entirely different reasons.

Chapter 2

"Ellsberg? I've Never Heard of Him"

Of the two and a half million words spread across the forty-three volumes of the Pentagon Papers, not a single one of them was "Nixon." The study, the brainchild of Robert McNamara, had been commissioned in 1967 as a postmortem of the Kennedy and Johnson administrations' push into Southeast Asia, designed to cut through a decade of government obfuscation and bureaucratic back-patting. When the *Times* published its findings, the gaping chasm between the government's rosy public statements—lies, really—and its dark internal assessments shocked the nation. The detailed indictment of the nation's military strategy, such as it was, astounded readers with the government's mendacity and cynicism, as the country had flushed a generation of blood and countless treasure into the jungles, rice paddies, and river deltas of Vietnam. "You know, they could hang people for what's in there," McNamara had said to a friend once. Giants of American politics and policy who had advocated for the war were all equally exposed and damaged—all, that is, except for the current occupant of the White House, who had instead spent the decade in political exile in New York.

His absence from the main story is why, presumably, the historical study caused Nixon little concern that Sunday as he read it among the wedding coverage. When Kissinger's aide Alexander Haig asked Nixon mid-day if he'd seen "this goddamn *New York Times* expose of the most highly classified documents of the war," Nixon admitted he hadn't even read the article.

"This is a devastating security breach of the greatest magnitude I've ever seen," Haig continued.

"Well what's being done about it?" Nixon asked, figuring that the simplest reaction would be just to hold the leakers responsible: "I would just start right at the top and fire some people." As Haig explained that the documents were years old and predated Nixon's administration, Nixon's enthusiasm waned. After realizing that his White House was exempt from the outrage, he told Haldeman Sunday they should "keep out of it." The only thing that really bothered him was the way the content had been released, not the content itself. As Ehrlichman said, "Had some process removed the Top Secret stamps from those pages, Nixon would have no objection to their publication."

*　　*　　*

Indeed, it first appeared that the scandal might skip the Nixon administration entirely; when Defense Secretary Melvin Laird appeared on *Meet the Press* that Sunday morning, just hours after the *Times* exposé was released, he wasn't even asked about it. Across the administration, officials shrugged; neither John Mitchell, William Rehnquist, or Robert Mardian, the three leaders at the Justice Department who might be concerned about a publication of national security secrets, apparently paid any special attention to the report on Sunday. Journalist Fred Emery recalls phoning a State Department official Sunday afternoon for reaction, only to be apologetically told that the source hadn't picked up his copy of the *Times* yet.

There was just one man inside the administration who was furious: Henry Kissinger. He fired up the president during a long telephone call from California. "It shows you're a weakling, Mr. President," the national security advisor admonished. "The fact that some idiot can publish all of the diplomatic secrets of this country on his own is damaging to your image, as far as the Soviets are concerned, and it could destroy our ability to conduct foreign policy."

Even though the *Times* didn't name its source, it didn't take long for official Washington to realize who had given the paper its intel. There were only fifteen copies of the top-secret study, and a former RAND analyst named Daniel Ellsberg had been peddling a photocopied version around Capitol Hill, trying to interest a leading Democratic foreign policy voice like William Fulbright or George McGovern in confronting the war's lies.

"Ellsberg? I've never heard of him," Nixon said, still not appearing to care as he heard the rumored source from Haig.

Kissinger, though, knew the name all too well—and his anger at the leak, in retrospect, seems to be not insignificantly driven by self-interest. He had served as a mentor to the young analyst and had enlisted him early in the Nixon administration in a separate study of what to do in Vietnam. "Henry had a problem because Ellsberg had been one of his 'boys,'" Haldeman recalled later. That the leaker could be so closely tied to Kissinger could cast suspicion on his staffing choices and decisions, doing untold damage to Kissinger's reputation with the president.* The next day, when Kissinger returned to Washington, Haldeman told Ehrlichman, "The two of them are in a frenzy."

On Monday morning, June 14, 1971, as the White House staff talked over how to respond to the papers, even the pugilistic Chuck Colson recalled being startled by Kissinger's rage. Coffee cups rattled as the national security advisor pounded his fist on the antique table, fuming, "These leaks are slowly and systematically destroying us." Turning to Haldeman, Kissinger said, "Bob, the President must act—today! There is wholesale subversion of this government underway."

Within hours, Kissinger had convinced the president to be outraged too. Nixon understood that his presidency would be won or lost in its foreign policy—he needed to achieve "monuments," he'd said after the 1970 midterm elections—and he'd been working hard in utter secrecy on two critical potential victories: bringing the Vietnam War to a close and developing a relationship with China, which had been closed to the

---

* Kissinger's version of his outrage at the Pentagon Papers, told in his memoirs, is decidedly more self-serving than the version that emerges from other memoirs and accounts. Kissinger, effectively, says all the outrage was Nixon's and that he "shared Nixon's views."

United States for a quarter century. He also had been working more publicly to pry open the Iron Curtain—becoming in 1969 the first president to visit a Communist country (Romania) and setting up a historic visit to Moscow itself for the summer of 1972, ushering in what he hoped would be an era of "détente" and a stable, peaceful international order. "Once this thing gets going—everything is beginning to fit together," Kissinger told him, optimistically.

The Pentagon Papers threatened all that. Not only would their grand triumphs crumble if leaked prematurely, the very contents of the study could unravel Nixon and Kissinger's careful diplomacy. Unpublished portions of the Pentagon Papers contained references to secret U-2 surveillance flights through Chinese airspace that, while no mystery to the Chinese, would cause public embarrassment if published and torpedo further talks with the closed regime.

By Monday afternoon, the administration had decided to go to war with the *New York Times* as well as the man who had leaked it the secret papers.

* * *

In a conversation with Kissinger and his attorney general, John Mitchell, that Monday, Nixon asked Mitchell for advice about crafting a strong White House response. The head of the Justice Department said, incorrectly, that his department and previous administrations had gone after other newspapers for similar actions—seemingly a green light for Nixon to do the same.

"What is your advice on that *Times* thing, John? You would like to do it?" the president asked.

"I would believe so, Mr. President. Otherwise, we will look a little foolish in not following through on our legal obligations and—"

"Has this ever been done before?" Nixon asked. "Has the government ever done this to a paper before?"

"Yes, we've done this before," Mitchell said confidently.

Soon after his conversation with Nixon, John Mitchell contacted the *Times* and asked in an official capacity that it cease publishing the study, citing national security secrets. The *Times* refused. In retaliation, Nixon quietly ordered that the administration break off all White House contact with the newspaper and its Washington bureau, headed by Max Frankel. "Don't give them anything," Nixon told Haldeman. "And because of that damned Jew Frankel all the time—he's bad, you know. Don't give him anything."

Following the president's direction, the Justice Department moved quickly to confront the paper legally, filing for a restraining order against the *Times* to prevent it from publishing additional sections of the Pentagon Papers. The *Times* accepted the restraining order, and court arguments were set for Friday, June 18. Friday morning, the *Washington Post* stunned the nation when it released its own stories based on copies of the study that it had obtained, one of the most significant decisions in the history of the paper—until then, it had never been a national player on the order of the *Los Angeles Times* or the *New York Times*. Katharine Graham, whose family had bought the *Post* out of bankruptcy in the Great Depression, had become the paper's publisher in 1963 after the death of her husband; two years later, she'd brought Ben Bradlee in as executive editor, and together they worked to burnish its reputation. The partnership between Graham—the glamorous, wealthy reigning doyenne of the D.C. social circuit—and Bradlee—rakish, handsome, devilishly fashionable with his signature French-cuff Turnbull & Asser shirts, and known for his close friendship with JFK—would be one of the most transformative in American journalism, and no single moment in their thirty-year career together would compare with the pressure, ambition, and risk that came with this one. The move coincided with the *Post*'s IPO, and the paper's lawyers and bankers feared that moving ahead with the reporting might sink the whole initial public offering. Graham said, simply, "Let's go. Let's publish."

Angered by Graham's decision, the government announced quickly it would move to restrain the *Washington Post* too. That strategy crumbled as soon as the *Boston Globe* began publishing excerpts as well, followed by the *Chicago Sun-Times*, and ultimately a dozen papers across the country. That weekend, Judge Murray Gurfein rejected the restraining order and allowed the *Times* to resume publishing, writing, "The security of the Nation is not at the ramparts alone. Security also lies in the value of our free institutions. A cantankerous press, an obstinate press, a ubiquitous press must be suffered by those in authority in order to preserve the even greater values of freedom of expression and the right of the people to know."

For days, the newspapers and the Justice Department battled in court in both New York and Washington, eventually reaching the highest court in the land. On June 30, a 6–3 Supreme Court issued a landmark ruling in favor of the freedom of the press, holding that the government had very limited ability to exert prior restraint on the media's ability to publish.*

The case—and the resulting public relations—was nothing short of a disaster for Nixon. In just a few short weeks, the administration's reaction had turned the Pentagon Papers from an airing of the dirtiest laundry of his predecessors into a self-inflicted wound, a prime example of Nixon's own secrecy and distemper.

What's more, Ellsberg had become a symbol of truth and patriotism as journalists and authorities confirmed his involvement. While the FBI raced to track the analyst down, he'd given an interview on June 23 to Walter Cronkite for the *CBS Evening News*, saying, "I hope that the truth that's out now—it's out in the press, it's out in homes, where it should be, where voters can discuss it, it's out of the safes and there is no way to get it back into the safes—I hope that truth will free us of this war." Five days later, he surrendered to federal authorities in Boston, walking arm in arm with his wife into the courthouse, where he was charged with theft and violation of the Espionage Act. More than 150 people cheered him on as he finally admitted to leaking the study.

Behind closed doors, Nixon's rage continued. Supreme Court Justice Potter Stewart, he railed, was a "weak bastard" who had been "overwhelmed by the Washington-Georgetown set." He ordered his aides to take matters into their own hands; if the courts wouldn't stand up for the country and shut down the leaks, they had to do it themselves. "We've got a counter-government here and we've got to fight it. I don't give a damn how it is done, do whatever has to be done to stop these leaks,"

* *The New York Times v. United States*, widely remembered as a seminal freedom of the press case, is far more ambiguous when viewed closely; the majority of six justices wrote six individual concurring opinions, each laying out slightly different tests and limits on the government's censorship capabilities.

Nixon told his aide Chuck Colson. "I don't want to be told why it can't be done. This government cannot survive, it cannot function if anyone can run out and leak."

It was a dangerous set of instructions to give Charles "Chuck" Colson, who represented the closest thing that existed in the White House to the President's id. Colson, his White House colleague Herb Klein said, "was one of the meanest people I ever knew," adding, "Nixon, on occasion, would be angry; he'd say, 'I think we ought to punch that guy on the nose,' and if your name was Herb Klein, or Bob Haldeman, or Bob Finch, we'd ignore it, and in a couple of days, he'd say, 'You never really did punch him, did you?' Colson's nature was to punch him twice." Many saw him as a whirling dervish of activity, schemes, and political machinations—"He always had about sixteen balls in the air at any one time, and he would not stop kicking them until he hit an absolute brick wall," his assistant Henry Cashen recalled later—but few missed the significance that Colson's office suite, Room 184 in the Executive Office Building, was right next to Nixon's chosen hideaway office.

A longtime Nixon fan and former campaign aide, he'd demonstrated early that he would do anything to please the president. One Friday afternoon, he noted an offhand comment by a frustrated Nixon that he wanted an executive order ready by Monday to fulfill a campaign promise and help the nation's Catholic schools—Haldeman, Ehrlichman, and others had been slow-rolling the request for months—but Colson, through a mix of force of will and procedural corner-cutting, managed to execute it, delivering an executive order to Nixon when the weekend was over. Nixon had finally found the accomplice he'd been looking for. "Within a short time, more egos were getting broken by Colson, who relished the bull-in-a-china-shop role that the president was encouraging him to play," his biographer wrote.

Colson carved out a role he described as "the president's liaison with the outside world," helping to translate Nixon to party activists beyond and vice versa. Unlike Nixon's other senior aides, whose loyalty to the Republican Party began and ended with Nixon personally, Colson was a forceful and committed conservative and wanted to shape the party's historic arc. He relished planting stories, favorable or unfavorable, and organized countless groups—Catholics for Nixon, Labor for Nixon, and so forth—seemingly able to instantly manufacture supportive telegrams, letters to the editor, or op-eds from activists and party leaders around the country, to both bolster Nixon's initiatives as well as pressure the White House toward action.

Haldeman had initially welcomed Colson's addition to the inner circle because the aide's presence freed up some of his own time—he hated talking politics with Nixon (and even more so hated listening to Nixon as he talked politics), whereas Colson, who wore thick-rimmed glasses and a perpetually bemused look, eyebrow seemingly half-cocked for a joke coming just around the corner, was happy to talk endlessly about it, trading gossip and political tidbits and Monday-morning quarterbacking recent developments. Only with time did Haldeman come to see the devil's bargain he'd made. "Chuck sat and listened, and wrote it down, and went out and did it," Haldeman lamented. Nixon speechwriter Ray Price once asked John Mitchell, "Who is Colson's constituency?" The attorney general's answer was blunt: "The president's worst instincts."

Colson managed to exist in the White House outside the normal organizational channels; no one was ever really sure what he and his two dozen staff were working on. His connection to so many of Nixon's most loyal—and needed—backers meant he had access to almost any conversation and a seemingly endless series of projects and secret missions; each project he kept organized on a separate yellow legal pad, such that he'd regularly appear in the Oval Office carrying seven or eight pads to discuss a myriad of projects. "We had a very good staff system, and the Nixon-Colson relationship cut across that system; it short-circuited it," Ehrlichman recalled. "Nixon bridled against the staff. The staff system, in a sense, required him to arrive rationally at decisions, where Colson did not, so he was able to vent his spleen, and had someone who would do things for him that, on judgment, the rest of the staff wouldn't have."

In fact, Nixon seemed to relish creating such adversarial and competitive staff relationships. He sometimes dispatched all three of his aides on the same project—as Haldeman would explain later, "I was the man for the straight, hit-them-over-the-head strategy. Ehrlichman, who loved intrigue, was given the more devious approach. And Colson was assigned the real underground routes." His speechwriting team existed in similar three-way tension: Pat Buchanan on the far right, Ray Price in the conservative middle, and William Safire on the more moderate end—each competing in their prose to win Nixon's favor and direct him.

Moreover, the less each aide knew about what the others were doing, the better, since Nixon compartmentalized and kept secrets as a standard practice. "Secrecy was a high principle—congenial, not only to his guarded personality but to his perception of the world," biographer Tom Wicker wrote later. "Most of us operated in watertight compartments, unaware of what Nixon was ordering our colleagues to do," Ehrlichman wrote later.*

Now, instructed by the president to stop the leaks, Chuck Colson's devious, ever-inventive mind began to churn.

---

* Kissinger's view was similar. "The relation of the various Nixon aides to one another was like that of prisoners in adjoining cells. They might hear something about the scale of the activity; proximity did not invite participation or intimate knowledge."

Chapter 3

The Chennault Affair

While Nixon's near-obsessive targeting of the press amid the Pentagon Papers scandal may have appeared reflexive—another battle in his lifelong war against the media—time has made clear it was more personal and more preventative. As the days after the initial leak passed, he became ever more worried that further revelations about the Johnson years and its Vietnam strategy might expose his darkest campaign secret.

As a politician, Nixon had always been up for spy games and deceit. "He just could not leave intrigue alone. He loved it; he loved politics; he loved the intrigue side," Ehrlichman recalled later.* Nixon's campaigns had always been accompanied by an abnormal level of dirty tricks, skullduggery, and outrageous allegations against his opponents; his own loathsomeness, in turn, had attracted such tactics against him from opponents who hated him as much as he them. For nearly his entire career, he had been dogged by a Democratic operative named Dick Tuck who had made pranking Nixon into a personal hobby. "It was easy to get combative," recalled an aide to Jerry Brown, Nixon's 1962 California

---

* As he began his first congressional race, against incumbent representative Jerry Voorhis, Nixon had scribbled down on one of his always ubiquitous yellow pads his to-do list: "Set up budget . . . office furniture . . . need for paid workers . . . call on newspapers, former candidates, leaders . . . arrange church and lodge and veterans meetings," and so forth. Then he added: "Set up . . . spies in V. camp."

gubernatorial opponent. "You're not running against a nice guy. You're running against a first-class son of a bitch."

Few campaign capers had gone so far as the mission Nixon, Kissinger, and John Mitchell had pulled off together in the closing months of the '68 presidential race. It is an episode that was deeply misunderstood in the contemporaneous period of Watergate; even today, the exact events that came to be known as the "Chennault Affair" remain hotly contested by historians, both because of the scant documentary evidence, much of which has emerged piecemeal from sealed archives decades after the fact, and the unreliability (and silence) of those involved.

The 1968 campaign had been one of the most tumultuous in U.S. memory. On the Republican side, Nixon had gotten into the race late, declaring his candidacy only on the final day of filing for the New Hampshire primary. The path to the GOP nomination had unexpectedly cleared for him, as Michigan governor George Romney dropped out and New York governor Nelson Rockefeller said he wouldn't run. Nixon romped through the primaries, only to see Rockefeller decide to reenter the race and attempt unsuccessfully, along with California governor Ronald Reagan, to deny Nixon the nomination at the Miami Beach convention. Alabama's George Wallace also staked a claim as a third-party candidate; standing as a proud segregationist, he aimed to block a majority winner in the electoral college and force the House of Representatives to decide the next president. The stalemate, he thought, would give him the chance to pressure the federal government to unwind its decade of efforts to desegregate the South amid the Civil Rights Movement.

As the fall began, the Democratic nominee, Johnson's vice president, Hubert Humphrey, faced a massive deficit both in polling and enthusiasm—barely ahead of Wallace in national numbers. Yet on September 30, 1968, the vice president broke from Johnson and called for a halt in the bombing of North Vietnam, saying he would take a "risk for peace." The change in tone and strategy worked, and Humphrey steadily closed the gap with Nixon every week through the end of the season.

Throughout the election year, the Johnson administration had been struggling to inch Vietnam peace talks forward in Paris and knew that it had to involve the president's possible successors in its efforts. Even before Nixon secured the nomination, Johnson invited him to the White

House for a briefing on the conditions he had set for suspending U.S. bombing, including North Vietnam respecting the Demilitarized Zone along its border with the South. The North Vietnamese had resisted LBJ's position, pushing instead for an unconditional bombing halt. He hoped that the candidate would either agree with his plan or at least respect the process so neither the South Vietnamese nor the North Vietnamese felt that by holding out through the fall, they'd get a better deal from a future Nixon administration.

Nixon, though, knew that a halt to the controversial bombing and the start of peace talks would be to Humphrey's benefit. Publicly, he deferred to LBJ, releasing an August statement saying the president's "emissaries in Paris must be able to speak with the full force and authority of the United States." Behind the scenes, however, he worked to undercut the U.S. negotiating position, keeping track of key developments in the Paris peace talks via Kissinger, who was engaged in his own campaign of subterfuge—advising Johnson's team even as he slipped details to Nixon's camp.* Kissinger at that point had established himself as one of the nation's top experts on the Vietnam War and had spent months in 1967 secretly trading messages with the North Vietnamese government to start the peace process.

In late October, the stalemate in the Paris negotiations began to break, as the North Vietnamese eased their hard line on an unconditional bombing halt, but just as the conversations began to inch forward, strings of intelligence both in the U.S. and abroad warned the Johnson team that Nixon was up to something. The National Security Agency had intercepted communications from South Vietnam's ambassador back to his government referencing conversations with the "Nixon entourage" and saying that the closer the U.S. got to a Nixon victory, the better the position South Vietnam was in. The intercept appeared to confirm a tip

---

* Due to his proximity to power, the Nixon camp thought they'd scored a big win with Kissinger's new back channel ("He's a hard-nosed son-of-a-bitch," campaign foreign policy aide Richard Allen remarked), but he was really playing all sides: The former Rockefeller advisor was simultaneously bad-mouthing Nixon to his friends and volunteering to turn over to Humphrey's campaign the opposition research Rockefeller had accumulated, what Kissinger called the "shit files." (As Kissinger told Zbigniew Brzezinski, Humphrey's foreign policy advisor, "Look, I've hated Nixon for years.")

that Johnson's national security advisor Walt Rostow had received from well-connected sources in New York that the Nixon camp was trying to block the peace talks from moving forward. LBJ and aides began to debate the explosive revelation that a presidential candidate—technically a private citizen—was attempting to influence the U.S. government's foreign policy by interfering in diplomatic negotiations. "This thing could blow up into the biggest mess we've ever had if we're not careful here," Secretary of State Dean Rusk warned.

On October 30, 1968, President Johnson called Georgia senator Richard Russell, a close advisor, to talk through the problem. "I've got one this morning that's pretty rough for you: We have found that our friend, the Republican nominee, our California friend, has been playing on the outskirts with our enemies and our friends both, our allies and the others. He's been doing it through rather subterranean sources." Johnson explained to Russell that as far as he'd pieced together, Nixon's plot had involved a "fellow named [John] Mitchell, who's running his campaign" and "Mrs. [Anna] Chennault [who] is contacting [South Vietnam's] ambassador from time to time—seems to be kind of the go-between."

Chennault, the widow of a dashing World War II general who had led a volunteer air force known as the Flying Tigers against Japan as it invaded China, had become a key player in the "China lobby" in Washington, D.C., where she'd relocated after Mao Zedong's Communist Revolution. Known as "Little Flower" to her friends and "the Dragon Lady" to nearly everyone else, the petite and beautiful woman had grown into one of the capital's top socialites, presiding over extravagant gatherings in her $250,000, 4,500-square-foot Watergate penthouse, with its private rooftop garden. She'd grown particularly close to Republican circles, who had spent decades flaying Harry Truman and Democrats for "losing" China. In 1968, she was Nixon's top female fundraiser.

For much of that year, she'd been carefully dancing between South Vietnamese ambassador Bui Diem and Nixon, arranging two secret meetings between them that remained unknown until the 1980s.*

---

* Nearly everything about the meetings remains incredibly hazy; a few snatches of sentences and some scribbled notes in Chennault's datebook are the only signs they existed at all.

As best as can be reconstructed, Chennault had first brought Diem to New York to meet the candidate in his apartment on a snowy February day—Chennault's memoir refers to it as a Sunday, but her desk calendar appears to show it was Friday, February 16—and they visited New York again in July, apparently to meet at Nixon's campaign headquarters. The second meeting was highly clandestine, perhaps secret from everyone but Mitchell; Nixon himself was concerned about the Secret Service finding out. It stretched more than an hour—hardly a perfunctory grip-and-grin.

The agendas of the meetings also remain sketchy; the only accounts that exist, from Diem and Chennault, appear to mix and match the events of the two meetings. According to Chennault, Nixon told Diem during their conversations that she would be his voice to South Vietnam: "Please rely on her from now on as the contact between myself and your government." Diem remembers Nixon saying something less definitive, but confirmed that he'd be in touch through both Chennault and Mitchell.

This communication channel evidently continued through the fall, though it's hard to say how frequently, as Chennault's normal involvement on the campaign fundraising side meant she and Mitchell were in touch regularly (daily, she claims). "Anna Chennault was an ideal intermediary, bright, resourceful, acting from deepest conviction, with only the drawbacks of being a bit too conspicuous and not always discreet in speech and action," concluded historian William Bundy, in his history of Nixon's foreign policy. On October 23, Diem cabled home an oblique message that seemed to reference the Nixon team: "Many Republican friends have contacted me and encouraged us to stand firm."

In those closing days of October, his suspicions aroused by Rostow's tip, LBJ ordered the FBI to place a wiretap on the South Vietnamese embassy, to surveil and report on everyone entering and departing the building, and to place a surveillance team on Chennault herself.* The dragnet immediately raised red flags, catching a conversation where a

---

* The FBI, though, declined a presidential order to place a wiretap on Chennault's phone; since she was so involved in Republican politics, the bureau worried about what it might overhear; as FBI deputy Deke DeLoach wrote Clyde Tolson on October 28, "If it became known that the FBI was surveilling her, this would put us in a most untenable and embarrassing position."

woman told the ambassador she'd stop by after a luncheon for Spiro Agnew's wife, followed by Chennault arriving at the embassy for a thirty-minute visit.*

Any attempt to confront Nixon was complicated by both political and security implications; the NSA couldn't exactly announce it was intercepting its ally's diplomatic cables. Instead, Johnson tried to warn him off through an intermediary, calling the Republican Senate minority leader, Everett Dirksen, and speaking in general terms about the plot. "It's despicable," Johnson spat. "If it were made public, it would rock the nation." He said, "I really think it's a little dirty pool for Dick's people to be messing with the South Vietnamese ambassador and carrying messages around to both of them." The campaign, Johnson declared, "better keep Mrs. Chennault and all this crowd just tied up for a few days."

That evening, on Thursday, October 31, around 6 p.m. LBJ assembled a private conference call with all three main presidential candidates—Humphrey, Nixon, and Wallace—to update them on the peace talk status. During the call, he made sure to deliver a casual, pointed warning against any domestic political interference, explaining that "some of the old China lobbyists . . . are going around and implying to some of the embassies and some of the others that they might get a better deal out of somebody not involved in this. Now, that's made it difficult and it's held things up a bit."

That night, Johnson gave a national televised address, trumpeting his peace talk progress—announcing his order "that all air, naval, and artillery bombardment of North Vietnam cease as of 8 a.m. Washington time, Friday morning." The peace talks would kick off the following Wednesday, the day after the election. It seemed a massive development, a rare sign of hope in a war that had dragged on and only worsened for years. That same night, Nixon hosted his own televised event from Madison Square Garden, a rally where he announced with his running mate Spiro Agnew, "Neither he nor I will destroy the chance of peace. We want peace." Soon after, though, Mitchell phoned Chennault with a very different message: "Anna, I'm speaking on behalf of Mr. Nixon. It's

---

* Chennault was hard to miss around town as she drove in a chauffeured maroon Lincoln Continental.

very important that our Vietnamese friends understand the Republican position, and I hope you have made that very clear to them."

Over the final five days of the presidential race, the Paris peace talks seemed to live and die almost by the hour. On Saturday, South Vietnam's president announced his country would boycott, refusing to be seated alongside an expected delegation from the Viet Cong. Nixon's team also spread anonymous—and false—allegations from a "Nixon confidant" that the campaigns had been reassured by Johnson that "all the diplomatic ducks were in a row," undercutting LBJ's credibility.

Johnson's anger only deepened when at 8:34 that Saturday night he got the latest FBI report on Madame Chennault, saying she'd "contacted Vietnamese ambassador Bui Diem and advised him that she received a message from her boss (not further identified) which her boss wanted her to give personally to the ambassador . . . 'Hold on, we are gonna win.'" Chennault had told the ambassador that her boss had just called from New Mexico, setting off a quick scramble by LBJ's national security advisor to figure out where Nixon was; they discovered that while Nixon hadn't been in the state that day, Spiro Agnew had, visiting Albuquerque. "The New Mexico reference may indicate Agnew is acting," Walt Rostow reported back to Johnson.*

Less than forty-five minutes later, the president was on the phone to the Republican Senate leader Dirksen again, laying out circumspectly the new evidence. "They oughtn't to be doing this," Johnson said. "This is treason."

"I know," Dirksen replied.

"I can identify them, because I know who's doing this. I don't want to identify it. I think it would shock America if a principal candidate was playing with a source like this on a matter this important," he continued.

As intended, Johnson's message to Dirksen was promptly passed along to the Nixon camp. Campaign aide Bryce Harlow wrote to Haldeman that

---

* There's no evidence that Agnew or anyone in his entourage was actually involved; a more plausible explanation, put forth by Chennault late in her life to her biographer Catherine Forslund, is that the FBI technicians misheard her say "New Hampshire," which was where John Mitchell was that particular day. The explanation that Chennault's orders were coming from Mitchell in New Hampshire is backed up by handwritten notes from Richard Allen, uncovered in the Hoover Institution Archives by journalist Shane O'Sullivan.

night: "LBJ called Dirksen—says he knows Repubs through D. Lady are keeping SVN in president position if this proves true—and persists—he will go to nation & blast Reps and RN. Dirksen very concerned."

Within twenty-four hours, Johnson also confronted Nixon directly by phone. Nixon denied it all; whatever Anna Chennault was doing, he said, it was freelance, unsanctioned, and he had no idea what she was saying.

On Monday morning, the FBI surveillance noted the *Christian Science Monitor*'s Washington bureau chief leaving the embassy and heading to the White House, where Rostow was told that the paper needed comment on "a sensational dispatch from Saigon . . . the 1st para of which reads: 'Purported political encouragement from the Richard Nixon campaign was a significant factor in the last-minute decision of President Thieu's refusal to send a delegation to the Paris peace talks—at least until the American Presidential election is over."

Through the afternoon, Johnson debated how to handle the story and whether to confirm it, aware that all their evidence came from secret intelligence and wiretaps. "I do not believe that any president can make any use of interceptions or telephone taps in any way that would involve politics," Dean Rusk advised. "The moment we cross over that divide, we're in a different kind of society."

Johnson agreed, and in the end the *Christian Science Monitor* story didn't run. The final polls were too close to call; Gallup had Nixon leading Humphrey 42–40, with Wallace at 14, and Harris had Humphrey up 43–40. Nixon would win by about seven-tenths of a percent in the popular vote. Even at the last minute, the Chennault allegations might well have tipped the election to Humphrey—and the wobbling on Johnson's Paris peace talks, seemingly the latest in a long series of false hopes and promises from the White House, almost certainly did tip the election to Nixon.

In the days after, intercepted reports from the Chennault back channel continued to come in. After another Friday conversation between her and Diem, seemingly about arranging a visit by now President-elect Nixon to Saigon, Rostow wrote, "I think it's time to blow the whistle on these folks."

Again, though, Johnson's team remained publicly silent. As Defense Secretary Clark Clifford had said during the Monday pre-election debate, it didn't seem "good for the country to disclose the story and then possibly have a certain individual elected. It could cast his entire administration under such doubt that I think it would be inimical to our country's interests." Journalist Jules Witcover later wrote that Humphrey's decision not to out Nixon's subterfuge in the final hours of the campaign was "either one of the noblest in American political history or one of the great tactical blunders. Possibly it was both."

On November 11, Johnson welcomed Nixon to the White House—"No visiting head of state of government has been given a warmer reception than the President gave Richard Nixon today," NBC News reported that day.

Kissinger, thanks in part to his loyalty and duplicity, was rewarded with his dream job of Nixon's national security advisor.

Until the day he died, Nixon would deny that he'd done anything wrong or had any improper communications with the South Vietnamese government. A garbled, inaccurate version of the episode was published in Teddy White's *Making of the President 1968* book in July 1969, blaming Chennault for meddling in the peace talks of her own accord—White reported that Nixon's team was appalled to learn that "she had taken his name and authority in vain" and repudiated the overtures instantly—but the truth, of course, was far from that. In recent years, however, Nixon biographer Jay Farrell found an apparent smoking gun: In Haldeman's notes of a conversation on October 22, Haldeman scribbled: "Keep Anna Chennault working on SVN." Later, he wrote, "Any other way to monkey wrench it?" Chennault kept her mouth shut—but she wasn't happy about it. Locked out of the administration despite her prodigious fundraising, she complained directly to President Nixon at an event.*

The gamble, though, had worked. Nixon won. And his deceit never surfaced. As Nixon's team began the move to Washington, John Mitchell asked Anna Chennault to connect him with her apartment building's management. He had come to like the building during his many visits

---

* In the 1980s, her friend Tommy Corcoran would tell the *Washington Post*, "People have used Anna scandalously—Nixon in particular. I know exactly what Nixon said to her and then he repudiated her."

to her penthouse. He and Martha ultimately purchased a $151,880 three-bedroom duplex in the Watergate.*

Later, when the burglary cover-up began to break open in the spring of 1973, Walt Rostow recognized exactly what had happened. The Chennault Affair was the scandal's clear precursor. "They got away with it," he wrote privately. "As the same men faced the election of 1972 there was nothing in their previous experience with an operation of doubtful propriety (or, even, legality) to warn them off; and there were memories of how close an election could get and the possible utility of pressing to the limit—or beyond."

*　　*　　*

Now, as the flood of revelations about the Pentagon Papers and the government's lies in Vietnam spread across the nation's front pages and provoked a nationwide call for government honesty, Nixon and Kissinger each wondered whether their earlier duplicity would be outed. In fact, in 1970, Haldeman had assigned Tom Charles Huston to collect and study the government's evidence and assess the political risk of the controversy around the "bombing halt" becoming public. Huston researched and wrote a twelve-page memo—parts of which remain classified to this day—and concluded that while the political calculations by Johnson to help Humphrey with the bombing halt were bad, Nixon's actions might be worse. "The evidence in the case does not dispel the notion that we were somehow involved in the Chennault affair," he wrote, "and while release of this information would be most embarrassing to President Johnson, it would not be helpful to us either."†

---

* Chennault ran into the Mitchells one afternoon in the elevator. "If I had only known what a beautiful woman my husband's been working with, I would have been so jealous," Martha joked.

† In preparing his report, Huston managed to get unusually thorough cooperation from FBI Assistant Director Sullivan because LBJ's surveillance and wiretapping operation in the Chennault Affair was the work of Deke DeLoach, Sullivan's competitor internally to succeed Hoover. The work had left Huston convinced Nixon worked to sabotage the peace talks. "Clearly Mitchell was directly involved," he said in a 2008 oral history. "It's inconceivable to me that John Mitchell would be running around, you know, passing messages to the South Vietnamese government, et cetera, on his own initiative."

As the Oval Office conversation continued in the wake of the Pentagon Papers, Nixon fretted about one of the rumors that Huston had collected in his research the year before: that there was another secret report—a Pentagon Papers sequel of sorts—about the so-called "bombing halt" and the peace talks. Huston's research had reported remarkably specific intelligence about the report (remarkable, in part, because there's no sign the report ever existed) and outlined who had copies, including Johnson's defense secretary, Clark Clifford, and another Pentagon official, Paul Warnke. Another copy was said to be at the Brookings Institution with a former Warnke aide, Leslie Gelb. "All these documents are top secret and I am amazed that they have been allowed to fall into the hands of such obviously hostile people," Huston wrote at the time.

"I need it," Nixon told Haldeman on Thursday evening as they met in the Oval Office with Kissinger, Ehrlichman, and Ron Ziegler.

"Huston swears to god there's a file on it and it's at Brookings," his chief of staff replied.

"Bob, now do you remember Huston's plan?" Nixon asked. "Implement it."

Kissinger chimed in with agreement: "Brookings has no right to have classified documents."

"I want it implemented," Nixon repeated. "Goddamnit, get in and get those files—blow the safe and get it."

Everyone in the room would have grasped immediately the significance of Nixon's mid-rant reference to "Huston's plan"—a mention not of the aide's research into the bombing halt but his *other* secret career-defining work at the White House, an attempt to jump-start the nation's domestic security apparatus and tackle the societal chaos and radical extremists who threatened the nation's tranquillity generally and the presidency of Richard Nixon specifically.

Chapter 4

The Huston Plan

Beyond the White House fences, America's streets convulsed with social change, as Vietnam's poison coursed through the nation's political veins and changing rhythms and expectations spilled over into peaceful protests and violent riots. The antiwar demonstrations that had dominated TV news in 1968 showed no signs of abating as Nixon's presidency began. In fact, they were intensifying at a rapid clip. The movement the press had taken to calling the "New Left," "a fomentation of hippies, student protesters, political agitators, and revolutionaries," as historian Melissa Graves explained, was battling the government for the nation's soul, equipped with a long list of demands. They wanted civil rights, as the promises of *Brown v. Board of Education* and LBJ's Civil Rights Act remained out of reach in cities from Birmingham to Boston, and women's rights and abortion rights, as the platonic ideal of the 1950s stay-at-home, aproned housewife went up in a giant bonfire of bras and burst of sexual liberation. On June 28, 1969, New York police raided the Stonewall Inn in Greenwich Village, provoking a week of violent riots in support of gay rights. As Graves explained, "A sliver of young people stood ready to spark a revolution through civil disobedience and, if necessary, violence." Or, as Steve Bull, one of Nixon's Oval Office aides, said, "If you didn't experience it back then, you would have no idea how close we were to revolution. It was a very violent time."

As the head of the government the new era sought to disrupt, Nixon found himself the direct target. "It is becoming more obvious with every passing day that the men and the movement that broke Lyndon B. Johnson's authority in 1968 are out to break Richard M. Nixon in 1969," David Broder wrote in the *Washington Post* in Nixon's first year. Nixon had run on a platform of "law and order," to restore peace not just overseas but at home as well. ("In the '68 campaign, 'law and order' became one word," recalled one campaign aide.)

The start of 1970 coincided with a worrisome rise of violence, both foreign and domestic. "The evolutionary circle of violent dissent spawned an ugly offshoot: the urban underground of political terrorists urging murder and bombing," Nixon recalled in his own memoirs. Airline hijackings swelled, terror groups formed, New Left radicals launched bombing campaigns, and American cities were overcome with bomb threats—New York City saw more than four hundred of them in one twenty-four-hour period during Nixon's first year. Dozens of police officers, nearly forty in all, were being targeted and shot down in the streets by snipers. Street crime too had soared; crime statistics are notoriously fuzzy, but murders—a crime usually well documented—rose more than 60 percent in the 1960s, and the FBI calculated that overall violent crime skyrocketed 130 percent.

White House aide Jeb Stuart Magruder recalled that the building in the early years of the Nixon administration seemed in "a state of permanent crisis," everything both urgent and important.* "The result was a highly-charged atmosphere, one that encouraged a siege mentality," Magruder said. That atmosphere permeating Richard Nixon's administration wasn't just metaphorical; amid the political turmoil, protests, and riots that marked so much of the late sixties and early seventies, there were days the White House became a literal bunker. One Saturday staffers were startled to find three hundred soldiers from the 82nd Airborne

---

* Alexander Butterfield, Haldeman's top deputy, once wrote a lengthy after-action memo to account for every decision and elapsed minute to explain how he'd waited nineteen minutes to inform Haldeman and Nixon of the shooting of presidential candidate George Wallace on May 15, 1972. "You're really working a crisis center all the time," John Dean said.

Division bivouacked in the basement cafeteria of the Executive Office Building, the out-of-sight last line of defense in case the war protesters outside broke through the ring of D.C. municipal buses that had been parked nose-to-nose outside.

If Nixon was under literal and metaphoric siege, then the general marshaling his response was John Mitchell. Mitchell, bitingly humorous, with mischievous eyes, had made his career and fortune in municipal bonds—a uniquely hard, Byzantine, and yet critical grease for local government that, as journalist Teddy White summarized, "though lucrative scarcely teaches a man high respect for public officials." He had a habit of not returning phone calls, a basic skill and grace, that baffled those who understood how much his inattention rankled politicians. A local D.C. TV host once asked him what his personal philosophy and guiding principles were: "Pragmatism," he said, simply. He maintained a certain Sphinx-like quality even to his closest aides.

The two men had forged a unique partnership in 1966 when Mitchell convinced Nixon during his time in the political wilderness to merge their respective law firms, creating a 120-lawyer powerhouse. Nixon had entered New York law during the darkest period of his life, following his defeat for the California governor's office in 1962, and Mitchell had been one of the only New Yorkers to welcome him. The two men had a strange relationship—sometimes warm, sometimes chilly—but Nixon generally had great admiration for Mitchell. (The respect was not always mutual; Mitchell sometimes referred to Nixon behind his back as "Milhous," the middle name he loathed.)

As his campaign manager in '68, Mitchell embraced the "Southern Strategy," stirring division and peeling off the right wing of the Democratic Party, setting a model that would guide the GOP until the present day by embracing a vision for a new race-based politics that united white Americans under an "emerging Republican majority." That idea, later outlined in a 1969 book by that title, authored by onetime Mitchell aide Kevin Phillips, explained in Phillips's words how "the more Negroes who register as Democrats in the South, the sooner the Negrophobe whites will quit the Democrats and become Republicans." It was ugly and poisonous to American politics, but—like the Red Scare—remarkably effective.

Preternaturally cool and self-assured, confident in himself to the point of extreme arrogance, Mitchell stood at ease in powerful circles in a way that Nixon himself never was. "Of all the public officials I ever met in my life, he cared less about what people thought about him than anybody," William Ruckelshaus said. (At the '68 convention, Senator Howard Baker introduced Mitchell to his wife, who warmly greeted him, saying, "Oh, I've heard of you, you are in Mr. Nixon's law firm." Mitchell's reply was as frosty as Mrs. Baker's was warm: "No, madam, Mr. Nixon has joined *my* law firm.") Even after Nixon ascended to the presidency, Mitchell seemed to keep the upper hand. "It was less fraternal and more paternal—with Mitchell, the younger man by a year, often seeming to be the President's father figure," journalist J. Anthony Lukas wrote.

After their victory, Nixon desperately wanted him to serve in the administration. Mitchell turned down the offer. His wife, Martha—a lively and troubled soul with a serious alcohol problem—was institutionalized at the time, and Mitchell wanted to tend to her. He would later say that he turned down the job of attorney general twenty-six times before giving in, agreeing to serve only if Richard Kleindienst, who had also worked on the campaign, was named his deputy.

Kleindienst would come to know all too well the unique challenges of working alongside the imperturbable and impenetrable Mitchell. Whereas most people in politics loved to talk, Mitchell preferred silence; in his years as a municipal bond attorney he had developed the ability to drink in others' desires and needs while sharing few of his own. "He was, and is, an unusually self-contained person," Kleindienst recalled. "He had a superior intellect and a retentive mind, and was a good listener." However, a specific management challenge grew from his soft-spoken and understated approach: Mitchell didn't give directions clearly, and staff sometimes left meetings thinking they had his assent when they didn't. As deputy attorney general, Kleindienst found it was often his role to follow up with staff after meetings "to interpret in unequivocal language what Mitchell really intended."

In his new role, Mitchell came to personify the Nixon administration's get-tough approach on the hippies, yippies, and dope-smoking flower children, "the prime advocate of no-knock laws, wiretapping, stop and frisk, [and] preventive detention," Lukas wrote. *Newsweek* featured him on the cover, dubbing him "Mr. Law & Order."* In November 1969, he watched from his fifth-floor balcony at the Justice Department on Pennsylvania Avenue as one mass protest convulsed the capital. Thousands streamed by his office, some holding a giant papier-mâché effigy of his face. When protesters noticed the looming presence of the attorney general, they went wild. "We screamed 'Fuck you Mitchell, fuck you Mitchell,' and threw at him whatever debris we could find," one protester recalled. "He looked down calmly from the railing, which was far too high for our missiles, holding his pipe, and with great deliberation gave us the finger right back."

His unfettered disdain for the New Left was an attitude that the president supported and encouraged. To Nixon personally—and his team broadly—the inner-city riots and the antiwar demonstrators who marched on the capital and threw rocks at his limo during the inaugural parade were just as much of a threat as the nation's drugs and murders. "We're going to enforce the law against draft evaders, against radical students, against deserters, against civil disorders, and against street crime," Kleindienst promised. "If we find that any of these radical, revolutionary, anarchistic kids violate the law, we'll prosecute."

And yet as Nixon's team girded for battle, they found themselves, unexpectedly, fighting alone.

J. Edgar Hoover, the powerful and longtime head of the FBI, had made it very clear he wanted nothing to do with fighting Nixon's enemies. Hoover had been the head of the FBI for nearly a half century, growing an underpowered and outgunned corner of the Justice Department into the nation's premier federal law enforcement agency and exercising its power against all manner of political enemies, from Nazis and Communists to

---

* In a surprisingly short time frame, Mitchell's Justice Department made a real impact: His anti-crime initiatives in D.C., which as a federal jurisdiction Mitchell exerted control over and where Nixon had ordered, "[Push] hard on law and order," led to a decrease in crime in 1970, the first in fourteen years. The Nixon administration pushed nearly thirty pieces of anti-crime legislation through Congress, led prosecutions against top organized crime leaders, and made inroads on narcotics. In 1972, the FBI reported the first national drop in crime rates since the 1950s. The department's efforts were both macro and micro; his Justice Department, working with a young aide named John Dean, even narrowed the circumstances where government witnesses could escape criminal prosecution through seeking immunity, a policy change that would ironically later be used against both of them.

civil rights leaders and antiwar protesters. "Edgar," as he was known to many presidents, was, columnist Jack Anderson explained, "10 percent lawman and 90 percent bureaucrat." Little information came out about the bureau beyond what Hoover and his legions of public relations specialists and ghostwriters allowed; his regular appearances on Capitol Hill always conveyed ferocity and thoroughness, and his force of suit-wearing, white-shirted, white male G-men (the only Black agents were Hoover's driver and steward) seemed the embodiment of postwar America.

Over decades in Washington, Hoover had become an American institution unto himself, outmaneuvering and ingratiating himself with every occupant of the Oval Office through his personal toxic stew of political intelligence, blackmail, and sycophancy. Nominally, he reported to the attorney general, but few had tried to seriously challenge him. The lack of supervision and boundaries had reared its head in recent years as the sixties protest culture intensified; the once progressive Hoover had steadily grown more reactionary, suspecting evil in all manner of political opponents, particularly Martin Luther King, Jr., whom he'd spied upon and, in one of the FBI's darkest moments, encouraged to commit suicide.

Hoover had been careful to strike up a friendship with Nixon early in his political career, in part because the director knew the bureau had rejected the future president's special agent application in 1937, just after he graduated law school.* They shared common cause in the 1950s fighting Communists like Alger Hiss—driving that case forward had required a long, delicate dance between the young congressman and the even then veteran FBI director—and they became regular dining partners in Washington. Unlike many others in D.C., Hoover had kept in touch during Nixon's eight years out of power, hedging his bets in case the failed candidate wasn't done, and when he'd arrived again in D.C. victorious after the '68 election, Nixon had every belief the two men shared a personal warmth and understanding of the nation's true enemies. LBJ had even assured the incoming Nixon in a private conversation during the transition, "Dick, you will come to depend on Edgar.

---

* Later, Hoover always brushed aside the rejected application, saying the bureau hadn't been hiring then, but actually the recruiter who interviewed Nixon thought he was "lacking in aggression."

He is a pillar of strength in a city of weak men. You will rely on him time and time again to maintain security. He's the only one you can put your complete trust in."

Nixon was in for a rude surprise. By 1969 Hoover had lost the energy and enthusiasm for the dirty work he'd done for (and to) a half-dozen presidents. He was now past the federal mandatory retirement age—his continued service came through annual presidential waivers—and he increasingly feared that any embarrassment or scandal would be used to ease him out of office and into obscurity. As his health declined, so too did the quality of the bureau's operations. When FBI reports arrived at the White House, they rarely seemed thorough or well executed enough to inspire confidence. "In general, the FBI investigative work I saw was of poor quality. The Bureau dealt excessively in rumor, gossip, and conjecture," Ehrlichman observed, and he told colleagues that he sometimes even sent back reports that seemed too sloppy. By the spring of '69, he'd grown so frustrated with Hoover that he'd hired his own private investigator, a former NYPD detective named Jack Caulfield, onto the White House staff.

Even more troubling to Nixon's White House was that the FBI seemed reluctant to deliver the intelligence he felt his due as president—and which Hoover had happily delivered to his predecessors. Whereas the CIA's authority was carefully delineated at its creation by the National Security Act of 1947, the FBI had been created in 1908 with a one-paragraph order from the attorney general, and its precise jurisdiction remained amorphous, guided by a hodgepodge of executive orders, presidential whims, and Hoover's preferences; this ambiguity particularly existed when it came to the bureau's work on matters of "national security" rather than criminal law enforcement. (Asked at one point about the origin of its authority to monitor political dissidents and combat espionage in the U.S., the bureau pointed to a Civil War–era court decision and a three-paragraph letter from FDR and the secretary of state during World War II.)

For decades, Hoover's agents had regularly spied aggressively on domestic dissidents and political opponents—in his paranoia, he drew little distinction between the two, assuming that anyone who opposed the U.S. government was either a Communist operative or at least funded, knowingly or unknowingly, by Communists. "Hoover wanted the FBI to be the world's elite law enforcement agency, and he stretched the legal limits of domestic intelligence in his effort to do so," historian Melissa Graves wrote.

Congress had always given Hoover a long leash, but it had begun digging into the FBI's activities more closely during the Johnson admin-istration—Senator Edward Long had held hearings on FBI wiretaps in 1965—and Hoover had been surprised when President Johnson didn't leap to the bureau's defense.* "When that support was lacking, Mr. Hoover had no recourse but to gradually eliminate activities which were unfavorable to the bureau and which in turn risked public confidence," the CIA's James Jesus Angleton said later. Hoover that year asked one of the bureau's top internal watchdogs, W. Mark Felt, to review the FBI's wiretap procedures and wind down unnecessary or particularly trou-bling investigations. Felt found the FBI had been running seventy-eight dubiously legal wiretaps, and cut the program in half, seemingly with little effect on national security. The following year, fearful of possible publicity and embarrassment, Hoover all but ended what the bureau called its "black bag jobs"—the illegal break-ins and spy operations he'd long quietly authorized, which were named after the black bags agents carried full of lock-picks, skeleton keys, and burglary tools.

When Mitchell arrived as attorney general, he tried to refocus the Justice Department and the nation's broader security apparatus on the threat from the New Left—encouraging prosecutions, restarting the department's Internal Security Division, creating a "campus rebel-lion" task force, pushing to infiltrate radical groups and populate them with informers, and marshaling a score of federal agencies, from the army to the Secret Service, to monitor suspected subversives. Even the CIA,

---

* Warrantless government wiretaps, including of domestic radicals, were allowed for national security purposes until a June 1972 Supreme Court decision found them unconstitutional. In an 8–0 decision, the court rejected the administration claims that surveillance of political dissidents was allowed without court approval for intelligence and national security purposes. "History abundantly documents the tendency of government—however benevolent and benign in its motives—to view with suspicion those who most fervently dispute its policies," Justice Lewis Powell wrote. "The price of lawful public dissent must not be a dread of subjection to an unchecked surveillance power." The decision was seen as a stunning setback for Nixon's Justice Department since by that point Nixon had appointed four of the justices.

which was supposed to be legally prohibited from domestic operations, began keeping an eye on various radicals.

To a certain extent, the FBI played ball—the bureau embarked on one of the largest surveillance efforts in its history, known as the Counter Intelligence Program, COINTELPRO for short, targeting both left-wing groups like the Weather Underground and the Black Panthers, as well as right-wing groups like the Ku Klux Klan—but Hoover still drew the line against more aggressive and legally dubious surveillance tactics that he'd routinely allowed in the past.

Amid growing frustration with the FBI's intransigence, Nixon had tried to jump-start his partnership and rekindle his old friendship with the director by making a vanishingly rare journey to Hoover's home for dinner; on October 1, 1969, he, Mitchell, and Ehrlichman spent a surreal night in Hoover's dining room, where the windows were decorated with multicolored lava lamps, and listened as the director regaled the presidential party with stories of the FBI's old successes. "Hoover seemed to me like an old boxer who had taken too many punches," Ehrlichman concluded.

The lack of cooperation grew only worse. In February 1970, in a fit of anger over a meaningless incident where an FBI agent had shared information with the CIA, Hoover cut off all intelligence cooperation with other government intelligence agencies. The method was not altogether surprising—the director had never played well with others in government and regularly forced out FBI agents whose public profiles threatened his own—but it quickly created an untenable problem for the U.S. government.

On March 6, 1970, three massive explosions rocked Greenwich Village in New York; responding firefighters and police were stunned when they realized that members of the radical extremist group the Weather Underground had accidentally triggered one of their own incendiary devices while assembling bombs in a townhouse basement, killing three of the would-be bombers.

On April 30, 1970, Nixon announced that the U.S. and South Vietnam would invade Cambodia—he preferred the word "incursion," not invasion—a move that escalated the nation's crisis to a boil. The war he'd promised to end was now worse—and larger—than ever, and fresh protests and riots started across the country. On May 4, ill-trained, poorly led, and scared National Guard troops opened fire on a nonviolent protest at Kent State University in Ohio, killing four students and wounding nine others. The photo of Mary Ann Vecchio kneeling over the body of Jeffrey Miller, her face frozen in a silent mid-scream, ran in papers across the country. Within days, millions of students staged a strike. "Fuck Richard Nixon," they chanted at the Washington Monument. "Fuck Richard Nixon."* The night of May 14, amid a student riot with fires and overturned cars, police at Jackson State in Mississippi opened fire on a dormitory, thinking a sniper was inside; two students were killed. In New York City, construction workers angry at the lack of patriotism displayed by a nearby antiwar protest swarmed down from a skyscraper project and beat the protesters—the police refused to get involved—sparking a pro-Nixon backlash that would lead to twenty-five thousand "hard-hats" marching on City Hall and lower Manhattan. Late that May, the Weathermen issued a three-page "Declaration of a State of War," promising that they would "attack a symbol or institution of American injustice" within two weeks.

The looming threat to the nation—and to Nixon—seemed obvious, but he was losing faith in the institutions designed to keep the nation safe. As the president would later calculate in his memoirs, from January 1969 through that spring of 1970, there were "over 40,000 bombings, attempted bombings, and bomb threats—an average of over eighty a day. Over $21 million in property was destroyed. Forty-three people were killed." America was at war at home—and as far as Richard Nixon was concerned, Edgar no longer appeared interested in battle. He desperately needed to break Hoover's intelligence freeze and get his security agencies working together. "Nixon became convinced that he was faced with a hostile conspiracy," Kissinger recalled.

---

* In one of the strangest moments of his presidency—or any presidency—Nixon went to the Lincoln Monument personally at 4 a.m. a few nights later, hoping to make peace with the protesters and accompanied only by a handful of terrified Secret Service and his aide Egil "Bud" Krogh, who had happened to be at the White House when a radio alert went out that Nixon was unexpectedly leaving the building. For an hour, he rambled on with the crowd, talking Vietnam, Blacks, travel, and even college football. "Most of what he was saying was absurd," a student noted later. That same night, across town, a briefcase bomb exploded outside the offices of the National Guard Association.

In June, the White House handed Tom Charles Huston, the twenty-nine-year-old staff assistant and onetime army intelligence officer who had previously dug into the reality of the "bombing halt," an even more sensitive assignment: Reform the nation's domestic surveillance apparatus. An Indiana native, Huston was one of the administration's true conservatives—he'd led the national group Young Americans for Freedom, one of the major players in the New Right movement, helping to draft its founding principles at William F. Buckley's house in 1960 and campaigning passionately for Goldwater in '64. An early backer of Nixon, he joined the White House to do its morning news summary, where he'd proved himself a resourceful researcher and gradually inherited the domestic security portfolio. That spring, he'd been working on coordinating the fight against foreign terrorists—particularly airline hijackings—and had watched the spreading domestic violence with concern, warning after the Greenwich Village explosion that "the most logical target at some point in time for these people is the President and the White House."

Huston's new assignment was consistent with how many ill-fated projects in the Nixon world unfolded: A seemingly loyal staffer was handed an assignment based on personal interest that strayed far beyond his established knowledge or experience. As Ray Price, Huston's supposed supervisor at the White House, would write later, the young, "intense, cadaverous" aide was "overly obsessed with such matters as internal security and insufficiently sensitive to civil liberties." He had already shown an interest in weaponizing the organs of government against political enemies: In 1969, he and Nixon counselor Arthur Burns had pressed the Internal Revenue Service to focus on radicals, leftist groups, and so-called ideological organizations, an effort that led to the creation of a secret team known as the "Special Services Staff," which compiled files on 8,585 individuals and 2,873 organizations, including the Urban League, the American Civil Liberties Union, and the National Council of Churches. "What we cannot do in a courtroom via criminal prosecutions to curtail the activities of some of these groups, IRS could do by administrative action," one White House memo explained.

Now, as a starting point, he summoned Hoover's deputy William Sullivan to his office in the Executive Office Building; there, Sullivan sat under a portrait of John C. Calhoun, the infamous defender of slavery and states' rights, as the young White House aide recited an all too long list of recent FBI failures, including violent protests at Columbia University and a bombing at a University of Wisconsin lab that killed a young professor. Sullivan, who had years of his own complaints about Hoover built up, decided quickly that he liked Huston. "It was as if he had said two plus two equals four. Huston was right, and we both knew it," the bureau official recalled. Sullivan had been pushing Hoover to reinstate the old black bag jobs for years and immediately seized the opportunity with Huston to recommend how to better target the nation's terrorists and radicals and even expand the FBI's legally questionable surveillance tactics.

On June 5, 1970, Huston convened a meeting in the Oval Office for the nation's intelligence chiefs, including Hoover and the heads of the National Security Agency and the Defense Intelligence Agency, so the president could read them the riot act. Using Huston's prewritten talking points and while Ehrlichman and Haldeman looked on, Nixon complained that he wasn't getting adequate domestic intelligence: "We are now confronted with a new and grave crisis in our country, one which we know too little about." The president said that college campuses and the youth of the era were "developing their own brand of indigenous revolutionary activism which is as dangerous as anything which they could import from Cuba, China, or the Soviet Union," and the government must act aggressively: "Our people, perhaps as a reaction to the excesses of the McCarthy era, are unwilling to admit the possibility that their children could wish to destroy their country."

Responding to the threat required a new national "threat assessment," Nixon said, including an understanding of what the security agencies knew and didn't know about what was happening on America's streets and a menu of options for improving situational awareness. As part of the effort, Nixon decreed that Hoover would chair a new Interagency Committee on Intelligence (ICI) and Huston would serve as the White House liaison, a role Huston grandiosely announced made him the intelligence equivalent of Henry Kissinger on foreign policy.

Afterward, Huston set to work with Sullivan on a memo that ultimately grew to forty-three pages and outlined a new approach for intelligence gathering and combating domestic subversives, including allowing agencies like the CIA and DIA, that both legally only focused overseas, to execute all manner of domestic operations. He also proposed reinstating the black bag jobs that the FBI had sworn off and ignoring prohibitions about opening Americans' mail and wiretapping telephones. "Present procedures should be changed to permit intensification of coverage of individuals and groups in the United States who pose a major threat to the internal security," he wrote. "Covert coverage [of U.S. mail] is illegal and there are serious risks involved. However the advantages to be derived from its use outweigh the risks."

Later, in a section on "Surreptitious Entry," Huston determined, "Present restrictions should be modified to permit selective use of this technique against other urgent and high priority internal security targets. . . . Use of this technique is clearly illegal: it amounts to burglary. It is also highly risky and could result in great embarrassment if exposed. However, it is also the most fruitful tool and can produce the type of intelligence which cannot be obtained in any other fashion. The FBI in Mr. Hoover's younger days used to conduct such operations with great success and with no exposure. The information secured was invaluable."

This wide-reaching vision for a domestic surveillance program complemented Nixon's own conviction that the nation's chief executive was entitled to broad powers that decided what was legal and what wasn't when it came to protecting the country. "He saw the president as above the law and empowered to do anything he or the intelligence community deemed necessary in furtherance of national security," historian Melissa Graves said.

On June 25, Huston presented his plan to the intelligence chiefs during a meeting in Hoover's office; everyone but Hoover agreed to sign off on it, but the FBI director was furious. "The hippie did this," he ranted after. "They're not going to put the responsibility for these programs on me." He had seen how Johnson had left him twisting on his own in the previous administration, and he wasn't going to take on such risk again without clear presidential authorization. He insisted on detailed footnotes of his various objections. Huston presented the plan to the president, who eagerly approved it—this was just the type of aggressiveness he wanted. Hoover, though, moved to sink the new organizational structure behind Huston's back, complaining to Mitchell, who, in turn, promptly shut it down. Just five days after Nixon approved the plan, his attorney general revoked it. The rejection embarrassed and infuriated Huston, who fired off a memo to Haldeman saying, "At some point Hoover has to be told who is President." But the battle, for now, was over. Huston, in short order, would be gone from the White House, leaving to return to the less treacherous world of an Indiana law firm.

The fallout—the damage to Nixon's relationship with Hoover, a schism between Hoover and Sullivan, and the never quite forgotten groundwork laid by the Huston Plan—would continue to reverberate for years. A copy of the abandoned memo was delegated to the White House's new counsel, John Dean, who inherited the domestic security portfolio from Huston. Dean placed it in his safe, where it sat like a time bomb, evidence that the Nixon White House repeatedly—and dubiously—explored the limits of legal activities aimed at its political opponents. As Senator Richard Schweiker would say years later: "Even though the Huston plan was dead, I believe it had nine lives."

*   *   *

John Dean had learned quickly that the key to power in the Nixon orbit lay in delivering political intelligence and keeping tabs on Nixon's enemies. John Ehrlichman had originally recommended Dean to be his successor as White House counsel that spring, as Ehrlichman took over the domestic policy portfolio; he'd spotted in Dean's work at the Justice Department the ability to handle an amorphous role that mixed legal guidance, reputational advice, and risk analysis. His new portfolio ranged from monitoring antiwar demonstrations and protests to presidential clemency requests, as well as, Haldeman added and smirked, "doing whatever you goddamn lawyers do for those who need you."

Both of his bosses at the Justice Department, Mitchell and Kleindienst, had warned Dean—strongly—against moving up Pennsylvania Avenue, counseling their young staffer to avoid what Kleindienst called "the zoo up the street." As Dean recalled later, "In an almost fatherly way, [Mitchell] suggested that the White House was not a healthy place," and yet he ultimately accepted for the same reason people of all walks have come to Washington for generations: ambition. "It was just too good a title, too good a potential to turn down at that age, and that stage of my career," he recalled later." His mind already raced with questions not only about the job but about its perks: Would he drive his Porsche to the office or be picked up each day in a White House limo?

By the end of July 1970, Dean had been ensconced at the White House, in a temporary, run-down office filled with discarded furniture, overlooking an asphalt courtyard, down the hallway from Colson. When Dean noted to Higby the dreariness of his new quarters, Haldeman's aide explained, "Bob hasn't decided where he wants to put you yet." Dean understood the message intuitively: "I was being tested and my performance would determine what I would get. I was at the bottom of the ladder, and instinctively I began to climb." For his first assignment, he was asked to defend Vice President Spiro Agnew against reports that he planned to cancel the 1972 election. Dean's tasking was written in the passive tense—"it was noted that this is a vicious attack"—and he quickly learned that the "note-r" in question was President Nixon himself. "No one had to explain to me why the President's name was not used," Dean wrote later. "He was always to be kept one step removed, insulated to preserve his 'deniability.'"

Dean soon came to be recognized inside the White House as the Nixon administration's Sammy Glick—a man in a hurry to get somewhere and be someone, but relatively agnostic about what or who. "He was extremely ambitious without portfolio," said Donald Santarelli, who had worked with Dean at the Justice Department. In fact, he had ended up in politics—working on Capitol Hill before he'd entered the Nixon administration—in part because he'd been cashiered from working communications law at a private Washington, D.C., law firm after only six months when his bosses discovered he'd been moonlighting with a firm client's competitor on a television license application. The episode demonstrated a certain pragmatic ruthlessness that his administration colleagues would come to know all too well. "I don't think that there was a moral compass there—or a great, overriding dedication to principle," White House and campaign aide Robert Odle said, recalling that he got used to participating in brainstorming meetings with Dean and others, only to see his and others' ideas suddenly circulating later under Dean's name. "He was a snake," Ray Price said. "An absolute snake," Haig said.

Many in the White House suspected that Ehrlichman had originally chosen Dean precisely because he was a comer; Ehrlichman, the theory went, wanted someone who would follow his lead, so he could maintain control of the counsel's office. (Santarelli warned Ehrlichman about his choice, "You have given him a charter that exceeds his abilities.") From the start, his new colleagues at the White House noted a certain flashiness in Dean—crisp tailored suits, Gucci loafers, the Porsche parked in the White House parking lot—that stood him apart from the traditional Nixon White House. "He lived a little fancier than the rest of us," Gordon Strachan, a young campaign lawyer who served as Haldeman's liaison, recalled. Ehrlichman observed, icily, that he "lived beyond his salary."

As his first assistant, Dean brought in another young lawyer, Fred Fielding, and the team began digging into the clemency petitions and conflict-of-interest questions that typically fell to their startup internal law firm, but they had bigger goals. "Word soon got around that the counsel's office was eager to tackle anyone and everyone's problems and do it discreetly," Dean recalled. As Dean gained his colleagues' and superiors' trust, he was pulled away from bureaucratic paperwork and into an ever-widening set of what he termed "intelligence requests," a motley assortment of questions about how best to counter or undermine critics of the White House. The cleanup tasks in the Nixon White House varied widely—ranging from digging for dirt on prominent antiwar protesters to investigating a comedian, "Richard M. Dixon," who resembled the president. One day, in the White House bunker off the East Wing, Dean and a small group of aides gathered to watch a pornographic B movie, *Tricia's Wedding*, about the first daughter's wedding to Ed "Cox"—done by actors in drag—to weigh whether the White House could move to suppress it. (They didn't have to—the movie was so bad, it disappeared on its own.)

The other staffer assigned to Dean, transferred from Ehrlichman, was Jack Caulfield, the former detective who handled an odd portfolio of discreet tasks for the White House. The Irish Bronx native Caulfield had worked with the NYPD's prestigious Bureau of Special Services and Investigations (BOSSI) from 1955 to 1966, overseeing the police department's protection of dignitaries and its intelligence operations against Communists, antiwar groups, feminist activists, civil rights agitators, and other perceived radicals and troublemakers. (The controversial unit was not known for respecting civil liberties or legal niceties as it conducted its surveillance, penetration, and intelligence-gathering.) After a strong performance as Nixon's security chief during the '68 campaign—no small feat in a year that saw Nixon campaign without incident across seventy-seven cities amid national riots and the dual assassinations of King and Bobby Kennedy—Caulfield had wanted to be the nation's chief U.S. marshal.* Instead, he ended up at the White House on Ehrlichman's staff as part fixer, part opposition research man, and part liaison to federal law enforcement agencies like the Secret Service—the most notable of his tasks being keeping an eye on the doings of Ted Kennedy, Nixon's possible rival for the '72 reelection.

Early on, Caulfield recruited another former NYPD BOSSI colleague, Anthony T. Ulasewicz, to be the president's personal private eye. Ulasewicz's "job interview" with Ehrlichman, such as it was, occurred in May 1969 in the American Airlines lounge at LaGuardia. The conversation, at first, didn't go well; the White House aide was put off by Ulasewicz's demeanor, which he interpreted as arrogance. "Your silence bothers me," Ehrlichman said. "I stay well-sealed, like a clam," replied the first-generation Polish cop, whose large, dough-faced head usually maintained a particularly blank expression. Ulasewicz noticed in their conversation how fascinated Ehrlichman seemed with the derring-do of secret investigations, and he proceeded to dictate his employment terms: He wouldn't do paperwork, refused to do any wiretaps, and payment had to come through a cutout. There should be no traceable ties between Ulasewicz and the White House.

Ehrlichman approved, and handed off the detective to Nixon's personal attorney, Herbert Kalmbach. Later, after the scandals around Nixon began to break open, the *New York Times* would name Kalmbach "the

---

* The Secret Service, which had only begun protecting presidents-elect in the 1950s, did not traditionally protect presidential candidates during the campaign, until Lyndon Johnson expanded its duties to include such protection after Robert F. Kennedy's assassination in the midst of the '68 campaign.

most mysterious figure among the strangely assorted cast of characters in the Watergate affair," but at the time he met up with Ulasewicz in D.C.'s Madison Hotel, he was all but unknown in Washington circles, except within an elite group who hoped to curry the president's favor.

Kalmbach had risen in Republican circles alongside his USC law school friend Robert Finch, helping Finch win the lieutenant governership of California before he went onto Nixon's cabinet as the secretary of health, education, and welfare. Kalmbach had been a prodigious fundraiser for Nixon's '68 campaign and served as deputy finance chair under Maurice Stans, but rather than join the Nixon administration after the election, he had chosen to remain in California to expand his law practice. After Nixon named him as his personal lawyer, Kalmbach's Newport Beach firm exploded in growth, attracting blue-chip businesses, like Marriott Hotels, United Airlines, and Travelers Insurance, who suddenly thought it useful to have the president's lawyer on retainer too. (As one local businessman said, "If you have business with Washington and you want a lawyer, you can get to Herb, but you can't talk to him for less than $10,000.") Kalmbach's role for Nixon—part attorney, part fixer—existed entirely behind the scenes; the only photo that seemed to exist of him came from a golf tournament, and his ability to conduct deals with a minimal paper trail was both impressive and unsettling. As the *New York Times* later wrote, "He handled Mr. Nixon's 1969 acquisition of his $1.4 million San Clemente estate so deftly that there exists no public record showing the President's interest in the trust-held property."

A big part of Kalmbach's role was safeguarding the Nixon campaign's cash kitty that paid for people like Ulasewicz. When the Nixon administration took office in 1969 and Stans started his role in the cabinet (as secretary of commerce), he turned over to Kalmbach the $1,668,000 remaining in the campaign's bank accounts—more than a million of which was stored in cash in safe-deposit boxes at the Chase Manhattan Bank in New York and the Riggs National Bank in D.C.; over the next two years, Kalmbach moved most of the cash west. From there, tens of thousands of dollars in cash moved from a bank in one tower of Kalmbach's office complex to another bank in a different tower, until the money was all but untraceable. Add in another $300,000 cash that had flowed to Nixon's coffers in his years in the White House, and by the time the

'72 campaign kicked off, Kalmbach was the trustee of close to $2 million that could be used at the discretion of a small number of Nixon aides for what they deemed "political purposes."*

At their Madison Hotel meeting, Kalmbach arranged to pay Ulasewicz out of those laundered and untraceable '68 campaign funds. Ulasewicz promptly created an alias, Edward T. Stanley, and explained how Nixon's team could contact him: Every day at 4 p.m., he would call a New York answering service, and if there was a message for Stanley, he would call Kalmbach. Then "Edward T. Stanley" got to work; all his tasks had one thing in common—getting even with Nixon's enemies and helping to wage the war that Hoover wouldn't.

One day in July 1969, Caulfield dispatched him to Martha's Vineyard within hours of learning that Ted Kennedy had been involved in an accident there on Chappaquiddick Island resulting in the death of a former aide, Mary Jo Kopechne. "Stanley," posing as a newspaper reporter, was standing on the island's Dike Bridge less than twenty-four hours after Senator Kennedy's car went off of it and was the first to speak with several relevant accident witnesses, but he didn't manage to uncover any key details. For months afterward, he regularly returned to the island, digging and searching, and in subsequent months, he traveled to dozens of states snooping on all manner of other Nixon irritants; he counted ninety-three distinct assignments, from antiwar protesters, to a Florida schoolteacher who harassed the president's daughter, to the drinking habits of House Speaker Carl Albert.

"It doesn't matter who you were or what ideological positions you took," one Nixon aide explained. "You were either for us or against us, and if you were against us, we were against you. It was real confrontational politics and there were a number of men around the White House who clearly relished that sort of thing."

---

* In 1970, the cash had been used to funnel $400,000 secretly to Albert Brewer, the Alabama Democratic gubernatorial primary opponent of the right-wing firebrand George Wallace, whom Nixon saw as a major third-party threat to his own reelection. Kalmbach made two $100,000 withdrawals from safe-deposit boxes in New York and Los Angeles, handing the money off to couriers he didn't know; Haldeman's brother-in-law also withdrew an additional $200,000 in New York.

*   *   *

The deeper into the first term Nixon got, the less he seemed to trust anyone around him—unsure even who his adversaries might be inside the White House. Even those he trusted the most, he didn't really trust that much, and by February 1971, he had decided he needed to take more aggressive action to secure his own historical legacy.

Alexander P. Butterfield was one of the nation's most accomplished air force pilots—ninety-eight combat recon missions in Vietnam—and looked the part. Strikingly handsome and personable, Colonel Butterfield had years before been UCLA's "Most Collegiate Looking Male," and had joined Nixon's White House after reading in a newspaper that his old college acquaintance, Haldeman would be a top White House aide. Through some sneaky networking, he managed to reconnect with the incoming chief of staff, who excitedly recruited Butterfield to his own staff based on the colonel's experience navigating Washington, and he had been in the White House since the start, attending Haldeman's very first staff meeting of the new administration at 8 a.m. on January 21, 1969.

It was days, though, before Haldeman would even introduce Butterfield to Nixon, and weeks before they achieved any sort of productive working relationship. Yet over time, Butterfield became a key functionary, the person Nixon could trust with the most delicate of tasks, and he was promoted to handle the minutiae of the daily Oval Office operations, privy to the president's biggest secrets. "Alex is the perfect buffer," Nixon told Haldeman one night.*

Butterfield studiously learned the rhythms of the presidential day; he was one of the few who understood that Nixon took an hour-long nap at 1 p.m. nearly every day in a cubbyhole room off the Oval Office and how the president would retreat at suppertime to his hideaway in the Executive Office Building next door, writing quietly on his ubiquitous

---

* One December evening in 1969, after an eighteen-minute pre-Christmas walk through the staff offices of the Executive Office Building, Nixon expressed his horror about how many of the career civil service staff serving the White House kept photos in their offices of previous presidents; one woman, who had been with the White House for decades, had two—*two!*—photos of John F. Kennedy on display. "I want all those pictures down today," Nixon ordered. By mid-January, Butterfield had prepared a report on the "Sanitization of the EOB."

yellow legal pads while he drank a glass of wine or Scotch and his butler served dinner. The room had been decorated in "politician casual," its soaring ceilings offset by a favorite lounge chair, brought down from the Nixons' New York apartment, and bookshelves packed with presidential biographies, multitudes of miniature elephants, and even a golf card showing a Nixon hole in one. Around 10:30 p.m., he'd take off his tie.

As his administration advanced, Nixon worried that his brilliant strategy and decisive leadership weren't being adequately captured for posterity; the notes that Haldeman, Butterfield, and others took in their meetings didn't record the full picture of what was happening in great moments. Considering his options, he found a solution that would help him write the most accurate and thorough memoir ever of his administration. "The president wants a taping system installed," Higby told Butterfield. "And Bob wants you to take care of it."

The move was a remarkable turnabout for Nixon; in the days after his election in 1968, he'd been shown on a transition-focused tour of the White House the private taping system used by Lyndon Johnson and squirmed. He'd ordered the Army Signal Corps to rip it out once he arrived in office.

The equipment's existence was to be of the utmost secrecy, Haldeman decreed—and that meant the military and the White House Communications Agency couldn't be relied on to handle it. Instead, Butterfield contacted the Secret Service's Al Wong, who headed its Technical Security Division, and talked through the parameters. The following weekend, while the president was off to Key Biscayne, Secret Service technicians carefully drilled five microphones up through the president's Oval Office desk and covered them in a thin layer of varnish. Other microphones were hidden in the lights atop the fireplace mantel. Everything fed into Sony 800B tape recorders hidden in a sealed compartment in the White House basement—and all of it, Wong explained, was voice-activated.

When Butterfield and Haldeman filled Nixon in on the new Oval Office accoutrement, Nixon said, "Who knows about that incidentally?"

"Just you, Alex, and I and Higby and that's it," Haldeman answered.

"Rose doesn't know about it?" Nixon asked, referring to his longtime secretary, Rose Mary Woods.

"No."

"Don't want Henry to know about it," Nixon added. "Ehrlichman?"

"No, absolutely not."

"This has got to be a well-kept secret," Nixon said. "Mum's the word."

Nixon's comment about not wanting Henry Kissinger to know about the taping system struck Haldeman as particularly notable, a sign that the president was afraid he wasn't going to get credit for his administration's successes. The Washington establishment was falling in love with Kissinger and seemed to be giving "their Henry" all the credit for things that went right with the Nixon policies, while laying the failures squarely on "that bastard" Nixon's shoulders. "We knew Henry as the 'hawk of hawks' in the Oval Office," Haldeman recalled dryly years later, "but in the evenings, a magical transformation took place. Touching glasses at a party with his liberal friends, the belligerent Kissinger would suddenly become a dove—according to the reports that reached Nixon."

The staffers agreed that no one else would know, beyond the small team of Secret Service techs who maintained the system, and Haldeman suggested that if they ever had to rely on the tape record to clarify or publicize a conversation, they could just pretend it came from notes. "Anytime that anything gets used from it, it's on the basis of 'your notes' or 'the president's notes,'" he said.

From February 16, 1971, until July 12, 1973, the recording system would capture 3,432 hours of conversation, providing, as demanded, a look at Nixon's mind and decision-making that was the most thorough and intimate view America has had of any of its presidents. It also would be the root cause of his downfall.

*   *   *

As that spring of 1971 unfolded, John Dean had overseen the White House command post during the May Day Tribe protests, an action during which hundreds of thousands of protesters descended on the capital and paralyzed the city's business; some 14,517 were arrested during the rest of the two weeks of running battles across the city from April 22 to May 6—including 7,000 in just a single day at their peak—all pushed and prodded into makeshift outdoor camps at RFK Stadium on the outskirts of Capitol Hill by police and federal agencies overwhelmed by the sheer scale of the demonstrations. These had been some of the darkest, scariest moments of the administration yet; Julie Nixon, a visiting Mamie Eisenhower, and others were sent screaming from a lunch in the White House family dining room when a tear gas canister was actually set off by security and filled the presidential residence with choking gas. Inside John Mitchell's Justice Department, army infantry set up machine gun nests to secure the building's long corridors in the event protesters managed to overwhelm the guards outside. Nixon decried the militants "who in the name of demonstrating for peace abroad presume that they have the right to break the peace at home."*

Dean monitored the federal response from the White House, submitting twice-hourly reports to the president from his war room as he collected dispatches from police and military units around the capital. ("Live bomb found suspended underneath Taft Street Bridge; deactivated by military bomb squad," Dean wrote at 1:30 p.m. on May 4. At 7 p.m., he reported: "Chief Jerry Wilson feels that the demonstrators have been broken in strength and spirit.") Dean and Ehrlichman had also flown over the city in a military helicopter, watching cars burn in Georgetown and fights break out between police and rock-throwing protesters.

As the White House team monitored the goings-on, Chuck Colson fluttered in and out. At one point Dean's colleague Fred Fielding joked that they should send oranges to the arrested protesters, mimicking Democrat Edmund Muskie, who often sent oranges to his campaign volunteers as a thank-you. "I'll do it," Colson said, running out the door. When he came back, Colson reported, "I sent the oranges and tipped off the press." The orange crate, dispatched to RFK Stadium, where the protesters awaited their fate in steel pens, read, "Best of luck, Senator Edmund Muskie."†

Running the May Day command post had been a heady experience for

---

* The court cases stemming from the incident would stretch on until the 1980s and lead to mass acquittals.

† When Haldeman related the oranges story to Nixon two days later, the president laughed. He loved this kind of stuff. "Damn Colson thing," Haldeman chuckled. "I don't know how the hell he does that stuff, but it's good. . . . He's going to get caught at some of these things. But he's got a lot done that he hasn't been caught at."

Dean, who had been the White House counsel for a year by the time of the protests and the subsequent Pentagon Papers scandal a month later. To him, it was the surest sign yet that he'd made himself useful and was on his way to being indispensable.

Now, two months later, the oddball team who worked in Dean's office—the White House detective and the off-the-books private eye— seemed perfect to tackle the plot germinating in Chuck Colson's mind to follow through on the president's order to burglarize the Brookings Institution and ensure Nixon's darkest secrets remained buried.

All they needed, Colson realized, was a little help from the CIA's most prolific novelist.

Chapter 5

Burglarizing Brookings

As his White House confronted the myriad betrayals in Washington following the publication of the Pentagon Papers in June 1971 and the societal unrest beyond, President Nixon told his staff they faced an environment just as poisonous as what he'd confronted as a young congressman when he went after that Communist traitor Alger Hiss. This time, with Daniel Ellsberg, he knew who his main enemy was: the Jews. (Ellsberg actually was raised a Christian Scientist.)

On July 3, he ordered Haldeman, "I want a look at any sensitive areas around where Jews are involved, Bob. See the Jews are all through the government, and we have got to get in those areas," he ordered. "The government is full of Jews."

"Most Jews are disloyal," he continued. "Bob, generally speaking, you can't trust the bastards. They turn on you." The White House couldn't stand for these betrayals. They had to destroy Ellsberg. "Don't worry about his trial," Nixon said. "Just get everything out. Try him in the press. Try him in the press."

As the days passed, his anger hardly dissipated. And neither, it turned out, was his order to burglarize the Brookings Institution a fleeting thought. He raised the subject again and repeated the orders again to a larger group. "They have a lot of material," he told a gathering of aides in the Oval Office that included Haldeman and Kissinger, as well as Attorney General John Mitchell and Defense Secretary Melvin Laird.

"I want Brookings—I want them just to break in and take it out," he reiterated. "Do you understand?"

"Yeah," Haldeman said. "But you have to have somebody to do it."

"That's what I'm talking about," Nixon said. "Don't discuss it here. You talk to Hunt."

The "Hunt" Nixon referred to was E. Howard Hunt, a CIA officer who had retired that spring and was helping out on Colson's team doing investigative work. "Helms says he's ruthless, quiet, careful," Haldeman said, offering an endorsement from CIA director Richard Helms.

"He's kind of a tiger," Colson said, chiming in. "He spent twenty years in the CIA overthrowing governments."

"I want the break-in," Nixon continued. "Hell, they do that. You're to break into the place, rifle the files, and bring them in. . . . Just go in and take it. Go in around eight or nine o'clock," he said, beginning to stray into actually planning the operation himself. "Clean it up. These kids don't understand. They have no understanding of politics. They have no understanding of public relations. John Mitchell is that way. John is always worried about is it technically correct? Do you think, for Christ sakes, that the *New York Times* is worried about all the legal niceties? Those sons of bitches are killing me."*

It wasn't even 9 a.m. the next morning before Nixon asked Haldeman: "Did they get the Brookings Institute raided last night?"

"No, sir, they didn't," Haldeman said, not acknowledging that not only had the mission not succeeded, it had not even been attempted.

"Get it done! I want it done!" Nixon said, banging the desk. "I want the Brookings Institute safe cleaned out."

Nixon wanted Haldeman to assign him a man to "work directly with me on this whole situation." Nixon picked up the conversation as soon as he could after lunch: "I think you need a team. This is a big job." He mused who might be right to lead, eventually saying, "Shouldn't Colson

---

* This conversation wasn't released until 1996, at which point Kissinger denied that he'd been present for the president ordering a break-in at one of the capital's most respected institutions. "I have no such recollection," he told a *San Francisco Examiner* reporter after having Nixon's recorded words read to him. "Nixon often said exalted things that people didn't think would have to be done."

be, when you come down to it, Bob?" Nixon added, "His instincts are particularly good."

Nixon further explained to Haldeman how desperate he was for better intelligence. "The FBI won't get into this sort of thing. They don't know how to handle it, Bob," he said. "I've got to get Huston or somebody fast. . . . I'll tell you what this takes—this takes 18 hours a day. It takes devotion and dedication and loyalty and devilishness such as you've never seen, Bob. . . . This is a hell of a great opportunity. . . . I want to track down every goddamn leak."

As Nixon saw it, his team weren't aggressive enough—they didn't grasp how messy politics needed to be: "John Mitchell doesn't understand that sort of thing. He's a good lawyer. It's abhorrent to him. John Ehrlichman will have difficulty. We have to develop a program for leaking out information—for destroying these people in the papers."

He knew exactly what he needed. "Let's have a little fun," he continued. "I really need a son of a bitch like Huston who will work his butt off and do it dishonorably. . . . I'll direct him myself. I'll pitch it. I know how to play this game."

Viewed years later, with a more complete understanding of the context, these words are hardly an incoherent, irrational rant by a man simply lashing out at his enemies. Nixon that week, as the Pentagon Papers unspooled in the nation's newspapers, airing the dirty secrets of his predecessors, was a man suddenly worried that one of his own great secrets might spill into public view too. "Nixon did have reason to believe that the bombing halt file contained politically explosive information—not about his predecessor, but about himself," scholar Ken Hughes concluded. "Ordering the Bookings break-in wasn't a matter of opportunism or poor presidential impulse control. As far as Nixon knew, it was a matter of survival."

Colson had a suggestion. "There's one guy on the outside that has the capacity and ideological bent who might be able to do all this," he told the president. "He's hard as nails. He's a brilliant writer. He's written 40 books on [espionage]."

Hunt, Colson said, was the right man to deal with the Brookings break-in. "He's here in Washington now. He just got out of the CIA, fifty. Kind of a tiger," Colson promised.

A tiger—yes, that was just what Richard Nixon required. And so it was that the Pentagon Papers, a scandal that might under another president have been overlooked entirely, would instead serve as the genesis for a major escalation in the administration's fight against its enemies.

*　　*　　*

At first glance, E. Howard Hunt seemed an unlikely clandestine operator—a father of four with a large house in suburban Maryland, complete with horses and stables, he split his time between being vice president for the Robert Mullen Company, a boutique D.C. PR agency, and consulting work with the White House, where he had a small office on the third floor of the Old Executive Office Building. It had been a late career switch for Hunt.

During a comparatively long World War II career, he'd seen service aboard navy convoys in the North Atlantic, as a war correspondent in the South Pacific, and as an officer with the U.S. Army Air Force, as well as a stint in China with the Office of Strategic Services, America's first crack at an intelligence agency. The field of intelligence at that time was less a profession than a lifestyle, an odd mix of derring-do steeped in patrician blue blood tradition—many of its founders came straight out of the old boys' network at Yale, Harvard, and Hunt's own Ivy League alma mater, Brown—and his training mixed lessons in killing, sabotage, and surveillance with steak dinners and martinis. After the war, Hunt worked with Ambassador Averell Harriman in Paris as Europe began rebuilding, and then joined the early days of the Central Intelligence Agency.* Over the next two decades, Hunt spent the peak of the Cold War and the global fight against Communism running covert assignments in Mexico, the Balkans, Japan, and Uruguay, among other stations abroad.

During that period, intrigue became not just his career, but an all-encompassing passion: He'd published his first novel, *East of Farewell*, about North Atlantic convoy duty, in 1942, to strong reviews, and

---

* Until the formation of the CIA, the U.S. had never had a meaningful intelligence capability—and certainly not in peacetime—and largely split such tasks between the FBI, the army, and the navy.

Hunt continued churning out potboiler novels under three different pen names—sometimes as often as twice a year—by writing for half the day on weekdays and then all day on weekends. (Not surprisingly, his four children remember him as a bit absent.) Unlike his fellow practitioners Ian Fleming and David Cornwell, who wrote under the pen name John le Carré, who defined for the world the esprit de corps of British intelligence and the great game of espionage, Hunt's books existed largely in obscurity—solid sellers, but rarely memorable and never a lasting commercial success.

In 1954, Hunt helped overthrow the Communist government of Guatemala—the first time since the Spanish Civil War that a Communist leader had been deposed—a success that earned him a key role in a subsequent operation, the Bay of Pigs invasion of Cuba. Living undercover at a CIA safe house in Miami's Coconut Grove with his family, Hunt worked with Cuban Invasion Brigade 2506, part of a team of exiles that the agency hoped would return to the island and trigger a national uprising that would remove Fidel Castro. Unlike the Guatemala coup, though, the Bay of Pigs was a costly disaster in both lives and U.S. prestige, one of the greatest embarrassments of the entire Cold War, but the ties and friendships that Hunt formed among the Cuban exiles would last and serve him again in a later chapter of his career.

Overall, Hunt was not well liked by his fellow intelligence comrades, and his agency career experienced the same middling success that his writing did; he never reached the upper ranks of the agency or held any major or high-profile postings. In fact, lost in the later shorthand biographies of Hunt was the crucial distinction that he'd never actually been a true covert operator for the CIA, only on the political side of the house—operating under State Department cover to work dissidents, assess political parties, and spread propaganda.

By his account, Hunt resigned as an intelligence officer in the CIA in 1965, when a copyright mix-up on one of his novels led to the possibility that the agency would be publicly linked to his writing. (Still, he continued on as a contract agent until 1970.) In 1968, Hunt, his wife, Dorothy—herself a onetime CIA employee who had met Hunt while they were both working in Paris after her previous marriage to a French marquis ended in divorce—and their family returned permanently to Washington, purchasing a horse country estate in Potomac named Witches' Island. His family, by tradition, ate dinner by candlelight each night, and their house was overrun by pets.

He immersed himself in Washington society with an eye toward a semiretirement career, and at a banquet for the Brown University Club during the Johnson years, he crossed paths with an accomplished D.C. lawyer named Charles Colson. The two men grew close, serving together as vice president and president of the alumni club. They talked regularly about Nixon as Colson became involved in his '68 presidential race, and later they lunched together at the White House, where Colson tried unsuccessfully to recruit the former CIA officer.

Instead, Hunt formally left the CIA on April 30, 1970, and began work the next day for the Robert Mullen Company, the PR firm that had long served to provide CIA cover for agents and officers overseas. Hunt's boss, Robert Mullen, understood that Hunt came with CIA Director Helms's "blessing," and Hunt sometimes served as the go-between for the agency and the firm.*

But as the nation's mood darkened in 1971, Hunt had reconsidered Colson's offer. He found that the anti-Vietnam rhetoric and protests rankled him—he had been outraged when students at his and Colson's alma mater turned their backs on Henry Kissinger as he received an honorary degree, and during the May Day Tribe protests Hunt had narrowly escaped injury himself when protesters rolled a telephone pole onto D.C.'s Canal Road as he drove by. Just weeks after the publication of the Pentagon Papers, Colson called Hunt to grill him on his feelings about Ellsberg and the leaked documents. Unsurprisingly, they were on the same page. "Ellsberg's deed seemed the culmination of the lawless mass actions that had taken place across the country during the previous years: chaos on street and campus, urban bombings and burnings, massive marches and nonnegotiable demands," Hunt recalled in 1974.

---

* Hunt's uncertain ongoing status with the CIA postretirement stands as one of the many nebulous and enormously strange CIA connections that permeate the Watergate story, leading some to wonder if Hunt was still reporting to the agency what he was doing for the White House. The numerous investigations after and years of further revelations have never shown this to be true—but they've also never produced clear evidence that Hunt wasn't feeding information to his old employer.

A few days later, Colson summoned Hunt to the White House: *His president needed him.* At $100 a day, Hunt became a part-time White House consultant, tasked with becoming an in-house expert on the origins of the Vietnam War, the Pentagon Papers, and how best to combat the evils being done to the president by his enemies. Immediately, the operative was enthralled by the whirl around his old friend. "Colson's phones were constantly ringing, appointments made and canceled, and invariably there were callers waiting in the outer office," Hunt recalled. "One had a sense that Colson was a dynamo around which spun large and powerful wheels."

To a certain extent, Hunt was closer to the center of power in retirement than he ever had been as a clandestine operator. It was easy too for him to imagine that his work now was in keeping with a career of service to the nation. It certainly beat writing the dreary corporate press releases of the Mullen Company. Still, it would only become more clear with time that excellence was never something E. Howard Hunt was destined for. "The way Hunt went about his new job could be called pathetic had it not been part of a scheme of extraordinary danger to the welfare of the United States," his biographer Tad Szulc wrote later.

*   *   *

The president couldn't have been clearer to Chuck Colson about his marching orders: "I don't want excuses. I want results. I want it done, whatever the costs." In response, Colson had Caulfield contact "Tony" Ulasewicz with instructions to scout the Brookings Institution on Massachusetts Avenue. (As a New Yorker unfamiliar with the capital—and in an age long before the internet—Ulasewicz's first stop after getting the assignment was the public library to look up what a "Brookings Institution" actually was.) Arriving later at its D.C. headquarters, he posed as a tourist to get past the lobby security guard and look around the think tank. He visited the personnel office to ask about open jobs, studied the security system, cased the vault on the top floor, and even talked with a janitor about the trash pickup schedule. "The security on the vault is tough," Caulfield reported back to the White House. "We'd have to get past the alarm system and crack the safe."

Colson suggested a plan: The operatives should start a fire at Brook-ings, then use the distraction to sneak into the building disguised as firemen themselves, and extract the needed documents from the safe. The idea, Caulfield felt, was impractical for myriad reasons, and he rushed to his boss John Dean's office to ask for help. "John, I'm no chicken, but this is insane—Tony can't go in there with a bunch of firemen. There are so many holes in this thing we'd never get away with it," he pleaded. "You've got to get me out of this."

After Caulfield left his office, Dean realized that he was now legally an accomplice before the fact. "It was out-and-out street crime," he thought. Nixon was spending the week that July in San Clemente and Dean called Ehrlichman, in California with him. "John, something's come up here that requires your firm hand," Dean said. "I can't talk to you about it on the phone."

That afternoon, Dean caught one of the regular air force courier flights, a C-135 transport plane, to the so-called "Western White House," Nixon's estate in San Clemente on the Pacific coast; in California, he laid out the troubled Brookings plan for Ehrlichman, who took in the information without reaction. He didn't let on that he'd been in the Oval Office when Nixon ordered the attack, or provide any of the background about the president's ongoing ire toward the think tank. Worried that the plan had spun beyond reason, he simply picked up the phone and called Colson while Dean stood in his office: "Chuck, that Brookings thing—we don't want it anymore. I'm telling Dean to turn Caulfield off," he said. After listening for a second, he said, "Right—goodbye."*

*　　　*　　　*

On his way west that day, Dean had been surprised to see Robert Mardian, the Justice Department's head of internal security, on board the same

---

* Notably, there's a slightly different version of this story that Dean told Nixon on March 21, 1973, as Watergate prepared to tumble down around them; Dean did not know that the conversation in the Oval Office was being recorded and proceeded to tell the president a version that more directly involved both Ehrlichman and Dean himself: "I flew to California because I was told that John had instructed [the Brookings burglary] and he said, 'I really hadn't.' It's a misimpression—for Christ's sake, turn it off.' And I did. I came back and turned it off."

courier flight; unbeknownst to both men, the Nixon administration's subterfuges were already beginning to conflict with each other. Mardian was on his own mission to the Western White House to disentangle how the government's prosecution of Ellsberg was colliding with the brewing, hidden civil war inside the FBI between Sullivan and Hoover.

Mardian, a navy veteran, former corporate lawyer, and son of an Armenian immigrant, had come into Republican politics with Goldwater and grown close to Mitchell on the Nixon campaign. The men became frequent golfing partners, and Mardian had started with the administration as general counsel to the Department of Health, Education, and Welfare before being promoted to assistant attorney general in 1970, in charge of what was known as the Internal Security Division—the unit formed in the 1950s to fight Communism, espionage, and subversion. There, in short order, he'd become one of the most visible—and passionate—defenders of the administration's "law and order" mission. ("You talk about wearing flags in lapels—this guy would have sewn a flag on his back if they'd let him," one of his Justice Department colleagues would later say.) At the start of his tenure, he had cleaned out many division lawyers and brought in aggressive new—usually crew-cut—attorneys who picked up thousands of draft-dodging cases from the Vietnam War; the balding Mardian liked to say that he could tell a man's political affiliations by the length of his hair.

His aggression instantly impressed his equally hard-line FBI counterpart, William Sullivan, who had continued—fruitlessly—to press the bureau to be more aggressive following the collapse of the Huston Plan. "Mardian," Sullivan later reported, "was a real fireball." His relationship with Hoover, though, soured fast. "Mardian is a goddamned Armenian Jew and I won't cooperate with any such person," Hoover steamed—but the director's increasing isolation meant his opinion mattered less than ever.

In fact, what had started as Nixon's mere annoyance and frustration with Hoover had tipped by 1971 into something more tense. The president had begun talking early that year about how to replace the director and ease him from the reins of the bureau; by February, Nixon's resolution had stiffened and he had told Mitchell and Haldeman that Hoover should be gone by the end of the first term. Not long after, when an FBI office in Media, Pennsylvania, was burglarized in March 1971, an opportunity seemed to present itself sooner than they might have imagined.

The files stolen from the Media Resident Agency had been turned over to the *Washington Post*, where reporters Betty Medsger and Ken Clawson were amazed to grasp for the first time the sweep of the bureau's widespread surveillance programs targeting New Left activists and radicals—their resulting exposé, drawn from the bureau's own documents, illustrated a sweeping program far more invasive and expansive than anything the public had imagined. As more than a thousand stolen documents trickled into public view, people recoiled at the bureau's targeting of Black activists, antiwar groups, and college students—including how it was recruiting informants as young as eighteen. Even the Quakers fell under the bureau's suspicious gaze. It was one of the first real, unvarnished glimpses into the FBI's work in American history, and many didn't like what they saw. "[The FBI] is the nearest thing America has to a police state," the *New Republic* editorialized. The leaked memos also made J. Edgar Hoover appear odd, dictatorial, and thin-skinned. Adding to the embarrassment was the fact that the bureau couldn't figure out the identity of the burglars, who had dubbed themselves the Citizens Commission to Investigate the FBI.

In April, as the burglary fallout spread, White House aide Pat Buchanan asked John Dean to work through how the FBI director could be replaced, by whom, and how long a Hoover successor might serve. The U.S. had never changed FBI directors before, so the procedures were unclear, and removing a man of Hoover's influence, regardless of the controversy, would not be easy. A *LIFE* magazine cover that month dubbed him the "Emperor of the FBI," portraying his visage in a marble bust, and during a party for Martha Mitchell, he joked to the crowd about how they might not recognize him in a tuxedo. "We emperors have our problems," he said. "My Roman toga was not returned from the cleaners." Martha, who playfully called him "Jedgar," joked, "When you have seen one FBI director, you have seen them all."

But behind the scenes, there was little humor to be found as the director's feud with Sullivan over the bureau's direction continued through the spring. In June, the two clashed over the Ellsberg investigation—Hoover wanted nothing to do with such a politically sensitive case, whereas Sullivan wanted it pursued tenaciously—and as of July 1, Hoover had effectively demoted Sullivan, creating a new number three post above his assistant director and installing an agent named W. Mark Felt in the role, as deputy associate director to assist Hoover's longtime number two, associate deputy Clyde Tolson, who was ailing himself and increasingly unable to fulfill his own duties.*

Mark Felt had spent six years heading the FBI's internal inspection division and was deeply loyal to Hoover, a respect that would last long past the man's death. He had consistently sided with the director over Sullivan in the ongoing feuds about the bureau's investigative posture, cautioning his colleague once, "Bill, the bureau can have only one boss."

Becoming Tolson's "deputy" meant, in most respects, serving as the bureau's actual operational leader and positioned Felt—at least in his own mind—as the heir apparent to be director of the FBI when and if Hoover ever left office. The list of possible Hoover successors had long been short—just three names, really: Felt, Sullivan, and former Hoover aide Cartha "Deke" DeLoach, but DeLoach had been largely removed from speculation during the Nixon years because of his close association with Lyndon Johnson, and he had retired from the bureau in June 1970 for a second career with Pepsi-Cola. Now, with Sullivan falling from favor, Felt stood all but unchallenged atop the bureau's hierarchy.

Hoover's demotion and reshuffling panicked Sullivan; he feared he might be fired outright and spotted an opportunity amid the Pentagon Papers case to ingratiate himself with Mardian and the Nixon White House and remind them of the secrets he kept. In early July, Mardian's prosecutors made a routine request that the FBI turn over documents pertaining to any "electronic surveillance information" about Ellsberg and others, like Mort Halperin, who were part of the Pentagon Papers dragnet, as they prepared their case against the leaker. The bureau checked its official files and responded that it had no relevant wiretaps or surveillance on Ellsberg or Halperin—which was true officially, but the file clerks didn't know about the special, illegal White House wiretaps ordered by Kissinger.

The Kissinger wiretaps, begun amid such presidential pique, had been no flight of fancy or momentary lapse in judgment; with an oft-rotating set of targets, the presidential wiretapping program had actually

---

* Inside the FBI, the reshuffling hit with the power of an earthquake. Sullivan had long existed in exalted air inside the bureau. Hoover typically referred to all of his aides by last name; Sullivan and Tolson were the bureau's only two leaders Hoover called by first name: Bill and Clyde.

continued for nearly two years, only ending on February 10, 1971. At that point, the FBI liaison at the White House collected all the wiretap summaries secreted away by Haig, Kissinger, Haldeman, Ehrlichman, and the president and returned them to Sullivan, who had hidden them away in his own safe. Now, all of a sudden, they seemed explosive.

Unofficially, Sullivan contacted Mardian to ask how he should handle the situation; the truth was there were at least fifteen separate monitored conversations that involved Ellsberg—some of which stemmed from a period when Ellsberg was Halperin's houseguest—all forgotten and hidden in Sullivan's office safe. Sullivan told Mardian that he was now concerned that Hoover might try to blackmail the president with the wiretap files if he mentioned the files to the director. Mardian reported the situation to his boss, Mitchell, and soon found himself sharing the courier flight with Dean.

Even before his arrival, the Nixon team in California had been debating how to handle the illegal wiretap files and whether they would have to be disclosed to the grand jury investigating Ellsberg. Ultimately, they assured themselves the taping program could remain hidden; after the meeting, Ehrlichman jotted down in his notes, "Re: grand jury—dont worry re tapes on discovery—re WHs."

In his own forty-minute meeting with Nixon and Ehrlichman on July 12, Mardian reviewed the status of the Ellsberg case and discussed the sensitive nature of the wiretap summaries, while Nixon and Ehrlichman underscored how unhappy they were with the Justice Department's progress on the Pentagon Papers case. "He was very upset," Mardian recalled later, and he'd tried to reassure the president: "I told him I was doing everything I could, within my legal powers, to nail him." As the head of domestic security left the meeting, Haldeman told him, coldly, "Mardian, you never come up with the right answers."*

Nixon ordered Mardian to get his hands on the files, deliver them to the White House, and verify that the FBI's files matched the White

---

* Mardian attributes this quote to Haldeman, although White House records don't show that the White House chief of staff was present for his meeting with Nixon; it's thus unclear whether Mardian was misremembering the speaker, who was actually Ehrlichman, whom he did meet with, or whether he spoke separately afterward to Haldeman, who was also in San Clemente at the time.

House's own logs of the wiretap summaries to ensure none was missing and vulnerable to possible blackmail. In their thinking, if the files existed at the White House, the Nixon administration could claim executive privilege and withhold the wiretaps if asked. Once back in Washington, Mardian met an agent from Sullivan's office, who handed the assistant attorney general a bulging, beat-up, olive-drab satchel, embossed with the initials "W.C.S.," which Mardian then took to the White House. There, Kissinger and Haig had their staff cross-check its contents before Mardian delivered it personally to the Oval Office. (He declined later, in interviews with FBI agents, to answer whether he had handed the satchel to Nixon directly.) Nixon had Ehrlichman take custody of the files, and he placed them in a special safe in his own office.

The entire episode underscored to the White House the possible treachery of Hoover and how poorly he was serving his commander in chief. Within hours of Mardian's departure from California, Ehrlichman began to build a team to do what the Justice Department seemed incapable of doing: stopping the leaks.

Chapter 6

The Plumbers

On a clear day, Richard Nixon could see sixty miles out into the Pacific, all the way out to San Clemente Island, from his perch at the vacation estate he had dubbed "La Casa Pacifica." At the start of his presidency, Nixon had sold his portfolio of stocks and bonds, to avoid any accusations of impropriety, as well as his New York apartment and invested the money instead in real estate, purchasing two vacation getaways, in Florida and California, to serve as his escapes from Washington.

He'd wanted a place near where he'd grown up and lived in California to serve as his presidential retreat, so after his election, a young Ehrlichman aide had driven up and down the Pacific coast scouting locations and eventually settled on a thirty-acre, Spanish mission–style estate, owned by the daughter of a Democratic Party finance chair. The fourteen-room tile-roofed hacienda opened into a courtyard with a central fountain, decorated with a statue of frogs and Cupid. Perched on a bluff adjacent to the Marine Corps base Camp Pendleton, the location was ideal too for security. Nixon purchased it using a series of Kalmbach-enabled questionable financial transactions with his wealthy friend Robert Abplanalp, and the U.S. government transformed it into a true presidential estate, installing advanced security and communications gear and converting outbuildings for staff and Secret Service quarters. Nixon stocked the house itself with books on presidents and politics, the only meaningful hobby interest he ever had, while friends paid for the construction of a three-hole golf course.

Thanks to presidential perks, the lush oceanfront property was a breeze to visit: a quick Air Force One flight to the El Toro marine base, then a marine or army helicopter to a nearby Coast Guard base and a short golf cart ride to the red tile roofs of the estate. Nixon spent nearly 200 days in San Clemente during his first term, another 150 in Key Biscayne—a full year away from the confines and structure of the White House.

It was from California on Thursday, July 15, 1971, that Nixon announced one of the foreign policy "monuments" he hoped would change the world: At 7:30 p.m. Pacific Time, speaking from the NBC studios in Burbank, he read a statement released simultaneously in the U.S. and in Peking, explaining that Henry Kissinger had held secret talks with Chinese premier Chou En-lai, and that he intended to visit China within the next year. It was a diplomatic triumph—a high point not just of his presidency but of a century of U.S. diplomacy. "We seek friendly relations with all nations," Nixon told Americans that night. "Any nation can be our friend without being any other nation's enemy."

Late that evening, after a celebratory dinner with the president at an L.A. restaurant, the White House staff helicoptered back to San Clemente from Burbank; shouting over the clattering rotors, Ehrlichman, Haldeman, and Kissinger turned back to the topic of leaks.

Ehrlichman insisted, over Kissinger's protest, that the national security advisor's aide-de-camp, David Young, help lead a new team dedicated to identifying and countering leakers. Young was Kissinger's boy wonder of the moment, in a high-pressure job that dealt with everything from the bachelor national security advisor's laundry to note-taking in high-level meetings with foreign leaders—the average tenure in the role was measured in just months. Haldeman smiled listening to Ehrlichman and Kissinger bicker—sticking a Kissinger man on the team was "bureaucratic genius," he thought, knowing "all too well how Henry would happily ignite a fuse, then stand off swearing that he knew nothing about it or had even been against it."

On Saturday morning, Nixon hosted a meeting to review his administration's plan to combat heroin in Vietnam—an increasingly complex military and domestic problem as drugs from Southeast Asia were funneled back to the streets of the U.S., sometimes even smuggled aboard air force planes—and Egil "Bud" Krogh, Jr., who headed the White House's narcotics portfolio, briefed the president on his just-completed two-week trip through the region. After, Ehrlichman, a longtime family friend, summoned the thirty-one-year-old Krogh to his office, closed the door, and handed over a bulky file.

Krogh had worked at Ehrlichman's law firm—even babysat for his children—and was part of the team the domestic policy advisor recruited to come to Washington to work in the White House. His friendly nickname, "Evil Krogh," a play on his actual name, was meant to be ironic and tongue in cheek—he was in fact straitlaced, having been imbued growing up with a strong sense of Christian Midwestern values, and had first come into the Nixon orbit working on a transition team focused on identifying, avoiding, and mitigating both real and perceived conflicts of interest with new administration appointees. He jogged five miles a day, usually on his White House lunch hour, wearing a gray sweatsuit. Once, in introducing Krogh at a party in D.C., the sardonic and self-aware Ehrlichman compared him to the beleaguered, overworked, and abused clerk in *A Christmas Carol*, saying, "He serves as my Bob Cratchit."

Ehrlichman now informed Krogh that he'd be in charge of the special team tasked with uncovering the conspiracy that surely lay behind the Pentagon Papers leak—so far, investigators hadn't found any links between Ellsberg's leaks and other New Left radicals or known Communists, but the president maintained there were surely bigger nefarious forces at work. "Nixon was sure that Ellsberg had not functioned alone," Krogh recalled. The president saw the battle against Ellsberg as akin to the one he'd fought early in his career against Hiss—another golden boy intellectual and card-carrying member of the foreign policy elite who had betrayed his country. As a starting point, Ehrlichman said the president wanted Krogh to read the Hiss chapter in Nixon's memoir *Six Crises*. Later, as Krogh read, a line on the book's page 40 leapt out: "[This case] involved the security of the whole nation and the cause of free men everywhere." The Ellsberg stakes could not be higher, the aide thought.

Krogh would be paired with Young, from Kissinger's National Security Council, and a third representative from Colson's team: Howard Hunt. In their first meeting, Krogh recognized why Hunt likely worked well at the agency; he was unassuming and able to blend into any group. He all but disappeared even as you were speaking to him. "Hunt was presented to me as a crackerjack CIA operative who knew his way around. I didn't know he was a clown. I didn't even know he was writing spy novels. They told me he could practice some good spycraft," Krogh told journalist Evan Thomas decades later. "What did I know?" The trio perfectly balanced the fiefdoms of the White House, giving everyone a stake in their success; the team's reports would go to Ehrlichman, who would pass them along to the president directly.*

They set up shop in Room 16 of the Executive Office Building, in the far southwest corner of the building next to the White House that housed most of the president's staff. The so-called Special Investigations Unit had its own secretary, Kathy Chenow, and Hunt had a special non-government phone line installed, with the bills sent to Chenow's home so they could make calls without any sign of government ties. Everything about their work seemed important and sensitive: Everyone on the team received a high-level security clearance; Krogh had a secure scrambler phone installed to communicate with military and intelligence offices, and the Secret Service secured the office suite with motion detectors; a large safe appeared to hold the secrets they collected. They kept track of their assignments and projects on a cork bulletin board, adding new leaks as they occurred, such as a summer *New York Times* article by Tad Szulc about tensions between India and Pakistan that the CIA feared would lead to the outing of one of its most senior sources in the Indian government.

Soon, they welcomed a new member: G. Gordon Liddy, whom journalist Fred Emery would later describe as "an exceptionally articulate man with rambunctious right-wing views." When they first met and shook hands, Liddy crushed Krogh's hand with his viselike grip.

---

* Unbeknownst to Krogh, he was hardly the top choice to lead such a sensitive assignment; speechwriter and Nixon muse Pat Buchanan had turned down the role, purportedly believing it to be too operational for his taste, and the internal rivalry meant that Nixon's supposed first choice, Colson, wasn't to be trusted by Ehrlichman and Haldeman. Meanwhile, Dean's role in shutting down the summer attack on Brookings left Ehrlichman doubting he had the stomach for such messiness. Ironically, as later events would show, Ehrlichman had it exactly backwards: In the months and years of messiness ahead, Krogh's conscience would act up long before Dean's did.

In recalling his childhood in Hoboken, Liddy, a self-styled tough guy, emphasized the bad—from beatings by his grandfather by day to dreams of ravenous giant moths out to get him while he slept by night—but he was hardly a hard-luck case; he came from a wealthy family who even amid the Depression employed a maid, and he grew up with fencing lessons and Latin tutors. He had long sought to prove himself tough and worthy on life's fields of honor—fourteen-year-old George had been disconsolate for a month following Japan's surrender in 1945 because World War II came to an end before he was old enough to fight—and he later found his dreams of combat glory similarly frustrated by a Korean War assignment to an army antiaircraft gun unit in New York City, where action came in the form of ogling passing women using the high-powered gun sights meant to track incoming Soviet bombers.

He'd eventually pursued law school and followed into the FBI his uncle, a distinguished federal agent who according to family lore was present at the shooting of John Dillinger (there's no sign in FBI records that he actually was). He'd loved the work, but not the pay, which stretched his large family—he and his wife had five children under the age of five before they reconsidered the rhythm method—and he left to work for a New York district attorney. Later, he tried politics, unsuccessfully running for Congress, and ended up at Nixon's Treasury Department working on law enforcement issues after serving loyally on the presidential campaign.

That first chapter of his D.C. career had demonstrated his unique willingness to fudge ethical lines: Upon starting as a political appointee, he used a special set of department badges—intended for use by CIA officers working undercover—to mock up his own "Treasury agent" credentials and grant himself permission to carry a gun. With an outsized ego and sense of his own capabilities, he tried for numerous senior law enforcement roles before finally winning a transfer to the White House in the summer of 1971 to work on a portfolio of "narcotics, bombings, and guns." Arriving at the White House the day after the Pentagon Papers broke, he soon found himself working with Krogh's SIU as well. "He projected a warrior-type charisma and seemed to possess a great deal of physical courage," Krogh recalled later. It didn't take long for outlandish stories about the new colleague to start circulating, like the time Liddy as a prosecutor fired a pistol in a courtroom to emphasize a point. He liked to boast to White House secretaries about how to kill someone with a pencil.

Hunt and Liddy hit it off immediately; Liddy appeared to have wandered right off the pages of one of Hunt's novels. "He seemed decisive and action-oriented, impatient with paperwork and the lucubrations of bureaucracy," Hunt recalled. They lunched together in the White House cafeteria and drank together after work at one of Hunt's two social clubs, the Army and Navy Club, just north of the White House, or the City Tavern Club in Georgetown. "They were narcissists in love with the romance of espionage," one Watergate chronicler said. Hunt especially loved his new role and hardly tried to hide it; he updated his own entry in the 1972–1973 edition of *Who's Who* to list the White House as his office address.

Liddy later recalled the unit's mission in grandiose terms for something where most of the staff were part-time: "Our organization had been directed to eliminate subversion of the secrets of the administration." He nicknamed their team the "Organisation Der Emerlingen Schutz Staffel Angehöerigen"—ODESSA, for short, a confounding moniker that pleased Liddy greatly despite (or perhaps because) it was the name of a long-rumored secret network of German SS officers after World War II. Even while Liddy marked the group's papers with the ODESSA name, the group would be known to history by a label given offhand by David Young's grandmother: When she asked him what he was doing in the White House, he explained, simply, "I am helping the president stop some leaks." She replied, proudly, "Oh, you're a plumber!"

The name stuck.

*　　*　　*

On July 23, the now five-member Plumbers had their first meeting. "A mood of manic resolve to carry out our duties drove us forward," Krogh recalled. The men were supposed to be concentrating on Ellsberg, but from the start, there were side projects: Nixon's circle had long suspected that John F. Kennedy was more culpable in the 1963 assassination of South Vietnam's president than anyone admitted, and Hunt was tasked with a ham-handed debriefing of a top CIA officer, who had overseen operations in Vietnam, to pry loose the full story of JFK's involvement in the coup that toppled and killed Diem. He came up empty.

Krogh and Young, meanwhile, began tracking what the White House considered to be a concerning leak printed in the *New York Times*, a July 23 article at the top of the front page. William Beecher had written a story about the ongoing Strategic Arms Limitation Talks (SALT) that enumerated the U.S.'s main proposals and its acceptable fallback positions—precisely the type of information that Kissinger thought could hurt the United States in its negotiations with closed regimes.

With the help of Al Haig, the Special Investigations Unit identified two potential leakers—a Pentagon staffer, William Van Cleave, and a Hill staffer, Richard Perle. When they showed Nixon the evidence that it was likely Van Cleave, the president grew angry; punching his right fist into his open left hand, he told Krogh and Ehrlichman that he couldn't stand for these leaks to continue. The encounter had a deep impact on Krogh, who increasingly saw his work as central to the nation's security; as he explained later, "The SIU was now operating with a whole new sense of mission."

That afternoon, fired up, Krogh convened another meeting in the West Wing's Roosevelt Room with Hunt, Mark Felt, Robert Mardian, and Pentagon general counsel Fred Buzhardt to discuss how best to tackle the next steps of the SALT leak investigation. The others were all in their weekend clothes; Mardian had been called off a tennis court. In their first outing as elite leak-fighters, the Plumbers found themselves stymied immediately by the bureaucracy; neither the CIA nor the FBI would cooperate and provide enough polygraph examiners to probe the leaks.

Krogh and Hunt walked out of the room with an important lesson in mind: The only people they could trust with their sensitive, vital work were themselves.

Days later, Krogh's team was back on the Ellsberg case—sifting through the FBI's Pentagon Papers reports, which included a notation that Ellsberg's psychiatrist in California, Dr. Lewis Fielding, had turned down two FBI requests for interviews. They suspected the doctor was trying to withhold relevant or sensitive information about his patient—perhaps exactly the kind of derogatory details they were looking for. Hunt and Liddy had a brainstorm and proposed a backup plan: They could break into Fielding's office and steal the doctor's records themselves; they'd done such "black bag jobs" in numerous cities both overseas and at home, they assured Krogh. "We felt a covert operation would be necessary and defensible," Krogh recalled. Krogh, in turn, went to Ehrlichman for permission and, through Ehrlichman, got an enthusiastic response from the president: "Tell Krogh he should do whatever he considers necessary to get to the bottom of the matter—to learn what Ellsberg's motives and potential further harmful action might be."*

*   *   *

On August 11, 1971, Krogh and Young drafted a two-page status memo on White House stationery about their "Pentagon Papers Project," outlining the status of the Justice Department's official grand jury investigation and their contacts with the FBI, as well as their less official probe of Ellsberg and all their other related targets, from his mother-in-law to a Princeton professor. "We have received the CIA preliminary psychological study [on Ellsberg], which I must say I am disappointed in and consider very superficial," they wrote. "We will meet tomorrow with the head psychiatrist Mr Bernard Malloy to impress upon him the detail and depth that we expect. We will also make available to him here some of the other information we have received from the FBI on Ellsberg. In this connection we would recommend that a covert operation be undertaken to examine all the medical files still held by Ellsberg's psychoanalyst covering the two-year period in which he was undergoing analysis."

Underneath, they provided a standard "Approve/Disapprove" box; Ehrlichman initialed a large "E" on the "Approve" line, then scribbled underneath "If done under your assurance that it is not traceable."

---

* In fact, if anything, Nixon was still worried that Krogh's Plumbers weren't going to be aggressive enough. On August 9, after a relaxing weekend on Maine's Minot Island, Nixon returned still fired up about the Pentagon Papers; the Democrats, he felt, were trying to bury the story of their party's shame. In his diary, Haldeman recorded, "The P's afraid that Krogh and our crew are too addicted to the law and are worrying about the legalisms rather than taking on the publicizing of the papers. His point here is not getting the *New York Times*; it's getting the Democrats."

Later in the memo, they noted that Howard Hunt wanted the FBI to ask British intelligence to double-check its telephone taps from the two years where Ellsberg was a graduate student at Cambridge University to see if it had evidence that during that time he'd been in contact with the Soviets. Underneath, again, Ehrlichman scribbled an "E" for "Approve."

As the leak probe he'd demanded churned along and entered a dangerous (and criminal) new phase, tipping over from a routine bureaucratic exercise into a conspiracy to violate the civil rights of an American citizen, Nixon focused his attention elsewhere, on history-making events: an exchange of secret letters with his Soviet counterparts that set the stage for a summit in Moscow with Soviet leader Leonid Brezhnev, a dialogue he and Kissinger worked by excluding the State Department and never informing Secretary of State William Rogers. Then that weekend, Nixon assembled a dozen top officials at Camp David in complete secrecy to plot upending the monetary system that had undergirded Western markets since World War II.

Sunday night, in a surprise national television address, Nixon announced that the U.S. was abandoning the "gold standard" that tied the U.S. dollar to gold reserves, and imposing a ninety-day freeze on wages and prices to arrest inflation, a step the administration believed would prevent a looming economic crisis. "We must protect the position of the American dollar as a pillar of monetary stability around the world," he told the nation.

Monday, the Dow Jones Industrial Average saw its largest gain ever, and the *New York Times*—that awful *New York Times*—praised him, writing at the top of its editorial page: "We unhesitatingly applaud the boldness with which the President has moved on all economic fronts."

This was the stuff he could do, the history he could make, the great leader Nixon could be when he was able to do things quietly and secretly, when there wasn't some son of a bitch out there spilling his strategy to the press. Statesmanlike victories on the global stage like these would power Nixon's reelection campaign. Secrecy and subterfuge were good for the country geopolitically—and good for the president politically.

Chapter 7

The Enemies List

While the Plumbers toiled away that August in Room 16, White House Counsel John Dean saw an opportunity to bring some order to the president's chaotic habits of documenting his political foes. Nixon compiled enemies lists like other people compiled grocery lists—frequently, numerously, and repetitively. "I'm sure he must have forgotten some of the people who did him wrong—because there were so many of them and he couldn't possibly remember all of them. He did have a remarkable ability, though, to keep most of them pretty well-catalogued," Haldeman said later. The efforts had begun at the White House in the first months of his presidency, as aides researched and delivered a comprehensive twenty-six-page catalog of the nation's press corps with biographies, editorial comments, and friendliness rankings. The list of "Those We Can Count On" was short, but "Those We Can Never Count On" ran on for nearly three full pages.

From that starting point, what aides called the "Political Enemies Project" eventually grew so expansive that they couldn't make sense of the various lists. Ultimately, more than two hundred people would populate the administration's constellation of foes, from political adversaries like Kennedy, Muskie, and Howard Hughes, to the Hollywood actors Gregory Peck and Steve McQueen, to sports star Joe Namath, to the leaders of national companies and organizations like the World Bank, Philip Morris, and—oddly—the National Cleaning Contractors, as well as all manner of establishment titans (the presidents of Yale, MIT, and Harvard Law) and media figures. "Am I wrong to assume that the 'Freeze List' is something over and above the 'Opponent' list'?" Alexander Butterfield wrote in a memo to Haldeman at one point. "If you will straighten me out on this matter, I will pass the word to Colson, Bell, Rose Mary Woods . . . and others who have a need to know." The vetting process was haphazard—the German-American international relations theorist Hans Morgenthau was included, evidently after being confused with former New York U.S. attorney Robert Morgenthau—and arbitrary—the worst offense of many of the "enemies" was a routine donation to a Democratic candidate.

In June, just days after the Pentagon Papers broke, aide George Bell compiled a seemingly definitive list of the administration's top "opponents," passing it along to other aides like Dean with a routine cover note that read, "Attached is a list of opponents which we have compiled. I thought it would be useful to you from time to time."*

On August 16, 1971, Dean tried to bring focus to the system, laying out "how we can maximize the fact of our incumbency in dealing with persons known to be active in their opposition to our Administration. Stated a bit more bluntly—how we can use the available machinery to screw our political enemies." There was no need, in Dean's thinking, for any "elaborate mechanism or game plan," the Political Enemies Project just needed a solid way to collect said enemies and then act. Dean proposed as a starting point that "key members of the staff (e.g., Colson, Dent, Flanigan, Buchanan) should be requested to inform us as to who they feel we should be giving a hard time." Then, a project coordinator should be assigned to "determine what sorts of dealings these individuals have with the federal government and how we can best screw them

* Bell's list ranged from the national director of the AFL-CIO's political department, to a top Muskie fundraiser, to the Democratic senator Scoop Jackson's administrative assistant ("We should give him a try. Positive results would stick a pin in Jackson's white hat"); Detroit congressman John Conyers was "emerging as a leading black anti-Nixon spokesman" and "has [a] known weakness for white females"; columnist Mary McGrory authored "daily hate Nixon articles"; New York mayor John Lindsay's top aide was a "first class S.O.B., wheeler-dealer and suspected bagman"; the *L.A. Times* managing editor Ed Guthman was a "highly sophisticated hatchet man against us in '68" and "it is time to give him the message." As to Morton Halperin, Bell wrote, "a scandal would be most helpful here." Actor Paul Newman supported "Radic-Lib causes." And CBS's Daniel Schorr was a "real media enemy."

(e.g., grant availability, federal contracts, litigation, prosecution, etc.)." Through much of the first term, the Nixon team had tried, with mixed success, to sic the Internal Revenue Service on various enemies—but the White House believed it could do much more. Dean recommended starting with a pilot project: Choose a small handful of names, "'do a job' on them," and see what the Nixon administration could stir up.

The very next day, CBS reporter Daniel Schorr, number 17 on George Bell's "opponents list," earned the specific enmity of the Nixon administration after reporting on the *CBS Evening News* that Nixon's promise to help Catholic schools was falling short. Schorr was summoned to the White House, and Haldeman told Higby to order the FBI to dig up dirt on him. Hoover misinterpreted the orders—to him, a White House request for a "background" investigation meant that the target was being considered for a possible political appointment, and bright and early the next morning, an FBI agent contacted Schorr while other agents fanned out across the country interviewing two dozen of his associates, relatives, and friends. Schorr grew alarmed; he reported the odd inquiry to his CBS bosses, who in turn contacted the FBI. By mid-afternoon, the whole exercise had been abandoned. The White House, embarrassed to be caught in its own muckraking, announced—implausibly—that Schorr was being vetted for a position on the Environmental Quality Council. Nixon was hardly chagrined, dismissing the whole episode in an Oval Office meeting later: "We just ran a name check on the son-of-a-bitch."

To Mark Felt, who had been tasked with executing the urgent, full-field investigation on Schorr, the episode proved a cautionary tale: These Nixon folks seemed far too comfortable deploying the FBI as a political tool—and when it backfired, they were far too comfortable letting it take the blame.

*　　*　　*

G. Gordon Liddy's official role at the White House focused on narcotics policy, so he split his time with the Plumbers along with work on firearms issues and heroin—never seeming too troubled by a role that involved law enforcement by day and lawbreaking by night. Liddy never seemed to doubt that fighting the nation's enemies meant fighting Nixon's enemies.

As Schorr faced Nixon's wrath, Liddy penned a long update on the Ellsberg project, describing the CIA's assistance so far as "disappointing" and how the FBI's work on Ellsberg "has been characterized by a lack of a sense of urgency." Shut out by the government's normal security agencies, the Plumbers and the White House forged ahead with their own operation against Ellsberg's psychiatrist. Needing disguises to execute their plan, they turned to the government's in-house burglary and concealment experts: Ehrlichman called the CIA's deputy director and explained that Hunt was a security consultant for the White House and would need help from time to time. Hunt, the White House aide explained, should be given "pretty much carte blanche" by the agency.

"I've been charged with quite a highly sensitive mission by the White House to visit and elicit information from an individual whose ideology we aren't entirely sure of," Hunt told his old colleague Deputy Director Robert E. Cushman, Jr., in a follow-up meeting. "We're to keep it as closely held as possible."

Hunt and Liddy met a staffer from the CIA's Technical Services Division at a safe house in southwest D.C. The tech went by the pseudonym "Steve," while Liddy introduced himself simply as "George," adopting his own operational pseudonym of "George F. Leonard." Steve equipped the White House aides with new identities—for Liddy, that meant not only a Kansas driver's license, but supporting "pocket litter" like a Social Security card and a lifetime membership card for the National Rifle Association, as well as a dark brown wig, new glasses, and a "gait-altering device" that slipped into his shoe.* Lastly, they were handed a concealed spy camera—a 35mm Tessina that slipped inside a compartment in a pouch of pipe tobacco, the underside of which had a special grill to allow easy photos.

On August 25, Hunt and Liddy took off for Los Angeles, flying on a government travel voucher, and checked into the Beverly Hilton, just a few blocks from the office of Ellsberg's psychiatrist, Lewis Fielding. The

---

* One of the oddities of disguises is that thousands of years of hunting-and-gathering evolution have made the human eye able from a far distance to recognize familiar people by their walk, meaning that for undercover agents, it's easy for a cover identity to be blown from afar, before wigs and glasses can even conceal an identity, hence the need for a different gait while undercover.

next day, they began surveillance in disguise; posing as tourists, they took photos of the building and the Volvo parked in the doctor's reserved spot, surveyed the building entryway, plotted escape routes, and scoped out Fielding's apartment, before returning to the office at the same time of night they planned to break in. Spotting cleaning equipment in the lobby, they waltzed in and found a Hispanic cleaning woman on the second floor; speaking Spanish, Hunt explained that they were doctors and needed to leave a message for their colleague. She unlocked the door to Fielding's office, and Hunt distracted her as Liddy pretended to leave a note while surveying the suite layout and office door. He breathed a sigh of relief: The lock would be easy for him to pick using his old FBI skills. Back outside, they monitored police patrols and traffic patterns, checking the building every fifteen minutes through the evening until midnight, when the cleaning woman left. Reconnaissance complete, they hopped a red-eye flight back to Washington. "Steve" met them at Dulles Airport to take their film to be developed by the CIA.

At the White House, they created a more formal burglary plan. Bud Krogh took only a day to approve the operation, just cautioning Hunt and Liddy not to participate in the break-in themselves. Hunt suggested enlisting some Cuban-Americans that he'd worked with during his CIA days around the Bay of Pigs invasion; they were discreet and had been trained in clandestine operations. And, as luck would have it, he'd recently reconnected with them.

On the tenth anniversary of the Bay of Pigs invasion that April, he'd traveled to Miami and visited the memorial for the failed operation. Using his agency cover name of "Eduardo," he'd set a meeting at the memorial with Bernard Barker, a former colleague. Barker, known as "Macho," was a longtime CIA agent and World War II veteran—he had spent a year in a German prisoner of war camp after his B-17 was shot down on a bombing raid—who had joined Cuban dictator Fulgencio Batista's federal police as part of his CIA role after the war. Together, they lunched at a Cuban restaurant with another operation veteran named Eugenio Martinez. "[Hunt] was different from all the other men I had met in the Company. He looked more like a politician than a man who was fighting for freedom," Martinez would recall later, using the unofficial reference for the CIA. "His motions are very meticulous—the way he smokes his pipe, the way he looks at you and smiles. He knows how to make you happy—he's very warm, but at the same time you can sense that he does not go all into you or you all into him."*

As conversations continued that summer, Hunt disclosed to the Cubans that he was working in the White House, putting together a team to operate where the CIA and the FBI couldn't and investigate a "traitor of this country who had given papers to the Russian Embassy," a reference to Ellsberg, who had been rumored—inaccurately—to have delivered a copy of the Pentagon Papers to the Soviets. Barker would be part of the team, and he needed two others: Was Martinez interested? "To me this was a great honor," Martinez recalled later, seeing the new offer as a reward and validation of his years of service to the CIA. In late summer, Hunt telephoned Barker from the Plumbers' office in Room 16 to officially recruit them into the Fielding burglary. They agreed on the upcoming three-day Labor Day weekend as the ideal date for the break-in.†

Inside the White House, memos and conversations focused on what information gathered during what was obliquely called "Hunt/Liddy Project #1" might be weaponized against Ellsberg. On August 27, Ehrlichman wrote to Colson, "On the assumption that the proposed undertaking by Hunt and Liddy would be carried out, and would be successful, I would appreciate receiving from you by next Wednesday a game plan as to how and when you believe the material should be used."

On September 1, a Wednesday, they met in Room 16, where Krogh gave Hunt and Liddy operational money; Colson had rounded up about

---

* One of the remaining mysteries of Watergate is whether Hunt's April trip—months before the Pentagon Papers and before he joined the White House—was truly as innocent and retrospective as it has been portrayed. Was Hunt still working for the CIA, and, if so, did he already have a mission in mind? "We did not think he had come to Miami for nothing," Martinez recalls.

† The CIA, meanwhile, was beginning to understand the Plumbers' operation and was concerned; "Steve," the technician, had developed their photos as instructed, but kept a set of copies for the agency, and the agency's deputy director, Cushman, called Ehrlichman to complain about Hunt's ongoing requests for assistance. The CIA was cutting them off, Cushman said, and Ehrlichman promised that he'd "restrain" Hunt.

$5,000 from an advertising firm that did work with the White House—monies that he would later repay out of campaign funds. From there, Hunt and Liddy were off to Chicago, where they intended to purchase the radio transceivers needed to coordinate the break-in. Krogh said goodbye with a simple request: "For God's sake, don't get caught!"

Given the green light, Barker passed the official word to Martinez: "Get clothes for two or three days and be ready tomorrow," he said. "We're leaving for the operation." The two Cubans met up at the Miami airport, joined by Felipe De Diego, another Bay of Pigs veteran and longtime CIA asset who now worked in Florida real estate. Martinez, who had never left Miami before, learned that they were headed to Los Angeles only once he got to the airport.

Arriving in L.A. after their stop in Chicago, Hunt and Liddy checked back into the Beverly Hilton and then split up to purchase the additional sundry equipment they needed—new cameras, tools, opaque plastic to cover the office windows from the inside, and rope in the event of an emergency escape from the second floor. Then they met up with their trio of burglars.

That afternoon, the Cubans disguised themselves as deliverymen and arrived at Fielding's office with a footlocker, addressed to Fielding, containing their burglary tools. The ever-obliging cleaning woman happily let them into his office, where they left the delivery before returning to Liddy's car and waiting. After she left for the night, the men approached the building to discover she'd locked all the doors behind her; they instead identified for the break-in a rear window concealed by shrubs. The Cubans entered, while Liddy—ever prepared for drama—stood watch outside with a Browning knife at the ready.

The group all met back at the hotel, where Hunt had readied a bottle of champagne. Once the debriefing began, though, it became clear that the operation had been far from successful. The Cubans had not located any files pertaining to Ellsberg, and the file cabinets had been visibly damaged. To cover up the now obvious burglary, they'd ransacked the suite to look like they were junkies searching for drugs. "There was nothing of Ellsberg's there," Martinez said later. Despite the apparent failure, the group went ahead with a champagne toast anyway. Liddy called Krogh, who "was so relieved that nothing had gone wrong, he wasn't concerned that we hadn't found anything."*

The next morning as the Cubans quickly left town, Liddy and Hunt took another trip to Fielding's home. Thinking the doctor might be keeping Ellsberg's papers there, Liddy snuck inside the building to photograph Fielding's door lock and scout his back porch. It would be useful reference if another attempt was needed. Flying back to D.C. under their assumed names, Liddy and Hunt boasted to the flight attendants how they had just been involved in a big national security operation; they "fuzzed up" the story of the break-in, but when it broke eighteen months later, the flight attendants recognized it enough to report the encounter to the FBI.

*   *   *

Back in the White House on Tuesday, Hunt tried to discuss his weekend activities with Chuck Colson, but was met with a terse refusal. "I don't want to hear anything about it," Colson said.† Liddy had more success reporting the operation to Krogh, showing him the Polaroids taken by the Cubans and the knife he'd carried to cover their entry. "To prove we had not spent the money on a party, we took photographs of the windows in Fielding's office; of the drugs we had strewn about," Liddy recalled. Krogh thought the whole presentation surreal—seeming to recognize for the first time the ethical and criminal line the president's men had

---

* There's an intriguing discrepancy in the Fielding burglary reports: Later, one of the burglars, Felipe De Diego, said that the burglars had found the Ellsberg file and successfully photographed it. Fielding too has said that the Ellsberg file was actually in the office that night, and when he arrived the next morning, it "looked as if it had been fingered," leaving open the possibility that either De Diego was telling the truth or that the burglars had raced past it without realizing. Liddy, years later, would wonder if Hunt and the burglars had done an end run around him: Did they actually find what they were looking for, photograph it, and take it back to the CIA? It would have explained the champagne toast. Fielding's filing cabinet today is in the possession of the Smithsonian.

† While it's never been established to have been part of their activities, it's possible this wasn't the only Ellsberg-focused burglary. In November, the office of the psychiatrist who treated Ellsberg's wife in Manhattan was burglarized and searched; blank checks were stolen, but a file cabinet containing the file on Patricia Ellsberg was also rifled.

crossed—but in the end didn't seem deterred. "Hang onto those tools and things, we may need them again," he told Liddy.

Ehrlichman reported the failed operation, obliquely, to Nixon the next day. "We had one little operation—it's been aborted—out in Los Angeles which, I think, is better that you don't know about," he told the president in the Oval Office, but reassured him, "We've got some dirty tricks underway. It may pay off." He'd experienced a brief flicker of doubt after the burglary, but quickly dismissed it—he recalled thinking, "Someone was betraying national secrets. Hunt and Liddy did what the FBI had been doing in such cases for years with the blessing of the attorney general and the president."

While the idea of breaking into Fielding's L.A. apartment was ultimately nixed—the risk versus reward seemed too great, given that no one even knew if the files were at the doctor's home—the team stayed focused on undermining Ellsberg in the public eye. Everyone seemed to have ideas for additional plots: Ehrlichman suggested breaking into the National Archives to steal files related to the Pentagon Papers that Democratic aides had deposited there, while the Plumbers considered drugging Ellsberg with LSD during a gala dinner in Washington so his bizarre public behavior would discredit him—they went as far as to work out how to infiltrate Cuban waiters to serve him soup laced with LSD mid-meal. The White House approved the operation, but not in time to execute it.

Meanwhile, Colson revived Jack Caulfield's plan to break into the Brookings Institution, giving Hunt and Liddy the go-ahead to formulate a plan. The problem, Liddy decided, wasn't that the previous scheme was a bad idea—it just wasn't ambitious enough. He and Hunt worked up a plan to purchase a used fire engine, outfit it with D.C. fire department logos, and staff it with the Cuban burglars disguised in uniforms and trained in basic firefighting. The fake engine would respond after a time-delayed firebomb exploded inside the think tank late at night; first on the scene, before the real D.C. firefighters arrived, the burglars would have time to enter the building, access the vault, and escape amid the confusion. The proposal was denied quickly—not because it was an insane, breathtakingly risky, and complicated illegal plot to be connected directly to the President of the United States. "Too expensive," Liddy recalled. "The White House wouldn't spring for a fire engine."

Beyond Ellsberg, the Plumbers pursued their own side projects, an in-house skunk works targeting the White House's enemies. Hunt continued his quest for evidence to pin the assassination of South Vietnamese President Diem on the Kennedy administration, but remained unable to find any incriminating evidence as he excavated the State Department's files—too many relevant diplomatic cables appeared suspiciously missing, Hunt concluded, so he forged his own cable, seeming to grant tacit permission for the assassination from Kennedy, and tried, unsuccessfully, to leak it to *LIFE* magazine.

*　　*　　*

That fall, the White House was increasingly concerned about the dysfunction at the FBI and asked Liddy to wade into its brewing internal cold war. The atmosphere of suspicion around the looming succession battle at the bureau had deteriorated rapidly through the summer and early fall and started to spill over into the media. "The appointment of W. Mark Felt has prompted much discussion within the agency and has raised speculation that Mr. Hoover has settled on the man he would like to replace him," the *New York Times* reported in late August. Felt clearly wanted the job, standing out amid an executive leadership who looked as if they had walked out of central casting of a 1930s gangster movie. "He had this quite flamboyant hair," recalled Nicholas Horrock, who covered the FBI for *Newsweek* at the time. "Mark dressed well and it was noticeable."

Six ramrod-straight feet tall, Felt was not well liked by his peers, who saw him as both icy and untrustworthy. "Some had dubbed him 'the white rat' for his thick mane of white hair and tendency to squeal whenever he thought it would help his own agenda," bureau historian Max Holland wrote. Angry over Felt's elevation and his own demotion, Hoover's longtime assistant director William Sullivan had been lashing out in a lengthy series of highly critical internal letters, laying out point by point and page after page how the bureau was falling short. In early September, Hoover had had enough. He instructed Sullivan to submit his application for retirement. Sullivan refused. On September 30, Hoover relieved the agent of his duties, pending his official retirement. In early October, Sullivan finally accepted defeat and left the bureau, pointedly leaving behind only his autographed picture of Hoover.

Days later, a column by Evans and Novak aired the long-building dirty laundry between Sullivan and Hoover, highlighting the "deterioration of the FBI" and saying the bureau was facing a "reign of terror." Longtime officials, they reported, were "heartsick" at the state of the nation's law enforcement agency and the drama "redouble[d]" a sense at the White House and Justice Department that Hoover "should go and go soon." To Felt, it seemed clear Sullivan was a key source—perhaps the only source—for the syndicated columnists, but it didn't bother him; as far as he was concerned, Sullivan's ignominious departure removed his only rival for the directorship after Hoover.*

As Sullivan imploded, Nixon continued to try to find the best way to encourage Hoover too to leave. He hosted Hoover for a breakfast on September 20—a rare event so private that it never even appeared on the White House's daily diary. They spent the better part of two hours talking, Nixon hoping he could convince Hoover to retire on his seventy-seventh birthday on January 1, but Hoover didn't take the bait and Nixon didn't have the heart—or the will—to push. "No go," Nixon told Haldeman later in the day. It surprised none of his staff that he couldn't bring himself to get rid of "Edgar." Nixon was awful at firing people. ("It was a little bit like killing the Thanksgiving turkey with a dull axe—hack away and back off and ask somebody else to do it," Ehrlichman observed.) Frustrated, Nixon whined to Mitchell in October, "He oughta resign," and enlisted Krogh to dig into the issue further.

Krogh, in turn, tasked Liddy with researching Nixon's next move. The former agent spent weeks talking to people inside and outside government. He delivered on October 22 a ten-page memo that quoted Tennyson and outlined the bureau's history, mission, and Hoover's impact, concluding that "years of intense adulation have inured Hoover to self-doubt." The need for change was obvious: "J. Edgar Hoover should be replaced as Director of the FBI. The question is when?"

---

* "It did not cross my mind that the President would appoint an outsider to replace Hoover," Felt wrote later.

While Liddy believed removing Hoover after reelection in '72 would be "no real problem," he argued for swifter action. "I believe it to be in the best interest of the Nation, the President, the FBI, and Mr. Hoover that the Director retire before the end of 1971," he wrote. "Immediate removal would guarantee that the President would appoint the next Director of the FBI, something akin in importance to a Supreme Court appointment opportunity." Yet the White House still couldn't see a safe path. Angering either Sullivan or Hoover seemed to bring its own risks, and Sullivan already knew too much about Nixon's behavior. "Sullivan was the man who executed all of your instructions for the secret taps," Ehrlichman reminded the president.

"Will he rat on us?" Nixon wondered.

"It depends on how he's treated," Ehrlichman replied.*

While they weighed the possibilities, Mitchell summoned Hoover's former deputy Deke DeLoach to Washington, asking him, "How can we get J. Edgar Hoover to leave office without him kicking over the traces?" The president seemed sure the director would "piss" all over whoever replaced him, making the successor's job untenable. Or worse—perhaps he would let loose the blackmail and slanderous accusations he'd gathered on so many U.S. officials. "We may have on our hands here a man who will pull down the temple with him, including me," Nixon said.

Even if the outcome stalled, Liddy's FBI plotting project helped establish the former agent as a rising White House star. In an Oval Office meeting that fall, Nixon commented to Ehrlichman, "That's a very good fellow, is it—Liddy? . . . Smart, isn't he?"

"Yeah, very," the aide replied.

"Must be conservative as hell," Nixon observed.

Liddy's memo impressed the president, Krogh reported back to Liddy, and Nixon said he wanted it to be used by staff across the White House as a model of how to brief the commander in chief. It seemed Liddy was ready for the next challenge. Krogh had just the project: helping to oversee a sweeping intelligence operation that would support the president's reelection efforts.

---

* Ehrlichman's concern would ultimately lead to the Nixon administration rehiring Sullivan the following year as the head of a seemingly prestigious new narcotics intelligence unit.

Chapter 8

Sandwedge

Jack Caulfield, the former NYPD officer assigned to John Dean's staff, wanted to parlay his experience as a political operative into his own outside political security and intelligence firm. He saw a major opportunity in the 1972 reelection campaign, and delivered to Dean that fall a twelve-page proposal for an extensive half-million-dollar operation to aid Nixon's effort.

Caulfield had dubbed it "Operation SANDWEDGE." He envisioned running the intelligence independent of the campaign or the White House (at least publicly), alongside a team that included Rose Mary Woods's brother, Joseph, who was a former Cook County sheriff, as well as two IRS officials and his colleague Tony Ulasewicz. Their firm, Caulfield said, would operate as the Republican equivalent to a storied dark-arts investigative firm that worked with Democrats and had been known as International Intelligence Inc.—Intertel, for short—founded by veterans of Bobby Kennedy's Justice Department. "Should this Kennedy mafia dominated intelligence 'gun for hire' be turned against us in '72, we would, indeed, have a dangerous and formidable foe," Caulfield wrote.

SANDWEDGE would help the Nixon campaign on everything from convention security to electronic eavesdropping, funded primarily by corporate "clients," who would give money knowing that it obliquely helped Nixon. The memo further outlined the "offensive capabilities" that the president's reelection campaign might require: "A) Supervise penetration of nominees entourage and headquarters with undercover personnel; B) "Black Bag" capability (discuss privately) including all <u>covert</u> steps necessary to minimize Democratic voting violations in Illinois, Texas, etc.; C) Surveillance of Democratic primaries, convention, meetings, etc.; D) Derogatory information investigative capability, world-wide; E) Any other offensive requirement deemed advisable." Reading over the plan, Dean smiled at the name—the sandwedge club was what a golfer used when in trouble.*

The idea of a political intelligence unit met with strong support inside the Nixon world. Gordon Strachan emphasized to his boss that they needed something like SANDWEDGE. "Ehrlichman and I believe it would be a good idea," he said, "but that it should be set up by Herb Kalmbach. John Dean would be the control point for all intelligence and in particular would supervise Caulfield's activities." Caulfield received $50,000 from Kalmbach for startup purposes, and as their first SANDWEDGE assignment, he and Ulasewicz outfitted a luxurious New York City apartment in which they hoped to lure and entrap some of the women who had attended the summer party on Martha's Vineyard with Ted Kennedy the night of the fatal Chappaquiddick incident.

Before long, the president's reelection effort began to debate not whether SANDWEDGE went too far, but if it went far enough. In a later memo to Haldeman, Strachan inquired if "intelligence shouldn't receive a greater allocation of time and resources than it is receiving now?" Haldeman scrawled an "H" across the option for "Yes more resources," adding "develop recs as to what." In fact, the main objection turned out only to be whether Caulfield was the right man to head a bigger, stronger intelligence effort. "I sensed that an Irish cop without a college education would not be entrusted with such a sensitive assignment in an Administration of WASP professional men," Dean recalled. John

---

* One oddity of Dean's recounting of 1971 and 1972 is that he consistently downplays his relationship and knowledge of Ulasewicz's activities, despite many of them closely following assignments from him. Caulfield also said Dean personally worked on Ulasewicz's contract, but in his memoir Dean said that he knew Caulfield's operative only as "Tony."

Mitchell stopped Dean after a meeting on another matter, and calling it "Operation Sandwich," Mitchell ordered, "I want a hold on it for now. I want a lawyer to handle it. If Caulfield wants to work for the lawyer, fine."

After discussion, Mitchell and Haldeman ultimately decided that the project should belong to the campaign's yet-to-be-determined general counsel. "How about Gordon Liddy?" Krogh suggested. "Gordon is a former FBI man and I'm sure he could handle any intelligence needs they might have." Liddy, Krogh explained, was just wrapping up his work analyzing the FBI's future, and Nixon liked his style. A few days later, Dean met Liddy for the first time and came away impressed. The man dressed dapperly, his hair groomed to perfection as if he'd walked straight out of a Vitalis hair tonic commercial, and obviously had a quick mind. "He bristled with energy," Dean recalled.

As soon as he was asked to take the role, Liddy went to Hunt's office and recounted the conversation with Dean and how he'd been asked to lead the intelligence operations. "Dean tells me there's plenty of money available—half a million for openers and there's more where that came from. A lot more," he told Hunt, adding that to be successful Liddy was sure he needed the help of the former CIA officer and his band of Cuban burglars: "I'll need you and Macho and all the rest of the guys if we're going to make this work."

✳   ✳   ✳

The sense that Nixon's White House was surrounded, inside and outside, with enemies and spies never seemed to abate. In December, journalist Jack Anderson—one of the capital's most feared and best-sourced muckrakers—published verbatim reports of a sensitive meeting the national security advisor had held on an unfolding crisis between India and Pakistan. Anderson's reporting made clear that Henry Kissinger had misled the nation and the world about the U.S. neutrality and that the government was secretly actively supporting Pakistan through the crisis.

It took David Young and the Plumbers a week to identify who they thought was the source of the Anderson leak: Charles Radford, a young navy yeoman working on the National Security Council, had admitted knowing the columnist. Radford worked for Admiral Robert O. Welander, the two of them encompassing the totality of the National Security Council liaison office for the Pentagon's Joint Chiefs of Staff.*

While the Plumbers hadn't been able to conclusively tie Radford to the story, he had admitted something even more troubling during a polygraph and subsequent questioning: He'd been regularly stealing some of the White House's most sensitive files and delivering them to Welander and the Pentagon. In fact, nearly everything that Kissinger dictated for his own staff had gone straight to the Joint Chiefs—Welander passed the stolen documents right to the chairman himself, Admiral Thomas Moorer. Radford added that he'd even rifled through Kissinger's personal briefcase. The young yeoman had carefully written the author, time, and date in the upper-right corner of each document, as well as where he found it, helping later readers at the Pentagon understand the chronology of unfolding policy debates.

Outraged that the Pentagon had been apparently running an espionage operation against the commander in chief, Ehrlichman and Young confronted Welander, prompting a startling hour-long confession. Amid the investigation, Young wanted to place a wiretap on Radford's phone, but Krogh felt squeamish. Seemingly he alone had grown uncomfortable with the Plumbers' clandestine work as the fall progressed. When Krogh objected to the wiretap, Ehrlichman brusquely told him he was removed from the Special Investigations Unit effective immediately. The White House ordered the FBI to begin listening to Radford's phone.

In the days ahead, there were hurried conferences among Nixon, Haldeman, Ehrlichman, and Mitchell as they weighed how to handle the military's betrayal and internal espionage uncovered by Young and the Plumbers. They contemplated prosecution; the idea that the Pentagon leadership was spying on the commander in chief during wartime seemed unconscionable.

"That is wrong—understand!" Nixon fumed.

---

* Radford had taken the White House role in the hopes that it would help him make the jump into the officer ranks and been instantly enthralled by the secret worlds now visible to him at the National Security Council. "I even stopped reading newspapers—that's how exciting it was—because the stuff in the newspapers was boring; they didn't know what they were talking about," he recalled later.

"No question about it, that the whole concept of having this yeoman get into this affair and start to get this stuff back to the Joint Chiefs of Staff is just like coming in and robbing your desk," Mitchell concurred.

Soon after, Mitchell confronted Moorer: "This ball game's over with." Moorer didn't exactly go to great lengths to plead his innocence, Ehrlichman explained later to Nixon: "I said, 'Well did you get a plea of guilty or a not guilty?' And [Mitchell] says, 'I got a *nolo contendere.*'"

Nixon quickly decided it would be better for everyone for the scandal to be buried. After all, he now held real power over the Joint Chiefs—men he had struggled to control since the start of his presidency. Moorer specifically would owe him big-time, knowing that Nixon could have ousted him in disgrace and didn't.*

The subterfuge and lack of consequences made Kissinger furious. He fired Welander, setting off an internal row with Al Haig. (Radford, for his part, was instantly reassigned to an obscure navy post in Oregon.) In the Oval Office later, Kissinger confronted Nixon: "I tell you, Mr. President, this is very serious. We cannot survive the kinds of internal weaknesses we are seeing." It was such an explosive and emotional outburst from Kissinger that after the national security advisor left, Nixon wondered aloud to Ehrlichman: Did Kissinger need psychiatric care?

Entering 1972, stress seemed sky-high for everyone in the White House. Anyone who doubted the tension in the building by month's end needed only to look at Henry Kissinger's hands. "I'd never seen fingernails bitten so close to the quick as Henry's were during that time," Ehrlichman recalled. In one Christmas conversation, Nixon seemed for a moment to recognize that the trouble all around him might be a product of the atmosphere he created. "Damn, you know, I created this whole situation this—this lesion. It's just unbelievable. Unbelievable," he repeated. "There have been more backchannel games played in this administration than any other in history"—but the moment of self-reflection was brief. Within days, he had reverted to his normal, brooding, paranoid self, seemingly angrier at Anderson for the leaks and breaking the story

---

* In a few months' time, Nixon nominated Moorer to a second term as chairman of the Joint Chiefs, a surprise extension that Nixon endorsed partly, as Ehrlichman would later say, because he had a "pre-shrunk admiral" under his finger.

of his administration's duplicity with India than he was with the Joint Chiefs spying on him. "I would just like to get a hold of this Anderson and hang him," Mitchell said in an Oval Office meeting as the internal turmoil wound down.

"Goddamn it, yes," Nixon said. "Listen, the day after the election, win or lose, we've got to do something with this son of a bitch."

* * *

The Radford incident, beyond simply underscoring the president's fear that his circles were populated by spies and adversaries, proved a fateful turning point for the administration.

In burying the episode quietly, the White House skipped over some uncomfortable, hard questions it uncovered about the loyalty of Kissinger's deputy, Al Haig. In fact, Welander specifically warned Ehrlichman and Young to look deeper into Haig's trustworthiness. "I think you have to talk to Al Haig on this," Admiral Radford had said. "It's been a two-way street," revealing Haig had been giving the military "game plans and so on." The warnings went ignored, and were never reported to Nixon himself, an oversight that allowed the ambitious Kissinger aide to continue to rise in the administration. Had Nixon seen the concerns about Haig then, John Mitchell said in 1986, "it would have taken and put Haig in a different light and probably . . . got [him] the hell out of there."

Beyond those questions about Haig's loyalty, the Radford episode also marked an end to the Plumbers era, given Krogh's removal as the team's leader and Liddy's transfer to the reelection campaign. The team's questionable legacy and dubious mission, though, would instead carry forward in new forms. Decades later, Krogh would write that their work that fall was "the first irreversible step by which a presidency ran out of control." The Plumbers had been meant as a tool to stop the White House's culture of leaking, secrecy, and paranoia, but rather than plugging the holes and ensuring Nixon a team worthy of trust, their six months of work had left a questionably trustworthy staff to fester and had further stretched (and broken) the ethical and legal boundaries of the White House's world. "It was like a culture taking root," Colson would later tell Nixon biographer Jonathan Aitken. "You could always get rewarded if you showed up at the White House with a bit of negative intelligence, so the puppies kept coming in with their bones."

That month, Gordon Strachan outlined to Haldeman how the Nixon campaign was building its own internal security and intelligence component in the wake of the Radford investigation. "SANDWEDGE has been scrapped," Strachan wrote. "Instead, Gordon Liddy, who has been working with Bud Krogh, will become general counsel to the Committee for the Re-Election of the President, effective December 6, 1971. He will handle political intelligence as well as legal matters. Liddy will also work with Dean on the 'political enemies' project."

In the final days of 1971, Jack Caulfield got a phone call from an official at the Republican National Committee. The party's security chief, Jack Ragan, who had helped Caulfield plant the unsuccessful bug on columnist Joseph Kraft's home, had enjoyed the libations a little too much at the RNC Christmas Party and ended up embarrassingly sprawled on the floor. "He has to go," the party's head of administration told Caulfield. A replacement was needed, so Caulfield asked Al Wong, the head of the Secret Service's technical division, for some retired agents who might be a good fit. Wong came back with a single name: A recently retired CIA officer who had overseen the agency's physical security at its headquarters in Langley, Virginia.

In early 1972, after an interview in Caulfield's office, James W. McCord started as the head of security for the Republican National Committee and the Committee to Re-Elect the President.

PART II

The Match

1972

Chapter 9

The Committee to Re-Elect

Gordon Liddy and Howard Hunt spent New Year's Eve 1972 together, with their wives, at Hunt's home in Maryland and then New Year's Day at the White House, in their old ODESSA conference room, beginning to sketch out the details of their campaign intelligence operation: "planting of our operatives in the staffs of Democratic candidates; surreptitious entries for placing of electronic surveillance devices and photographing key documents such as lists of donors and drafts of position papers with an eye for interstaff rivalries that could be developed into disruptive strife; the capacity to neutralize the leaders of anti-Nixon demonstrations; the exploitation of sexual weaknesses for information and the promotion of ill-feeling among the Democratic candidates to keep them as divided as possible after the nomination." From there, they began compiling another list of the required skills and roles they would need to fill—from lock-pickers and eavesdropping experts to burglars and prostitutes.

It would be an expansive—and expensive—effort, but Liddy had little reason to doubt the campaign could deliver. John Dean, after all, had promised a half million dollars for openers, and it was clear to everyone associated with the White House that the reelection campaign would be unprecedented in scope and scale. "My sense of purpose as I realized the opportunity I'd been handed pumped me so full of adrenalin I never felt tired," Liddy recalled. "In January, 1972 promised to be the best year I'd ever had."

There wasn't a great deal of mystery to Liddy's new secret mission on the campaign. A few days after he started on the reelection effort, Liddy stopped back at the White House to complain to John Dean: The deputy campaign director, Jeb Stuart Magruder, was going around introducing him as "our man in charge of dirty tricks." As Liddy said, "Magruder's an asshole, John, and he's going to blow my cover." Dean, annoyed, called Magruder: If you've hired someone to carry out your dirty tricks, it's best if you don't advertise that fact.*

Liddy's transfer to the Committee to Re-Elect the President came just as the campaign effort began to hit its stride. Known to most by its unfortunate acronym, CREEP—its own staff preferred CRP—the name had been chosen in part because of the unique air of distaste that surrounded Nixon himself in the public's mind. It was based, in part, on Rockefeller's slogan "Elect Governor Rockefeller Governor," but going a step further to remove the name of the candidate entirely. People, polling showed, wanted to support reelecting the president—as long as they weren't specifically reminded that man was Richard Nixon. "The poll results suggested a campaign that would say to the voter not 'You like Nixon' but 'You need Nixon,'" Magruder wrote later. There was no warm, friendly "We Like Ike" air around Nixon's reelection; the campaign slogan too would skip the candidate's name: "Now More Than Ever."†

The team had agreed to largely forgo the Republican Party apparatus and build their own, one that they knew would be entirely loyal and responsive to Nixon, and when they opened CREEP's new headquarters at 1701 Pennsylvania Avenue NW, inside the First National Bank building across from the White House, the goal was to be an intimidating, shining model of modern politics. CREEP's offices, with burnt-orange carpeting and ubiquitous electric typewriters, shared the building with Nixon strategist Murray Chotiner and were on the same fourth floor as

---

* Magruder, in his telling of the story, says he announced Liddy as the campaign's "supersleuth."

† As Nixon geared up for the reelection, he also installed a friendly—and feisty—leader atop the Republican National Committee: Bob Dole. While he's remembered today as a kind and warm political icon, a man best known for celebrating the last of the World War II veterans, Dole at the time had a reputation as just about the most partisan and hard-nosed political brawler Nixon could find to lead the RNC.

the Washington office of Mudge, Rose, Guthrie, and Alexander, Nixon and Mitchell's former law firm. The building also housed the Finance Committee to Re-Elect the President. Nixon had planned to entrust the two halves of his reelection to John Mitchell, as CRP director, and Maurice Stans, as finance chair, but he saw no need to rush either the attorney general or the commerce secretary out of the cabinet before election season, and so the temporary leadership consisted of Magruder as deputy director to oversee planning and operations and Hugh W. Sloan, Jr., as treasurer, to handle the budgeting and finances. On the outside, it fell to Kalmbach to lead the fundraising efforts and cajole and collect donors' money.

The highly charged, take-no-prisoners environment of the Nixon White House would turn out to be a particularly poor fit for Magruder, whose role at the center of the Nixon orbit seemed to exist solely because of his general malleability and willingness to follow the instructions of his superiors. ("He was the white-collar hustler as weakling," journalist Teddy White would write later, in what still ranks as one of the kinder descriptions of an empty vessel of a man, all too ready to fulfill others' ambitions, taskings, and visions.) He'd ended up at the campaign not because of his strength of leadership but precisely because of his lack of any—he'd do precisely what Haldeman and Mitchell told him to do with a minimum of fuss.

Stans, who had served as Nixon's treasurer in the '68 campaign, faced a Herculean task of raising even more money for '72. An accountant by training and demeanor, he styled his closely coiffed hair and carefully tailored suits and seemed to consider persnicketiness a professional virtue. Stans's fundraising target seemed to grow by the month. The $34 million that had powered Nixon just four years earlier was now dwarfed by CREEP's anticipated $52 million budget. "The committee was afloat and awash with money, enough to over-fertilize the imagination and ambitions of the most balanced minds," Teddy White wrote.

The vast resources were necessary, in part, because Nixon hardly felt a shoo-in for a second term. He was seen in many circles as a placeholder president, an accident of the Democrats' remarkable collapse three years earlier. Thanks to Wallace splitting the vote in '68, Nixon had been elected with 2.5 million fewer votes than he'd received in his unsuccessful

1960 presidential campaign; for someone like Nixon—*especially* for someone like Nixon—it was hard not to take personally that the equivalent of
the entire population of South Carolina or Connecticut had turned against
him. The 1970 midterm elections had not been encouraging either, with
the GOP losing twelve more seats in the House and eleven governorships.
Republicans feared that Nixon did not appear on track to win any of
the nation's ten largest states in 1972. He needed a victory—and a big
one, the kind that would prove to all those who had ever doubted him,
snickered at him, and insulted him that he was indeed a transformational
figure. "The victory over Humphrey had been far too close for comfort,"
Nixon wrote in his memoirs. "I decided that we must begin immediately
keeping track of everything the leading Democrats did. Information
would be our first line of defense."

As he wrote, "I vowed that I would never again enter an election at a
disadvantage by being vulnerable to them—or anyone—on the level of
political tactics." In '72, the gloves would be off.

*　　*　　*

Jeb Stuart Magruder had come into the White House orbit in the summer
of '69. Named for his father's favorite Confederate general, Magruder had
an inauspicious and roguish family background for someone working at
the highest levels of government—his great-grandfather had smuggled
shoes for the Confederacy during the Civil War, and his grandfather had
been prosecuted and sent to jail for a bank fraud tied to the construction
of cargo ships in World War I. His own career had been characterized by
a strange brew of seemingly unbound but aimless ambition, repeatedly
reaching for the biggest thing he could but lacking the self-discipline
to make it a success.

A native of Long Island, Magruder had flailed through two years at
Williams College in Massachusetts before taking time off in the hope
that the military would help him mature; he was booted out of Officer
Candidate School just weeks before graduation for skipping class to take
a colonel's daughter out in his new Chevrolet. He ended up spending
his desultory army stint guarding the Demilitarized Zone in Korea just
after the end of the war there. The experience launched a fascination

with politics and government, and he majored in political science when he returned to Williams.

Following college, he dropped out of IBM's training program after just a few days, heading west to California after a bad breakup, to marry a Berkeley student and take a job selling paper goods in Kansas City. A traditional, moderate conservative in the spirit of Eisenhower, he'd volunteered for Nixon in '60 and, after a move to Chicago, become a ward chairman in 1962 for a bright, ambitious congressional candidate named Donald Rumsfeld, chaired the district for Goldwater in '64, and then abruptly quit a part-time role managing the campaign of a sheriff to again head west. After some work with the Nixon presidential campaign, he was invited into the administration by Secretary of Health, Education, and Welfare Robert Finch; Finch's aide L. Patrick Gray had worked to identify the right job, though not at the assistant secretary level Magruder coveted—only to have Magruder turn it down when offered. Instead, he'd landed at the White House, where he'd helped reshape the administration's approach to handling the press.

In the fall of 1969, Magruder authored what would come to be known infamously as the "rifle and shotgun" memo, encouraging the Nixon team to stop "shotgunning" wildly at each individual press attack and instead aim for larger, more targeted game with the tools they had at their disposal—the IRS, for example, could be used against individual reporters, as a pressure point, and the FCC and the Justice Department should use their regulatory capabilities to pressure the networks and media owners. "The possible threat of antitrust action I think would be effective in changing their views," Magruder wrote.

The strategy was quickly adopted by the office of the vice president. In a national televised address, Nixon's snarling attack-dog running mate Spiro T. Agnew blasted the press as "a tiny, enclosed fraternity of privileged men elected by no one and enjoying a monopoly sanctioned and licensed by government."* Agnew's remarks catapulted his previously low profile to the front ranks of the administration, and he

---

* As Nixon biographer Tom Wicker wrote, "Nixon found Agnew a shallow malcontent within the White House, but appreciated the public acclaim he had aroused for views the president shared."

was instantly seen as a threat by the TV networks, whose broadcast licenses were overseen by the government. CBS President Frank Stanton called the speech an "unprecedented attempt . . . to intimidate a news medium which depends for its existence on government license."[*] Agnew was thrilled by the outrage: "Gangbusters!" he told speechwriter Pat Buchanan. A few days later, they had teamed up again for Agnew to attack the *Washington Post* and the *New York Times* in a speech to an Alabama chamber of commerce. Agnew's fiery and fierce anti-media, anti-elite rhetoric soon became his stump speech calling card, earning him the affection of conservative groups across the country and keeping the base fired up for Nixon.

While many political observers saw Magruder's deputy campaign director role as a move by Haldeman to have his own man in Mitchell's office overseeing the campaign, the truth seems more that both Mitchell and Haldeman saw in the weak-willed Magruder someone who would execute their vision with a minimum of fuss or conversation as they continued to run the White House and the Justice Department. This was evident when Magruder received one of his first campaign assignments. Besides votes, reporters, and campaign stops, Magruder was also tasked with overseeing one of the most consequential elements of Nixon's reelection: John Mitchell's wife.

*   *   *

A native of Pine Bluff, Arkansas—as her oversized drawl of a voice never let anyone forget—Martha Mitchell had grown in the first term of the Nixon administration into perhaps the first national conservative celebrity pundit, the second most requested speaker for Republican audiences, behind only the president himself. Voluble, outspoken, and full of southern pride, Mitchell lived her life confident that rules didn't apply to her; friends cited examples all the way back to her civilian days in the military's chemical weapons service in World War II,

---

[*] Stanton's words were notable because he was hardly a radical media voice; during the earlier Eisenhower-Nixon administration, he had been close enough to the government that he'd served as a secret, wartime censorship-czar-in-waiting.

when she converted an empty office into a full-fledged kitchen without authorization.*

She and John had fallen deeply, intensely, and incongruously in love in the mid-1950s, a second chance for both of them as their first marriages fell apart. They saw each other almost every night in New York, dining out on Chinese, and both rushed their divorces; just eleven days after John's was final in 1957, they married in Elkton, Maryland. Whereas Martha's first wedding, in 1946, had been the largest ever seen in Pine Bluff, her second go-round was far simpler—just her and the groom at a local court office. While friends noticed their care for each other—"John gloated in the love and affection Martha showed him. It was interesting to watch him at a party; he'd stand around, smoking his pipe, never taking his eyes off Martha. He seemed to worship her," a friend said— their dynamic contained a certain level of complication and drama, with John supporting her publicly but often working behind the scenes to undermine her efforts.†

She had not been a big Nixon fan to start—and to hear her tell it, her husband wasn't either—and she'd unhappily weathered the time John spent on the '68 campaign. Scotch became such a regular part of her day that she checked herself into a psychiatric hospital to dry out. Yet she'd excitedly embraced John's nomination as attorney general, and their initial period in Washington was wonderful. They moved into their new $150,000 duplex in the Watergate, and FBI agents accompanied them everywhere, much to Martha's delight. She was also the only cabinet wife to have a full-time government chauffeur. (She attracted some scandal when news photographs showed FBI agents helping her iron a dress and serving the Mitchells' daughter breakfast in bed.) Her husband considered the luxuries to be a fair trade. As his former secretary later recalled, John thought "being a Cabinet wife would give Martha

---

* She became such a fascinating celebrity to America that there were two full-length biographies published in the 1970s about her life, even though her husband—the first and only attorney general ever to serve time in prison—waited more than forty years before a single biography was written about him.

† One oft-told story was how when she expressed an interest in joining him on his regular golf outings, he purchased his left-handed wife right-handed clubs, insisting that she learn to golf that way; furious and fumbling in her lessons, she quickly gave up.

everything [she] desired. And it did, with one exception—John Mitchell. She needed him. She was tremendously insecure and she had this great dependency on him."

Her national profile had begun to rise in November 1969, following a *CBS Morning News* interview where she'd blasted the "liberal Communist" antiwar protesters. The remarks ignited a firestorm, but Nixon himself loved it. He wrote her a three-sentence note on his personal presidential stationery: *Dear Martha, Don't let the critics get you down—Just remember they are not after you—or John—but me—I appreciate deeply the loyalty and courage you and John have constantly demonstrated. We'll come out on top in the end. RN.* In the months ahead, her controversial and always conservative remarks became a balm to Nixon's "silent majority" base. She had it out for justices, educators, politicians, liberals, activists—even the nation's hairdressers. Margaret Mead? "She caused a lot of trouble." The Supreme Court? "Eradicate it!" Richard Nixon himself? "Sexy!" she declared. In an age where most high-ranking wives were still listed officially as mere extensions of their husbands, the idea of Martha making news under her own name was almost its own social revolution.

As spectacularly and colorfully opinionated as she was attired, her relationship with the Washington press corps existed with a certain symbiosis, as reporters quickly learned that she made great copy. "She suddenly became this folk hero," White House speechwriter Pat Buchanan remembered. Her long, rambling, opinionated phone calls at all hours of the day and night became legendary—and they were often highly revealing, since her habit of eavesdropping on her husband's telephone calls at their apartment and rifling through his papers at home meant she was usually remarkably well informed.

By the early 1970s, she was receiving hundreds of pieces of mail per day and had been given her own press secretary.* "No woman in public life has achieved so quickly the national awareness of Martha Mitchell," a pollster group concluded. In a newspaper article in December 1971 about suggestions for Spiro Agnew's gag Christmas gifts, the humor piece listed "For Martha Mitchell, a brand-new Princess phone. For John

---

* Her press aide, Kay Woestendiek, struggled to keep up with the incoming requests, leading Martha herself to answer the phone sometimes as "Mrs. Woestendiek's secretary."

Mitchell, a padlock for a brand-new Princess phone." She became so famous that she was named to Gallup's national list of the world's ten most admired women.

At CREEP, Magruder and his team referred to Martha as "The Account," stealing the phrase from the advertising world, a client to keep pleased, active, and engaged. In time, he came to understand it would be a round-the-clock effort: She and John would sit at home drinking in the evening—they rarely ventured out of the Watergate, in part because of Martha's fear that John would be assassinated by one of the era's New Left radicals—and John would eventually retire to bed, leaving her awake and drunk, turning to the phone and anyone she could reach in the middle of the night for companionship.*

When one White House aide complained about her constant distracting comments—in September 1970, during a game of gin rummy and bridge with the press on Air Force One, she told the press, "The Vietnam war stinks," and continued, "The war would have been over 16 months ago if it hadn't been for Fulbright"—Haldeman quickly shot it down. "She's the best thing we've got going for us to keep the conservatives pacified," he said. Appearing on the TV show *Laugh-In*, Martha deadpanned, "John and I have the perfect arrangement. He runs the attorney general's office and I run the rest of the country."

*   *   *

Over several weeks that winter of 1972, as Magruder monitored Martha, Hunt and Liddy crisscrossed the country trying to build a covert campaign team. The two men treated themselves well on the road—traveling

---

* Her Watergate neighbor and regular confidante Anna Chennault had a different interpretation: "It was not that she drank too much, but that people simply couldn't believe how she could say some of the things she did without being drunk," Chennault wrote in her own memoir. "The label of an alcoholic was a convenient one for a high government official's wife who expressed unpredictable opinions." Similarly, Magruder's wife, Gail, recognized in Martha an all-too-familiar figure: The Nixon administration was filled with men whose ambition led to hurtful neglect of their families, people who sought power instead of love—her own husband included. "My heart went out to her," Gail told Jeb at one point. "She was so bouncy and funny, but she was like a child, always seeking your approval. She might have been entirely different if she'd married a warmer man, instead of one who froze her out of his life."

first-class, staying in the nicest rooms at the fanciest hotels, and recruiting over meals at top restaurants, justifying the lavish expenses because, as Liddy would explain, "[potential recruits] must believe that money is no object to their employers if they are to accept the risk of that kind of employment." Beyond the money, though, Liddy wanted to signal that he would weather whatever was necessary to protect the identities of those who joined his team. At dinner in California with a woman he hoped to recruit as a potential plant in the Democratic campaign, he asked her to hold out her lit cigarette lighter, then placed his palm over the flame, locking eyes with her as his flesh blackened and smoked. (Shaken by the demonstration of loyalty, the woman declined Liddy's offer.)

In Miami, he and Hunt again tapped Barker and their Cuban network to build a squad of counterdemonstrators, interviewing a dozen men who impressed Liddy with their toughness. Between them, Hunt bragged to his partner, the men had killed twenty-two, including two hanged from a garage beam. At the end of their conversation, the leader spoke in Spanish to Barker, who laughed. "He called you a falcon—," Barker translated back to Liddy, clutching his hands like talons, "the bird other birds fear." (The name would become Liddy's self-appointed code name for that year's operations.) Hunt also recruited a locksmith who could serve as the team's covert-entry specialist, a man who had once been part of Cuban dictator Fulgencio Batista's secret police. Liddy was so pleased by the viciousness of his new colleagues that he pulled Bud Krogh aside when they crossed paths outside the White House and told him, "Bud, if you want anyone killed, just let me know."

By the end of January, they had a plan and a budget totaling a million dollars. "I knew exactly what had to be done and why, and I was under no illusion about its legality," Liddy recalled later. The radical left had declared war on his country.* When it came time to present the plan to John Mitchell and top Nixon advisors, Liddy knew they couldn't exactly turn to the local neighborhood office supply store, so instead, they turned

---

* Once, passing a Vietnam War protester holding a candle on the streets of D.C., Liddy claims to have grabbed the man's wrist and used the protester's memorial candle to light his cigar. Ignition completed, he allegedly said, "There, you useless son of a bitch, at least now you've been good for something."

to the CIA's in-house graphics department. One January day at precisely noon, Liddy was told to stand on a certain street corner near the White House, and a CIA technician handed him a wrapped set of oversized charts.

On January 27, materials in hand, Liddy walked into the Justice Department. Inside the attorney general's office, he set his charts up on an easel before Mitchell, Magruder, and Dean, and began to outline what he had dubbed Operation GEMSTONE.

First up was Operation DIAMOND, Liddy's plan to undermine, attack, and defeat demonstrators attempting to target the Republican National Convention by kidnapping the leaders of the movement, drugging them, and holding them in Mexico until the event's completion. Liddy labeled the kidnapping plot *Nacht und Nebel* ("Night and Fog"), after a 1941 directive from Hitler to disappear resistance leaders, and explained that it would be carried out by, as he told Mitchell, "an *Einsatzgruppe*," his special action group whose twenty-two kills Hunt had boasted about.

"Where did you find men like that?" Mitchell asked, removing his pipe from his mouth.

"I understand they're members of organized crime," Liddy replied.

"And how much will their services cost?"

"Like top professionals everywhere, sir, they don't come cheap."

"Well, let's not contribute any more than we have to to the coffers of organized crime," the attorney general said, returning his pipe to his mouth.

The gems and rocks kept unfurling as one CIA-designed chart after another described schemes and plots to upend the opposition party's ability to compete in a free and fair election. There was Operation RUBY, an effort to seed spies into the Democratic campaigns, and Operation COAL, meant to stir up division in the primary campaign by laundering money to the campaign of Shirley Chisholm, the first Black candidate for a major party's presidential nomination; Operation EMERALD would equip a jet airliner as a specially modified chase spy plane to follow the Democratic nominee across the country and eavesdrop on the campaign in the air, while Operation QUARTZ would do the same on the ground. CRYSTAL proposed outfitting a luxury houseboat at the Democratic National Convention in Miami with additional spy equipment, while prostitutes employed under Operation SAPPHIRE would seduce party

power brokers and lure them back to the houseboat's king-size bed.*
Four different "black bag jobs" fell under Operation OPAL (known as
OPAL I through OPAL IV), break-ins similar to the Ellsberg psychiatrist
operation that would target the campaign offices of Democratic candidates Edmund Muskie and George McGovern, as well as the convention
headquarters in Miami. GARNET proposed false-flag demonstrations
on behalf of Democratic candidates, meant to provoke public outrage,
as well as attempts to disrupt Democratic events, fundraisers, and generally spread disorder through the fall election. Lastly, there was TUR-
QUOISE, an effort by Cuban operatives to sabotage the air-conditioning
system in the main hall of the Democratic convention, forcing the nominee to address the packed delegates inside and the nation beyond in
one-hundred-degree Miami summer heat.

The meeting marked a critical escalation for the ethically questionable
administration; all of the dubious schemes, hijinks, and bad ideas until
then had emerged seemingly from genuine—albeit clearly misguided—
desires to protect national security. Now, in Mitchell's office, a tide was
turning: a dangerous new intensification and widening of Nixon's war
that would target domestic politicians as if they were true enemies of
the state. It was as illegal as it was un-American.

After his initial comment on DIAMOND, Mitchell said nothing
through the rest of the presentation, puffing steadily on his pipe and
reacting only with a smile to the idea of the overheated convention hall.
When Liddy had finished, the attorney general paused for a while, refilling
and relighting his pipe. Finally, he spoke, but the man in charge of enforcing the nation's laws didn't exactly offer a resounding condemnation.†

---

* Liddy had argued extensively over which women would be most enticing to Democrats:
Hunt and Barker kept wanting to recruit dark-haired, "sultry" Cuban women, while Liddy
preferred fair-skinned; after reviewing only photographs provided by Frank Sturgis, he had
identified two Anglo-Saxon women he felt confident could seduce discerning men of power.

† It's unclear the extent that John Mitchell ever actually endorsed the theoretical concept of
GEMSTONE. As Magruder noted later, Mitchell was rarely prone to direct confrontation,
and Dean remembers Mitchell winking at him midway through Liddy's presentation—perhaps acknowledging that it was far outside the bounds. Kleindienst, his deputy at the Justice
Department, cited Mitchell's major "limitation" as his "soft-spokenness and his tendency to
understate his view." As Kleindienst said later, "I frequently found it necessary, after a staff
meeting, to interpret in unequivocal language what Mitchell really intended."

"Gordon," Mitchell began, "a million dollars is a hell of a lot of money, much more than we had in mind. I'd like you to go back and come up with something more realistic."

As a heartbroken Liddy gathered his things, Mitchell spoke again: "And Gordon?"

"Yes, sir?"

"Burn those charts," the attorney general commanded. "Do it personally."*

$*$ $*$ $*$

On February 4, just barely a week later, the men reconvened in Mitchell's office. This time, Liddy presented a scaled-back plan on regular paper typed up by campaign secretaries. It cut some of the most expensive items—like the houseboat and the spy plane—and trimmed the number of illegal break-ins, but kept much of the rest of the program. Mitchell weighed the proposal and said he'd think about it. Dean, who had arrived late to the meeting, was shocked that Mitchell actually was willing to accept a scaled-down plan in some form—the attorney general's objection to the January GEMSTONE presentation truly was only about its scale and cost, not a philosophical objection toward dirty tricks.

The White House lawyer spoke up. "Excuse me for saying this—I don't think this kind of conversation should go on in the attorney general's office," he said. The meeting broke up awkwardly. Afterward, he recalls telling Liddy, "Gordon, I don't think you and I should ever talk about this subject again." It was an ambiguous comment—less a forceful repudiation of illegality than a potential precaution for operational security—and Dean would reflect later, "I left, annoyed by my weakness, but thinking positively about what I had accomplished."

According to his later accounts, Dean filled Haldeman in on the concerning meeting, but the chief of staff seemed largely focused mentally on the upcoming, high-stakes trip to China. "Bob, this stuff is incredible, unnecessary, and very unwise," Dean recalled saying. "No one at the White House should have anything to do with this." Haldeman agreed,

---

* In Dean's memoir, he attributes this remark to himself, not Mitchell.

and according to Dean, that was the end of his own involvement in the political intelligence portfolio he'd worked so hard to gain.

When Dean first crossed paths with Liddy, he'd been put off. At that time, Krogh had offered advice. "Liddy's a romantic," he said. "Gordon needs guidance. Somebody should keep an eye on him." Instead, as Liddy's schemes got wilder, nearly everyone in the Nixon world seemed to draw further away from him.

Most importantly, nobody firmly told him no.

* * *

Perhaps one of the reasons that Liddy's plan didn't attract the eyebrow raises it should have is that the Nixon campaign already had a variety of dirty tricks and intelligence gathering operations underway. As Nixon himself recounted in his memoirs, "I wanted the leading Democrats annoyed, harassed, and embarrassed—as I had been in the past."

Throughout the White House and the campaign, aides focused heavily on disrupting and raising questions about Ed Muskie, the Maine senator they saw as the most formidable Democratic opponent. One aspect of Liddy's overall GEMSTONE project was what came to be known as RUBY I, a covert operation he'd inherited from Magruder when he arrived at CREEP in January. The previous August, Magruder—under pressure from the White House—had planted a spy in Muskie's campaign under the guidance of John Buckley, a government employee at the Office of Economic Opportunity.

Elmer Wyatt "volunteered" as a cabdriver for the campaign, running menial errands and eventually becoming Muskie's courier for interoffice mail between the campaign and his Senate office. For more than seven months, from September 1971 through April 1972, Wyatt and Buckley intercepted key documents, photographed them, and delivered them to CREEP and the White House; after first attempting to photograph the documents in the backseat of Wyatt's car, they eventually rented an office at 1026 17th Street NW and purchased high-tech photographic equipment to more clearly capture the images. Some of the intercepted material—itineraries, draft press releases, and more—was used internally, but other items were retyped by CREEP secretaries on plain paper and leaked to reporters.

After Hunt started working with Liddy, he met Buckley on D.C. street corners more than a dozen times to hand off rolls of film; the two men never knew each other's name—Buckley went by "Jack Kent," and Hunt used his "Ed Warren" alias. Wyatt was paid $1,000 a month by the campaign, an expense both Magruder and Mitchell viewed as a low-stakes answer to the calls from the White House for more aggressive action. "Mitchell's attitude struck me as ambivalent," Magruder recalled later. "I think he saw $1,000 a month as a cheap way to get the White House off our backs." (The RUBY operation was, in Magruder's mind, a clear—and early—example of what he called the White House's "slippage problem," that rather than simply saying no to bad ideas, Nixon's team cultivated a culture of answering with a "half-loaf.")

Beyond the internal campaign spy, Magruder had sought through the fall more innovative ways to mess with Muskie and his fellow Democratic candidates. Most of all, he wanted Nixon to have his own Dick Tuck. Tuck, Nixon's own "political hobgoblin," as the *Washington Post* would call him, had first met then Congressman Nixon in 1950, when he was running for the U.S. senate and came to speak at UC Santa Barbara, where Tuck, a Democrat, was a student. Asked by a professor to organize Nixon's speech, Tuck maneuvered the event into a large auditorium with a small audience, gave a long-winded and energy-draining speech of his own, and then impishly introduced Nixon by saying that the congressman would speak about the International Monetary Fund. Nixon, off-kilter and embarrassed throughout, afterward demanded Tuck's name and promised, "Dick Tuck, you've done your last advance."

Over the years ahead, though, Tuck had continued to pull all manner of low-grade pranks on Nixon and other Republican candidates. Tuck's escapades, what William F. Buckley once called "glorious improvisations," were mostly juvenile and harmless—arranging for garbage trucks with "Dump Nixon" on the side to drive by the 1956 Republican convention and for an elderly woman wearing a Nixon button to hug the candidate in front of TV cameras the morning after his 1960 TV debate with John F. Kennedy and tell him, "Don't worry, son. He beat you last night, but you'll do better next time." His most famous stunt came at Nixon's expense amid the gubernatorial campaign in 1962, as Nixon had been dogged by questions about a large loan from industrialist Howard Hughes to his brother Donald. The candidate appeared in San Francisco's Chinatown among smiling children holding signs in English and Chinese, and Nixon's team failed to realize that the Chinese characters spelled out, "What about the Hughes loan?" He posed, happily, with the signs until someone pointed out the Chinese meaning, at which point he tore one up on camera.*

To fight fire with fire, Magruder began a low-stakes and at first anodyne effort at CREEP to make life harder for the Democratic candidates on the trail. At campaign stops for Muskie and others, Magruder and his colleague Herbert Porter lined up crowds of Republican supporters to appear, chanting and carrying Nixon signs. They also recruited a man named Roger Greaves, code name SEDAN CHAIR, to engage in their own "dirty tricks," enlisting him as a campaign gremlin to steal the keys from idling motorcade vehicles or the shoes that campaign workers left outside their hotel rooms overnight for a shine. "He is ready, willing, and most able. Any ideas?" Porter wrote Magruder on November 17, 1971. Greaves, who was paid a salary of $2,000 a month, recruited some hostile picketers for various Democratic rallies and then quit in early 1972. Magruder, though, told Porter that Mitchell wanted a full-time prankster.

They soon found Roger Stone, a young student at George Washington who talked Magruder into hiring him. Herb Porter enlisted Stone, who was working as a scheduler in the campaign office, to find someone who could work in "two or three of the primary campaigns as kind of an eyes and ears." (Stone later recalled that he was told there should be a "prankster" element to the recruit as well.) After asking around the campaign, he identified a possible partner—a Kentucky campaign worker who had done similar work in a recent gubernatorial race.

Stone, adopting the alias Jason Rainer, traveled to Louisville and hired Michael McMinoway as a spy for $1,500 a month, telling him that "Rainer" represented "a group of concerned citizens that were interested in the outcome of the 1972 presidential election." Over the months ahead, McMinoway worked for a variety of the Democratic challengers,

---

* Afterward, Tuck learned he'd misspelled the signs, which actually said "What about the huge loan?"

pretending to be a volunteer and gradually advancing his responsibilities through what he called "hard work and seemingly helpful efforts." He enthusiastically embraced assigned tasks—just happening to slightly screw them up: During one phone bank for Humphrey, he reversed the prepared call texts, so Black voters heard the messages meant for union voters and vice versa, and duplicated the day-shift phone bank lists with the evening shift, so voters became annoyed at the repeat calls. "Some [volunteer block] captains have already quit because of the repeated calls," he reported to Stone. He told volunteers they weren't needed when they were, and hired the least competent volunteers he could find. In Wisconsin, helping Muskie, McMinoway convinced his team that rather than distribute campaign literature, they should hit the bar and drink.

McMinoway—known internally to CREEP as SEDAN CHAIR II—provided Stone with a variety of internal campaign documents, from schedules to campaign finance records, which Stone passed onward to Porter, Magruder, Strachan, Haldeman, and Mitchell. His intelligence was referred to in CREEP memos only as coming from "a confidential source."

In February, Hunt and Liddy picked up a rumor that the publisher of the *Las Vegas Sun*, Hank Greenspun, possessed some dirt on Muskie. They began researching how to access the safe in the corner of Greenspun's office, and teamed up with one of billionaire recluse Howard Hughes's security men; they'd heard that Hughes was also interested in liberating some documents from Greenspun following a falling-out. The elaborate forced-entry plan fell apart when Hughes's team refused to provide a required plane and Muskie's political threat faded that spring.

One of the potential areas of concern about what might have been in Greenspun's safe stemmed from his close association with Jack Anderson, the columnist whose December reporting on the India-Pakistan tensions had led the Plumbers to uncover the Joint Chiefs' spying on the White House. Anderson was one of the nation's most powerful journalists. In an age when syndicated newspaper columns carried enormous weight, pushing insidery Washington reporting far beyond the capital, Anderson reigned king. His daily column, "Washington Merry-Go-Round," ran in a thousand newspapers nationally and was read by one in five Americans, and he led a team of eager muckraking assistants whose fingers seemed to extend into every office in the capital. "Whether it's a peccadillo or a state secret, the Washington Merry-Go-Round is interested," Anderson wrote.*

Nixon's government had grown increasingly alarmed that winter about Anderson's excellent sourcing. In a January column, he'd bragged about reading the CIA's daily reports to the White House during the India-Pakistan tension. The CIA that month took the unprecedented step of starting what would ultimately be a three-month surveillance operation to identify his sources. As many as sixteen CIA officers—spread across eight cars as well as a fixed photographic observation post by his office—watched Anderson (code-named BRANDY in the agency's operation) as well as his cowriter Les Whitten (code-named CORDIAL), his secretary Opal Ginn (SHERRY), and two of his reporters, Brit Hume (EGGNOG) and Joseph Spear (CHAMPAGNE).

What no one realized was that these eyes would be in place as one of Nixon's largest scandals took shape, monitoring Anderson as he uncovered yet another secret the Nixon administration hoped to hide.

---

* At one point, he'd gotten into a high-profile flap with J. Edgar Hoover after his reporters had started going through the FBI director's trash—a common-enough investigative technique by the bureau that its leader didn't appreciate being turned against him.

Chapter 10

The Dita Beard Memo

From the start of the administration, Nixon's Justice Department had been different. The U.S. Justice Department is meant to occupy a unique role in the federal government—a cabinet department that simultaneously exists as part of the executive branch while also standing apart, beholden to the letter and spirit of the Constitution. Since its formation under Ulysses S. Grant, the department's goal has been equal justice under the law, with prosecutions pursued without fear or favor, with an attorney general intended to serve not as the president's top lawyer, but the nation's. Traditionally, presidents tried hard to craft a department leadership that appeared free of routine politics.

Nixon chose a different path. Not only did he appoint his campaign leader to head the department, a man who had never worked there or even as a prosecutor at any level, but he filled seven of the top eight positions with campaign staff or defeated political candidates.* The choice for the department's number two, Richard Kleindienst, was almost as incongruous, epitomizing the new type of conservative partisan Nixon had tried to populate his administration with as he arrived in 1969. A

---

* Oddly, given his focus on "law and order" during the campaign, Nixon seems to have given little overall thought to staffing the department. At one point after the '68 election, when it looked like Mitchell was going to refuse the job of attorney general, Nixon offhandedly offered it to Ehrlichman, someone even less qualified.

former Goldwater campaign aide fluent in Navajo from growing up in Winslow, Arizona, Kleindienst was aggressive but inexperienced. He had been learning on the job since he started—surprised at one point when he was told that there were ninety-three U.S. attorneys and an equal number of U.S. marshals spread across the country.

The appointments worried department veterans. "When the attorney general was the president's campaign manager, the deputy attorney general was a campaign field director, and three assistant attorneys general recently ran for office, you are politicizing things, no matter what kind of face you try to put on it," Lyndon Johnson's deputy attorney general Warren Christopher had warned.

Some of the department's early moves under Nixon had seemed to herald just that type of politically beneficial decision-making: It waved away charges against twenty-one GOP finance chairs who had violated campaign reporting rules outlined in the Corrupt Practices Act, and it dropped a potential bribery case involving a Maryland contractor and multiple U.S. congressmen. Then there was the antitrust case against El Paso Natural Gas Company, a client of Mitchell and Nixon's law firm; in the administration's first week, the Justice Department suddenly abandoned the suit.

Mitchell and Kleindienst additionally seemed to have little appreciation of department culture. Kleindienst turned out to be a tough-talking and sometimes boorish manager and insisted the department's lawyers begin recording their days in quarter-hour increments and tracking their incoming and outgoing telephone calls for review. Day to day, he ran the organization as Mitchell found himself juggling three full-time jobs in 1970 and 1971—attorney general, reelection campaign manager, and senior Nixon advisor—in addition to the demanding challenge of his wife.

As winter progressed, Mitchell finally had to move to the campaign full-time, and he announced on February 15, 1972, that he'd resign as attorney general effective March 1. Martha had fought the move as hard and long as she could, fearing the loss of status and perks that came with being a cabinet spouse—she'd even enlisted Bebe Rebozo for help to undo her husband's reassignment—but at every turn she was told that Mitchell was precisely what the president needed to win his reelection. "Mitchell knew that it was his manifest destiny to run Nixon's last campaign," campaign aide Robert Odle recalled. Martha didn't see why he had to choose. She argued, not wrongly, "He's been running it from there ever since CREEP started."

The departure touched off a fateful series of musical chairs: Nixon nominated Kleindienst to succeed Mitchell, and another loyal Nixon aide, L. Patrick Gray III, to succeed Kleindienst. (As Mitchell stepped down, Kleindienst hailed him as "the greatest attorney general that the Department of Justice has had in its 100-year history.") The Senate moved in late February to take up Kleindienst's and Gray's fairly straightforward nominations. While Gray didn't have any law enforcement experience, the onetime navy submarine officer had worked on Nixon's '60 and '68 presidential campaigns, worked in the Health, Education, and Welfare Department during the administration's first year, and later landed at the Justice Department heading the civil division. The Senate initially appeared ready to approve both men, but as their joint confirmation hearings wrapped up on Wednesday, February 23, Senator Ted Kennedy asked for the odd proviso that the committee have a week to ready its confirmation of Kleindienst.

The confirmation hearings were only a minor story as Nixon's historic trip to China dominated the world's headlines—a week of grandiose diplomacy, pomp, circumstance, touring, and elaborately staged photo ops as the president opened up the closed world of the Chinese empire to Western cameras. On the evening of February 28, Nixon arrived back at the White House triumphant, greeted by his family, vice president, and other luminaries, and addressed the nation from Andrews Air Force Base about his momentous, first-of-its-kind journey.*

He went to bed that night at 11:52 and woke up the next morning to the biggest (but not the last) scandal of his administration.

---

* The reaction to the China summit was overwhelmingly positive, but Kissinger still noticed in his boss a distinct level of discomfort. "We encountered the curious phenomenon that success seemed to unsettle Nixon more than failure. He seemed obsessed by the fear that he was not receiving adequate credit," Kissinger observed. "It conveyed a lack of assurance even during his greatest accomplishments. It imparted a frenetic quality to the search for support, an endless quest that proved to be unfulfillable."

＊　　＊　　＊

As Richard Kleindienst read the newspapers that next day, he suddenly knew why Ted Kennedy had asked for a week's delay in his nomination: Since the fall, Jack Anderson had been digging around on the Nixon administration's suspicious handling of a controversial merger by the conglomerate ITT. Now he appeared to have the goods on the attorney general nominee, and the Democratic senator clearly had been tipped off.

The controversy dated back to the earliest months of the Nixon administration; following the also suspicious abandonment of the El Paso Gas case, the Nixon Justice Department had seemingly been set to crack down on other oversized companies, appointing the well-respected and hard-nosed Richard McLaren as its head of antitrust enforcement—the lone non–Nixon aide or losing politician among the department's eight senior officials. He appeared beyond reproach and immediately took a firm line, warning publicly against any merger among the nation's two hundred largest firms or within already concentrated industries.

That public warning, however, apparently meant little to the International Telephone and Telegraph Corporation, which had grown in prior years into one of the world's largest companies and the nation's archetypal conglomerate. CEO Harold "Hal" Geneen's vision had made him the Napoleon of American industry, growing the company from $800 million in annual revenue to more than $7 billion, accumulating 390,000 employees in more than 300 subsidiaries throughout 67 countries around the world, and weaving together big brands like Sheraton Hotels, Avis Rent-a-Car, the maker of Wonder Bread, and the home-builder Levitt & Sons, as well as all manner of smaller companies, ranging from cosmetics to auto parts to book publishing. Growth largely came through a steady stream of mergers and acquisitions, as many as five a month, and repeatedly triggered the government's antitrust fears—at one point, the government had blocked ITT from purchasing the ABC television network.＊

＊ The company's sheer scale seemed to offer it an ability for what was known in antitrust circles as "reciprocity," that is, steering customers or company spending from one subsidiary to another in a closed anticompetitive loop; four out of five of ITT's Levitt home buyers, for instance, also purchased their life insurance through ITT's insurance companies.

In April 1969, ITT forged ahead with the largest merger in corporate history, attempting to purchase the Hartford Insurance Company. There was reason to believe it could push past government concerns: ITT had built out an almost unparalleled network of well-connected lobbyists and former officials, including a former CIA director and onetime secretaries-general of both NATO and the United Nations, and spent liberally on campaign contributions.*

Within days of the proposed Hartford merger, McLaren wrote privately to Mitchell, "If [the] Antitrust [Division] is ever to take action to prevent such a restructuring of the market, this acquisition of a leading firm by the largest conglomerate is the one to challenge." He asked for permission to seek a temporary restraining order to litigate the question before the merger was completed, but Mitchell turned him down. Only after the merger became official in November 1969 did the Justice Department finally file multiple antitrust lawsuits, challenging not just the Hartford purchase but also ITT's simultaneous purchase of Automatic Canteen, a vending-machine giant, and Grinnell, the dominant manufacturer of fire sprinklers.

For the better part of two years, the government and ITT jockeyed over the lawsuits. McLaren saw them as key to protecting competition amid a wave of mergers that had seen 110 of the nation's 500 biggest companies swallowed up since the mid-1960s, but in July 1971, the Justice Department made a surprise announcement that it was settling the case. ITT, the government agreed, would keep Hartford, but sell off other components, including Avis, Canteen, and its Levitt home-building work. Nearly simultaneously, McLaren resigned from his post and was nominated and confirmed quickly to a federal judgeship in Chicago—a process that normally takes months but was magically accomplished by the administration in just hours. "I immediately smelled a rat, but could find no evidence that the judgeship was tainted," Ted Kennedy later recalled.

Columnist Jack Anderson had also taken notice and was further convinced of backroom dealings as news trickled out that fall that ITT had

---

* It was also no stranger to hardball politics; later revelations would show that in 1970 ITT, worried about the nationalization of one of its Chilean companies, had tried to fund the overthrow of the Chilean government.

made a $400,000 donation in June to the Republican National Convention. Anderson suspected there was even more to the story—after all, the head of both the Justice Department and the president's reelection campaign were one and the same. He also learned Connecticut regulators had only approved the deal after the company promised an expensive new build-out of offices and a new ITT-Sheraton Hotel in downtown Hartford.

Through the fall, Anderson's reporters dug deeper and his column hinted at nefarious doings; one published in December said an "aura of scandal" hung over the merger and included details about how Connecticut's insurance commissioner had met secretly with company officials, as well as a scoop that the Securities and Exchange Commission was investigating suspicious stock sales that benefited ITT executives.

On Tuesday, February 29, the morning's papers carried Anderson's latest report. For the last week, his colleague, a lanky twenty-nine-year-old named Brit Hume, had been confirming the authenticity of a June 1971 memo leaked to them on the first day of Kleindienst's hearing. The memo from an ITT lobbyist named Dita Beard appeared to explicitly outline a quid pro quo between the Justice Department lawsuit and the RNC donation. "Our noble commitment has gone a long way toward our negotiations on the mergers eventually coming out as [CEO] Hal [Geneen] wants them," she'd written. "Certainly the President has told Mitchell to see that things are worked out fairly. It is still only McLaren's mickey-mouse we are suffering. . . . If it gets too much publicity, you can believe our negotiations with Justice will wind up shot down. Mitchell is definitely helping us, but cannot let it be known." Her memo ended with a simple request: "Please destroy this, huh?"

Anderson followed up his Tuesday scoop with additional reports on Wednesday and Friday, revealing a previously unknown series of meetings between Kleindienst and an ITT director in April 1971. Realizing his nomination was in jeopardy, Kleindienst pleaded with the chair of the Senate Judiciary Committee, James O. Eastland, to restart the hearing. "[Kleindienst] insisted that he had never talked to Mitchell or anyone else at the White House about the ITT case," Kennedy later recalled. "He was lying."

On March 2—one day after Mitchell officially stepped down to begin his work on CREEP—the judiciary committee relaunched what would become the Senate's longest confirmation battle in history, a process that would stretch through the end of April and involve more than 20 days of hearings, 32 witnesses, 193 exhibits and pieces of evidence, and a transcript that would reach 1,791 pages. The hearings and the ITT controversy would all but paralyze Mitchell during his first month on the campaign.

By the time the Senate reconvened on March 2, Dita Beard had disappeared. Robert Mardian called Mark Felt to locate her and serve her with a congressional subpoena to appear before the Senate—soon, a team of twenty-four FBI agents, spread across five states, were on the hunt. At the bureau, Felt worried again about the FBI getting pulled into the administration's shenanigans: "I did not like the assignment, which smelled of politics."

*　　*　　*

Until that fateful February, Dita Beard had been an under-the-radar power player—the sole registered lobbyist for ITT in the capital and a fifty-three-year-old, twice-divorced native Washingtonian with a strong joie de vivre, kept all too busy raising five children as a single parent. Succeeding wildly in D.C. despite its dominant male influence, she earned a reputation of being able to out-drink, out-shoot, out-play, and out-curse just about any male colleague. "Falstaffian," one newspaper described her in a headline a few days into the scandal.

She'd first confirmed the memo as authentic in an initial meeting with Hume at her office on February 24, then later that night summoned him to her home, where during a two-hour, tear-filled follow-up interview she explained the ITT PR team wanted her to disavow the whole thing. "But that would be a lie and she wouldn't lie like that," Hume wrote in his interview notes to Anderson. "I finally began to press her to tell if there been an agreement of this kind. She was weeping now. She nodded yes. I asked her if it was negotiated by her. Again, a yes nod. With Mitchell? Again, yes, nodding."

ITT, in an strategy session at its Park Avenue headquarters in New York, quickly settled on a three-pronged attack: Undermine the memo,

Beard, and Anderson.* The Senate seemed willing to cooperate: Its initial list of new witnesses were all administration voices, like Mitchell, Kleindienst, and McLaren, who all testified that there had been nothing untoward about the process. Kleindienst demurred, saying yes, he'd had contact with an ITT executive, but had simply referred the man to McLaren's office. McLaren, for his part, said he'd reversed himself after being convinced by ITT's pleas that divesting itself of Hartford Insurance might cause large, negative ripple effects in the economy. The testimony was so one-sided and surface-level that Anderson and Hume ultimately insisted they be allowed to testify too.

When Beard finally resurfaced, it was in a Denver hospital, where she was reportedly being treated for heart problems. Back in D.C., her longtime doctor seemed to break every medical ethic by testifying at length about his patient's drinking and bouts of "distorted and irrational behavior." "Her thoughts do not flow in a logical order. She would become so disoriented that she would be incapable of a legal act, such as signing a will or a letter," he told lawmakers. The message that her memo wasn't to be trusted was clear, but cross-examination by senators in the hearing revealed that the doctor had visited the Justice Department twice just prior to testifying and had never reported any concerns to ITT during his regular, corporately mandated reports on her health.

The pressure on Beard herself was also high; on March 6, the company withheld her expected $15,000 annual bonus—a third of her annual compensation. Through it all, the White House worked closely with ITT to defuse the scandal and smooth Kleindienst's confirmation. Colson dispatched Hunt to interview Beard in the hospital, wearing his CIA-provided red wig and traveling under his cover name "Edward T. Hamilton." He took an envelope of cash from Liddy, met with Beard's daughter in D.C., and flew to Denver, where he told Beard he was a "friend of Hal's," the ITT CEO. In an extended interview watched over by her physician, Hunt pressed her on whether her memo was real or a forgery and reassured her that the missing bonus was "doubtless a

---

* Ironically, one of ITT's first responses to the scandal was to hire Intertel to lead its own internal investigation and damage-control efforts, the same Kennedy-linked political intelligence firm that Jack Caulfield had hoped to emulate with his SANDWEDGE plan the year before.

misunderstanding." Far from being fired, Hunt promised, her job at ITT was secure and waiting when she felt better. Hearing that she'd be financially taken care of had an instant, profound effect on her memory. "Her recollection seemed to have improved, for she now told me she could not have typed the memorandum," Hunt reported. He phoned Colson with updates throughout the three conversations and, after getting what he needed, told Beard that ITT planned to take care of her hospital bills too.

Back in D.C., Colson and the White House worked with Hunt's employer, the Robert Mullen Company, to draft a public statement on ITT's behalf. On March 17, a new lawyer for Beard, paid for by ITT and sharing an office with a Republican Party committeeman, announced that the memo was a "forgery, a fraud, and a hoax."

The next day at the White House, aides talked Nixon through planting their own forgery with Anderson, with the aim of discrediting his reporting. "Don't we have some spurious stuff that we can give to Jack Anderson?" Haldeman asked.

"I got just the scheme for that," Colson said.

They then discussed how to soil the reporters with allegations of homosexuality. "Do we have anything on Hume?" Haldeman asked. "I thought there was some taint on him."

"We're doing a check on him. We don't have it yet," Colson replied.

"It would be great if we could get him on a homosexual thing," Haldeman said.

Nixon recalled an old rumor he'd heard: "Anderson, I remember from years ago: he's got a strange, strange habit out of—I think [Anderson's colleague Drew] Pearson was [homosexual], too," the president said. "I think he and Anderson [were]."

Soon, the inner circle's conversations turned even more sinister. One day, Colson pulled Hunt into his office and Colson explained, Hunt would later recount, that Nixon was "incensed" over the "son of a bitch" Anderson's ongoing publication of leaks. The columnist "had become a great thorn in the side of the President." It was time, Colson said, to "stop Anderson at all costs." Hunt was "authorized to do whatever was necessary" to assassinate Jack Anderson. "I assumed, as I usually do with Colson, that he was either reflecting the desires of the Chief Executive, or else that as a prescient staff officer, was attempting to find a solution to a problem that was troubling his chief," Hunt later said.

Hunt immediately teamed up with Liddy, confiding that he'd received word from "my principal," the code he always used to refer to Colson, that they had to do something about the reporter. He explained that Anderson had crossed the line in airing the nation's secrets. "As a direct result of an Anderson story, a top U.S. intelligence source abroad had been so compromised that, if not already dead, he would be in a matter of days," Liddy recalled being told. "Something had to be done."

Over lunch at the Hay-Adams Hotel on March 24, across Lafayette Park from the White House, Hunt and Liddy met with Dr. Edward "Manny" Gunn, a recently retired CIA physician, and spoke in broad hypotheticals about how an accident might befall their victim. Anderson's name was never used in the conversation; instead Liddy presented a hypothetical case where they were seeking to remove someone who was compromising the identity of intelligence sources, but by midway through the conversation Liddy assumed Gunn had seen through the thin cover story and guessed the would-be target's identity. Hunt wondered whether a massive dose of LSD, spread across a steering wheel, might lead to a car crash. Gunn thought it unlikely to work, and instead suggested staging a fiery crash; Liddy and Hunt said they weren't sure they had access to a driver necessary to initiate such an event. They discussed and rejected options like trading out the victim's aspirin for poisoned pills, fearing the risk that a family member or visitor would end up taking the medicine instead. Finally, they settled on a run-of-the-mill mugging, turned wrong. Washington was experiencing an epidemic of street crime, and it seemed easy to imagine that even a famed columnist might coincidentally be cut down for his wallet and watch. At the end of lunch, Hunt handed Gunn a $100 bill from CREEP's coffers for his time.*

---

* It's never been clear who directed what during this episode or who knew what when; the lunch with Gunn is discussed at length in Liddy's memoir, and while Hunt and Gunn confirmed the lunch meeting in later Senate testimony, they indicated that the only goal had been to discredit Anderson (or, in Gunn's testimony, an unknown person) by making him seem incoherent and that the trio never discussed at lunch killing Anderson. Colson, for his part, denied ever giving an order to Hunt to kill Anderson.

While awaiting a final "go" order from the White House—an order that ultimately never came, for reasons that were never clear—Hunt and Liddy discussed how best to affect the fatal mugging of Anderson and settled on using Barker's Cuban team. "Suppose my principal doesn't think it wise to entrust so sensitive a matter to them?" Hunt wondered.

"Tell him, if necessary, I'll do it," Liddy replied.

Years later, Liddy explained what was going through his mind as he volunteered to kill an American reporter on an American street on the orders, supposedly, of the American president: "I know it violates the sensibilities of the innocent and tender-minded, but in the real world, you sometimes have to employ extreme and extralegal methods to preserve the very system whose laws you're violating." Liddy's observation, given in a 1980 *Playboy* interview, is as concise a summary as we've ever seen of the mindset that led Nixon's men so corruptly and thoroughly into more chaos.

✳   ✳   ✳

As the White House tried to salvage Kleindienst's nomination, Mark Felt received a phone call and visit from Pat Gray. The head of the Justice Department's civil division was up for deputy attorney general alongside Kleindienst, and helping to coordinate the defense in the newly reopened hearings. They'd never met until then, and when they did, Felt took stock of the man who had demanded to see him on short notice: tall, close-cropped hair, weather-beaten face. "He was a strong and vigorous-looking man," Felt assessed.

Gray handed the FBI executive an envelope containing what he said was the original Beard memo—given by Anderson to the Judiciary Committee, who had then passed it to Gray. "It is very important to know whether it is authentic," Gray said, and pleaded for the FBI laboratory to examine it. Felt sent the letter to the lab for analysis, only for Gray to recall it and retrieve it barely an hour later. After several days of back-and-forth, the FBI laboratory still hadn't had much of a chance to assess the memo, although it had not been typed on the same typewriter Hume used. John Dean got involved too, telling the FBI that ITT and Intertel had collected documents typed on Beard's machine at various points over the preceding year and that ITT's own examiners guessed that the document had been written in January 1972.

On Saturday, March 18, Felt informed Dean that the FBI's document experts had determined the memo was identical to others typed on the same ribbon in or around June 1971. Dean asked Felt to not state that publicly; Felt refused, and Dean ordered him to check with Hoover, who also declined to alter the FBI report. Over the next forty-eight hours, the FBI, the Justice Department, and the White House argued, even as further tests backed up the bureau's conclusion. "Though the findings were not categorical, they made a strong case that the original Beard memorandum was prepared on or about June 25 and that it was authentic," Felt recalled. ITT tried to present new "evidence" of the forgery, only to have the FBI's examiners refute it. Dean called repeatedly, pushing for the report to be changed before it was delivered to Congress, but Hoover moved ahead. Dean, Felt recalled, was furious. The shenanigans had also begun to worry Gray; he stopped by Felt's office to report that Senator Eastland had heard of all the White House backroom dealing and was now questioning Gray's nomination too. "It might be enough to block my own confirmation," he said, fearfully.

Finally, on Sunday, March 26, Beard herself testified in a special Judiciary Committee hearing convened at her hospital bedside in Denver. "I did not write, compose, or dictate the entirety of the memorandum which Mr. Hume presented to me in the Washington office of ITT last month," she told the visiting senators. Instead, she charged, some unknown force or person had forged additional, incriminating statements around innocent passages pulled from an authentic memo she'd written in the summer of 1971. She'd been confused during Hume's original questioning, she explained, because she obviously recognized some of the memo as her own writing and mistakenly believed that the whole thing must have been hers. Asked why she'd confirmed the Mitchell deal that night to Hume at her house, she brushed it off, saying, "If I did, it must have been toward the end of the evening, when I was upset." Her story didn't hold up under questioning, but as senators pressed and her alibi seemed set to unravel, she began to moan. The hearing ended when doctors intervened, cleared the room of the visitors, and her lawyer announced she was experiencing a heart attack.*

Later, Beard gave an interview to CBS's Mike Wallace, and a week after her dramatic heart attack, she checked out of the hospital and disappeared for good. Two Denver doctors later said there was no medical sign she'd ever experienced heart problems at all, before or during her hospitalization.

Back at the White House, a worried Colson wrote to Haldeman recommending that Kleindienst's nomination be withdrawn. The ITT scandal was too costly on multiple fronts, he wrote, not the least of which was the distraction it was causing Mitchell as he was supposed to be taking the reins of the campaign. However, even more than the opportunity cost of the scandal, "there is the possibility of serious additional exposure by the continuation of this controversy." He explained that there were material facts unknown to Mitchell or Kleindienst—including deeply incriminating documents that outlined the president's involvement in the ITT lawsuits and the commitment from ITT to the Republican convention well before the antitrust case was settled. "This memo put the A.G. on constructive notice at least of the ITT commitment at that time and before the settlement, facts which he has denied under oath," Colson warned.

Kleindienst also had kept silent about how the president himself had interfered directly, at one point ordering the deputy attorney general to shut down the prosecution. In April 1971, Nixon had called Kleindienst at his office. "I want something clearly understood, and, if it is not understood, McLaren's ass is to be out within one hour. The IT & T thing—stay the hell out of it. Is that clear? That's an order," Nixon said. "The order is to leave the goddamned thing alone." At the time, Kleindienst had protested Nixon's order to Mitchell, who had smoothed the objections so the case could move forward. Altogether, the administration's former

---

* The surreal experience would be among the most memorable in Ted Kennedy's long Senate career. "[Beard was] a crusty, fast-talking woman in her early fifties who sprayed jumbled thoughts in salty language at us as she alternately sucked on cigarettes and gulped from her oxygen mask," he recalled.

attorney general—and current campaign manager—as well as its attorney general nominee had committed perjury, and other top administration officials had supported it. They couldn't risk that becoming public.

Despite the risks, the White House pushed forward with the nomination, and the cover-up held. The stark denials from administration witnesses mixed with the obfuscation and confusion around the authenticity of the memo worked; public interest waned, and the story fell from the front pages of the nation's news coverage. The cover story, as thin as it was, seemed to satisfy the Senate, though Anderson was outraged—convinced, he wrote later, that "the only people who were falling for this planned confusion were those who wanted to be deceived."

In late April, the Senate hearings ended; the Judiciary Committee reapproved Kleindienst's nomination, this time by a vote of 11–4. Looking back on the episode, the lesson of the ITT scandal was clear to Kennedy, one of those four dissenting votes: "[ITT] was the true beginning of Watergate," he wrote in his memoir. "Nixon now felt the heat of curiosity from congressional Democrats and the party's leaders. His instinct was to dive more deeply into the murk."

That same month, the CIA finally wound down its surveillance of Anderson—having never found a meaningful clue as to who his sources were. On April 14, 1972, still caught up in the closing chapter of the ITT scandal, he received a letter from a New York entrepreneur and source named William Haddad. As Anderson recalled later, "He wrote that a private investigator had told him of plans to tap the telephones of the Democratic National Committee."

Anderson did nothing with the tip.

Chapter 11

"He's Our Hitler"

I f Nixon's "La Casa Pacifica" was the "Western White House," then Bebe Rebozo's compound in Key Biscayne operated for the Nixon administration as something akin to a "Camp David South," a luxurious and sun-drenched presidential retreat. The son of a Cuban immigrant cigarmaker, Rebozo had made himself into a wealthy banker and real estate investor through strong hustle amid the booming postwar Florida real estate market—a fortune that was aided along the way by his friendship with Nixon, and in turn was put at Nixon's disposal.

The main Key Biscayne compound, on the exclusive island off Miami, was actually a mix of buildings and properties belonging to Rebozo, Nixon, and their other friend Robert Abplanalp, some of which had been turned over to the Secret Service and White House communications offices. All told, Nixon himself would visit more than fifty times as president, often retreating even from his retreat, heading farther out, to Abplanalp's private island, known as Grand Cay, in the Bahamas. When Nixon himself wasn't there, Rebozo welcomed the president's inner circle too, and as the turbulent March of the ITT scandal wound up, John Mitchell decided that a Florida escape was just what he needed to reset and refocus.

When he and Martha arrived at Rebozo's estate, she was none too pleased to discover she had to share her vacation with a steady stream of reelection campaign staffers—all seeking decisions on the logjam of campaign issues. One was Jack Caulfield, who was now working as a CREEP security guard for Mitchell and was "sitting around the swimming pool, in his bathing trunks, with his gun at his side." Later, Martha became even more upset when Caulfield left and handed his gun over to Fred LaRue, a campaign staffer who had previously killed his father in a hunting accident. This wasn't exactly the relaxing, air-clearing, mind-clearing getaway she'd anticipated.*

On March 29, Jeb Magruder arrived from D.C. with two briefcases full of accumulated campaign materials, plans, strategies, and memos for Mitchell to review and approve; among them was Liddy's latest revised version of GEMSTONE. They spent two days reviewing more than thirty sets of plans and strategies, debating items like the direct-mail program and Pat Buchanan's plan to set up "truth squads" to police the statements of the Democratic candidates. (Martha kept interrupting their meeting, passing through to complain: "I don't know why they have to be here when we're on vacation.") The Liddy plan came up last.

GEMSTONE had languished for weeks, amid the distraction of the ITT scandal, and as a result tensions had risen between Magruder and an increasingly frustrated Liddy.

"Why don't you guys get off the stick and get Liddy's budget approved?" Colson had demanded in a phone call one night to Magruder.

"We'll get to it as fast as we can—you know the problem with Mitchell," Magruder replied.

That spring, a growing number of senior aides, including Fred LaRue and Robert Mardian, had joined the campaign too, and as the staff grew and Liddy's ambitions hung in suspension, the general counsel and deputy campaign director clashed. Liddy thought almost as little of Magruder, the "pipsqueak" campaign leader, as Magruder thought of the "bantam rooster" former FBI agent. They had many strange encounters. "Jeb, did you know I have a gun that will shoot underwater?" Liddy asked at one point.

---

* LaRue was sort of an odd duck around the campaign; he served as Mitchell's alter ego and, as Dean would note, even looked like a younger, thinner Mitchell. Fabulously wealthy from oil money, he had been a dollar-a-year White House consultant before taking a pay cut to volunteer for the campaign. "He had been serving in the administration out of curiosity mingled with a sincere desire to be of help," Dean would observe. "He had no ambitions that I could discern, nor any enemies."

"Gordon, when are you going to be shooting anybody underwater?" Magruder said, dubiously.

"I might have to sometime," he replied. "You never know what might happen."*

A final falling-out had occurred when Magruder confronted Liddy by the CREEP elevators about some overdue campaign reports. "The delay is causing me problems—if you're going to be the general counsel, you've got to do your work," he said, putting his hand on Liddy's shoulder.

"Jeb, if you don't take your arm off my shoulder, I'm going to tear it off and beat you to death with it," Liddy replied coldly.

Within a few days, Liddy had transferred away from CREEP to be general counsel for Maurice Stans's finance operation, which was housed in the same building at 1701, on the second floor. There, Liddy impressed his colleagues with his competence and dedication to the campaign's underlying legal work. Stans remembered him sitting each day in their six-person management meetings, helping to devise a way for supporters to donate appreciated stock without tax consequence to themselves or the campaign. "He did a good job; he was a good lawyer," he recalled. "There was never a suggestion by him, or anybody else, that something should be done that was illegal."

And yet, day by day, Liddy awaited approval for GEMSTONE. One afternoon, amid their infighting, Magruder went to the White House to meet with Strachan and complain about Liddy; he was reassured of the importance of Liddy's intelligence work, whenever it got fully underway. "Liddy's a Hitler," Strachan said, "but at least he's our Hitler."

Later, all three men involved in the Florida meeting at Rebozo's villa would give different versions of how the conversation unfolded: Mitchell said he rejected the Liddy plan outright; in LaRue's memory, Mitchell said, noncommittally, "This is not something we have to decide now"; and Magruder maintained that Mitchell okayed the operation outright. Martha, who had eavesdropped on the conversation through the kitchen

---

* At another point, Liddy seized on an offhand comment from Magruder, complaining about Jack Anderson, and announced—perhaps facetiously—to Magruder's aide as Liddy left the office that he was off to kill Anderson on Magruder's orders. Flustered, Magruder backpedaled. Liddy replied, "Well, you'd better watch that—When you give me an order like that, I carry it out."

intercom, later recalled to a friend, "There was no question if they were doing the dirty tricks—only the amount of money to be spent. They used terms like categories: how much to spend on people, on wiretapping, and other various and sundry things. They also discussed who was in charge of what, who would do this, and who would do that." According to Magruder, Mitchell asked at one point, "How do we know that these guys know what they're doing?"

Regardless of how they got there, Magruder felt a certain momentum to Liddy's scheme through the spring. Nixon had been asking for just this sort of aggressive intelligence operation for years. Colson wanted it, and Strachan had told Magruder that Haldeman was fine with the plan if Mitchell was. (Magruder later said, "It was another of what I called [Mitchell's] throwaway decisions, made under pressure to please the White House.") It was, in some ways, the ultimate example of the Nixon "slippage" problem: Liddy had come in asking for a lavish kidnapping and sabotage fund and had been negotiated down to "just" a smaller wiretapping and burglary fund. He'd gotten away with a quarter loaf—even though it was a quarter loaf too much. "Once you accept the premise of no-holds-barred intelligence-gathering, G. Gordon Liddy is what you wind up with," Magruder wrote later. Mitchell set a limit of $250,000—a rounding error on the campaign's overall budget—and they briefly discussed the plan's best wiretapping targets. "It was agreed that Liddy should go ahead with the wiretapping of Larry O'Brien's office at the Watergate, then we'd see about the other possible targets," Magruder recalled.

Subterfuge sorted, Magruder went to play tennis.

It seems quite likely that Magruder's account of Mitchell approving the plan—one given in his memoir and under oath to investigators—is wrong. It seems just as likely—perhaps even probable—that Magruder, tired of Liddy pestering him and under pressure from the White House, just gave the go-ahead to the scaled-back plan himself after Mitchell put off the decision again. Mitchell consistently denied ever okaying the GEMSTONE plan, although he did admit in testimony later that he understood the plan proposed illegal activities.

But there's no doubt that *someone* okayed the scaled-back GEMSTONE plan after the Florida conversation; the following day, Strachan wrote to Haldeman, "Magruder reports that 1701 now has a sophisticated political intelligence-gathering system with a budget of 300," seeming to misquote the $250,000 budget actually approved.*

*   *   *

While Magruder, Mitchell, and LaRue met to plot the campaign's summer and fall strategy, the finance arm of the reelection effort sprinted to lock in large cash donations ahead of a new political fundraising disclosure law.

Up through the early 1970s, the nation had little history of attempting to limit or demand transparency around political donations and campaign funding—and even less history actually enforcing the few prohibitions that did exist. President Theodore Roosevelt had first pushed for a prohibition on political contributions from corporations as part of his progressive agenda at the start of the century; Congress had later, in the 1940s, added prohibitions on donations from unions. Yet as late as the 1960s, the campaign rules, Lyndon Johnson had said, were still "more loophole than law."

In early 1972, Congress finally passed the Federal Election Campaign Act, which required regular, quarterly disclosures of donors and expenditures and established the first federal campaign watchdog, a new Office of Federal Election in the Government Accounting Office. Signing the bill that January, Nixon touted its new transparency: "By giving the American people full access to the facts, of political financing, this legislation will guard against campaign abuses and will work to build public confidence in the integrity of the electoral process."

Behind the scenes, though, during the eleven weeks before the law took effect, his campaign raced to hide as much money as it could. The

---

* The other piece of the puzzle is the approval of the planned burglary. The House Judiciary Committee would accept Magruder's version that Mitchell ordered the Watergate break-in during the Key Biscayne meeting. LaRue, a Mitchell loyalist, would tell writers Len Colodny and Robert Gettlin in later interviews that he vividly remembered the Key Biscayne conversation and that since Mitchell didn't approve the Liddy plan in the first place, they definitely couldn't have selected a wiretapping target. LaRue in 2003 told journalist James Rosen, "Basically, the guy that's lying is Magruder." Another primary reason to doubt Magruder's timetable is that it took nearly a month until Magruder told Liddy to target the Watergate—an oddly long time to hold back a seemingly critical instruction, had it indeed been given that day in Florida.

campaign's lawyers identified a particularly useful loophole whereby the old disclosure regulations expired on March 10 and the new ones didn't start until April 7. For just under a month, there were almost no rules at all. It was a period that was perfect for Nixon—as incumbent he was all but assured the nomination—and a disaster for the Democrats, who were still engaged in a multi-way primary with no front-runner to coalesce fundraising around.

By that point, the president's Newport Beach lawyer, Herbert Kalmbach—who had developed a lucrative business as a prodigious fundraiser and connector between corporate America, wealthy Republicans, and the Nixon world—had focused on maximizing the CREEP war chest for nearly two years and had already delivered in a big way. (By the time all was said and done, Nixon's '72 operation would raise some $69 million, more money than had been spent in the '64 and '68 presidential campaigns combined.) Long before the election year had rolled around, Kalmbach—later with the help of Stans—leaned hard on deep pockets, crisscrossing the country to meet informally with corporate leaders and influential Republicans.

In every one-on-one meeting, donors knew that Kalmbach sitting across from them represented the manifestation of the president himself. Nixon's top ten contributors would pledge more than $4 million total; roughly a fifth of Nixon's haul came from just its top one hundred donors. On November 18, 1970, Nixon sat down to an 8 p.m. dinner at the White House with Kalmbach, Attorney General Mitchell, and five businessmen. The group—which included Pittsburgh banking magnate Richard M. Scaife and an Illinois insurance executive, Clement Stone—enjoyed themselves for more than three hours, never once talking about campaign fundraising, before the president stood up from the table at 11:25. Only after he left did Kalmbach raise the big question: How much would the guests like to contribute to the president's reelection? Together, they pledged $7.5 million.

During another dinner, in New York in 1971, with George Spater, the CEO of American Airlines, Kalmbach suggested the airline make a $100,000 contribution to the campaign; Spater said he could put together $75,000. He felt he didn't have much choice—his airline was in the midst of a merger with Western Airlines, and just weeks before their dinner, the Nixon cabinet had split over whether to approve the deal, and Spater knew that Kalmbach, in his legal work, also represented rival United Airlines. The executive moved quickly to deliver the promised donation; American Airlines executives collectively gave the campaign $20,000 personally, and $55,000 from the company laundered through a "special commission" paid to the Swiss bank account of a Lebanese businessman. The businessman, in turn, withdrew the money in cash and returned it to American Airlines executives in New York, where it was placed in an envelope and delivered to Nixon's team.

In other meetings, Kalmbach was even more direct; while U.S. presidents had long offered ambassadorships to major supporters, Nixon's campaign turbocharged their offers in exchange for contributions. Nixon thought he knew precisely how much a good diplomatic post—and the lifetime privilege of being addressed as "Ambassador"—was worth to the nation's well-heeled. "Anybody who wants to be an ambassador must at least give $250,000," he told Haldeman in the White House. "The contributors have got to be, I mean, a big thing, and I'm not gonna do it for political friends and all that crap." Over the course of his first term, nearly $2 million had flowed in from donors who later received diplomatic posts abroad. At one point, hearing that Cornelius Vanderbilt Whitney was set to be named an ambassador, Nixon marveled, "It was a great sale. He gave a quarter of a million dollars."*

Sometimes—illegally—the trade was specific. J. Fife Symington, Jr., unhappy with his first-term post as ambassador to the new country of Trinidad and Tobago, traveled to California to meet with Kalmbach. He asked for a "European post," and Kalmbach suggested that Symington, whose wife was heir to the Frick steel fortune, might think about a $100,000 donation. Symington replied that he could do it, but would need to be promised a great ambassadorship from Haldeman himself. Kalmbach left their lunch and called staff at the White House, who tracked down Larry Higby, who was in Chicago with Haldeman and the president that day. Higby called back soon after: "Herb, the answer is

---

* Later, Whitney's nomination ran into trouble and Nixon withdrew it to avoid risking exposing the cash payment. Haldeman reported, "He'd have to reveal his financial support. He'd have to lie or reveal it. And that would be a mess, too." Nixon offered Whitney a refund.

go." Kalmbach returned to the lunch table and wrote out an agreement: *$100,000 for Spain or Portugal.* At another meeting, department store heiress Ruth Farkas was quoted $250,000 for the ambassadorship of Costa Rica; at a sit-down with Kalmbach, she said, "I am interested in Europe, I think, and isn't $250,000 an awful lot of money for Costa Rica?" In a follow-up conversation, Kalmbach explained that Europe cost $300,000. "Done!" she said. Her nomination as ambassador to Luxembourg was sent to the Senate six days after the final check of her $300,000 donation arrived for the reelection campaign.

Nowhere else fundraising-wise, though, would Kalmbach and the Nixon campaign have more success than with the nation's dairy and milk producers. Since Nixon had taken office, the dairy industry had been lobbying to increase the price supports paid to farmers; the Associated Milk Producers, Inc., had spent years organizing and consolidating power to become a political force. Kalmbach had told AMPI in 1969 that "contributions would be appreciated," and in August of that year, an industry lawyer had flown to Dallas, retrieved a briefcase with $100,000 cash in it, and flown to California to deliver it to Kalmbach. The money went into the campaign's stash in safe-deposit boxes. Over the next two years, extensive conversations about the industry's key priorities continued with a variety of Nixon aides, but little movement was made. Even a follow-up pledge of another $2 million failed to yield the results farmers wanted. Progress only began when the group retained Nixon's longtime advisor Murray Chotiner in March 1971, at a then large $60,000 annual fee.*

With Chotiner now in the picture, Nixon brought together the administration's top agriculture leaders on March 23, when they revisited the price levels set by the Department of Agriculture. That afternoon, Chotiner and Treasury Secretary John Connally suggested the dairy producers do even more for the campaign; the industry rushed to buy tickets for the next night's Republican "Kick-Off 1972" fundraising dinner at the Washington Hilton. AMPI executives used the organization's plane

---

* Chotiner, a consultant to Nixon since his first congressional campaign, had long been one of Nixon's most loyal aides and one of the most notorious practitioners of the political dark arts. Nixon's pre–White House hatchetman remained a valuable—if dwindling—figure in his presidential circles.

to fly to Louisville at 4 a.m. to gather up checks. The next night, after the fundraising dinner—attended by Nixon, Agnew, RNC chair Bob Dole, and the heads of the GOP's congressional and senate fundraising efforts—a dairy representative and Chotiner met Kalmbach across town at the Madison Hotel and reaffirmed that the industry was going to contribute $2 million to the president's reelection. The payoff was fast: The next morning, March 25, a press release from Agriculture Secretary Clifford Hardin announced an "upward adjustment" in milk price supports, changing levels that had been set just two weeks earlier.

The only question remaining was how to funnel such a huge amount of money to the campaign without raising eyebrows. As Kalmbach later testified in a twist of Orwellian doublespeak, "We were trying to develop a procedure . . . where they could meet their independent reporting requirements and still not result in disclosure." Their creative solution was to channel the money in very small donations, under $3,000, through a network of hundreds of new campaign committees created in D.C. by John Dean and Robert Bennett—the head of the PR firm that employed Howard Hunt—all with instantly forgettable names like the Committee for Political Integrity, Americans Dedicated to Stable Growth, Organization of Sensible Citizens, Americans United for Safer Streets, Volunteers for Good Government, the Committee for a Better Nation, and the Committee for Adequate Political Information. Nearly a quarter million dollars flowed from the milk producers through to the Nixon organization.

Despite the best efforts of the campaign and the White House to disguise the contributions, reporters noticed the wave of questionable new political groups; upon examination, the accompanying paperwork proved sloppy and suspicious.* Suspicions would dog the campaign for months.

---

* The address for one turned out to be a nightclub, and there were overlapping committee executives. A September 1971 *Washington Post* article reported its suspicions: "[The] Organization of Involved Americans has its address at [D.C. attorney John Y.] Merrell's office in Washington and another, Americans United for Political Awareness, at his home in Arlington. He heads one, he said, and his wife is chairman of the other. But he wasn't sure which was which." When contacted by a reporter, Merrell had asked, "I'm just curious—how many are there?" He laughed when the *Post* reporter said they'd uncovered more than sixty. Another D.C. consultant said he'd never heard of Americans for a Sensible Agriculture Policy, which was registered to his office address.

Millions of dollars flooded through the Nixon campaign in the first days of April, as the campaign rushed to both collect and distribute donor money ahead of the deadline on the 7th. The campaign employed a half-dozen couriers to collect cash, racing around the country in a frenzy so great that in one city Sloan later recalled, "We couldn't even pick up a $50,000 contribution." All told, they collected more than $11 million in untraceable money—some $5 million of which came in a final, frenzied sprint in the forty-eight hours before the law kicked in.

Although Hugh Sloan held the money as treasurer, he had little control over it, handing it out at the orders of Kalmbach, Mitchell, Stans, and others. The first disbursement went out in April to a Republican congressional candidate in Maryland named William Mills—other monies went to Kalmbach's own cash fund and to start funding Liddy's activities—but not all of the incoming donations were even converted to cash before heading out; some incoming checks went directly to Liddy, donations that would, with time, help bring down the Nixon presidency. (The money to Mills, meanwhile, would later come with an even higher price.)

*　　*　　*

On Monday, April 10—the first business day after the new campaign finance laws kicked in—Laurence Richardson, the president of a conglomerate known as the International Controls Corporation, appeared in Maurice Stans's office carrying a briefcase with $200,000 in cash. The money, intended to be anonymous, was the culmination of a yearlong lobbying campaign by ICC, whose founder Robert Vesco had run into trouble with the Securities and Exchange Commission in the U.S., as well as other authorities overseas. Vesco—a young, fabulously successful New Jersey businessman who considered himself tightly tied to Sears and GOP power brokers—had been increasingly desperate to use his connections with the Nixon administration to shut down the probes and increasingly frustrated when his scheming didn't seem to deliver.

In March, Vesco and Richardson had met with Stans at his 1701 Pennsylvania Avenue NW offices. Vesco was convinced that if he could just get an audience with the head of the SEC, they'd be able to talk out the problem mano a mano—surely that was the type of thing Nixon's team could arrange. Stans politely redirected, saying that maybe John Mitchell could help, then returned to the matter of a donation to the reelection campaign. "I want to be in the front row," Vesco told him, proposing a $500,000 donation. Stans had outlined the new law and suggested that the first $250,000 be paid by April 6 to avoid disclosure. There was no doubt in Vesco's mind what his money was buying. "Tell Stans to get that fucking SEC off my back," Vesco had told Richardson as Richardson prepared to deliver the cash. The money helped Vesco get a hearing with John Mitchell himself, who placed a call to the SEC to set up a meeting with Vesco's representative.

Even though the Vesco money hadn't met the deadline, Stans processed the donation anonymously at CREEP anyway, handing it off to Sloan. As Sloan would later recall, Stans instructed him to list the donation under John Mitchell's initials; it went into the ledger as "JM."*

In his role as the campaign finance committee's counsel, Liddy found himself totally consumed by the early-April rush for money. In just days, he helped set up new committees to spread around untraceable donations, collected checks in the offices of the Robert Mullen Company—Hunt's employer—raced to New York to bag another $50,000 donation, and traveled onward to Detroit, Buffalo, St. Louis, and Chicago to affect the final collections.

Sorting out the how and the who of all the campaign's money proved challenging. Throughout the campaign finance committee's office, cash piled up in office safes. At the White House on April 6, Haldeman's liaison to CREEP Gordon Strachan asked Alexander Butterfield to recommend someone to hold some of the questionable cash. Butterfield tapped a friend, Virginia management consultant Leonard Lilly, and handed off $350,000 in cash, packed inside a briefcase, in the lobby of the Key Bridge Marriott in Arlington, Virginia. The money represented a sizable chunk of the leftover 1968 funds overseen in the slush fund by

---

* Sloan's account actually changes, subtly and importantly: Before a grand jury later, he first said Stans instructed him, "For the time being, list it under John Mitchell's name," but at trial he said the instruction was "John Mitchell wants it listed under the initials 'JM' for the time being."

Herbert Kalmbach. Lilly placed them in an Arlington safe-deposit bank for quick use if and when needed.*

Sloan also asked Liddy if he could convert to cash a series of signed traveler's checks that had been donated to the campaign; Liddy flew to Florida and met with Barker, who arranged for a Cuban banker to get the cash. Soon, Sloan returned again—first with a $25,000 check from a Minnesota businessman named Kenneth Dahlberg, dated after the deadline, and then with a pile of four checks drawn on a Mexican bank. Each time, Liddy helped turn the checks into cash. Much of it came back from Barker's contact in crisp, brand-new, sequentially numbered $100 bills.

*   *   *

Once the frenzied finance deadline passed, Liddy was able to launch the plans he'd spent all winter concocting. He asked Sloan for the first down payment on GEMSTONE's funds, requesting $83,000 out of the $250,000 he'd been authorized. Sloan handed the money over in hundred-dollar bills, stuffed in a manila envelope, coincidentally some of the same sequentially numbered $100 bills Barker had laundered through his Miami bank contacts.

GEMSTONE's first move, Liddy decided, would be to leverage RUBY II. A few months earlier, in March, Hunt had recruited a new campaign spy, a young Utah college student named Thomas Gregory, to begin working in Muskie's campaign headquarters in D.C., on the foreign affairs policy team. Dubbed "RUBY II," Gregory was charged with typing up regular reports about information he'd gleaned while working for Muskie and delivering them during weekly rendezvous with Hunt in a downtown D.C. drugstore. As the Democratic campaign evolved and Muskie faded, though, Strachan told Liddy that Haldeman wanted Liddy's "capability" to shift its focus to McGovern. ("George McGovern was the perfect political opponent, Nixon felt, far to the left of center.

---

* Later, after the scandal had broken wide open, *Washington Post* editor Barry Sussman interviewed Butterfield and listened to him describe the odd scene of counting the money; Sussman asked: Didn't this whole episode feel peculiar, even wrong? Not at all, Butterfield explained: "When you work in the White House for the President of the United States, the last thing you think of is that you might be involved in wrongdoing."

If we did our job, McGovern would leave Nixon most of the moderates and independents," Ehrlichman wrote later.) Hunt asked Gregory to move over to the McGovern campaign, which he promptly did, and Roger Stone urged McMinoway—aka SEDAN CHAIR II—to move over to McGovern's campaign. McMinoway relocated to California and continued to report each day to Stone by phone.

According to Liddy's scaled-back GEMSTONE budget, the operation had funding for four surreptitious break-ins—operations Liddy code-named OPAL—and he began planning to target both McGovern's headquarters and the Democratic convention in Miami. The break-ins were manpower-intensive, and expensive. When Liddy added up the costs of a break-in—including a bonus of a month's salary for Hunt and McCord, payments and round-trip first-class airfare from Miami for the Cuban burglary team, as well as hotels, car rentals, and more—each OPAL operation came in around $10,000.

As Liddy's various operations were getting underway, Magruder finally passed along the detail—supposedly decided in Key Biscayne—that Liddy was to burgle and bug the Watergate offices of Democratic Party chair Lawrence O'Brien. "Get in there as soon as you can, Gordon—it's important," Magruder said. Liddy was not pleased; the Watergate hadn't been on his original list, and adding it would use up the last of his contingency funds, almost even before he'd started work.

*　　*　　*

While he was attorney general, John Mitchell had had five FBI agents watch over him and his family, and now that he was out of the cabinet, he continued to worry about the safety of his family—especially given Martha's public profile on the campaign. The idea of Jack Caulfield or Fred LaRue sitting around the pool in Key Biscayne with a gun didn't seem sustainable, and he insisted that James McCord find a long-term solution. Until McCord could hire a permanent bodyguard, he began escorting the Mitchells' daughter, Marty, to and from school himself.

In early May, McCord located a former FBI special agent named Alfred Baldwin and asked him to come to D.C. to discuss working for CREEP as a bodyguard—the request was urgent; Baldwin, McCord said, should fly down that night.* Baldwin was initially underwhelmed by the idea of guarding Martha Mitchell, but McCord explained it was the starting point for a higher-profile permanent role in the government after the election. The next day, McCord handed Baldwin a .38-caliber revolver, a holster, and $800 cash for expenses, and sent him along on a six-day trip with Martha to Detroit and New York. He was to receive a salary of $70 per day.

The bodyguard and protectee didn't hit it off; it was his first and last trip with Martha Mitchell. "Al Baldwin is probably the most gauche character I have ever met in my whole life," Martha complained, explaining he'd even taken off his shoes and socks in her suite at the Waldorf-Astoria, walking around barefoot "in front of everybody." After flunking his test assignment with Martha, Baldwin was quickly reassigned by McCord; don't worry, McCord promised, they had some other operations underway.

*   *   *

The same May Monday that McCord hired Baldwin, J. Edgar Hoover walked out of the FBI headquarters for the final time. On May 2, 1971, the emperor of American law enforcement died overnight at home alone. Mark Felt was at his desk around 9:45 a.m. when another FBI official called to simply announce, "He's dead." Felt assumed at first the announcement was about his boss, the ailing Clyde Tolson; then the official clarified, "Hoover's dead."

The body was readied immediately in a D.C. funeral home, so the director could lie in state the following day at the Capitol. In death, the controversial figure was lauded across Washington. "Mr. Hoover almost singlehandedly transformed the FBI into the superlative law enforcement agency it became," Gerald Ford memorialized, while the *New York Times*'s full-page obituary decreed, "If there is such a thing as

---

* How and why McCord chose Baldwin specifically has always been a bit of a puzzle and mystery: He said he chose Baldwin through the bureau's Society of Former Special Agents, but despite no shortage of retired agents local to D.C., McCord selected Baldwin, who lived in Connecticut, meaning that CREEP constantly had to pay travel and lodging for him. Equally odd, Baldwin had seemingly no relevant surveillance experience.

a cumulative total, [he was] the most powerful official in the long span of the American Government."

Felt was relatively confident he would be named the FBI's director—after all, he'd been effectively running things for nine months already—but Nixon saw a moment he had long wanted to construct a more malleable FBI, one where he could install the servant and partner he'd never had in Hoover. Unbeknownst to Felt, he was never a serious contender on that list.

Nixon settled instead on L. Patrick Gray III—a loyal candidate who had been in his mind for the role since at least the previous fall. Nixon decided he would not name Gray the permanent director of the bureau; instead, Gray would be announced as the "acting" director, to serve through the election. By skipping an immediate confirmation battle, Nixon hoped to avoid dredging up for congressional Democrats the bureau's many recent controversies and sins. Besides, by May, as Nixon watched the Democrats begin to flounder on the other side of the presidential race, he felt more confident about a successful reelection. Gray's nomination to be deputy attorney general still lingered in the Senate, held up amid the Kleindienst-ITT scandal, but the Senate seemed poised to confirm him as soon as the Kleindienst controversy died down, meaning that presumably they'd be happy to confirm him as FBI director too post-election.

Kleindienst announced the temporary pick just twenty-six hours after the news of Hoover's death. Nixon wanted to "name a man in whom he has implicit personal confidence," Ron Ziegler told reporters. "I think you will find that Patrick Gray is not a political man."

Felt was stunned. How could Nixon do this to the FBI, betraying its agents by installing an outsider? Soon, his shock and surprise gave way to an even stronger set of emotions that flooded him: bitterness, disbelief, and a desire to right the wrong done to him. If Gray was going to be a temporary seat-warmer, then there was still time to sink him and win the top job.

The FBI's first director had reigned for forty-eight years; Nixon's choice would barely last forty-eight weeks.

*   *   *

As plans came together for Hoover's elaborate funeral, Nixon's team sought to provide a final strange service to the former director: An antiwar protest, led by figures like Daniel Ellsberg and Jane Fonda, had been scheduled outside the Capitol while Hoover was supposed to be lying in state. Based on instructions funneled to him from Colson to Magruder, Liddy asked Hunt to bring Barker and his team to D.C. to protect the casket.

Barker hurried to Washington with his core Cuban team—Frank Sturgis, Eugenio Martinez, and Felipe De Diego—and met Hunt and Liddy at the Robert Mullen Company office. Liddy introduced himself using his George Leonard alias and showed Barker photographs of the leading antiwar figures, like Ellsberg, and asked the team to circulate through the crowd, heckle speakers, and seize any Viet Cong flags protesters displayed. Then, if there was any run at Hoover's casket, they should attempt to slow or fight the crowd.*

Despite Liddy's fears, no real trouble materialized and the protesters never tried to storm the Capitol; the only drama came when Frank Sturgis traded punches with one protester and was escorted from the scene by police. Their task complete, Liddy seized the opportunity to plan for his OPAL break-ins while the would-be burglary team was in town.

That night, Liddy, Hunt, and Barker's team cased McGovern's headquarters on Capitol Hill, studying the street lighting outside, and then Liddy took them to the new target Magruder had added to the OPAL list.

"That's our next job, Macho," he told Barker, pointing to the Watergate.

---

* Liddy's explanation that the Cubans came to Washington to "protect Hoover's casket" has always had doubters, who wonder if instead Liddy brought the Cuban team to D.C. on such short notice to launch an operation to retrieve and seize Hoover's private, secret files, which were supposed to be hidden at his house. Nixon did appear to have immediate interest in securing the files: When he heard Hoover was dead, he asked the White House to locate Hoover's former deputy Deke DeLoach immediately to help identify the location of the rumored files, which contained highly sensitive materials on top officials Hoover kept as both political protection and potential blackmail material. The files never surfaced, so perhaps the snatch-and-grab operation was aborted and the "casket protection" became a ruse.

Chapter 12

Third-Rate Burglars

Richard Nixon considered the chance to appoint an FBI director as consequential as that to pick a Supreme Court justice. Two of his court nominations had been debacles of their own—Nixon had been the first president in decades to have two nominees rejected back to back—but his choice of an FBI director proved an even worse decision than his failed court choices: He'd picked the wrong man, gambled on the wrong political strategy, and—without knowing it—angered the wrong alternate candidate.

Under different circumstances, L. Patrick Gray III might have jibed well with the culture created by the bureau's legendary founder. Resourceful and service-minded, a Texan child of the Depression, he'd spent four years trying to win an appointment to the Naval Academy, and finally achieved it in 1936. Unable to afford the travel to Annapolis, he talked his way onto a tramp steamer as an apprentice, teaching the shipmaster math in trade for lessons on seamanship and navigation, landed in Philadelphia, and hitchhiked to the academy, where he later became the starting quarterback. He did six combat submarine patrols in World War II and three more in the Korean War, becoming a star of the navy, destined perhaps even to become the service's chief of naval operations had he not retired to be Vice President Nixon's military advisor.

It was a great résumé, but he still knew absolutely nothing about the FBI. As its acting director, he was all but destined to fail. Gray was an unknown to the bureau, unfamiliar with its ways, and a mystery to its leadership—a figure who commanded little respect or loyalty from the bureaucracy or the rank-and-file. "The plain truth of the matter was that I just did not know enough about the customs and traditions of the FBI, its inner workings, or the background and character of its senior executives," he wrote in a posthumously published memoir.*

From the start, Gray mistakenly trusted Mark Felt, and he rapidly named him the acting associate director—the bureau's number two—elevating him to a uniquely powerful and valuable role that involved translating the bureau to its new director and vice versa. Gray drowned in the volume and velocity of the bureau's work—inheriting a massive paperwork machine that had long churned to keep J. Edgar personally up to speed on all aspects of the FBI's work—and asked Felt to dial back the decisions that came to the director's office. He quickly turned over the day-to-day operations almost entirely to Felt.

Within days of Gray's arrival at the FBI in May, Felt began to play a dangerous, manipulative game—undermining his boss behind the scenes as he pledged loyalty to his face. With Gray just a temporary caretaker until the election, in either outcome Felt believed he might benefit: If Gray stayed postelection, the deputy seemed loyal enough to become the permanent number two; if Gray failed, Felt would again be best positioned to take over.

The bureau was in an especially delicate position in the wake of Hoover's death; it had literally never existed without Hoover in charge, and everyone in Washington—and much of America beyond—wondered how and if it would remain up to the task without his careful eye.

Here too Felt found opportunity. In the first few weeks after Hoover's death, he moved quickly—and cautiously—to deliver information to the press anonymously that helped preserve the FBI's integrity and defuse criticisms of the bureau. In mid-May, Arthur Bremer shot and wounded fiery presidential candidate George Wallace at a shopping center in Laurel, Maryland, emptying a revolver at the Alabama governor, hitting him

---

* The title, *In Nixon's Web*, seemed to leave little doubt whom he ultimately came to blame for his predicament and the ignominy that would befall him in the role.

multiple times and leaving him paralyzed from the waist down. Bremer was wrestled to the ground after and arrested.

Many wondered if more sinister forces were behind Bremer's shooting. "Felt sensed that the incident could blow into a violent political storm, fanned by conspiracy theories on both the left and the right," wrote his co-biographer John O'Connor decades later. (At the White House, Colson actually tried to enlist Hunt to snoop in Bremer's apartment and determine his political leanings—or perhaps even plant some pro-McGovern materials that would undermine the Democrats.) The FBI, though, moved fast on its investigation and while it found that Bremer had also stalked Nixon that winter, unsuccessfully attempting to shoot him before settling on Wallace instead, the bureau didn't believe Bremer was part of any larger plot. He just wanted fame.

Felt leaked details about the thoroughness of the FBI investigation to a young *Washington Post* reporter he knew named Bob Woodward, enabling the cub reporter to write a series of authoritative stories about how the bureau had concluded that Bremer was a strange, crazed loner.

For Woodward, the series was a critical scoop, bolstering his career and profile inside the paper. For the FBI, the leaks helped rebut a conspiracy theory and trumpet the bureau's ongoing effectiveness post-Hoover.

Everybody won. And Felt realized he had a powerful new tool to wield in his covert fight for the bureau's top job.

Now he just needed Pat Gray to screw something up.

*   *   *

All through the spring of 1972, CREEP security director James McCord had stockpiled electronic equipment under Liddy's guidance—advanced eavesdropping tools, walkie-talkie radios, tape recorders, and more. Now, as they planned their first missions in the OPAL covert-entry program, the cache of spy toys would finally be put to use, and he had just the guy to help monitor the bugs: Al Baldwin, the onetime Martha Mitchell bodyguard, was enlisted to help surveil the Democratic National Committee at the Watergate. He moved Baldwin into a room at the Howard

Johnson Motor Inn across the street, rented in the name of McCord's consulting firm, McCord Associates.

When the DNC had moved into the sixth floor of the Watergate, some objected because it was too fancy for the workingman's party. The six-building complex consisted of a hotel, two condo co-ops, and two office buildings and had become the capital's priciest address as its buildings opened in the 1960s and early 1970s. An underground parking garage offered space for twelve hundred cars, and the shopping center boasted a post office, a bank, and a supermarket, as well as a florist, a salon, and other amenities. Mrs. Herbert Salzman, the neighbor of Senator Abe Ribicoff and his wife, bragged, "If it only had a tennis court and a movie theatre, I don't think I'd ever have occasion to leave the place."

The ambitious, grand complex, originally envisioned as D.C.'s answer to Rockefeller Center, had taken years to wind through the District's planning and zoning approvals, evolving and shrinking as it sought to make the best use of an awkward ten-acre site squeezed between Rock Creek Parkway and the new John F. Kennedy Center for the Performing Arts. The design, its Italian backers explained, was meant to embody "the sophistication and dedication of the 'new Washington,'" marking the postwar growth of the capital as it had transformed from a sleepy southern city, largely abandoned during the humid summers, into a world capital as strategically and historically relevant as Paris, London, or Rome. Prices ranged from $17,500 for a studio up to over $200,000 for one of the seven penthouses; bidets came standard in most condos.*

After the '68 election, the residential complex became a who's who of the Nixon administration: The Mitchells, RNC head Bob Dole, Commerce Secretary Maurice Stans, Transportation Secretary John Volpe, the chair of the Federal Reserve, Arthur Burns, and even Nixon's secretary, Rose Mary Woods, all moved in, joined over time by the postmaster general and his deputy, Nixon's chief of protocol, the head of the U.S. Information Agency, the director of the U.S. Mint, and all manner of

---

* Not everyone loved the new design, set among the capital's standard white marble buildings. *Washington Post* critic Wolf Von Eckardt wrote that the Watergate's aesthetic was as appropriate as "a strip dancer performing at your grandmother's funeral."

other administration aides. The concentration of power became known as the "Republican Bastille."

The day-to-day reality, however, proved less glamorous than advertised: Many residents complained their condos had been furnished with faulty appliances, and Martha Mitchell lamented how "this place was built like low-income housing—it's the cheapest equipment you ever saw." The marketing materials had also played up the sophisticated surveillance and security system (the *Washington Star* reported, "Intruders will have difficulty getting onto the grounds undetected."), but Rose Mary Woods had returned home from an early 1969 international trip with the president to find her condo burglarized and a suitcase of jewelry stolen. "It's really tragic," Ron Ziegler said. She took to storing her remaining jewelry in her safe at the White House.

✳   ✳   ✳

The Watergate wasn't supposed to be Liddy's first operation, but planting electronic surveillance inside the McGovern headquarters had been more difficult than the operatives had imagined. They'd schemed through the spring about how to access the building using their campaign mole, Thomas Gregory, and Gregory, Liddy, and Hunt surveilled the headquarters in Liddy's green Jeep, discussing how best to sneak inside. Later, Gregory actually got McCord—posing as a visiting uncle—into the campaign offices to walk around and imagine the best opportunities for electronic bugs. McCord scouted the offices of campaign leaders Frank Mankiewicz and Gary Hart and determined he could be in and out in about five minutes.

On their first attempt, Liddy and Hunt had Gregory hide out in the building's furnace room until nighttime so he could let McCord in to plant his bugs. Unfortunately, the hideout was discovered and Gregory only barely managed to escape with some quick talk. The close call worried Gregory ("The youth was becoming a bundle of nerves," Hunt recalled), and so the team adjusted their plans, imagining instead how to break in through the campaign's rear door, where there was no guard. Liddy, with Frank Sturgis standing watch one night, used an air gun pistol to shoot out the street floodlights near the back door.

Momentarily stymied by McGovern's building, the team moved forward instead with targeting the DNC offices at the Watergate.* In late May, the six Cuban members of the GEMSTONE burglary team recruited by Hunt—Barker, Martinez, Sturgis, Virgilio Gonzalez, Felipe De Diego, and Reinaldo Pico—arrived in D.C. and spent four days touring the capital and familiarizing themselves with the area around the Watergate. One night they even went as a group into the building, signed in with the guard, and walked up to the door of the DNC offices to check them out; undetected, Hunt made a clay impression of the lock.

Their scouting determined that an underground corridor linked the hotel and the office complex, so they rented a hotel banquet room near the corridor for May 26 and planned to fake a corporate event that would last until the complex emptied out for the night. They believed they had a narrow window to execute a break-in: According to McCord and Hunt, an alarm on the corridor stairwell kicked in at 11 p.m. McCord and Baldwin's observation post across the street would allow them to see when the DNC offices were empty for the night; after the entry, it would serve as a listening post once the bugs were installed.

On May 26, the team checked in as guests at the Watergate Hotel and proceeded to dinner.† They dined in the Continental Room on shrimp cocktail and filet mignon, drank Cutty Sark Scotch, and smoked cigars. As the others left around 10:30 p.m., Hunt and Gonzalez stayed behind in a closet, but party staffers were still at work in the DNC at the 11 p.m. cutoff. Adding insult to injury, the night guard then locked the banquet

---

* For reasons that have never been fully explained, John Dean evidently was separately interested in the Watergate that month too. On May 18, Tony Ulasewicz had met Dean at the White House. (He'd taken an instant dislike to the president's counsel, whom he thought looked like a mannequin in a men's shop, and "dismissed him as a slick operator.") Dean thanked him for cooperating earlier in the year with some work by Liddy—a figure Ulasewicz only knew as "Mr. George"—and explained that the campaign had plans to stir up some trouble for Democrats. A few days later, Caulfield told the private investigator that Dean wanted the Democratic National Committee at the Watergate scoped out, a mission that appeared separate from Liddy's operation.

† The fact that the Cubans were in town four days early for the scheduled break-in has long puzzled Watergate historians; in most other operations, the always cost-conscious Liddy brought them into town the same day or just a day before operations. Historians have long wondered if there had been plans for another operation, executed covertly or aborted prematurely, that would explain the long D.C. visit.

room doors and trapped Hunt and Gonzalez inside overnight. Hunt, nevertheless, was in good spirits when he finally managed to escape the next day—arriving in Liddy's Watergate Hotel room and laughing about how he'd urinated into a partially empty bottle of Johnnie Walker Scotch. "I can see Larry O'Brien now, with a puzzled look on his face, saying, 'Funny, if I didn't know this was Scotch, I'd swear it was piss!'" Liddy laughed.*

The second night's attempt didn't go much better. Gonzalez struck out, unable to pick the lock at the DNC's entrance; Barker reported that they'd tried unsuccessfully for forty-five minutes before aborting the mission. Gonzalez said he didn't have the right tools, and Liddy, annoyed, ordered him to return to Miami, get the tools, and come straight back—amazingly, Gonzalez did just that, making a same-day round trip to Florida that enabled them to make a third, successful attempt Sunday night. Inside the offices, Barker photographed two rolls' worth of film, documenting papers spread across O'Brien's desk; McCord reported that he'd successfully installed the necessary bugs. On Monday morning, May 29, Liddy reported to Magruder that the Watergate had been successfully burgled.

The Keystone Kops nature of the mission continued in the next few days. The team's local D.C. photography contact was away, so Hunt had to fly to Miami to have a Barker contact develop the prints—that "contact" ended up just printing the photos at a commercial photo store. As they waited for the prints to arrive, Hunt and Barker went over plans for their honey traps for Democratic politicians, plans to bug key locations, and efforts to rouse embarrassing protesters during the upcoming convention.

Back in D.C., Liddy and McCord realized as the week progressed that the bugs planted inside the Watergate had failed—one didn't appear to be transmitting at all, and the other, while it could be heard in Al Baldwin's observation post, appeared to be on a phone line filled with unimportant calls. Liddy reviewed each day's logs with an increasing sense of dread; he dictated some edited, intercepted transcripts to his secretary

---

* This joking exchange does not appear in Hunt's recounting of the night, but as we'll see later on, it's possible that much of the widely accepted story about how the failed break-in on the 26th unfolded is a lie.

Sally Harmony, passing the details on to the campaign leadership "for informational purposes only," and Mitchell was furious when Magruder showed him Liddy's transcripts. The intercepts, he said, were simply "shitty." On Friday, June 9, Magruder called Liddy to complain. "Not to my surprise he said that the content of the logs to date was hardly worth the effort, risk, and exposure we had gone to," Liddy recalled.* What could they do about the broken bug?

To placate his boss, Liddy explained that he planned to hit the McGovern headquarters the weekend of June 17—perhaps while the team was in town, they could also go back to the Watergate and attempt to fix the faulty bugs. Hunt blanched at the new plan.

"Looks like high risk, low gain to me," he told his partner.

"The Big Man wants the operation," Liddy pleaded, implying it came from the former attorney general. "Look, we're soldiers in this thing, Howard. If I've got a future, it's in government, and when the Big Man tells me to do something, either I do it for him or he gets someone else who can."

On Monday, June 12, Magruder summoned Liddy again, this time to insist that the burglary team prioritize photographing every document they could find. "Take all the men, all the cameras you need," he said. The team was determined to do it correctly: McCord sent Baldwin to the DNC offices to ask for a tour, pretending to be the nephew of a former Democratic Party chair, John Bailey of Connecticut. Remarkably, he was able to get a tour that included "his uncle's" old office, now Larry O'Brien's. Afterward, Baldwin drew a detailed office floor plan for the burglars from memory.

*   *   *

Looking back, the timing of the DNC operation appears uniquely odd. CREEP's intelligence operation, dirty tricks, and espionage—begun in

---

* Mitchell denied all of this, saying it's a "palpable, damnable lie." Magruder's version had Mitchell confronting Liddy directly, which is not backed up by Liddy's book, but the sum and substance of the phone call from Magruder on June 9 in the book is similar to the message Magruder says Mitchell said.

desperation and anxiety a year before when it seemed possible Nixon would face a serious Democratic challenge—seemed completely unnecessary by June 1972. Nixon's presidency was soaring, from the reopening with China and the Soviet Union diplomatic victories overseas to the audacious economic moves at home. The Democratic candidates seemed to be collapsing, and the shooting of George Wallace had removed even that third-party electoral threat. Nixon had a full nineteen-point lead in polling, and his approval rating had climbed from 49 to 60 percent. At the beginning of June, he had returned from overseas in dramatic fashion, ending a trip to a Moscow summit, with secondary stops in Austria, Iran, and Poland, by flying from Warsaw to Andrews Air Force Base and then helicoptering directly to Capitol Hill to address a special joint night session of Congress.

The entire reelection apparatus was going strong. Martha Mitchell had kept up almost weekly campaign trips, making appearances in Indiana, Illinois, Virginia, Michigan, Nebraska, and Pennsylvania, as well as two trips to New York, eight social events in Washington, and hosting a cocktail party and a dinner at her own house. On June 14 she predicted to reporter Helen Thomas that Nixon would win big—there was nothing but sunshine and rainbows ahead for the campaign, she said. Her own GOP speaking schedule was already booked full, with three or more appearances every week through November. "I am going to rock and roll," Martha told Thomas.

The next day, she appeared at a Flag Day gala, accepting the Distinguished Citizen's Award from the Lions Club, and then she and John left for California. Both Mitchells planned to accompany Pat Nixon to a fancy Hollywood gathering of "Celebrities for Nixon," while the president himself headed for Florida, where he'd deposit his aides in Key Biscayne, and then retreat to his friend Robert Abplanalp's island.

Columnist Jack Anderson was headed out of town that day too, scheduled for a speech in Cleveland, and at D.C.'s National Airport he recognized an old face in the crowd. Years earlier Anderson had written about Frank Sturgis's role in fighting Fidel Castro, a period during which Sturgis had introduced him to his colleague Bernard "Macho" Barker, and Anderson had listened as they regaled him with stories of "Eduardo," their shadowy CIA boss. ("They were a collection of romantics, forever seeking adventure, forever misadventure," the reporter recalled.) Now Sturgis introduced Anderson to his traveling companion, Eugenio Martinez. Anderson casually asked what brought them to Washington. "Private business," Sturgis said, tersely. The interaction ended there—Anderson headed off to Cleveland, and Sturgis, Martinez, and the other Cubans headed to the Watergate to meet "Eduardo," aka Howard Hunt.

*   *   *

When Hunt and Liddy met up that night at the Watergate, they first discussed a small hiccup to the weekend's plans: Earlier in the day, Thomas Gregory had informed Hunt and McCord that he had cold feet about participating further in the McGovern operation. "This is getting too deep for me," he said. It was a hit, but they decided that losing their inside man shouldn't be cause to abandon the operation. As soon as they wrapped up the Watergate, they would move ahead with the McGovern break-in.

That night, the burglar team managed to squeeze in a lobster dinner in the Watergate Hotel restaurant, before the Cubans returned to their hotel room. There, they created a makeshift command post and kept practicing their technique for photographing documents. Around 10 p.m., McCord reported that he'd taped open the entrance doors for the parking garage—a common technique used by maintenance and repair that wouldn't draw much attention if discovered.

While they waited for the last lights at the DNC to go out, Sturgis fetched some Coca-Cola and Hunt and Liddy walked outside for a snack. When they got the all clear, McCord joined them in the hotel from the listening post. He told them that on the way over he'd stopped by the garage doors and noticed someone had removed his tape, so he'd reinstalled it. Warning bells went off for Hunt—"Let's junk it," he said—but Liddy and McCord were insistent. They needed to prove the team's worth, and Liddy didn't have an endless supply of money to keep paying the burglary team for more days and nights of work.

The team headed off, and Hunt and Liddy settled in to watch a movie on the TV; a car radio antenna sat on the balcony outside, a wire stretching back to their walkie-talkie to communicate with the burglars and with Al Baldwin, who manned the listening post across the street at the Howard Johnson's.

*   *   *

Frank Wills, a Savannah, Georgia, native, had bounced around a series of what he saw as deadbeat jobs—his asthma had ended his most promising one, on a Ford assembly line in Detroit—before landing a midnight-to-dawn shift as the lone overnight security guard at the Watergate for $80 a week. By June 1972, he'd been doing the job for a year and there had been a grand total of a single attempted burglary, so he carried nothing more potent than a can of Mace. As he patrolled the night of the 16th, the Black guard was already thinking about his next career move, as his employer had just promoted over him a white colleague at the security company who had started after Wills.

On his first pass that night through the complex, he noticed a garage door with a piece of tape holding it open. He removed it, unconcerned—assuming someone had been moving during the day and forgotten it. After, he headed across the street for a bite to eat. When he came back a half hour later, he noticed the piece of tape had been replaced. Someone else was inside the building, he realized in a panic, probably not far away. Wills rushed back to the lobby and called the D.C. Police's Second Precinct for help.

In the classic movie version of *All the President's Men*, the officer responsible for the corner of the city that included the Watergate was off refilling his squad car with fuel when the dispatch came through. The truth, however, uncovered in 2012 by historian Craig Shirley, is much more dramatic: Shortly after midnight, the officer in that car had taken a break at PW's Saloon, on 19th Street NW, a new bar that had quickly become a favorite of on- and off-duty cops. One of the owners, Rich Lacey, was working the bar and poured the officer a bourbon and Coke; since it had been a quiet night, the officer lingered and had another. When the officer's walkie-talkie finally squawked with the burglary report, he was in no condition to respond. "Tell them that you're out of fuel and you got to go back and refuel before you can respond," Lacey suggested. "Somebody else will take the call."

That someone else turned out to be three undercover officers, dressed as hippies and driving a light blue 1972 Ford, Car 727. Sergeant Paul W. Leeper and Officers John B. Barrett and Carl M. Shoffler had also had a quiet night; the most excitement they'd seen was when they tried to warn two women in Georgetown about suspicious men nearby who might be purse-snatchers. (The women had responded "Narc!" and given them the middle finger.) They heard the dispatcher's open plea, "Any detective car or any cruiser anywhere, [see] guard at the Watergate Hotel . . . in reference to the possible suspicious circumstances," and drove to meet Wills and search the building. The ordinary blue Ford pulling up was unremarkable to Baldwin, still on lookout across the street.* In fact, he didn't note any unusual activity until the undercover officers had made it to the sixth floor. Finally seeing movement and lights, puzzled, he radioed McCord to ask how the burglary team was dressed.

"We're wearing suits and ties," McCord replied.

"Well, you've got a problem because there are hippie-looking guys who've got guns," he reported back.

It was already too late.

"They've got us," came a quick radio from inside the Watergate. The police officers were into the DNC offices.

"Hands up," the undercover officers shouted—only to be shocked when five sets of hands popped up from behind desks across the floor.

"I must admit that when I saw those ten hands go up, I thought, *Well, I expected one and I've got five; how do I know there isn't a sixth one behind me with a .45 aimed at my skull?*" recalled Sergeant Leeper. "I turned around very slowly, but there wasn't." The police were even more puzzled as they took in the full scene before them—a politically sensitive location, older-than-usual burglars wearing fancy attire and surgical gloves, carrying sophisticated surveillance equipment and rolls of $100 bills. They told the men they were all under arrest.

---

* For whatever reason, the burglary team would say later that they'd never contemplated that the building security guard would call the police upon suspecting a break-in. Instead, they had carried the $100 bills into the building, figuring that if they were confronted by a low-paid hourly guard, they could easily bribe their way out.

While Hunt and Liddy listened in growing horror as further on-scene narration came from the listening post (". . . *Police wagon pulling up at the entrance, also some marked police cars . . .*"), they realized Barker had a key to the hotel room they were in and quickly packed up what they could; Hunt slipped the car antenna down his pant leg, and they retreated to his Firebird, parked on the street outside. Hunt drove Liddy four blocks, to his own Jeep. "I'll be in touch tomorrow," Liddy said.

Then Hunt doubled back to the Howard Johnson's listening post and instructed Baldwin to evacuate. "It's all over," he said. "Pack up and get going." As Hunt left, he saw the burglars being led out of the building. "It all seemed so damned final," he recalled later.* He drove to the White House and put all the electronic equipment he could into his office safe. He took out $10,000 cash and phoned a former Mullen Company colleague, Douglas Caddy: "I hate to wake you up, but I've got a tough situation and I need to talk." Next he raced to the Mullen offices to call Barker's wife in Miami and explain that her husband had been arrested. Finally, he went to Caddy's apartment. While the lawyer boiled water for instant coffee, Hunt explained that he'd had an operation at the DNC go bad and asked if Caddy would go represent the burglars and bail them out. "I'm not a criminal lawyer, Howard—you know that," he said. "I don't have the faintest idea where police take arrested men." Caddy phoned his law firm partners to learn more about D.C.'s arrest procedures, and determined the burglars were probably at the D.C. jail.

Hunt went home as dawn lightened the sky, took a sleeping pill, and went to bed. In that moment, he was not particularly concerned; in the short term, he figured Caddy would successfully bail the men out and they could all disappear. If Caddy's efforts failed, Liddy had likely already informed the White House leadership and they could intervene. The whole operation, he thought, had been authorized by Attorney General John Mitchell, so a quick telephone call from Mitchell's successor, Kleindienst, to the D.C. police chief would surely spring the men, no questions asked.

* As a reward for his vigilance, Wills was given a raise, after taxes, of 40 cents a week.

Liddy, on the other hand, had gone straight home, knowing exactly how much trouble lay ahead. McCord was a former government employee; his fingerprints were on file. His alias wouldn't hold. As he climbed into bed around 3 a.m. next to his sleeping wife, Fran, she stirred. "Anything wrong?" she asked.

"There was trouble," Liddy answered bluntly. "Some people got caught. I'll probably be going to jail."

Across D.C., word of the strange events at the Watergate spread. The burglars initially identified themselves as Raoul Godoy (Gonzales), Gene Valdez (Martinez), Edward Martin (McCord), Edward Hamilton (Sturgis), and Frank Carter (Barker). The crew had thirty-nine rolls of film, a stand to photograph documents, bugging equipment, and twenty-four sequentially numbered $100 bills, as well as two keys for the Watergate Hotel, to Rooms 214 and 314. Realizing this would not be an ordinary case, the police summoned a top prosecutor from the U.S. Attorney's Office.

Beyond simply the fact that the burglars were wearing suits, prosecutors raised their eyebrows when a lawyer named Douglas Caddy arrived at the precinct, saying he represented them. As far as the police knew, none of the burglars had made any phone calls noting they'd been arrested—so who had sent over a lawyer?

*   *   *

The puzzle that the arresting officers faced that morning—what were these well-dressed burglars doing inside the offices of the Democratic National Committee?—has never actually been satisfactorily answered. What were the burglars actually looking for? Who ordered them into the building? And who on the burglary team knew what? It's still hard to know. The basic question of the burglary's motive remained—and has remained—an open question that bothered even key players in the scandal: In 1979, John Ehrlichman and his wife, Christy, happened to run into James McCord in the Seattle airport, where Christy blurted out, "Why did you fellows break into the Watergate?" We still don't know. No one was ever charged with ordering the break-in, nor has anyone ever confessed or presented conclusive evidence one direction or another about what the burglars hoped to accomplish that night.

There are generally five distinct theories that have coalesced around the events of June 17, though it is possible that more than one can be true at the same time. They are so different—conflicting in some directions, overlapping in others—that even with extensive research and parsing, the general motives are difficult to establish, especially when paired with the group's tendency for sub-schemes and subterfuge. The decades of silence—and, in recent years, death—of participants mean it's almost certain never to be fully explained.

The least complicated theory is the official one: The Watergate incident was a simple, stunningly incompetent burglary conducted by bumbling campaign aides with overeager imaginations and the end goal of bugging the office or telephone of Democratic Party Chair Larry O'Brien. The official version in some ways makes the most sense: It's clear that the Nixon White House was deeply paranoid, expected the worst from its enemies, and often assumed that everyone else was engaged in the very dirty tricks it was doing itself. Liddy, Hunt, and McCord all had overeager imaginations and, at best, were poorly supervised by the Nixon operation, and it's hardly a leap to imagine them launching an ill-conceived and poorly executed operation of dubious value.

Where it gets trickier is whether the burglars were trying to uncover dirt on the Democrats, or find out what dirt the Democrats had on Nixon and his team. While there's no shortage of dirt the burglars may have hoped to uncover (if they had any specific ideas at all), speculation in the years since has generally focused on three separate theories—one about financial improprieties and the upcoming Democratic convention in Miami, another on sexual blackmail, and a third about illegal foreign campaign donations.

The most straightforward "hidden dirt" theory is that the burglars were looking for both financial improprieties on the Democrats, potentially stemming from the ITT controversy earlier that spring, as well as trying to uncover whether the Democrats might be plotting to disrupt the Republican convention—just as CREEP was planning to do to the Democrats.

Jeb Magruder and John Dean have both explained over the years that they believe the White House was motivated by anger at the ITT controversy and the sense that Democrats were cutting similar deals over funding their Miami convention. Dean outlined his theory as part of a new 93-page afterword when his memoir republished by a small publishing house in 2009 and pointed to a note Haldeman scrawled in March 1972 after a conversation with Nixon: "Do some [checking] on where the Democratic money for Miami is coming from." In the days after, Nixon—much as he'd obsessed over the Brookings break-in during the Pentagon Papers—repeatedly asked for updates on what he called the "Miami investigation." As Dean saw it, "The Nixon administration had been hammered, day in and day out, for months, and been badly stung by the Democrats' charges" over the ITT financing. They were desperate to strike back and felt the Democrats surely had their own shenanigans to hide. Indeed, in later testimony, Hunt says he instructed the Cuban burglars to "photograph everything that was available with particular reference to any papers with financial figures and computations on them, anything that looked like contributors."

This theory, at least, was the one later reported to Nixon himself. During a January 3, 1973, conversation in the Oval Office, when Nixon wondered aloud "what the Christ [were the burglars] looking for?" Haldeman replied, "They were looking for stuff on two things. One, on financial. And the other on stuff that they thought they had on what [the Democrats] were going to do to screw us up, because apparently a Democratic plot." (Haldeman then added, cautiously, "I don't know any of this firsthand—I can't prove any of it, and I don't want to know.")

G. Gordon Liddy, though, later settled on a different motive and theory. According to Liddy's telling, Magruder on June 12 asked Liddy to have his team reenter the Watergate, try to fix the bug, and photograph everything they could get their hands on. At that point, Magruder gestured to his own file drawer, where Liddy knew Magruder kept the campaign's sensitive, derogatory information on Democratic candidates, and told Liddy, "I want to know what O'Brien's got right here."

Liddy, in his memoir, is under no misapprehension about the burglars' mission that night—he even italicizes the mission for readers: *"The purpose of the second Watergate break-in was to find out what O'Brien had of a derogatory nature about us, not for us to get something on him or the Democrats."*

So what might the burglars be digging for? The sexual blackmail theory focuses on two of the enduring mysteries of the break-in—why the team was targeting the phone of Spencer Oliver, a relatively obscure official who worked with the party's state chairs, and why burglar Eugenio Martinez was carrying a key that fit the desk of Ida Maxwell "Maxie" Wells, Oliver's secretary at the DNC. Why Martinez had Wells's key has never been explained—nor has anyone ever explained how the burglars procured the key in the first place. In fact, it would take weeks before the FBI even determined that the key Martinez was carrying opened Wells's desk, and apparently no one ever asked the twenty-three-year-old secretary what would have been of interest inside her desk. "We wouldn't be sitting around again with all the puzzling and all the mysteries had we taken the time to find out what that key was about," one of the arresting D.C. police officers, Carl Shoffler, later said in an A&E documentary.

John Dean argues the Oliver bugging was a simple mistake: The burglars thought they'd targeted Larry O'Brien's office because they didn't understand the DNC office layout until after the first burglary. But in the 1991 book *Silent Coup*, Len Colodny and Robert Gettlin offered their own answer, piecing together a new theory that the break-in was tied to a high-priced escort service linked to Democratic officials—one that may or may not have involved the woman John Dean ultimately married.* The Colodny/Gettlin theory notes contemporaneous news reports of a ring of high-end escorts that involved a D.C. lawyer named Phillip Mackin Bailley, who was involved in a call-girl ring based at the nearby Columbia Plaza apartment complex and who faced his own legal peril that spring during the period just before and after the break-in, and claims that John Dean's then girlfriend, Maureen Biner, was friends with a woman named Erika "Heidi" Rikan, a fetching blond German immigrant who Colodny and Gettlin maintain was a high-priced D.C. escort at the time. As a later court opinion summary explains, "the implication of Colodny and Gettlin's narrative is that the June 17, 1972, Watergate break-in was ordered by Dean so that he could determine whether the Democrats had

---

* Parts of this theory were also developed in an earlier "revisionist" history of Watergate, Jim Hougan's *Secret Agenda*, which came out in 1984 and was the first Watergate narrative to have access to large portions of the FBI's files, given out under the Freedom of Information Act, and which is a mix of crack observation and investigation and hard-to-source rumor. The *Washington Post* called it a collection of more "working hypotheses than prudent conclusions."

information linking Maureen Biner to the Bailley/Rikan call-girl ring and whether they planned to use such information to embarrass him."

Their theory holds that the Democratic National Committee was connected to the Columbia Plaza call-girl ring and that inside Wells's desk was a photo portfolio of Rikan's escorts that visiting Democratic officials could view before arranging liaisons using the phone in Spencer Oliver's out-of-the-way office. Baldwin, who manned the listening post, would later explain that he had intercepted telephone calls that were "primarily sexual" and "extremely personal, intimate, and potentially embarrassing," but prosecutors at the time suggested that such intimate calls were just DNC secretaries talking to their boyfriends.

When *Silent Coup* was published, it sparked enormous controversy. Both John and Maureen Dean vigorously denied any and all of the allegations and John Dean called the book "absolute garbage." The *Washington Post* at various times called *Silent Coup* "a byzantine piece of revisionism" and one of "the most boring conspiracy books ever written" despite its "wild charges and vilifications." Sam Dash, the later chief counsel for the Senate Watergate Committee, called the book "a fraud . . . contradicted by everything on the White House tapes and by the evidence"—yet the book spent weeks on the bestseller lists and was embraced by Watergate figures like Liddy and Ehrlichman. The work spawned multiple, long-running libel and defamation lawsuits between the authors, Dean, Liddy, Wells, and others; the resulting claims, counterclaims, depositions, and trials stretched for years and eventually the Deans and the publisher reached an out-of-court settlement. Another lawsuit, by Wells against Liddy, ended in a mistrial in 2006.

A third theory about the secrets hidden inside the DNC centers around illegal foreign campaign finances. The Cuban burglars, some of whom spoke little English and seemed genuinely befuddled by the purpose of the whole mission, believed they had been recruited to uncover the Democratic Party's links to Fidel Castro, but the evidence that has since emerged shifted instead toward shadowy contributions to Nixon's own campaign. As it turns out, the Chennault Affair wasn't the only foreign-influence subterfuge that the campaign had pulled off in the closing weeks of the '68 election: There was also the "Greek Connection," where the campaign accepted about a half million dollars from the brutal

Greek military junta, money funneled from the Greek intelligence service KYP, providing a critically needed infusion of cash as Humphrey closed the polling gap through that fall.

Greek journalist Elias Demetracopoulos, who had been forced into exile by the military, had suspected something was fishy when in the fall of 1968 the Nixon campaign suddenly publicly embraced the junta, and he later uncovered how KYP had collected a total of $549,000, mostly in large-denomination bills, and funneled it in three tranches via Nixon's vice finance chair Thomas A. Pappas, a Greek-American Boston businessman; one payment went to Mitchell, two to Maurice Stans. Demetracopoulos reported what he knew to Lawrence O'Brien in '68.

While Lyndon Johnson decided not to make a public issue of the illegal donation in the closing days of the election, the ticking time bomb of the Greek donation "caused the most anxiety for the longest period of time for the Nixon administration," wrote Watergate historian Stanley Kutler.* In 1971, a House committee tried to look further into the donations, prompting Nixon's longtime backroom brawler Murray Chotiner to visit Demetracopoulos and demand that he lay off Pappas or risk deportation; John Mitchell delivered a similar ultimatum.† Could it be that when Magruder asked Liddy to find out what derogatory information O'Brien kept hidden in his desk on the Nixon campaign, he was talking about the documentation of the "Greek Connection"? But if that's what he meant, why didn't he specifically explain that goal to Liddy?

Other longstanding questions and theories about the burglary center

---

* Christopher Hitchens, in his book *The Trial of Henry Kissinger*, provides compelling evidence that the Nixon administration's vendetta against Demetracopoulos might have gone even further than just time: The Greek junta in the spring of 1974, when the Nixon administration was in its final months and the junta was actually in its final weeks, plotted to kidnap and likely murder Demetracopoulos, smuggling him out of the country on a Greek submarine at dock in Virginia. One of the top officials at the Greek embassy later wrote to Demetracopoulos that Henry Kissinger was fully aware of the plot, but a congressional investigation into the allegation and the CIA's work with the Greek junta was shut down at Kissinger's request.

† Behind the scenes during this period there was also heavy government surveillance on Demetracopoulos, including by both the CIA and the FBI, with reports funneled to Henry Kissinger's National Security Council, including attempts to link the Greek journalist to Daniel Ellsberg.

around whether some of those involved in the operation set out to torpedo it from the start. Some wonder if the CIA, whose presence loomed large over the entire escapade, purposefully sabotaged it—perhaps either to sink Nixon or to protect its own role in the Bailley call-girl ring. After all, there were two agency retirees involved, McCord and Hunt, and Hunt also worked for a PR firm known to be an agency cover, and Eugenio Martinez was actively on the CIA payroll, a $100-a-month asset who reported to his case officer through his year of hijinks with Liddy and Hunt—not to mention that the other burglars had their own involvement in past CIA plots. The agency also seemed at various levels and points to have had unique insight into what Hunt and the others were planning, given the photos it helped Hunt develop from the Fielding operation and the GEMSTONE charts it helped Liddy make.

Were Hunt and/or McCord still working for the agency, either formally or informally? Did one or both of them have their own secret agenda? Researchers digging into the burglary years after the fact found notable inconsistencies in Hunt's telling of how the first attempts to break into the Watergate unfolded, details that initial investigators did not pay close attention to—the failed banquet dinner, for instance, almost certainly didn't unfold the way Hunt told Liddy it did.*

In particular, there are questions about James McCord's movements the night of the burglary. The other burglars noted he seemed to disappear at odd moments from the group ("McCord did not come in with us [when we first entered]," Martinez would note later. "He said he had to go someplace. We never knew where he was going."), and an associate of McCord's, Lou Russell, a private detective and CREEP security guard who had once been the lead investigator for the House Un-American

---

* Hunt's memoir says that the banquet wrapped up around 10:30, when a guard told them to close up, and that he and Gonzalez were stuck in the Continental Room until after 11 p.m. when the alarm on the corridor stairway kicked in, but in the 1984 book *Secret Agenda*, journalist Jim Hougan uncovered that there was no guard on duty before midnight who could have told the burglars to wrap up their dinner at 10:30 p.m.; the banquet waiter apparently didn't leave work until 12:30 a.m.; and the building's guard log—written, as it were, by the same overnight guard, Frank Wills, who would discover the burglars on the 17th—noted on his 1 a.m. rounds, "Contineal [*sic*] Room Open / Having Meeting Cont / Room Close at 2:10 a.m." Nor, according to the Watergate's head of maintenance, was the corridor door alarmed in the way that McCord and Hunt say stymied their efforts.

Activities Committee, may have been that evening across the street at the Howard Johnson restaurant—coincidentally, he maintained until his death in 1973. Did McCord have a "sixth man," a hidden accomplice or lookout that night, unknown to his fellow burglars?

The FBI was never able to tie Russell to the burglary, but there were long rumors that he had been involved in the Columbia Plaza call-girl ring—or perhaps even that the call-girl ring was a CIA operation to amass blackmail material on prominent Washingtonians and visiting diplomats. As the *Washington Post* later—dismissively—summarized this "sixth man" theory, "This secret CIA operation involving the prostitutes was so sensitive that McCord and Russell set out to sabotage the break-in at Watergate to insure that the other Watergate burglars wouldn't stumble across it." Indeed, whether McCord, who demonstrated little skill in his operations, would have likely been the agent of a major CIA plot seems dubious. But questions about the CIA's tense relationship with Nixon have lingered. In the heart of the scandal to come, Senator Howard Baker would say, "Nixon and [CIA Director Richard] Helms have so much on each other, neither of them can breathe."

The final remaining theory claims that the Democrats and/or the D.C. police had advance knowledge of the burglary and sprung their own trap. That a squad of undercover vice officers responded to the burglary—a team that included Officer Carl Shoffler, who had been intimately involved in numerous cases about the D.C. prostitution scene—was quite the coincidence, and over the years, multiple sources of varying levels of credibility have come forward to say that Shoffler, who unexpectedly volunteered to work an unscheduled shift that evening, had been tipped off about the possibility of action at the Watergate. Was Shoffler in cahoots with McCord or Hunt in actively sabotaging and exposing the burglary? If so, to what end? Or perhaps the Democrats got wind of the operation themselves (after all, Jack Anderson had received a tip earlier that spring that such nefarious doings were underway) and sprung the D.C. police on the burglars to embarrass the president?

The evidence for and against each of these theories has filled entire books in decades since—not to mention thousands of pages of depositions and civil lawsuits—but all remain frustratingly inconclusive, each their own version of the "lone shooter" vs. "grassy knoll" debates around

JFK's assassination. It's also possible (perhaps probable) that parts of multiple theories are all true at the same time: It could be a bungled burglary, designed either to facilitate or cover up improprieties, that the CIA wanted to sabotage by tipping off the D.C. police. And it could be true that Liddy thought the burglary had one purpose, while Hunt and/or McCord double-crossed him with a second mission, and all the while the Cubans were kept in the dark and told a third goal entirely. Or it might be exactly what White House Press Secretary Ron Ziegler dubbed it soon thereafter: "a third-rate burglary."

Regardless of the underlying motive or motives, one thing is clear: By the time dawn rose in Washington, the cover-up had begun.

Chapter 13

"A Crime That Could Destroy Us All"

A s investigators and prosecutors rushed to uncover what they could about the bizarre break-in at the Watergate, Liddy and Hunt moved to hide everything they could. Around 7 a.m. Saturday, Liddy drove to a Texaco station to begin damage control; using a pay phone, he tried to call Magruder, but the White House switchboard informed Liddy that Magruder was in California with Mitchell. Realizing it would be several hours before he could speak to campaign leadership, he went to the CREEP offices. "I also had a lot of material in my office that was now white-hot and had to be destroyed immediately," he recalled, and he began to feed his GEMSTONE files and the receipts from his various operations into the office shredder a few pages at a time. As the office filled up with other staff, he ran into Hugh Sloan between his office and the shredder. "Our boys got caught last night. It was my mistake, and I used someone from here—something I told them I'd never do," Liddy told the campaign treasurer. "I don't know how much longer I'll be able to keep my job."

Mid-morning, Liddy learned that Mitchell was scheduled to speak imminently at a California press conference and raced to the White House Situation Room to use a secure phone. Operators located Magruder at breakfast in the Polo Lounge with the LaRues, Porters, and Mardians;

Liddy explained that Magruder should hurry to the closest secure phone at a nearby missile base. The annoyed deputy campaign director protested, and instead called back from a pay phone outside. Then Liddy shared news of the arrests. "You used McCord?! Why, Gordon, why?!" Magruder sputtered. Later, Magruder called Liddy back at the CREEP offices and told him to have Kleindienst intervene.*

Magruder then went to Mitchell's hotel suite, where he relayed the story to the campaign director. "That's incredible!" Mitchell exclaimed. Magruder then spent the day successfully avoiding telephone calls from the two men he feared the most: Haldeman and Haldeman's aide, Gordon Strachan. (Amazingly, the two men wouldn't speak until Sunday.) Initially Magruder—like Hunt—seemed confident that the problem would be contained, but as hours passed, he grew less sure. From California, he called his aide Bob Reisner and asked him to remove the GEMSTONE file in Magruder's CREEP office, as well as other sensitive documents. "This was a crime that could destroy us all," Magruder recalled thinking.

Across Washington, officials learned more details. The FBI's overnight watch supervisor had alerted Mark Felt, who hurried into the office at 8:30 a.m. on Saturday. "This thing has all kinds of political ramifications," Felt said. "The utter stupidity of it baffled me. What could anyone find at the Democratic National Committee that would be worth the risks?"

For years, John Dean maintained that he didn't learn of the burglary until Sunday; the White House counsel had been in the Philippines, part of a U.S. delegation to an international narcotics event, and he tells in his memoir how he experienced "two Mondays," flying back from

---

* This story has "evolved" from the early years of Watergate investigation. Liddy's (highly detailed and entertainingly written) memoir was not published until 1980, long after the political repercussions and after the criminal statute of limitations had expired for the acts involved. Liddy said the phone call ordering him to find Kleindienst came from Magruder, but Magruder argued it came from Robert Mardian. Magruder's memoir seems among the less reliable of the Watergate memoirs, while Liddy's, if anything, seems to perhaps overinflate Magruder's culpability. What does seem clear, though, is that Mitchell was never consulted, as Magruder originally implied.

Manila on Monday the 19th, crossing the international date line, and landing back in San Francisco on Sunday the 18th. It was there that, by his account, he spoke to Fred Fielding for the first time, learned of the burglary, and flew immediately back to Washington. He also claimed not to have known of McCord's involvement until Sunday night, when he arrived in D.C. and met with Fielding.*

Haldeman had been on the hotel terrace in Key Biscayne with Higby Saturday morning when Ziegler interrupted with the first wire service reports of the arrests. "Watergate historians have already supposed that the heavens fell when those in the President's party in Florida learned the break-in had been discovered," Haldeman later recounted. "Quite the reverse is true. My immediate reaction was to smile. *Wiretap the Democratic National Committee? For what?* The idea was ludicrous." He says he assumed immediately it was a Chuck Colson operation, the president's "impresario of 'hard ball' politics." Higby had the same thought; he told Haldeman, "I'll bet they're Colson's gunners."

Nixon on the other hand was furious. Haldeman shared the news around 11 a.m., and the president promptly called Colson, telling the aide he threw an ashtray across the room. "The whole thing made so little sense," he recounted thinking in his memoir. "Why? I wondered. Why then? Why in such a blundering way? And why, of all places, the Democratic National Committee?"

Yet even as word spread among the White House staff, there were

---

* At least that's the story Dean told to the Senate Watergate Committee and in his memoir. However, in *Silent Coup*, Len Colodny and Robert Gettlin tracked down Dean's travel partner, another U.S. official, and traced the flights that they were on, and reported that they believed Dean actually left Manila as early as he could Sunday and experienced two Sundays—a critical difference pointing to an earlier role for Dean in the Watergate cover-up than he ever allowed at the time. Dean disputes their conclusion and argues they are misreading his travel documents. Whenever he found out about the burglaries, one of Dean's first moves was, apparently, to reenlist his old intelligence operatives, Jack Caulfield and Tony Ulasewicz. Ulasewicz got a phone call on the morning of the 18th from Caulfield—who, given the timing, seems likely to have spoken to Dean during the White House counsel's layover in San Francisco—saying that Dean wanted the private eye in D.C. pronto, ready to take on any necessary tasks. Ulasewicz initially resisted—he said he wanted no part of a cover-up—but eventually relented, checking into the Roger Smith Hotel for two days, never to receive a phone call or mission.

doubts that the president's inner circle were as innocent as they would profess. Alexander Butterfield heard about the burglary on the radio during his daily drive in to the White House, and when he arrived at the Oval Office, he said to Nell Yates, one of Nixon's favorite secretaries, "You know, don't you, that he had to have done this?"

"Of course," she replied, not pausing for a moment.

They spoke for another moment before Butterfield concluded, "I can't imagine anything happening in this administration that the president and/or Haldeman haven't approved."

*   *   *

Richard Kleindienst had not even been attorney general for a full week when word reached him via a call from the head of the Justice Department's criminal division, Henry Petersen, that the Watergate had been burgled.* With little other information, the attorney general headed on with his day's plans: the annual members golf tournament at Washington's elite Burning Tree Golf Club.

During lunch in the club dining room, he looked up from the table to see Gordon Liddy and CREEP press secretary Powell Moore motioning to him from the passageway to the locker room. Kleindienst had only met Liddy once, during a meeting on narcotics policy. When Kleindienst walked over, he noticed the aide was agitated. "I've got to talk to you at once," Liddy said. "Where can we talk in private?"

Inside the locker room, the story tumbled from Liddy's mouth. "John Mitchell sent me from Los Angeles to inform you that some of the persons arrested last night at the Watergate Hotel might be employed by the White House or the Committee to Re-Elect the President—and he wants you to get them out of jail at once!"

Kleindienst was taken aback, but doubted that such a direct request had been made. "What in the hell are you talking about, Liddy?" he said.

---

* After the prolonged ITT controversy, he had been confirmed by the Senate on June 8 and sworn in on June 12.

"John Mitchell knows how to reach me; I don't believe he gave you any such instructions."*

According to Liddy's memory of the conversation, he then told Kleindienst, "I know—there's no way you can ever try to do it without it getting out. Then what happens to you?"

"Me?!" Kleindienst spat back, according to Liddy. "Fuck what happens to me! What happens to the President if I try a fool thing like that? It's the Goddamnest thing I ever heard of."

Dialing from the locker room phone, Kleindienst called Petersen. His instructions were clear: "Henry, I don't know what this is all about, but those persons arrested last night are to be treated just like anyone else."†

Frustrated, Liddy returned to the CREEP office to complete his shredding. That afternoon, he heard more bad news: Hunt's name had apparently been inside the notebook of one of the burglars. The FBI had already attempted to interview Hunt at home, but he'd declined until he had the chance to speak to his lawyer.

*   *   *

As the day progressed, the D.C. federal prosecutors assigned to the break-in, Chuck Work and Earl Silbert, set about obtaining search

---

* Kleindienst's intuition was almost certainly correct. While it seems clear Magruder had invoked Mitchell's name in the order to Liddy that Saturday morning, further investigation has made it clear that Magruder didn't speak to Mitchell beforehand. According to the logs of Mitchell's bodyguard, onetime FBI agent Steve King, Magruder didn't meet with Mitchell that Saturday until 9:55 a.m. PT, nearly 1 p.m. ET, whereas by all accounts Liddy had already driven to Burning Tree and was standing in the club dining hall by around 12:30 p.m. ET. The question of whether Mitchell did order Liddy to find Kleindienst is not entirely an academic one: When prosecutors later charged Mitchell, Mardian, and others with conspiracy and obstruction of justice, they listed the Burning Tree conversation as the first "overt act" of the conspiracy. So who invoked Mitchell's name and ordered Magruder to dispatch Liddy?

† While Kleindienst says he recalls telling Petersen that his phone call was prompted by the presence of Liddy, Petersen said that the attorney general never mentioned Liddy's name and that it was months before anyone at the Justice Department became aware of the conversation at Burning Tree.

warrants for the burglars' hotel rooms.* When the arresting police officers, Sergeant Leeper and Officer Shoffler, were finally granted access, they and other D.C. police found mysteries aplenty: spy equipment, sequentially numbered $100 bills, and, among some other papers, various letters and mail mentioning someone named "E. Howard Hunt," as well as the burglars' address books, which also included entries for Hunt, one noting "WH" and another outright saying "W. House."

Investigators initially thought one of the burglary motives might be jewelry theft and assigned the case to the FBI's C-2 squad, the Washington Field Office's "street sweepers" who handled "miscellaneous crimes," ranging from migratory bird violations to crimes on the capital region's many military posts. FBI Special Agent Angelo Lano was the first on the scene, which made him the "case agent," a post he would hold through the scandal's conclusion. He'd handled several of the Watergate complex's domestic burglaries already, including the jewelry theft from Rose Mary Woods. "I never solved any of them," he recalled years later. "The Watergate had simply become my beat."

Soon investigators hit their first big clue when they realized that the burglar who called himself Edward Martin was actually someone named James McCord—and, confoundingly, he appeared to work for the president's campaign. The bureau, meanwhile, searched its files for Howard Hunt and found it had recently run a background investigation for someone of the same name who was up for a job at the White House.

As questions compounded, Lano brought in his colleague Daniel Mahan, a twenty-nine-year-old agent known for being a skilled interviewer, and dispatched him to the D.C. jail to speak to the burglars. "They clearly didn't look like ordinary knuckleheads," Lano recalled. They gave up nothing—when Martinez was asked about the purpose of the burglary, he replied, "That's the $64,000 question, isn't it?"

Interviewed by another Spanish-speaking agent, Paul Magallanes, Martinez remained enigmatic. "We're working for the same man," Martinez said. "You work for the government. We work for the government. And we're going to be taken care of."

---

* In the federal capital, the 140 federal prosecutors are also responsible for trying "local" crimes, meaning that the run-of-the-mill burglary was still being run by the U.S. Justice Department.

Who did Martinez mean? the FBI agent asked. "By the man—the president," the burglar said. "We work for the president, just like you do."

∗   ∗   ∗

News of the burglary began to circulate in the media after the Democratic Party's deputy chair, Stan Griegg, called Lawrence O'Brien to inform him his office had apparently been the target. O'Brien was in Miami, preparing for the summer presidential convention, and Griegg explained that he had been to the jail to look at the suspects, but didn't recognize them. "Neither Stan nor I knew what to make of the break-in," O'Brien recalled. The DNC's lawyer, Joseph A. Califano, Jr., however, knew someone who might. He also happened to be the lawyer for the *Washington Post* and called his other client to pass along a tip.

Around 8:30 a.m. Saturday morning, the paper's city editor, Barry Sussman, enlisted the *Post*'s legendary police reporter, Alfred Lewis, and a relatively new reporter named Bob Woodward to dig deeper. Lewis's job was to hang around police headquarters and local precincts and call in tips and stories to the paper's rewrite desk; despite having worked for the paper since before World War II, his colleagues weren't sure he'd ever written a story himself. After thirty-five years on the beat, he was almost more cop than journalist—he even often wore a regulation blue police sweater—and that day, he marched right into the Watergate alongside a police official he knew, swirling past the media and cameras waiting outside. Soon, he was inside the DNC office suite and used one of the party's phones to call Sussman with some details. It was clear this was more than just a weird crime story. "One of the men had $814, one $800, one $215, one $234, one $230," Lewis dictated. "They seemed to know their way around; at least one of them must have been familiar with the layout."

As Lewis gathered details at the scene, Woodward began working the story from the newsroom. He'd been at the paper just about nine months. Having just left the navy and suddenly dreading the prospect of starting law school, he had in August 1970 approached the *Washington Post*'s metro editor, Harry Rosenfeld, about becoming a reporter, showing up at the paper's headquarters at 15th and L Streets NW and prowling the building until he found Rosenfeld. Rosenfeld firmly rebuffed Woodward's interest, pointing out he'd never even worked on his college newspaper, and quizzing him on the basics of journalism. Woodward flunked. Still, something about the young man's audacity piqued Rosenfeld's interest, and he offered Woodward a two-week tryout, a test Woodward also flunked; he tried to research and write a dozen or so stories over the two weeks and succeeded at none. Rosenfeld told him to go learn the ropes at a small newspaper, suggesting a suburban Maryland weekly run by a former *Post* editor. "Though I had failed the tryout completely—it was a spectacular crash—I realized I had found something I loved," Woodward recalled later. "The sense of immediacy in a newsroom and the newspaper was overwhelming to me." He joined the *Montgomery County Sentinel*, learned the basics of reporting, and a year later, Rosenfeld hired him onto the *Post* staff.* He started as the *Post*'s lowest-paid reporter, making $165 a week, working the night cops beat, from 6 p.m. until 2 a.m., running from crime scene to fire across the city. By June, he felt he was ready for bigger things and had just finished his first major investigative series, looking at the assassination attempt on George Wallace.

As Saturday unfolded, Sussman enlisted another reporter, Carl Bernstein, to gather biographical information on the burglars.† The team soon figured out that four of the burglars were from Miami's Cuban-American community, and Sussman—a heavyset, thirty-eight-year-old newspaper veteran from Tennessee who had been at the paper for nearly a decade—dispatched a reporter accompanying Nixon to Key Biscayne to talk to the exile community in Florida.

Mid-afternoon Saturday, Woodward headed to the courthouse for the burglars' preliminary hearing, where he had several confounding exchanges with Douglas Caddy and Joseph Rafferty, the lawyers who

---

* His final hiring interview at the *Post*, with executive editor Ben Bradlee, came on Friday, September 3, 1971, the same weekend that Howard Hunt led the burglary of Ellsberg's psychiatrist.

† The reporter's sudden appearance was not surprising. "Bernstein also had an unnerving habit of somehow materializing in the newsroom day or night or on a weekend when a big story was breaking and muscling his way unassigned into the coverage of it," Len Downie, who would later edit the Watergate coverage, once wrote.

seemed to be representing the burglars. Caddy said he'd met one of the defendants, Bernard Barker, during a gathering at the city's posh Army-Navy Club—not exactly a normal hangout for a burglary suspect—and had been called by Barker's wife around 3 a.m. when she hadn't heard from her husband.

When court came to order around 3:30 p.m., Judge James Belsen asked the burglars their professions. "Anti-communists," Barker said, speaking for the group as the others nodded.

McCord, when asked the same question, replied he was a security consultant.

"Where?" the judge asked.

"I've recently retired from government service," he said, his voice soft.

"Where in government?"

"CIA," he all but whispered.

Woodward, sitting toward the rear of the room, muttered out loud: "Holy shit."

He raced back to the newsroom to add his reporting to the paper's main story, which would run on the front page of the Sunday edition under Alfred Lewis's byline. A second story profiled Wills, the security guard, and a third by Bernstein and the reporter in Key Biscayne provided what details they could gather about the suspects. Altogether, ten *Washington Post* reporters contributed to those first reports. "As we read it over, no one could fail to be impressed by the extraordinary mystery at hand," Sussman recalled.

Not every news organization, though, saw a major story. At the *New York Times*, the assignment desk decided the burglary wasn't even worth calling the D.C. bureau's designated weekend writer.* Instead, one of the paper's young minority interns, Nat Sheppard, wrote up the story; it ran on page 30.

---

* As Harrison Salisbury, a Timesman who authored a major history of the paper, wrote later about why the *Times* originally missed Watergate, "Nothing was more un-chic than to stay in grubby Nixonian Washington over a weekend from June 15 to September 15. Nobody worth knowing possibly could be in town."

*　　*　　*

Unaware of the burglary, Martha Mitchell woke for the day in California around eleven and headed to the beauty parlor. As she went about her day, she noticed a certain franticness and moodiness to the staff—at one point, returning to the Mitchells' suite in the Beverly Hills Hotel from a photo shoot, she saw John sitting, glumly, with the LaRues and the Mardians, all drinking—but the evening's campaign party, headlined by Pat Nixon with stars that included Zsa Zsa Gabor, Jimmy Stewart, Clint Eastwood, and John Wayne, proved a triumph. At the end of the night, she found John still too consumed by meetings to absorb her complaints that the first lady had snubbed her at the party.

On Sunday, the Magruders left abruptly for D.C., but the Mitchells and others headed south to Newport Beach and the Newporter Inn, one of the Nixon staff's favorite resorts during trips to the Western White House.* That afternoon, John and Martha sat together, pleasantly talking in the sitting room of their resort villa; John explained that he needed to return to Washington, but that she should spend a few days relaxing with their daughter. He would leave Steve King, their bodyguard of the moment, to stay with them. ("Those were the last decent words we ever had together," she later said.) That evening, everyone tromped to another Nixon fundraiser, but Martha still heard no mention of a burglary. As she said later, "They had me at a brunch, they had me at a cocktail party, they had me at a reception and a dinner all day Sunday. They kept me going all that day."

That Sunday morning, the AP reported for the first time that one of the burglars, James McCord, was the security coordinator for the president's reelection campaign, and John Mitchell issued a swift and stern statement from California: "The person involved is the proprietor of a private security agency who was employed by our committee months ago to assist with the installation of our security system. He has, as we understand it, a number of business clients and interests, and we have no

---

* Coincidentally, Acting FBI Director Gray was also at the Newporter, having given the commencement address at Pepperdine on Saturday. He'd gotten word from D.C. about the break-in, but left the investigation in the hands of Mark Felt. Sunday afternoon, he ran into Fred LaRue at the pool. "That Watergate thing is a hell of a thing," the Mitchell aide commented.

knowledge of these relationships. We want to emphasize that this man and the other people involved were not operating on either our behalf or with our consent. There is no place in our campaign or in the electoral process for this type of activity, and we will not permit or condone it."

Martha was still none the wiser.

On the other side of the country, the official word was that Nixon was "ignoring" the incident and "taking no interest." After the ashtray-throwing phone call to Colson, he'd continued on with his weekend, ensconced on Bob Abplanalp's private island, far from his top aides, and he didn't return to Key Biscayne until noon on Sunday and didn't head back to D.C. until late Monday. In between, he talked repeatedly with Colson, Haldeman, Haig, Kissinger, and others weighing the evolving situation and dealing with other presidential business.

There's reason to believe the White House's interest was deeper and more troubled than it let on. According to Pat Gray's 2008 memoir, Ehrlichman phoned Henry Petersen at the Justice Department Sunday afternoon to urge the head of the criminal division to wrap up the case pronto. "That's it," the White House aide told Petersen. "You have the burglars—close it out in the next 24- to 48-hours."

"Screw you," Petersen replied, according to Gray. "We're not going to."

Ehrlichman certainly understood how important it was to keep Watergate bottled up. As he recalled later, "We had one hundred and some days until the '72 election. If we could keep it out of the White House for that length of time, he'd be home free."

* * *

Back at the *Post*, Woodward and Bernstein focused Sunday on learning more about the burglars. It was the first time the two had ever worked together on a story, and they didn't exactly have a warm relationship. Although just a year apart in age, they came from radically different backgrounds. While Woodward had come to journalism late, Bernstein had started early—he'd been at the *Post* for six years, most recently covering Virginia, and had begun as a $44-a-week copyboy at the crosstown-rival *Washington Star* at sixteen and, after dropping out of college, became a reporter full-time at nineteen.

In their own way, the two men represented the nation's political drift and divide. Woodward was the son of an Illinois judge, a Yale graduate, and a registered Republican, a true product of the conservative establishment, while Bernstein had a full head of long, shaggy hair indicative of his general disregard for authority.* Woodward had voted for Nixon in '68 and there seemed no doubt that Bernstein didn't.

Their distrust was immediately mutual. Woodward knew Bernstein's reputation around the office as someone who weaseled his way onto others' stories to score a big byline. Bernstein had heard Woodward's writing was atrocious. The office joke was that English wasn't even the Yale grad's first language. (Bernstein said later, "I didn't really think a lot about most Woodward stories. I thought they were from the wham-bam school of journalism, making a lot out of very little.") Bernstein by comparison was a flowery, energetic writer, a hearty practitioner of the "new journalism" style then evolving in magazines like *New York* and *Esquire*.

Their first day reporting alongside each other that Sunday was tedious. They dug through the phone book and the so-called "criss-cross" directory, which listed telephone numbers by address, to find neighbors who might know McCord. One attorney they reached thought he knew a family who knew McCord—their name was something like Westall. After returning to the phone book and trying five similar names, Woodward reached Harlan Westrell, who, seemingly oblivious to the news, happily began filling in details about McCord's background and provided other names for the reporters to try.

That night, Woodward drove out to Rockville and knocked on the door of McCord's suburban home. Lights were on inside, but no one answered. As he thought through the information he'd collected that day, one fact stuck in his mind: Westrell and three others who knew McCord had all alluded to him being a "government man," the type who followed orders and would never have carried out an action like the Watergate burglary without proper authorization from superiors. *If so, whose orders might McCord be following?*

---

* Bernstein's colleagues knew him as someone who was always borrowing a cigarette or a dollar, with no expectation of ever returning the favor.

The news of Tricia Nixon and Ed Cox's wedding ran the same day that the *New York Times* began publishing the Pentagon Papers—leaked by Daniel Ellsberg, who quickly earned the ire of the Nixon White House. *(Ellsberg photo by JP Laffont)*

John Mitchell became one of Nixon's closest advisors in the White House, and his wife, Martha, one of the administration's loudest defenders. *(Mitchells photo by David Hume Kennerly)*

Clockwise from upper left: H. R. Haldeman, John Ehrlichman, John Dean, and Charles Colson would form the centerpiece of the administration's drama.

Nixon's office in the Old
Executive Office Building
became his daily hideaway
for quiet solitude.

Nixon traditionally ate the
same minimalist lunch everyday,
including cottage cheese flown
in weekly from his favorite
California dairy.

As president, he nearly
always seemed to be taking
notes on his ubiquitous
yellow pads.

The "Western White House" in San Clemente, with the Pacific visible out the windows, served as the Nixons' escape from D.C., where they walked—often alone—on the beach.

The Nixon house in Key Biscayne also became an important retreat, enabled by Nixon's two closest friends, Bebe Rebozo and Robert Abplanalp.

15

Nixon's 1968 victory turned out to be a squeaker, and his duplicity with Anna Chennault—shown in the Oval Office with aide Henry Kissinger—became a key source of later stress.

16

17

Vice President Spiro Agnew was chosen because of his ties to the most conservative corners of the party, and the fierce attack dog would later become the center of his own scandal.
(Photo by David Hume Kennerly)

By the time Nixon arrived in office, he found he could no longer rely on the FBI's longtime director, J. Edgar Hoover.

Nixon turned to Tom Charles Huston to help remake—unsuccessfully—the nation's domestic intelligence apparatus.

Mark Felt (*right*), with his wife, Audrey, was fiercely loyal to J. Edgar Hoover and expected to succeed him as director.

21

22

23

Clockwise from upper left: White House aides
Jeb Magruder, Egil "Bud" Krogh, Jack Caulfield,
G. Gordon Liddy, and Alexander Butterfield.

25

24

* * *

Early Monday morning, around 3 a.m., the *Post*'s night cops reporter, Eugene Bachinski, was—incredibly—allowed a look at the burglars' property himself. Writing down as many telephone numbers and names from the address books as he could, he spotted the odd notations for someone named Howard Hunt, labeled "W. House" and "W.H." The inventory also listed four other items seemingly linked to Hunt, including "two pieces of yellow-lined paper, one addressed to 'Dear Friend Mr. Howard,' and another to 'Dear Mr. H.H,'" as well as a bill from the Lakewood Country Club and an unmailed envelope from Hunt to the club with his check for the same amount, $6.36.

Following up on Bachinski's leads later that morning, Woodward tried the White House switchboard and asked for Hunt. There was no answer at the first extension the operator tried, but then she helpfully suggested, "There is one other place he might be—in Mr. Colson's office." The secretary who answered in Colson's office referred Woodward to Hunt's office at the Mullen Company PR firm. Neither seemed the least bit wary of someone trying to contact Hunt at the White House—that, Woodward realized, meant they were used to him being there.

In fact, unbeknownst to Woodward, Hunt had actually shown up at work that day, stopping by Colson's office with a warning. He told Colson's secretary Joan Hall, "That safe of mine upstairs is loaded."

"I sort of thought it might be," Hall replied.

With that, Hunt left the White House complex for the last time and headed across the street to the Mullen Company office, where Woodward finally reached him and asked why Hunt's name was in the address books of two Watergate burglars. "Good God!" Hunt exclaimed. "In view that the matter is under adjudication, I have no comment," he hurriedly said before hanging up.*

---

* Confoundingly, Hunt in his memoir places this telephone call from Woodward as occurring Saturday morning, hours after the burglary, saying that it was the first thing to happen to him after waking up that day. Woodward's timeline seems almost certainly correct instead. Hunt's version of the seventy-two hours following the burglary seems generally to mix up and collapse the time certain events occurred. Liddy's account also seems confused during this time window at points; he places the Woodward-Hunt call incorrectly on Sunday afternoon.

Over the rest of the afternoon, Woodward researched Hunt and McCord. He tracked down the latter's military affiliation, calling different Pentagon offices until a personnel officer nonchalantly confirmed that the burglar was an air force reserve lieutenant colonel, attached to a special team that worked with the civilian Office of Emergency Preparedness—the forerunner agency of FEMA that dealt with the nation's doomsday plans. He helpfully gave Woodward the names of fifteen people listed in McCord's unit. When Woodward reached one, he learned their work involved compiling lists of domestic radicals and developing censorship plans in the event of a national emergency.

Woodward found equally strange information about Hunt; the White House confirmed he had worked on some projects, although it said Hunt hadn't done anything since March. When Woodward called Robert Bennett, the head of the Mullen Company, Bennett volunteered, "I guess it's no secret that Howard was with the CIA." That was certainly news to Woodward. *Now two people tied to the burglary had known CIA ties?*

In the initial stages of the newspaper's inquiries that weekend, Woodward also tried calling a source he'd relied on from time to time in reporting: Mark Felt. Woodward and Felt had met in the first year of the Nixon administration; Woodward, then a young navy officer, had run into the FBI leader while on a routine courier mission delivering documents from the Pentagon to the White House. Both men had been sitting, waiting, outside the Situation Room on the lower level of the West Wing. Woodward immediately noted Felt's "command presence, the posture and calm of someone used to giving orders." Woodward introduced himself; they were, Woodward would recall, "like two passengers sitting next to each other on a long airline flight with nowhere to go and nothing really to do but resign ourselves to the dead time."

Despite Felt's best efforts to remain disengaged—Woodward remembers how the agent's trained eyes seemed to surveil around them every detail of the West Wing—the navy officer slowly drew him into conversation about his job and the world at large. "I peppered him with questions," Woodward recalled. That chance, begrudging encounter led Woodward to consult Felt from time to time about his career; occasionally, he even visited Felt's house in Virginia. As he'd started at the *Post*, he'd continued the relationship, though Felt insisted that he never appear in the paper as a source. Now, reached about the Watergate burglary, Felt held Woodward to their agreement; none of what he said could be used in the paper, but he could confirm that Woodward was on the right track: The FBI considered Hunt a key suspect.

The next piece fell into place when Sussman dug into Colson, who appeared tied to Hunt. One of the paper's other editors recognized the name: He was a special counsel to Nixon and known, the editor explained, as a "hatchet man." When Sussman pulled Colson's file from the *Post* library—a folder filled with clippings that mentioned his name—he found a *New York Times* article from June 1970 entitled "Seldom Seen Aides Protect Nixon's Political Flank" that described Colson as one of the "original back-room boys—the operators and the brokers, the guys who fix things when they break down and do the dirty work when necessary."* Together, the reporters and editors pulled together the scarce details they had into a story that ran the next day, headlined, "White House Consultant Linked to Bugging Suspects."

---

* *All the President's Men* misidentifies the *New York Times* article as running in February 1971.

Chapter 14

"Boys Will Be Boys"

For Dean, Monday morning, June 19, was spent trying to assemble the pieces of the weekend disaster. First, he spoke with Ehrlichman, who asked him to start monitoring the case through the Justice Department and for a report to be forwarded to the presidential party in Key Biscayne. Ehrlichman added that Colson seemed to all but deny knowing Hunt. "Chuck sounded like he hardly knew the man, said he hadn't seen him in months," Ehrlichman said. "Why don't you have a little chat with him and find out what you can?" Dean knew immediately Colson was dissembling—Hunt had been centrally involved in the ITT mess and been dispatched to Dita Beard's bedside—and asked his associate Fred Fielding to pull Hunt's White House personnel records. They had to answer a key question before moving further: *Who was exposed to what?*

Around 11 a.m., Dean summoned Liddy to the White House; when Liddy arrived, they went for a walk.* Both men were silent until they went outside and found a park bench by the Ellipse.† "Am I correct in

---

* Magruder had already run into Liddy at the CREEP offices Monday morning and told him, "Gordon, let's face it—you and I can't work together. Why don't you talk to Dean? He's going to help us on this problem."

† Many details differ slightly in their accounts between Dean and Liddy, right down to Liddy's appearance: Dean says Liddy was unshaven and rumpled, where Liddy's memoir makes a point of explaining he was wearing a fresh suit and had shaven that morning.

assuming you're the damage control action officer for this problem?" Liddy asked, ever the Walter Mitty operative. "If you're the action officer, then you need to know it all." Dean, exhausted already, nodded.

First, he asked who in the White House knew of the operations—Colson? "Fucking Magruder," Liddy replied. He promised that McCord and the others wouldn't talk, but as he began to fill Dean in on the full scope of their covert activities, including the Fielding burglary, Dean began to get nervous. Liddy added that the jailed men would expect "support," as he put it, "the usual in this line of work—bail, attorney's fees, families taken care of, and so forth." While the White House counsel would deny saying it later, Liddy recalled Dean promptly confirming, "That goes without saying—everyone'll be taken care of."

As they walked back, Liddy suddenly turned to Dean: "Look, John, I said I was captain of the ship when she hit the reef, and I'm prepared to go down with it. If someone wants to shoot me, just tell me what corner to stand on, and I'll be there, okay?"

Dean's head snapped around. After a moment, realizing Liddy was serious, he stammered, "Well, uh, I don't think we've gotten there yet, Gordon."

The two men continued on, discussing the unfolding FBI investigation; Liddy offered tips about what to ask the bureau for in order to closely monitor their unfolding case. Then Dean brought up Hunt. "I think he'd be better off out of the country. Does he have someplace to go?" he asked. "The sooner the better."

As they parted ways outside the Executive Office Building, Dean said, "Gordon, I don't think it's a good idea for me to be talking with you anymore."

"Sorry about the way things turned out, John," Liddy said, extending his hand.

"It sure is a mess," Dean replied, taking Liddy's hand listlessly.*

---

* The conversation between Liddy and Dean stands out as an intriguing one; Dean starts the meeting by insisting he is the main point of contact going forward, then pumps Liddy for all the information he has to give, learns that Liddy has no suspicion that Dean himself is involved, and then ends the meeting seeming to wash his hands of the whole matter. If one's goal was to quietly learn of the potholes and trouble spots ahead to avoid, all to mastermind the ongoing cover-up, it would be hard to better script the interaction.

Afterward, Liddy called Hunt, introducing himself on the phone by his alias in case anyone was listening, and gave instructions to walk outside and turn left. Once he was confident Hunt wasn't being tailed, Liddy intercepted him. They walked south, down toward the National Mall. He told Hunt that there were orders from "across the street" that he should head overseas. Hunt didn't like it, saying it made him look like a fugitive. "Let's get a lawyer for me, Gordon," he countered, but ultimately agreed that he would use the $1,500 left in GEMSTONE funds to depart immediately. "Go as far as you can on that, and I'll get more money to you somehow," Liddy promised.

Within forty minutes, Dean called Liddy: *Ehrlichman said to cancel Hunt's move.* Liddy caught an annoyed Hunt at home and relayed the news. "A 180 on a thing like leaving the country in 45 minutes doesn't exactly inspire confidence we're dealing with people who know what the hell they're doing," Hunt said.* Unsettled from the conversation and tired of reporters hounding his family at home, Hunt left town anyway, first to New York City and then to California to stay with an old CIA colleague.

*   *   *

In press reports, security professionals scoffed at the seemingly amateur nature of the odd break-in, labeling it a "Mickey Mouse operation"—but the deeper reporters dug, the less the burglars appeared to be random thieves. One *New York Times* journalist, Tad Szulc, even knew the arrested Cuban exiles. Szulc dug into Hunt's history, tying him publicly to the Bay of Pigs invasion, and quickly reported how Miami Realtor Bernard Barker was a Cuban CIA agent known by the code name "Macho." In

---

* While Hunt's memoir, published in 1974, includes a similar recounting of the exchange with Liddy, Dean's memoir, published in 1976, tells a slightly different version—one that shifts the timetable to the afternoon and responsibility for the "get out of town" order to Ehrlichman. Dean says that later that afternoon, during a meeting in Ehrlichman's office with Colson, the White House's domestic policy advisor told Dean to tell Liddy to tell Hunt to flee. Dean's account provided one of the reasons Ehrlichman would later be charged with obstruction of justice, but he would deny giving the order for Hunt to flee and the evidence is at least circumstantial that he never did.

fact, Szulc wrote, "A reconstruction of the backgrounds of those allegedly involved in the raid on the Democratic headquarters suggested that all at different times had had links with the C.I.A. and anti-Cuban operations."

As the political intrigue of the break-in became clear, DNC Chair O'Brien called for a full FBI investigation to answer "the ugliest questions about the integrity of the political process that I have encountered in a quarter-century of political activity." He swiftly filed a million-dollar civil suit against CREEP for compensatory and punitive damages. Speaking in California during a visit to the San Francisco field office, Acting Director Patrick Gray brushed aside worries, saying the FBI had all the jurisdiction it needed to launch an investigation, and adding, "I foresee no difficulty in conducting an objective investigation."

At first, it seemed like the FBI's main problem would be too *many* leads. When the burglars' photographs appeared in papers across the country that weekend, tips flooded in and the number of agents assigned to the case swelled from five to twenty-six by week's end to manage them. One tip proved useful immediately: The manager of the Howard Johnson Motor Inn across from the Watergate had recognized the photo of James McCord and told agents he'd rented a room to the suspect that spring; McCord stuck out because after a few days, he'd switched rooms to a higher floor; there had also, the manager explained, appeared to be a second man staying in McCord's room. It didn't take the FBI long to connect the dots back to Al Baldwin, who evidently had spent a lot of the time calling his mother back in New Haven.

As suspicions and questions mounted, Mitchell and Republican National Committee Chair Bob Dole both released statements denying having anything to do with what the press was calling the "Watergate caper." Ron Ziegler continued to dismiss not only any presidential tie, but even any presidential interest in the case, saying Nixon hadn't even discussed the burglary with anyone like Mitchell. "I'm not going to comment from the White House on a third-rate burglary attempt," he said, in a line that would prove to be one of the most famous—and infamous—in the entire scandal.

Contrary to Ziegler's confident dismissal of the caper, aides at the White House were deeply concerned and desperate to figure out who knew what and when. Nixon's inner circle was among the most baffled.

("McCord, Hunt, Liddy—none of these names meant diddly to me. I had never met—and still have never met—McCord, Hunt, and Liddy," Haldeman recalled years later.) On Monday afternoon, Dean updated Ehrlichman on some of what he knew, including the GEMSTONE meetings with Mitchell, and Dean noticed Ehrlichman seemed to perk up when he heard the former attorney general was involved. Maybe, Ehrlichman seemed to think, Mitchell could be made the fall guy for the break-in.

When they brought in Colson to discuss Hunt in depth, Ehrlichman and Colson each seemed to outperform the other about their ignorance of Hunt's White House work. "He's not been working for me for months," Colson said, as nonchalantly as possible; later, as Colson explained that Hunt had a safe in his office that someone should check out, Ehrlichman was shocked: "You mean to tell me he even had an office here?!" The group ultimately decided that Dean should take custody of the safe's contents. After the meeting broke up, Dean's secretary handed him a note: "Meeting. 6 p.m. Mitchell's Watergate Apartment." It was the first time he'd even been invited to the inner sanctum of "Mr. Mitchell," and the inclusion made his chest swell; he was on his way to being a trusted insider.

At the end of the day, Ehrlichman finally filled in Haldeman. "It's CRP all the way," Ehrlichman reported. "Believe it or not, according to Mr. Dean, on this one Colson is clean." Haldeman marveled. Colson, the White House chief of dirty tricks, had by a miracle managed to miss the one trick that exploded, he thought. To Haldeman, based on Dean and Ehrlichman's reports, the task ahead was clear: *Contain the break-in to CREEP, don't let it slop over to the White House. Hold it to as low a level as possible. Furnish as little political ammunition to the Democrats as we can.* "To me, it sounded very simple at the time," he reflected later.

That scheme, though, quickly grew more complex. As Haldeman and Nixon discussed the fallout, the chief of staff explained that it wouldn't be easy to hang the burglars out to dry entirely. ("The problem is that there are all kinds of other involvements," he said, nodding presumably to the Fielding burglary and other Plumbers operations.) Instead, containing the fallout meant the White House needed to go to the source and shut down the investigation itself.

According to Haldeman's memoir, Nixon first raised in a phone call that Monday night what would end up being the two keys to the cover-up and the administration's eventual downfall: hush money and the CIA. "These people who got caught are going to need money," the president explained. "I've been thinking about how to do it," and he had found a solution: Play up the anti-Castro angle. That would help them raise money from defense funds for the Cubans in and around Miami, as well as encourage the CIA to help block further investigation because of their ties to the agency's shadowy operations. "Tell Ehrlichman this whole group of Cubans is tied to the Bay of Pigs," Nixon added.

Later, when Haldeman passed along the president's message, Ehrlichman refused. "I want to stay out of this one," he told the chief of staff, separating himself from an environment he had played a significant role in creating. From that moment, "almost by osmosis, it seemed, John Dean took over," Haldeman recalled. It was exactly what the young counsel wanted. As Haldeman wrote in his memoir, "Dean was for a long time, as he admits, having fun."

＊　　＊　　＊

That same night, across town at the Watergate condos, Fred LaRue greeted Dean at Mitchell's door and led him into the second-floor den to meet with Mitchell, Magruder, and Mardian, all freshly back from California. (Mitchell grumbled about how cramped their jet had been.) LaRue, whose primary function appeared to be serving as Mitchell's professional, full-time friend, melted away to smoke his pipe in silent observation. Before long, Magruder left for an evening tennis game with the vice president, saying breezily, "I'll leave the crisis to you gentlemen."

The remaining group took stock of developments. Mardian had been golfing over the weekend in California when he found out about the burglary from Magruder, instantly recognizing trouble: "Burglary is bad enough—you might get away with it—boys will be boys, but bugging is disastrous." Dean, though, still saw little peril. In fact, he loved the feeling that seemingly every power center of Nixon's world—Ehrlichman, Colson, Mitchell, presumably even Haldeman—was relying on him to fix this. "I was learning what the job really meant," he remembers thinking.

"I was a refuge, a shoulder, a brain, a counsel. I was about to arrive." The conversation that night, however, didn't go much further; it kept being interrupted by phone calls about Martha.

Mitchell's wife, still in California, was angry, confused, and agitated. Her husband's ruse had worked and she hadn't heard news of the burglary until reading the Monday papers, by which time John and the rest of the Nixon crew were safely back in D.C. "Jesus Christ—I jumped out of bed like a sheet of lightning," she recounted later. From the published reports, she discovered her husband had evidently hidden from her that he'd released a statement about McCord's involvement on Sunday before leaving town. Martha immediately saw the statement distancing CREEP from McCord for what it was: a lie. She knew McCord all too well—he'd been driving Marty to school just a few weeks earlier!—and knew how deeply he'd been engaged in the campaign. Neither her secretary nor her bodyguard Steve King would offer much more information, and when she started phone-banking CREEP officials, they brushed her off too. According to a later FBI report, King said that Martha was drinking straight gin through the day. "Those bastards left me out here without telling me anything," she complained.

By the time she reached John back at their Watergate apartment, she was frantic. Upset after interrupting the plotting session with Dean, LaRue, Mardian, and Mitchell, she tried to light a cigarette, but the pack of matches exploded in flames in her right hand. The doctor who was summoned to treat her badly burned hand gave her a sleeping pill, and she drifted off to sleep in a haze.

Magruder had his own run-in with flames that evening in Washington. As the deputy campaign director later recalled, he asked Mitchell on his way out to meet Spiro Agnew for tennis what to do with the GEMSTONE files retrieved from the CRP office over the weekend. Mitchell, he said, told him, "Maybe you ought to have a little fire at your house tonight."* After his tennis game, Magruder did just that;

---

* Notes taken by prosecutors during a later debriefing of Magruder say the idea to destroy the documents was Magruder's to begin with, another case of Magruder's story seeming to change later to better indict Mitchell. He only apparently "remembered" that Mitchell gave the order on his fourth interview with prosecutors.

sitting in front of his fireplace around midnight, he fed document after document, photograph after photograph, into a roaring fire on a warm June night. He was surprised by how brightly the photographs flared; they looked like Christmas trees. "What in the world are you doing?" his wife interrupted him.

"It's all right," he said. "It's just some papers I have to get rid of."

Chapter 15

"Stay the Hell Out of This"

B y Tuesday, Nixon's first day back at the White House post-burglary, the cover-up had already kicked into high gear. Distrust and disbelief inside the president's orbit had spread, and anonymous sources speculated to reporters that the campaign was more involved than initially reported. "Bob Dole and I were talking on the day of the arrests and agreed it must be one of those twenty-five-cent generals hanging around the committee or the White House who was responsible," one GOP source told Bernstein. "Chotiner or Colson. Those were the names thrown out." Even Nixon himself didn't seem clear who did what; in his first recorded White House conversation about Watergate, he asked Haldeman, "Have you gotten any further word on that Mitchell operation?"

"No, I don't think he did [know]," the chief of staff said.

"I think he was surprised," Nixon agreed.

Mitchell indeed seemed as confused as anyone. As Mardian and LaRue filled him in on the various threads of Liddy's operation, the campaign director seemed to be "sincerely shocked," but decided not to share what they learned with the president. ("To this day, I believe that I was right in not involving the president," Mitchell said the following year. "I still believe that the most important thing to this country was the reelection of Richard Nixon.")

Amid the intrigue, few in the White House paid much attention to what would, with hindsight, turn out to be Tuesday's most consequential political development: Far from Washington, in Brooklyn, a political newcomer named Elizabeth Holtzman shocked the establishment by defeating a fifty-year incumbent, Emanuel Celler, in the congressional primary for the state's 16th District. The thirty-year-old Phi Beta Kappa graduate of Radcliffe—who had worked for Mayor John Lindsay's Parks Department and installed the first rubber padding on the ground of the city's playgrounds—eked out victory by just 610 votes among 31,000 ballots.* While the race attracted headlines—both because Celler was the most senior congressman ever to lose a primary and because Holtzman would become the youngest congresswoman ever elected—the biggest ramification of the upset would only become evident months later.

The defeat of the stubborn and arrogant eighty-four-year-old dean of the House freed up his slot as chair of the Judiciary Committee and opened the door to a new leader, Pete Rodino, whose name would a year later become all but synonymous with the burglary itself. "If the impeachment process had gone to the Judiciary Committee under Manny Celler, it would have died there," Democratic leader Tip O'Neill wrote later. No one understood it that night, but as Jimmy Breslin wrote later, "The primary election between Holtzman and Celler could be considered one of the most meaningful elections the nation has had."

*   *   *

Out of an abundance of caution, staff members began destroying any relevant documents that might solidify ties to the White House. "Make sure our files are clean," Haldeman told Strachan. Strachan began shredding, while Colson had an aide chase down and destroy as many copies as he could find of the page in the White House telephone directory that listed Hunt as working for him. Liddy, meanwhile, scoured his life for further links to the break-in after he put on the suit he'd worn the night of the burglary and discovered a Watergate room key in the pocket; he

---

* A main controversy of the race hung on a Celler speech opposing the Equal Rights Amendment, where the veteran congressman said, "There is as much difference between a man and a woman as between lightning and a lightning rod—and between a chestnut horse and a horse chestnut."

even gathered up the hotel soaps he'd brought back from the Fielding burglary and other mischief-scouting trips to Miami and tossed them into the Anacostia River. At CREEP, he shredded the remaining sequentially numbered $100 bills, slipping them between other sheets of paper so passing colleagues wouldn't think he'd gone mad.*

Around two-thirty that afternoon, Colson joined Nixon in the Oval Office for a rambling, roving conversation about possible political risk, controversy, and strategy that would stretch more than an hour. "Now I hope everybody is not going to get in a tizzy about the Democratic committee," Nixon began.

"It's a little frustrating—disheartening, I guess is the right word," Colson replied. "Pick up that Goddamn *Washington Post* and see that guilt by association," he added, referring to that morning's article on Hunt. "They say, 'Were you involved in this thing?'" Colson continued. "Do they think I'm that dumb?"

Nixon fell back on one of his firmest convictions: He was only doing to others what they were doing to him. "A lot of people think you oughta wiretap," he said. "They probably figure they're doing it to us, which they are." A few moments later, he pointed to the irony of McCord, the CREEP expert hired to prevent bugging, getting caught bugging someone else. "That's why, uh, they hired this guy in the first place, to sweep the rooms, didn't they?"

Ultimately, Colson advised that the White House should minimize Watergate, if not ignore it entirely, unlike their response in the ITT controversy, which had rapidly escalated to Senate hearings. "Mistake would be to get all of them zeroed in on it," he said. "Make a big case out of it." As Colson saw it, "These fellas are just in there trying to win the Pulitzer Prize."

"The hell with it," Nixon said. "Let me say it flatly—we're not going to reach to it that way." His strategy would be clear: "At times, I just stonewall it."

---

* James McCord's wife burned a selection of his papers, as well as a bag of typewriter ribbons from CREEP's headquarters, later in the week too, some in the presence of a former McCord CIA colleague, Lee Pennington, Jr. When this news came out, the head of security, Howard Osborn, was forced into retirement.

"Stonewall" would become the official playbook. Publicly deny, deny, deny—and quickly offer a lot of the money to the central players for their loyalty and silence.

The White House team could sense that each passing day worried Howard Hunt and his associates, who all genuinely expected the administration to sweep the incident under the rug. To their mind, they were covert operatives for the president, carrying out what they were told were national security missions for the White House, but the president seemed unable to save them or shut down the press coverage.

An early phone call between the burglary conspirators did little to assuage concerns. "It's ballooning all over the place," Liddy had said.

"Everything's come apart," Hunt agreed. "There hasn't been any response at all."

By the end of their conversation, Liddy was worried. Hunt sounded isolated and worried that he was being abandoned; he needed money and a lawyer. His fear endangered a successful cover-up.

On Wednesday, five days after the break-in, Liddy took matters into his own hands. He wrapped $5,000 around each leg, tucked into his socks, and flew to Los Angeles, purportedly on CREEP business. Instead, he visited Hunt at the home of a onetime CIA colleague, where Hunt was hiding, to hand over $1,000 to help Hunt line up a lawyer. Liddy promised that everyone would be taken care of "company-style," a reference to the CIA, and asked Hunt to head to Miami to check in with Barker's wife and reassure her similarly. "She's going bananas," Liddy said. As they parted, Liddy said, "This may be the last time I'll see you for a while."*

On Thursday, June 22, Richard Nixon made his first public statement on the Watergate issue: "The White House has had no involvement whatever in this particular incident." The phrasing left reporters across Washington wondering: If not this "particular" incident, were there others that the White House had been involved in?

---

* On Thursday, Hunt flew to Florida, but according to his account, Barker's house was surrounded by reporters and he couldn't reach Barker's wife by phone, and so he abandoned the trip to return to California.

That suspicion, that there might be fire behind the smoke surrounding the burglary, lingered, but by mid-week, the still-unfolding story collided at the *Washington Post* with the vagaries of running a metro newspaper: City editor Barry Sussman explained to Bernstein that he had to go back to his regular Virginia beat—the paper needed him back covering the commonwealth. Bernstein pounded out on his typewriter a five-page memo about the strange unresolved questions around the break-in, pleading to be left on the case and speculating it might be directly tied into the reelection campaign's leadership.* Grudgingly, his editors kept him on the story. "As it happened, what often seemed like rash, early judgments by Bernstein proved almost invariably to be correct," Sussman recalled.

While the news stories of Woodward and Bernstein would attract the nation's attention and history's spotlight, the reporting duo were hardly the only *Washington Post* staffers focused on the president. For years, Nixon had been tormented by the paper's biting political cartoonist, known as Herblock, whose shadowy, long-jowled caricature of Nixon had done so much to ingrain the president's dark side in the public's mind. Just a few days after Watergate, Herblock turned his attention to the burglary too, penning a cartoon that showed a guard throwing a burglar out of the Democratic Party's national headquarters as Nixon, Kleindienst, and Mitchell all looked on. The caption read: *Who would think of doing such a thing?* Publisher Katharine Graham said later, "He was well ahead of me and of the news side of the paper."

*   *   *

Away from the public eye, the FBI investigation progressed rapidly. By June 21, agents had already had a big break, tracing the cash in the burglary to Bernard Barker and a series of bank transactions in Miami. Further investigation of Barker's deposits uncovered that the money

---

* His precise theory, that Nixon's longtime dark-arts maestro Murray Chotiner was behind the operation, actually proved false; in fact, as Metro editor Harry Rosenfeld later said, "His was the one name that never appeared in Watergate."

had appeared to come from Nixon campaign donors. By the end of the month, they'd interviewed a Minnesota Nixon finance leader named Kenneth Dahlberg, who had played a major role in both the '68 and '72 campaigns, as well as a Mexican corporate attorney who appeared to have been gathering cash for the campaign.

As Angelo Lano and his team dug, they correctly suspected that they weren't getting the full story and total cooperation from the White House, but no one could figure out what was being hidden. Oddities proliferated. When he and Daniel Mahan interviewed Chuck Colson, with Dean sitting in to observe, Dean expressed surprise that Hunt had an office in the White House complex; later, when Dean turned over what he said were the contents of Hunt's safe, Lano realized Dean had ordered the safe opened three days *before* the FBI interview. Lano accused Dean of lying, but it wasn't clear to anyone why.

What they didn't know was that Ehrlichman had called FBI Acting Director Gray on Wednesday morning and said, "John Dean is going to be handling an inquiry into this thing for the White House. From now on, you're to deal directly with him." By eleven-thirty, Dean was in Gray's office, explaining that he intended to sit in on all FBI interviews of White House staff. Gray thought it a reasonable request—after all, the only staffer the FBI had interest in at that point was Chuck Colson, who had hired Hunt. "None of us in the FBI had any inkling that the Watergate conspiracy ran anywhere near the senior people in the White House," Gray later recalled.

For his part, Henry Petersen had also promised the White House counsel that there would be "no fishing expedition"; Dean remembered him offering an assurance that Silbert and the federal prosecutors would not stray into the president's campaign and the dirty laundry of the Republican Party. "He's investigating a break-in," the assistant attorney general said, according to Dean. "He knows better than to wander off beyond his authority into other things."

In multiple meetings on the 21st and 22nd, Dean and Gray discussed how to handle the case, though Dean already had privately settled on a two-part strategy: The White House and CREEP would have Hunt and Liddy take the fall, arguing that the two men had been rogue, redirecting funds meant for other purposes to criminal activity, and then CREEP would stop the FBI from tracing the burglars' funds back through to campaign donors, a thread that could very easily lead to all manner of other scandals and campaign-related crimes.

The first part seemed easy enough to pull off, and the germ of the second came together as Gray filled Dean in on how the FBI had traced the money that had ended up in Barker's wallet. The FBI director laid out the various theories the bureau was exploring: (1) a legitimate or illegitimate CIA operation; (2) a political espionage and intelligence scheme by people associated with the Republican Party or the president's reelection campaign; (3) a Cuban right-wing mission; or (4) some kind of setup by a double agent. All seemed likely and unlikely in their own ways. "We just could not see any clear reason for this burglary," Gray recalled later.

Dean warned the FBI director that if he started tracing that money too closely, he might find himself upsetting the CIA. Gray doubted that; agents had raised the suspicion and he had already called CIA Director Richard Helms to ask if the D.C. police had stumbled into an agency operation.* Helms expressed equal confusion and said that as far as anyone would admit there was no known CIA role. Gray explained to Dean that until there was a clear CIA link, the FBI was going to pursue all leads aggressively, albeit sensitively. He suggested that going forward, Dean communicate directly with Mark Felt, who would be kept up to date on all aspects of the probe.

Debriefing the Gray-Dean conversation later that night with Mitchell, the Nixon team spotted the outlines of a new plan: *The cloak of "national security" could bury the investigation.*

The White House strategy came together Friday morning, June 23, during a 10:04 conversation between President Nixon and Haldeman in the Oval Office. The two men saw opportunity in the avenue suggested by the FBI: If they could get the CIA—perhaps the deputy director, Vernon Walters—to wave Pat Gray off, they might be able to block the whole thing. "The way to handle this now is for us to have Walters

---

* As Lano recalled the early theories, "[Head of the FBI Washington Field Office] Bob Kunkel asked me candidly who I thought was behind the burglary. I must admit that at that point I believed that it was a botched CIA operation."

call Pat Gray and just say, 'Stay the hell out of this—this is business here we don't want you to go any further on it,'" Haldeman said. "That would take care of it." The chief of staff further added that Gray would comply and even happily enlist his own deputy in shutting the case down.

"He'll call Mark Felt in, and the two of them—Mark Felt wants to cooperate because he's ambitious—he'll call him in and say, 'We've got the signal from across the river to put the hold on this.' And that will fit rather well because the FBI agents who are working the case, at this point, feel that's what it is—this is CIA." Through Haldeman's comments, Nixon grunted his usual assents. What they said in that recorded conversation would soon become the central mystery and hinge of the entire Watergate scandal. The comments left little doubt of the intent; Nixon's team intended to use the organs of government to cover up their own rogue operation, mislead investigators, and throw the cloak of national security over what was really a political mission. "The scheme . . . relied on Nixon's cherished powers; not only was it a clever move, it was a power move—the kind Nixon preferred," journalist Tom Wicker observed later. Whatever else had transpired until that moment—from the Chennault Affair to the Huston Plan to the Fielding burglary to the Brookings plan—a new Rubicon had been crossed and a fatal wound for the administration now created, left to fester.*

*   *   *

After the Oval Office conversation with Nixon and Haldeman, Ehrlichman summoned Helms and his deputy, Vernon Walters, to the White House. Walters, a talented army linguist who had served as a presidential translator and worked with Nixon during his vice presidency, was new to the job and the agency—just six weeks into being the number two

---

* Whether Nixon and Haldeman ever really thought of this conversation again over the next year is unknown—nor is it clear in the moment whether either man registered the depth of the corruption of their scheme. John Ehrlichman, who didn't know about the conversation, would later come to believe that at least Nixon did and that it ate away at him over the months ahead, becoming to the president the beating, pulsing telltale heart of Edgar Allan Poe.

at Langley.* The men arrived at 1 p.m. and were ushered into Ehrlichman's office.

Walters recalled the conversation with Nixon's team in a memo written five days later: "Haldeman said that the 'bugging' affair at the Democratic National Committee Hqs at the Watergate Apartments had made a lot of noise and the Democrats were trying to maximize. The FBI had been called in and was investigating the matter. The investigation was leading to a lot of important people and this could get worse. He asked what the connection with the Agency was and the Director repeated that there was none. Haldeman said that the whole affair was getting embarrassing and it was the President's wish that Walters call on Acting FBI Director Patrick Gray and suggest to him that since the five suspects had been arrested that this should be sufficient and that it was not advantageous to have the enquiry pushed especially in Mexico, etc." Helms got tense and reacted with opprobrium to the suggestion; he explained he'd already talked to Gray and assured the FBI that the CIA wasn't involved. ("There was turmoil in the room," Haldeman would recall in his memoirs.) Haldeman repeated his request, telling Walters to go see Gray. "I'm just following my instructions, Dick," the chief of staff said. "This is what the president told me to relay to you."

Walters finally agreed. "I had been in Washington for six weeks at this point and it simply did not occur to me that the chief of staff to the president might be asking me to do something illegal or wrong," he wrote later. "I genuinely believed that Haldeman had some information that I did not have." That afternoon, Walters met with Gray and encouraged the FBI to drop the Mexico element of its probe. Gray, with some hesitation, agreed.

* Walters and Nixon had developed a special bond during a 1958 trip to Venezuela, where a crowd had attacked Nixon's motorcade in Caracas. The crowd tried to overturn the vice presidential limo and shattered its windows in what at the time was called the "most violent attack ever perpetrated on a high American official while on foreign soil." Secret Service agents had been prepared to open fire on the crowd, but Nixon told them not to shoot unless he ordered. Walters, then a lieutenant colonel, was with Nixon in the armored passenger compartment, which the crowd almost managed to breach, and ended up with a "mouthful of glass particles, and calmly picked them out, spitting blood," according to a *Los Angeles Times* account of the attack.

Back at CIA headquarters, Walters began to ask around if there was some covert operation in Mexico he wasn't aware of. There wasn't. As further pressure came from the White House, he realized the agency was being used for political purposes and began to document his conversations and the executive branch's abuse of power. In an agency that all too frequently found it easy to lose files it found historically or politically inconvenient, Walters created a lethal paper trail of his own. Memo by memo, conversation by conversation, they went into Walters's personal safe.

*   *   *

John Dean also had his own plans for Pat Gray, relying on the procedural knowledge of FBI investigations that Liddy had given him. He met the acting director near Gray's residence in Southwest D.C. and they walked to a bench overlooking the Potomac. During the meeting, he demanded that the FBI furnish him with its raw interview reports, known as "302s" in bureau parlance.*

Gray initially tried to refuse, explaining that the raw files were incredibly closely held and never given to anyone outside the bureau, but eventually succumbed to his discomfort and had Dean promise he was asking on behalf of the president. (As Gray justified it to himself, the president was the head of the executive branch and so could see any document created within it.) Dean enthusiastically confirmed, and soon after, Gray delivered the files personally—a total of eighty-three investigative reports through October, about half of all the FBI's investigative materials in the case. "I was totally aware of what the bureau was doing at all times," Dean said later.

Dean also used Gray to hide some of the existing conspiracy material. After the contents of Hunt's safe had been delivered to the White House counsel's office a few days after the burglary—workers wheeled in several dollies' worth of material—Dean had sorted it all in the presence of Fred

---

* Unbeknownst to Gray, Dean had already asked for such documents from Petersen and Kleindienst and been rebuffed—he was told it was wildly inappropriate for the president's counsel to be seeing raw FBI interview reports.

Fielding.* As Dean and Fielding cataloged, they realized much of the haul was troublesome, just as Hunt had promised. "Holy shit," Dean had said to Fielding as they looked over everything from a briefcase of McCord's electronics to Hunt's work forging State Department cables to implicate the Kennedy administration in the assassination of South Vietnam's president.

They sorted the documents into three piles. Dean surreptitiously kept the seemingly most incriminating documents for himself: In his own safe, tucked underneath Richard Nixon's estate plan, he placed two "operational" Hermès notebooks Hunt had kept throughout the work of the Plumbers and GEMSTONE that recorded meetings, conversations, plans, and details.

While they handed over all the innocent contents to the FBI and Lano's team directly, Dean decided to pass other sensitive files directly to Gray. By turning over the most explosive documents to Gray directly, Dean and Ehrlichman figured that if they were ever asked under oath, they could truthfully say they "turned over everything to the FBI." During a meeting in Ehrlichman's office, Dean made clear to the FBI leader that this special sensitive set of files shouldn't be turned over to investigating agents. "I distinctly recall Mr. Dean saying that these files were 'political dynamite,' and 'clearly should not see the light of day,'" Gray testified later. After receiving the files from Hunt's safe, Gray took them home and hid them under a pile of shirts in his closet.†

---

* Most ominously, the safe contained a small pistol—which made headlines and worried Dean, but which Hunt would explain later he'd brought into the office amid a rash of street crime earlier that year.

† While Dean took advantage of Gray's naïveté, Gray seemed to understand he was doing something wrong in handing over the interview reports to the White House; he never told his assistants he was doing so and pulled them covertly from a complete copy of the Watergate case files he insisted on keeping in his office in order to stay up to date.

Chapter 16

"Keep My Mouth Shut"

I n California, Martha Mitchell's mental condition deteriorated fast. She had been relegated far from Washington as a brewing scandal engulfed her husband and the campaign, and she was in pain, tending to her bandaged hand by smoking heavily and drinking glass after glass of Dewar's. By the moment, she became angrier and angrier—at CREEP, at Nixon, at John, all of them. They'd abused her and kept her in the dark about the activities at the committee, even as she had served as its most popular public face. "I would have understood it," she said later. "Even if I hadn't been a member of the committee, John owed me some explanation of what was going on." And yet she couldn't reach him; everyone at CREEP seemed to be dodging her calls as the week continued.

The night of Thursday, June 22, Fred LaRue answered when she dialed her own apartment at the Watergate. Furious, she relayed a message for John: *She was never coming back to Washington, unless her husband quit politics that moment.* She told LaRue her next call would be UPI reporter Helen Thomas, a threat she followed through on. "I've given John an ultimatum. I'm going to leave him unless he gets out of the campaign," she ranted to Thomas. "I'm sick and tired of politics. Politics is a dirty business."

No sooner had the words been spoken than Thomas heard Martha shout, "You get away—just get away!" before the phone line went dead. Thomas tried to call back, repeatedly, and finally tried the hotel

215

switchboard operator, who told her Mrs. Mitchell was "indisposed." Panicked and confused, Thomas called John Mitchell at the Watergate, who brushed it off. "That little sweetheart," he said. "I love her so much. She gets a little upset about politics." The United Press article chronicling the late-night call ran in papers coast-to-coast the next day; the *San Francisco Chronicle* titled it, simply, "What Martha Said She Told John," no last names needed.

Though John had assured Thomas that Martha was fine, she was anything but. By her account, Steve King had charged into the room, pushed her over, and torn the phone off the wall. (Someone—perhaps Fred LaRue—had called King and told him to keep her from making calls.) Martha rushed to her daughter's room to reach another phone, but King followed, again pushed her away, and disconnected that phone as well. Then he pushed her back into her own bedroom and shut her inside. When Martha went out onto the balcony to escape, King reappeared; they struggled as he hauled her back in and kicked her.*

At some point the next morning, she made it downstairs, but King again caught her as she tried to exit the villa's glass patio door; they struggled again, and Martha's left hand was cut seriously. A doctor and nurse arrived to give her stitches, only to be surprised that there were also a half-dozen men, apparently security, all over the villa too. (Martha would later claim that there were both Secret Service and FBI agents watching her, and one of the mysterious men introduced himself to the doctor as part of the team who "guard the president.")

Frantic and fearful, Martha resisted treatment. The security men held her down as the doctor administered a sedative. "They pulled down my pants, and shot me in the behind," she recalled later, incredulously. She tried repeatedly to escape, and each time was blocked by King or others. Finally, she was carried back up to her room. Through it all, the Mitchells' eleven-year-old daughter, Marty, wandered through the villa, confused and worried.

---

* Steve King, who would go on to be a prominent Republican businessman in Wisconsin and serve as President Trump's ambassador to the Czech Republic from 2017 to 2021, has denied generally some of the encounter with Martha Mitchell but mostly held to silence about what transpired during his work with Martha. As King told the *WisPolitics* blog in 2006, "Neither you nor anybody else will ever get me to talk about the matters of the Mitchell family."

When word of the grave situation reached her husband, John enlisted Herbert Kalmbach, who lived nearby, to help: "If you've ever done anything for me, Herb, do this for me now." Kalmbach sought medical advice, and that night, his secretaries monitored the villa and again prevented Martha from placing telephone calls.

Finally, John dispatched two friends from out east to retrieve his wife, and the following day, they and Martha headed for New York—she held fast on her refusal to return to Washington. By the next night, she was ensconced in Suite 543 of the Westchester Country Club, where she finally got ahold of Helen Thomas on Sunday night. "If you could see me, you wouldn't believe it," she told the reporter. "I'm black and blue. I'm a political prisoner." She was done with politics, done with Washington. "I love my husband very much, but I'm not going to stand for all those dirty things that go on."

The resulting article set off a fresh media firestorm. Reporters flocked to Westchester, and the *Daily News*'s Marcia Kramer scored an interview, spending hours listening as Martha recounted the harrowing preceding days while pacing the room in a rumpled suit and wild hair, smoking and crying. As an experienced crime reporter, Kramer was used to disheveled witnesses and alarming scenes, but even she was taken aback by Martha's bruises and appearance. The next day's *Daily News* screamed: "'I'M A PRISONER OF GOP': MARTHA."

John Mitchell's team denied everything. "It's all news to me," he said. "Everyone knows that Mrs. Mitchell has her private personal problems," an aide added. The *Washington Post* didn't mention the story at all. The relative shrug with which Washington greeted the wife of the attorney general–turned–presidential campaign chair declaring herself a prisoner and saying that she was tired of all the "dirty things that go on" is a testament to how thoroughly the city had already written her off. She wasn't a power player; she was entertainment.

*   *   *

While the newspapers were fixated on Martha's drama, that same weekend the twenty-six FBI agents working on the Watergate case were summoned to Gray's office at the Justice Department for an unusual 11 a.m. meeting on Saturday, June 24. They thought it might be an *attaboy*—perhaps an award and bonus for the hard, fast work on the case so far. Instead, Gray berated them angrily for a leak to *TIME* magazine. Sandy Smith, one of the nation's top crime reporters, had been doggedly pursuing the burglary over the preceding week and called Gray Friday night to inquire whether the FBI director was trying to prematurely shut down the Watergate case. Gray's fury rose steadily as he listened to Smith, who seemed to have well-sourced details about the case's early days and Gray's discouraging of the Mexican money trail investigation. The acting director, taking notes on the conversation as it progressed, had scribbled in capital letters the words he feared most: *SOMEONE IN THE FBI IS TALKING ABOUT THE DETAILS OF THE INVESTIGATION.*

Now he wanted answers—and a scalp. "I want that agent, or those agents, to step forward. I want their credentials, their weapons, on the table," he spat. No one moved. "What we need in the FBI are dedicated professionals, not a bunch of little old ladies in tennis shoes," the acting director continued, calling the team a bunch of "yellow-bellied singing canaries." The agents were humiliated; even when the head of the Washington Field Office, Robert Kunkel, tried to interject, the director shut him up fast. "We were just frozen," recalled Agent Magallanes.

The meeting backfired spectacularly. What might have worked for Gray in his military career aboard a submarine failed with his new bureau agents, who saw before them not a tough commander but a figurehead questioning their integrity. The meeting, which agents would later jokingly call the "Saturday Morning Massacre," would be Gray's only encounter with the Watergate squad—and it didn't even reach its intended target. Decades after the fact, it would become clear that the actual FBI leaker to Smith was almost certainly Mark Felt, who wasn't even present for Gray's dressing-down. The leak to Smith was, according to the cowriter of Felt's memoir, intended as a "warning to Gray that if he allowed a Watergate whitewash, his career would be in public tatters."

In any case, the investigation continued, and Angelo Lano finally sent a memo to Gray and headquarters outlining the main roadblocks: Lano argued agents needed to move quicker to interview key sources like the lookout, Al Baldwin, Hunt's White House colleagues David Young and Young's secretary Kathleen Chenow, and even Mitchell himself.

The memo sat, unread, for three days while Gray traveled to field offices around the country.* When he finally read it, the acting director was apoplectic; he summoned Felt, Kunkel, and Lano to FBI headquarters, along with the head of the bureau's criminal division, Assistant Director Charles Bates. Lano defended the memo. "The facts set forth were true," he recalled. "After I insisted that investigators were accustomed to conducting a complete and thorough inquiry, Gray backed off, indicating that he would urge Dean to move up the interviews."

In hindsight, Felt was clearly the source of Gray's woes. In theory, he could have pushed the FBI investigation forward as Gray's proxy while he was out of town, but he had held the big decisions to hurt the acting director on all sides, undermining him to the bureau's investigators, underscoring his absences, and pushing ultimate responsibility for the investigation onto his shoulders. It left the acting director in the untenable position of either angering his agents by turning down the requests or angering the administration he desperately wanted to please by approving them—altogether, quite a bureaucratic sleight-of-hand.

On June 26, a week after the burglary, the FBI was able to justify a more active investigation when agents found in burglar Eugenio Martinez's address book a reference to a "George" listed with a D.C. telephone number. It didn't take agents long to end up with G.—George—Gordon Liddy. This was a significant revelation: While the bureau had deduced that Hunt had been traveling on White House business under the alias "Warren," a second mystery traveler known as "Leonard" had yet to be identified. The notation made agents suspect Liddy, a key clue in their

---

* Gray's frequent travel underscored how ambitious but stunningly out of his depth and ill-suited he was for his vital role; he seemed to fixate on all the wrong things. Gray had decided that key to winning the respect of the FBI he knew so poorly was visiting as many of the bureau's field offices as he could; he kept up a heavy travel schedule, one that seemed inviolate and one that often kept him far from Washington. It seemed fitting he'd been in California when the original burglary occurred, because he always seemed to be jetting off to Puerto Rico, Cincinnati, Miami, or some other field office at an inopportune time. He traveled to fifty-eight of the FBI's fifty-nine field offices in his first six months. Mark Felt even called him "Three-Day Gray," due to the absences. (Other news reports from the era noted his nickname as "Two-Day Gray," so it's unclear whether Felt misremembered the mocking name or, for whatever reason, adopted his own.) The fact that Gray did most of his travel on expensive, leased military jets—out of a concern for the era's wave of hijackings—didn't help his regal profile inside the bureau.

developing theory that the burglary had ties to CREEP personnel. The only issue was that CREEP insisted on having its own lawyers monitor its staff interviews with the FBI, just as Dean supervised interviews with White House staff. Even though the official position of the committee and the White House was that everyone should cooperate fully and that anyone who didn't would face termination, the presence of Dean or a campaign lawyer all but ensured that no one truly spoke openly. Without that access, the puzzle pieces only abstractly fit.

On June 28, Lano's colleague Daniel Mahan and another agent, Donald Stuckey, tried to interview Liddy at the CREEP offices, but the general counsel refused to speak with them. It set off a particularly odd charade, as Fred LaRue summoned Liddy to his office and officially fired him for not speaking to the FBI—even as everyone involved understood that Liddy's silence was in CREEP's best interests. In the same termination meeting, Liddy handed back the last $8,500 of GEMSTONE funds to the man who had helped him orchestrate the cover-up. Then Liddy and Maurice Stans headed to a final lunch together at the White House. As they dined, Stans asked what his former colleague would do next.

"Keep my mouth shut and go to prison," Liddy replied.

"That's shouldn't be necessary," Stans said, still not apparently grasping the gravity of the situation.

"Believe me, sir, it is," Liddy replied.

*   *   *

In the days since the break-in, Nixon had come to believe—likely incorrectly, as history would show—that John Mitchell had approved the burglary and related dirty tricks. With Haldeman, the president determined that the risk of allowing Mitchell to stay as the campaign director was too great. He had to go.

The onetime attorney general, who had been in charge of the campaign less than four months, came to the White House on June 30, where in as gentle a way as they could, Nixon and Haldeman pushed him to promptly resign. "The longer you wait, the more risk each hour brings. You run the risk of more stuff, valid or invalid, surfacing on the Watergate caper,"

Haldeman said. "As of now there is no problem there. As of any moment in the future there is at least a potential problem."

"I'd cut the loss fast," Nixon added. "I'd cut it fast. If we're going to do it, I'd cut it fast." Martha's very public unraveling, they argued, was the perfect humanitarian excuse to step out of any possible Watergate spotlight. Mitchell should just say that his wife's health and stability require his attention. Everyone would believe it. "A hell of a lot of people will like that answer—they would," Nixon said encouragingly. "And it'd make anybody else who asked any other question on it look like a selfish son-of-a-bitch, which I thoroughly intended them to look like."

It was one of the saddest moments of Watergate, a turning point that could have averted the disaster to come. Nixon, shy and desperate as always to avoid personal confrontation, couldn't take the opportunity to have a real conversation or inquire about the truth—even with one of the closest and most trusted aides in his world, a man who perhaps had no more foreknowledge of the burglary than he did.

Mitchell followed the direction, announcing soon after, "I have found that I can no longer [carry out the job] and still meet the one obligation which must come first: the happiness and welfare of my wife and daughter." As Nixon and Haldeman predicted, most newspapers took Mitchell's departure at face value. "Investigation today turned up no evidence that any pressure had been applied to Mr. Mitchell to resign," the New York Times reported under a top-of-the-front-page headline reading, "Mitchell Quits Post, Putting Family First."

Mitchell gamely would repeat the cover story throughout the summer; in a follow-up interview with the New York Times a week later, he discussed his new life in the Mudge Rose law firm offices just fifty paces from the old CREEP offices and underscored that he was following his wife's desire to leave politics behind. "If my own investigation had turned up a link between this committee or the White House and the raid, I would have been less inclined to leave. I would have wanted to stick around and clear it up," he told the reporter. During another interview, conducted while riding to New York on an Amtrak train with Martha, he took his pipe from his mouth and pointed to her: "She spent a million dollars last year and now I have to earn it."

*   *   *

On June 30, as Mitchell made his forced exit, Mark Felt orchestrated his next leak: He handed a young reporter at the *Washington Daily News*, the capital's afternoon tabloid, a scoop about the contents of Hunt's safe. The story was headlined, "Searchers Turn Up Map of Dem Watergate HQ in Nixon Aide's Desk," and outlined the many suspicious items found in Hunt's office—information known only to the FBI, John Dean, and Fred Fielding. Dean promptly called Felt and Gray to complain. "He was very, very unhappy about that," Gray recalled later, but the acting director reassured the White House counsel that he had put Felt on the case. His deputy had investigated and reported that the leak didn't come from the FBI.

The article on Hunt's safe would end up being the *Daily News*'s only Watergate scoop; it shut down publication in early July. Whether, if it had continued publishing, the paper would have become Felt's preferred source of leaks, rather than *Post*, will never be known.

Chapter 17

The Arrival of Mr. Rivers

Howard Hunt resented the way the press was portraying him as a fugitive. He wasn't hiding from investigators; he was just dodging reporters. As he lay low in Los Angeles in the aftermath of the burglary, he read in multiple newspapers how the FBI was searching for him across the country and around the world. "I was rumored to be simultaneously in Spain and Mexico while reports from Europe indicated that I had been seen strolling the boulevards of Paris," Hunt would later recount. The retired CIA officer certainly understood that you could get cut loose in a scandal or if an operation went bad—after all, he'd watched the U.S. government abandon Cuban freedom fighters on the beaches during the Bay of Pigs—but his frustration had only grown. He had kept his CIA affiliation secret his entire life, and now the government was openly discussing his covert activities. He'd been fired by the Robert Mullen Company, the announcement made before he was even told, and his fellow burglars were still in jail, the high-powered legal help they had all expected nowhere in sight. Tired of waiting for news in L.A., he headed for his wife's cousins in Chicago; once safely ensconced with family, he had them call Dorothy and suggest, nonchalantly, that she come for a visit. The career CIA spouse understood the subterfuge immediately and left to see her husband for the first time since the weekend of the burglary.

After some time together, Hunt lined up a Washington lawyer for himself and returned to D.C. on July 3. If the White House would cast him aside as a friend, he would have to be their enemy. That lawyer, William Bittman, then contacted Silbert and said Hunt was happy to meet with prosecutors whenever desired, no subpoena necessary.*

Dorothy Hunt was also infuriated by her husband's treatment. Unable to get answers from the burglars' lawyer Douglas Caddy or to reach Liddy at all, she had shown up at CREEP's offices and chewed the ear off a campaign attorney. CREEP, in Hunt's words, "blanched." As it turned out, unbeknownst to the Hunts, John Dean had already been frantically working to line up payment for the burglars.† First, he had tried to pressure the CIA to support the burglars, encouraging the agency not only to post bail and cover the legal fees but even perhaps pay them salaries if they went to prison. Deputy Director Vernon Walters balked—he had grown suspicious of the White House motives and didn't want to further involve the CIA. He told Dean that if the agency paid the burglars, that information would surely become public. As Walters recounted in a later "memcon," a memorandum of conversation, he told Dean that "the agency would be completely discredited with the public and the Congress and would lose all value to the President and the Administration." He explained that any order to pay the burglars would have to come from "the highest level," a clear reference to Nixon himself, and not just from a deal struck with a White House aide.‡

Without access to official funds, Dean turned to Herbert Kalmbach and the Nixon campaign war chest. Dean, who seemed to be getting quite used to covert park bench meetings, summoned Kalmbach to D.C., and

---

* Hunt's biographer, Tad Szulc, would write that the onetime CIA officer's post-burglary behavior was "a story of deceit, lies, blackmail, and disloyalty toward virtually everybody with whom he had been associated."

† Whether these payments—both living expenses and legal fees—were "hush money" versus merely payment due for services rendered would become a fierce point of contention in the months ahead.

‡ John Dean's own memoir *Blind Ambition* fails to mention any of the three conversations he had with Vernon Walters about pressuring the CIA to pay hush money to the burglars. In fact, Walters's name doesn't even appear in Dean's book at all. Dean did speak of the meetings, though, before the Ervin Committee.

they spoke at length in Lafayette Park, where Dean explained the need for money. "Kalmbach gulped and made sour faces upon learning of his assignment, but he accepted it," Dean recalled.*

Finally, cash began to flow. Soon after Dorothy's visit to CREEP, Bittman received an anonymous phone call from someone who identified himself only as "Mr. Rivers" and asked to be connected with "the writer's wife." Bittman knew immediately the caller meant Hunt. "You're the only writer I know," he told the prolific novelist. A quick check with CREEP assured Bittman and Hunt that "Mr. Rivers" was an authorized campaign representative. He soon called Dorothy directly, telling her to leave the house and be at a specific telephone booth in Potomac Village within thirty minutes. The phone in the booth rang on time, and "Mr. Rivers" asked Dorothy to contact the other burglars' families and collect estimates of their monthly living expenses and legal fees.

"Mr. Rivers," as it would turn out, was Tony Ulasewicz, enlisted by Kalmbach during a meeting at the Statler Hotel in D.C. on June 28. "Dean thinks you're the man to deliver the money," Kalmbach had told him. Ulasewicz had been initially reluctant to get involved—he didn't trust Dean—but Kalmbach reassured him. "Kalmbach was still the President's attorney and was a man I trusted without hesitation," he recalled later.† Kalmbach also seemed to be in way over his head, and the former detective took pity on the lawyer. "He was being given a part to play in a drama he had no business performing," Ulasewicz thought. He walked out of the hotel room with $75,100 from Maurice Stans, hidden inside a hotel laundry bag.

Over multiple trips between D.C. and New York—and what Ulasewicz felt were far too many rounds of coded telephone calls—he parceled out the money. First up was $25,000 as a retainer to Bittman, deposited in

---

* Dean, notably, would tell the Senate Watergate Committee that permission to use campaign funds came from Mitchell during a meeting on June 28; the meeting, apparently, never happened. Later investigations would turn up that Mitchell was actually in New York on the day Dean says they met to plot the hush money.

† "I didn't trust Dean at all. He was going to park himself in the most secured area he could find and deceive anybody he had to in order to save his hide." Perhaps true to Ulasewicz's impression, Dean denies that using the private investigator was his idea—he says Kalmbach recommended Ulasewicz.

a brown envelope next to the pay phone in the lobby of his office building. Then, Dorothy Hunt provided the requested estimates of monthly living expenses, what the conspirators referred to as "scripts" from the "players." "Let's multiply that by five to cut down on the number of deliveries," Ulasewicz advised her. The number struck Dorothy immediately—there were just five months remaining until the presidential election. The first delivery seemed set to buy silence and prolong legal proceedings at least until the other side of the campaign.

Ulasewicz next instructed Dorothy to go to National Airport, where a locker key would be taped under a specific pay phone. Inside the locker, she would find a blue bag filled with cash—although it turned out to be just three months of payments, not five. It seemed like Liddy's promise that everyone would be taken care of "Company-style" was coming true.

Liddy received his own coded call ("This is your publisher, Mr. Waters, I'm gonna publish your manuscript. I wanna talk to you about your royalties") and during a similar National Airport exchange retrieved a package filled with eighty $100 bills, about three months' salary.

In the days, weeks, and months that followed, Ulasewicz handed out about $26,000 to Liddy and another $154,000 to Dorothy Hunt to pass along to the other Watergate conspirators.

The private eye found himself making so many calls from so many pay phones that the heavy piles of quarters he carried everywhere wore through his pants pockets. Instead, he finally took to wearing a bus driver's coin changer on his belt.

* * *

With the public unaware of the reverberations unfolding inside the White House and CREEP, newspapers with few exceptions continued to treat the Watergate burglary as an oddball local crime story rather than a national political scandal.

Even as details emerged about Hunt and CREEP, political insiders weren't exactly surprised that some people tied loosely to Nixon's team had stumbled into such an episode. Columnist Joseph Kraft reminded readers that in every one of his elections, Nixon had faced stories of "smear charges, knees in the groin, and thumbs in the eye" and outlined how the president "set a tone that positively encourages dirty work by low-level operators." Kraft concluded, "Solid, practical reasons argue that Republican leaders were not directly connected with anything as inept as the recent attempt to enter Democratic headquarters. But you don't hear anybody saying that President Nixon and John Mitchell couldn't have been involved because they were too honorable and high-minded, too sensitive to the requirements of decency, fair play, and law."

As odd as so many details of the break-in seemed, the news reporting over the first two weeks indeed didn't add up to much more than Kraft's initial supposition. With every passing day, the burglary faded from the news, lost amid the broader focus on the presidential race and the Democratic National Convention in mid-July. "The story died like a fourth of July skyrocket, leaving a few flickers of its train" journalist Harrison Salisbury wrote.

Woodward headed home for a family vacation on Lake Michigan, and Bernstein went back to covering Virginia politics, so unhappy with his place at the paper that summer that he was angling for a job at *Rolling Stone* and met with the magazine's cofounder Jann Wenner. (Luckily for Bernstein, Wenner dragged his feet on making a job offer. "I would've gone in a song," Bernstein said later.) With his family, Woodward tried to explain the would-be presidential scandal to his father, a Republican through and through. His dad urged him to still vote for Nixon in the fall.

*   *   *

Though the press had seemingly lost interest, FBI special agent Angelo Lano and his colleagues were still on the case. They chafed at being blocked by Gray from investigating the Mexican money trail and pressured the acting director to let them move ahead, until he finally called the CIA's Vernon Walters in early July and explained that he would approve additional Mexico-related interviews unless the agency requested otherwise in writing. Walters arrived in Gray's office the next morning to discuss the matter face-to-face.

As Walters recounted in a memcon that same day, he told Gray, "I had a long association with the President and was as desirous as anyone of protecting him. I did not believe that a letter from the Agency asking the FBI to lay off this investigation on the spurious grounds that it would uncover covert operations would serve the President. Such a letter in the current atmosphere of Washington would become known prior to election day and what was now a minor wound could become a mortal wound." Walters explained that he'd write such a letter only under a direct order from the president. If pushed, he was prepared to resign.

Gray confided to Walters that he'd thought about resigning too, but believed the move would raise too many questions. They agreed that the cover-up seemed to stem from mid-level White House officials "who had acted imprudently," and that they couldn't compromise their own organizations to protect Dean, Ehrlichman, Haldeman, or even Mitchell. When the meeting concluded, Gray walked Walters to the door.

Later, the acting director called Nixon directly, still unable to imagine that the president himself would be involved in the cover-up. "Dick Walters and I feel that people on your staff are trying to mortally wound you by using the CIA and the FBI and by confusing the questions of CIA interest in, or not in, people the FBI wishes to interview," he explained.

"Pat, you just continue to conduct your aggressive and thorough investigation," Nixon said, as nonchalantly as he could manage. Only later did it occur to Gray that the president hadn't asked for any details or evidence leading the charge.

Even as Gray and Nixon spoke, the campaign's wall of silence was already cracking. On July 1, FBI agent Magallanes received a phone call at home from Peggy Gleason, a CREEP employee he'd unsuccessfully interviewed the day before at the campaign offices. She explained she was calling from a pay phone—she feared she might be being followed—and had more she wanted to say to the FBI than the monosyllabic answers she'd provided when she'd been supervised by a CREEP lawyer. Following her conditions, Magallanes hurriedly picked her up in his personal car, along with his partner Charles Harvey. The trio spent two hours driving around the capital, talking. When the car got too hot to bear, they retreated to a Holiday Inn, where Gleason spoke for seven more hours about what had transpired inside CREEP both before and after the break-in.

A few nights later, Gleason recruited another colleague, Judy Hoback, a campaign accountant, and the two women joined the agents for a long, get-to-know-each-other dinner in the lounge of the Key Bridge Marriott. As Gleason explained, Hoback was a single mother and wanted to be sure she trusted the agents before risking her career to help them. They won her trust, and at her Bethesda house later that night, she revealed what she knew, talking until 3 a.m. about the oddities of the campaign's financing, its plentiful cash reserves, and McCord and Liddy's involvement.

The interviews with Gleason and Hoback were incredibly valuable, but paled in comparison to a bomb dropped on July 5 by Al Baldwin: He and the U.S. Attorney's Office struck a deal for testimony and guaranteed immunity. The Watergate lookout talked. And talked. And talked. For hours, he outlined his odd ten-week employment arc with CREEP, culminating in manning the listening post at the Howard Johnson. The first conversation he heard, he said, "was in regard to a man talking with a woman and discussing their marital problem." He added that he had also eavesdropped on the conversations of R. Spencer Oliver, the coordinator of the DNC's state chairs, from 8 a.m. to 6 p.m. daily, according to McCord's instructions, and prepared logs that McCord picked up each evening. He explained that he had no idea he was doing anything illegal; the imprimatur of McCord and CREEP, headed by the former attorney general, had reassured him every step of the way that it was a legitimate operation—right up, that is, until the arrests.

The agents had their perps and their first big witness, but continued to be stumped by their motive. Multiple FBI searches in the days after the burglary had found no listening devices in the DNC at all; no bug on Spencer Oliver's phone nor one on the phone of Larry O'Brien, which made some wonder if the burglars had actually been removing the bugs—not installing them. The FBI agents found Baldwin's almost ludicrous explanation of his recruitment and employment strangely reassuring. Given the burglars' backgrounds, they'd continued to wonder whether the D.C. police had intercepted a rogue CIA mission, but Baldwin's tale—which wouldn't be publicly known until the fall—seemed consistent with the idea that they were, indeed, investigating just a "third-rate burglary" and not a sophisticated covert op. "He gave us some very valuable evidence," recalled prosecutor Earl Silbert. "He became a critical government witness."

By July 12, thanks to Baldwin, Gleason, Hoback, and others' testimony, the FBI believed it was ready to arrest Hunt and Liddy for masterminding the break-in. Instead, however, Silbert and the two other prosecutors assigned to the case, Seymour Glanzer and Donald Campbell, asked the bureau to wait and let the Justice Department continue with a grand jury indictment.*

With the grand jury, the prosecutors decided to zero in on just two aspects, the burglary and wiretapping at the Watergate—an approach the FBI team found annoyingly narrow, given all the other tantalizing leads about misdeeds and misappropriated money they were stumbling upon.† In a lengthy summary of its investigation assembled on July 21, the FBI warned that it had been told by CREEP staffers that the campaign's leadership was systematically keeping the truth from investigators and sending bureau agents on irrelevant "fishing expeditions" meant to distract them, but the depth of the cover-up was already even more worrisome than investigators realized. CREEP treasurer Hugh Sloan resigned quietly in mid-July, appearing to realize for the first time the true shadiness of some of the practices and people he'd been working alongside over the previous year.

Now, without him and Liddy, Magruder sought out Bart Porter, who headed the campaign surrogate program, and explained that he needed help making the cover story stick. "Your name was mentioned as someone we could count on," Magruder said. CREEP's strategy was to pretend that the sums of money given to Liddy were reasonable given the above-board, respectable programs he was supposed to have been working on. Would Porter be willing to tell the grand jury that the money given to Liddy had helped finance surrogate operations and protect against radical demonstrators?

"I need some time to think about that, Jeb," Porter replied, though in the end, he agreed, and together they formed a plan: CREEP would admit to and apologize for shoddy bookkeeping—*who knew that Sloan*

---

* As Silbert recalled, "In our view, [Liddy] and Hunt considered themselves James Bond types, super sleuths and big macho-male types."

† Frank Wills, the office security guard, was shocked to enter the grand jury hearing and find a veritable sea of Black faces staring back at him. "Man, I never was so surprised in my life," he recalled. "Most of the members of the jury were Black. I couldn't count five white persons in the room."

could just hand out cash money like that without documentation or receipts!—but maintain that it had nothing but the best of intentions for Liddy's operations, armed with an outline of legitimate and logical security projects that they thought Liddy had been pursuing on the campaign's behalf.

Despite the new cover story, Magruder fretted. "I was beginning to sense that I was in a very lonely and vulnerable position," he recalled. When interviewed by the FBI in late July, he played as dumb as he could, telling the agents that McCord was just acting as a "soldier of fortune" and any legitimate political operative would know that "real information of value" would come from a campaign headquarters, not the party headquarters. In the final paragraph of the agents' notes of the encounter, they wrote, "MAGRUDER explained that the $250,000 authorization which he had made for intelligence gathering was justified . . . [by] the information which LIDDY had furnished regarding the San Diego convention site."

Kleindienst, the attorney general, Petersen, the head of the criminal division, and Gray, the FBI director, all seemed content to accept the cover story at face value. Through the summer, witness after witness paraded through the grand jury, as subpoenas rained down on everyone from Liddy to Stans, but few cracks appeared in the case, and under pressure from Petersen and Kleindienst, the prosecutors didn't seem inclined to push further. Throughout, the department's leadership seemed overly deferential to the campaign and White House officials, allowing them to testify in private rather than before the grand jury, among other accommodations. "My own feeling was that Henry didn't want to make a fight," Silbert said later.

Gray at one point even brought Felt and other FBI leaders into his office to ask whether the case could stop at the five burglars, plus Hunt and Liddy. "Can the investigation be confined to these seven subjects?" the acting director asked.

"We do not have all the evidence yet, but I am convinced we will be going much higher than these seven," Felt said. "These men are the pawns. We want the ones who moved the pawns."

Gray's reticence to move beyond the initial conspiracy targets made Felt believe the department's leadership was guilty of "silent obstruction," leaving only one path to push the investigation through—the press.

Chapter 18

The Dahlberg Check

By the end of July, as the prosecutors settled on a narrow investigation, it seemed clear that whatever other dirty laundry might be hidden amid the president's reelection campaign would likely remain that way until at least November. The election would continue, and votes would be cast with no knowledge that anything unbecoming had unfolded in the midst of the campaign, much less that a bizarre local D.C. burglary potentially had ties to the Oval Office—until July 22, when the story roared back to life. That morning *Newsday* reported that Liddy had been fired from the campaign for refusing to cooperate with investigators. Later that week, the *New York Times* heightened the drama when it broke a major new revelation on its front page from one of its White House writers, Walter Rugaber.

Rugaber, a savvy young political journalist, had been suspicious of the Watergate operation as soon as he heard that CREEP's security director was involved. "From the moment McCord was identified I was confident it could not be anything but a Nixon operation," he said later. Rugaber had come to the D.C. bureau in 1969 after covering the Civil Rights Movement in Georgia and Alabama, and found covering the White House beat "just dreadful." The Nixon team was secretive and iced him out even before the *Times* imbroglio over the Pentagon Papers, leaving him to get scrappy to find information. This ultimately benefited his reporting, when he realized that the key to unraveling the burglars' story would be found in Miami. His colleague Tad Szulc had already tried with a run of stories focusing on the Cubans' CIA connections, but Rugaber doubted that angle actually amounted to much. After Szulc's trail went cold, Rugaber set out to uncover the paper trail he assumed might link the Cubans to Nixon's orbit.

Early in July, he flew to Florida to dig around, striking up an odd alliance with Richard Gerstein, the Democratic state's attorney in Miami's Dade County, who was personally and professionally curious whether the Watergate plot had roots in his jurisdiction. The reporter's hunch mixed with the subpoena power of a prosecutor made for a powerful combination. Gerstein gathered Barker's phone records, and Rugaber took to calling each number in turn; he knew he'd struck pay dirt when one call was answered: "Committee for the Reelection of the President?"

On July 25, the *New York Times* published Rugaber's first report that Barker's Miami phone had called the CREEP offices more than a dozen times from March to June—specifically dialing an extension that reached the office Liddy shared with another lawyer, Glenn J. Sedam, Jr. When the *Times* asked Sedam about it, he denied speaking with Barker, presumably meaning that Liddy had been the intended recipient. One call to Liddy's office from Barker's phone had come the day before the break-in. Reached at home, Liddy told the paper he would have "no conversation with the press on any subject at all."

Rugaber's scoop spurred the *Washington Post* to reassemble their Watergate team—managing editor Howard Simons, annoyed, cornered city editor Barry Sussman with the *Times* in hand and demanded, "Why didn't we have that?"* And by the end of the day, Woodward and Bernstein

---

* Almost from the start, Simons—the person Joe Califano had called first thing that Saturday morning after hearing about the break-in at the DNC offices—drove the first months of the *Post*'s coverage. "[Simons was] the day-to-day agitator, the one who ran around the newsroom inspiring, shouting, directing, insisting that we not abandon our inquiry, whatever the level of denials or denunciations," Woodward would say later, though Simons, all but written out of the movie version of *All the President's Men*, was turned into a weak-willed supporting character buoyed along by Ben Bradlee's enthusiasm for the story. Bradlee, in his own memoir, wrote that his relationship with the managing editor was "never the same" after the movie. Simons was hardly the only key player hurt by the later mythologizing of Woodward and Bernstein: Barry Sussman, the city editor who also dogged the story for months and originally enlisted the two reporters in the first place, was written out of the movie entirely. "I don't have anything good to say about either one of them," he said to "Woodstein" biographer Alicia Shepard decades later.

were back on the beat until further notice—though in its own way, the assignment of two young, inexperienced reporters amid a newsroom filled with respected veterans still indicated how little attention the *Post* expected to get out of the scandal.

Bernstein immediately wanted to start digging into the money trail too. He reached out to Gerstein, and on his own made arrangements to visit Miami. On July 31, he boarded a plane to Florida and opened his morning copy of the *Times* to find Rugaber's latest scoop, datelined from Mexico City: "Cash in Capital Raid Traced to Mexico." Investigators, Rugaber revealed, had traced the burglars' sequential $100 bills to two bank withdrawals by Barker in Miami, on May 2 and 8, that totaled $89,000. The withdrawals matched precisely the total amount of four deposits Barker had made earlier, on April 20, of bank drafts from Banco Internacional in the amounts of $15,000, $18,000, $24,000, and $32,000, all of which appeared to come from a prominent Mexican corporate lawyer, Manual Ogarrio Daguerre.

Bernstein called back to the *Post* newsroom as soon as he landed and asked Sussman whether he should head to Mexico City. In what Bradlee's biographer Jeff Himmelman would call "arguably the most important decision made by any *Post* editor during the initial phase of Watergate," Sussman told Bernstein to stay in Miami and dig into what he could find there.* The reporter spent the rest of the day trying to coax information out of the state's attorney; he ultimately not only confirmed that the four checks were exactly as described in the *Times*, but also learned of a fifth check, from someone named Kenneth H. Dalhberg, for $25,000, that Barker had also deposited.

Gerstein's investigators hadn't been able to figure out who Dalhberg was, but some guesswork and archival research by Woodward, Bernstein, and the *Post*'s librarians managed to identify him. Dahlberg, they determined, lived in Minneapolis and had headed the '68 Nixon campaign's efforts in the Midwest. Dahlberg seemed baffled how his check had ended up in the Miami bank account of a Watergate burglar. "I don't have the

---

* "Whatever you said about Bernstein," Ben Bradlee said decades later, after Bernstein would spend decades living in the shadow of the prolific scoop-machine Woodward, "Bernstein made the first key connection of the money."

vaguest idea about it," he told Woodward over the phone. "At a meeting in Washington of the committee, I turned the check over either to the treasurer of the committee [Hugh W. Sloan, Jr.] or to Maurice Stans himself." It seemed that the president's reelection money had somehow been laundered through Barker's account in Miami.* The article ran in the next day's paper under what would soon be the most famous dual byline in journalism.

Until then, Woodward and Bernstein had been all but competing with each other, each keeping his own hunches, scoops, and sources under wraps, not trusting that the other wouldn't run with the story and steal credit. As they pursued Dahlberg, though, Woodward requested that Bernstein's byline also be featured, despite him being in Miami, and all future Watergate stories would be co-bylined. Colleagues soon came to see a pattern in the duo's style: Woodward would tear speedily through a first draft of a story to establish the basic facts and outline, then Bernstein, the better writer, would work it through to a more polished version. They would argue—loudly—in the newsroom over individual word choices and phrasing, arguments that regularly grew so heated that one or the other would throw up his hands and walk away. Their finished drafts always seemed to arrive at the last minute before deadline.

The Dahlberg story marked one of the first moments in the *Post*'s coverage when the paper broke new revelations and moved the story forward, rather than just following leads already developed by government investigators or another paper. Based on the reports about the Dahlberg check, the federal elections division of the government's watchdog, the Government Accounting Office (GAO), began an audit of the Nixon campaign, the first ever carried out as part of the new federal campaign finance law that had taken effect on April 7.

*   *   *

* Rugaber forever regretted decamping to Mexico City rather than chasing the fifth check or handing news of it over to other *Times* reporters to follow. He had expected the Miami investigators to keep it quiet until he returned to Miami and thought he'd have time to run it down separately. "It was, as Rugaber said, the smoking pistol, the precise bit of irrefutable fiscal evidence, the link in the paper chain which he had been certain would connect the burglars with the White House," Harrison Salisbury wrote later.

Publicly, the White House continued to project an attitude of genial cooperation with investigators throughout the summer. "The President's view is that all those who are asked to cooperate should cooperate," Deputy Press Secretary Gerald Warren told reporters in early August. But in the Oval Office and the Executive Office Building, Nixon's team spent that month concocting an elaborate series of lies, suborning perjury, and constructing half-truths to obfuscate the campaign's darkest corners. Though Nixon was still confident in the efforts thus far to stonewall the case ("I'm not that worried about it, to be perfectly candid with you," he told Haldeman on August 1. "After all, Mitchell's gone, and as we've all pointed out, nobody at a higher level was involved"), he spoke openly to Haldeman of the "considerable cost" of keeping Hunt quiet. "They took a hell of a risk and they have to be paid," the president lamented. "That's all there is to that." The hush money was worth every penny, and they just had to hold strong.

In mid-August, Magruder was called before the grand jury. Heading into the testimony, it seemed highly likely that the deputy campaign director would be indicted (and he would have been had he told the truth), but on August 15, he and Dean met in the White House counsel's office to prepare his answers. There had been more and more stories spreading about Liddy and his antics, and the White House was trying to make clear Liddy acted alone without prompting the former aide to reconsider his silence. Magruder paced as Dean tested him and rehearsed for three hours with the toughest questions he might face from prosecutors.

As it turned out, Dean's questioning was tougher than that by the prosecutors. As Campbell sat off to the side, taking notes and doubling back to check facts, figures, and timelines, Silbert interrogated Magruder for two hours, seeming to Magruder to steadily lose steam and interest. Magruder emphasized how big and sprawling and expensive the Nixon operation was compared to Liddy's tiny operation—*sure, $250,000 might sound like a lot of money, but it wasn't to CREEP*—and he explained how the distraction of the ITT scandal had meant Mitchell's campaign controls weren't as tight as they should have been through the spring. All in all, he sold the cover story about Liddy's legitimate activities and walked out of the grand jury apparently trouble-free. Dean kept in close—inappropriately close—contact with Henry Petersen, and the next day, Dean called Magruder to tell him that the campaign official was no longer a target. He had escaped; that night, Magruder got roaring drunk at Billy Martin's Tavern in Georgetown with Fred LaRue.

Nixon fared just as well with every passing week. "As the cover-up progressed through July and August, I was struck by its tremendous political success," Dean recalled. That August, Democratic candidate George McGovern had stumbled through his own embarrassing episode as he named Thomas Eagleton his running mate, only to drop the Missouri senator nineteen days later when questions arose about past electroshock therapy treatments he'd undergone for clinical depression in the 1960s.* Sargent Shriver, the Kennedy family member and former director of the Peace Corps, was named the new vice presidential nominee, only after McGovern's first two choices, Hubert Humphrey and Ed Muskie, both embarrassingly turned him down.

The Democrats also couldn't make Watergate stick to Nixon's campaign—though not for a lack of trying. The party had sensed real opportunity with their civil lawsuit against CREEP ("Forget about the burglaries. The story is the money. Keep your eye on the money," the DNC's lawyer, D.C. legal titan Edward Bennett Williams, told reporters that summer), and suspicions only grew as the case's early stages progressed. After one of the first hearings, Williams loudly proclaimed in the courtroom to CREEP's lawyer Kenneth Parkinson, "Until you made your argument, I thought you guys were innocent."

Williams and the DNC legal team deposed the burglars and even tracked down Baldwin weeks before his involvement became public. John Mitchell's deposition went especially poorly; the former attorney general simply refused to answer questions, got up, and left the office. "I can tell when a guy is lying and these guys are lying and covering up," Williams declared afterward. Yet the civil suit stalled—first the judge, Charles Richey, required the depositions remain sealed, negating the ability of damaging information to be wielded as a political weapon outside the courtroom, and then as the fall began and the election neared, Richey

---

* In fact, the scoop about the Dahlberg check, which seemed to link the bugging incident to the president's reelection campaign, was buried even on the *Post*'s front page by the eight-column banner headline that day: "Eagleton Bows Out of '72 Race; McGovern Weighs Replacement."

paused further investigation and depositions until after the election—which effectively neutered the case's aim to expose information before the nation voted.

At every turn, bad news seemed buried by good news. In late August the *Washington Post* reported that the GAO audit had identified a campaign slush fund at CREEP; the same night at the Republican convention in Miami, Nixon was formally nominated as the party's presidential candidate. The three-day event, hurriedly relocated from San Diego to Florida after the ITT affair earlier in the spring, was chaired by the House minority leader, Gerald Ford, and featured a speech by Pat Nixon, the first convention speech ever by a Republican first lady. The nomination underscored what a pivotal political figure Nixon had been in the twentieth century; his fifth appearance on his party's presidential ticket tied the record held by FDR.

Soon after, however, the campaign took some direct hits. The day after Nixon's acceptance speech, Maurice Stans was questioned in his Doral Hotel suite by the local state's attorney about the Barker funds, while that same day in Washington, two Houston oil executives met with the federal grand jury to answer questions about the campaign financing operation. In the next morning's newspaper, the *Times*'s Rugaber laid out more details about how the money-laundering operation unfolded: The mysterious $25,000 check from Dahlberg had originated with a prominent Democratic donor, Dwayne O. Andreas, head of the powerful agricultural conglomerate Archer Daniels Midland, and all or nearly all of the other mystery $89,000 originated in Houston with Democratic donors who wanted to hide their identity by providing cash ahead of the year's April campaign finance reporting deadline. Oil executives had "sacked up" the cash and taken it to Washington to deliver to the campaign, while Dahlberg flew to Miami, collected the $25,000 in cash from Andreas at a golf club, and delivered it to Washington.

Adding insult to injury, the GAO released its preliminary audit of the Nixon reelection effort, laying out what it said were eleven "apparent and possible" violations of the new federal campaign finance law amid questionable transactions totaling at least $350,000. The auditors announced that they had referred the possible violations to the Justice Department for potential prosecution. They were horrified by what they uncovered, telling Woodward at one point that the Nixon campaign was "a rat's nest behind the surface efficiency of computerized financial reporting."

Representative Wright Patman, the head of the House Banking Committee, was troubled by the GAO's report, calling it "chapter one of what must be a top-to-bottom investigation of all the allegations involved in the Watergate incident and the closely related areas of political fund raising." He told reporters that he also had concerns about the ability and willingness of the Justice Department and its "strongly partisan" Attorney General Kleindienst to follow up on the questions raised by the GAO, and urged the appointment instead of what he called a "special prosecuting team" to look into the matter independently. "Anything less can only destroy the public's confidence in the nation's democratic processes," he declared. Despite the outrage in Washington, however, the opposition could not translate it to the general population. As the DNC's O'Brien recalled later, "Our efforts to make Watergate a campaign issue failed. The American people had tuned out Watergate."

On August 29, Nixon held a press conference out in San Clemente, quickly brushing aside a leadoff question related to the campaign fund. Maurice Stans, he said, was "an honest man and one who is very meticulous" and would easily and quickly remedy any "technical violations [that] have occurred." He also dismissed the need for a special prosecutor, noting the aggressive investigations already underway by the FBI, the Justice Department, the Senate Banking Committee, and the Government Accounting Office, all of which had "total cooperation" from the White House.

Then Nixon added an unexpected twist: "In addition to that, within our own staff, under my direction, counsel to the President, Mr. Dean, has conducted a complete investigation of all leads which might involve any present members of the White House Staff or anybody in the Government. I can say categorically that his investigation indicates that no one in the White House Staff, no one in this Administration, presently employed, was involved in this very bizarre incident."

"We are doing everything we can to take this incident and to investigate it and not to cover it up," Nixon continued. "What really hurts in matters of this sort is not the fact that they occur—because overzealous people in campaigns do things that are wrong—what really hurts is if you try to cover it up." Nixon's words surely ranked as among the most brazen—or least self-aware—statements ever by someone actively involved in the very behavior he condemned.

Dean, watching the press conference on TV in his San Clemente hotel room, "damn near fell off the bed" when he heard the president's remarks. He had not only not conducted an investigation, he had actually devoted the last seventy-two days to architecting the cover story—but in the moment Dean cared little that Nixon had just lied. Instead, he was ecstatic—the president had mentioned his name on national television, the latest sign of his rising power and influence. His hard work was getting recognized. That summer, he even received a coveted official upgrade, allowed access for the first time to Washington's true inner sanctum of officialdom: He was now allowed to dine in the White House's executive mess.

Chapter 19

The Patman Probe

S peaker of the House Carl Albert hadn't paid much attention to the
original burglary at the DNC offices, except to note that one of the
burglars, James McCord, had once lived in his congressional district in
Waurika, Oklahoma. The diminutive five-foot, four-inch congressional
leader known as the "Little Giant," the first House speaker born in the
twentieth century, had been wary of Nixon since they had been freshman
congressmen together in 1947. He had considered the California representative personally friendly—perhaps second only to Lyndon Johnson
in his total absorption in politics—but possessed by an obvious dark and
paranoid side. "That command early [of politics] was tied to the lowest
form of partisan tactics," Albert wrote later. It was with this behavior in
mind that, as summer progressed and the financial oddities around the
burglary accrued, Albert asked Wright Patman's Banking Committee
to investigate.

Patman had come into Congress six months before the Crash of 1929;
by the time the Watergate investigation rolled around, the seventy-nine-
year-old had served in the U.S. House of Representatives for a fifth of the
entire history of his country. In the process, he had earned a reputation as a
pugnacious loner and financial industry watchdog.* "To Wright Patman,"

---

* When Patman eventually died, in 1976, he was the fourth longest serving member of
Congress in history.

the *New York Times* explained, "the root of all evil was the concentration of economic power in the hands of a small number of bankers, business executives and government officials." "He's something of a crank," the *New Yorker* added, "but he's an intelligent and knowledgeable crank."*

From the start, Patman saw the markers of a financial conspiracy in the sequential currency carried by the Watergate burglars—and the subsequent reports about the Dahlberg check had only deepened his sense that something was terribly amiss. He also—like Albert—had a mistrustful relationship with Nixon, who had first won election to Congress in 1946 by defeating one of Patman's friends, the incumbent Jerry Voorhis. It had been a bitter, dirty campaign during which the future president had accused the loyal New Dealer of being a secret Communist.† Ever since, Patman had warily eyed Nixon's win-at-all-costs approach to politics.

In August, Patman dispatched committee investigators to trace the campaign slush funds that had financed the burglary. A key step was meeting with Maurice Stans himself at the CREEP offices, but almost immediately, the interrogation derailed. "As soon as we asked the question, he and his lawyers would go to this [side] room . . . and it was like a clown car in there. There must have been 20 people in this little tiny room," investigator Curtis Prins later recalled. "They were all in suits and ties, and you could tell that they were people who were connected to something bigger than just the Committee to Re-Elect the President."After consultation, Stans would return and decline to answer the question. The investigators left frustrated.

As summer ended, the FBI too was increasingly frustrated by the Justice Department's seemingly inadequate investigation; agents pointed at the GAO reports and wondered how no request had come from the Justice Department to pursue the leads further. The sense that the FBI was being stonewalled fueled a steady drip of leaks, which further aggravated the administration and led to calls for Felt and Gray to demand a crackdown.

---

* In 1932, after a battle with Herbert Hoover's treasury secretary Andrew Mellon, Patman had actually introduced an impeachment resolution.

† Accusing the labor union CIO's political action committee, which supported Voorhis, of harboring Communist principles, Nixon courted the women's vote by handing out twenty-five thousand thimbles that said, "Nixon for Congress / Put the needle in the PAC."

Someone was leaking prodigiously to *TIME*'s Justice Department reporter Sandy Smith, as Smith first reported the existence of the "plumbers," and *TIME* warned readers the "Watergate Caper" was morphing into something larger and more sinister. "The case had begun to resemble a dinner party at which the silverware starts disappearing. A certain taut silence has descended," the magazine wrote.

Gray himself was puzzled. Sometimes it seemed as if information was appearing in the press within hours of the FBI learning it, but mostly there was a noted lag in the public scoops. "The 'revelations' in newspaper and magazine stories were four to eight weeks behind their original discovery by the federal investigators," Gray would later note. If someone had been studying the news reports, however, a pattern would have emerged: The leaks were less about the "what" of the investigation and more about the "how."

Whoever was providing journalists with information seemed to care more about hurting Gray than hurting Nixon.

One weekend in late summer, Bob Woodward drove to Felt's house in Fairfax, Virginia, about thirty minutes outside D.C.; Felt wasn't exactly happy to see the reporter, but they ended up having a long talk, during which the FBI executive outlined the circumstances under which he'd be willing to cooperate more deeply with Woodward's reporting. The stakes, Felt said, "were much higher than anyone outside perceived," and necessitated serious caution. They worked out a system where Woodward would contact Felt when needed, but only for background information, not for quoting or reference.* He'd only confirm what Woodward had already gathered, guide reporting, or help provide analysis—not volunteer any new details, leaving the power in his hands. This approach also allowed Felt to go to other outlets and scatter the information around to reporters like *TIME*'s Smith.

The control Felt and his loyal FBI coterie had over the investigation's information flow also kept suspicion away from him; certain stories required a certain level of clearance or knowledge, and might expose his role if he wasn't careful. In fact, during that August ground-rules meeting,

---

* Felt had been upset earlier that spring when Woodward had seemed to too clearly point to a high-level FBI source in his reporting on George Wallace's attempted assassination.

he neglected to mention two major developments that the FBI was sitting on that weekend about the burglary and subsequent cover-up: the White House's pressure campaign on the CIA to help cover up the break-in and Al Baldwin's revelations about CREEP's activities. That news of Baldwin's existence took so long to surface particularly provides insight into Felt's media manipulation; he didn't consider his leaks a patriotic act, nor was he in a hurry to break news. His only goal was highlighting how Gray was harming the bureau. By deciding when to get involved, he gave himself plausible deniability, and could rage against certain leaks in his official capacity while lying about his own involvement.*

Baldwin's role in the burglary finally became public at the end of the summer amid a flurry of early-September trouble for Nixon. Lawyers for the DNC and Lawrence O'Brien's civil suit tracked down the co-conspirator themselves and interviewed him in Connecticut. The DNC lawyers were astounded at his story, and to bring attention to the Republicans' misdeeds, O'Brien began to speak publicly about Baldwin and the larger bugging operation behind the burglary, first in mid-August and then expounding further at a September 7 press conference. Finally, O'Brien's legal team—who, after all, were also the *Post*'s legal team—gave even more detail to Woodward and Bernstein, who published a front-page story on Baldwin on September 11.

Felt, of course, knew he wasn't a source for the Baldwin story, and he cunningly seized the opportunity. Throughout the summer and fall, the FBI hierarchy seemed to misunderstand the news reporting they were reading, believing that stories like Baldwin's were being pulled directly from their own internal reports, known as "302s," that summarized interviews. ("It did not occur to them that an article might appear to have come from a 302 because the same person interviewed in the 302 had also talked to reporters and said the same thing," historian Max Holland observed.) In the wake of Woodward and Bernstein's story on Baldwin, Felt wrote in a memo, "The article which appeared in

---

* Years later, when it became clear how hard the Nixon White House had leaned on the CIA, news that never came through the "Felt channel," Woodward would explain, "It was too high. It was held too close. Too few people knew. We couldn't get that high." Similarly, when Watergate historian Max Holland asked Woodward why Felt never told him about Baldwin, the *Post* legend would say, simply, "The answer is, I don't know."

the *Washington Post* this morning appears to have been taken from the FD-302 of our interview with former SA [Special Agent] Baldwin. . . . [The Washington Field Office] should forcibly remind all agents of the need to be most circumspect in talking about this case." Also in early September, frustrated by such leaks, Silbert asked the FBI to conduct a sweep of his office and the grand jury room for electronic bugs. Mark Felt again signed off on the memo; no bugs were found.*

The leaks continued.

A day after the Baldwin story, Patman distributed on September 12 the first report from his House investigation to fellow members of the Banking Committee—a move he hoped would be the jumping-off point for a wider, more thorough investigation ahead of the November election. He explained that the committee had to look into the "wanderings of Republican campaign funds," including the $100,000 or more that had apparently moved back and forth between Texas and Mexico. The supposedly confidential internal report quickly leaked to Jack Anderson and the *Washington Post*, and the resulting headlines on September 13 led to a major rift in the committee as the Republican members suddenly grasped the political danger to the president ahead of the election. They need not have worried, as it turned out. The committee's first, eighty-three-page report would turn out to be almost its last report as well.

---

* Days later, though, a bug did turn up in an unexpected place. Technicians were summoned to the DNC offices at the Watergate on September 13 to inspect the malfunctioning telephone in Spencer Oliver's suite. They discovered an antiquated bugging device on the line. How and when the bug had been placed there remained a mystery. Did the FBI techs miss it during their earlier, repeated searches? Was it installed sometime after the summer searches, perhaps with the intention of being found? Experts who spoke with the FBI suspected that the bug was so antiquated and crudely placed that it had been installed specifically to be found—perhaps the DNC itself had installed the bug to aid its own civil suit against the president and CREEP? The bureau went so far as to open a new case on the Oliver bug, believing it to be wholly unconnected to the June 17 burglary.

Chapter 20

"A Hell of a Story"

Two days after Patman's initial report, on Friday, September 15, 1971, the government's long-anticipated indictments landed, a near-total strategic victory for the White House, CREEP, and the cover-up. The prosecutors zeroed in solely on the five burglars, plus Liddy and Hunt—the narrowest case possible, though the Justice Department stated officially, "We have absolutely no evidence to indicate that any others should be charged." Attorney General Kleindienst called the proceedings "one of the most intensive, objective, and thorough investigations in many years," and CREEP's chair, Clark MacGregor, hubristically demanded a public apology from those who had suggested the campaign's direct involvement.

To anyone who had closely followed the story, however, the indictments were baffling, mentioning none of the campaign finance violations and none of the accusations about the $89,000 from Texas or the $25,000 from Minnesota that had found their way into Barker's bank account. There was also no reference to the $350,000 slush fund that Stans had apparently used to fund Liddy's operations. It was as if the money intended for the Nixon campaign had just coincidentally ended up in the burglars' bank account—and then their pockets—as they broke into rival campaign offices.

Earl Silbert announced the indictments in the courtroom of U.S. District Court judge John J. Sirica, a scrappy and streetwise boxing aficionado who carried his pugilist style onto the bench. Sirica, whose grandparents had emigrated from Italy, had settled in D.C. in 1918, living above a shoemaker's shop on the spot where the FBI's new headquarters was now under construction along Pennsylvania Avenue. He'd hoped to be a boxer—and even won his first professional bout—but his parents cajoled him into the law. He'd worked both as a criminal defense lawyer and a prosecutor before starting his own practice in 1934, scrounging moderate success and living almost hand to mouth for fifteen years before joining the showy firm of Hogan and Hartson. In 1957, he was sworn in as a federal judge—a post he'd received after helping the Eisenhower-Nixon ticket in 1952 and 1956 bolster support in the Italian-American community. His friend and onetime best man, world heavyweight champion Jack Dempsey, attended the swearing in ceremony.

As a judge, Sirica was not exactly well respected, "regarded near the bottom in depth of legal knowledge, more a Sancho Panza than a Solomon," the *Post*'s Barry Sussman later recalled. "Sirica had the looks, manner, and speech mannerisms of a bus driver."

As the D.C. court's chief judge, Sirica, however, oversaw grand juries and could take on major trials as they interested him. That summer, he had presided over a grisly murder trial before the DNC burglary caught his eye. He assigned himself to it, explaining to colleagues that it might be preferable to have a Republican-appointed judge presiding to avoid any appearance of a Democratic-backed witch hunt. Court observers suspected something else was at play: Sirica loved publicity, and the Watergate case was sure to be a spectacle. The formal arraignment of the seven Watergate defendants that September indeed resembled a circus, with crowds of media and camera flashes. Liddy, when it came his turn to face the authorities, surrendered his passport, and his mother put up the $1,000 necessary for him to make bail.

Inside the White House, Nixon's team celebrated their good fortune. Their cover-up might just work. That Friday evening, the 15th, around 5:30 p.m., Dean was invited into the Oval Office to discuss the day's events with Nixon and Haldeman. It was a rare opportunity for Dean, and he entered to find Haldeman and the president slumped down, reclined in their chairs. The casual reception thrilled him; it was another sign that he was now part of the inner circle.

The president looked at Dean through the "V" of his feet crossed upon his desk. "Well, you had quite a day today, didn't you? You got Watergate on the way, huh?" Nixon said in greeting.

"Quite a three months," Dean replied.

As the conversation progressed, they praised the good initial press, wondered if the case had been stopped in its tracks, and gossiped about the FBI investigation and political ramifications. "Three months ago I would have had trouble predicting where we'd be today," Dean said. "I think that I can say that 54 days from now that not a thing will come crashing down to our surprise."

The president also seemed mostly pleased. "The whole thing is a can of worms," Nixon told Dean. "A lot of this stuff went on. . . . But the way you've handled it, it seems to me, has been very skillful—putting your fingers in the dikes every time that leaks have sprung here and sprung there." He railed about the double standard that he saw his campaign being held to by the public and the Democrats. "We have not used the power in this first four years, as you know," he said.

"That's true," Dean replied.

"We have never used it. We haven't used the Bureau and we haven't used the Justice Department, but things are going to change now."

"That's an exciting prospect."

"It's got to be done. It's the only thing to do."

"We've got to," Haldeman chimed in.

"We've just been God damn fools—for us to come into this election campaign and not do anything with regard to the Democratic senators who are running?" Nixon continued. "They're crooks, they've been stealing, they've been taking [unintelligible]. That's ridiculous. Absolutely ridiculous. It's not going to be that way any more."

Later, Dean brought up one of the biggest challenges he saw on the road ahead: Patman's investigation in the House. "Whether we will be successful or not in turning that off, I don't know," the lawyer said. "We've got a plan whereby Rothblatt and Bittman, who are counsel for the seven that were indicted today, are going to go up [to Capitol Hill] and visit every member and say, 'If you commence hearings you are going to jeopardize the civil rights of these individuals in the worst way, and they'll never get a fair trial.'"

Dean explained that he also wanted to enlist House Republican leader Gerald Ford in blocking the Banking Committee's work. "Jerry Ford is not really taking an active interest in this matter that is developing, so Stans can go see Jerry Ford and try to brief him and explain to him the problems he's got," he said. "Then the other thing we are going to do is we're looking at all the campaign reports of every member of that committee because we are convinced that none of them have probably totally complied with the law either. If they want to get into it—if they want to play rough—some day we better say, 'Well, gentlemen, we think we ought to call to your attention that you haven't complied [with] A, B, C, D, E, and F, and we're not going to hold that a secret if you start talking campaign violations here."

As they weighed the options, Nixon ultimately agreed: "Jerry's really got to lead on this. He's got to really lead."

"Jerry should—damn it," Haldeman added.

The meeting wrapped up with Nixon giving a final order: "Tell Ehrlichman to get Brown in and Ford in, and then they can all work out something—but they ought to get off their asses and push it. No use to let Patman have a free ride here."

As Dean left the Oval Office, he couldn't help but think about a moment in the meeting when a phone call from Clark MacGregor, who had taken over the campaign from John Mitchell, interrupted them. As the president hung up at the end of the call, he told MacGregor, "Get a good night's sleep—and don't bug anybody without asking me, okay?"

Nixon laughed at his own joke.

*　　*　　*

Then, thanks to the dogged work of the press and the vengeful mouth of Mark Felt, the idea that the Justice Department's indictments would resolve the entire Watergate affair did not last through the weekend. Led by Harry Rosenfeld and Barry Sussman, the *Post* had stayed focused on the story even as other newspapers dipped in and out (Sussman was relieved of his role as city editor to focus entirely on Watergate) and they watched as Woodward and Bernstein poured long hours into tracking the story, an assignment made easier by the men's lack of spousal attachment—Woodward's first marriage hadn't survived his stint in the navy, and Bernstein, who had married another *Post* reporter who had subsequently gone to work for the government, was in the process of getting a divorce. Effectively without a home life, they were able to devote hours of nights and weekends to reporting that many colleagues (and particularly competitors at other outlets) were unwilling or less able to.*

Although Robert Redford and Dustin Hoffman would later make their work look glamorous, the team's investigative reporting process was usually "lonely, frustrating, tedious, and emotionally draining work," wrote Len Downie, who edited many of the later Watergate stories. Sussman grew used to the sight of Woodward grabbing a toothbrush and toothpaste from his desk drawer late at night and padding off to the bathroom to brush his teeth. Bernstein, who had long seemed to live a nocturnal existence in the newsroom and was never great on life's administrative details—he famously once forgot a company rental car for weeks in a parking garage—found he was falling behind on paying bills because he was rarely home enough to get them.

Their work continued unrelentingly through the fall, and as the government's own investigations into Watergate expanded, so did possible sources. Woodward and Bernstein each kept separate lists of people they called routinely twice a week to probe for new information. Often a source would only feel more comfortable talking over time, while others would provide small nuggets that added up week to week. Ultimately there were hundreds of people they called regularly. "Don't you guys work together?" a source asked Woodward at one point. "I just this minute hung up on Carl." The notes and details of those conversations gradually were organized into file folders sorted by person and subject, filling four cabinets in the *Post* newsroom.

For sources who were too sensitive to call by phone—or those they had no existing relationship with—the reporters often tried home visits. They would leave after the newspaper's early edition deadline at

---

* Woodward's social life at the time was equally Watergate-focused too: That summer, he'd started dating a young CBS reporter named Lesley Stahl, who had been assigned by the network to cover the scandal. She was one of the only other reporters in the courtroom on June 17 for the burglars' arraignment.

7:45 p.m.—Bernstein by bicycle and Woodward in his small 1970 Volkswagen Karmann Ghia coupe—and knock on doors across Washington and its suburbs. At the time, it was a novel reporting technique. "Reporters didn't do that then," CBS newsman Bob Schieffer recalled. "Washington was a place where everybody played by the rules. You dealt with people in the office. . . . Watergate was when the stakeouts first started." The door-knocking was often fruitless, but it paid off often enough—and big enough—that it became a regular part of their reporting. "It was like selling magazine subscriptions—one out of every thirty people will feel sorry for you and buy one," Bernstein would say later.

Still, it wasn't popular. Nixon's campaign manager Clark MacGregor complained to the *Post*'s Ben Bradlee, about the disruptive evening visits to CREEP staff, calling it harassment. "Well how did they harass them?" Bradlee asked.

"They knocked on the doors of their apartments late at night, and they telephoned from the lobby," MacGregor said.

"That's the nicest thing I've heard about either one of them in years," Bradlee replied.

The deeper the reporters went into the world of the president's reelection campaign, the more they continued to be puzzled by how cursory the Justice Department's investigation of the burglary seemed to have been. Key witnesses hadn't been questioned at all, and those who had often hadn't been asked seemingly central questions. Most questioning had happened at the campaign offices, under the eyes of campaign lawyers. It was almost as if prosecutors were going out of their way to encourage the campaign staff to clam up and not cooperate.

After seeing the narrowness of the September 15 indictments, Bernstein called a Justice Department official and wondered out loud why the charges seemed to ignore all manner of evidence already exposed by the press and the GAO. "It can safely be said that the investigation for the present is at rest, in a state of repose," the source said. "It seems highly unlikely that it will be reopened."

The next day, Woodward broke Felt's rule about telephone contact, calling him to discuss a new story reporting that the FBI knew senior campaign officials had been involved in funding the Watergate burglary. "Too soft," Felt said. "You can go much stronger." As they talked,

Felt also confirmed a lead Bernstein had picked up from the campaign bookkeeper: A $350,000 cash slush fund kept in Maurice Stans's office safe had financed not just Liddy and the Watergate bugging but "other intelligence-gathering activities." When the reporters went to the Nixon campaign for comment, the campaign's statement did not seem to deny the details: "No one employed by this committee at this time has used any funds [for purposes] that were illegal or improper." Given the wide number of departures, resignations, and firings from the campaign since the burglary, the fact that the campaign would only state that no *current* employees were responsible for such actions left a lot of wiggle room.

The *Post* story the following morning led with the news that fifteen "principal assistants" under Mitchell had "access to the secret fund of more than $300,000 earmarked for sensitive political projects," further revealing that "only one accounting of the special fund—a single piece of lined ledger paper listing the names of 15 persons with access to the money and the amount each received—was maintained. It was purposely destroyed shortly before April 7, the date that the new campaign finance law requiring detailed accounting of election funds took effect, the sources told the *Post*."

During a follow-up visit, the campaign bookkeeper told the reporters how upset she was about the injustice of the indictments. "I went down in good faith to the grand jury and testified and obviously the results are not there," she said. Before long, the reporters pieced together that Liddy, Magruder, and Bart Porter had gotten large cash payouts from the Stans slush fund. "Everybody got $100 bills," their source admitted.

To be sure he was on the right track, Woodward called Felt for the second time that weekend, but realized instantly the call was a mistake; their conversation was ominous, and Felt was clearly worried. The constant stream of leaks was causing immense pressure inside the FBI, so this would have to be the last time they spoke by phone, the FBI executive told him. "Let's just say I'll be willing to put the blossoming situation in perspective for you when the time comes," Felt said.

The *Post*'s resulting story, "2 Linked to Secret GOP Fund," carried an on-the-record denial from Magruder—one of the first and only times that a CREEP official had directly addressed allegations—and only increased the paranoia inside the administration and the FBI. Special Agent Paul

Magallanes later recalled reading the story and again thinking the reporters must have access to FBI records. "Oh my god," he thought. "That's
my interview."

Not satisfied, Woodward and Bernstein chased a tip about how campaign treasurer Hugh Sloan had resigned because he was uncomfortable
with the subterfuge. Sloan, a source told them, "wanted no part of what
he then knew was going on." That Monday night, Bernstein knocked
on Sloan's door in McLean, Virginia, the picture of domestic bliss. The
house was part of a tidy new development of Tudor-style homes, and
Sloan's wife was pregnant, due any day. "I haven't talked to the press,"
Sloan told Bernstein, and explained that he refused to be quoted. The
reporter reassured him he would never be identified in any of the *Post*'s
stories as a source, and over the course of a long conversation, he let loose,
filling in extensive details about the campaign's suspicious spending and
the post-burglary cover-up, including the bombshell that a half-dozen
ledgers documenting all the pre–April 7 campaign donations had been
destroyed after the burglary.

The revelations served as the core of a follow-up story that week
outlining "a massive 'house-cleaning' in which financial records were
destroyed and staff members were told to 'close ranks' " after the break-in.
The *Post* reported that the campaign's political coordinator, former assistant attorney general Robert Mardian, and its special assistant to the
director, Fred LaRue, a former White House counsel to Nixon, had led
the effort.

Less than a week after the neat and tidy burglary indictments, the *Post*
had reported a whole new series of charges, which if true would amount
to a broad conspiracy to obstruct justice. The campaign, for its part, only
said, "The sources of the *Washington Post* are a fountain of misinformation."
Mardian told the *Los Angeles Times* that the "house-cleaning" story was
"the biggest lot of crap I have ever heard in my life."

Toward the end of September, Woodward and Bernstein sat for another
long conversation with Sloan at his house, a few days after his daughter
was born. Sitting in the living room, the men were struck by how Sloan's
house was still packed with White House mementoes; even though the
thirty-two-year-old had resigned from the campaign in disgust, Sloan still
prominently featured a framed, inscribed Christmas card from Nixon.

Over two hours and three cups of coffee, he explained how he had regularly called Mitchell at the Justice Department to approve disbursements from the CREEP slush fund. The Mitchells had continued to loom in the background of the scandal—Martha's treatment in California had been the topic that month of meaty coverage in *Parade* magazine—and many questions circled about John's role in the run-up to the break-in. Now Sloan was apparently confirming that the attorney general had knowingly authorized illegal campaign activities.

As the reporters readied the story for publication, pushing the print edition's late deadlines, Bernstein called the Mitchells' hotel suite at the Essex House in New York around 11:30 p.m.

John Mitchell answered and Bernstein introduced himself. "Sir, I'm sorry to bother you at this hour, but we are running a story in tomorrow's paper that, in effect, says that you controlled secret funds at the committee while you were attorney general," he said.

Mitchell let out a long exclamation, "Jeeeeeeeeesus. You said that? What does it say?" As Bernstein started to read the first few paragraphs of the story, Mitchell let out several more elongated "Jeeeeeeeeesus"-es. After the third paragraph, he interrupted. "All that crap, you're putting it in the paper? It's all been denied. Katie Graham's gonna get her tit caught in a big fat wringer if that's published. Good Christ! That's the most sickening thing I ever heard."

The two went back and forth for a few moments, Mitchell's reactions more guttural than substantive, at one point again seeming to threaten the reporters with a massive lawsuit and invoking the paper's top attorney, Edward Bennett Williams: "You fellows got a great ballgame going. As soon as you're through paying Ed Williams and the rest of those fellows, we're going to do a story on all of you."

Finally, he cut off the conversation: "Call my law office in the morning."

Bernstein was simultaneously frightened and invigorated. He knew he had to get the former cabinet officer's reaction into the story, so he and the night editor called Ben Bradlee at home. Bradlee, in bed, wondered if he needed to call Graham herself to okay such a colorful quote involving her. *Was Mitchell drunk?* He double-checked that Bernstein was confident of the answer, had properly identified himself, and had good notes. Finally, he okayed it, instructing Bernstein: "Leave everything in but 'her tit.'"

Kay Graham laughed off Mitchell's comments when the story ran the next day, but as the fall unfolded further she and the *Post* executives grew nervous about how their peers ignored their reporting. They were impressed by the staff's work, but worried how the scandal had all but disappeared from the *New York Times*; after Walter Rugaber's ground-breaking reporting on the financial trail behind the burglars, the paper seemed to lose interest. "We thought, 'If this is such a hell of a story, where is *The New York Times?*'" Graham recalled. "Here we were alone with this . . . cow mess walking down a street and nobody came near it." Kissinger at one point even called her to warn her against further reporting—it was overblown, he promised.

Only two other reporting teams, at the *Los Angeles Times* and at *TIME* magazine, consistently seemed to be on the beat; the *Los Angeles Times* had assigned three of the city's best-respected (and most feared) investigative reporters to investigating the fallout from the break-in: Jack Nelson, Ronald Ostrow, and Bob Jackson. Nelson, in particular, had a track record of speaking truth to power—a newspaper veteran, he had covered the Civil Rights Movement, including the "Bloody Sunday" march in Selma, Alabama, and gone after J. Edgar Hoover and the FBI for bungling an investigation of the Ku Klux Klan in Meridian, Mississippi. (Hoover had retaliated with a smear campaign labeling Nelson a drunk, but as the reporter later quipped, "What they didn't realize is that you can't ruin a newspaperman by branding him a drunk.")

Nelson had worked the Watergate beat full-time that fall, especially after the paper's national editor, Ed Guthman, had come away from the Miami convention with a sinking feeling about the president's reelection effort. He saw the total security lockdown Nixon's crew commanded in Miami and felt there was something sinister, menacing, and arrogant about CREEP's approach to politics. He had been dismayed when the paper's owner, Otis Chandler, pulled him aside after a fall meeting to explain that the editorial board would be endorsing the president. Even coming from the normally conservative paper, the move upset Guthman. *Had they even been reading his own reporters' coverage of Watergate?*

At one level, the owners were probably right: America didn't seem to care about Watergate. Nixon's reelection campaign barreled along and

looked better poised by the day for a runaway victory against McGovern.*
Senator Hugh Scott, the Republican minority leader, seemed accurate
when he chided the press, "Nobody is paying any attention to what you're
writing," but as October began, Jack Nelson was hard at work trying to
land his biggest Watergate scoop yet—an interview with Al Baldwin.

After hints of a burglary participant came from Larry O'Brien's early-
September press conference, Ron Ostrow had managed to uncover the
witness's name and locate Baldwin in Connecticut. Nelson quickly
ensconced himself nearby and began to court the onetime accomplice.
Soon, other reporters caught on too and hordes of news organizations
began to descend on Baldwin.† Over days, Nelson patiently laid out the
case that the West Coast paper was the best home for a tell-all. In fact,
speaking to the press would offer Baldwin critical protection. Did he
really want to trust himself solely to the Justice Department when the
White House was involved so closely?

Baldwin initially hesitated because he was under subpoena to Patman's committee—but one afternoon Nelson happened to be meeting
with Baldwin's lawyers when they heard Patman had lifted his subpoena.
Nelson agitated to meet with Baldwin that night—there was no time to
lose. Over five hours and a sandwich dinner at one of the lawyers' homes,
Baldwin finally disclosed the full story of the Watergate burglary to a
reporter for the first time, taking Nelson step by step through the same
story he'd told FBI agents in early July—how McCord had recruited him,
his dealings with Liddy and Hunt, his time monitoring the wiretaps and
his courier trips to CREEP with eavesdropping logs, and the night of
the break-in itself.‡

---

* The *Los Angeles Times*'s Nixon endorsement was later seen as such a mistake that Chandler
ended the practice; the paper didn't endorse another presidential candidate for thirty-six years,
until Barack Obama.

† "Everyone wants to talk to Al," Baldwin's lawyer said to Woodward as the *Post* courted him
too. "Ugly fuckers, you reporters."

‡ Baldwin said he was sure that Mitchell himself knew of the break-in, but he couldn't provide
any proof, so Nelson believed they couldn't publish that particular detail. Nelson just couldn't
believe that the attorney general would be involved in such an outlandish scheme.

As their meeting wound down, Baldwin approached Nelson with a special request: He had a girlfriend in Wisconsin he wanted to impress—could Nelson refer to him as a "husky ex-Marine"? Nelson took stock of the pudgy former lieutenant, an apparent lesser light of one of Connecticut's proudest political families—Baldwin's great-uncle served as the state's governor, senator, and chief justice of its Supreme Court—and thought, *What the heck, every story has its price.* Baldwin would be described in his national newspaper debut as a husky ex-Marine.

The men met the next day to go over the story again, as Guthman rushed Ostrow north to New Haven to help. The entire conversation was tape-recorded—a decision that would cause the *Times* no end of problems in the months to come—and Nelson stayed up until 3 a.m. dictating it to editors in Los Angeles, only to be awoken four hours later with an urgent call from Baldwin's lawyer: Watergate prosecutor Earl Silbert had somehow been tipped off to Nelson's scoop and wanted to block the story. Around noon, Judge Sirica—sick at home in bed that day—rushed to sign a preexisting request from Hunt's lawyers for a gag order, apparently spooked by both the impending Baldwin story and an attempt the previous day by Bernstein to pry information from FBI agent Angelo Lano. His order enjoined the Justice Department, the defendants, their lawyers, witnesses, and even potential witnesses, like the victims, from making "extrajudicial statements to anyone, including the news media." Silbert angrily read the order over the phone to Baldwin's lawyers in Connecticut, and then called the *Los Angeles Times* to advise against publishing.

The paper moved forward and under a dual byline on October 5, Nelson and Ostrow revealed the first direct link between the burglars and the Nixon campaign, filling column after column in the paper's main news section with Baldwin's tale, including how he had delivered "sealed sets of eavesdropping logs to the Committee for the Re-Election of the President less than two weeks before [the burglary]." (Baldwin said he couldn't remember whom he had handed them off to, but he knew it wasn't one of the seven people who had been indicted.) Yet it was the paper's second story, written using Baldwin's own words in an as-told-to format, that carried the real power: "An Insider's Account of the Watergate Bugging" began with the moment the burglars were busted, "Across the street in the Democratic National Committee I could see men with guns and flashlights looking behind desks and out on the balcony," and filled an entire page opposite the editorial page. Anyone who started it would devour the entire thing.

The story rocked Washington. Nelson's scoop, wrote David Halberstam, was "perhaps the most important Watergate story so far, because it was so tangible, it had an eyewitness, and it brought Watergate to the very door of the White House."*

*   *   *

Even if the White House was having a hard time bottling up the press, it managed to successfully stonewall Wright Patman's investigation. Following Nixon's order that the congressman not have a "free ride" in his inquiry, John Dean had helped organize a coordinated campaign to block the Banking Committee's investigators. First, the Justice Department's Henry Petersen urged that the legislative probe be shut down to avoid interfering with the forthcoming trials. ("This was supremely cynical," Dean wrote in his memoirs. "We were trying to make Liddy, Hunt, McCord and the Cubans the scapegoats for all of Watergate at the same time we were blocking Patman with boundless professions of concern for their civil liberties.") Then, the Nixon team also questioned Patman's own ethics, alleging Communist ties and pointing out that the congressman

---

* The *L.A.Times* decision to publish underscored the impracticality of Sirica's sweeping gag order. The *Post* also objected that it appeared to prohibit reporters from covering any aspect of the case that didn't unfold in open court and would even block George McGovern from mentioning the case on the campaign trail. Under immense pressure and facing heavy criticism from Capitol Hill, the judge eventually softened it, making clear it did not apply to the news media or to Congress.

The article also touched off another major First Amendment fight in Sirica's courtroom: Hunt's lawyers subpoenaed the tapes of Nelson's interviews with Baldwin, hoping to find inconsistencies between his statements to the *L.A. Times* and his court testimony. When the *Times* refused to turn over the tapes, Sirica summoned its Washington bureau chief, John Lawrence, to court and ordered him held in contempt. Two deputy U.S. marshals whisked the reporter, visibly pale and scared, from the courtroom without the chance to even say goodbye to his wife. He was jailed in the courthouse's basement for several hours while an appeals court reviewed the case, ultimately ordering him free pending a full appeal. Eventually, Baldwin's attorneys released the *Times* from its confidentiality agreement and allowed the paper to turn over the tapes for review, defusing the crisis and ensuring that Lawrence, a father of four, wouldn't spend Christmas in jail.

had received $1,500 for a speech at a Wall Street event arranged by Elias Demetracopoulos, the exiled Greek journalist and known Nixon enemy, whom the Nixon team charged was a "dangerous foreign agent."

They saw another opening when Patman sought subpoena power to compel witnesses to appear at hearings examining the financial shenanigans around the break-in. "This is a serious case—one which goes right to the heart of our system of government," Patman said, citing Nixon's own August plea to clear the air around Watergate. "It is obvious that there will be no 'clearing of the air' unless this committee issues subpoenas and conducts open hearings."*

When the issue came up for a vote on October 3, John Dean and House minority leader Gerald Ford outmaneuvered Patman, uniting Republicans against the subpoenas and even managing to turn a number of Democratic votes through varying degrees of political pressure and blackmail, including Brooklyn representative Frank Brasco, a normally solid critic of Nixon. At the vote, Brasco spoke about the importance of preserving the burglars' right to a fair trial—using almost word for word the defense that Dean had earlier outlined for the president in the Oval Office. "Politics should stay out of justice," he said, sounding almost as if he were a member of Nixon's defense team. Patman lost his bid for subpoena power 20–15.†

The chairman was furious. "I predict that the facts will come out—and when they do, I am convinced they will reveal why the White House was so anxious to kill the committee's investigation," Patman ranted to his fellow committee members. "The public will fully understand why this pressure was mounted." He then sent letters to Dean, Mitchell, MacGregor, and Stans, and asked them to voluntarily testify during an

---

* Bowing to Petersen's pressure, Patman sidestepped subpoenaing any of the indicted Watergate defendants.

† What was not yet known was that three of the six Democrats who defected were themselves the center of various political corruption probes—or possible probes—by the Justice Department. Nelson Rockefeller had helped orchestrate a meeting between Mitchell and Brasco, during which Brasco promised he'd stay out of the Watergate inquiry. Another member, Representative Richard Hanna, was already in the FBI's sights for illegal contributions from a South Korean businessman. This scandal, which would come to be known as Koreagate, would burst into public view only in 1976.

October hearing. He knew it was a long shot, and his colleagues agreed; Georgia GOP representative Ben Blackburn scoffed to reporters, "It would be absolutely crazy for a witness to appear." When the designated hearing date arrived, none of the witnesses or their lawyers appeared. Instead, Patman directed questions for an hour at four empty chairs in the committee room, each labeled with a name tag for an absent witness. "This is a sad spectacle, a massive cover-up," Patman said.

A photo of the hearing scene ran on the front page of the *Washington Post*, a Quixotic publicity victory that marked the final attempt to uncover the truth of Watergate before the November election. It ran alongside another Woodward and Bernstein story that would help turn the tide of the unfolding story.

Chapter 21

"I Can't Talk About Segretti"

I n early October, during one of his routine call-arounds, Carl Bernstein phoned the FBI's Watergate case agent, Angelo Lano, who quickly declined to speak and hung up, before calling back ten minutes later. He instructed Bernstein to meet at a nearby drugstore, and the two ended up sitting at the counter, drinking coffee. Though the reporters didn't know it, the White House's ongoing protests about press leaks allegedly stemming from the FBI had taken a toll; in late September, the head of the FBI's Washington Field Office, Robert Kunkel, had been transferred to St. Louis, in part because Gray suspected him of leaking or failing to adequately control leaks. (Subsequent evidence has indicated that Kunkel was indeed likely a key part of the "Felt faction" feeding anti-Gray storylines to reporters.) The investigative agents at Lano's level knew they weren't the ones leaking, but remained confounded about the press access. Lano had received special permission from prosecutors to meet Bernstein in the hopes of figuring out who the paper's high-level sources were. "You guys are causing big trouble. Our reports are showing up in the paper almost verbatim," Lano said.

The reporter and agent talked about the case, each interrogating the other; Lano seemed particularly interested in the *Post*'s revelations about Mitchell's control over Nixon's secret funds, which didn't square with the FBI's knowledge.

"The only person who knows I'm with you is my boss," Lano said, after they left and were walking along by the White House. Then he added, "Nobody believes the case stops with the seven who were indicted. The question is why did it stop there?"

One clue arrived days later, amid the final weeks of the campaign, through a rare random tip. The caller reached Bernstein and explained that his friend, an assistant attorney general in Tennessee named Alex Shipley, had been asked to help the Nixon campaign the year before. "Essentially the proposal was that there was to be a crew of people whose job it would be to disrupt the Democratic campaign during the primaries. This guy told Shipley there was virtually unlimited money available," the caller told Bernstein.

When the reporter reached Shipley, the Tennessee lawyer confirmed the tip and began telling an almost outlandish story about being approached by someone named Donald Segretti in June 1971 and invited to join a political espionage team. Segretti seemed to have plenty of money—Shipley said he flew around the country all the time—but he was always suggesting lowbrow pranks, like having a fake group called the Massachusetts Safe Driving Committee award a medal to Ted Kennedy as a way to needle the senator over Chappaquiddick or calling a venue where a Democratic candidate was scheduled to hold a rally and telling the organizers the event had been postponed. It was all simply about wreaking "havoc," Segretti told Shipley. As Woodward and Bernstein dug, a few other former colleagues of Shipley and Segretti—everyone involved seemed to have served together in the Judge Advocate General's Corps in Vietnam—verified Segretti had been involved in something strange. Bernstein also used a confidential source at a credit-card company to confirm that as the primaries unfolded Segretti had hopscotched across the country through 1971, stopping in key political states like New Hampshire, Florida, Illinois, and California.

The *Post* sent a West Coast freelancer named Robert Meyers to stake out Segretti's apartment in Marina del Rey—the lawyer appeared to have gone off on a business trip, according to neighbors—and finally after a week Meyers noticed that a matchstick he'd lodged in Segretti's front door had fallen out, indicating it had been opened. That afternoon—the same day the *Los Angeles Times* published the Baldwin scoop—Segretti answered the door, and Meyers began questioning him about his political espionage operation. "This is ridiculous," Segretti replied midway through the questions. "I don't know anything about this. This all sounds like James Bond fiction."*

Yet it didn't appear to be fiction as Bernstein and Woodward kept digging in D.C. The reporters uncovered hints that the Justice Department was aware of Segretti, and that his activities were part of the larger Watergate inquiries. He also appeared tied to the "USC mafia" in the White House, which included fellow graduates Ron Ziegler, Dwight Chapin, and Bart Porter, who had been one of the administrators of the campaign's slush fund. That couldn't just be a coincidence. "I can't talk about [Segretti]," a Justice Department official told Bernstein when he called. "Political sabotage is associated with Segretti. I've heard a term for it, 'ratfucking.' There is some very powerful information, especially if it comes out before November 7."

Intrigued, Bernstein called another Justice Department official, who immediately exploded when he raised the subject of "ratfucking." The source sputtered, "I was shocked when I learned about it. I couldn't believe it. These are public servants? God—it's nauseating. You're talking about fellows who come from the best schools in the country. Men who run the government. The press hasn't brought that home. You're dealing with people who act like this was Dodge City, not the capital of the United States."

The source explained that Bernstein's question tied back to a bizarre episode in February in which the *Manchester Union-Leader* had published an unverified letter alleging that Ed Muskie had referred to French-Canadians with the slur "Canucks." The letter had exacerbated tensions between the conservative New Hampshire paper and Muskie, leading to salacious reporting about Muskie's wife, and ultimately defined the doomed campaign when the candidate, standing in the snow, appeared to break down in tears as he defended his wife and attacked the paper's publisher as a "gutless coward."

Bernstein began to wonder out loud how high up these efforts went: *Was Mitchell involved?* "He can't say he didn't know about it, because it

---

* The conversation is rendered slightly differently in Barry Sussman's account: He says Segretti dismissed it as "This is material for a good novel."

was strategy—basic strategy that goes all the way to the top. Higher than him, even," the Justice Department official said. As Bernstein hung up, the phrase struck him: There were at a maximum two or three people who were "higher" than Mitchell—perhaps Ehrlichman, definitely Haldeman, and definitely the president. *Was the president of the United States the head ratfucker?*

*　　*　　*

Back in the newsroom, Sussman suggested to Bernstein that he try drafting a story to make sense of the various tidbits the reporters had assembled across the country. "Why don't we put it on paper, see what it looks like, and talk about it then?" Sussman said. He also pulled Woodward aside with instructions to meet his special source.

The identity of Woodward's source remained a mystery to the other editors and reporters on the Watergate chase; Woodward called him simply "my friend." Finally, managing editor Howard Simons nicknamed him "Deep Throat," a reference both to the source's insistence on operating on "deep background" and to the then popular pornographic film of the same name that celebrated a character's wide-open mouth.

Making sense of the Segretti story was precisely the type of lead where Deep Throat seemed useful, and so Sunday night, October 8, Woodward arranged to meet with Mark Felt in person. On the way, Woodward switched cabs twice and was dropped off several blocks away from their parking garage rendezvous location. When he arrived around 1:30 a.m., Felt was already standing there, smoking.

They talked straight through until morning, a conversation that finally allowed Woodward to grasp the full scope of the story he had been chasing. "Remember, you don't do those 1,500 [FBI] interviews and not have something on your hands other than a single break-in," Felt pointed out. "They are not brilliant guys, and it got out of hand."

He sketched out an operation that was unprecedented and sinister but also, at a basic level, routine and naive. As Bernstein's source had indicated, Mitchell was certainly involved. "Check every lead," the FBI official told Woodward. "It goes all over the map, and that is important. You could write stories from now until Christmas or well beyond that. . . . Not one of the games was freelance. This is important. Everyone was tied in."

Woodward was incensed by his source's vague allusions, and at one point, he grabbed Felt's arm in frustration. Felt relented. "You can safely say that fifty people worked for the White House and CRP to play games and spy and sabotage and gather intelligence. Some of it is beyond belief, kicking at the opposition in every imaginable way," he continued. "It's all in the files. Justice and the Bureau know about it, even though it wasn't followed up."

As the reporting team convened later in the day at the *Post*, Woodward recounted Deep Throat's revelations to his stunned colleagues. "Our understanding of Watergate had taken a quantum leap," Sussman recalled later. Then they got to work. The story, sourced to "information in FBI and Department of Justice files," ran on the front page of the *Post* Tuesday, titled, "FBI Finds Nixon Aides Sabotaged Democrats."

"FBI agents have established that the Watergate bugging incident stemmed from a massive campaign of political spying and sabotage conducted on behalf of President Nixon's re-election and directed by officials of the White House and the Committee for the Re-election of the President," Woodward and Bernstein wrote. It was a uniquely carefully worded piece—the verb "established" covered a lot of ground and made clear that the FBI hadn't exactly "concluded" that there was a massive campaign, but that its interviews had suggested as much. (Gray, reading the piece that morning, scribbled in the margins next to the lead sentence: "Have we?")

The operation, the reporters explained, ran the gamut from "following members of Democratic candidates' families and assembling dossiers on their personal lives; forging letters and distributing them under the candidates' letterheads; leaking false and manufactured items to the press; throwing campaign schedules into disarray; seizing confidential campaign files; and investigating the lives of dozens of Democratic campaign workers." The Nixon campaign delivered its typical response: "The *Post* story is not only fiction but a collection of absurdities"—but when pressed on the specifics, they refused further comment, saying "the entire matter is in the hands of the authorities."

Woodward, even in the heat of Watergate, would call the Segretti reporting their "largest and most significant story," but while the core of it was accurate, its most shocking detail—that Segretti's dirty tricks team consisted of more than fifty operatives—was inaccurate. No evidence would ever emerge that Segretti's efforts encompassed nearly that many people. It was possible that he had contact with fifty people over the course of the campaign, but he'd never had anything like fifty people involved in his trickster-ing and pranking. An FBI follow-up memo labeled the allegation "absolutely false," and for months, Simons would bug the reporters to find the "other 49."*

After the article ran, Dean called Gray to complain—again—about the leaks. Then, that evening, Dean's colleague Fred Fielding visited the FBI director to pick up yet another batch of raw FBI investigative reports for Dean to peruse on his own.

*   *   *

Even though the identity of Deep Throat would not become public for another forty years, Nixon already knew his name. On the afternoon of October 19, after a haircut in the White House barbershop, the president retreated to his hideaway office in the Executive Office Building to spend nearly three hours "chewing the cud" with Haldeman and, later, Colson, including his ongoing frustration with Watergate leaks: "You know, materials are leaked out of the FBI. Why the hell can't Gray tell us what the hell has left?"

---

* The Segretti headlines and their intense focus reporting-wise through the fall of 1972 in some ways also represented an all but unrelated branch from the main Watergate story; not only was Segretti's work almost entirely preceding and unrelated to the hard-core efforts of Liddy's GEMSTONE team, but he was even operating independently from Magruder's other trickster-ing efforts. Segretti, in fact, likely intersected the "dirty tricks" operation run by the operative Magruder had nicknamed "SEDAN CHAIR." As it came out later, they both—unaware of the other—had targeted a Muskie speech at Nixon's alma mater, Whittier College. A dozen chanting Nixon picketers had confronted Muskie at the speech, organized by Roger Greaves—the SEDAN CHAIR operative—even while Segretti passed among the audience handing out literature about Muskie's conservative position on abortion, which he assumed would (and did) rile up the student audience.

"We know what's left and we know what's leaked and we know who leaked it," Haldeman said, surprising the president.

"Is it somebody in the FBI?"

"Yes, sir," the chief of staff said. "The FBI doesn't know who it is. Gray doesn't know who it is. And it's very high up."

"Somebody next to Gray?"

"Mark Felt," Haldeman said.

"Now why the hell would he do that?"

"It's hard to figure," Haldeman replied. "Then again, you can't say anything about this," he cautioned, "because we'll screw up our source, and the real concern is Mitchell is the only one that knows this. And he feels very strongly that we should—we'd better not do anything."

"Do anything? Never!" the president agreed.

"If we move on him, then he'll go out and unload everything. He knows everything that's to be known in the FBI," Haldeman continued. "He has access to absolutely everything."

They talked for some time longer, discussing the challenges and delicacies of confronting Felt, and whether they should warn Gray. Haldeman explained that he'd already brought up the matter with Dean, but the lawyer didn't believe Felt had committed any crimes by leaking.* They also speculated about Felt's motive. "Maybe he's tied to the [Ted] Kennedy set? Maybe he's playing this game, building himself up?" Haldeman suggested at one point.

Then Nixon's darkest side emerged. "Is he a Catholic?" the president asked. "Find out. Find out."

"I think he's Jewish," Haldeman wondered out loud.

"Christ! I'm not going to put another Jew in there. Mark Felt is certainly a Jewish name. Well, that could explain it, too," the president said.

---

* It's not clear from the conversation whether Haldeman had any sense of the scale, depth, or breadth of Felt's leaks; in fact, the *Post*'s reporting is never mentioned in the conversations about the topic, although they do specifically discuss Felt's leaks at that moment to Sandy Smith at *TIME* magazine. Woodward, in his own 2005 book, *The Secret Man*, assumes Nixon's conversations were about him and the *Post*, but there's evidence that the source Haldeman cited actually was a lawyer related to Time Inc., Roswell Gilpatric, a former Kennedy Pentagon official, who told Mitchell.

As the conversation continued, they considered a transfer to a new field office to get Felt out of Washington, but Nixon ultimately agreed that the reward was not worth the risk. "I don't want him to go out and say the White House tried to squelch him and all the rest," the president said. "It's hard to think what would make him do that, but there may be bitterness over there that we didn't put Felt in the top spot." With almost a sense of Machiavellian admiration, Nixon added, "That's a hell of a way for him to get in the top spot."

The debate recommenced the following day, and Nixon brought Ehrlichman in. A plan was formed to keep Felt in check: They would issue their own leak about Nixon considering Felt as the permanent director postelection—a dangle that presumably would shut him up until any decision was made. As Haldeman wrote in his diary, "We found the FBI leak, and that it's at the next to highest level. . . . [Nixon's] concerned that we not do anything that blows it up at this time, but that we try to turn off any further activities so that it doesn't get any worse."

Back at the Justice Department, Kleindienst was hearing the same rumors about Felt from Mitchell. "He's leaking, Pat, and we know it," the attorney general told the FBI's Gray. Kleindienst had suggested to Gray five times already that he fire Felt, and Colson apparently offered similar warnings: "There are leaks in the FBI from the old guard." When confronted, Felt denied involvement and offered his own scapegoat. "[*TIME* reporter] Sandy Smith talked to Charlie Bates," Felt told Gray, naming the head of the FBI's criminal division. "He says his source is someone in the Department of Justice and it's the same as Bernstein and Woodward's."

A few days later, Smith was back in the pages of *TIME*, with some of the most explosive and damaging allegations yet against Gray and the Nixon team: "While the White House has tried to ignore some unpleasant FBI findings in the Watergate case, it has used the agency in an unprecedented way to aid the Nixon campaign." The article outlined an effort by Ehrlichman and Gray to boost the president's campaign message on criminal justice, and published a teletype to twenty-one FBI offices asking for help, because Gray had wanted to be sure that Ehrlichman could "give the president maximum support" on the campaign trail.

Playing both arsonist and firefighter, Felt told his boss, "The president was on the ceiling about this leak, and Kleindienst thinks it's someone who's after you."

Felt was, of course, talking about himself.*

* * *

As the election neared, the *Washington Post* team had, in Barry Sussman's words, "run out of gas," with no new developments post-Segretti and no stories to chase. "What scared me was that the normal herd instincts of Washington journalism didn't seem to be operating," Howard Simons said. An October Gallup poll still showed that 48 percent of Americans did not even recognize the word "Watergate," let alone have any sense of what it encapsulated, and even though the *Washington Post* team had written fifty-one stories on the scandal, the TV networks all but ignored it, struggling to find compelling "pictures" that conveyed its magnitude.

CBS's Daniel Schorr was one of the few TV reporters who seemed invested. Schorr had interviewed Al Baldwin after the lookout had spoken to the *Los Angeles Times*, and found his oceanfront interview in Connecticut chilling, listening as the onetime FBI agent banally recounted an executive burglary plot as if it were a routine case debriefing. "It was from Baldwin that I first got a sense of one of the great evils of Watergate—the way the aura of law and order was given to a conspiracy against law and order," the correspondent recalled. Schorr, trying to explain the drama for TV audiences, had done more walk-throughs of the Watergate building than he cared to count, so to get new video, he'd finally settled on filming stakeouts as the various civil lawsuits around the case proceeded—trying to grab a few seconds of witnesses passing him on the street while he asked questions. Witnesses hated the TV gauntlet. As he arrived one morning that fall, John Mitchell grumbled, "How is Larry O'Brien's press corps?"

---

* In another instance that winter, Felt made a stink about a leak he knew he wasn't responsible for and fingered prosecutor Campbell as the likely source, and used the opportunity to rail about the shoddiness of the reporters covering the scandal. "[Woodward and Bernstein's] stories have contained much fiction and half-truths," Felt wrote to his deputy, Robert Gebhardt.

On Wednesday, October 25, Schorr was waiting outside a D.C. law firm on 19th Street NW when Hugh Sloan and his lawyer arrived for a deposition. He asked the men about that morning's big Woodward-Bernstein story, "Testimony Ties Top Nixon Aide to Secret Fund," which had alleged none other than H. R. Haldeman himself as the fifth person "authorized to approve payments from a secret Nixon campaign cash fund, according to federal investigators and accounts of sworn testimony before the Watergate grand jury." The article said all five people who controlled the fund had been named in Sloan's testimony, but when Schorr asked, Sloan's lawyer was clear: "We categorically deny that such a statement was made by the grand jury."*

Hearing the denial later that morning, Woodward felt sick. *Had they made a huge error?* The reporters gathered their editors, each seemingly more stricken than the next at the news of the potential mistake. It was, Bradlee said later, "my lowest moment in Watergate."

The story indeed had been garbled; throughout their reporting, Woodward and Bernstein had relied on strict multiple-source rules, ensuring information was checked and cross-checked to extrapolate what they came to call the "best obtainable version of the truth." With the Haldeman story, however, they'd relied on a series of odd, opt-in and opt-out confirmations that confused their own sources and misinterpreted vague responses from Felt, Sloan, FBI special agent Angelo Lano, and a fourth Justice Department official.[†]

The Haldeman revelation, the reporters knew, would be huge—a link to the top level of the White House, from someone giving information to the grand jury. Looking over the story before it headed to press, Bradlee had insisted on going over the verbatim conversations with each source. "The numbers [are] getting terribly terribly heavy," he intoned, feeling the significance of their reporting. When reached for comment, Haldeman's denial, "Your inquiry is based on misinformation because

---

* Sloan was testifying as part of a Common Cause lawsuit trying to compel the disclosure of the "anonymous" pre–April 7 Nixon campaign donors, using the mechanism of the Foreign Corrupt Practices Act.

† In a later, lengthy statement to the FBI, Lano gives a different account of the conversation than the version of the conversation in *All the President's Men* recalls, outlining it as far more hostile than Bernstein does and in which he provided far more ambiguous and less useful answers.

the reference to Bob Haldeman is untrue," seemed pro forma and didn't raise any alarms. They knew the stakes were high, especially as news came that RNC chair Bob Dole had blasted the paper that same evening during a speech in Maryland, attacking the press generally and the *Post* specifically—fifty-seven times.

The day the Haldeman story was published, Woodward and Bernstein were meeting with their literary agent and editor to talk about turning their Watergate reporting into a book—the project that would ultimately grow, through many twists and turns, into *All the President's Men*—but the excitement of the meeting was deflated by the reporters' fears of a potentially massive screwup. At the White House, Ron Ziegler blasted the *Post* and its reporting, calling it "shabby journalism," "absurd," and a "blatant effort at character assassination."

After lunch, Woodward reached Sloan's attorney. "Your story is wrong," he said. "Wrong on the grand jury." The conversation grew heated. Woodward, desperate, tried to figure out how and where they had erred. He asked Sloan's lawyer if they owed Haldeman an apology. The attorney said he didn't think so. Woodward breathed a sigh of relief. Perhaps the gist of their story was right, but the sourcing had been misattributed.

In a rash move, Woodward and Bernstein rushed to federal court to find and confront Lano. The agent smiled when he saw them. Bernstein was incensed. "This is no fucking joke," he snapped. The reporters threatened to talk to Lano's boss if he didn't explain where they screwed up. Woodward waved the notes from Lano's Monday-night conversation with Bernstein at the FBI agent. "I'll deny everything," Lano said angrily. "I can't even be seen talking to you two bastards." He added a final "Fuck you" before walking away.

Down the hall, the reporters spotted prosecutor Don Campbell and confronted him.* Campbell angrily read over the notes of Lano's conversation and stalked off, reminding the reporters that it was against the law to monitor a conversation across state lines (Woodward had been

---

* In their book, they don't identify Lano by name and identify Campbell as "one of the agent's superiors" but FBI records released later make clear it was Lano and Campbell. The FBI records also show that prosecutors Campbell and Silbert were both present for the ensuing conversations, but the presence of both is not mentioned by Woodward and Bernstein.

listening in on Bernstein's conversation on another extension without telling Lano). The situation escalated quickly; Lano found them again in the hallway and ordered them to remain in the building. They panicked and left, calling their editor from the street, before returning to confront investigators one more time.

They found Lano and Campbell in Silbert's office and threatened to name Lano as their source unless the prosecutor and the FBI agent cleared up the mistake. "You're getting no answers from here," Silbert said with finality. The showdown was, in Woodward and Bernstein's own words, one of the most "unprofessional" moments of the entire multiyear escapade, one that could have resulted in serious legal trouble for almost everyone involved, not to mention major ethical problems for the reporters—outing an anonymous source to the source's boss was just about the worst sin in journalism.

Back at the newsroom, they chewed over with editors what had gone wrong. "You don't know where you are," Bradlee told them. "You haven't got the facts. Hold your water for a while." He then sat down at his typewriter and tried, repeatedly, to craft a statement to release to the other news organizations now clamoring for clarity from the *Post*. *Fuck it*, he thought, as he finally typed a simple statement: "We stand by our story."

Around 9 p.m., Bernstein finally reached Sloan by phone. He explained that, yes, his issue was just with the sourcing. "I never said it before the grand jury," he said. "I was never asked."

The next night, Woodward signaled for a parking garage meeting with Deep Throat. "Well, Haldeman slipped away from you," the FBI leader said, kicking the wall. "When you move on somebody like Haldeman, you've got to be sure you're on the most solid ground. Shit, what a royal screw-up!"*

---

* Unbeknownst to Woodward, Felt had had a front-row seat to the previous day's drama at Silbert's office; some combination of Lano and Silbert had immediately reported the incident to their higher-ups, and by the end of the day, a four-page memo and eight-page statement from Lano was on Felt's desk, to be dispatched to Kleindienst, Gray, and other Justice officials outlining the incident. Woodward and Bernstein's insistence that Lano was their source was "an outrageous lie," which Lano would swear in an affidavit. "Bernstein and Woodward have obviously gotten themselves into an extreme bind because of their false story and they are seeking to make SA Lano their scapegoat," the memo explained. Across the top, Felt scrawled, with his trademark elongated initial, "original delivered to AG at home evening of 10.26.72."

Newspapers across the country covered the subsequent White House denunciations. The following Sunday, McGovern cited the reporting on a morning talk show and Agnew criticized the *Post* on another channel, while *TIME* (presumably with the impeccable sourcing of Sandy Smith) reported in its new issue the Haldeman news was false. In response, Bradlee assigned Woodward and Bernstein to write a story clarifying the error. The duo explained they were "incorrect" in saying Sloan identified Haldeman before the grand jury, but that their "federal sources" had indeed confirmed "once more that Haldeman was authorized to make payments from the fund."

Disaster had been averted, but the short-term damage was real. Across town at the *New York Times*, the *Post's* missteps on the Haldeman "scoop" reaffirmed its decision to stay out of Watergate. As D.C. Bureau Chief Max Frankel said later, "They were writing stuff that we couldn't have gotten into the *Times*. Judged by what they printed we couldn't feel they had a solid hold on the story, particularly when they broke the Haldeman story."

That fall, as the election neared, Walter Cronkite joined his CBS colleague Daniel Schorr in the belief that Watergate deserved to be a national news story and made a final on-screen effort to attract attention—an extended, two-part segment that tried to explain the swirling, complicated scandal. Cronkite's interest in the story meant a great deal. He was the embodiment of journalistic gravitas and integrity—in fact the term "anchorman" had been invented in 1952 to describe precisely his role—and one of the evening broadcast's best producers, Stanhope Gould, carefully constructed a lengthy segment that explored the break-in, the political espionage, and Segretti's dirty tricks.

Cronkite loved the first segment—which ran to a full fourteen minutes, an eternity in a TV newscast that lasted just twenty-two minutes each night—even though by TV standards it was boring, repetitive, and complicated. (Gould reasoned the repetition was necessary in such a complex saga.) CBS executives balked at devoting so much time to a single piece, but Cronkite pushed ahead and aired it on Friday, October 27, just days after the Haldeman blowup.

"At first it was called the Watergate caper," Cronkite began. "Five men apparently caught in the act of burglarizing and bugging Democratic headquarters in Washington. But the episode grew steadily more sinister: No longer a caper but the Watergate affair, escalating finally into charges of a high-level campaign of political sabotage and espionage, apparently unparalleled in American history." The segment was highly produced, with photos of the main players and carefully labeled sourcing, painting the first national picture of what Schorr called "a kind of extra-legal shadow government, existing side by side with the constitutional government."

Chuck Colson complained immediately, calling the head of CBS, and over the weekend the network battled for hours over whether to air the planned second segment. It decided to move forward, but as a compromise ultimately aired just nine minutes of the second segment on Tuesday night the 31st, cut down from the originally planned fourteen. Even in truncated form, Cronkite's involvement shifted the national attitude, and validated the *Post*'s work. When she saw CBS executive Bill Paley at a party soon after, Katharine Graham ran to his side and kissed him. "You saved us," she exclaimed; Paley, who had borne the brunt of Colson's diatribe and all but ordered the second segment truncated or shelved, froze in dismay at Graham's embrace.

As the final days of the campaign ticked away and Patman's investigation seemed to fade from view, Walter Rugaber penned a pre-election analysis of what the *New York Times* called "the Watergate mystery" and the mix of "generally accepted fact, reasonable guesswork, and simple assertion" that united the three threads thus far seen publicly: the burglary and wiretapping allegations, the campaign's financial shenanigans, and Segretti's political mischief. From many thousands of words written over many months, Rugaber made the most important point in just two sentences: "There are still no definitive, conclusive answers to either of the key questions posed by the Watergate affair from the beginning: What are the limits in assessing blame? What were the intentions and actions of those involved?"

The questions would linger, unanswered, right through Election Day.

Chapter 22

Landslide

When Nixon's greatest life triumph arrived, he marked it alone, in serious pain. The campaign trail push to Election Day had been exhausting—Chicago, Tulsa, Providence, Greensboro, and Albuquerque—before finally finishing with a rally in Ontario, California, just a few miles from his boyhood home, on Saturday, November 4.

Speaking without notes in a speech that went on for too long, he tried to sum up all that he had learned and seen as president, from America's streets to the four overseas capitals he had been the sole commander in chief to visit: Peking, Moscow, Bucharest, and Warsaw. The rally inspired him. Thirty thousand people or more spilled out before the stage, stretching off as far as he could see, and the din of their enthusiastic cowbells and honking horns extended even farther. "I believe that we have the chance—and this is our goal—to make the next four years the best four years in America's history," he told them all. "This, of course, not only is the last rally of this campaign that I will speak to, it is the last time I will speak to a rally as a candidate in my whole life, and I want to say to all of you here who worked on this, to all of you who took the time to come, thank you very much for making it probably the best rally that we have ever had."*

---

* On election eve, he'd written in his diary on his first-term accomplishments—Peking, Moscow, and more: "The only sour note of the whole thing, of course, is Watergate and Segretti. This was really stupidity on the part of a number of people."

Early Tuesday morning, he arrived to vote for himself one final time, at Concordia Elementary School. Then it was back to Washington; there was no real doubt about the victory ahead, and the mood aboard Air Force One, the *Spirit of '76*, was, one observer remarked, "like coming from an easy win at a football game." Everyone ate Mexican food and drank champagne. Ziegler joked that the next day the *Washington Post* would carry the headline "McGovern Sweeps D.C." in its largest font, with a subhead that read "Nixon carries nation."

At home in the White House, Nixon ate dinner with his wife, daughters, and their husbands. Then mid-meal, he grimaced. He had broken a crown. He was examined for a half hour by the White House dentist, then went, alone, to the Lincoln Sitting Room to await telephoned updates from the campaign's election-reporting teams stationed in the White House lobby and at the Shoreham Hotel. His family, aides, and friends gathered in the Residence's reception room to watch the results. Nixon turned down an offer for a portable television set.

By night's end, he had swept every state but Massachusetts and D.C.; McGovern conceded, and Nixon addressed the nation from the Oval Office for two minutes at 11:54 p.m. before setting off for a victory party at the Shoreham. Colson remembered looking around the ballroom that night with an ominous feeling: "There was no air of triumph here," he wrote later. "The faces before us were unsmiling." Back at the White House, later, Nixon rejected draft after draft of a telegram to McGovern. "He could show no charity in his hour of his greatest triumph," Colson recalled.

Wednesday's *Washington Post* put it simply: "Nixon Wins Landslide Victory." The byline belonged to famed political correspondent David Broder, who wrote in his lede, "Richard Milhous Nixon yesterday won re-election as President of the United States in a landslide victory rivaling the greatest of American political history."

The word "Watergate" never once appeared in the 2,800-word story.

* * *

With the next four years and a national mandate secure, Nixon proceeded to move ahead with the second half of his victory plan: building a new administration from the ground up. "Nixon believed that second terms were worse than first terms, because the same people do the same work, and they are tired and lose their creativity and energy," then secretary of the treasury George Shultz explained. He was intent on avoiding the mistakes presidents usually made after winning reelection, and so in his moment of triumph, Nixon moved with alacrity to dismiss everyone.

In a series of postelection meetings where most aides expected to be covered in a geyser of gratitude for their hard work, he instead demanded resignations. The suddenness and discourteousness of the move struck even his senior staff, like Kissinger, as "appalling" and "degrading." Shultz too was crisp in his reaction: "It was cruel." There was, however, one administration appointee the White House moved quickly to reassure he was safe from the ax: Henry Petersen. As Dean said on the phone to Haldeman, "There's one guy we can't afford to piss off—one guy we need, who's been helpful, concerned, and who's been watching out after our interests." Dean reached Petersen just after Kleindienst had told the Justice Department's leadership they were all to resign, and he recalled hearing an audible sigh of relief as Petersen learned he was excluded.

Nixon ordered the rest of the White House staff to prepare what they called a "spent volcano" analysis, a job-by-job examination of who had fire left. "This is the time to face up to our mistakes in personnel and to get some new committed, hard-charging, capable people in key jobs," Nixon aide Fred Malek explained. Analysis in hand, Nixon retreated to Camp David with his inner circle to sit in judgment. The president had fought the bureaucracy throughout his first term; his second, he would control it—or as he said, "every goddamn Cabinet officer . . . and every damned agency head." For days and then weeks, military helicopters shuttled applicants and supplicants back and forth from Washington. Many were offered second chances; others were pushed aside.

As Nixon had promised that crowd in California, the next four years were going to be his—and America's—best years yet. As one Nixon aide bragged, "During the first term, we stopped their revolution, now we can move forward with our own."

Amid Nixon's larger administration shake-up, the White House cover-up machine continued to churn along, quietly reshuffling aides and trying to keep the hush money flowing to the burglars. Dean stayed busy, carving time out of his postelection honeymoon to debrief Segretti in Palm Springs, an hours-long conversation he recorded for Haldeman. At the White House, he also hosted a series of discussions with what he'd later call the "middle-level cover-up group," aides like LaRue and CREEP's lawyers Kenneth Parkinson and Paul O'Brien (no relation to the DNC's O'Brien), as well as with Colson, Ehrlichman, and Haldeman, about how to lock down remaining loose ends. Looking over the amounts of the hush money payments, O'Brien was shocked. "I think I'm going to switch sides," he joked. "Any of you guys have any break-ins you want me to do?"

Among the moves they settled on was rewarding Jeb Magruder with a job at the Commerce Department at the highest rank that didn't require Senate confirmation. Egil "Bud" Krogh, whose ouster from the Plumbers in 1971 had saved him from public exposure to the scandal, was promoted to undersecretary of transportation—a job that did require Senate confirmation, but he simply denied any knowledge of Watergate in his testimony, which was technically, if not wholly, accurate. Dwight Chapin, who had been Segretti's contact, headed for the private sector, as did Chuck Colson, who had long hoped to build his own law practice as the Republican equivalent of the Democratic power broker Clark Clifford. ("Colson can be more valuable out than in," Nixon said. "Basically in, he has reached the point that he is too visible.") Gordon Strachan, whose knowledge of the Liddy operation was seen as the administration's biggest threat, was transferred away from the White House and given a top job at the U.S. Information Agency. ("[Dean] said the important thing is to keep him in the government, keep him where he doesn't feel that he's been cut off at all, and just let him roll," Haldeman reported to the president during a conversation at Camp David.)

The plan worked for now, but as he moved each chess piece around the board, Dean became increasingly aware of his own exposure. "I took a sweaty tour through the obstruction-of-justice laws. What I found obliterated any notions I might have entertained that I had been protecting myself," he recalled in his memoir.

Howard Hunt was feeling equally jumpy as he and his lawyers reviewed the evidence supposedly seized from his White House safe;

he realized that Dean must have hidden away Hunt's operational note-books—the only documents, in Hunt's mind, that could have provided exculpatory evidence of how his actions were guided by direct orders from the White House leadership. As the trial neared, postelection, Hunt pressured the prosecutors for the whereabouts of the missing safe contents; Silbert, genuinely confused, asked the White House aides who had opened Hunt's safe whether Hunt was telling the truth. When the prosecutor's questions reached Dean, the lawyer—who continued to maintain that he'd turned over all necessary documents to the FBI—wiggled out of answering and flagged down a passing Henry Petersen. "Henry, I've got to talk to you," Dean said, putting his arm around the head of the Justice Department's Criminal Division. "Some of the documents were politically very embarrassing and we sent them straight to Pat Gray. If there are missing documents, he's got them."

"Oh shit," Petersen said, realizing the legal jeopardy prosecutors now faced. "You're not serious?"

"I don't have any idea how to handle that if I get called to testify," Dean said, his implication clear: If this wasn't resolved, it could lead to a witness-stand accusation from the White House that the FBI was obstructing justice. The ploy worked. As Dean recounted in his memoir, "I heard nothing more about being called as a witness."

The missing evidence underscored to Hunt the sense that he again was being cut out of the picture. He and his wife had grown frustrated with the stop-and-start payments from "Mr. Rivers," which never seemed to show up as needed—and when they did, the sum was always less than required.*

At one point in October, Dorothy had appealed directly to Colson's office for funds to pay attorneys, and the next month it was Hunt's turn to beg. At a prearranged time on November 14, he dialed Colson from a pay phone. "Commitments that were made to all of us at the onset

---

* In September, Ulasewicz had decided he wanted nothing more to do with the payments and returned the remaining money to Kalmbach, who in turn enlisted Fred LaRue to handle the payoffs. Later, in an ashtray in Dean's White House office, LaRue, Dean, and Kalmbach burned the ledger Kalmbach had kept of his payments.

have not been kept, and there's a great deal of unease and concern on the part of the seven defendants," he warned. "This is the long haul and the stakes are very, very high." *Money was expendable, men weren't*, he said. Colson tried to deny being involved at all. Hunt and his wife began to fear that with the election behind them, the promises from Nixon's team might drift away.

"I left the telephone with a distinct feeling that the White House had washed its hands of us," he recalled in his memoir. Ten days later, with no sign of progress, Dorothy told McCord the defendants appeared to be on their own.

*   *   *

On November 11, just a week after the election, Bernstein caught up with Segretti too. Out of a job, struggling to figure out how to make his car payments, scared, and rather pathetic, the five-foot-four USC grad hardly seemed a master covert operator. His family and friends were being hounded by reporters; investigators from Senator Ted Kennedy's subcommittee, which had launched its own Watergate probe, were calling left and right. "Hi, Carl. I wondered when we'd meet up with each other," Segretti said when they met, and he explained that everything had to be off the record. "I don't understand how I got in over my head."

As Segretti recounted his experience, Bernstein realized that the aide seemed more naive than anything. "What I did was mostly nickel-dime stuff," he told Bernstein and Ronald Meyers, the *Post*'s West Coast free-lancer, as they sat in his living room. "With fifteen cents or a quarter every once in a while." Bernstein stayed for five days, but was unsuccessful convincing Segretti to go on the record.

The reluctance was hardly surprising. No one appeared eager to take on Richard Nixon postelection, at what seemed like the peak of his power, and especially not by name. "Everybody dried up," Howard Simons recalled. "Who was about to talk with Nixon taking 49 states out of 50? So we were anxious."

Later that month, still struggling to advance their reporting, Woodward and Bernstein tried a new avenue to uncover what prosecutors knew and searched for members of the grand jury willing to talk about what had occurred during the closed-door proceedings. After consulting with Bradlee and the *Post*'s lawyers, they had determined that the secrecy oath sworn by grand jurors placed the burden on the juror—reporters were not prevented from asking questions. "No beating anyone over the head, no pressure, none of that cajoling," Bradlee warned as he gave the men the green light. "I'm serious about that—particularly you, Bernstein, be subtle for once in your life."

The first step was identifying and locating the jurors, whose identities had thus far been kept secret. Woodward decided that a low-key approach might be the easiest, so he took a cab to the D.C. courthouse, went to the clerks' office, and nonchalantly asked for a list of all jurors who had been called in recent months. He knew the Watergate's grand jury had begun in early June and the foreman had an Eastern European–sounding name, and using those parameters he quickly identified the likely group. The clerk, unsure if anyone was even allowed to be seeing the orange cards each juror filled out with personal details—name, age, occupation, address, phone numbers—cautioned the reporter that he couldn't take notes. Woodward carefully started memorizing four cards at a time, then making an excuse to run outside and jot down the information he could remember. It took more than an hour and several furtive escapes for Woodward to compile the twenty-five names and their contact details.

Back at the office, the *Post* team went over the list and tried to establish which jurors seemed most likely to talk: *Priscilla Woodruff, age 28, unemployed? Naomi Williams, 56, retired teacher and elevator operator? Julian White, 37, janitor at GW?* They eliminated government workers and military personnel—too likely to follow the rules—and tried to imagine who among the generic names and occupations might be outraged enough at what they'd learned to speak to a reporter. Everyone involved with the exercise was nervous and wary of being caught; they might not be technically breaking the law, but it still didn't feel right.

Over the weekend of December 2 and 3, Woodward and Bernstein approached a half-dozen grand jurors. Most played dumb, saying they knew vaguely about the case—"Watergate?" one supposed juror replied innocently. "I heard about it on the television, all that break-in business and stuff; there's no place safe in this city"—while others were more direct. One juror told Woodward that he'd taken two sacred secrecy oaths in his life: one to the Elks and one as a grand juror. He didn't intend to violate either.

Monday, with nothing to show for their efforts, the two reporters were summoned to Bradlee's office. "The balloon is up," the editor told them. One juror had reported Woodward and Bernstein's cold call to prosecutors. "Sirica is some kind of pissed at you fellas," explained the *Post*'s top lawyer, Edward Bennett Williams, adding that he'd been working hard all day to keep the judge from sending the reporters to prison.

When the paper promised that there would be no further attempts to speak with the grand jurors, Silbert and the prosecutors backed off. "I settled on a stiff lecture in open court," Sirica recalled; on December 19, with Woodward and Bernstein nervously sitting in the audience—both men dressed up in case they were arrested on the spot—the judge explained that a "news media representative" had approached the grand jurors, a matter he saw as "extremely serious" given their "sacred and secret" obligation. The other reporters present that day, unaware of the behind-the-scenes drama at the *Post*, were baffled by Sirica's angry tirade: Who had done what? After the hearing, Woodward and Bernstein tried to sneak out before anyone could figure it out.

Though the men may have felt lousy, their behavior may have been worth it: They had actually gotten one grand juror to talk—a lot—but it would take nearly forty years before the reality of that weekend's hunt became clear.

In 2010, Bradlee biographer Jeff Himmelman found a contemporaneous memo in the former editor's personal files from Bernstein dated Monday, December 4—the very day that Sirica confronted the *Post* and demanded it cease contacting grand jurors—recounting a conversation the reporter had with a source who would appear in *All the President's Men* by the mysterious moniker "Z." The source, hidden in plain sight for all those years, had a long, fruitful, and meaty conversation with Bernstein that unfolded across pages 211 to 213 in the reporters' memoir of the scandal and was described as a "woman [who] was in a position to have considerable knowledge of the secret activities of the White House and CRP." According to the book's telling, the conversation with Z occurred sometime after the grand jury episode, when the reporters "returned to more conventional sources," but Himmelman discovered in the memo that Z was actually a grand juror—a source so helpful Woodward would later cite her as one of his most important sources, apart from Deep Throat.

"Your articles have been excellent," the woman told Bernstein, according to their book, when he knocked on her door. She refused to speak with him but then slipped him her unlisted telephone number under the door and said, "I don't trust a soul."*

In a follow-up phone conversation that evening, Z explained that she felt the truth had not come out in the indictments and investigation. Like Deep Throat, she was hesitant to directly provide new information, but happy to point them toward previous clues and nuggets in their reporting that should be examined more closely. In the book, Bernstein portrays her wisdom as so smart that she "sounds like some kind of mystic," but there's little doubt in the Bradlee memo that Z is a grand juror. Bernstein noted in the memo that her unlisted telephone number "checked w. grand jury list number." She also told Bernstein, "Of course I was on the grand jury," and refused to answer other questions because "I took an oath."

When Himmelman published his discovery of the memo in April 2012, Woodward and Bernstein pushed back hard. In a five-hundred-word statement released to their own *Washington Post*, they dismissed it as inconsequential: "If Jeff Himmelman thinks his discovery of a December 4, 1972, memo on Watergate is a significant revelation, he is wrong," they wrote. "To the best of our recollection, someone contacted Carl and said there was a person, a neighbor, who had important information on Watergate. Carl went and interviewed the woman . . . [and] did not know she was a member of the Watergate grand jury when he arrived at her home." They added, "The interview with her had been of little consequence because she was not telling us much more than we already believed," which is why the episode garnered

---

* In the book, Bernstein says the Z conversation took place around 8 p.m.; if the date of the memo is to be believed, either it recounts a conversation from earlier that weekend, or Bernstein went out to track down yet another grand juror hours after the paper was chastised by a federal judge.

just two pages in *All the President's Men*, and why they had forgotten it further until 2010.*

Ultimately, as frustrated with their progress as Woodward and Bernstein were that November, they didn't need to wait long. Even as Nixon plotted his triumphant second term, the forces set in motion by the summer's break-in had acquired their own natural momentum. The scandal was set to break wide open just at the peak of Nixon's power.

* * *

Nixon had promised that he would make the *Post* pay for its meddling, and after the election, he began the squeeze. "There ain't going to be no forgetting, and there'll be Goddamn little forgiving," the president promised in one conversation with Ehrlichman that November.† Colson had plotted through the fall to attack Katharine Graham's bottom line, writing a colleague to ask, "Please check for me when any of the Washington Post television station licenses are up for renewal," and in short order, "citizen groups" backed by Nixon supporters challenged two of the Washington Post Company's TV licenses with the FCC—targeting stations in Miami and Jacksonville—a dire threat that caused the paper's stock to drop by half after the president's reelection as his fury became evident.

Another plot, uncovered later in Ehrlichman's notes at the Nixon

---

* It might be a believable excuse, but it wasn't entirely accurate. Thirty pages after the Z mention in the book, Woodward goes to meet with Senator Sam Ervin as he begins work leading the Senate's new Watergate Committee in January 1973, and turns over in his mind who would be most useful for the Senate probe: "Information from Deep Throat and Z and some other bits and pieces might help the investigation, conceivably could even send it on its way." There are a handful of other references to her over the rest of the book, like "the riddles of Z" on page 243 and "Z's statements" on page 251, that make clear her information and directional advice stuck with the reporters for weeks as the story unfolded, and that her involvement was not contained to just a two-page aside. As Himmelman concluded, "Maybe the moral of the story is that nobody gets to come out of the great mud bath of Watergate with his hands entirely clean."

† To Nixon, part of the paper's affront stemmed from just how "dumb," in his words, the underlying DNC burglary was. "Tying it to us is an insult to our intelligence," he told Ehrlichman. His aide responded, "We don't mind being called crooks, but not stupid crooks." Interestingly, in that same November 1 conversation, Nixon still appears unsure if the burglary was a Mitchell operation. "If he did [it], he's stupid," Nixon said.

archives, had suggested that conservative titan Richard Mellon Scaife buy the newspaper away from the Graham family; since it was publicly traded, if he offered enough, they'd be all but forced to sell. Nixon, though, didn't want to stop at the *Post* itself. One night, in a classic example of his "Alice-in-Wonderland off-with-their-heads" orders, he called Colson and told his aide to figure out how to force Edward Bennett Williams, to give up his role as president of the Washington Redskins football team.

Both Bradlee and Graham felt the enormous pressure of tackling a president at the peak of his power. Williams encouraged Bradlee through the darkest moments as the paper pursued the case, telling him, "Ben, the kids have got to be right because otherwise why are the Nixon people lying to you so goddamn much? If they're clean why don't they show it?"

As measured as she tried to be in public, publisher Katharine Graham recalled, "I was feeling beleaguered. The constant attacks on us by CRP and people throughout the administration were effective and taking a toll." At the many social events she hosted and attended, friends like columnist Joe Alsop and even Henry Kissinger tried to warn her to tread carefully. She was personally incensed when Bob Dole alleged in his attacks on the paper that the aggressive reporting was encouraged because Graham "hate[d]" the president. She wrote Ehrlichman directly. "What appears in the *Post* is not a reflection of my personal feelings," she said. "I would add that my continuing and genuine pride in the paper's performance over the past few months—the period that seems to be at issue . . . proceeds from my belief that the editors and reporters have fulfilled the highest standards of professional duty and responsibility."*

That December, Graham crossed paths with Woodward at a luncheon reception. It was the first time she really knew who he was. As Bradlee's biographer would write, "She had bet the paper on two reporters that she couldn't distinguish from each other until after their most important reporting had already been done."

---

* Graham actually ran into Bob Dole on a flight to the West Coast a few weeks after the election, and he casually dismissed the caustic remarks he'd made about her and the paper. "Oh you know, during a campaign they put these things in your hands and you just read them," he said. Graham was shocked; as she recalled in her memoir, "His reaction amazed me, dismissing so lightly something that had had such a powerful effect on all of us at the *Post*, especially me."

*   *   *

At the end of November, Liddy and Hunt, with their lawyers, met to discuss the lack of financial support from the White House. Hunt said he was increasingly embarrassed that the Cubans appeared forgotten; he had recruited these men—a recruitment based on their long, shared history—and vouched to them the import of their collective mission. As Liddy recalls the meeting, Hunt said they should start upping their demand for more money. Liddy stalked out, saying, "I just want everyone in this room to understand one thing: I am not for sale."

On December 8, 1972, Dorothy Hunt flew to Chicago to see her family, the same cousins Howard had hid out with that summer. Hunt was in his study, working on finishing his latest novel, *The Berlin Ending*, when his son arrived home from school and burst into the study, panicked. "Papa, in the car radio coming home I heard Mama's plane crashed and she's dead!" he shouted.

United Airlines Flight 553 had crashed while attempting to land at Chicago's Midway Airport; forty-three of its sixty-one passengers died, including Hunt's wife. News headlines quickly began to trumpet how investigators had found $10,000 cash in her purse.

By Hunt's account, the death of his wife of nearly a quarter century crushed him emotionally, sending him into a deep depression. He realized he wouldn't be able to withstand the mental stress of a trial, especially without her or the White House's support. "The government was still concealing the only documentary evidence that might establish I had been acting in good faith," he wrote later, referring to his operational notebooks and files that had been hidden by John Dean and Patrick Gray. Hunt began to consider pleading guilty.

Meanwhile, appearances to the contrary, the warnings about the money from Hunt rattled the White House, which started to put pressure on John Mitchell to sort out the cover-up, even as the co-conspirators remained unsure of everyone's role in their joint conspiracy. "We all know who should have handled this. Goddamn it, it was Mitchell and he wasn't handling it," Nixon fumed on December 11 to Ehrlichman and Haldeman. "John Mitchell has a serious problem with his wife. He was unable to watch the campaign and as a result, underlings did things without his knowledge."

"The minute you dump on Mitchell indirectly by saying he didn't have a chance to watch the underlings, the underlings are going to produce their diaries and show Mitchell was in 18 meetings where this was discussed, ratified, approved, authorized, financed," Ehrlichman cautioned.

"Was he?" Nixon said, still curious and confused about who had done what when in the conspiracy.

"I gather so," Ehrlichman replied, himself still unsure months later about who had known what and done what when.

*   *   *

As the year ended, McCord also stewed. He didn't like where he saw the burglary trial was heading; first, it seemed that the whole caper was going to be laid at his doorstep, the break-in some kind of rogue effort. When he protested through his defense counsel that he wouldn't keep quiet if that thesis was borne out, fresh leaks appeared to instead posit that the burglary was a CIA operation. That angered him even more. He had spent his entire life in service to his country and was a fanatical patriot, loyal to the agency above almost all else. He had imagined that he was continuing his service to his nation—and his attorney general and president—with his work at the Watergate and couldn't stomach the idea his bosses in the caper were trying to slander his former employer.

On December 28, 1972, he penned a private letter to Jack Caulfield warning that the White House should tread carefully if it was to blame the CIA and its director, Richard Helms. "If Helms goes and the Watergate operation is laid at CIA's feet, where it does not belong, every tree in the forest will fall," he warned. "It will be a scorched desert. The whole matter is at the precipice now. Just pass the message that if they want it to blow, they are on exactly the right course. I'm sorry that you will get hurt in the fallout."

Around the same time, acting FBI director Patrick Gray stood before the trash incinerator in his Stonington, Connecticut, home, and fed into a roaring fire, one page after another, the documents from Howard Hunt's safe that had been passed to him by Dean and Ehrlichman. He had flipped through some of them, and reassured himself that the files appeared to have to do with the Kennedy administration and the assassination of the South Vietnamese president. They were unconnected to Howard Hunt or the Watergate burglary, surely. "The clear implication of the substance and tone of [Dean and Ehrlichman's] remarks was that these two files were to be destroyed and I interpreted this to be an order from the counsel to the President of the United States issued in the presence of one of the two top assistants to the President of the United States," he testified later.

* * *

After months of the *Post* wondering why the paper of record continued to ignore their scoops, the reporting machine of the *New York Times* was finally focused on trying to get into the Watergate story itself; its editors and reporters in the Washington bureau were beginning to gather each day at 10 or 11 a.m. to discuss the day's news and what angles the paper should try to chase.

One day that month, *Times* photographer Mike Lien poked his head into the morning meeting and said that he'd been out drinking the night before with some Secret Service agents. "They told me something interesting: They said the president has a whole taping apparatus in the Oval Office—it's run by the Secret Service. They tape everything that goes on there," Lien explained. His tip was met with only silence. "Thanks a lot," someone finally said.

No one bothered to follow up the tip.

PART III

Brushfire

January–June 1973

Chapter 23

"Something Was Rotten"

History turns on the unexpected. In the opening months of 1973, as the 93rd Congress commenced in the Capitol, Thomas P. O'Neill was settling into his new role as House majority leader. O'Neill had been born in Boston's "Old Dublin," and just two generations removed from Ireland he looked every bit the part—the red face, bulbous nose, and *Bahstan* accent. "With the full blood of Cork City in his face," Jimmy Breslin wrote, he had gained influence in the rough-and-tumble world of Boston Irish politics, first understanding the power of patronage and political machines when his father was the Cambridge superintendent of sewers.*

In 1971, O'Neill had become the House's majority whip, the third-highest position in the body, and expected to spend the traditional decade or longer biding his time in the shadow of the new majority leader, Hale Boggs.

Then, just three weeks before the November election, the Cessna carrying Boggs through Alaska with the state's sole congressman, Nick Begich, had disappeared in the great expanse of the Last Frontier, crashing somewhere during a flight from Anchorage to Juneau. After nearly a hundred planes searched for forty days, nothing had been found. The

---

* On snowy days, men would line up outside the O'Neill door to get a token that would allow them to shovel out the city for pay.

unexpected vacancy in the House leadership propelled O'Neill—known as "Tip" to most of the country but as Tom to his closest friends—to the role just below the speaker himself.*

The transition marked a serious change for the House, elevating one of the great retail politicians of the twentieth century at just the moment when sensing the mood of the nation would prove critical. The House itself was also in flux, as a younger generation of congressmen—and a rising number of congresswomen—advocated for a more responsive and active legislature. It was a moment perfectly suited for O'Neill, who understood power innately—the illusion of it, how it ebbed and flowed, and what made men move.

He had witnessed plenty of hardball politics and thought he knew the world of dirty tricks inside and out, which is also how he knew that Nixon's campaign had gone beyond the accepted bounds. In fact, he had suspected something was off about the president's reelection effort for a year.

His suspicions had started with George Steinbrenner, a wealthy Ohio businessman who had revitalized a family shipping company on the Great Lakes. Steinbrenner had begun to dabble in sports and theater and chaired the Democrats' major annual fundraising dinner in 1969 and '70, so O'Neill noticed immediately when the shipping magnate didn't make his annual party donation in 1972. Steinbrenner refused to discuss the issue over the phone and instead came to see O'Neill in person. "Tip, it's terrible," he lamented. "They're holding the lumber over my head." Over the course of the conversation, Steinbrenner revealed that his shipping company was under pressure from the federal government on various fronts—safety standards, working conditions, antitrust, and more—and that he'd been told the problems might disappear if he cooperated with the Committee to Re-Elect the President.

Steinbrenner told O'Neill how CREEP had maneuvered him into a corner: He had first visited Maurice Stans, then been sent on to Herb Kalmbach. "I'm a Democrat, but I'll give you twenty-five thou," Steinbrenner had offered, only to be met with a quick rejection. Kalmbach

---

* The hope-against-hope for Boggs's miraculous return meant that for months O'Neill presided from an office that still featured Boggs's home-state Great Seal of Louisiana on its ceiling.

handed him instead a sheet of paper with the names of sixty loosely affiliated pro-Nixon organizations, the names of which all seemed innocuous and interchangeable, and wrote in the top-left corner an enigmatic code, "33@3, 1@1," which Steinbrenner instantly grasped: He was expected to donate $100,000 to the campaign, split among the maximum $3,000 contributions to any thirty-three different Nixon committees. Kalmbach added that all donations had to be in before April 7, 1972, the deadline of that new campaign finance law after which donors' names would be public.* "They had practically blackjacked them," O'Neill recalled later.

Around the same time, O'Neill noticed that other prominent donors had fallen silent, only to appear in "Democrats for Nixon" ads, and one of O'Neill's longtime Boston friends, Tom Pappas, a top GOP donor, even bragged to the House leader about how the campaign had set a $25,000 minimum for its donors. "Tom didn't reveal any dirty secret, but he didn't have to. A $25,000 minimum? That was unheard-of," O'Neill recalled. "The conclusion was inescapable: what we had, plain and simple, was an old-fashioned shakedown." Then, of course, had come the break-in and all the other strange reports circulating in the press.

Still, as 1973 began, O'Neill was hardly eager to dive into investigating the campaign; as partisan as he was, he was also institutionally disinclined toward investigations—viewing them as unnecessary noise and friction in what was supposed to be a still mostly collegial political environment. Nevertheless, he sensed that more would come and that the further revelations would lead to more trouble. "I was convinced that something was rotten in Washington," he recalled later. O'Neill went to Speaker Albert and used the "i-word" for the first time in January: "The time is going to come when impeachment is going to hit this Congress," O'Neill said. "We better be ready for it."

The would-be congressional players all shared O'Neill's initial reluctance to dig deeper. Neither Albert nor Pete Rodino, the also relatively

---

* What only came out later was that in addition to Steinbrenner's own $75,000 in donations, he structured an additional $25,000 in donations by laundering the money as bonuses to his firm's executives, who then turned around and donated the money to Nixon. The checks—including eight from other employees, all dated April 6 or April 7—had been rushed out from American Shipbuilding's offices and carried by hand by a company employee who flew to Washington to deliver them in time to the campaign.

new chair of the House Judiciary Committee, was eager to act. Impeachment was a nuclear option, used just eleven times ever—mostly against federal judges—and hardly any member of Congress remembered the most recent trial, in 1936. The Republican House minority leader, Michigan's Gerald Ford, had tried to lead an impeachment crusade against liberal Supreme Court justice William O. Douglas in 1970, charging he had ties to underworld gambling interests, but a six-month investigation by the House Judiciary Committee had gone nowhere, as the move was mostly seen for what it was: politics.

Impeachment of a president seemed even more unthinkable; it had been more than a century since the last time Congress had impeached a president, and the only historical exposure most members on Capitol Hill had to that case, against Andrew Johnson, came in John F. Kennedy's blockbuster book, *Profiles in Courage*, in which he had held up Kansas senator Edmund Ross as a hero for voting to acquit Johnson and save his presidency. "By 1973, the history books had come to agree that [Johnson's impeachment] was a shameful, politically motivated, tasteless event in American history," wrote UPI's Howard Fields. It was hardly an encouraging scenario as the members weighed their own role in history, and Rodino discouraged any such talk.

"You're not a lawyer," Rodino cautioned O'Neill. "You're only going on intuition, and you can't prove a thing you're saying."

For now, O'Neill would watch and wait. But he knew what was coming.

*   *   *

Richard Nixon turned sixty on January 9, and in a birthday-themed interview, he explained that his formula for living was simple: *Never slow down.* True to form, he started 1973 fighting hard on all manner of fronts—including a Christmas bombing campaign against Vietnam that had provoked protests at home and a battle in Congress over the president's right to "impound" assigned appropriations, that is, ignore Congress's priorities and refuse to spend money it had allocated for specific purposes. The postelection effort to remake the executive branch, as devastating as it had been to staff morale, had centralized power at the

White House to an almost unprecedented degree, purging the cabinet of personalities, stumbling blocks, and dissenting voices, and installing in their place what historian Arthur M. Schlesinger, Jr., labeled that spring "the most anonymous Cabinet within memory, a Cabinet of clerks, of compliant and faceless men who stand for nothing, have no independent national position and are guaranteed not to defy Presidential whim." Schlesinger hadn't meant it as a compliment, but Nixon would have seen it as such.

There had also been a massive sea change in American politics; less than a month apart, Harry Truman and Lyndon Johnson, the Democratic Party's two lions, both died, bringing a close to the postwar liberal consensus of the New Deal and the Great Society. Nixon—the first time this had happened in decades—was the sole president alive, and he seemed ascendent. Gallup showed him with a national favorable rating of 68 percent, the highest in four years.

There was still, however, the small issue of the Watergate break-in.

* * *

The morning after Nixon's birthday, the burglary trial finally began, more than six months after the break-in—delayed, in part, because Judge Sirica had pinched a nerve in his back. Public and media interest in the trial was huge, but it still seemed a sideshow, hardly something that could affect Nixon or his presidency. "My instincts told me that if the truth came out, things could be difficult for some of the president's friends and assistants," Sirica recalled, but never did he imagine that damage would reach the Oval Office.

Even before opening arguments, it was clear the proceedings would be unsatisfying to nearly everyone involved; Silbert and the prosecutorial team made clear that they wouldn't offer a satisfying motive for the crime, nor spend much time examining who ordered the break-in or why. "The indictment they had prepared was very narrowly drawn," Sirica recalled later. "Technically, they didn't have to prove a motive, only that the seven men were guilty of the charges against them. But the public was growing more and more suspicious. There had to be some reason these men had gone into the Watergate. Why not develop it?"

The seeming reticence of the prosecutors to dive deeper into a mystery they clearly hadn't cracked belied their generally strong reputations. "Earl the Pearl" Silbert was known for his particularly polished presentations; his mother joked that her Harvard Law School grad son was so meticulous that he even perfectly lined up the heels of his shoes in his closet. The forty-six-year-old Seymour Glanzer, the oldest of the assistant U.S. attorneys on the case, was equally scrupulous. In addition to Watergate, he had been working on a federal government case aimed at forcing the soda industry to drop sugar from diet ginger ale—a move to protect diabetics—and so spent much of the investigation sitting in an office stacked with cartons of various ginger ales. Donald Campbell, whose bald head and freckled face was dominated by his red mustache, had come to the case as one of the government's top wiretap experts, even sitting on the Justice Department panel that oversaw such investigative requests. He kept the team's detailed Watergate calendar, marking down with his silver ballpoint pen every date that witnesses mentioned, trying to make sense of what happened when.

Investigators had continued to run down leads from the burglary straight through December, tracking down every telephone call they could and crisscrossing the country to interview potential witnesses. In December, in Utah, they had located Thomas Gregory, the college student who had been a spy for CREEP in the McGovern campaign and had knowledge of the earlier May burglary at the Watergate. "That really strengthened our case because he could also identify Liddy," said Silbert. "It was one of those cases from a prosecutor's point of view—you have good evidence, you simply have to win it."

The day the trial began, away from the courtroom, Katharine Graham lunched with Woodward and Bernstein. The two reporters had desperately wanted to cover the trial themselves, but the paper's editors felt they were too close to the story; the trial was instead assigned to the *Post*'s normal court reporter, though Woodward and Bernstein would alternate sitting in the audience to keep an eye out for stray details that could help their reporting. That day at lunch, Graham asked the reporters, "I mean, are we ever going to know about all of this?"

Chapter 24

Guilty Pleas

E very seat in D.C.'s largest ceremonial courtroom was full as the trial officially opened on January 10, 1973. Jury selection had lasted just two days, during which a pool of 250 was whittled down to 12 jurors and 6 alternates, ranging from a taxicab telephone operator to an ink maker at the government's Bureau of Engraving and Printing. Each had been sent home with deputy U.S. marshals to pack a suitcase before returning to the courthouse for sequestering on its upper floors.*

Everyone was in position. The government's three prosecutors—Silbert, Glanzer, and Campbell—sat on Judge Sirica's left, opposite two tables filled with the defendants and their attorneys. Sketch artists crowded the galleries, trying to capture the drama of the grand room for newspaper readers and television viewers at home.

To start, Silbert spoke for more than an hour, outlining the case and the barest hints about the money trail—Sirica's ears pricked up when the prosecutor stated the government could only account for about $50,000

---

* A story related by Liddy in his memoir underscored the haste with which the jury was chosen: Most of the potential jurors were questioned en masse, as the individual questioning seemed to take too long, and in the trial's second week Sirica learned that one of the selected jurors barely spoke English and, when questioned by Sirica, had to rely on the Cubans' lawyer to translate to Spanish. Sirica was embarrassed to discover behind closed doors that he'd selected someone clearly unable to communicate in English, dismissed the juror, and sealed the record of the hearing to hide his own mistake.

of the $235,000 it had identified Liddy receiving from the campaign. ("[It] signaled to me that Earl Silbert and the prosecutors hadn't yet found out the full story," Sirica recalled.) Though Silbert laid out as evidence of wrongdoing a half-dozen other operations, including the placement of Thomas Gregory as a spy in Muskie's campaign headquarters, the government's ultimate theory remained that Liddy had been a rogue agent. "Liddy was the boss," Silbert repeated multiple times, seemingly content to argue that somehow a widespread and expensive operation had unfolded entirely without official sanction or supervision beyond a mid-level staffer.

Confusingly, Silbert also argued that the Cubans and Hunt were at the DNC that night solely for the money Liddy offered; the burglary's pay was a bizarre motive, and Sirica found himself frustrated already by the time he recessed the court for lunch. This trial, he thought, was a joke.

The afternoon provided a bit more drama; after opening statements from the lawyers representing McCord and the Cubans, Hunt's lawyer made an announcement: Since his client's efforts to negotiate had been thwarted, he instead was going to plead guilty to everything.

The next day, when Hunt stood before Sirica to plead guilty to all six charges facing him, the widower appeared fully broken. "He was a pathetic figure standing there, a former CIA agent, a man of some literary talent who had produced a small library of spy novels, the father of four children, and a resident of a posh Potomac suburb," Sirica recalled. Speaking before the courthouse, a defeated and fatigued Hunt said, "Anything I may have done I did for what I believed to be in the best interests of my country."

Friday morning, word reached Sirica that the Cubans wished to plead guilty too. The trial was recessed, and Sirica spent the rest of the day going back and forth with the Cubans and their attorneys.

These sudden changes of heart appeared all the more suspicious following back-to-back stories in the *New York Times* that weekend by Seymour Hersh, the reporter famous for his coverage of the My Lai massacre, alleging that the burglars were being paid "by persons as yet unnamed."

The story had formed after Hersh cultivated Frank Sturgis as a source. He had heard the burglar, a former Marine and Cuban freedom fighter, had been circulating a possible book project in New York literary circles, and secured a dinner meeting at Joe's Stone Crab in Miami. After the meal, Sturgis asked to borrow Hersh's rental car. Hersh agreed—if Sturgis told him the whole story. The result of the dinner and car loan was published on the *Times* front page. "One of the defendants, Frank A. Sturgis, acknowledged that payments continued after his arrest but also said that his funds had been sharply reduced the last few months," the *Times* reported. "Another closely involved source said that payments to the four men now ranged from $400 a month up."

It was a blockbuster scoop—one of the biggest of the entire scandal—but one that the *Times* as an institution seemed almost reluctant to publish. "[It was] a newspaper that hated to be beaten but didn't really want to be first. It was scared to death of being the first on a controversial story that challenged the credibility of the government," Hersh's D.C. editor, Bill Kovach, recalled years later.* Despite the paper's hesitation, it printed a second story on Monday, in which Hersh quoted a source saying that the burglars were under "great pressure" to plead guilty and that "a substantial promise of money had been made to the men" if they did so. The new details seemed to confirm *TIME* magazine's weekend reporting that the burglars might be secretly paid $1,000 a month through their jail sentence if they stayed silent.†

With the payoff stories the talk of everyone in the courtroom, Sirica accepted the guilty pleas and tried to quiz the four Cuban defendants about their motives and the money involved. All of them dodged his questions; at one point, Barker told him that he received the money in the mail in a blank envelope. "I'm sorry, I don't believe you," the judge chided, but he soon surrendered. The burglars weren't going to say anything.

So it was that by the start of the first full week of the trial, just two of the seven defendants remained: McCord and Liddy. Whereas Sirica

* As part of its recognition that it needed to compete more strongly on the story, the *Times* had deployed Hersh to D.C. and set him loose. The sneaker-wearing reporter fit so awkwardly into the literally buttoned-up *Times* team that the D.C. bureau chief, Clifton Daniel, gave him a box of Brooks Brothers shirts and sweaters.

† That Monday morning, Hersh was surprised to receive a telephone call from Woodward, thanking him for the big story on the hush money; the *Post* had been feeling out on a limb, particularly after the sustained postelection attacks from the administration, and the newly aggressive coverage from the *New York Times* had helped to provide cover and solidarity.

had hoped that the public trial might force the conspiracy behind the burglary into view, the combination of Silbert's limited theory of the case, the *New York Times* reporting, and the guilty pleas made clear that not only would this not be a venue for truth, but that the cover-up was actually both still strong and ongoing.

* * *

The sudden guilty pleas and hush money revelations came even as the White House continued its high-stakes back-channeling to keep the conspirators silent. The Saturday night before the trial began, Liddy had received a phone call at home. "Gordon, I think you'll recognize my voice," John Dean had said, without further identifying himself, and proceeded to lay out how much the White House needed Liddy's silence—both at the trial and amid Bud Krogh's looming confirmation hearing. "I want to assure you; everyone's going to be taken care of," Dean promised. "First you'll receive living expenses of $30,000 per annum. Second, you'll receive a pardon within two years. Three, we'll see to it you're sent to Danbury prison [a relatively comfortable minimum-security facility in Connecticut]; and fourth, your legal fees will be paid."*

"You said 'pardon,'" Liddy sought to clarify. "You know the difference between a pardon and a commutation?"

"I do," the White House counsel responded, "and it's a 'pardon.'"

Liddy promised he'd stay quiet, but took notes from the conversation and immediately handed them over to his lawyer.

On Monday afternoon, as the trial began, Nixon had stewed with Colson about the ongoing problems: "God damn hush money, uh, how are we going to [unintelligible] how do we get this stuff?" (The exchange, not released until years later, indicated he may have known about the money being paid to the burglars far earlier than he let on.) He and Colson debated how cleanly and quickly they could get clemency for Hunt, appealing to Americans' sympathy for his lifetime of service to the CIA, the death of his wife, and the need for him to help stay at home and care

---

* Dean's version of this phone call, told in his memoir, is decidedly more innocent than the version recounted by Liddy.

for a disabled child. "We'll build that son of a bitch up like nobody's business," Nixon ordered.

Over the days ahead, though, it became clearer that the walls around the burglars might crumble. The first crack appeared when McCord approached Bernard Barker and said that he was unwilling to be a scapegoat. He wanted Barker to cooperate with prosecutors alongside him. "This is too big for someone like me," Barker said, advocating silence. "When something is this big, leave it alone." But McCord couldn't. The former CIA officer appeared to genuinely believe the work he was doing for the reelection campaign was authorized and protected by the president himself. "Jimmy was not prepared for things to go wrong; the appearance of power caused these people to think that they had connections and would not have problems, so they broke down," Barker later explained.

Before long, word of McCord's plan reached Dean, who in turn called Jack Caulfield, the former White House investigator who had begun a new job as the head of criminal enforcement for the Treasury Department's alcohol, tobacco, and firearms bureau just days before the trial started.

Over a public pay phone line, Dean asked Caulfield to pass along an oblique three-part message to the Watergate burglar: *A year is*[n't] *a long time; your wife and family will be taken care of; you will be rehabilitated with employment when this is all over.* Caulfield, now one of the nation's most senior federal law enforcement officials, balked; this was a dangerous and inappropriate request. Dean settled on using Tony Ulasewicz as the anonymous cutout instead. Ulasewicz called McCord and reported back that the burglar had seemed satisfied with the message; a day later, McCord asked to see Caulfield in person back in Washington.

Through Ulasewicz, they made plans to meet at an overlook on the George Washington Parkway across from D.C. in Virginia. It was below freezing as an angry McCord slipped into the passenger seat of Caulfield's car. "I have always followed the rule that if one goes, all who are involved must go," Caulfield recalled him saying. "People who I am sure are involved are sitting outside with their families." Why should they be free if he wasn't? "I can take care of my family; I don't need any jobs," McCord told Caulfield. "I want my freedom."

Caulfield felt a wave of disgust and regret wash over him. He and McCord had been friendly, and had even talked at one point about going into business together after the election. It was partially on Caulfield's recommendation that McCord had become involved with the GOP at all. He told his former colleague that he thought the message from the White House was sincere. McCord asked who had given Caulfield the message; he only said it was the "highest level of the White House."

As the conversation ended, McCord left Caulfield with a final message: Twice in September and October, he had called foreign embassies in Washington—telephone numbers he knew were wiretapped by U.S. intelligence—and explained to attachés that he was a figure in the Watergate trial and wanted a visa to travel.* Similar illegal wiretaps had helped sink Ellsberg's prosecution; if the government and his lawyers could plot a motion to dismiss the case over the intercepted telephone, he could walk away free.

The next morning, a Saturday, Caulfield met with Dean at the White House to explain that McCord seemed more interested in freedom than clemency, and relayed McCord's threat. Then Dean, seemingly off-kilter, surprised Caulfield, hinting that the case had spiraled into a very sensitive area and might do real damage to the president—the offer of clemency, he stressed, was genuine and came from the highest level. Caulfield knew from his own time in Dean's office that the reference probably meant at least Ehrlichman, if not Haldeman or even higher.

Caulfield arranged to meet McCord again Sunday night at the same overlook. It was warmer, and two men walked together down a path toward the Potomac. They spoke for only ten or fifteen minutes, and McCord still wasn't satisfied. When Caulfield called Dean that night to report no progress, Dean was clearly frustrated. There wasn't going to be anything done with the embassy wiretaps, he said. This was all in McCord's hands now.

*   *   *

* One of these phone calls went to the Chilean embassy; there's an odd thread of Watergate that seems, often, to return to Chile, across the burglars, ITT, and other parts of the scandal, perhaps hinting at some deeper connections or further, still-uncovered plots and geopolitical intrigue.

With the opening days' initial crowds dissipated, the trial picked back up in Sirica's normal second-floor courtroom the week of January 15. The prosecutors began in earnest, calling Thomas Gregory and Baldwin to tell their stories about CREEP's odd capers. Baldwin's appearance on the stand prompted perhaps the sole interruption of the trial's steady march, eliciting an exchange all but forgotten by history and even mostly overlooked and misunderstood at the time: As Baldwin started to testify to his activities in the listening post, Charles Morgan—a civil rights lawyer representing DNC official Spencer Oliver and others—moved to suppress any discussion of the contents of the conversations that Baldwin overheard.

The reaction stemmed from a lunch when Silbert had explained to Morgan and an associate that he intended to show how the burglary was linked to efforts to blackmail Oliver. Morgan wanted to keep any mention of his client or the overheard telephone calls from appearing at trial, so he and Sirica worked out a procedure in advance that allowed him, despite the fact that he wasn't otherwise involved in the criminal trial, to lodge the objection to Baldwin's testimony—effectively speaking from the courtroom audience. Sirica, as planned, denied the request, but suspended the trial so that an appeals court could immediately hear Morgan's argument; the appeals court agreed with Morgan, locking away any details of tapped conversations, which remain sealed to this day. With the motion went the last—and potentially only—chance to know whether, in fact, the burglary and wiretapping plot had included a sexual motive.

At the end of the week, the court—and the nation—paused to watch Nixon's inauguration. The sequestered jury watched the parade on television from a private room in the courthouse that Sirica arranged. It was a day of triumph for the president; the *Washington Post*'s twenty-two-page special section, "The Nixon Years," did not mention Watergate once. The inaugural director was none other than Jeb Stuart Magruder himself.

To mark the occasion, Nixon gave each member of his cabinet and his top aides an inscribed four-year desk calendar, with each day counting down to the end of his second term on January 20, 1975. His inscription read, "Every moment of history is a fleeting time, precious and unique. The Presidential term which begins today consists of 1,461 days—no more and no less. Each can be a day of strengthening and renewal for America; each can add depth and dimension to the American experience.

The 1,461 days which lie ahead are but a short interval in the flowing stream of history. Let us live them to the hilt, working each day to achieve these goals."

The calendars would soon be useless. Nixon had just 566 days left in his presidency.

*   *   *

The trial's third week focused on officials from the Committee to Re-Elect the President: Robert Odle, the campaign's head of administration, as well as Herbert Porter, Magruder, and Sloan. The trial produced almost nothing of drama; prosecutors asked all the right questions, and campaign officials gave all the right, innocent answers. Liddy, who knew more about what had transpired than just about anyone in the courtroom, amused himself with rating the prosecutors' responses to various witnesses. "[Silbert] swallowed the perjury of Jeb Magruder whole but wouldn't believe poor Hugh Sloan who was doing his best to tell the truth," he recalled.

"Mr. Magruder, did you ever give Mr. Liddy any assignment concerning the Democratic National Committee?" Silbert said.

"No," the deputy campaign director replied.

Sitting at his bench, Sirica grew ever more frustrated. The handsome, well-dressed campaign official in the witness box looked every bit the model of a respectable young executive—"smooth as silk," he recalled—but he just couldn't accept the logic. The campaign really expected everyone to believe that amid this highly efficient, tightly run campaign, they were just handing out gobs of cash with zero questions and zero accountability? "It didn't make sense," Sirica recalled. "I just didn't believe these people. The whole case looked more and more like a big cover-up."

Unsatisfied by Silbert's prosecutorial efforts, Sirica started to intervene by questioning witnesses himself, without the jury present. From the start, Sirica had been more an activist and participant than many judges. His rulings through the fall, including the October gag order and the jailing of the *Los Angeles Times* bureau chief, had drawn widespread criticism that he was erratic. Similarly, his early behavior at trial drew unfavorable and uncharitable comparisons to the Illinois federal judge

Julius Hoffman, who oversaw the trial of the antiwar protesters known as Chicago Seven and had been blasted for his unconcealed distaste for the defendants—yet as the Watergate trial progressed, America found itself as frustrated and puzzled by the trial as the judge was, and courtroom observers sensed an earnestness to Sirica's desire for the truth. With each passing day, Sirica's incredulity from the bench became not only palatable but welcomed.*

"What was the purpose of turning over $199,000 to Liddy?" he asked Sloan on one such occasion.

"I have no idea," Sloan replied.

On and on they went, question after question, forty-two in all, with the former CREEP treasurer providing no meaningful answers. Sirica had struck out.

On January 29, Silbert gave his closing argument, repeating his assertion to the jury that "[McCord] and Liddy were off on an enterprise of their own." The defense, for their part, hardly offered much of one. Liddy and McCord seemed content to sit there and be made the scapegoats.

After hearing from sixty witnesses, it took the jury just ninety-eight minutes to reach a verdict. Both defendants, guilty on all counts. Liddy had expected nothing less; that morning, he'd kissed his wife goodbye as she dropped him at court. "Take it easy, kid," he told her, expecting— accurately—he'd be in jail that evening.

Judge Sirica set bail at $100,000. "I am still not satisfied that all the pertinent facts that might be available"—he said as he handed down the order—"I say *might* be available—have been produced before an American jury." He set a March 23 sentencing, already knowing the seven defendants would receive stiff prison terms. "I would frankly hope, not only as a judge but as a citizen of a great country and one of millions of Americans who are looking for certain answers, I would hope that the Senate committee gets to the bottom of what happened."

With the trial over, John Dean began to worry about what would happen if more inquiries were opened. He dug out Hunt's two Hermès notebooks from his safe and fed them into his office shredder. "Destroying

---

* "Watergate was kept alive in the early months because of the determination of Judge John Sirica to get to the truth," the DNC's Lawrence O'Brien recalled later.

the notebooks was only a small addition to a whole string of criminal acts I had committed, but it seemed to me to be a moment of high symbolism," Dean said later. "[It] shredded the last of my feeble rationalizations that I was an agent rather than a participant—a lawyer defending guilty clients, rather than a conspirator."*

Dean was hardly the only one with an ominous mood. As the month's events changed perceptions across the capital, Ehrlichman scribbled a note to Haldeman: "There is something rancid about the way things are going just now."

---

* The Hermès notebook episode is an important, illustrative case study of how Dean reckoned with his own role. He went to great lengths to hide the notebooks—they were, as far as Hunt and Dean agree, the only items from Hunt's safe that were neither turned over to the FBI routinely nor part of the special "sensitive" files handed directly to Gray (and ultimately destroyed by him). Presumably that means that Dean studied the notebooks carefully enough at the start to realize they were too sensitive to hand over even to Gray, but then he purported to forget about them in his safe until Hunt started about them—at which point he misled both Silbert and Petersen about their whereabouts and existence. Then he purported to forget about them again until he destroyed them post-trial—then forgot about that act of destruction weeks later when he began to cooperate with investigators. He only "remembered" destroying the notebooks in November 1973, after he had already settled his own criminal case, at which point he told prosecutors a far more innocent story than what was later published in his memoir—for instance, he said in the memoir that he "leafed through them" before destroying them, whereas he told prosecutors he "did not look at the contents and cannot recall what might have been in them."

Chapter 25

The "Country Lawyer" Enters

U.S. senator Sam Ervin hadn't been present when his Democratic colleagues launched the process that would transform him into a household name. Instead, he had been stuck at home in North Carolina, felled by a January storm, when his party's caucus voted to appoint a special "select" committee on Watergate. They also decided that he would be the one to lead it.

Like Tip O'Neill on the House side, Senate Majority Leader Mike Mansfield had resisted a formal congressional inquiry into the brewing presidential scandal. The summer before, he'd quickly dismissed the idea that the president was involved in the odd caper at the DNC offices, and "when Watergate jokes were going around, he wouldn't listen to one, or repeat one, for love nor money," his aide Peggy DeMichele later recalled. Gradually, though, he'd come around to the need, as reports grew more detailed, and more serious. The trial clearly hadn't delivered the answers the American people wanted—and it seemed necessary for Congress to step in.

Like the House, the Senate had recently been experiencing its own political shift. For decades, the Democratic bloc in Congress had been split between the northern urban machines, like the Irish of Boston and Chicago, and the unapologetically segregationist southerners, until Lyndon Johnson's civil rights push upended the status quo. The South was shifting Republican, but many of the Hill's top committees were still ruled by Dixiecrat politicians like James Eastland and Sam Ervin, the two men who respectively led the committees that seemed most apt to investigate the burglary cover-up—Judiciary and Government Operations. Mansfield was resistant to his options: Each committee was both large, filled with unwieldy egos under the best of times, and populated by men who had been targeted by Nixon and his campaign's "dirty tricks": Ted Kennedy was a high-profile member of Judiciary, while "Scoop" Jackson and Ed Muskie sat on Government Operations.

Ultimately, he settled on building a new committee around Ervin. A former state associate supreme court justice, the North Carolina senator had judicial experience, a reputation for being nonpartisan, and—most importantly—harbored no apparent higher ambition. A self-proclaimed "country lawyer," he held an intense interest in constitutional rights and civil liberties, as well as possessing a sharp legal intellect that he'd regularly deployed through the fifties and sixties to protect Jim Crow laws and segregation. Ervin had done battle with the Nixon administration already over issues like "impoundment," an obscure but fraught separation-of-powers fight over the president refusing to spend monies appropriated and directed by Congress, but "I knew he'd be fair-minded," Mansfield said later.

For the committee itself, Mansfield carefully selected members who would likely not use the perch for personal political gain. Formally known as the "Select Committee on Presidential Campaign Activities," Ervin's panel ultimately included three other Democrats—Hawaii's Daniel Inouye, New Mexico's Joseph Montoya, and Georgia's Herman Talmadge—as well as three Republicans—Tennessee's Howard Baker served as the ranking member, alongside Florida's Edward Gurney and Connecticut's Lowell Weicker. It was as close to an assemblage of honest brokers as one could likely find in the U.S. Senate. The group was approved in early February by a unanimous, bipartisan 77–0.*

---

* Nixon, for his part, was wary of Ervin from the start. He told Dean in a February 28, 1973, meeting, "Ervin works harder than most of our Southern gentlemen. They are great politicians. They are just more clever than the minority—just more clever!" Ervin, though, had low expectations going into the whole project. "I suspected the committee might discover by its investigation that some overzealous aides of President Nixon had overstepped the bounds of political decency," he recalled later. "It was inconceivable to me at that time, however, that President Nixon was personally involved."

The same afternoon Sirica debated bail for McCord and Liddy, Ervin began the work of assembling his team. First, he summoned Sam Dash, a criminal law professor from Georgetown Law School. Dash had written a well-respected treatise on eavesdropping and seemed a solid candidate to lead the committee staff. As the men met at the Capitol, Dash was immediately struck by the North Carolina senator—big and jovial, with a ruddy face, he played his background as a simple country lawyer to the hilt, but led from a solid core.

"This Watergate investigation is a mighty important assignment. It has to be the most thorough and objective inquiry ever made by the Senate," Ervin explained. "It must be broad enough to cover everything that needs to be looked into, and the committee must be given all the powers necessary for such a broad investigation." Together, Ervin, Dash, and assorted advisors reviewed the draft resolution Ervin planned to bring to his senate colleagues for authorization. He was impressed with Dash's suggestions, which strengthened the committee's mandate as well as its investigative powers, and on February 20, he offered him the role of chief counsel.

For the first month, Dash's only workspace was a spare conference table in the office of Ervin staffer Rufus Edmisten, who had been recruited to serve as deputy chief counsel. The arrangement became untenable, as the committee staff juggled job interviews, media interviews, and document gathering, and soon they were given use of the Senate auditorium, to partition into the necessary offices.

On the Republican side, ranking member Howard Baker had chosen a Tennessee lawyer named Fred Thompson to be Dash's counterpart. Thirty years old, he had spent three years as an assistant U.S. attorney before working on Baker's campaign staff in 1972. Thompson was summoned to Washington with just a day's notice and spent the intervening night at the Vanderbilt University library reading through news clips about the scandal. "The only names I could recall without prompting were Howard Hunt and Gordon Liddy, and my only reaction to the case had been a vague feeling that every political campaign has a few crack-pots who cause embarrassment," he recalled. "Watergate may not have seemed like much of an event in Nashville, but I soon discovered that in Washington the scandal and the Watergate committee were the biggest action in town."

As the two lawyers met for an initial lunch at the Monocle, a famed and favorite haunt close to the Senate side of Capitol Hill, Dash appraised Thompson and his thick drawl. "Physically, he seemed to dominate the room—he was tall, big-boned and husky. He had a broad, handsome face and a full head of thick brown hair that curled down to the back of his neck," Dash recalled. Thompson explained he would commute back and forth to Nashville for the duration of the investigation. He then surprised Dash by saying that he expected them to be done by summer, even though the committee had until February 1974 to complete its work. "We're not going to need a year," he confidently told Dash.

Dash was dubious; he saw at least three investigations looming, each of which seemed daunting and time-consuming: the break-in itself, the campaign of dirty tricks, and the broader questions around illegal campaign finance practices, and he had recruited associate counsels from across the country to lead those three task forces: James Hamilton, a trial lawyer at one of D.C.'s top firms, Covington and Burling, would head the break-in team; Terry Lenzner, a former Justice Department lawyer in the Civil Rights Division, would lead the dirty tricks task force; and Dave Dorsen, the deputy chief of investigations for New York City, would oversee the investigators examining campaign financing.* At Ervin's suggestion, the committee had also named a forensic accountant and former FBI agent–turned–Kennedy family aide, Carmine Bellino, as its chief investigator. Bellino had worked for Jack Kennedy before helping his brother target Jimmy Hoffa during Bobby's tenure as attorney general; more recently, he had worked with Ted in the early stages of his subcommittee's own Watergate probe. "Bellino appeared easygoing and kindly in private conversations, but he gave me the impression that inside he was tough as a pine knot," Thompson recalled. "He was seldom seen and he conducted his part of the investigation—accounting was his specialty—by himself."

Despite the scope of the investigations ahead, expectations were modest. "I don't believe any senator or staff member believed that this would end up implicating the president or his senior officials. At most it might lead

---

* Hamilton passed for the diversity hire: Unlike Dash, Dorsen, and Lenzner, all Harvard Law grads, Hamilton had gone to Yale.

to legislation to prohibit unfair campaign practices," task force leader Terry Lenzner recalled later. At one of the early closed-door committee meetings, Republican member Lowell Weicker speculated responsibility for the burglary might trace back to Haldeman. The room was aghast. "Mind you, he wasn't even accusing the president—but to think that he was virtually accusing the president's right-hand man! Most of us were incredulous," recalls Donald Sanders, a former FBI agent and veteran of the Hill who served as the Republican deputy counsel on the committee.

There was also not much of a track record at that time of congressional investigations; high-profile inquiries were more the exception than the norm, and they had little playbook to draw from.* To start, Lenzner had asked the staff to collect every employee list they could find from the White House, RNC, and CREEP and begin building "satellite charts," to see who around the main investigative targets might have relevant information. In an age before Google and online databases, retrieving biographical information on potential witnesses and targets often involved poring over microfilm and newspapers. Investigators spent time cloistered in the Library of Congress, while Dash and Thompson often spent several hours a day at the Justice Department, reading the FBI's investigative files.

Somewhat counterintuitively, the committee had decided that starting the investigation and congressional hearings by focusing on the break-in itself might not prove fruitful. The end of the public trial meant there wasn't much more to immediately dig into. To maximize their opportunity and impact, the committee's first subpoena went to Donald Segretti with the hope of jump-starting an inquiry into the Nixon campaign's political dirty tricks.

As the committee staff began their targeted work, one of Dash's first meetings was with Bob Woodward. He wanted to propose what he called an "unusual arrangement," in which the reporter would share investigative leads with the committee with no expectation of receiving information in return. "Bob agreed to help," Dash later recalled, but "this

---

* One member of the Ervin Committee, James Hamilton, would actually go on to write the definitive history of congressional investigations, *The Power to Probe*, a book that underscored how few real analogues there were to the work Ervin set forth to accomplish. Hamilton cites, for instance, previous examples about Congress's attempt to investigate the debacle at Bull Run at the opening of the Civil War.

relationship never proved productive." In fact, he added, "It wasn't long before our knowledge of the facts far exceeded Woodward's."

∗   ∗   ∗

In early February, John Ehrlichman summoned John Dean to California, where Nixon was spending the weekend and his inner circle wanted to privately discuss how to handle the impending Senate probe. Haldeman, Ehrlichman, Dean, and a fourth White House aide, Robert Moore, convened at Haldeman's villa at the La Costa Resort Hotel for more than twelve hours of discussion. Though the group had successfully navigated the FBI investigation so far, they understood that the Senate was a fundamentally different beast—the committee had broad jurisdiction and an uncertain set of members, none of whom was under the president's control, and several of whom were relative unknowns. When he read through the congressional directory entry on Senator Inouye, Ehrlichman explained his name was pronounced "Ain't no way," then joked, "Ain't no way he's going to give us anything but problems." Only Gurney, they decided, could be counted on to help the White House.

With time, they refined a strategy: Nothing but full cooperation in public, but behind the scenes the White House would box in the Senate inquiry and push the message in the press that the committee was a partisan sham. As their conversation wound down, Ehrlichman raised a big question: Would the original seven Watergate defendants remain silent? No one really knew, but Dean mentioned that the defendants were still asking for more money. In response, Ehrlichman issued clear instructions that Mitchell should be told it was his responsibility to raise the money to keep the defendants quiet.

Later, Haldeman handed Dean several memos that all but explicitly laid out how the White House would continue to block the truth about the burglary and the campaign's activities.* "The coverup had become a way of life at the White House, and having made it to this point, those involved were becoming careless and more open about it," Dean recalled.

---

* In the days ahead, Haldeman even twice contacted local GOP officials in North Carolina in an attempt to uncover dirt on Ervin that could be used to discredit the Senate inquiry.

Ehrlichman, who had long tried to avoid the Watergate fallout, walked out of the meetings worried; their situation seemed precarious. As he recalled, "I heard enough to trouble me deeply."

Inside the Oval Office, the president was also beginning to express more explicit concern. On February 13, Nixon told Colson, "When I'm speaking of Watergate . . . this tremendous investigation rests unless one of the seven [defendants] begins to talk. That's the problem." The conversation picked up again the next day: "We gotta cut our losses. My losses are to be cut. The President's losses got to be cut on the cover-up deal."

"This is a tough one—because there's so many players, and so God damn sad I think of those seven guys—" he said.

"So do I," Colson interrupted.

"—who are involved, you know, Jesus Christ, they did it with good intentions," Nixon continued. "I guess they must have known that they had to take this kind of risk."

*   *   *

James McCord, who indeed believed he'd only ever had good intentions, was vacillating about whether to fold. He hadn't given up hope that the White House would intervene in his case, even with the guilty verdicts in hand.

McCord and Caulfield met a third and final time at their chosen George Washington Parkway overlook, before driving off together through rural Virginia. They talked, as friends, for an hour or two, expressing regret about the situation McCord now found himself in, about their families, and about Caulfield's new law enforcement role at the Treasury Department. From time to time, they cycled back to Watergate. It gradually became clear to Caulfield that McCord was going to break his silence. He didn't know when or where or how, but as he'd promised, McCord wasn't going to take the fall for the burglary.

As their conversation ended, Caulfield offered his friend advice. "Jim, I have worked with these people, and I know them to be as tough-minded as you and I. When you make your statement, don't underestimate them," he said. Then, he paused, and offered his own counsel: "If I were in your shoes, I would probably do the same thing."

Chapter 26

"Twist Slowly,
Slowly in the Wind"

The catastrophic miscalculations that would finally crack Watergate wide open began in February 1973 with Nixon's decision to nominate Patrick Gray as permanent director of the FBI. Gray had narrowly avoided being replaced in Nixon's victory-tour purge of "spent volcanoes." Nixon had intended to send him to a non-Senate-confirmed role in the Office of Emergency Preparedness or the Arms Control and Disarmament Agency, and replace him at the bureau with D.C. police chief Jerry Wilson. But before they could implement the moves, Gray was suddenly hospitalized for more than six weeks with a recurring gastrointestinal problem, leaving Mark Felt in charge of the bureau. By the time Gray recuperated and returned to work in January, Nixon's calculus had changed and the Wilson plan was shelved.

By February 1973, with the Senate inquiry looming, loyalty now seemed paramount. "[Gray] is a guy we can tell to do things and he will do them," Ehrlichman said to the president. Plus, they figured Gray could help in his confirmation hearing by emphasizing what a thorough investigation into Watergate the bureau had conducted.* In that same

---

* Writing in his diary, Nixon said, "It is a true story of a thorough investigation and this of course knocks down the cover-up. As I emphasized to Ehrlichman and Haldeman and Colson, but I am not sure that they all buy it, it is the cover-up, not the deed, that is really bad here."

February 14 conversation, Ehrlichman told Nixon for the first time about how he and Dean had turned over Hunt's sensitive files to Gray for him to hide. "[Gray] has some guilty knowledge in connection with the Watergate," Ehrlichman said, adding confidently, "That'll never come out."

On Friday, February 16, Nixon met with Gray and told him he would be officially nominated for the FBI's top job, though the conversation's primary topic ended up being the president railing about the scandals engulfing him. "This country, this bureaucracy—Pat, you know this, it's crawling with, Pat, at best, at best unloyal people and at worst treasonable people," Nixon said. "We have to get them, break them."

Nixon made clear that the first target to break was Mark Felt, whom he suspected of fueling the Watergate press coverage with his polygamous leaking. In January, after seeing a *Washington Post* story that Nixon suspected came from the FBI deputy, he'd complained to Haldeman, "The point you ought to make about this . . . Gray's got to—it seems to me—he's got to get Felt off of this [case]"—and now, he lectured Gray directly. "The only problem you have on Felt is that the lines lead very directly to him, and I can't believe it, but they lead right there," the president said. "It would be very, very difficult to have Felt in that [number two] position without having that [leaking] charge cleared up. And, incidentally, let me say this—this is also a directive—you should take a lie detector test on him."

Gray left the Oval Office meeting shaken; he had achieved his dream of leading the bureau, but in the process had seen an ugly side of a man he'd known and respected for more than a decade. "For thirty minutes, he lectured me on leaks, lie detector tests, cracking the whip, and developing a ruthless style of leadership," he wrote later. "Nixon was not Nixon."

To prepare for his confirmation hearing, Gray quickly convened the bureau's top Watergate investigators on February 23 to review progress and ensure he could explain the status to inquisitive senators. The meeting turned sour fast when Gray confessed to his investigators that he'd been giving their reports directly to John Dean.

"You did *what?!*" Angelo Lano asked, sputtering in anger. The others in the room looked on, aghast. Gray tried to defend himself, explaining that Hoover had routinely passed information to the White House, but Lano objected. "When you're investigating the people at the White House, you don't tell them you're investigating!"

Suddenly, for Lano, it all began to click—Dean had always seemed to be a few steps ahead of the investigators because he was, indeed, a few steps ahead. He left the meeting and went directly to Silbert. "We were screwed from the beginning, Earl," Lano told his colleague. "Pat Gray had given John Dean everything."

As the proceedings began at the end of February, it became clear the senators overseeing Gray's confirmation felt similarly wary about the acting director. Many perceived (accurately) that he had been selected out of his loyalty to the president, and while Gray tried to highlight his active leadership of the bureau and pointed to the progressive policies he'd implemented—like starting to hire female agents—the inquiries from senators constantly veered back toward Watergate. Gray stumbled with almost every exchange.

Realizing the danger he faced, Gray made a desperate, wild offer to reassure the senators of his independence and strength: He would make available to any interested senator the same investigative files he had delivered to Dean. ("What's the matter with him? For Christ's sake, I mean, he must be out of his mind," Nixon said, hearing of the gambit.) Two special agents brought the files to Capitol Hill to be examined as desired, prompting rare shared condemnation from both the Nixon Justice Department and the ACLU (the latter protested the airing of unproven rumors in the files regarding people who hadn't been charged with a crime).

Back at FBI headquarters, Felt believed he stood a good chance of taking over the bureau if Gray's nomination tanked; despite the punishment meted out to other suspected leakers inside the bureau, he'd managed to remain in Gray's good graces. As part of a final push to secure his own ascendance, Felt gave *TIME* a tip about the Kissinger wiretaps, airing a scandal that Felt hoped would ensure his former rival William Sullivan couldn't sneak his way back into the bureau. He badly miscalculated. As it turned out, Felt was effectively the only person who knew of the wiretaps outside of those directly involved; the revelation became just a blip at Gray's hearing, but would metastasize through the spring into a larger scandal that would sink Felt himself.

Undistracted by the Kissinger wiretaps, the Senate settled on another target: John Dean. "Until February 28, 1973, Dean had lived publicly at the periphery of Watergate—a White House aide who had reportedly investigated the bugging incident for the President, never seen, seldom if ever in mind," recalled the *Post's* Barry Sussman. Within the first few hours of Gray's hearing, Dean—and his activities with the acting director—became the focus of attention.

Under questioning, Gray admitted he had regularly sent investigative reports to the White House via Dean, allowing the president's staff access to files that Hoover had previously guarded. Then came the admission that Dean had also sat in on FBI interviews. Senators were shocked by Gray's apparent naïveté, and their suspicions grew as Dean also came up in questioning about the ITT matter, with Gray testifying that the White House counsel had been involved with the Dita Beard memo.

Though Gray kept citing the "presumption of regularity"—that as an agency head he had to operate as if his government colleagues were simply doing their jobs as expected—the senators were dumbfounded that the head of the FBI could so easily assume that Nixon's staff couldn't have possibly been involved in Watergate. As Senator Robert C. Byrd said, "Everything is accepted at face value, without question, without the slightest iota of suspicion."*

The increasingly hostile exchanges made the White House realize Gray was a lost cause and stoked fears that his testimony might result in calls for Dean and Ehrlichman to testify too. "It makes me gag," Dean said on the phone to Ehrlichman in early March. The silver lining, though, was that Gray's disastrous hearings refocused Watergate attention away from the White House itself. Maybe there was value in just letting his nomination linger? "I think we ought to let him hang there," Ehrlichman concluded. "Let him twist slowly, slowly in the wind."†

---

* Even as Gray seemed generally open and honest—perhaps too honest at points, volunteering information beyond what the senators were asking—he knew real trouble lurked too. After his third day of hearings, he called Ehrlichman and pleaded for Dean to "stand awful tight in the saddle" about the documents from Hunt's safe—that secret couldn't come out.

† Nixon, in another conversation, came to the same conclusion, believing that the beating Gray was taking meant he wouldn't be as willing to do the president's own bidding once in office. "After going through the hell of the hearings, he will not be a good director as far as we are concerned," the president determined.

Any potential benefit to the administration disappeared on March 7, when Gray nonchalantly confirmed that Kalmbach and Chapin had been involved with Segretti's operation, and that it had been paid for by anonymous CREEP funds—revelations that cut against long-standing denials from the White House and unleashed a furor at the press briefing: "Ron, since both Mr. Kalmbach and Mr. Chapin either do or have worked for the President of the United States and you are the president's spokesman, let me just ask you this direct question," one reporter queried, "just this simple question: Which man is lying?"

*   *   *

Throughout that spring, Watergate steadily became a more substantial part of the president's day and his world; through February, March, and April, Ehrlichman alone would recall participating in dozens of conversations on the subject. Dean too moved further into the president's orbit; late February marked the first of what would ultimately be dozens of telephone calls and meetings between the two men—a notable change in tempo considering the counsel had, until then, met with the president precisely once.

More than ever, the Nixon operation found itself wound up in the lies and distrust of its key players. Few within the inner circle, least of all the president, really understood who was culpable for what. Nixon still seemed to think Watergate was a Mitchell operation, while Haldeman told him he suspected the blame fell to Colson. Colson, for his part, pointed the finger at Haldeman and Dean, warning Nixon, "This could stretch into the White House."

"You mean Bob and John?" Nixon replied.

"Yes," Colson said.

Layer upon layer, meeting upon meeting, lies compounded and questions spread. Nixon biographer Stephen Ambrose later studied the transcripts of that winter and spring and observed, "One of the things that stands out is the amount of dissembling that went on." There was a giant psychology experiment underway, a high-stakes "Prisoner's Dilemma," where no one was willing to be honest or confront one another, even though the only real path they had out of the mess would have been a coordinated defense. Instead, they lurched forward, conversation to conversation, never really understanding each other's guilt. As Mitchell's biographer James Rosen would later write, "This was Watergate: an endless clash of memories over the substance of meetings and telephone calls featuring a revolving cast of self-interested men, most of them lawyers."

While nearly everyone—including Nixon himself—was a lawyer, none of them was really an expert in criminal law, making it harder to assess their own vulnerabilities. At one point, they discussed calling in Henry Petersen, to "hypothetically" discuss the case. Dean loved the idea of presenting a "wild scenario" to the head of the Justice Department's Criminal Division, not dissimilar from a law school case study, but Haldeman offered another approach: ask for literary advice. "My friend is writing a play," he suggested, and needs to depict an accurate scenario. In the end, they struggled to see how to speak candidly with the nation's head criminal prosecutor without making themselves vulnerable. Not even swearing Petersen to secrecy on behalf of the president would work, because that would imply the president was in on the game.

On Saturday, March 17, Nixon and Dean met—Dean's first time in the Oval Office without a necktie—and their conversation meandered through the early days of the GEMSTONE plan, Dean's own role in the cover-up, and the president's ongoing desire to launch a counter-scandal that would distract and dismay Democrats. Again, Nixon raised his favorite bugaboo—the tapping of his campaign plane in '68 by Johnson that J. Edgar Hoover had warned him about as president-elect, an incident he continued to believe would show the world "everybody bugs" and that CREEP's dirty tricks were no more than that which had been done to him.

"It's your view the vulnerabilities are basically Mitchell, Colson, Haldeman—indirectly, possibly directly—and of course, the second level is as far as the White House is concerned, Chapin," Nixon said, leaning back in his chair.

"And I'd say Dean, to a degree," the counsel added.

"You? Why?"

"Well, because I've been all over this thing like a blanket," Dean said.

"You were in it after the deed was done," Nixon argued. "You have no problem. All the others have participated in the goddamned thing, and therefore are potentially subject to criminal liability."

As they talked, it became clear that it would be impossible to single out a Magruder or other top official and lay all the blame at one doorstep. "Can't do that," Nixon lamented.

That night at dinner at the Kleindienst house, Marney—the attorney general's wife—cracked a joke at the glum-looking Dean: "If they send you to prison, I'll bake cookies for you and come visit you every week." The look of terror that spread across Dean's face made Marney, Richard, and Dean's wife, Mo, suddenly realize it wasn't funny.

"After nine months, the hot torch of skepticism had finally burned through our story that Liddy had done it on his own," Dean recalled. "Even the President could no longer lie about it convincingly." Through repeated conversations in the subsequent days—both private ones in the White House and public exchanges with the press—Nixon felt the pressure building on his administration for an accounting of its role in and knowledge of the bugging scandal. Too many people now seemed to know too much. Dean at one point was warning a colleague, who he figured was in the dark, about the trouble ahead, and his colleague volunteered he knew about the "Ellsberg thing." The exchange made Dean worry even more.

The president understood that the best way to defeat the Ervin Committee would be to ensure that it never got up a head of steam in the first place, and so his team settled, with time, on two layered defenses: first, a broad claim of "executive privilege" that would shutter the committee's ability to conduct an independent inquiry or compel the White House to participate, and, second, publishing the mythic "Dean Report," which would cleanse the administration and defuse any public interest. "I wanted to talk with you about what kind of a line to take," Nixon told Dean on February 28. "I think we ought to cooperate in finding an area of cooperation."

The doctrine and operation of "executive privilege," the idea that under the constitutional separation of powers presidents could prevent disclosure to Congress or the court of confidential communications and presidential advice, remained ill-defined at the time.* While more than a dozen presidents had blocked a variety of congressional requests over the years, Eisenhower had been the first to explicitly lay out the idea that a commander in chief needed to receive confidential advice without fear of later subpoena or inquiry. "There is no business that could be run if there would be exposed every single thought that an adviser might have, because in the process of reaching an agreed position, there are many, many conflicting opinions to be brought together," he had argued. "If any commander is going to get the free, unprejudiced opinions of his subordinates, he had better protect what they have to say to him on a confidential basis." Nixon had already begun exploring the tactic as a shield in January amid a minor kerfuffle about the firing of a Pentagon analyst who had complained about cost overruns of the C-5A transport plane. Behind closed doors, he had ordered Ehrlichman to "have the most godawful gobbledygook answer [about executive privilege] prepared . . . something that will allow us to do everything that we want." In March, Nixon explained publicly why he saw it as okay for agency and department heads to testify before Congress but needed to resist calls for testimony from White House aides.

"In the performance of their duties for the President, those staff members must not be inhibited by the possibility that their advice and assistance will ever become a matter of public debate, either during their tenure in government or at a later date," he said in a statement. Otherwise, the candor with which advice is rendered and the quality of such assistance will inevitably be compromised and weakened. What is at stake, therefore, is not simply a question of confidentiality but the integrity of the decision-making process at the very highest levels of our government."

Nixon promised too that "executive privilege will not be used as a shield to prevent embarrassing information from being made available but will be exercised only in those particular instances in which disclosure would harm the public interest."

---

* One of the few times that it had been tested since the early years of the republic was actually in the Alger Hiss case, when Truman had invoked its amorphous cloak in refusing to turn over the administration's loyalty files to Congress and the committee of a young Richard Nixon.

Absent such testimony, he knew reassuring the public required coming clean about Watergate—hence the need, in his mind, for a "Dean Report" absolving the White House of any responsibility.

The only problem was it didn't exist; his White House counsel had not only never conducted an investigation of the White House's role in Watergate, but even worse Dean—more than almost anyone around the president—knew that the White House was decidedly not innocent when it came to the bugging scandal.

Nixon didn't see why that inconvenient truth should prevent Dean from releasing just such a "thorough investigation" now. He desperately wanted to go on the offensive and still believed that the administration could successfully muddy the waters around its wiretapping debacle by publicizing the allegations that Johnson had spied on Nixon's campaign in '68. Dean funneled the information to Senator Barry Goldwater's staff and hoped for controversy as the Ervin Committee started, but to no avail.*

*   *   *

On Tuesday morning, March 20, Dean met with Ehrlichman and relayed the latest demands from Hunt: $75,000 to support his family, plus another $50,000 to cover his legal fees. Finding money to pay off the burglars was proving challenging; it was a lot of cash and the campaign had quickly used up the untraceable money left in its various secret safes.

---

* Amazingly, though, because of the rough game of "FBI telephone" that had played out in '68, Nixon never pieced together that the core of the allegations of LBJ bugging his campaign traced back to Nixon's own Chennault Affair plot. His own campaign plane had never been bugged; the FBI, after hearing (or perhaps mishearing) references on its Chennault wiretaps to Chennault's "boss" in New Mexico, had tried to search telephone records of phone booths around the Albuquerque campaign stop of Spiro Agnew's campaign plane. (As previously mentioned, it's most likely that the FBI actually mistook "New Mexico" when Chennault actually said "New Hampshire," which is where John Mitchell had been at the time, meaning that the game of telephone was even more convoluted.) The FBI investigation hadn't been a political intelligence operation—it had been probing Nixon's own apparently treasonous behavior. Nixon was so deep into so many conspiracies that he didn't realize that his attempt to get out of one might actually lead the world straight to another.

In early March, Mitchell and the Nixon team had ultimately arranged to get funds from the Republican fundraiser and Greek grocery magnate Thomas Pappas—"sort of one of the unknown J. Paul Gettys of the world right now," Haldeman had called him—the same Boston businessman whose comments had helped spark Tip O'Neill's sense that something was off in Nixon's fundraising.

In return for providing the needed cash, Haldeman told Nixon that Pappas had requested that the Nixon administration leave in place the current ambassador to Greece, rather than shuffling him onto another post. "No problem," Nixon said. "I'm just delighted."

A few nights later, Pappas had attended a White House reception that included top Nixon fundraisers, and he and the president spoke briefly. The next day, Nixon had him into the Oval Office. "I want you to know that . . . I'm aware of what you're doing to help out in some of these things that Maury's people and others are involved in," Nixon told Pappas, referring to CREEP's top fundraiser, Maurice Stans. "I won't say anything further, but it's very seldom you find a friend like that, believe me."*

Now they turned to him again on the Hunt issue. Ehrlichman told Dean to call Mitchell in New York and order him to get the money. John Dean called him that night to follow up: "Can I report any progress? Is the Greek bearing gifts?"

At 7:30, Dean returned home to a dinner party already in progress, and found the phone ringing: the president, again. They spoke for thirteen minutes, Nixon extolling the apparent virtues of a "Dean Report." Dean suggested instead they meet the next day. "We could probably do it, say, around ten o'clock," Nixon said. The meeting was set. Dean gulped down the last of his first drink before he was even off the phone.

The pressure felt unrelenting.

---

* Nixon went on to assure Pappas that the senior campaign officials were innocent in the whole caper, saying "a few pipsqueaks down the line did some silly things," and expressing his ongoing amazement that anyone would bother with the DNC. "They don't know a goddamn thing. I thought it was the most [stupid] thing. But, you know, amateurs. That's what it is."

* * *

On Wednesday morning, sitting in front of the Oval Office desk at 10:12, Dean bared his conscience to the president of the United States. "The reason I thought we ought to talk this morning is because, in our conversations, I have the impression that you don't know everything I know, and it makes it very difficult for you to make judgments that only you can make on some of these things," he began. Over the following 103 minutes, he explained how the administration had become so entirely caught up in a web of its own making.

"There's no doubt about the seriousness of the problem we've got. We have a cancer within—close to the Presidency, that's growing. It's growing daily. It's compounding, it grows geometrically now because it compounds itself," Dean explained. "It basically is because (1) we're being blackmailed; (2) people are going to start perjuring themselves very quickly that have not had to perjure themselves to protect other people and the like. And that is just—and there is no assurance—"

"That it won't bust," the president finished.

The lawyer continued through a sanitized—and particularly friendly to his own interests—debrief, from the early proposals by Jack Caulfield for SANDWEDGE through to Liddy and GEMSTONE and the meetings in Mitchell's offices. "Liddy laid out a million-dollar plan that was the most incredible thing I have ever laid my eyes on. All in codes, and involved black bag operations, kidnapping, providing prostitutes to weaken the opposition, bugging, uh, mugging teams. It was just an incredible thing," Dean said, making sure to exonerate himself and implicate Magruder as a naif who wouldn't have known better that Liddy's schemes were all over the line.

Nixon took in the information with remarkable cool, asking few questions but clearly concentrating. After completing the narrative, Dean circled back to discuss what he called the "soft spots" of the investigation and the administration's cover-up. "This was something that just could have been disastrous on the election if it had—all hell had broken loose, and I worked on a theory of containment," Dean explained. "I was totally aware what the Bureau was doing at all times. I was totally aware of what the Grand Jury was doing. I knew what witnesses were going to be called. I knew what they were going to be asked, and I had to."

Nixon interjected, "Why did Petersen play the game so straight with us?"

"Because Petersen is a soldier. He played—he kept me informed. He told me when we had problems, where we had problems, and the like," Dean said. "He believes in you. He believes in this Administration. This Administration has made him—uh, I don't think he's done anything improper, but he did make sure the investigation was narrowed down to the very, very fine criminal things, which was a break for us. There's no doubt about it."

Finally, Dean turned to the issue of the hush money and how Caulfield and others had raised the possibility of presidential clemency with McCord and Hunt, in exchange for their silence. "Hunt now is demanding another $72,000 for his own personal expenses; another $50,000 to pay his attorneys' fees—some $120,000. Wants it—wanted it—by the close of business yesterday," he said, adding that Hunt also now was explicitly threatening Ehrlichman and Krogh.

Suddenly the Oval Office conversation took a surprising—and ominous—turn. "It'll cost money. It's dangerous. Nobody, nothing—people around here are not pros at this sort of thing," Dean began. "This is the sort of thing Mafia people can do: washing money, getting clean money, and things like that, uh—we're—we just don't know about those things, because we're not used to—we are not criminals and not used to dealing in that business."

"That's right," Nixon said.

"It's a tough thing to know how to do," Dean concurred.

"Maybe we can't even do that."

"That's right," the counsel replied. "It's a real problem as to whether we could even do it. Plus there's a real problem in raising money. Mitchell has been working on raising some money—feeling he's got, he's one of the ones with the most to lose. But there's no denying the fact that the White House, and uh, Ehrlichman, Haldeman, Dean are involved in some of the early money decisions."

"How much money do you need?" the president asked, bluntly.

"I would say these people are going to cost, uh, a million dollars over the next, uh, two years," Dean guessed.

"We could get that," Nixon said. "On the money, if you need the money, I mean, you could get the money. You could get a million dollars. And you could get it in cash. I know where it could be gotten."

Once again, confronted with a decision point that was clearly illegal, the president did not condemn or reject the possibility, but instead chose to advance the scheme himself. There was no question that the hush money would continue—the debate was only over where it would come from and who would deliver it. The answers emerged quickly: Mitchell should handle it, to keep the circle as small as possible. "He's working— apparently he talked to Tom Pappas," Dean said.

"I know," Nixon said.

To Dean, it was a remarkable admission—until that moment, he had thought only he, LaRue, Mitchell, and Ehrlichman knew about the conversation with Pappas.

The rest of the conversation took on an entirely different tone. As Nixon ran through his own "soft spots," Dean mentioned that Ehrlichman might face criminal liability over the Ellsberg burglary, explaining that the Justice Department had copies of the photos Liddy and Hunt had taken in Los Angeles, and Nixon interjected, "Oh, I saw that— the picture." Dean, again, was shocked. Nixon had clearly been better informed at almost every step of the conspiracy than his counsel had believed.

"I think we've got it buried, there is no telling when it's going to pop up," Dean said. "I don't have a plan of how to solve it right now, but I think it's at the juncture that we should begin to think in terms of, of how to cut the losses; how to minimize the further growth of this thing; rather than further compound it by ultimately paying these guys forever."

"That's worth it—at the moment," Nixon said. "Suppose the worst, that Bob is indicted and Ehrlichman is indicted," he continued. "And I must say, maybe we just better then try to tough it through. You get my point. . . . Say we're going to go down the road, see if we can cut our losses, and no more blackmail and all the rest, and the thing blows and they indict Bob and the rest. Jesus, you'd never recover from that, John."

"That's right," Dean agreed.

"It's better to fight it out instead," the president said, his mind clearly set. "Time is of the essence."

A few moments later, Nixon buzzed for Haldeman. When he arrived, the president suggested that Dean, Ehrlichman, Haldeman, and Mitchell convene to have the same conversation among themselves. "We've got to see what the line is—whether the line is one of continuing to run a, try to run a total stonewall, and take the heat from that, having in mind the fact that there are vulnerable points there," he explained.

Haldeman chimed in: "That's where your dangers lie, is in all these stupid human errors developing."

Nixon agreed: "Bob, let's face it, the secretaries know, the assistants know. There's a lot of the, many of the damn principals may be hard as a rock, but you never know when they're going to crack. But we'll see, we'll see. First you've got the Hunt problem. That ought to be handled." As they prepared to wrap up, Nixon made a final point: "No problem, we could, we could get the money. There is no problem in that. We can't provide the clemency. The money can be provided. Mitchell could provide the way to deliver it. That could be done."

As Nixon stood up from his desk, Dean left and ten members of the Soviet women's gymnastics team marched in, visiting as part of a goodwill tour. Nixon tried to crack a joke. "I watched the Olympics on television. I noticed you always land on your feet. That is what our politicians always try to do," he said to the group, before adding, perhaps thinking of the meeting he'd just concluded, "Not always with success."

*   *   *

Nixon had immediately seen the peril of Dean's confessional. There wasn't any corner of the scandal that Dean could show without potentially exposing everything. "What the hell is he going to disclose that isn't going to blow something?" Nixon asked Ehrlichman just hours after Dean's talk. It was the fundamental problem with everything—Watergate was never a one-off burglary. It was the Gordian knot of scandal, unable to be untied neatly or at all.

Later that day, the president sought out Rose Mary Woods. In a tape of a mysterious and often oblique conversation that wasn't released until 1997, it's clear that Woods was a key collaborator, holding on to some of the seemingly ubiquitous cash that the campaign had amassed.

"We may have a need for substantial cash," Nixon said. "How much do we have?"

"I still have that hundred," Woods replied. "I'm so worried. They called earlier, and I said it had been used for a special project, so that there'd be no record."

"And you have some other as well?"

"Yes, I don't know. I would have to look," she said. "I'd have to get in the safe. I don't remember."

"But it's a sum you can take? We may have to call on that," the president said. "We have to use it for certain purposes."

"Nobody here knows I have it."

"Well I know—and nobody any place else knows," Nixon said.

In the end, the money didn't need to come from Woods's hidden slush fund. The Greek had brought a gift, but only a partial one. That night, a final envelope with $75,000 cash was delivered to Hunt's lawyer, monies intended to support his family and his legal fees for two years, but which still fell well short of the $120,000 he had needed. Hunt totaled up the money with a sinking realization: "I could count on no further assistance."

* * *

The day after Dean's "cancer on the presidency" meeting, Pat Gray sat, again, at the witness table for another day of hearings on his confirmation. When his turn to ask questions came, Senator Robert C. Byrd doubled back over the matter of Hunt's safe, pointing out how Dean had expressed surprise about its existence to the FBI even after he had actually had it opened by government technicians. "He lied to the agents, didn't he?" Byrd asked.

"I would say, looking back on it now and exhaustively analyzing the minute details of this investigation, I would have to conclude that that probably is correct—yes sir," Gray replied.

Frantic, Dean called Gray during the hearing's mid-day break and pleaded with him to change his testimony; the answer was devastating to the White House counsel's credibility. Gray refused.

That afternoon, Ehrlichman gave Nixon the final word: "Gray is dead on the floor." The Senate never reconvened Gray's confirmation hearings.

Gray eventually wrote to the president and asked that his nomination be withdrawn; he intended, instead, to stay on as acting director until a replacement could be located and confirmed.

Dean, wounded, began to consider his options. *Could he save himself, even if it meant torpedoing the rest of his colleagues?* He met that day with Mitchell, Haldeman, and Ehrlichman—a tense and guarded conversation about the unraveling conspiracy—and the four of them later met with Nixon himself to discuss how to move forward. "What words of wisdom do we have from this august body?" Nixon asked as he surveyed his top aides standing around his desk.*

After nearly two hours of conversation, they agreed to still pursue the multilayered defense they'd already settled on that spring: fight on executive privilege, which could delay hearings on the case by eighteen months or even perhaps the entire second term, and then publish a White House report that made clear no one was involved. "I don't give a shit what happens," Nixon said. "I want you all to stonewall it, let them plead the Fifth Amendment, cover up or anything else if it'll save it—save the plan. That's the whole point." Continuing to Mitchell, he added, "Up to this point, the whole theory has been containment, as you know, John."

Dean should get going on writing the report that day, Haldeman suggested. Ehrlichman agreed: A successful report would make clear that the president himself and the top staff were innocent of culpability and foreknowledge of the dirtiest tricks.

"You think we want to go this route now?" Nixon asked later. "Let it hang out, so to speak?"

"It's a limited hang out," Haldeman clarified.

"It's a limited hang out," Dean agreed.

"It's a modified limited hang out," Ehrlichman chimed in.

As Dean then explained, "What it's doing, Mr. President, is getting you up above and away from it. And that's the most important thing."

"Oh, I know," Nixon said. "But I suggested that the other day and remember we came down on the negative on it. Now what's changed our mind?"

---

* Amazingly, the meeting that afternoon—as Mitchell's biographer James Rosen noted—was the only time the five central participants in the Watergate story ever met together in person.

"The lack of alternatives—or a body," Dean said. Everyone laughed.

"We went down every alley," Ehrlichman agreed.

Maybe, Ehrlichman suggested, Mitchell could apologize? "John says he's sorry he sent those burglars in there, and that helps a lot," the aide suggested.

"That's right," Nixon said.

"You are very welcome, sir," Mitchell said, taking his ever-present pipe from his mouth and bowing for the room.

Everyone laughed.

Chapter 27

"Perjury Occurred"

John Sirica's courtroom filled to capacity on Friday, March 23, for the 10 a.m. sentencing of the Watergate defendants. A surprise awaited. To make sure the right people were in the room to witness it, the judge had called Sam Dash earlier in the week. "I think you should be present in the courtroom when I sentence them," he'd told the Senate counsel. "What I plan to do should be of special interest to you and the committee. That's all I can say, you understand."

As Sirica took his seat on the bench, he made an announcement: "Prior to the beginning of the sentencing scheduled for this morning, I wish to put a certain important matter on record in open court. On Tuesday, March 20, of this week, a letter addressed to me from one of the defendants, James McCord, was delivered to me by a probation officer. After reading the letter I had it sealed in the presence of my court clerk and placed it in his custody." Sirica turned to the clerk: "Mr. Clerk, would you please unseal the letter and hand it to me at the bench?"

Gasps of astonishment peppered the courtroom as Sirica read the letter aloud. McCord's statement explained the dilemma he faced—torn between answering the court's queries, potential further investigations by the Senate and others, and his and his family's safety. And yet, he wrote, "Be that as it may, in the interests of justice, and in the interests of restoring faith in the criminal justice system, which faith has been severely damaged in this case, I will state the following to you at this time which I hope may be of help to you."

What followed were six jaw-dropping revelations:

1. There was political pressure applied to the defendants to plead guilty and remain silent.
2. Perjury occurred during the trial in matters highly material to the very structure, orientation, and impact of the government's case, and to the motivation and intent of the defendants.
3. Others involved in the Watergate operation were not identified during the trial, when they could have been by those testifying.
4. The Watergate operation was not a CIA operation. The Cubans may have been misled by others into believing that it was a CIA operation. I know for a fact that it was not.
5. Some statements were unfortunately made by a witness which left the Court with the impression that he was stating untruths, or withholding facts of his knowledge, when in fact only honest errors of memory were involved.
6. My motivations were different than those of the others involved, but were not limited to, or simply those offered in my defense during the trial. This is no fault of my attorneys, but of the circumstances under which we had to prepare my defense.

As Sirica concluded reading, the room erupted into absolute chaos; reporters raced for the lobby telephones to call in the breaking news, while others simply sat in shock.

When the situation settled, Sirica stated that he was tabling McCord's own sentencing in light of the letter, before perfunctorily sentencing Liddy to more than six years in prison and the other five burglary defendants to the maximum possible punishments. The Bureau of Prisons, he added, would study the prisoners and report back to him on their cooperation with other investigations. With that information, he would adjust their sentences accordingly.

Hearing and then reading a copy of the McCord letter back at the *Washington Post*, Ben Bradlee breathed his first true sigh of relief since the previous summer. "For the first time really, I felt in my guts that we were going to win," he wrote later. "Winning would mean all the truth. Every bit. I had no idea still how it would all come out, but I no longer believed Watergate would end in a tie."

*   *   *

By the time Sam Dash made it back to Capitol Hill, he already had a message from McCord asking to meet. He immediately went to the office of McCord's lawyer, Bernard Fensterwald, bringing along his colleague and investigator Hal Lipset. ("I was too embarrassed to let McCord or Fensterwald know that I did not have any other investigators at the time," he recalled later.)

Sitting in Fensterwald's law library, McCord hardly seemed to Dash like some kind of rogue secret agent—more an ordinary, albeit determined, middle-aged businessman. McCord explained that he didn't trust the FBI or the U.S. Attorney's Office—both reported up a chain of command to the White House—and preferred to deal directly with the Senate committee. Then, he and Fensterwald asked for a copy of the Watergate trial transcript, so that the burglar could review it and accurately pinpoint the problematic testimony he'd outlined in his letter to Sirica. They promised to work that evening and the next day before meeting again to go over more specifics. "For the time being, I thought it best to let McCord disclose information at his own speed," Dash recalled.

The next day, Saturday, the men gathered again and spoke at more length. McCord handed over a poorly written memo, which Dash read silently to himself. "I, in addition to my own sworn testimony, am prepared to give the Senate Watergate Committee supportive information and/or leads to convince them beyond a reasonable doubt that the statements I have made in the attached memorandum are true and correct," it began. As it went on, McCord outlined specific allegations against Jeb Magruder, claiming he'd perjured himself by testifying on January 23 that he'd had no knowledge of the bugging operation at the Watergate prior to the June arrests: "Mr. Magruder knows the names of others knowledgeable of and involved in the Watergate operation sequence. One of such persons was John Dean of the White House staff. Had Magruder answered truthfully the question propounded above at page 1422 of the transcript and made full disclosure of the names of others involved, he would have named Dean."

Dash absorbed the information—senior officials in the White House and the president's reelection campaign had been involved in the break-in—and instinctively decided to keep it private, even from Lipset, who was sitting nearby.

Avoiding naming names verbally, Fensterwald and McCord explained that McCord's role and knowledge of the larger conspiracy was quite limited. "I've got one slice of it," he said. "I think Mr. Hunt has the other slice you want—the biggest slice."

"Will Hunt talk to us?" Dash asked.

"That depends on a lot of things in the next few days—what he's thinking about, what he reads in the paper, what he sees. I suspect that will affect him greatly," McCord replied.

Fensterwald pushed for Dash to make their conversations public, arguing that everyone should know McCord was cooperating and be worried. Afterward, as they headed back to Capitol Hill, Lipset told Dash he agreed. "The whole cover-up depended on a wall of silence," he said. "If we let out that McCord is talking, there are going to be some pretty scared characters around town who may be able to make some bigger cracks in the wall."

*   *   *

That Friday, March 23, had started out bad enough for John Dean. The morning newspaper headlines blared Gray's accusation from the previous day's Senate hearing, "DEAN PROBABLY LIED," and reporters were camped out at his house. Then, mid-morning, came word of McCord's letter and courtroom bombshell. At 12:44 p.m., the president called; they discussed and eventually agreed that Dean should hole up at Camp David for the weekend.* As he and his wife, Maureen, rode up into the Catoctin Mountains, Dean's imagination wandered to the possibility of

---

* In his memoir, Dean makes the Camp David suggestion sound completely out of the blue, but it had been an extensive and explicit part of his Thursday-afternoon conversation with Haldeman, Ehrlichman, Mitchell, and the president.

fleeing—surely John Mitchell and the president could arrange him a covert flight to a Latin American country, where some wealthy businessman would allow him to live in a grand villa in exile while he shouldered the blame back home for Watergate?

At 3:28 p.m., Nixon and Haldeman called again to discuss Dean's weekend assignment, compiling the "Dean Report." He started the next morning, following instructions that it would "incriminate no one other than Liddy." He asked Fred Fielding to round up additional documents from his White House office and send them up to Camp David, along with Dean's secretary, on Monday. By Sunday afternoon, though, he had reconsidered. The lies were too deep. Dean realized he should make an effort to come entirely clean with the president—"The truth might persuade him, once he saw it written down," he later recalled thinking.

On Sunday afternoon, more bad news arrived: Ron Ziegler called to say the *Los Angeles Times* was about to publish a story that Magruder and Dean had had advance knowledge of the Watergate burglary.

The next morning, Sam Dash was stunned by a phone call from Carl Bernstein relaying the same news: "The *LA Times* reported this morning that McCord named Magruder and Dean to you as having advance knowledge of the Watergate bugging. Did McCord make that statement to you or was the *LA Times* just guessing?" Dash declined comment, but as he listened to the *Washington Post* reporter, his mind began to churn. Only four people had known the names McCord had given them—McCord, Fensterwald, Ervin, and himself. Who had leaked? He was certain it was McCord and his lawyer, hoping to force the investigators toward quick action.*

The *Los Angeles Times* article on March 26 was the start of a cascade of near-daily headlines, developments, scoops, and leaks that brought the story consistently to the front pages and opinion pages of the nation's newspapers and magazines; that week, Watergate even occupied the cover of *Newsweek*. "News leaks of massive proportions occurred," recalled Barry Sussman.

The White House, for the moment, decided to stand by Dean, but agreed Magruder was on his own. According to Dean's memoir, Haldeman

---

* Indeed, this was precisely what had happened: McCord had spent three hours at his house spilling the full story out to the *Los Angeles Times*'s Robert Jackson.

told him in a phone call that morning, "We've been protecting Mitchell and Magruder too long, and it got us into this mess," and then reviewed in great detail what Dean knew and when. The conversation with the chief of staff was painful, but not hostile. Haldeman, Dean knew, was taking careful notes. Following the *Los Angeles Times* report, Dean issued a statement saying he was exploring suing the newspaper for libel, but he was less sure of his innocence behind the scenes and began to arrange his own criminal lawyer.

Fear spread. That Monday, Martha Mitchell called the *New York Times*: "I fear for my husband," she said. "I'm really scared. I have a definite reason. I can't tell you why. But they're not going to pin anything on him; I won't let them."

Indeed, "pinning" Mitchell was exactly what the White House was planning to do. On March 27, Nixon, Haldeman, and Ehrlichman discussed how to force the former campaign director to admit to authorizing the whole thing—and that the buck stopped with him. "What is Mitchell's option?" Nixon asked aloud during the morning meeting in the Oval Office. "Does Mitchell come in and say, 'My fault. . . . My memory was faulty. I lied'?"

"No, he can't say that," Ehrlichman replied.

"'Without intending to, I may have been responsible for this, and I regret it very much, but I did not intend that—I did not realize what they were up to'?" Nixon continued brainstorming. "'They were talking—we were talking—about apples and oranges.' That's what I think he would say. Don't you agree?"

"He authorized apples and they bought oranges, yeah," Haldeman agreed.

"Mitchell is never going to go in and admit perjury. You can talk about immunity and all the rest, but he's never going to do that," Nixon said.

"They won't give him immunity anyway—I wouldn't think—unless they figure they could get you. He is as high up as they've been," Haldeman said.

"He's the big enchilada," Ehrlichman seconded.

*　　*　　*

In the wake of the *Los Angeles Times* leak, McCord and his lawyer feigned fierce outrage, telling Dash that McCord now would only speak under oath directly to the committee itself. Much to Dash's chagrin, the senators loved that idea. "They were sitting on the hottest committee in the Congress and a sensational witness like McCord was irresistible," he recalled. Thompson immediately sensed the change among the committee members after the *Los Angeles Times* story too. "It was the first solid indication that Watergate indeed might turn out to be something more than a 'third-rate burglary,'" the Republican counsel explained.

The resulting private meeting between the Senate committee members, McCord, Fensterwald, Thompson, and Dash quickly turned into what Dash called a "disaster." Ervin's office was packed, as a score of senators, staff, and lawyers lined a long table with McCord and filled in along the walls behind. Both sides—investigators and conspirator—were unprepared, and neither trusted the other. "His testimony was damaging, but the parts of it that incriminated Mitchell, Magruder, and Dean were all hearsay from Liddy," Thompson recalled. Expecting a friendly conversation as a willing witness, McCord found himself under skeptical cross-examination from a committee unwilling to offer the immunity he wanted.

Inquiries were now unfolding in parallel; after his messy private testimony to the Senate, McCord went back to Sirica and the U.S. attorney to ask for immunity and the chance to testify to a grand jury. He was still concerned about whether to trust the Justice Department, but he was eager to get on the record somewhere. For weeks, Dash was relegated to reading leaks of McCord's grand jury testimony in the newspapers. Still, with its new structure in place and its investigative staff finally expanding, the Senate committee began making real progress. It had followed up on McCord's suggested witnesses, summoning, to corroborate certain meetings and conversations, aides and secretaries to Magruder and Liddy, some of whom had never been questioned by the FBI or spoken to the grand jury.

An important lead emerged when one CRP secretary located a duplicate copy she'd kept of Magruder's appointments calendar from the campaign and presented it to the committee. Scanning through the green diary, Senate investigator Jim Hamilton zeroed in on two entries documenting meetings between "A.G.," Liddy, and Dean, on January 27 and February 4, 1972, potentially the conversations McCord had referenced during which the campaign intelligence and dirty tricks operation had been presented. Further testimony from campaign aides seemed to back up the theory; some remembered Liddy walking around sometime in January 1972 with an awkward, oversized wrapped package of what appeared to be charts, and another Magruder aide, Robert Reisner, recalled a scramble—probably in February 1972—to find Liddy an easel for a meeting in Mitchell's office. He then told the Senate investigators that Magruder had warned him about cooperating with the committee, saying, "People's lives and futures are at stake," and complaining that Reisner was going to reveal the story about asking for an easel. "How come you remember an easel? There wasn't an easel," he said Magruder told him.

It was one of many indications that the Watergate conspirators were growing concerned— Magruder, especially. Magruder went to the White House on March 28 to ask Dean and Mitchell whether they'd stick with their established narrative about the GEMSTONE meetings from the previous summer. Haldeman gathered the men together, only to reiterate, "I don't want to get involved with this," before leaving them alone in Dwight Chapin's empty office.* When Mitchell and Magruder finally pressed Dean on what he would say, the lawyer said that if called to testify before the Senate or the grand jury, he would tell the truth. Magruder pleaded with his former colleague; it was Dean, after all, who had counseled Magruder through perjuring himself before the grand jury the previous summer—was he really now going to hang Magruder out to dry? As Magruder later observed, "The chronology of the affair proves that he was about ten days smarter than I was."

Paranoia grew among all the co-conspirators; Dean, Ehrlichman, and Haldeman were by then covertly taping their own conversations with each other and with others, hoping to capture self-exonerating statements and incriminating admissions. The conversations and tapings, though, sometimes proved more complicating than clarifying. During a meeting

* Magruder's book recalls the meeting as being in Higby's office.

with Ehrlichman, unaware he was being taped, Mitchell explained he had nothing to hide. "I really don't have a guilty conscience. I didn't authorize these bastards." Ehrlichman was flummoxed. If Mitchell hadn't, who had?

*　　*　　*

When McCord finished with the grand jury, he returned to Capitol Hill to work with Dash and Thompson's investigation. During long sessions in their makeshift Senate interrogation room, G-334, McCord laid out everything he knew. Dash was impressed, noticing "a sense of stoic dignity," and observing, "I developed a genuine affection for Jim McCord." It gradually became clear McCord's misguided patriotism had led him into the Watergate the previous June and that he had actually believed he was on a mission on behalf of the attorney general. When Dash asked whether he would have participated in the break-in had he known he was only working for Liddy, McCord replied sharply and indignantly: "Never!"

As Dash and his staff continued to make progress, Ervin's committee agitated for public hearings. At a mid-April meeting, Dash said he expected it would take another month to be ready, and so hearings were set to begin May 15. There was already a fear among the committee that Nixon would use executive privilege to block his aides from testifying. "Frankly, under the regular rules of evidence we have the right to draw negative inferences from the president's withholding of information," Ervin said in one meeting. "If the president won't let his aides testify under oath, I think the public can conclude that he is unwilling for the people to get the truth about Watergate."

To try to curb the committee's investigative attempts, the White House floated submitting written answers to questions, and Nixon advisor Leonard Garment suggested that Nixon's aides would simply refuse to answer questions that touched on executive privilege or national security. "Nonsense," Dash replied. Thompson echoed the objection: "If the members of the committee ask a White House aide, before a nationwide television audience, if he and the president discussed plans to break into the Watergate and you claim executive privilege for that answer because it's a private communication with the president, you're ruined."

In early April, Attorney General Kleindienst appeared before an all-but unprecedented joint session of three House and Senate committees to debate the question of executive privilege. "Executive privilege is a constitutionally founded, historically accepted, and vital principle of American government," the attorney general argued. According to his argument, the shield could protect the president from having any executive branch employee testify if he didn't want them to do so. Senators balked. It was clear each side was drawing its lines for battle.

*   *   *

On the morning of April 3, Dean finished laying out the situation for his new criminal lawyer, Charles Shaffer. "What do you think?" the White House aide asked. He didn't get the warm, consoling answer he'd hoped.

"John, you're in big trouble. Serious trouble," Shaffer said. "I'm not worried about pre–June 17, but *post*–? There, as far as I'm concerned, you're guilty as hell of conspiring to obstruct justice."

They agreed that Shaffer would go meet with prosecutors Silbert and Glanzer, both of whom he knew from previous cases, and see what the investigators had planned, a move he made subtly but did not entirely keep a secret. In fact, Dean told Haldeman, who was in San Clemente with the president, that he'd begun talking to a lawyer, couching the move as a way to assess the liability for all the co-conspirators. ("I think Shaffer can help us find out how good a case the prosecutors have against Mitchell and Magruder," he said.)

Over the next few days, the prosecutors and Shaffer worked out a plan to allow Dean to begin speaking to them "off the record," a minuet that would give each side a chance to test and assess the other. It was the first real break, besides McCord, that Silbert had had in months. Through the spring, Sirica, Silbert, and the grand jury had kept searching for more answers without much success. Hunt and the burglars had been brought to the courthouse, given so-called "use immunity" to encourage their testimony, and subjected to hours of examination, but Liddy had refused to participate; he was held in contempt of court, with even more prison time added to his sentence, but he held strong to his promise to take the fall for the operation.*

Now that Dean was ready to spill, the investigators felt renewed hope. The White House counsel scheduled his first session with prosecutors for Sunday the 8th, hours before the president and his aides were set to return to the capital. He held off informing Haldeman until the last minute, reaching the chief of staff just as the presidential party was heading for Air Force One and while Dean himself was already in Shaffer's Maryland office awaiting the prosecutors' arrival. Haldeman was, as expected, taken aback by the news the White House counsel was starting to meet with prosecutors. "Remember that once the toothpaste is out of the tube, it's going to be very tough to get it back in," he warned.

As the meeting between Dean and the prosecutors began, Shaffer laid out the ground rules: *No notes, nothing that could be held against Dean later, nothing about conversations with the president.* Then Dean began to talk. Listening for a few moments, Shaffer interrupted his client's pablum brusquely: "This is not the Dean Report you're giving these men with all the self-serving bullshit. I want you to tell these guys the ugly realities."

Chastened, Dean course corrected, starting over with a more detailed and honest account that stunned the prosecutorial team. "He's the one who first told us, with specifics, about the cover-up," Silbert later recalled. "Payments being made. Perjured testimony being given to the grand jury by Magruder and others. John Mitchell's involvement. His own involvement. Magruder's involvement. Ehrlichman and Haldeman's involvement, but initially not the president." Even though they could tell there were still elements of the story to explore, the prosecutors found him credible. "The thrust of what he was saying was not something that one would make up, so in that sense we accepted it," Silbert recalled.

---

* In fact, Liddy in some ways seemed to relish his time in a revolving series of prisons—including the D.C. jail—where he took to counseling fellow inmates with his own freelance legal advice, a development appreciated neither by prosecutors nor defense attorneys. He also attracted no shortage of fights and masculine posturing; at one point, anticipating the damage that Hunt might do if he testified to everything he knew, Liddy said he scouted out a plan inside the jail to kill Hunt in case he got such an order from the White House. (No order came, nor is there any evidence that any such order was ever even contemplated.)

They talked for two hours before Shaffer's phone rang with a radio-relay call from Air Force One for Dean. It was Higby with a brusque order. "Be in Wisdom's office at 1600 hours for a meeting with Wisdom and Welcome," Haldeman's aide commanded, using the White House code names for Ehrlichman and Haldeman. As scared as Dean was by the call, he was also relieved: It gave him an excuse to wrap up the meeting with Silbert and Glanzer before his story got further into the cover-up.

The White House meeting that afternoon proved anticlimatic; the knowledge that Dean was now shifting loyalties seemed to make everyone—including Dean—nervous and more forgetful. It was clear no one could trust any of the others going forward.

The next evening, Dean picked up the meetings with the prosecutors. Soon, he was talking about the hush money.

Then he was talking about Pat Gray.

*   *   *

Nixon seemed to sense that the walls were collapsing. Early Monday morning in the Oval Office, he and Haldeman plotted their defense strategy, wondering aloud whether Magruder would be a big enough fish to satisfy prosecutors. Haldeman began: "The editorial drumbeat now is building to say that throwing Dean and Magruder to the wolves is not—"

"—Satisfactory, yeah," the president finished the sentence. "You're guilty until proven innocent," Nixon lamented. As they continued, it seemed to them that Mitchell was almost certainly going to fall; as campaign chair, he simply had too much culpability for too many decisions.

The next point to tackle was the growing body of evidence the White House had been inadvertently gathering on itself. As he discussed with Haldeman, the president had become acutely aware of the political damage that might be found in his White House tapes.* "The hell with Dean," Nixon grumped to Haldeman, weeks of fraught conversations churning in his head. "Frankly, I don't want to have in the record discussions we've had in this room on Watergate. You know we've discussed a lot of that stuff."

---

* This series of conversations wasn't released until 1997, following a long push by historian Stanley Kutler.

Over the course of several conversations that day, in roundabout, elliptical terms, the chief of staff and the president seemed to edge closer to a decision to destroy the tapes that had been being recorded for nearly two years. Nixon hoped they could be exculpatory, but Haldeman argued it would be insufficient to prove innocence—someone could just argue that conspiratorial discussions could have taken place in another room, out of range of the microphones.

"Who you going to prove it to?" Haldeman said. "Could also argue that, you know—"

"—that we destroyed stuff?" Nixon finished the sentence again.

"Well, you discussed that," the chief of staff reminded him.

Later in the day, Haldeman said they should hold on to the important national security conversations, "Pull out what we want, and get rid of the rest of it."

"And we want to get rid of the rest of it," Haldeman repeated.

"That's right," Nixon agreed.

In the end, though, Haldeman did nothing. In his diary that night, he recounted how "We had a long discussion about the monitoring facilities in his offices. He wants them all taken out, but then he later changed his mind and said to leave them in on a switch basis. He's obviously concerned about having everything covered and wants to set up some kind of limited means of coverage." Nixon's reaction and concern was right—but years too late.

The tapes lived on.

* * *

During the first week of April, Magruder met alone with Mitchell at the former attorney general's D.C. law office. Mitchell pleaded with Magruder to stay strong, but the onetime campaign subordinate knew he couldn't hold out for much longer. He jetted to Bermuda to line up a criminal lawyer—his desired attorney had been attending a conference on the island—and told Fred LaRue and Bart Porter it was time for him to come clean, suggesting they do the same. "The whole thing had become ridiculous. I was up to my ears in a criminal conspiracy," Magruder recalled. "My story hadn't a chance of surviving." On April 10, he fully opened up to his lawyers, their reaction echoing that of Dean's attorney. "Jeb, you've got no choice. It's just a matter of time before they know the whole story and right now, they need us," his lawyer Jim Sharp advised. "We should go to the prosecutors and make the best deal we can."

Just days after Dean, unbeknownst to Magruder, began cooperating, he did too, arriving on Silbert and Glanzer's doorsteps on Thursday, April 12. The sequencing would prove significant: John Mitchell's biographer James Rosen argues that one reason Magruder's confessions consistently pointed the finger at Mitchell rather than Dean might simply be timing. The prosecutors were no longer interested in making a case against Dean—they wanted Mitchell or even bigger fish. "Dean was as involved [in Watergate] as I was," Magruder reiterated in 1990. "I made it clear to Silbert that Dean was in from the beginning, but Silbert didn't care . . . because Dean was already in their pocket."

Magruder and his lawyers began trying to negotiate reduced charges right from the start. After a number of telephone calls, details, and proposals, they reached the agreement they were hoping for: a single felony-count indictment for his perjury the summer before, a reduced charge that would hold a maximum sentence of five years in prison, which would likely be about a twenty-month term. The deal was struck officially on a Friday night, while Magruder and his wife, Gail, were at a dinner party for an admiral. On the drive home, Magruder finally informed Gail of the trouble he was in and the full scope of his Watergate involvement.

The next morning, Dean began to jot down a long list of who he thought might be indicted: Mitchell, Magruder, Strachan, Haldeman, Ehrlichman, Dean, LaRue, Mardian, O'Brien, Parkinson, Colson, Bittman, Kalmbach, Ulasewicz, Stans, maybe even the sources of the hush money themselves. It was a stunning list—nearly every top figure from the entire administration.

Even as they talked with Dean and Magruder, the D.C. prosecutors—Silbert, Glanzer, and Campbell—hadn't told their boss or anyone at Main Justice about their secret meetings. By that weekend, though, they knew it was time. "It was too much to hold on to," Silbert recalled. "The significance was too enormous." On Saturday night, April 14, they met with Henry Petersen, D.C. U.S. attorney Harold Titus, and a few other top aides and outlined what they'd learned in their secret conversations.

When they were finished, Petersen, who had worked in the department since 1947, stood up and poured himself a drink. His sharp, craggy face, which appeared to have been carved from granite, indicated shock. He had worked for years alongside Mitchell—contrary to the cold, almost heartless reputation the man had cultivated publicly, he was well liked and respected by many of his colleagues.

Petersen called Kleindienst, who had been out at the annual White House Correspondents' Association dinner.* Around midnight, the group reconvened at Kleindienst's house. "When we arrived at his home, Kleindienst told us that he had been shedding some tears . . . over John Mitchell," Silbert recalled. Indeed, Kleindienst recalled the conversation as "the most distressing narrative I had ever heard."

The next day, Kleindienst went directly to Nixon. As they spoke, Nixon said he felt the D.C. U.S. Attorney's Office was doing a fine job, but that an outside voice might be needed to oversee the investigation. Lawmakers had begun calling for a special prosecutor as the allegations against the administration multiplied, but Nixon saw an opening for less an independent prosecutor and more an independent supervisor—one who would ensure Silbert pursued the investigation adequately and brought any needed indictments before closing the matter for good.

Kleindienst realized that he needed to take himself out of the case as a starting point, and handwrote a letter to Petersen recusing himself from the investigation, placing the responsibility for the case on him. That afternoon, he suggested to the president that he resign as head of the Justice Department. "Absolutely not," Nixon said.

*　　*　　*

Even if the president wasn't ready to throw Kleindienst aside, it was clear the scandal had fully engulfed the White House. Leonard Garment had been helping to lead an effort to excavate the truth about the spreading

---

* Kleindienst already had heard via Ehrlichman before the dinner that Magruder was cooperating. "Would [his new testimony] be inconsistent with his testimony before the grand jury?" the attorney general had asked the White House aide. "Dramatically inconsistent," Ehrlichman replied.

scandal and the staff's culpability. "The slow march of administration witnesses to the prosecutors had become a footrace," Garment recalled. A veteran litigator from the Nixon, Mudge, Rose law firm, Garment had spent the administration's early years as a White House counselor on issues relating to Native American affairs and the arts, two beloved subjects, but found himself pressed into Watergate service that spring as the scandal spread.*

He had little reason to doubt that the cover-up and guilt stretched into the White House's upper ranks. Over the weekend, he cornered Kissinger for a lengthy update; the national security advisor was taken aback by the dire prognosis—a housecleaning was necessary. "Whoever was the culprit, in Garment's view, only radical surgery and the fullest admission of error could avert catastrophe," Kissinger wrote, recalling the meeting. "The scale of wrongdoing made it impossible to imagine . . . [Haldeman and Ehrlichman] were unaware," Kissinger thought, and quickly followed that thought with a darker one: "If Haldeman and Ehrlichman were involved, it was nearly inconceivable that the President had been completely ignorant." Looking back, Kissinger would cite that weekend as "the moment when all hopes for a period of healing dissolved."

The very trio that Kissinger and Garment worried about—Nixon, Ehrlichman, and Haldeman—indeed spent much of the weekend debating just how far-reaching that housecleaning would have to go. They spoke for nearly six hours altogether. Options dwindled. Nixon worried too much was slipping into view. "It's just a question of putting together all the facts," Nixon said. "And there it'll be."

They needed, Ehrlichman said, to get someone to tell Mitchell, "The jig is up." Dean, they agreed, was finished. "He's to go," the president said. But by then it didn't seem clear that even sacrificing Mitchell and Dean would end the conflagration.

"You've got a really—a punchy decision, which is whether you want me to resign or whether you don't," Haldeman said, offering himself up for the sacrificial pyre. "That's one you've got to figure out. The problem

---

* "I was the last senior White House staffer who (a) had a license to practice law and (b) was not a potential indictee," Garment wrote, explaining how he came to the role.

with that is if I go on the basis of the Segretti matter, you've got to let Dean go on the basis of his implication, which is far worse."

For now, everyone stayed.

*   *   *

On Sunday the 15th, Glanzer and Silbert met with Dean again at his lawyer's office in Rockville, Maryland. They talked for hours, and then as the conversation was wrapping up—Silbert was already standing in the doorway—Dean, prompted by his lawyer, revealed for the first time the details of the White House mission to target Ellsberg's psychiatrist. "We had already heard a lot of shocking disclosures," Silbert recalled. "This was another of major magnitude." Suddenly, everything started to make sense. "We realized that the Ellsberg break-in and its implications was a dominating—a critically important—motivation for the Watergate cover-up," Silbert explained. The White House must have been terrified that if Hunt and Liddy started cooperating on Watergate, they'd lead investigators back to Ellsberg. The prosecutors drove straight to Petersen's house to give him the new information.

Dean spent the rest of the day dodging calls from the White House, refusing at one point to speak even to Ehrlichman. Later that evening, though, the red White House phone at Dean's house rang repeatedly until he finally picked it up.

Nixon himself was on the other side of the line.

At 9:17, Dean walked, dejectedly, into the president's private office in the Executive Office Building to find him sitting in a smoking jacket. "I hope someday you'll know I was being loyal to you when I did this," Dean said. "I felt it was the only way to end the cover-up."

They spoke for nearly an hour, as Nixon had Dean walk through the vulnerability of top aides like Haldeman and Ehrlichman. "You think their problems are that bad, eh?" Nixon said at the end.

"I'm afraid so, yes. I think they are at least as bad as my own," Dean replied. "I'm convinced all of us have serious legal problems."

"Are you prepared to resign?" Nixon asked. Dean said he was.

The president asked that he avoid speaking of their conversations and to stay away from national security concerns like the Kissinger wiretaps.

"Those newsmen's wiretaps and things like that—those are privileged, John," he warned.

As their conversation progressed, it became clear to Dean that Nixon intended to maintain that the first time he'd heard the depths of Watergate was the day when Dean had declared it a cancer on the presidency. "That's when you brought the facts in to me for the first time, isn't it?" Nixon said.

Four minutes after Dean left, Ehrlichman and Haldeman entered Nixon's office. They talked together for nearly another hour, stretching past 11 p.m.

The next morning, when Dean walked into the Oval Office at 10 a.m., Nixon's assistant appeared with two letters for him to sign: one, a letter requesting an indefinite leave of absence; the other, a letter of resignation. Dean balked.

If he was going to resign, he wanted to write his own letter.

*   *   *

That same Monday, Magruder called Mitchell in New York. "I'm sorry, but I've got to think of my family, and I don't have any other choice," he said apologetically.

"I understand," Mitchell said, adding that he would deny everything: "You understand, of course, that I'll have to go the other way."

"I understand that," Magruder said. "Good luck, boss."

"Good luck, Jeb."

Chapter 28

"What Meat Do They Eat?"

There was a delicate moment, Senator Lowell Weicker would later recall, in the spring of 1973 when it wasn't clear how serious or thorough the Ervin Committee would actually be—or how close it would get to the truth. The committee was an odd mix of personalities, not all obviously interested or seemingly up to the historic task ahead. Joseph Montoya, for one, never seemed that engaged—committee investigator Terry Lenzner peeked at Montoya's desk after watching him write intensely during a briefing only to discover that the New Mexico senator had been practicing his signature. Ervin, long set in his rhythms as a committee chair, struggled to adjust to his new colleague Daniel Inouye, a Japanese-American who had lost his right arm to a grenade in Italy during World War II; Ervin routinely polled the committee by asking them to raise their right hands, only to quickly stammer, "Except you, Danny."

The committee's two rank-and-file Republicans, serving with ranking member Howard Baker, each played their own distinct and—to Ervin—infuriating roles. Whereas Gurney clearly wanted to be Nixon's chief defender, Weicker was interested because the investigation appealed to his good-government instincts, and he conducted his own parallel investigation with his own aides and interviews, which was ripe with a constant stream of friendly press leaks.*

---

* Grudgingly, though, Baker came to view his fellow Republican's efforts as correct.

At the staff level, there first appeared to be a vast gulf between the two lead counsels in experience and public profile. With nearly twenty years of age between them, Thompson had actually used Dash's classic book *The Eavesdroppers* as a resource for his own law school dissertation, but the two men were more evenly matched than initially expected. Though Thompson had worked in politics, Dash was avowedly non-partisan, and what the Republican lacked in his profile in the legal community, the folksy six-foot, five-inch lawyer more than made up for with his personality, energy, and oversized presence in meetings. Leaving one heated committee session where Thompson had clashed with Dash's staffers, Howard Baker started to laugh: "I don't think he's afraid you'll overpower him with your intellect as much as he's afraid you just might beat the hell out of him."

The Ervin Committee staff inherited the files from Patman's House committee, as well as the those dug up by the investigators from Ted Kennedy's Administrative Practices Subcommittee.*

Before long, they made an incredible discovery: The Nixon reelection campaign, in its hubris, had carefully assembled and turned over its files the previous November to the National Archives, thinking they would be a valuable resource for future academics or politicians. Now, as the Senate probe was underway, investigators realized no one appeared to have swept or sanitized the 1,100 boxes and 32,000 pages preserved for history, which included all the White House political memos cc'ed to Jeb Magruder. "The Nixon White House probably put down on paper more of its ideas and activities, lawful and unlawful, than any other administration in the country's history," Dash later recalled. For the first time in a congressional inquiry, the staff used a computer to track the materials; the computer tapes and microfilm made cross-referencing testimony or inquiring about the events of a given day simple. Investigators were wowed.

---

* It would forever be a sore point to Speaker Carl Albert that the Senate got the glory of the Watergate investigation and left the House to play catch-up. "[We] had more jurisdiction than the Senate did," Albert said later in an oral history. "We were going to do it if they didn't, you know, but [Ervin] had run out and got it."

In early April, Ervin called a rare press conference to address the president's arguments about executive privilege.* Standing in the large Senate Caucus Room, with reporters all but crammed to the rafters—one photographer literally was shooting film atop a twenty-foot ladder—the senator held forth for more than thirty minutes about the history of executive privilege, a speech more law school lecture than sound bite, and decried the administration's resistance to open testimony.

"What meat do they eat that makes them grow so great?" Ervin asked as he railed against Nixon's haughtiness. Presidential aides weren't royalty or nobility—they and their boss answered to the American people who paid their salaries, he declared. The president was trying to stretch executive privilege "way out past the stratosphere," brandishing Supreme Court opinions that undermined the president's argument. The position, he said, wasn't executive privilege—"It's executive poppycock. It's akin to the divine right of kings, which passed out of existence in America in the Revolution."

The fiery, homespun conference began Ervin's transformation into the president's star inquisitor. "The jowls jiggled. The eyebrows rolled up and down in waves. The forehead seemed sieged by spasms," *TIME* magazine described in its cover story on "Senator Sam" that followed his performance. "Yet the lips continuously courted a smile, suggesting an inner bemusement. The words tumbled out disarmingly, softened by the gentle Southern tones and the folksy idiom. But they conveyed a sense of moral outrage."

*   *   *

It was common practice in journalism to routinely monitor the early editions of major competitors, and on the evening of Monday, April 16, word came into the *Post* newsroom that the front page of the next day's *Los Angeles Times* would contain a startling announcement: "The White House will make a dramatic admission within several days that one or

---

* His aides said at the time it was only the third of his career; he wrote in his memoir it was just his second.

more high level officials bear some responsibility for Watergate-type political espionage."

Woodward, contacted with the news at home by the *Post*'s night editor, rushed to the Madison Hotel, following the protocol he'd earlier established with Felt in the event of a need to contact the source in an emergency. From the hotel, he called Felt's home, said nothing when the FBI leader answered the phone, and hung up after ten seconds. Felt knew the signal meant to call Woodward back at a predetermined Madison phone booth. "You don't have to tell me why you called," he told the reporter when they connected. "You'd better hang on for this—Dean and Haldeman are out, for sure. They'll resign. There's no way the president can avoid it. Several are talking—go find out."

That next day, the *Los Angeles Times* prediction was confirmed when Nixon announced in the White House briefing room that there had been "major developments" in Watergate—words that, if anything, actually were an understatement. "On March 21, as a result of serious charges which came to my attention, some of which were publicly reported, I began intensive new inquiries into this whole matter," Nixon said, reading from a five-minute prepared statement that he'd worked on frantically that afternoon with Ehrlichman and Haldeman. He then recounted—in general terms—his meetings with Kleindienst and Petersen, stating, "I can report today that there have been major developments in the case concerning which it would be improper to be more specific now, except to say that real progress has been made in finding the truth."

The president continued on to explain that he, Ervin, and Baker had reached an agreement on ground rules for White House participation in the Senate investigation that, in his mind, preserved the separation of powers and executive privilege. Finally, he promised that if any member of his administration was indicted, the person would be suspended immediately, and that he hoped no past or present member of the administration would be given immunity. Nixon, who had devoted dozens of hours over the preceding week to the cover-up, concluded with a strong statement: "I condemn any attempts to cover up in this case, no matter who is involved."

On Capitol Hill, Dash immediately wondered whether Nixon's seemingly noble desire to prosecute his administration to the fullest extent contained more sinister and self-protective reasoning: If conspirators were cut off from negotiating for immunity, that would likely serve to insulate Nixon himself.* Dean, listening in his White House office, had the same thought: The immunity line was directed at him. The president was circling the wagons, and Dean wasn't inside. He gathered up a boxful of Watergate papers and went home, leaving the White House perhaps for the last time. Shortly after, he issued a statement of his own: "Some may hope or think that I will become a scapegoat in the Watergate case. Anyone who believes this does not know me, know the true facts, nor understand our system of justice."

The president's announcement changed the entire tenor of the scandal, the White House's posture, and the press corps's interest. As a starting point, White House press secretary Ron Ziegler announced that all previous statements about the bugging incident were "inoperative."

Around midnight that night, Nixon wondered aloud on the phone to Kissinger whether he would need to step down. "Goddamn, I think of these good men," he said. "It's going to splash on a lot of them."

"The major thing now, Mr. President, if I may say so, is to protect the Presidency and your authority," Kissinger replied.†

"If we can we will, and if we don't, what the hell," Nixon said. "Maybe we'll even consider the possibility of, frankly, just throwing myself upon the sword—"

"No!" Kissinger interrupted.

"—and letting Agnew take it," Nixon continued. "What the hell!"

"That is out of the question, with all due respect, Mr. President. That cannot be considered," Kissinger declared. "It is impermissible to touch the President. That cannot be permitted, at any price."

---

* Indeed, when the tapes of that afternoon's Oval Office conversation came out, that was exactly what Nixon, Haldeman, and Ehrlichman had intended. "We're cognizant Dean's going to make a case against this Administration," Nixon had said. "God damn if he'll get immunity!" The president called Kissinger too, and said he wanted to put "the fear of God into any little boys [who sought immunity]."

† The national security advisor had a certain amount of sympathy for what he saw as the simple naïveté of Ehrlichman, Haldeman, and the others caught up in the scandal. "They had not thought of their conduct as a 'cover-up' but as a means to protect an elected Administration that still had much left to accomplish from opponents working against the national interest as they perceived it."

As they finished talking, Kissinger said encouragingly, "You have saved this country, Mr. President. The history books will show that, when no one knows what Watergate means."

Off the phone, Kissinger had a darker thought. As he recalled, "We had all become passengers in a vehicle careening out of control in a fog."

* * *

As the Nixon aides turned on one another, Dash and the Ervin Committee worried that if the prosecutors started bringing new indictments it would derail their own hearings. "How can you possibly expect the defendants to get a fair trial if we put out all the evidence against them on live TV?" investigator Dave Dorsen asked.

"That's the damnedest cave-in talk I've heard!" Terry Lenzner shot back. "I thought that's why the Ervin committee was created—because Congress didn't want to trust the Watergate investigation to the Justice Department."

In the days ahead, Dash and Thompson met with Silbert and his two deputies to ask for guidance on how to proceed: *Would public hearings interfere with the government's prosecution?* But the truth was the Justice Department had just as little understanding of how to proceed as the Senate committee—and, unlike the Senate, the Justice Department leaders were scared for themselves and their jobs. After one meeting with the prosecutors, Thompson chuckled to Dash: "Sam, didn't they look like three scared possums? Hell, they could have given us some hints. They just don't want to cooperate." The hearings, Ervin decided, would go on as planned.

As April unfolded, the Senate investigators were piecing together all manner of evidence about the bugging plan, the existence of Liddy's GEMSTONE plans, and Magruder's involvement. Hugh Sloan, for his part, appeared before the Senate investigators in Room G-334, their offices in the basement of the Dirksen Senate Office Building, and laid out the payments given to Liddy, his concerns when after the burglary Magruder tried to get him to commit to a fake cover story for the payment, and how he'd resigned from CREEP.

Few details astounded the Senate team as much as the ones provided by Liddy's secretary, Sally Harmony. She confirmed there had been actual printed GEMSTONE stationery; the investigators tracked down the printer, who provided a sample sheet, complete with a blue "Gemstone" logo, along with the outrageously conspicuous brown envelope Liddy had also commissioned—modeled on the government's own envelopes for classified materials, right down to the red hash marks around the four sides. The front included one-inch-tall red capital letters saying "SENSI-TIVE MATERIAL," as well as instructions to "Handle as Code Word Material" and "Exdis" and "No Disem," spy shorthand for "Executive Distribution" and "No Dissemination." It hardly seemed the low profile one would normally want to keep while carrying out a criminal conspiracy. "The only thing Liddy appeared to have omitted in this childish effort to proclaim his master spying were neon lights," Dash observed.

Then too came revelations uncovered during a late April meeting with Lenzner in Herbert Kalmbach's Los Angeles law office. Kalmbach outlined how John Dean had recruited him after the break-in to raise money and deliver payments for the burglars to support their families and cover legal expenses, the lawyer thus removing any remaining ambiguity about this being some sort of rogue operation—he had checked Dean's payment request directly with Ehrlichman, he told the Senate investigators, and the White House aide told him to proceed. Dash rushed Kalmbach to D.C. for further testimony. He recalled, "Kalmbach's tale sounded like a combination of comic opera and the sinister activities of La Cosa Nostra."

The lawyer further explained how, with Dean's help, he'd recruited Tony Ulasewicz to be the actual bagman; they'd worked out code names for the various defendants and communicated among a set network of telephone booths. As Kalmbach grew wary of the task, he had gone directly to Ehrlichman to ask if he needed to continue. He recounted pleading to Ehrlichman whether the work was needed and aboveboard: "John, I'm looking right into your eyes. I know Jeanne and your family, you know Barbara and my family. You know that my family and my reputation mean everything to me." Ehrlichman, Kalmbach said, confirmed the payoffs were important and necessary.

As Dash came to know the president's onetime personal lawyer, he found himself almost pitying the fallen aide. "Kalmbach was a sorry figure, stripped of the power and influence gained from his association with Nixon," Dash noted. "Despite his activities in the cover-up, I could not help feeling sympathy for him."

* * *

Across Washington, people were wrestling with the implications that the White House itself might have been involved in the scandal. On *Meet the Press*, Massachusetts Senator Edward Brooke said he thought it was "inconceivable" that Nixon himself didn't know about the bugging at the Watergate, and the network reported a Gallup poll showed 41 percent of the nation felt the same. One night that week, Fred Thompson wrote in his journal, "The focus is on the president now. The word 'impeachment' is beginning to creep into Capitol Hill conversation. . . . Many believe the entire White House staff will go. The key issue is now crystallized: When did the president first know? Presumably after the break-in." He began to wonder what was to him the unthinkable: *Did the president participate in the break-in or the cover-up himself?*

Indeed, despite his seemingly strong statement about getting to the bottom of Watergate, Nixon continued the rush to control the damage, which was fast spreading. As part of that, he tried to wave the Justice Department off any inquiry into the Plumbers and their anti-Ellsberg efforts; when Petersen telephoned to say prosecutors had learned from Dean of the burglary of Ellsberg's psychiatrist, Nixon told him crisply, "That is a national security matter," and that Petersen should "stay out of [it]." Across the spectrum, risks seemed to be growing, not lessening.

On April 22, at 8:24 a.m., John Dean awoke to a ringing phone; he'd worked until about 4 a.m., outlining the events of Watergate and organizing his notes and memories for the prosecutors. It was the president, calling from Florida. All week, Nixon, Haldeman, and Ehrlichman had been rushing to understand what Dean was doing—"Don't know what the son of a bitch is going to say," Nixon said one night. "He's obviously very upset. He's just lashing out. Goddammit . . . I'm at a loss . . . that goddam Dean"—but that morning, on the phone, Nixon pretended everything was fine.

"Good morning, John," Nixon said, "I'm just calling to wish you and your wife a happy Easter." They spoke for fifteen minutes, a bizarre and through-the-looking-glass conversation where both parties danced around the final rupture both knew was coming. Nixon tried to reassure Dean he was still a part of the team. They spoke about the looming scandal, the immunity challenge, and Dean counseled the president to be careful about obstruction himself. "You should talk to Henry Petersen," he said. Nixon agreed.

"Well have a nice day, John," the president said.

Dean replied, "Thank you, Mr. President. I hope you have a nice day, also."

The two men would never speak again.

Chapter 29

"Voice of Doom"

In late April, Earl Silbert stealthily cornered Paul Friedman, the administrative assistant U.S. attorney, in the cafeteria of the D.C. courthouse and asked if the lawyer could start looking into the question of whether the Justice Department could investigate and prosecute the president of the United States. The case had simply gotten too big and too complex, and its targets too powerful. The mission, Silbert stressed, would require the utmost level of secrecy.

The various threads of Watergate filled entire pages in the newspapers, and the uncertainty and stress of the unfolding investigations were wearing down senior members of the administration. Reporters staked out the homes of Magruder and Dean. Americans who had long overlooked the story were now hungry for details. *TIME* magazine began running cover stories—its first was on Patrick Gray on March 26, the first of nearly three dozen Watergate covers to unfold over the months and years ahead—and, in an era where an average issue sold 245,000 copies, the Watergate covers began to top 280,000 copies sold, then 300,000. It was a major turnabout; Nixon's Man of the Year issue in 1972, post-China, post-Moscow, post-victory, had sold below average, just 214,000.* "Only

---

* One of *TIME*'s senior editors, Jason McManus, sensed where the story was going mid-April, cabling his colleagues: "If Mitchell really planned Watergate from the outset, if Mitchell and Dean bribed those caught into silence, if Kalmbach was in on the espionage, is it really credible that Nixon was not involved?"

in his disgrace was Richard Nixon a hot commodity," reflected David Halberstam.

On April 26, Jeb Magruder resigned from government, his ties to Watergate too much of a distraction for his new role in the Commerce Department. The next day, in Los Angeles, the judge presiding over Daniel Ellsberg's trial for leaking the Pentagon Papers disclosed that Hunt and Liddy had burglarized the psychiatrist's office, soon to be followed by revelations that Ellsberg had been the target of government eavesdropping. (Later, the judge officially dismissed all charges against Ellsberg saying the "improper" government conduct "offended a sense of justice.") The irony was obvious: The Nixon White House's attempt to punish the leaker of the Pentagon Papers backfired and resulted in Ellsberg going free entirely.

During a spring meeting with Attorney General Richard Kleindienst about quotidian budgetary matters, Representative Pete Rodino asked perfunctorily how the attorney general was doing—only to be surprised by a dark response. "Let me tell you something, Pete," Kleindienst said. "You have no idea what I'm going through, because every Friday when I come home from the office, I tell my wife, 'Darling, we got through another week without being indicted.'"

On the same Thursday that Magruder resigned, the *New York Times*' Walter Rugaber scooped further news that acting FBI director L. Patrick Gray III had destroyed the documents given to him by Ehrlichman and Dean, a story publicized by Ervin Committee member Lowell Weicker. Across the administration, everyone was sprinting for the lifeboats, and Gray had confessed his role to Weicker after hearing that Dean was cooperating with prosecutors—a sign, to him, that other high-ranking White House officials would be in trouble too. Gray wanted to make sure he ended up a witness, not a defendant. "I could not accept the fact that we in the FBI—and the American people—had been lied to so blithely," he recalled later.

As the blockbuster report traveled through the city, the *Post* tore up and redid its front page. Managing editor Howard Simons looked stricken as he sat in the newsroom, drawing hard on a cigarette. "A director of the FBI destroying evidence? I never thought it could happen," he said.

Friday morning, Gray called Mark Felt and asked that the bureau's leadership be assembled. Once in front of his staff, with tears in his eyes, he announced he was resigning, turning to a naval metaphor for explanation: "I was the captain, and I had let my ship run onto the rocks." The next day, his resignation and departure was just one of five separate stories on the front page of the Saturday *New York Times* regarding what the paper called "the intensifying Watergate crisis."*

On Friday, Mark Felt finally achieved his dream of becoming acting FBI director—a role that lasted just two hours and fifty minutes before Nixon named William Ruckelshaus the new interim director.[†] The Nixon White House had been thinking about someone to nominate in place of Gray throughout the month and, at one point, Ehrlichman tried to recruit Matthew Byrne, the judge overseeing the Ellsberg trial in California—a remarkably odd and improper conversation that, even though it was unsuccessful, would contribute to the aura of misdeeds. Now, they tapped the head of the EPA, Ruckelshaus, who had been working in his garden on a day off when he was summoned by the president and unexpectedly handed the reins to the bureau; Nixon's new choice had one simple request about Watergate before he agreed: "No matter who is involved there would be no sparing of anyone."

*   *   *

With Dean now in the spotlight, the White House returned to its Liddy defense, painting him as a power-hungry lone wolf. Jack Anderson ran a lengthy column that seemed almost certainly sourced from Chuck Colson's or John Ehrlichman's office, accusing the president's counsel of ordering Hunt out of the country after the burglary and saying that the president's "faith in Dean began to waver" in mid-March. Dean worried more as Anderson quoted Ervin Committee sources saying that

---

* Gray never really recovered from the humiliation of his FBI exit; he left it to his sons to pack up and clean out his office. Unfortunately for him, though, he had years of further FBI scandal ahead to weather.

† Felt, in his brief tenure, managed to put a single stamp on the bureau: He did away with the practice of "accountability logs," paper records of who saw certain sensitive documents, logs that often ended up far eclipsing in length the underlying document.

investigators believed he had lied in statements to the FBI, raising the potential of perjury charges.

The growing media attention only worsened Nixon's paranoia. On April 25, John Ehrlichman broached the I-word to the president. "I think it's entirely conceivable that if Dean is totally out of control and if matters are not handled adroitly that you could get a resolution of impeachment," the aide warned. "My own analysis is that what he has falls far short of any commission of a crime by you . . . so far as I know."

Over the next seventy-two hours, Nixon became totally consumed managing the changing situation—there was Dean, Pat Gray, the hush money for the burglars, the Ellsberg trial. He might even need to ask for the resignations of his own two top aides; each problem seemed intractable and each outcome unacceptable. Meeting with Haldeman, Nixon said, "You, Ehrlichman, and I have got to put the wagons up around the President on this particular conversation [the March 21 "cancer on the presidency" talk with Dean]. I just wonder if the son of a bitch had a recorder on him? I didn't notice any but I wasn't looking."

Haldeman listened to the tape of the March 21 conversation himself, trying to find the words that would clear the president. Nixon laid out his strategy: We need, he said, to keep "one jump ahead of the fucking sheriff." Defiantly, he said he welcomed the fight ahead.

"Now if he's going to have this pissing contest . . . all right, bring it out and fight it out and it'll be a bloody goddam thing, you know in a strange kind of way that's life, isn't it?" Nixon said. "[It'll] be rough as a cob and we'll survive. . . . Despite all the polls and all the rest I think there's still a hell of a lot of people out there . . . you know, they, they want to believe, that's the point, isn't it?"

Day after day, he stewed. He asked his aides, incredulously, "Do you think the people of the United States are gonna impeach a President because of *John Dean?*" At another one, still incredulous, he said, "My god—what the hell have we done to be impeached?"

He felt as if he alone were holding the free world together—and safe—and yet still all his ravenous domestic enemies could do was attack him. "The press has got to realize, that whatever they think of me, I'm the only one at the present time in this whole wide blinking world that can do a goddamn thing—you know—keep it from blowing up," Nixon complained. "Look, if we went in with sackcloth and ashes and fired the whole White House staff . . . that isn't going to satisfy these goddamn cannibals. They'd still be after us. Who are they after? Hell, they're not after Haldeman or Ehrlichman or Dean; they're after me, the President. They hate my guts."

By that weekend, it was time for action. At Camp David, Nixon hosted a seemingly endless stream of staff and strategy sessions. On Sunday morning, he called Haldeman back in D.C. and said he needed to see his top aides immediately and have them resign.

Haldeman, in turn, called Ehrlichman. "Voice of doom," he explained. "We go to Camp David today." The men met at the Pentagon helipad shortly and flew north. Ehrlichman was furious—"Goddamnit—he's not going to tie us in one bag with Dean," he fumed. They each met in Aspen Lodge with the president to hear their fate; one of the key breaking points between Haldeman and Nixon would come later, when the chief of staff realized Nixon had used the same maudlin speech and lines on both men separately: "Last night before I went to bed, I knelt down and this time prayed that I wouldn't wake up in the morning. I just couldn't face going on."

In an attempt to soften the blow, he offered large figures of financial support he could provide to help the aides and their families, offering $200,000 at one point and $300,000 at another. (Bebe Rebozo had also volunteered that he and Abplanalp could raise money for the men.) Both turned him down. Ehrlichman, now even more bitter, replied, "Just explain all this to my kids, will you? Tell them why you had to do this."

The meetings shook Nixon. Asking his chief of staff and top aide to resign was "the toughest thing I've ever done in my life," he said. "I had done what I felt was necessary, but not what I believed was right." It was a rare moment when Nixon's hidden anguish broke through to the surface, Julie Nixon later said, and Kleindienst too recalled the president looking absolutely grief-stricken as the attorney general walked in to discuss his own departure. As Kleindienst left, after tendering his resignation, Elliot Richardson walked in.

Richardson, the fifty-two-year-old defense secretary, had held thirteen different government jobs in Massachusetts and Washington, climbing steadily as he sought to reach his ultimate goal: governor of

Massachusetts. An archetypal Boston Brahmin, he was descended from the original Puritans, a *Harvard Lampoon* editor in college who had joined the army as a combat medic in World War II and landed on Utah Beach on D-Day. After the war, Richardson had been president of the *Harvard Law Review* in law school and clerked with liberal legend Felix Frankfurter before becoming a prosecutor himself.* Relentless and polished, Richardson loved Beethoven sonatas and doodled his way through meetings—always paying careful attention—and then crumpled up his paper to shoot baskets into the trash can. "It had come to be the cliché about Richardson that he resembled the stiff, square-cut comic-strip character Clark Kent," the *New Yorker*'s Elizabeth Drew observed. About the wildest thing anyone ever accused Richardson of, Drew said, was that he was an "uninhibited dancer."

Before arriving at Camp David, Richardson had already been told by Secretary of State William Rogers that Nixon intended to make him attorney general, Richardson's third cabinet job of 1973, since he'd spent two-and-a-half years as secretary of health, education, and welfare before moving to the Pentagon on January 30.† Richardson tried to beg off and talk Rogers out of the switch, but he was told it was too late: There wasn't time to locate another acceptable appointee.

That Sunday, amid a beautiful crisp spring sky, tucked a world away from Washington in the Catoctin Mountains, the two men talked Watergate. Richardson, Nixon said, was to pursue the investigation wherever it led, "even to the presidency," and he understood that a special prosecutor might need to be appointed. The choice was Richardson's, Nixon said, but he offered some suggestions: retired judge Joseph Edward Lumbard, establishment lawyer John McCloy, and a young Richardson lieutenant, Wilmot Hastings. Finally, as the meeting wrapped up, Nixon leaned forward, all but pleading with his cabinet secretary. "I had no knowledge of any of this," he said. "You must believe that, or you can't take this job."

---

* Frankfurter thought so much of Richardson that he had recommended his former clerk to become president of Harvard at thirty-three.

† Richardson, who would go on to be Ford's secretary of commerce, and George Shultz are the only two Americans to hold four different cabinet posts.

And then he said something, a warning, that Richardson would find himself returning to again and again in the months ahead: "Be extremely careful of national security interests, otherwise I don't give a goddamn," he said. "Above all, protect the presidency—not the president."

In that moment, Richardson saw a president, raised in genteel but pinching poverty, still striving unnecessarily to prove himself to contemporaries who had always looked down on him. "I wish somehow deep down inside yourself you could come to believe you have really won," Richardson told him. "The American people are rooting for you to succeed."

Nixon, Richardson recalled later, said nothing.

*   *   *

On Monday, April 30, John Dean was in New York, being grilled by a grand jury investigating John Mitchell and Maurice Stans for their role in the brewing scandal over controversial investor Robert Vesco's contributions to the Nixon campaign. James Polk, a reporter for the *Washington Star-News*, had reported early in 1973 about how Vesco had funneled money into the reelection effort through Mitchell and Stans and all but explicitly asked for the Nixon aides to make some of his legal troubles go away; Vesco's associate had delivered the unreported $200,000, saying, "Sure hope that we might get some proper help somewhere along the line, if possible." (The revelations would ultimately earn Polk a 1974 Pulitzer Prize.) It was there, in New York, where Dean received a midday telephone call from his secretary at the White House, who informed him that he'd been fired by the president.

News of the shake-up trickled through the capital. At the *Post*, Howard Simons interrupted Ben Bradlee in a meeting: Ehrlichman and Haldeman were resigning, along with Kleindienst; Dean was fired. Bradlee had his feet on the desk and had been tossing a plastic basketball at a hoop on the other side of his office. "How do you like them apples?" the editor yelled with surprise. *His boys had been right.* "The white hats win!"

"Don't gloat," Simons replied.

That night, President Nixon addressed the nation on television from the Oval Office, saying, "I want to talk to you tonight from my heart on a subject of deep concern to every American." The address mixed bluster, performative outrage, and righteous indignation about the assaults by his own staff on the "integrity of the White House itself." Recent weeks, he explained, had made clear that the longstanding denials by key aides of their own role in the break-in were wrong. He had held faith in people undeserving of it. Worried that he wasn't getting the truth, Nixon explained he had ordered a renewed investigation and fresh answers—and what he had learned from that investigation proved deeply troubling and led him to the unfortunate conclusion to clean house, ousting Haldeman, Ehrlichman, and Dean.

In a remarkable twist of the facts, Nixon blamed himself for the atmosphere of the 1972 campaign as he'd been distracted by pursuing world peace around the globe. "I decided, as the 1972 campaign approached, that the Presidency should come first and politics second. To the maximum extent possible, therefore, I sought to delegate campaign operations, to remove the day-to-day campaign decisions from the President's office and from the White House," he said.

Change now, though, was necessary. From this point forward, Nixon pledged, he would focus again on restoring the integrity of the presidency. "Some people, quite properly appalled at the abuses that occurred, will say that Watergate demonstrates the bankruptcy of the American political system," he said. "I believe precisely the opposite is true. Watergate represented a series of illegal acts and bad judgments by a number of individuals. It was the system that has brought the facts to light and that will bring those guilty to justice—a system that in this case has included a determined grand jury, honest prosecutors, a courageous judge, John Sirica, and a vigorous free press. It is essential now that we place our faith in that system—and especially in the judicial system."

With the housecleaning complete, it was time for a fresh start. "I must now turn my full attention—and I shall do so—once again to the larger duties of this office," he concluded. "I owe it to this great office that I hold, and I owe it to you—to my country."

About an hour later, he spoke to Haldeman. "It's a tough thing, Bob—for you, for John, the rest, but God damn it, I never want to discuss this son of a bitch Watergate thing again. Never, never, never, never," he said. "You're a strong man, God damn it and I love you and I love John. . . . Keep the faith, keep the faith. You've got to win this son of a bitch."

Chapter 30

The End of Mark Felt

For Richard Nixon, the year had begun with such promise—even peace in Vietnam!—but on the morning of May 1, at 8 a.m., he arrived in the Oval Office as isolated and alone as he had ever been. There was no pop-in from Haldeman, no brief chat with Ehrlichman, no phone call from Mitchell. Even for a man who preferred solitude, it was lonely. Outside, the spotlight on Watergate burned brighter than ever and now centered on the White House itself.

In the wake of Ehrlichman and Haldeman's resignations, FBI agents had moved to secure their offices. Under orders from their new boss, William Ruckelshaus, a half-dozen agents from the Washington Field Office at the Old Post Office Building were dispatched to the White House, where they briefly argued with the Secret Service about whether they could bring their guns into the executive mansion. The agents, armed, took up posts in the narrow West Wing hallways with orders to stop anyone from removing anything from either office; other agents secured Dean's office in the Executive Office Building. Ruckelshaus and Richardson had agreed that they wanted to avoid the chaos and trouble that had come from Hunt's safe the previous year following the burglary— better to seal the offices immediately.

Soon after they arrived, Nixon passed through the hallway. When he realized what was happening, he grew furious. *How could such good men like Bob Haldeman and John Ehrlichman be disrespected like this and treated like common criminals?* Special Agent Bill O'Reilly watched, astounded, as Nixon seized the agent outside Ehrlichman's office and shoved him down into a nearby chair, saying, "It's bad enough I have to see you fuckers—I don't want you in my way." The president stormed off, only to return, chastened, about a half hour later to apologize, explaining how much stress he was under.

Later that morning, Haldeman himself arrived, walking past O'Reilly into his office, and he began gathering up papers from his desk—when O'Reilly protested, Haldeman shouted back. The scene escalated, with Haldeman promising, "You sonofabitch, I'll have your job," and O'Reilly explaining that if the former White House chief of staff tried to leave the office with his briefcase, he'd be arrested. Finally, Leonard Garment arrived with an FBI supervisor to assess the situation. He looked at Haldeman with an air of disappointment. "Bob, it's been all this time, and you've had plenty of time—you should have shredded this shit by now. And if you haven't done it by now, it's the FBI's turn."

At an afternoon Cabinet meeting that day, Nixon confronted Kleindienst over the FBI's presence; the attorney general, who had submitted his resignation but planned to stay until Richardson's confirmation, was flabbergasted. He had had no idea about the FBI operation. The president's tirade about Kleindienst's incompetence, malevolence, and disloyalty continued at length until Kleindienst stood and walked out of the White House for the last time. "You're wrong about me, sir," he said as he left.

*   *   *

As chaos engulfed his surrounding offices, White House spokesman Ron Ziegler faced an angry press corps; the resignations and Nixon's televised address had made very clear that Ziegler had misled, actively lied, or been ignorant of the actual facts time and again since June 17, casting doubt on accurate reporting and scoops by Woodward, Bernstein, and others. Now he apologized: "Where we're wrong, we're wrong," adding, "I would apologize to the *Post*."

"Mistakes were made in terms of comments," he added after a moment, sheepishly and passively.

It was part of a brief victorious moment for the paper. The Pulitzer Prize board had been planning to recognize another newspaper that spring—the *Post*'s Watergate reporting package hadn't even been one of the five original finalists for its highest Public Service award—but instead re-voted in the wake of the dramatic McCord letter. It said in its citation, "The *Washington Post* from the outset refused to dismiss the Watergate incident as a bad political joke, a mere caper." Beyond just Woodward and Bernstein, the Pulitzer board credited the broader work of editorial board writers Roger Wilkins and Philip L. Geyelin and the biting cartoons by Herblock satirizing the burglary and resulting cover-up.*

After months of tentativeness, the press corps surged into full scandal mode, chasing every morsel and rumor they could. The anonymous—and even less than anonymous—sources of Watergate suddenly broke into public view, using press leaks to compete for deals with prosecutors. Seymour Hersh later recalled that he had written forty-two articles about the scandal for the *New York Times*, all but two on the front page, between April 19 and July 1, "an unimaginable explosion of news as Nixon was being fed to the wolves by his friends and enemies." On May 2, he published a three-level banner headline in the *New York Times*: "Watergate Investigators Link Cover-Up to High White House Aides and Mitchell." Underneath, a subhead said, "6 May Be Indicted." On May 3, another three-level headline trumpeted, "Investigators Term G.O.P. Spying A Widespread Attempt to Insure Weak Democratic Nominee in 1972." A May 5 story linked a senior Nixon attorney to the destruction of campaign data, and on May 6, Hersh wrote a three-column story headlined "C.I.A. Officials Summoned to Explain Agency's Role in Ellsberg Break-In Plot." The next day, another three-column headline: "Marine Corps Head Linked to C.I.A.'s Authorization for Ellsberg Burglary."

---

* Woodward and Bernstein were initially angry that the paper had entered the "Public Service" category, which alone among Pulitzers is given to the newspaper rather than individual reporters, but Bradlee aggressively argued back that the paper had staked its reputation on their work. "The paper had its cock on the chopping block," he told them. Bradlee was furious in his own way with the Pulitzer board: Amid the horse-trading that accompanied re-awarding the Public Service prize to the *Post*, the board stripped *Post* reporters of two other Pulitzers they were supposed to be awarded: Woodward and Bernstein's victory came at the expense of their colleagues Bob Kaiser and Dan Morgan, who were meant to win for foreign reporting, and Bill Claiborne, who had been set to win the local spot news prize.

Hersh developed a special technique to get past secretaries and ensure his calls got returned, barking, "Tell him I'm writing a story about that son of a bitch he was involved with." Message recipients would inevitably then answer the phone call to understand which "son of a bitch" was involved, given that in Watergate there were so many possible candidates. For Gordon Strachan, Hersh had a more specific tactic—he'd become convinced the aide played a key role in the whole scandal, and he tried to prey on his conscience, calling his office daily to leave the same message: "Tell Strachan to watch the *New York Times* tomorrow."

After having had the story all but to themselves for so long, Hersh and Woodward "became particularly fascinated with each other" that spring, recalled one of Woodward's editors, Len Downie. The competitors met with Bernstein for dinner at a Chinese restaurant, where they roasted the Washington establishment. Hersh and Woodward began playing tennis together at the Arlington YMCA from ten to midnight on Thursdays, followed by pizza nearby and war stories from the Watergate beat, the fun color tidbits that didn't make the papers—like how Charles Colson regularly tried to leak Hersh other non-Watergate stories to distract him from the scandal.*

In fact, as the scandal cracked open—the McCord letter, the Gray hearing, and the Dean testimony, all rapidly intensifying toward the summer Senate hearings—the power dynamics and relationships all over the capital had begun to change. "This was a turning point in the relationship between the White House and the press," wrote journalism historian Alicia Shepard. "Never again would White House reporters be so trusting or respectful of a press secretary pushing the administration's agenda." All the reporters who had contributed materially to advancing the scandal over its first year, from *TIME*'s Sandy Smith to the *Times'* Walter Rugaber to the *Los Angeles Times* duo to Woodward, Bernstein, and Hersh were White House outsiders, people who had little reason to trust the Nixon denials and little reason to brush up against Henry Kissinger at fancy parties. Now they held the keys to the kingdom.

---

* The rivalry, though, only teetered on the friendly; once Bernstein stopped by the *Times* bureau and left a note on Hersh's desk saying he'd rifled his competitor's files. Hersh, interviewing a source one day, learned that Woodward was due to stop by later and left a note: *I was here first.*

It was a shift lost on neither Woodward nor Bernstein. "There has been an obscene affection in Washington for the official version of a story," Woodward said. "Big-name reporters were merely stenographers. Watergate has proved that that is not enough."

*   *   *

On May 3, at the Washington Press Club's annual roast charity dinner, Howard Baker took on the role of the Republican toastmaster, standing in front of a room containing nearly every major player on both sides of the Watergate investigation. "It's a little hard to just come off the campaign trail with echoes of 'four more years' ringing in your ears and get used to the new popular chant: 'not less than two, nor more than ten years' [in prison]," he deadpanned. The crowd roared. Later, as Fred Thompson navigated through the packed ballroom, he passed Ron Ziegler and his wife seated at one of the dinner's round tables and introduced himself. Ziegler lit into him about Baker's softball jokes. Finally, Thompson extricated himself: "All right, Ron," he said. "I'll deliver the message."

The next day, on May 4, Haldeman and Ehrlichman appeared before the Senate staff; Dash had steeled himself for a hostile encounter, knowing the men's reputation, but was surprised to find the two aides warm and respectful. Jim Hamilton whispered at one point, "I like these fellows. Maybe they won't tell us everything they know, but they're certainly not the ogres they've been made out to be."

Both claimed to have nothing useful to share and maintained "to have never been around when any Watergate event occurred or was discussed," Dash recalled. Haldeman claimed that after the burglary, he hadn't even spoken to anyone about it in passing. Matter-of-factly, they laid all the blame on Dean. The conversations, Dash found, provided valuable insights into the reelection campaign's culture and work, despite the men's avoidance of any major details. At one point, the committee counsel asked Ehrlichman to explain an unfamiliar phrase: What did the former advisor mean when he said that Mitchell had "stonewalled" him?

"Stonewall? That's easy. He just denied knowing anything. It was like talking to a stone wall," Ehrlichman replied.

After the witnesses left, Dash and Hamilton agreed: They had been repeatedly, albeit very politely, lied to. There was no way to square the Washington reputation of Haldeman and Ehrlichman—men who supposedly commanded absolute power in the White House, spoke for the president in all manner of settings, and were charged by Nixon with navigating the hardest political questions—with these allegedly disconnected foot soldiers consumed by the nation's other business. Dash cracked a smile, deploying the word they'd learned that day: "Jim, I have the feeling that we have been stonewalled."

That same day, Senator Weicker unexpectedly showed up in Dash's office to report that he'd spent the previous evening talking to Dean. "He's told me a fantastic story," Weicker said, handing over three pages of typewritten notes that outlined for the first time the extreme nature of Liddy's plans for his original GEMSTONE intelligence operation—kidnappings, prostitutes, and recording devices galore. When Ervin and Dash reviewed Weicker's memo later, the committee chair instantly understood its importance. "Just think Sam, this is only a small part of it," he said to Dash. "Our hearings are going to stun the American people."

*　　*　　*

His fall from insider to pariah complete, Dean began to more fully open up to his lawyer about two elements of the case he'd been reluctant to address while still working for Nixon: the specious "national security" argument for the administration's schemes—including the forty-three-page Huston Plan that Dean still had a copy of—as well as the president's own involvement in the cover-up. After Dean related the March 21 "cancer on the presidency" meeting to his counsel, Charlie Shaffer simply said, "That's the damndest conversation I've ever heard."

Over the days ahead, as Dean hid out at a Maryland beach house away from the eyes and cameras of the Washington press corps, Shaffer negotiated carefully between Silbert and Dash—playing the prosecutors against the Senate investigation. There was no shortage of investigators and lawyers interested in speaking with Dean; the growing number of other lawsuits and investigations spawned by Watergate, including

Common Cause's effort to force the disclosure of the Nixon campaign donors and a House investigation of ITT, all also wanted time. As part of the negotiations, Dean took the most sensitive—and potentially explosive—documents and placed them in a safe-deposit box, since he was no longer supposed to be in possession of classified or presidential materials; Shaffer then delivered the key to Judge Sirica. Sirica, in turn, passed them to the prosecutors and the Senate committee.

Dash knew that Dean would be a critical witness for Ervin's committee, but the White House aide insisted on being granted immunity if he was going to speak publicly. "I'll be goddamned if I'm going to sit down and be the only one to go and take the whole rap for this thing," Dean told Dash in their first meeting.

In conversations with Dean at Shaffer's townhouse, Dash finally grasped how much worse the situation was than he'd realized. "The burglary at the Watergate was just the last of a series of similar acts over a period of years sponsored by the White House. It was really not unusual, in light of what had been going on," Dean had explained to him. "A way of life had developed in the White House which made a burglary or an illegal wiretap acceptable and almost normal behavior."

He talked and talked, his dry monotone and command of the details instantly adding credibility as he spoke; they talked night after night, as Dash wrote furiously on a yellow pad, interrupting regularly to ask clarifying questions. The longer the conversation went, the more Dean's memory blossomed, as questions jogged his thoughts. Dash continued to be impressed; the story got stronger and more detailed, which Dash knew was the sign of a reliable witness. Dash reported to Ervin that Dean appeared worthy of immunity. "I couldn't break his story," Dash explained, "and he provides enough supporting details that naturally fit together to persuade me he's telling the truth."

As his mid-May deadline to start the public hearings drew near, Dash still hadn't settled on how to structure them. All around him, Washington eagerly awaited news of his strategy—the TV networks had not originally planned to carry the hearings live, but the ouster of the president's inner circle had instantly transformed their interest. Now it seemed to Dash that he not only had to convince a Senate committee, but the American people watching at home too. He saw the hearings as a critical moment for the country and an important civics lesson in accountability.

Whereas most had suggested that he should start out with the big-name witnesses—like Mitchell or Haldeman—Dash settled on the reverse. After all, there was a story to build. "It was my plan to start out with little-known witnesses, who would provide the details necessary for the public to understand the background roles and activities of the major witnesses," Dash explained.

Thompson was taken aback when he saw his counterpart's proposed witness list; it stretched across dozens of names. "You want to produce 40 witnesses in the Watergate break-in phase alone?" he asked with incredulity. "Why, Sam, that would keep us in public hearings until September, and we wouldn't have touched the dirty tricks phase or the campaign financing phase." He and Baker offered an alternative: limited, short hearings—a few days on each phase of the investigation, wrapping up around the end of June—and then the summer to write the final report. The GOP proposal was rejected in an early May hearing. The die was cast; the public hearings of the Senate Watergate Committee would be meaty, substantive, and carefully crafted by the expert staff.

Dash was ready to fight.

*   *   *

With the top ranks of his White House decimated, Nixon needed new leadership—and fast. He and Haldeman knew only one man seemingly capable of stepping into a White House under fire: Kissinger's former aide, General Alexander Haig, Jr. At the moment, he seemed destined to be the next chairman of the Joint Chiefs. Instead, he was relocated to the White House as Nixon's new chief of staff.

Haig had been a below-average student at West Point and an average army officer, but he possessed an above-average political acumen. His time on Kissinger's staff in the early years of the Nixon administration had accelerated his rank from colonel to four-star general in just four years, skipping over 240 more senior officers. The promotion pace surely stunned even Haig himself, but it mirrored the wishes of his commander in chief: Nixon wrote the army in 1970 that Haig was "a phenomenal individual with outstanding judgment and leadership ability." A year later, in 1971, Kissinger similarly endorsed Haig in an evaluation as "the most outstanding flag officer in the Armed Forces."

On May 2, the forty-seven-year-old received the call; by May 4, he was fully ensconced in a White House confident that the worst of Watergate was now behind it.* As would become clear with time, Haig, as a career military man, neither understood America nor Washington. He believed that he could stay above the fray, and that his boss was innocent. ("The original crime was stupid, and the idea that it was possible to cover it up was more so," Haig recalled thinking. "I thought that Nixon was just too smart to be involved.") He didn't realize the position defending the president would put him in, but Nixon did. The president knew in his heart there would be no escape for Haig. "We were in for a long and bloody struggle, and for Haig it would be like volunteering to return to combat with no guarantee of the outcome and with no medals at the end," he reflected later in his memoirs.

As his first order of business, Haig rapidly reorganized the White House structure. "The changes were fundamentally that Al controlled everything—everybody and everything," Larry Higby explained later. "Al was trying to manage the whole thing personally." It was a change Nixon's circles would come to resent; even though Haldeman had been a powerful chief of staff, his actions and behavior were always seen as being in service of the president himself, while Haig seemed to set himself up as a separate, independent power center, akin to a "first minister"—over the course of the next year, as Nixon retreated deeper mentally and physically

---

* Haig's calculating nature was apparent in how he navigated accepting the White House; since federal law prohibits active-duty officers serving in civilian government roles, in order to preserve his military commission he tried first to get a Pentagon ruling that he was just being detailed to presidential duty. When that sparked outrage on Capitol Hill, including from Barry Goldwater, he announced he would resign his military commission—effective four months *after* taking over at the White House, a delay that would tip him over the next level of retirement pay and increase his pension by $3,000 a year, a paperwork sleight-of-hand that similarly drew fierce criticism on Capitol Hill.

while Watergate consumed his presidency, some would joke that Haig became the nation's "37½th president."*

His next step involved strategy. In one of their first conversations, Nixon debriefed Haig on the political landscape they faced and how he felt Dean's goal was to force a resignation. "My God," Haig replied. "It's unthinkable. It's unthinkable."

"Only one person [is] trying to do that—you realize that—that's Dean, and goddamn him," Nixon continued. "One disloyal President's counsel—a lawyer, of all people!—not just a Henry Kissinger walking out, you know, as a disgruntled person, people will understand it. But the President's lawyer? Jesus Christ."

"Well, he's a sniveling coward," Haig said.

"I think we can destroy him—we must destroy him."

"Have to."

"We never can allow this to happen—even if I was guilty as hell, but I'm not [unintelligible]. I was dragged into this, son of a bitch, because of stupid people—well-intentioned stupid people," Nixon said.

"That's something entirely different," Haig agreed. "Here we've got a vicious little coward who's trying to protect his ass at any cost."

"And therefore he's got to be destroyed," Nixon said.

Within a week, Haig had recruited J. Fred Buzhardt as the White House's legal counsel on Watergate matters. ("He's a hell of a competent guy," Haig promised Nixon during an Oval Office chat. "He's a hard-working guy and he knows the town. He knows the Hill.") Buzhardt, known behind his back as "Buzzard," was a South Carolinian who had once worked on Senator Strom Thurmond's staff as a military advisor, where he'd helped argue against Hawaii's admission to statehood on racial grounds. Later, he had served in the Nixon administration as the general counsel at the Pentagon, where he'd worked the Pentagon Papers case and argued against prosecuting Ellsberg. When he joined Nixon's team, the *Charlotte*

---

* The fact that Haig was one of Watergate's most prodigious leakers, ensuring his story was told in the kindest light, certainly did much to influence history's view of his tenure. Then and now, pundits and historians debate what exact level of influence Haig held, with theories running the gamut from a well-meaning military leader who stepped into a power vacuum to steady the country in crisis to a Machiavellian conniver who shielded himself from consequences as he maneuvered Nixon out of office.

Observer quoted one of his former Thurmond colleagues: "He's the kind of guy who could steal your underwear without ever disturbing your pants."*

Soon after Buzhardt's appointment, Haig and Nixon rounded out the new team with two more appointments: Melvin Laird, Nixon's longtime congressional friend and onetime defense secretary, who would fill the role formerly played by Ehrlichman as a wide-ranging confidant and domestic political and policy advisor, and Bryce Harlow, who would serve as the White House's liaison to Capitol Hill, a role that would prove ever more crucial as the executive and legislative branches neared a collision over Watergate.†

On May 10, John Mitchell was indicted in New York, along with former commerce secretary and Nixon finance leader Maurice Stans. Both men were charged with obstruction of justice in the investigation into New Jersey financier Robert Vesco and his $200,000 donation to the Nixon campaign. In the entire history of the republic, only one former cabinet official had ever been indicted, convicted, and sent to prison: interior secretary Albert Fall, during the Harding administration and the Teapot Dome scandal. Now two former cabinet secretaries had been indicted in a single day. Mitchell's law firm moved quickly to remove his name from its door. "They couldn't wait to get rid of him," Martha noted, darkly. The charge was a serious hit for the White House, adding to its legal and public jeopardy.

Nixon ranted in a conversation with his former chief of staff, Haldeman. "All this crap about the President should resign—"

---

* Elliot Richardson, meanwhile, received a similar assessment from one of Buzhardt's former Pentagon colleagues that would ring true only months later in hindsight: "If you need a job done with no traces, Fred Buzhardt is your man. He can bury a body six feet under without turning a shovelful of dirt."

† The new role was a hard sell for Laird, less so for Harlow; Laird was worried about returning to what he called "that jungle," having felt distrusted by Nixon as defense secretary despite their personal friendship. But the congressional leadership, including Gerald Ford, lobbied Laird hard for help. Laird's wife remained steadfast that it was a bad idea. "She thought President Nixon was lying about the Watergate cover-up," Laird recalled to his biographer. Nixon, ever ungrateful, grumbled even as Laird returned: "[He's] somebody to go out and leak everything," Nixon complained to Haig. "He loves to do that." Most of the new team Nixon recruited would quickly fumble. As Kissinger recalled, "Nixon was too shattered to reach out genuinely. . . . Without specific assignments they proved of little help."

"Don't even listen," Haldeman interjected.

"—Nobody should even raise such things," Nixon continued. "If I walk out of this office, you know, on this chickenshit stuff, why it would leave a mark on the American political system. It's unbelievable. . . . The other thing—if they ever want to get up to the impeachment thing— fine. . . . If they get to that—the President of the United States!—my view is then fight like hell."

*   *   *

After nearly a yearlong high-wire act of Machiavellian manipulation, Mark Felt's secondary career as a prodigious leaker would unravel in May, ironically thanks to a bombshell report for which he had not been the source. On the first anniversary of Pat Gray's first day as acting FBI director, a *Washington Post* article by Woodward and Bernstein expanded on earlier reports about the Kissinger wiretaps, hinting that the panic over covering up the burglary stemmed in part from the fears that revelations would spill over into previous Nixon administration misdeeds.*

A few days later, John Crewdson published in the *New York Times* the first deep, authoritative account of the Kissinger wiretaps, a story that given the deluge of Watergate news engulfing the capital was relegated to page 18, with the spillover jump of the Vesco indictments. Crewdson's reporting was richly detailed, filling two columns and a quarter of the entire page, and—known to anyone familiar with the background—came directly from the most knowledgeable anonymous source possible: William Sullivan, the FBI official who had led the program.

In response, William Ruckelshaus kicked off a high-level inquiry with a special team of agents, dispatched to hunt down the truth about the wiretaps, as well as any remaining evidence from the program—evidence they eventually found in John Ehrlichman's old office file cabinets, right where it had sat since Sullivan turned it over to Nixon himself in the fall

---

* The core of the article's revelations—that *Times* reporters Hedrick Smith and Neil Sheehan had been wiretapped by Liddy and Hunt over the Pentagon Papers—had been delivered to Woodward in February, but was wrong in almost every respect; Hunt and Liddy had nothing to do with the wiretaps, and the wiretaps on Smith and Sheehan had nothing to do with the Pentagon Papers.

of '72. It was an effort to show Ruckelshaus's determination to restore public trust, but Felt and the bureau remained dubious.

The onetime EPA administrator had not exactly been welcomed warmly by the bureau's leadership; Felt labeled Ruckelshaus's first day "Blue Monday," realizing for the first time that the FBI would never have a leader promoted from within its own ranks. He had drafted and assembled a telegram to the president, supported by more than seventy other FBI officials, calling for a permanent selection of a "career professional."

What he didn't know was that Ruckelshaus had been warned not to trust the deputy he'd inherit at the bureau and, particularly, Felt's propensity for leaks ("Yes, the president mentioned it to me when he asked me to become the director of the FBI," Ruckelshaus told Watergate historian Max Holland in 2007), and so he was being watched carefully from the director's suite, and the investigation of Crewdson's sourcing would lead quickly to Felt's denouement—a series of events Holland re-created in full for first time only in 2012. In fact, as Holland pieced together, Felt's downfall began just hours after the *Times* story appeared.

A man identifying himself as "John Crewdson" called Ruckelshaus and said that the anonymous source was none other than Felt. He told the FBI director that he didn't normally out his sources, but that he was "just very concerned about the situation in the country."*

Word spread; as Al Haig reported to the president that day, "Bad guy. Now last night he gave the whole thing . . . to the *New York Times*."

"Felt did?" Nixon said.

"Yeah. Now he's got to go. But we've got to be careful as to when to cut his nuts off," Haig cautioned. "He's bad."

Moments later, he continued. "According to Elliot [Richardson], they're sure. And as a matter of fact, I talked to Bill Sullivan yesterday, and what Felt is doing is trying to kill Bill Sullivan so he can be director

---

* Crewdson denied ever making the phone call when asked in 2008, which according to him was the first time he'd ever heard of it. The most likely scenario is that both men are telling the truth; Ruckelshaus wouldn't have known Crewdson's voice and, presumably, was set up by someone, perhaps in Sullivan's camp, who saw the story as an opportunity to sink Felt and knew enough about the secrecy surrounding the wiretap chapter to know that Felt could have been suspected of being the leak.

of the FBI. These guys are just unbelievable," Haig said, in wonder. "That place is riddled and rotten."

The solution was simple: "Fire his ass."

And Ruckelshaus did—quietly.

The following Monday, the interim FBI director announced the results of his probe of the Kissinger wiretaps, explaining that the bureau had uncovered seventeen such wiretaps between 1969 and 1971 and had located the logs in Ehrlichman's office safe. That day too he confronted Felt. To underscore that his own information was impeccable, he made up a story that an old fraternity brother who was now a *Times* editor had called the previous week to double-check that Felt would be in a position to know the information in Crewdson's story. The men argued; Felt named Sullivan as the likely source, but did admit that he'd spoken to Crewdson the previous week—though only to correct mistaken information the *Times* reporter already had. As the conversation wrapped up, Ruckelshaus asked Felt to turn in his keys to the office.

The next morning, Felt's letter of resignation was waiting on Ruckelshaus's desk. That same month, William Sullivan retired from the Justice Department, finally accepting that he'd never lead the bureau either. The cold war to succeed J. Edgar Hoover had ended with his most devoted soldiers' mutually assured destruction, but not before they helped unleash the forces that would ensure Richard Nixon's undoing.*

* * *

One year after the original break-in, what had begun as a possible jewelry theft investigation now encompassed a whole host of public subplots—the Huston Plan, Sullivan, the Kissinger wiretaps, ITT, Donald Segretti and CREEP's dirty tricks, and Vesco, among others. With their list of

---

* It wouldn't be long before Nixon announced he would nominate Kansas City police chief Clarence Kelley as the bureau's new director. Standing in the Oval Office with the police officer and Attorney General Richardson beside him, Nixon said, "We picked the best man in the country for the position." That standard, even if true, seemed unnecessary; as one Justice Department official anonymously told the *Times*: "This agency is so much on the ropes at the present that they will be happy with most anybody."

problems quickly growing, the Nixon team scrambled to prevent other scandals from spilling out—especially they wanted to avoid any public mention of the Pentagon spy ring that had been using Yeoman Radford to steal secrets from Kissinger's National Security Council.

On May 16, the day before the public Senate Watergate hearings kicked off, Nixon huddled with Buzhardt and Haig to discuss Senator Stuart Symington's Armed Services Committee investigation into the Huston Plan. "Don't it seem like we always have problems?" Nixon lamented. The men had spent much of the day meeting and talking in various configurations, including five meetings of all three together. There was plenty of other drama amid the domestic and foreign challenges that spring and summer—inflation had doubled to nearly 9 percent over the course of 1973, challenging consumers and businesses and threatening the national economy—but for Nixon, inside the bubble of the White House, with a shrinking circle of advisors, there was only Watergate.

As the clock swept past 9 p.m., Nixon ranted to his lawyer and his chief of staff in the Oval Office. "We have to realize they're not after Bob or John or Henry or Haig or Ziegler. They're after the President. Shit! That's what it's all about. You know that—they want to destroy us."

Haig nodded in agreement. "What they're hung up on—they're really in a dilemma up there. They want to get you and yet they don't. And that's tough for them too."

"You know, it's ridiculous that the President of the United States has to spend his time for the last almost two months worried about this horse's ass crap. Unbelievable!" Nixon concluded.

That same Wednesday night, across the Potomac, Felt and Woodward met again in their designated parking garage. Woodward had no sense of the internal drama that had gone down at the FBI, nor that his inside source had delivered his resignation to Ruckelshaus Tuesday morning. He imagined that recent developments would have been a moment of great satisfaction and triumph for the FBI official—Nixon's crookedest aides had been thrown, disgraced, from office, and penetrating congressional hearings were about to start—but instead, Felt seemed angry and worried, almost manic. He paced and spoke for only a few minutes before disappearing, warning of how Nixon had tried to enlist the CIA in obstructing Watergate and saying, almost out of nowhere, "Everyone's life is in danger."*

In shock, Woodward summoned Bernstein. Together, they went to Bradlee's house at 2 a.m. for a parley. "What the hell do we do now?" Bradlee asked. No one knew what to make of Deep Throat's bizarre performance.

That next morning, Bradlee picked up the *New York Times* only to discover on its front page that as he and his reporting duo had been caucusing on his lawn, Seymour Hersh had been finishing the next big scoop in the wiretap story. Apparently, after Ruckelshaus's public announcement about the wiretaps that Monday, Sullivan had asked Hersh to lunch, after which Sullivan stood to leave, and told Hersh he had left something behind. On Sullivan's seat, Hersh found a manila envelope filled with the original seventeen Nixon administration wiretap requests, sixteen of which the reporter was stunned to see had been signed by Kissinger himself. The requests included the names of the FBI technicians who had placed the wiretaps, and Hersh quickly began to call around to confirm his scoop. When he reached Kissinger, the national security advisor gasped when he heard what Hersh possessed. There was no doubt the documents were authentic.

As word of Hersh's scoop spread within the Nixon White House, Al Haig called Hersh to plead for the *Times* story to be killed or held. "You're Jewish, aren't you, Seymour?" asked the White House chief of staff, who had overseen the wiretapping program himself in 1971 as Kissinger's deputy. Haig grasped at one of the only straws he had left: "Do you honestly believe that Henry Kissinger, a Jewish refugee from Germany who lost thirteen members of his family to the Nazis, could engage in such police-state activities as wiretapping his own aides?"

*　　*　　*

That month, Symington's hearings on the Huston Plan ultimately uncovered the "memorandums of conversations," or "memcons," that Vernon

---

* Even in his *Secret Man* book, published after Felt's outing, Woodward doesn't mention the internal drama at the FBI nor its possible relevance to Felt's sudden bout of paranoia, simply noting that Felt informed him at that meeting that he was retiring.

Walters had written in the days after the burglary, as Haldeman, Ehrlich-man, and Dean had tried to block the unfolding FBI investigation—the first hints that White House aides had tried to lever the CIA as part of a cover-up. Pat Gray, who was also beginning to speak with the Ervin Committee and sharing for the first time the pressure the FBI had been under to shut down its investigation, was among those shocked by the revelations in Walters's memos; he'd never known that Walters had been dispatched directly from—and by—the White House to lean on him. "It was a bombshell," the FBI director wrote later in his memoir. "I was incensed."

The Walters revelations soon became the focus of even another set of congressional inquiries, this time by Representative Lucien Nedzi's Special Intelligence Subcommittee. Nedzi's hearings stretched through the summer, bringing forth as many questions about the administration's scheming and plotting as they resolved. In the end, the committee was unconvinced that it had gotten to the bottom of the White House, CIA, and FBI subterfuges. "To be charitable, the best that can be said for [the CIA's explanation] is that it is rather strange," the committee concluded.* Piece by piece, the outlines and full scope of the Watergate cover-up were coming into view.

---

* The CIA director who had weathered Nixon's push in the summer of '72, Richard Helms, would come to be criticized for not more clearly and forcefully speaking up to confront the White House pressure publicly, and indeed, his motives throughout the administration remain questionable and complicated. Helms's biographer, Thomas Powers, later assessed, simply, "Helms hoped to keep the CIA out of this, not just out of the break-in, but out of the line of fire. . . . Helms did not want Nixon to think of him as an enemy."

Chapter 31

"A No-Win Job"

The Capitol bears few rooms more historic than the Caucus Room in the Russell Senate Office Building, where the Ervin Committee's Watergate hearings convened publicly for the first time on May 17, 1973. The French-inspired room, with rich wood, dark black-veined marble, and gilded rosettes stretching across the ceiling, had hosted hearings on the sinking of the *Titanic* and on the Teapot Dome scandal, as well as Estes Kefauver's historic 1950 inquiry into organized crime and Joseph McCarthy's infamous hearings on Communism. But despite its legacy—or perhaps because of it—the room by the early 1970s looked somewhat shabby. "It had the appearance of a grand old downtown railroad terminal suddenly restored to use, mobbed with people, but unrenovated," recalled the *Post*'s Watergate editor Barry Sussman, noting the chipped paint and tattered curtains as the latest historic hearings began.

As Sam Dash entered the room that Thursday, it was packed with nearly four hundred observers—including celebrities like Norman Mailer and Dick Cavett. The press settled in as cameramen fine-tuned the lighting and angles, while the committee counsel immediately felt a mix of awe and inadequacy, worried that the first five days of scheduled proceedings—during which time they expected to hear about the structure and operations of the Committee to Re-Elect the President and from both the arresting police officers and burglars about the Watergate break-in itself—might not live up to expectations. Fred Thompson, for his part, couldn't get over how blinding the TV lights were for those sitting on the dais; the room's acoustics were quite poor too, and it would hard for many people to hear the unprecedented admissions about to be made.

To begin, each senator framed the hearings in grand terms, both positive and negative. "If the many allegations to this date are true, then the burglars who broke into the headquarters of the Democratic National Committee at the Watergate were, in effect, breaking into the home of every citizen of the United States," Ervin said in his introduction. "And if these allegations prove true, what they were seeking to steal were not the jewels, money, or other property of American citizens, but something more valuable—their most precious heritage: the right to vote in a free election."

Gurney, for his turn, struck his own distinctly partisan note, warning that the inquiry's "rocking of the boat by Watergate" risked a "catastrophic effect upon the institution of the presidency." Weicker, full of the moral indignation he'd displayed throughout, wondered aloud whether the committee would have the stomach to follow the path wherever it led. "The gut question for the committee and country alike is and was how much truth do we want?" he asked. "The story to come has its significance not in the acts of men breaking, entering and bugging the Watergate but in the acts of men who almost—who almost stole." It was a slow and esoteric way for the proceedings to begin—Jules Witcover, writing in the *Washington Post*, declared the next day, "If you like to watch grass grow, you would have loved the opening yesterday of the Senate select committee's hearings on the Watergate and related campaign misdeeds"—but the drama began in no time.

On the second day of testimony, McCord himself took the stand and spoke about how he'd been offered clemency for his silence, recounting the surreal series of meetings with Caulfield at the George Washington Parkway overlooks.* The story astounded the committee, and helped the investigators begin to piece together what Tony Ulasewicz, Kalmbach, and others had also said about the hush money, but it also underscored

---

* Caulfield had taken a leave of absence earlier that month from the Treasury Department when the *Los Angeles Times* first broke news of his clandestine meetings with McCord.

the challenge ahead: Every one of the players seemed to be involved in so many shady activities that it was hard to keep a narrative straight—it would be hard to confine witness testimony to just one line of questioning at a time. The committee agreed to recall witnesses multiple times to tell different slices of their story at the appropriate moment.

When McCord's story was corroborated by Caulfield and Ulasewicz, the whole tenor of the hearings shifted. "Presidential involvement in Watergate could be inferred," Dash recalled. Whereas just weeks earlier it had appeared that the campaign finance questions and dirty tricks of the reelection might be the centerpiece of the hearings, now everyone understood: The burglary and its cover-up were the main event.

Perhaps even more surprising was the apparent shifting perspective on Sam Ervin. From the start, Fred Buzhardt, citing the constitutional watchdog's history of running boring, impenetrable hearings, had been certain that the committee chair would bungle his moment in the spotlight. "He's our biggest asset, Ervin," Buzhardt had promised Nixon—and yet as the first days unfolded, it became clear they had misjudged their new opponent.

In the wake of McCord and his colleagues' disclosures, Ervin yielded to the instincts of Dash, who conducted much of the meaty questioning himself—rather than the traditional congressional approach of allowing members to lob unrelated questions at witnesses one by one. It was equal parts horrifying and fascinating, showing the excavation of facts in real time. In a profile of the Georgetown professor–turned–Senate investigator the week the hearings began, Dash's wife, Sara, had explained that her husband loved archaeology, telling the *New York Times*, "If he ever retired, I think he'd go dig."

*   *   *

While Ervin's hearings continued on Capitol Hill, the Nixon administration faced the bizarre challenge of presenting a nominee for a cabinet office currently under investigation. Elliot Richardson's Senate confirmation as attorney general had not been as smooth as he'd imagined—especially since the job was not one he particularly wanted. Leading the Justice Department was, by almost every measure, a step down from his current role heading the Pentagon, and from the first moments of Senator James Eastland's opening statement at his hearing, Richardson found himself off-balance.

"Did you ever hear of the Watergate affair?" the judiciary chair asked, by way of greeting. The room erupted in laughter.

"Yes, Mr. Chairman," Richardson replied.

"All right—now, if you are Attorney General, what are you going to . do about it?" Eastland continued.

Richardson promised that he would "undertake that responsibility determined to pursue the truth wherever it may lead. I have examined my conscience on that score. I am satisfied that I am prepared to do that without fear or favor, and with regard solely to the public interest."

"What about a special prosecutor?" Eastland said, raising the idea that had been growing in popularity in the preceding weeks. Within moments, the topic of Richardson's nomination itself was all but shelved as the hearing devolved into a discussion about the charge and independence of such a role. Richardson had no intention of giving up full control of the case and pushed for a special assistant attorney general to lead the investigation autonomously, making clear that he would not fire any special prosecutor unless his actions were "arbitrary, capricious, or irrational." Several senators pushed for more—suggesting Congress adopt the model used in the Teapot Dome scandal, when Congress itself had appointed independent prosecutors.

Robert C. Byrd of West Virginia made clear that unless Richardson embraced the committee's suggestions for a special prosecutor, he would halt the nomination at once. Eventually, everyone agreed Richardson would set to work immediately finding an independent investigator; he needed a trial attorney, an experienced fact-finder—and fast.

The White House suggested two former Democratic governors, Pat Brown and Warren Hearnes, both of whom Richardson rejected. Meanwhile, his own first four choices—federal judge Harold Tyler, former deputy attorney general Warren Christopher, and retired New York state appeals court justice David Peck—turned him down or took themselves out of the running. It was an embarrassing series of setbacks for a man who wasn't even confirmed yet as attorney general, and he was forced to stop ranking his choices so there was no "scorecard on refusals." "The smart ones knew there was a mess of trouble in this thing," Richardson's aide Wilmot Hastings said.

Finally, Richardson reached Harvard Law legend Archibald Cox during a lecture series at the University of California. The former U.S. solicitor general under President Kennedy, Cox hadn't been on any initial candidate lists, but the deeper into the field Richardson got, the more his name had come up. He had worked as a labor arbitrator and built a national reputation helping to respond to student protests at Columbia and Harvard during the peak of the antiwar movement, experiences where Richardson knew he'd shown "unfailing fairness and firmness." He didn't have that central characteristic of trial experience, but he had integrity, which seemed just as critical. (The fact that Cox had worked for three Democratic presidents didn't hurt either.) Over the phone, Richardson asked if the law professor was, in his word, "available?"

Cox knew he didn't want to be. "This is probably a no-win job," he told his wife, Phyllis. "I'll be damned by everybody." And yet, he knew someone had to do it. He was late in his career, tenured at Harvard Law, with no ambitions for public office. It might as well be him. As his wife later said, "I know Archie will love it. It appeals to his old-fashioned sense of being called by the nation."

Two days later, on May 18, Richardson announced that if he was confirmed, he would name Cox to a $38,000-a-year job as special prosecutor. "This is a task of tremendous importance," he said. "Somehow, we must restore confidence, honor and integrity in government." Both men touted that they'd come to an amicable understanding about Cox's independence, agreeing on terms "word for word."* One of those terms, perhaps most importantly—and most presciently—was the conditions under which Cox could be fired: Richardson could only do so personally, and only for "extraordinary improprieties."

---

* It wasn't quite that simple—there actually were several rounds of suggestions and negotiations over the job's specific scope and mission, but it was all amicable and Cox did effectively get everything he requested—including specific authority not just to investigate the burglary but to investigate White House misdeeds and personnel generally; Cox sensed from reading the newspapers that there were aspects of the case, like ITT and the Ellsberg burglary, that might not be directly related to the DNC burglary but were part and parcel of similar behavior.

On Monday, May 21, as Mitchell and Stans pleaded not guilty in New York to the charges in the Vesco case, Cox appeared in Washington alongside Richardson at the would-be attorney general's confirmation hearing. Time and again, Cox emphasized that he was comfortable with the level of independence he'd have from Richardson. "The only authority he retained is the authority to give me hell if I don't do the job," Cox said of Richardson. "Let's face it, I'll have the whip hand."

"And you won't hesitate to use it?" asked Senator Robert C. Byrd.

"No sir," Cox promised.

The next day, Leonard Garment appeared in the White House Press Room to release a massive four-thousand-word statement from the president, responding to the first days of hearings, with equal parts national apology and political defense. The statement had grown out of days of labor by Pat Buchanan, Haig, Garment, Buzhardt, and others who had drafted versions around a conference table in presidential writer David Gergen's office, delivering them to Nixon in his hideaway, and then waiting patiently as he edited and revised in solitude.

In an echo of his April 30 speech, where he professed that the root cause of Watergate grew out of how much he cared for the country and how seriously he took his duties as president, Nixon again argued that he'd had only the best intentions—it was his staff who had "gone beyond my directives" and that he "should have given more heed to the warning signals I received along the way about a Watergate coverup and less to the reassurances." As soon as he'd realized what Haldeman, Ehrlichman, Dean, or others might have done, he had acted quickly. "I had no prior knowledge of the Watergate operation," the president said, the first in a list of seven points he wanted the nation to understand, continuing:

2. I took no part in, nor was I aware of, any subsequent efforts that may have been made to cover up Watergate.

3. At no time did I authorize any offer of executive clemency for the Watergate defendants, nor did I know of any such offer.

4. I did not know, until the time of my own investigation, of any effort to provide the Watergate defendants with funds.

5. At no time did I attempt, or did I authorize others to attempt, to implicate the CIA in the Watergate matter.

6. It was not until the time of my own investigation that I learned of the break-in at the office of Mr. Ellsberg's psychiatrist, and I specifically authorized the furnishing of this information to Judge Byrne.

7. I neither authorized nor encouraged subordinates to engage in illegal or improper campaign tactics.

At least six of those points would later prove lies.

Altogether, it was a powerful statement—one featured prominently in banner headlines the next day, juxtaposed with photos of McCord and Caulfield testifying to the Ervin Committee—and served its purpose well. The Senate, Richardson, and Cox all felt reassured by the president's words; Cox, especially, was buoyed by the lines about waiving executive privilege. "The assumption was that I would get to see everything," he recalled later.

Thursday, after the Senate confirmed his nomination as attorney general, Elliot Richardson gave his farewell press conference at the Defense Department and made clear that his priority in his new job was to restore the nation's trust in its law enforcement. "A kind of sleaziness has infected the ways in which things have been done," he said from behind his Pentagon desk, as he doodled stars on the scratch pad before him. "I think there is an opportunity to restore confidence through finding ways in which the law enforcement process can be made to be, and perceived to be, scrupulous in the ways in which it carries out its job."

On Friday the 25th, he was sworn in at the White House by Chief Justice Warren Burger, after which he and President Nixon greeted the two hundred guests into a State Dining Room reception. "The attorney general would be happy to see those of you who do not have any matters pending before the courts at the moment," Nixon quipped.

The room roared with applause.

In private, though, Nixon didn't see much to joke about. The scandal was now more than just a distraction from the nation's business; it was becoming a literal threat to his legacy. Even as Richardson was sworn in, the Richard M. Nixon Foundation announced that the plans and fundraising for a presidential library were being shelved as the majority of the seven trustees who were supposed to build the permanent monument to his career were now implicated in the cover-up: Ehrlichman, Haldeman, Mitchell, and Kalmbach.

At the White House, the president's darkness was starting to appear inescapable, his grumblings about resigning more constant. "Wouldn't it really be better for the country, you know to just check out?" he'd asked Haig the night before Richardson's swearing-in. "I can't fight the damn battle, you know, with people running in with their little tidbits and their rumors all that crap." Later that night, with his family, he asked, "Do you think I should resign?" His daughters Julie and Tricia Nixon rejected the premise outright; Pat Nixon was circumspect too. She saw Ervin as a mortal danger and could only watch the Senate hearings in half-hour doses. "The hearings [were] just like a snake about to devour people," she told a friend.

That night was the last time he'd mention resignation to his family until August 2, 1974.

*   *   *

That same Friday morning, the front page of the *New York Times* announced Magruder would plead guilty and cooperate with prosecutors. Next to it was another headline, a tragic reminder of the long reach of the still-widening Watergate scandal: "A House Member Apparent Suicide."

A longtime congressional aide, William Mills, had won his seat after its occupant, his boss Representative Rogers Morton, was named Nixon's interior secretary in 1971, but it had been a tough fight; the mid-cycle special election struggled for money, given the short timespan it had to raise funds. Morton had turned to CREEP for help. In April 1971, his assistant took the first distribution from the piles of campaign cash that had accumulated in Hugh Sloan's safe and delivered the $25,000 gift to Mills's campaign—money that was never reported on either federal or state disclosure reports.

Maryland authorities had begun investigating the slush fund cash after the Government Accounting Office investigation uncovered and made public questions about the donation earlier that week. With Watergate dominating the national headlines and the newspapers filled with stories of people making deals with prosecutors, Mills evidently feared that his political career was over—or worse.

He was found dead in an Eastern Shore barn, near his horses, after shooting himself with a twelve-gauge shotgun. Among the seven different suicide notes Mills left, authorities said, was one lamenting "he had done nothing wrong but said he couldn't prove it, and so there was no other way out." Mills, a World War II army veteran and a proud member of the Elks and the Rotary Club, left behind a wife, a twenty-four-year-old daughter, and a sixteen-year-old son.

Chapter 32

"A Russian Novel"

If Richardson's swearing-in featured grand White House ceremony, Archibald Cox's was the opposite, only a low-key ceremony at the Justice Department that reunited the various chapters of his career. His bow ties would become famous over the course of the next five months, but for that day, he had borrowed a standard red, pin-striped necktie from his brother. He was sworn in by FDR's solicitor general, his first boss in Washington, as Robert Kennedy's widow, Ethel, and Senator Ted Kennedy both looked on from the audience.

It was clear immediately that Cox would have to triangulate his own position among at least four other centers of gravity in the Watergate case—the existing prosecutors and Judge Sirica's grand jury, the Ervin Committee, the president, and the Justice Department itself—and catch up on his reading. As he and Phyllis relocated to Washington, he filled his briefcase every trip with sensitive reports and case files. Two U.S. marshals traveled alongside him and came home with him each night, not to protect him, but to secure the papers. As his wife recalled, "I fed them and watched them watch Archie."

In D.C., Cox started to build an organization that would be known as the Watergate Special Prosecution Force. He was joined by two Harvard Law colleagues, James Vorenberg, a onetime McGovern policy advisor, and Philip Heymann, a former solicitor general colleague who, twenty years Cox's junior, was all but a son to him. At their first meeting in Room

1111 of the Justice Department, the small team was far outnumbered by the press waiting outside. James Doyle, a *Washington Star* reporter recruited as the special prosecutor's new spokesperson, took stock of his new boss, dressed in signature bow tie and suede Wallabee shoes. "Prosecutors are supposed to have the instincts of a shark; this one seemed more the dolphin. High-pitched voice. Very intelligent," he recalled later.

Cox understood precisely the incredible power and national trust being vested in his new role. Just days after his appointment, he confided in Vorenberg that he felt he was "being asked to play god."

"It's sort of playing St. Peter, isn't?" Vorenberg clarified.

"I'd be content to settle for that role," Cox agreed. "He doesn't pass the judgments."

Their first night in the office, the team asked Henry Petersen to stop by and talk to them about the case. Over hours—sometimes collegially, sometimes testily—Cox asked for documents and quizzed Petersen on his meetings with the president, Mitchell, Kleindienst, and Gray. At one point, he asked the assistant attorney general: "Did you ever get a report from the president of what Dean told him?"

"That report is on tape, but I didn't want to hear it," Petersen replied. "The president said [on April 16] I could hear it if I wanted to, but I couldn't listen to that tape because we were dealing with Dean and his counsel."

"Do you mean Dean's conversation with the president is on tape?" Cox said, startled.

"So I've been told," Petersen said.

They kept talking, and Petersen's defensiveness finally overwhelmed the meeting, as Cox wondered aloud how thorough the summary he was getting of Petersen's conversations with Nixon and the other officials could be. "I'm not very good at cross-examining presidents," Petersen finally grumbled.

"No, I doubt any of us are," Cox replied.

Cox also met with Earl Silbert, Seymour Glanzer, and Donald Campbell, the three D.C. prosecutors who had handled the Watergate case up until then, who had been making noise publicly about quitting in the days leading up to Cox's arrival. The trio, who had weathered nearly a year of harsh criticism about their handling of the investigation, argued that they'd now nearly solved the case and just needed time to wrap it up; in their eyes, the addition of a special prosecutor was an insult—and too late to be of any help. They told the press the case would be done in sixty days if they remained in charge.*

Publicly Cox gave them a vote of confidence, but he still began to formulate his own team, calling first upon James Neal, the Nashville federal prosecutor who had won a conviction of Jimmy Hoffa in 1964 while Cox was solicitor general. "Jim, I desperately need a trial man to get on top of this case," he pitched, initially agreeing that Neal could work for just two weeks. (He ended up staying indefinitely, much to the consternation of his small Tennessee law firm.)

Cox's next stop was Sam Dash; the two men had known each other for years—Cox had been the Senate investigator's labor law professor at Harvard Law—and the special prosecutor now hoped he could convince his former student that the Senate should now step back from its investigation and give him space to work, indict, and try defendants. "It doesn't seem to make any sense that there should be two investigations, does it?" But Dash resisted; America didn't yet have a reason to trust the Justice Department and it needed to continue its own search for answers. Despite rounds of effort with Dash, Ervin, and even, later, after pressing Judge Sirica to weigh in, Cox was unable to stop the Senate hearings.

The last of Cox's initial meetings came on June 6, with the toughest audience of all: Nixon's three-member defense team: Fred Buzhardt, Leonard Garment, and Charles Alan Wright, the newest addition to the team, who had been brought in to focus on the case's special questions about presidential powers. Garment had assumed Dean's role as the president's personal White House counsel, whereas Buzhardt was solely focused on the Watergate case, and Wright even more specifically focused on the constitutional questions raised by the scandal and resulting investigations.

They met, awkwardly and tensely, in the Special Prosecutor's Office, where Cox raised the topic of Petersen's odd conversation with the president on April 16. He wanted the tape of the conversation between

---

* The night after Cox's hearing before the Senate, Silbert had dictated to his diary, "I have had [it] with the case. I think this case is nothing but problems and we have compromised on integrity, been questioned, we have no supporters, we have no credibility."

Nixon and Dean if it existed, as well as Petersen's documentation of that meeting. Buzhardt rapped his West Point ring on the meeting table and said the president would turn over no such thing, dismissing the "tape" that Petersen and Nixon discussed as an after-the-fact Dictabelt recording of the president's own recollection of the exchange.* A request was also made for nearly a year's worth of White House meeting and call logs, detailing the president's interactions with top aides, which would be invaluable in determining who was present for what conversations and which witnesses could testify to what. The lawyers at least agreed to think about it.

During their first days organizing the Special Prosecution Force, Vorenberg for his part kept popping into the office of Glen Pommerening, the department's acting administrator, to discuss hiring staff, locating offices, and purchasing equipment, sketching out a nearly $3 million budget and mission; they would need to set up five distinct task forces to investigate different groupings of allegations—the burglary and cover-up, the Plumbers and government abuse of powers, the finances of the Nixon reelection campaign, and the dirty tricks, as well as a team to run the ITT probe, which Richardson on June 8 announced he was also moving to Cox's office. Vorenberg's estimate was that Cox needed about forty lawyers—five senior task force leaders and a dozen solid, veteran mid-career lawyers, experienced in investigations and prosecutions, plus perhaps two dozen junior workhorses. Recruiting such a team, on the fly, was no small challenge, and the operation would eventually be larger than all but six of the nation's ninety-three U.S. Attorneys' Offices.

At one point, Vorenberg looked up at the walls of Pommerening's office, decorated in standard government fare, with photos of the department's leaders: There was Nixon, Mitchell, and Kleindienst. "This is the first case I've worked where the potential defendants' personally autographed pictures are on the office walls," he noted.

*   *   *

---

* Cox doubted Buzhardt's version in the moment, and it would later be clear that Buzhardt certainly misled, if not outright lied, in the exchange at the Special Prosecutor's Office that day.

As Cox got to work, Washington's headlines were dominated by the parade of witnesses making their way through Sam Ervin's committee.* As the story unfolded, "it began to take on the characteristics of a Russian novel," the *New Yorker*'s Elizabeth Drew wrote. "It became a major effort just to keep the names straight." Under oath, Tony Ulasewicz displayed to investigators the busman's coin changer he'd attached to his belt as he hustled around in the summer and fall of '72 arranging hush money payments, while Howard Baker couldn't get over the seeming caricature of an investigator before him. "Who thought you up?" Baker asked Ulasewicz. "I don't know—but maybe my parents," the president's onetime private eye shot back. Everyone laughed.

While most of the scandal's major players—like Haldeman and Ehrlichman—had decamped from Washington, Magruder and his wife had decided to stick it out in the capital, where their children were in school. Reporters often accosted the kids as they headed out in the morning. The onetime campaign leader had quietly taken up some part-time marketing consulting work around the heavy schedule of depositions, interrogations, hearings, and grand jury appearances required by prosecutors and congressional investigators, and finally appeared before the Ervin Committee on June 14 with a great deal of trepidation. "It was like going to church to make your confession—but in front of a hundred million people," he recalled.

Dash was struck by the man's hypocrisy and playacting. Behind closed doors in a prep session the day before his public testimony, the deputy campaign manager had cataloged his crimes and the broader conspiracy with relative disinterest ("He appeared totally insensitive to the nature of these offenses and to their impact on the country"), but now before the cameras, Magruder was suddenly contrite. His telling of the campaign's scheme implicated virtually all of the White House's major figures except the president himself, naming Mitchell as the head of the campaign espionage program and Dean as the architect of the cover-up.

---

* At one point amid the hearings, Haldeman crossed paths in the Dirksen Senate Office Building with the Democratic prankster Dick Tuck, the longtime Nixon campaign trail nemesis who had inspired CREEP's efforts to set up its own dirty tricks operation. "You S.O.B., you started this!" Haldeman muttered. "Yeah, Bob, but you guys ran it into the ground," Tuck shot back.

"No witness in my experience has affected me the way Magruder did," prosecutor Jill Volner later recalled in her memoir. "I was stunned by the ease with which he dissembled, even as he tried to clear himself. He was a slippery confabulator, and I came to the conclusion, based on our many hours of conversation, that he had no moral center."

*   *   *

While his former colleagues faced the spotlight, John Dean had spent weeks that spring honing a lengthy opening statement that would lay out for the committee the full arc of how the Nixon administration had lost its way. Dash quickly rejected the first draft. "This won't do," the investigator told the former White House aide. "You put your finger on everybody but yourself, John. When you told me the story before, it was very clear to me that you were as much a part of the cover-up as the others. In fact, you were directing a large part of it." Charlie Shaffer agreed, confronting his client. "You've got to tell every last fucking thing you did, no matter how bad or lousy it sounds or how distasteful it is to you to admit it."

Revelations about what Dean would say steadily leaked into the press; on June 3, dual stories in the *Washington Post* and *New York Times* headlined the depth of the collusion between the president and his counsel: "Dean Said to Tell of 40 Meetings with Nixon in '73," the latter declared on Sunday's front page. Monday's paper then headlined the CIA's fears from the days after the burglary that it was being dragged into the cover-up, a "potential political bombshell."

Nixon hated what he read. "Dean, I felt, was re-creating history in the image of his own defense," Nixon wrote later in his memoirs. Trying to counter the counsel's torrent of revelations, Nixon began to dive into his secret tape recordings himself with his aide Stephen Bull, listening, plotting, and fuming.

That week, as everyone waited for Dean's testimony, Dash's office received an anonymous threat printed in large block letters: *JOHN DEAN WILL NEVER BE A WITNESS. HE WILL BE DEAD.* After consulting with Cox, they decided that U.S. marshals would provide round-the-clock protection for the witness—transporting him to and from the Capitol and sitting behind him during his testimony.

Finally, on the morning of June 25, amid an especially packed Caucus Room, Ervin gaveled the committee to order. Thompson, in his seat, was fuming; he'd only been given Dean's book-sized opening statement and fifty accompanying documents that morning—hardly enough time to digest and respond.

"Counsel will call the first witness," the North Carolina senator instructed.

"Mr. John W. Dean, the third," Dash responded.

Sucking on throat lozenges and refreshing himself with water, John Dean began reading from his carefully worded prepared statement. "The Watergate matter was an inevitable outgrowth of a climate of excessive concern over the political impact of demonstrators, excessive concern over leaks, an insatiable appetite for political intelligence—all coupled with a do-it-yourself White House staff, regardless of the law," he began. "The fact that many of the elements of this climate culminated with the creation of a covert intelligence operation as part of the President's re-election committee was not by conscious design [but] rather an accident of fate." From there, he unfurled the wild tale, sweeping from the Huston Plan to the Brookings burglary plot to Operation SANDWEDGE and on through the Committee to Re-Elect the President.

It took the entire first day for Dean to get through all 245 pages of his opening remarks—his head down, peering through his tortoiseshell eyeglasses, and speaking directly into a phalanx of microphones, with his wife, Maureen, perched over his shoulder in a striking yellow outfit. "The effeminate Pretty-Boy image he projected in the news magazines is wrong," observed essayist Mary McCarthy. "Horn-rimmed glasses, small face, small neatly set ears, hair growing thin at the crown, he appears more like a history or economics professor at a Middle Western university looking up from a carefully prepared lecture text."

As part of the testimony, the committee also released a cornucopia of documents Dean had turned over; at one point, CBS reporter Daniel Schorr found himself reading for the first time, live, Dean's August 16, 1971, memo on Nixon administration "priority enemies" list. In front of a national television audience, he reached "#17: Schorr, Daniel. Columbia Broadcasting System, Washington. A real media enemy." He did his best to read onward without a pause. "I do not know how well I carried off my effort to appear oblivious," Schorr recalled, "but I count this one of the most trying experiences in my television career."

The scene captivated the nation. "The worst fears of most Americans, which had been building by speculation, were now realized," Dash recalled. The *Washington Post* ran the next day six full pages of excerpts from Dean's testimony, the most space Sussman had ever seen the newspaper devote to a single subject.

The prosecutors who had talked with Dean through the spring were equally stunned. He'd always been vague about specifics with them, but now to the Senate, he had given a precise, corroborated, and almost minute-by-minute rundown of the entire scheme. The four days of follow-up questions did little to shake confidence in Dean's memory or his accounting of the events. Polls showed 70 percent of Americans believed the president's former lawyer.*

As he emerged at the public center of the scandal, however, Dean's centrality to events raised fresh suspicions with former Hill colleagues. Jerome Zeifman, Rodino's counsel on the Judiciary Committee, recalled working with Dean on the committee before he went to the administration and described him as cautious and ambitious by nature; he wasn't one to act unilaterally, without authority and cover. "I know damn well that if Dean had his fingers in the cover-up, John's mentality is such that he made goddamn certain that the president would know John Dean was covering [Nixon's] ass," Zeifman told his colleague Frank Polk. "John Dean is not loyal to anybody or anything other than his own career."†

---

* As Dean testified, far from the hearing room, Lyndon Johnson's national security advisor Walt Rostow handed the head of the LBJ Library a sealed envelope marked with a big "X." It was labeled "Eyes Only." He asked that it be sealed for fifty years; inside, it turned out later, were the files, wiretaps, and memos relating to the Chennault Affair. Rostow understood in that moment as Dean began testifying how the Chennault Affair tied into the mentality of the scandal he was watching unfold on television, and he clearly knew the important relevance of the Chennault Affair to Nixon's conduct as president, but rather than raise it in the allegations in a moment when they would have altered the trajectory of the ensuing scandal, he chose instead to bury the evidence for decades. "He left us no explanation," wrote historian Ken Hughes, who authored a 2014 book on the subject.

† Committee staff were surprised too by how the press lionized Dean as a noble man of conscience. "I never saw him that way," investigator Terry Lenzner recalled later. "His main motive, understandably, was self-preservation."

On Dean's fourth day of testifying, Senator Weicker stated how disgusted he had been by what he heard from Dean and the behavior he'd seen from the president's camp. "Conspiracy to obstruct justice, conspiracy to intercept wire or oral communications, subornation of perjury, conspiracy to obstruct a criminal investigation, conspiracy to destroy evidence, conspiracy to file false sworn statements, conspiracy to commit breaking and entering, conspiracy to commit burglary; misprision of a felony; filing of false sworn statements; perjury; breaking and entering; burglary; interception of wire and oral communications; obstruction of criminal investigation; attempted interference with administration of the Internal Revenue laws; and attempted unauthorized use of Internal Revenue information," he summarized, seeming to even surprise himself with the sheer scope of perceived White House crimes.

"I say before you and before the American people that I'm here as a Republican," the Connecticut senator said before a packed room. "And I think I express the feelings of the 42 other Republican Senators and the Republicans of Connecticut and the feelings of the Republican party far better than those who committed illegal, unconstitutional and gross acts."

He continued, his jaw firmly set, "Republicans do not cover up. Republicans do not go ahead and threaten. Republicans do not go ahead and commit illegal acts. And, God knows, Republicans don't view their fellow Americans as enemies to be harassed."*

With Dean's testimony complete, the hearings adjourned ahead of the July 4 congressional recess and were set to begin again in mid-July when Mitchell, Haldeman, and Ehrlichman would take the stand. House Majority Leader Tip O'Neill was now sure of one thing: Nixon was done. "Tip realized he was going to have to act after he heard John Dean," *TIME* magazine's Neil MacNeil recalled later. The rest would just be process and politics.

With Rodino's assent, his committee staffers Zeifman and Polk called to request a meeting with their Senate counterpart. "I want to impress upon you, Mr. Dash, that this meeting has to be kept very, very

---

* The next morning, Weicker found Chuck Colson at his office door, there to defend himself and Nixon, in an exchange that grew heated. When Colson said he was proud of his work for the president, Weicker blasted: "How could you be proud after the disservice you've done him?"

confidential," Zeifman said, his voice barely above a whisper, as he closed the door when they convened. "What I'm about to say to you must be considered as a hypothetical matter. Our committee has taken no action whatsoever, not even a suggestion of an action. Only Chairman Rodino has talked to me. He wanted me to raise with you—hypothetically, mind you—the question of what help your committee can give our committee in an impeachment inquiry against the President of the United States?"

Dash, taken aback, plotted his response carefully, but assured the House staffers that Ervin would surely want to provide "the fullest cooperation possible." That said, Dash reminded them, Senator Kennedy had specifically prohibited, with an amendment, the Senate committee from investigating the president. The next step, they agreed, would be for Rodino to write a formal letter to Ervin asking for cooperation and information.

It was a huge moment, one that had previously seemed unthinkable, but it was clear that the tide was turning, beginning with one of the proceedings' most unmoveable men.

✳   ✳   ✳

With Dean's testimony still rippling through the American public, Cox's team knew it needed to find a first domino to fall—one that would pressure conspirators and set the tone and scale for the punishments to come. Fred LaRue, they agreed, would be the easiest target. He'd first spoken to prosecutors that spring without an immunity deal, and his culpability in the hush money payments was clear. James Neal pressured LaRue and his lawyer to fold, and as Dean's testimony wrapped up, LaRue pleaded guilty to a single count of conspiracy to obstruct justice. As soon as the plea was before Judge Sirica, prosecutors knew who they'd go after next: Magruder, then Dean.

Watching from the White House, Fred Buzhardt had grown increasingly concerned as he rushed to formulate the best defense he could, closeting himself with some of Nixon's recorded tapes. As he listened, he worried. His client sounded guilty. Buzhardt heard a lot that seemed to be obstruction of justice at a minimum—perhaps worse. Buzhardt, though, didn't know who to tell or what to share; the strictures of attorney-client privilege precluded commiserating with most of his White House colleagues.

One night, after work, he stopped by the house of his former Pentagon boss and now White House colleague Melvin Laird. Buzhardt and Laird went into the basement, and Buzhardt opened up. "The president was involved in the cover-up," he said. "I've listened to some of the tapes, and he was in the cover-up right up to his eyeballs from the beginning."*

There was only one legal strategy ahead: delay.

---

* In the sole biography of Laird, Dale Van Atta's *With Honor*, Laird recounts how "the morning after" Buzhardt's confession, he confronted Nixon in person about the president's culpability. However, as historian Ray Locker traced, the timing of such a confrontation, if it ever happened, must have come later than Laird remembers, as Nixon was away from Washington in San Clemente from June 23 to July 9.

PART IV

Firestorm

July–December 1973

Chapter 33

"We Need You Today"

At the dawn of the summer, the special prosecutor's team moved into two floors of a private office building downtown at 1425 K Street—it was important optics-wise to Cox to be outside the offices of the Justice Department—and began filling the space with its growing staff.

Cox found the hardest role to fill was his deputy; none of his top five choices either wanted the role or seemed to match the profile needed.* Finally, they settled on Hank Ruth, a veteran of New York City mayor John Lindsay's administration. Cox and Ruth met for lunch downtown and noted right away how different they were. "Cox tends to be all optimism and dogma in his conversation. Ruth, who has a penchant for irreverent one-liners, spices his idealism with a dose of cynicism," recalled Jim Doyle. "The two men shared one bond: Both thought the job was a loser, and both thought it had to be done."

Beyond the deputy, the rest of the team leadership came together rather quickly: James Neal headed the Watergate cover-up team himself, joined by two young, talented, and ambitious lawyers, Richard Ben-Veniste and Jill Volner, a Columbia Law School grad who had been the first female attorney to work in the Justice Department's organized

---

* Cox's first choices included a legendary Boston Republican attorney, James St. Clair, and a Justice Department veteran, John Doar. Both men would be drawn into the case in the months ahead anyway.

crime and racketeering section, where she'd helped prosecute a teamster boss and a boxing promoter who was fixing fights.* William Merrill, a veteran of Robert Kennedy's presidential campaign, led the Plumbers team; Tom McBride, a veteran organized crime prosecutor, took over the campaign finances team; Richard Davis, a federal prosecutor from New York, oversaw the dirty tricks task force; Joseph Connolly, a rare devout Republican on the team, was named the fifth task force leader, charged with the ITT investigation that was merged into the special prosecutor's work.

Recruiting was rushed. Volner interviewed on Cox's second day, and told Vorenberg she could start in a month, once she'd transitioned her other Justice Department cases. "We need you today," he countered and made clear he had the power to make such an instant transition possible.

Vorenberg also recruited Philip Lacovara, a deputy solicitor general, who turned down leading a task force to instead appoint himself Cox's counsel—figuring that the team would need someone focused on the legal theories and maneuvering of the whole office. "He was one of those people who finished everything—high school, college, exam papers, legal briefs—in half the time it took other people," Doyle later recalled. Lacovara's role put him right below Cox's deputy, Ruth. "I am number two-and-a-half," he would joke.

The team Cox assigned to the burglary case itself—Neal and a young, twenty-nine-year-old assistant prosecutor named George Frampton, Jr.—journeyed daily over to Silbert's offices to review the overflowing file cabinets generated by the first year's investigation, indictments, and trial. Each night, they then reported back to Cox on their progress and analysis. Once they felt up-to-speed in June, Cox informed the original D.C. prosecutors—Silbert, Glanzer, and Campbell—that he no longer

---

* Volner's presence, the only woman on the Watergate task force, caused wonder and confusion throughout the investigation. On her first day on the job, she and Neal met with Jeb Magruder. Not yet thirty herself, Volner was struck by how young the thirty-eight-year-old campaign aide looked; when Neal asked if anyone wanted coffee, Magruder turned to Volner and said, "I'll take mine black." Neal, chomping as usual on a cigar, drawled, "Not very smart, insulting a major player in deciding the terms of your plea agreement." Instead, George Frampton, the junior prosecutor on the team, fetched everyone's coffee.

needed them. In stiff but cordial letters, exchanged publicly, the trio formally requested to withdraw from the case and argued how well they'd performed in the Watergate investigation. Cox, in turn, thanked them for the work and "invaluable" help with the transition. From that point forward, Neal, Ben-Veniste, Volner, Frampton, and an appellate lawyer named Peter Reint would carry the Watergate burglary case; eventually two others would join too, creating an eight-person team to take on the president.

The Nashville litigator Neal was a stark exception to much of Cox's Watergate Special Prosecution Force, most of which came from the toniest circles of the Eastern Establishment, had graduated from Ivy League law schools, and had been schooled in the tight confines and regimented process of federal procedure as prosecutors or Justice Department attorneys. Neal, by contrast, had little patience for legal theory. "He had a short attention span for anything he regarded as peripheral to the guts of the case—namely, that small core of evidence he could use to most effectively at trial convince a jury of the defendants' guilt," recalled Ben-Veniste and Frampton. Enduring Neal's work sessions, during which he smoked enormous Jamaican cigars within an ever-thickening cloud of haze, came to be something of a test of human endurance for his task force attorneys.

From the start, security in the office was tight; the suites always had an odd, timeless twilight to them, as the blinds and drapes were always kept closed to prevent eavesdropping or spying. The prosecutors knew that any leaks could have major consequences, and so Doyle was confounded (and worried) when the *Washington Post*'s John Hanrahan somehow managed to put his hands on two internal memos in the office's first weeks in operation. After the second memo appeared in the paper, Cox called *Post* editor Ben Bradlee. "If you ever tell anyone I told you this, I'll deny it, but Archie, you've got a trash problem," Bradlee said. Evidently, while the office had arranged for its trash to be incinerated, the actual process for disposing of their office waste was less secure: The building used transparent plastic bags and the contents were easily visible on the loading dock, awaiting pickup, to anyone walking by.

Soon thereafter, a massive shredder appeared in the office.

*   *   *

Nixon's ranch in San Clemente had for some time been his escape, and as the scandals around him deepened, he spent longer and longer stretches out at the so-called Western White House. During an extended Fourth of July escape, the family walked on the beach and watched movies like *The Railway Children* and *Rebel Without a Cause*. Then, one morning, Nixon opened the *Los Angeles Times* to see that, in what he viewed as an egregious personal attack, Archibald Cox's team was investigating the propriety of his vacation home.

Nixon erupted, angrier than he had been about almost any Watergate revelation so far; he had worried about Cox from the start (*Jack Kennedy's solicitor general?!?!*), and the new reports seemed to indicate the worst. This wasn't about finding the truth concerning the DNC break-in, this was about hunting the president—however, wherever, and whenever he could.*

Nixon ordered Haig to call Richardson and check on the report. The chief of staff and the attorney general spoke multiple times that morning, and Haig, huddled in San Clemente with Ziegler and the president, called Richardson back a second time at 1:05 p.m. ET. On a third telephone call, Nixon himself interjected to demand that Richardson get a retraction from Cox within half an hour or else he'd fire the special prosecutor.

Richardson weighed the best response and considered for a moment whether to resign—especially if Nixon moved ahead with a threat to fire Cox. He called the special prosecutor, who calmly explained that the San Clemente request was no more than a general gathering of old newspaper articles on the subject. As a matter of fact, the topic of the president's estate had come up at Cox's most recent press conference, and he hadn't known enough to even answer the questions. Richardson argued the president's San Clemente house didn't fit within Cox's purview. "I disagree," Cox said, "but I'm at a disadvantage since I don't know the allegations or the facts." He assured Richardson there was no

---

* "[Cox] seemed like a scholarly, calm objective professional, but he was in fact a fairly conventional Nixon hater," Len Garment wrote later. "The organizing objective of these investigations was to bleed Nixon to death."

"investigation," but also made clear he thought the attorney general's intervention was troubling. "Elliot, do you really think it's proper for you to call me up like this?" he said. "It will do neither of us any good if you advertise the fact that you called me the first time that something hostile to the president appeared in the press."

Finally, Cox agreed to issue a brief statement confirming that all he was doing was reading about San Clemente. Speaking to reporters, Ron Ziegler labeled any allegations of financial improprieties "malicious, ill-founded and scurrilous." In Washington, Sam Dash announced that the Watergate Committee would recall Dean to testify about Nixon's personal finances and the San Clemente estate.

As the responses crisscrossed the country, Richardson wondered, just barely a month into his role, whether he could survive the pressure ahead. He had been perfectly happy—enthusiastic even—in his role as defense secretary, but now he found himself in an unprecedented, and obviously perilous, position, overseeing investigations of not only the president, but the vice president as well—as it turned out, federal prosecutors from Maryland were building a case against Spiro Agnew, who they believed had accepted bribes in the White House complex. They'd been in Richardson's office that very day outlining their case, as Haig kept phone-banking him about the *Los Angeles Times* story.

The president's behavior more broadly through the summer had simply confounded Richardson; loyalty ranked almost equal in his mind to integrity, and he felt deeply loyal to Nixon and wanted his president to succeed.* He kept seeing opportunities for Nixon to take the offense—at one point, he wrote a lengthy memo suggesting a "Federal Code of Fair Campaign Practices" to make illegal many of the dirty tricks that Segretti, Dick Tuck, and others had carried out over the years, a move he thought would win favor with the country and show how seriously Nixon wanted to move past the scandal—but the suggestions, despite follow-up, went nowhere. "The President, it seemed, could not or would not take positive steps to restore confidence in his administration and

---

* In fact, he'd moved ahead with appointing Cox in part out of just how loyal he felt to Nixon, knowing that absent an arm's length investigation "the struggle to preserve my independence would be painful."

himself," Richardson wrote later. "I charged this off to an error in judgment. I should, of course, have realized that Richard Nixon was more likely to be guilty than stupid."

The truth was that he had little insight into the case that would define his tenure as attorney general; the president had quickly cut him off from conversations about Watergate, as Richardson had made clear that he didn't see his role as serving as a presidential defense attorney, and the freedom he'd granted Cox meant the special prosecutor didn't share much with him. As he'd say later, "I never did know much about Watergate."

*   *   *

Each day, as the Watergate Special Prosecution Force passed into their office, they walked by a government security poster in the hall that warned of leaks; with a picture of a telephone wired to dynamite, it announced "Loose talk is explosive . . . Anytime." The regular warning seemed to have little impact. The same day Cox quashed the San Clemente eruption, CBS's Daniel Schorr reported the outlines of an eighty-page status memo that Silbert had written upon his departure, including the recommendation that Haldeman, Ehrlichman, Mitchell, and Dean face indictment and that Gray and Strachan be offered plea deals. Their defense lawyers promptly protested the leak, saying it prejudiced any future jury, and Cox was equally outraged—seeing the move as undermining his leadership, a feeling that seemed to spread across Washington that summer. "Archie Cox is a bit of a softie," journalist Teddy White warned Doyle as he started. "You'll find that he gets pushed around by his staff." A Democratic senator similarly complained to *Newsweek*, "He's too quiet. He just doesn't seem to be turned on to his job."

His staff, though, found such snap judgments mistaken. They never doubted their boss's "diligence and judgment," recalled Stephen Breyer, the future Supreme Court justice who worked on the ITT investigation task force, and Ben-Veniste and Frampton, in their joint memoir, concluded, "Cox's predominant characteristic, one sometimes mistaken for arrogance, was his overwhelming sense of the importance of distinguishing right from wrong." Twice the age of many of his prosecutors, Cox ran the office with the aplomb of a law professor, trusting his team and stoking debate, ultimately falling back on what he called "Lincoln's Rule": Everyone on staff got one vote, but his vote counted more than everyone else's combined. This was to protect against an important generational and philosophical divide he had identified: his young, ambitious team had mostly come of age amid the turmoil of the 1960s, and were naturally more distrustful of power and institutions. They saw their investigation as a standard prosecution case—albeit one with particularly high-profile targets—while Cox, a child of the Great Depression and product of the upper ranks of the Justice Department, saw Watergate as an institutional problem, not just a legal one.

The Force came to intimately know the witnesses and headline-grabbing names who had found themselves in the eye of the storm. Hunt struck them less as a superspy and more the anti–James Bond, and Ben-Veniste took an intense disliking to him, finding his answers squishy and self-serving. The Cubans earned sympathy as pawns in the conspiracy, and Barker and Martinez were respected for their CIA service. But as the team heard from LaRue, Magruder, and Mitchell about the March 30, 1972, meeting in Key Biscayne where Mitchell was said to have approved the GEMSTONE plan, none of the accounts lined up. "Each of the three 'witnesses' claimed that the other two did all the talking at the meeting," recalled Ben-Veniste and Frampton. "We reckoned that must have been one of the quietest campaign meetings in history."

As they investigated, the prosecutors understood that the president merited a higher-than-usual standard of evidence; they knew, for instance, that Nixon might have technically committed a crime known as "misprision of a felony" when he failed to tell the Justice Department about the cover-up at the time that, according to his telling, he first learned about it in March and April, but no one expected such an obscure charge to be brought against a president. Instead, they knew they needed to find places where Nixon had taken affirmative actions to advance a conspiracy, initiate a felony, or obstruct justice.

And they had to work with hard evidence. "Guilt or innocence in the political-corruption case often hinges on very small differences in testimony, on fine interpretations of motive and intent," Ben-Veniste and Frampton later explained. In fact, political corruption cases are almost by definition among the hardest prosecutors face, because they almost always involve a high-profile—and often well-liked—figure, respected and rooted in the community and able to advocate loudly for himself in the press. Nixon epitomized all those challenges and more—he was even still, technically, their boss as employees of the Justice Department.

Relatively late into the summer, it wasn't clear that there would be any meaningful charge against or even investigation of Nixon himself. When Cox asked Jim Vorenberg to assemble a strategy memo outlining all the evidence prosecutors had uncovered against the president, the resulting document found little beyond circumstantial evidence, growing primarily out of Dean's testimony. "More frustrating than the lack of hard evidence was the absence of any obvious line of investigation by which additional facts could be uncovered," Ben-Veniste and Frampton recalled.

One morning Cox came in looking particularly tired. "I'm afraid I didn't sleep much last night," he said, when questioned by Doyle. "I was worrying about witness Nixon."

"If you think you had a bad night, imagine what kind of nights he's having," Ben-Veniste replied.

*   *   *

Though Woodward and Bernstein had missed much of the spring and summer's Cambrian Explosion of scandal revelations while racing to draft their book on the first year of Watergate—the manuscript that became *All the President's Men*—other journalists more than picked up the slack. In July, Seymour Hersh began reporting in the *New York Times* about the fake Pentagon bookkeeping system that had obscured the fourteen months of illegal B-52 bombing of Cambodia. The matter quickly spurred new congressional hearings, which confirmed that the administration had concocted an elaborate double-entry system, known to only a small number of high-ranking officials, to enable a grand lie about the use of one of the military's most prized assets.* The revelations touched off another congressional probe by Stuart Symington's Senate Armed Services

---

* A year later, Nixon's effort to have the U.S. Air Force lie about its missions would be cited in a fourth article of impeachment by the House of Representative as an egregious abuse of power; that specific article, ultimately, was not adopted by the House.

Committee, which had previously been digging into the Huston Plan. The illegal operation dating back to 1969 clearly implicated two of the newly arrived White House staff—Al Haig, who had been Kissinger's deputy on the National Security Council during the Cambodia operation, and Melvin Laird, who had then been defense secretary—placing even Nixon's newly arrived help under scrutiny.

Then another big scoop broke open: John Crewdson and fellow *Times* man Christopher Lydon flew to Indiana to interview Tom Charles Huston. As he talked to them at his quiet law office, a world away in many respects from the White House, they asked if he still had a copy of his 1970 "Huston Plan" to remake the U.S. intelligence world. He paused for a moment, shrugged, and pulled it out of his files, nonchalantly handing the reporters one of the most sensitive documents of the entire Nixon presidency. The blockbuster ran two days later.

The deeper into the scandal investigators and reporters got, the more CREEP's financial tricks and shenanigans began to move to the center. Crewdson struck more journalistic gold when he convinced an FBI source to let him peruse thousands of pages of the bureau's investigation on Segretti's "dirty tricks"—he walked out of the Justice Department with his briefcase packed with sensitive files and returned them later to his source—and built his find into two stories neatly tying together Segretti, Magruder, CREEP, and the White House. Relying on "informed sources," Crewdson explained on the front page of the paper on July 9 how "the Republican party's effort to sabotage Democratic Presidential candidates in 1972 was a two-pronged operation approved by some of President Nixon's most influential aides, directed in part by White House officials, and financed with more than $100,000 in unreported contributions to the Nixon campaign."

Around the same time, Archibald Cox announced that American Airlines had come forward to admit the substantial, illegal contribution its CEO George Spater had orchestrated to CREEP as part of its attempt to win approval for a pending merger with Western Airlines. Spater explained in a statement how he'd felt pressured by Kalmbach to play ball. "I knew Mr. Kalmbach to be both the President's personal counsel and counsel for our major competitor [United Airlines]," Mr. Spater said in a statement. "I concluded that a substantial response was called for."

Cox encouraged other companies that had made similar illegal donations to come forward voluntarily, stating, "It is fair to say that when corporate officers come forward voluntarily and early to disclose illegal political contributions to candidates of either party, their voluntary acknowledgement will be considered as a mitigating circumstance in deciding what charges to bring."

Across the country, dozens of corporate executives who had played ball with CREEP the year before gulped.

*   *   *

On July 10, John Mitchell finally returned to Washington to testify publicly before the Ervin Committee. Mitchell had made quite clear in press statements that he wasn't going to take the blame for Watergate, nor would he allow Nixon to be blamed for it either. "Somebody has tried to make me the fall guy, but it's not going to work," he told UPI.

Behind closed doors with the committee staff, he had been clearly nervous—the toll of that spring, both professionally and personally, was weighing on him, particularly after Martha had engaged in an hours-long running battle with the press camped outside their New York apartment, throwing a doorman's cap at one reporter and striking another twice. "You are part of the Communists," she'd screamed—and in the committee room Ervin's chief aide, Rufus Edmisten, watched as the former attorney general's hands trembled when he tried to light his pipe. Edmisten finally leaned forward and offered to hold the lighter. "Young man, that was very kind," Mitchell said.

When his time at the witness table arrived, Mitchell said virtually nothing at all. "Throughout his long testimony before the committee he sat placidly smoking his pipe, finding it difficult to recall the details of practically any event, and claiming a lack of knowledge of most relevant facts," Dash recalled. Nothing the committee could throw at him rankled him. "He gave the impression that 15 years of hearings would not alter his story," Thompson recalled.

As Mitchell confirmed that he'd met frequently and repeatedly with Nixon, Ervin pressed him, "Did you at any time tell the President anything you knew about the White House horrors?"

"No sir, I did not," Mitchell replied.

"Did the President at any time ask you what you knew about Watergate?" Ervin asked, and Mitchell again declined, leaving the senator to quip, "If the cat hadn't any more curiosity than that it would still be enjoying its nine lives—all of them."

"I hope the President enjoys eight more of them," Mitchell shot back. The former attorney general again made clear he considered nothing more important than the president's reelection. All other goals—including, it seemed, fully informing Nixon about the work of his own campaign—had taken a backseat.

After Mitchell's first day of testimony, Baker, Thompson, and others were debriefing when a secretary interrupted them: Martha was on the phone. She'd been watching the proceedings while on a visit to Mississippi, drinking a steady stream of Bloody Marys as she did. When Thompson picked up, she told him to pass along her compliments to Baker about how well the first day had gone. "You tell Howard to get John so mad tomorrow that he will just blurt it out—just blurt the truth all out," she told Thompson.

"Blurt out what Mrs. Mitchell?"

"You know—you know what I mean," she said. "You know what he's doing, you know who he's protecting—just get him so mad he'll tell the truth."

Nearly everyone shared Martha's observation: Mitchell clearly knew more than he would say. "No attempt was made to lend some minimal plausibility to his denials, to his repeated 'I don't recall' concerning crucial incidents," wrote essayist Mary McCarthy. "The weariness and boredom of his voice suggested that all this was ridiculous, preposterous, but also that he could not take the trouble to work up a lie that someone might conceivably believe."

The Senate select committee gathered again on July 12 and confronted a letter from President Nixon refusing to provide the committee with any of the documents it had requested. "The way I see it," Ervin said, "the President can't use executive privilege to deny us these papers. They deal with political matters or criminal activities in the Watergate affair. Executive privilege is supposed to protect as confidential only those conversations between the President and his aides which assist the president in carrying out his statutory or Constitutional duties. None of the papers we want has anything to do with the President's lawful duties."

Weicker chimed in, adding, "The only language the President will understand is a subpoena from this committee." The senators, though, were wary of so instantly provoking a showdown between the branches of government.

That afternoon, Nixon and Ervin spoke on the phone for sixteen minutes; Ervin's office was crowded with staff and senators, all listening to his end of the conversation and eagerly interpreting the chairman's bushy, twitching eyebrows. They could tell the conversation wasn't going well long before Ervin curtly finished by saying, "I'm sorry we can't work this out."

On the other end of the line, Nixon was in a particularly foul mood, suffering that day with what his doctors would eventually diagnose as pneumonia. As he hung up with Ervin, he continued to rant in the Oval Office to Haig and Kissinger about Ervin's request: "I'm glad I was so tough on him—hard—what he and Weicker asked is disgraceful."

"Disgraceful," Haig concurred.

As they spoke, Nixon dug in harder. "Ervin wants Dash to come down and look over the papers and determine which ones would come out. I said, 'Not on your life. There ain't gonna be no papers that come out,'" Nixon said. "Let him sue. Christ, they—If the Supreme Court wants to decide in its wisdom to help destroy the Presidency, the Supreme Court destroys it. I'm not gonna destroy it."

Next, the president went off on Ervin directly: "I'm not going to allow this slick Southern asshole to pull that old crap on me. He pretends he's gentle and he's trying to work things out—bullshit!"

The seething continued through the afternoon; an hour later, on the phone with Haig, Nixon labeled Howard Baker a "simpering asshole" and said he intended to fire Archibald Cox: "I am so disgusted with Cox in the press that I'm about to let him go next—next week anyway. I don't know if it's right or if it's wrong, but believe me here, we're fighting a desperate battle."

Foul and ill-tempered, he shifted to the topic of selecting federal judges—saying he wanted to find the "toughest, meanest right-wing" nominees, and then delineating his second most important criteria: "No

Jews. Is that clear? We've got enough Jews. Now if you find some Jew that I think is great, put him on there. Put a Black Jew? But you gotta do something in this damned office—what the hell are we here for?"

An hour later, he was once again ranting to Kissinger, "The hell with [Ervin's committee]. I'll sit on those papers. If I have to burn them, I'll burn every goddamned paper in this house. You realize that? Every paper in this house before I'll hand them over to that committee. . . . We'll have a Constitutional crisis. If we do, it'll be a goddamn, ding-dong battle and we might—if we lose, I'll burn the papers." And he concluded, "I would never turn these papers over to a court, never give them over to the committee."

Kissinger concurred. "Ninety percent of this stuff they are talking about goes on all the time," he told the president.

"Keep, keep fighting," Nixon replied.

Then, his condition worsening, Nixon headed quietly to a nearby navy medical clinic for a chest X-ray, then returned to the White House to prepare to head to the Bethesda Naval Medical Center for a few days' treatment and rest.

At 8:41 p.m. that night, Nixon called his secretary, Rose Mary Woods, to tell her he was heading into the hospital. "I told Ziegler to make the announcement because I said it's the only time in his career he will hear the press corps clap," Nixon grimly joked.

"Oh those bastards—they won't clap," Woods replied.

That exchange comprised the final words of some 3,700 hours of conversations and telephone calls that the White House taping system captured.

Chapter 34

Butterfield's Bombshell

Alexander Butterfield had spent nearly all of the first Nixon term watching the president up close as Haldeman's chief assistant, his desk mere feet from the Oval Office itself, but in the second term he'd consumed the Ervin hearings from afar, watching from the tenth floor of the Orville Wright Federal Building at 800 Independence Avenue NW, the headquarters of the Federal Aviation Administration, where he'd been installed as the nation's head aviation leader. It was a plum gig for a combat fighter pilot and recipient of the Distinguished Flying Cross, one he'd been enjoying thoroughly, but he had a sinking feeling about the storm clouds on the horizon. As one of the only people in the capital—one of the only people in the world, really—who knew that there were tapes of every conversation in the Oval Office, Butterfield understood the implications of John Dean's testimony. *God, if they only knew*, he thought.

Butterfield had been asked by Eugene Boyce of the Senate Watergate Committee staff to come in for what was expected to be a routine interview on Friday, July 13. The Senate investigators had been working through their "satellite charts," the maps of the minor figures around the major ones—Dean, Mitchell, Ehrlichman, Magruder, and Haldeman—and Butterfield was next on their list.

Before he left the house that day, he and his wife, Charlotte, discussed how he would handle the delicate question of the tapes if it came up.

He thought it unlikely—no more than a one-in-a-million chance—but he told her, "I think the best thing for me to do is wing it if I can, if the question is oblique or vague." If the question was direct, though, he had to tell the truth. "I can't get caught up in this thing," he said. Charlotte suspected it was an easier decision than he let on—she was sure her husband was going to find a way to mention the tapes. Whatever loyalty or gratitude he had once had to the nation's chief executive had long since evaporated. The man had abused him and too many other aides for too long.*

Butterfield's interview in Room G-334 was considered so routine that no senators attended; Democratic investigator Sam Armstrong and deputy Republican counsel Donald Sanders led the questioning, joined by two other investigators and a stenographer. The interview was physically uncomfortable—it was oppressively hot inside the room—and the committee's work space was a mess, as janitorial crews were prohibited for security purposes from cleaning it.

Armstrong, a longtime friend of Bob Woodward's, had gotten the job on the committee after Dash had tried to recruit the *Washington Post* reporter and, rebuffed, asked instead for the smartest person Woodward knew. Now, as he started in on Butterfield, he was instantly impressed by the former aide's military manner and steel-trap memory. "With his hands folded in front of him, he considered each question carefully," Armstrong recalled later. "He looked directly at me; he spoke in calm and even tones."

The committee staff had an agreement not to interrupt each other's examinations, so Sanders sat for three hours in silence, listening intently and taking notes as Armstrong walked Butterfield through the operations and flow of the Oval Office. During the session, Sanders remained puzzled about the conversation summaries they kept reviewing, which seemed too detailed to be reconstructed from later recollections or notes. *Was it possible they were reading actual verbatim transcripts? But from what?* When

---

* Butterfield's motives at this moment would become a point of debate in the years ahead. He had been hired based on his old friendship with Haldeman, but in Haldeman's own 1978 memoir, he wrote that Rose Mary Woods believed that Butterfield had been planted as a spy at the White House by another agency, just as Yeoman Radford had been. Her theory was CIA. "I have to agree she may have a point," Haldeman concluded.

it was his turn to question Butterfield, Sanders asked a blunt question: Why would the president take John Dean to a certain corner of the Oval Office to have a sensitive conversation?

"I was hoping you fellows wouldn't ask me that. I've wondered what I would say. I'm concerned about the effect my answer will have on national security and international affairs," Butterfield replied. "But I suppose I have to assume that this is a formal, official interview in the same vein as if I were being questioned by the committee under oath?"

"That's right," Sanders replied.

"Well, yes, there's a recording system in the White House."

The words hit like lightning—and for the next forty minutes, Butterfield laid out how the system worked, where the microphones had been installed, and who had access to the tapes.

By the time they were done, it was about 6:30 p.m. Everyone involved knew this was a game-changer. Sanders raced to track down Fred Thompson at a nearby Capitol Hill pub and found his boss having drinks with a reporter. As casually as he could, he joined the two and ordered a beer. Eventually, Sanders asked to speak to Thompson outside and filled him in. Thompson immediately called Baker.

Armstrong and his colleague Gene Boyce, who had also been in the Butterfield interview, meanwhile, went to find Dash, catching him just as he was leaving for home to celebrate Shabbat with friends. They pushed Dash back into his office: "Sam, Nixon taped all his conversations—apparently including those with Dean." Dash stood frozen for a moment. "Let me call Sarah," he then said. He was going to be late for dinner.

The team needed to get Butterfield's revelation out in public testimony fast—he was set to leave the following Tuesday for an aviation treaty negotiation in the Soviet Union. They worked through the weekend to line up an appearance, but the aide was deeply reluctant to be the public source on the taping and repeatedly asked the committee to subpoena another person who would have knowledge of it.* The lawyers told him it was impossible.

---

* Dash also met with Dean that weekend to explain that the committee believed there was a record of Dean's conversations with the president; Dash wanted to surprise his star witness with the news to test whether the former White House counsel would suddenly grow concerned about the accuracy of his testimony. Dean didn't flinch.

On Sunday, while Nixon was still in the hospital, Butterfield called Len Garment at the White House and told him of what was about to befall the administration; Garment was as stunned as anyone to learn about the tapes. The White House had no strategy for this. Haig immediately ordered the taping system shut down.*

Monday, Butterfield was getting his hair cut at 11:15 a.m. when he was told he would be expected to testify that afternoon. If he wasn't in Ervin's office by 1 p.m., the Senate would send U.S. marshals looking for him.

Since Sanders had uncovered the taping system in questioning, Dash and Thompson agreed that the Republican committee members would get first crack at Butterfield. "This is going to be quite a blow to the administration, and I don't want the minority on the committee to look like it got caught with its pants down, when in fact it played a key role in discovering the tapes," Howard Baker explained to his Democratic colleagues.

When the committee convened at 2 p.m. that Monday the 16th, spectators were surprised to hear Butterfield's name announced as the next witness. (As everyone gathered, Dash leaned over into the audience and whispered to his wife, "We've got a bombshell for you.") Following a half-dozen opening questions, Thompson got to the meat: "Mr. Butterfield, are you aware of the installation of any listening devices in the Oval Office of the President?"

"I was aware of listening devices, yes sir," Butterfield said. In subsequent exchanges, the two walked through each of the recording devices, its location and operation, and purpose. There were recording systems not only in the Oval Office, Butterfield revealed, but in the Executive Office Building, the Cabinet Room, and the president's most used phones, including in the Lincoln Sitting Room in the residence and the

---

* While Haig would later maintain that the Butterfield revelations were the first time he understood the existence of the taping system, there had been at least two conversations since he took over as White House chief of staff where Nixon had mentioned its existence, on May 8 and 11—so it's unclear if Haig just didn't really register those exchanges or was lying, later, when he said he didn't know about it. "Just between us, I have a record of everything [Kissinger] said here, at Camp David, the Lincoln Sitting Room, the EOB, everything. Everything! Everything in the national security arena has been recorded," Nixon told Haig on May 11.

president's cabin at Camp David. "There was no doubt in my mind they were installed to record things for posterity, for the Nixon library," the former aide explained. "The President was very conscious of that kind of thing." Most of those in the president's orbit, he added, didn't know that the tapes existed.

Now it was Dean's turn to watch Butterfield on TV. As he heard the aide's testimony, Dean breathed a big sigh of relief. "I was no longer the sole accuser," he recalled thinking.

*　　*　　*

From the start, Cox and his team had been more annoyed than anything by the televised spectacle of the hearings. The manipulation, the strategy, and the drama—not to mention the information spilling into public view—complicated their work, witness-wise and investigation-wise.

But Butterfield's blockbuster—that was something else.

Activity in the office all but stopped as the special prosecutor's team watched the day's hearing. Cox's executive assistant, a mustachioed, one-time Olympic speed skater named Peter Kreindler, stood watching the small TV kept on Doyle's desk. As he tamped the tobacco in his pipe, he kept repeating, "Can you believe that? Can you believe *that*?" Minutes later, inside Cox's sparse office, he and Lacovara absorbed the news that apparently a tape existed—or had existed at one point, at least—of every meaningful conversation in the Watergate conspiracy. It changed everything.

Until then, as convincing as Dean had been as a witness and as well as he had withstood cross-examination from the prosecutor, his impact had been muted because he had stood so alone. The president, Mitchell, Ehrlichman, and Haldeman had all maintained that the lawyer was lying when he said they'd known of the break-in or participated in any cover-up, and until now there'd been no way to resolve that dispute. "Suddenly, a debate that appeared to turn solely on the credibility of various conflicting witnesses—with Dean far outnumbered—could be resolved through uniquely probative evidence," Lacovara recalled.

There was no way, Cox knew, that Nixon was going to hand over the tapes without a fight. Luckily, his team already had a leg up: Investigators had recently received the President's Daily Diaries for June 15, 1972, through April 30, 1973, after a small battle with the White House: Buzhardt had been stalling the special prosecutor's request for weeks, but had gotten spooked when he heard that Cox was calling a press conference (the event was only to introduce his latest hires) and sent over the files. Those documents, which listed the minute-by-minute log of the president's movements, phone calls, and meetings, would now be key in reconstructing what conversations Cox's office should fight for next. Cox, after talking it through, had a simple message for his aides: "Let's get started."

Cox immediately requested the White House disclose the precise location of the tapes and identify their custodian. Buzhardt responded that they were being held by the Secret Service, but were under the president's sole custody. Cox grasped immediately the meaning of Buzhardt's wording: There was no way to get the tapes without fighting over executive privilege. For its part, the Ervin Committee officially issued two subpoenas, one for tapes and one for records—the first congressional subpoenas for presidential materials ever—and met with a similar response from Buzhardt. Any attempt to access the tapes would have to go through the president, and the power and privileges of the presidency.

A fight it would be. But where to start? "The immediate problem was to pinpoint a small number of tapes that the courts would be hard-pressed to deny the special prosecutor," James Doyle recalled later. "The trick was to pick not those tapes which common sense told you would be most revealing but those which would help make a strong-but-narrow point in court—that these conversations were important criminal evidence in the cover-up investigation and ought to be turned over despite the normal traditions of presidential confidentiality."

On July 18, Cox sent Buzhardt an artful letter requesting eight specific tapes, all informed by the Presidential Daily Diaries and carefully chosen because either they were fantastically suspicious—like the first meeting post-burglary between Nixon, Haldeman, and Ehrlichman—or because a participant had already spoken publicly about the contents of the meeting, which would weaken any confidentiality claims and give Cox ground to investigate their truthfulness and whether perjury charges would be warranted.* Ultimately, the goal was to fight for what they were most likely to win. As Doyle explained, "Once you convinced the courts that some of these tapes were indispensable to justice it would be easier to go back for more."†

* * *

Richard Nixon had been stunned by the public revelation of his secret taping system when he received word at the hospital of Butterfield's testimony. "I had believed that the existence of the White House taping system would never be revealed," he recalled in his memoirs—at the very least, he had felt confident no staffer would confirm its existence to anyone outside the White House without invoking executive privilege.‡ The idea that Butterfield had just up and mentioned it when asked was appalling. These conversations, recorded surreptitiously, represented the literal and figurative inner sanctum of the presidency, as close to the thoughts in a commander in chief's head as possible. Protecting them and ensuring they avoided public scrutiny required the full weight and power of the office—not just for Nixon, but for all who would come after.

For the moment, no one seemed to know what to do with the tapes. Haig, Buzhardt, and Garment met with the president at his bedside. "Destroy the tapes," Buzhardt recommended, a surprising response for a lawyer. (Spiro Agnew, in another meeting, took it a step further, suggesting that the president do so in a bonfire on the White House lawn.)

---

* Moreover, Cox explained in his letter that providing the tapes to him, for the purposes of a grand jury investigation by the Justice Department, avoided any questions about separation of powers that might be relevant had the Ervin Committee requested the tapes.

† Cox's office wasn't even originally sure how to write their demands. "We could not even make up our minds whether the legal pleadings should say, 'the United States move for such-and-such action' or 'the Government moves . . .' or 'the Special Prosecutor moves . . . ,'" Ben-Veniste and Frampton recalled. Who was who when you're investigating the commander in chief?

‡ Larry Higby had testified the week before, on July 5, and had sought advice from the White House about what to say if asked about the taping system; he was told to claim executive privilege, but managed to make it through the interview without being directly confronted on the question.

The other staff, however, weren't so sure; Garment cautioned that anyone who destroyed the tapes was almost certainly staring down an obstruction of justice charge, and Nixon doing it himself might well be an impeachable offense.

Nixon wasn't sure he wanted the tapes gone in the first place either; perhaps, he thought, they could protect him. "We know that Dean lied and the tapes proved that," Nixon told Haig, according to the White House chief of staff's memoirs. "We don't know what other lies may be told by people who are trying to save themselves. Who knows what Ehrlichman might say or even Bob Haldeman? The tapes are my best insurance against perjury. I can't destroy them."*

Outside the hospital suite, public speculation ran rampant: Why would the president record himself while under investigation for wrongdoing—and why would he keep proof? No one will ever know for sure why Richard Nixon never destroyed the Oval Office tapes, but there are two prevailing theories. The first is precisely what he intimated in the hospital: He actually wanted—even needed—the tapes. Nixon had hoped for years to use the recordings to his advantage (Tip O'Neill recalls at one White House meeting listening to Nixon speak boldly and grandly, as if he were speaking directly into history, and wondering if somewhere there was a recording device), and the president had long counted on the tapes to secure his legacy, particularly to secure himself from people like Kissinger who said one thing inside the Oval Office and another outside. He had an administrative record to be proud of, one where he felt he changed the course of the nation for the better. The tapes were what would someday convince others of what Nixon already saw.

The second theory is that, by the time he realized that the tapes might—or would—become public, Nixon thought them too politically explosive to hide. "[Nixon] didn't believe he could survive their destruction," Pat Buchanan said years later. "I think he could have. There

---

* Since one of the first actions Haig took after Butterfield's revelations was to shut down the White House taping system, it's worth noting that from here on out in the Nixon presidency, there are no further verbatim records of what's said. Instead, the words of the president and his advisors are all filtered through memoirs, testimony, and news accounts. So maybe Nixon said this—or maybe he didn't.

would have been another fire storm and it would have been over: The tapes would have been gone."

Garment's view was more sanguine. As the president's lawyer saw it, "[Nixon] relied in the end on the simple, traditional mental safeguard against certain disaster: Hope." Garment recalled an old tale of a Russian peasant who gets money to feed his family by promising the Czar that he can get a dog to talk within a month; if he fails, he'll be killed. The peasant's wife berated him for the deal, but the peasant explained, "Keep calm. The Czar is a busy man and may forget. He may get sick and die. There may be a war. And who knows—maybe the dog will talk!"

Nixon, Garment realized, was crossing his fingers and betting the dog would talk.

* * *

Nixon, still pale, left the hospital on July 20 and rejected calls for his resignation as "just plain poppy cock," insisting, "What we were elected to do, we are going to do, and let others wallow in Watergate, we are going to do our job."

On Monday, July 23, Haig called Elliot Richardson with an official answer: Nixon was going to publicly refuse to release the tapes. He had a warning for the attorney general too. "The President is uptight about Cox. He wants a tight line drawn. No further mistakes, or we'll get rid of Cox," Haig said.*

Publicly, Nixon's team argued that Cox didn't even have standing to ask for the tapes in the first place. Article II of the Constitution vested the president with overseeing the executive branch and all aspects of its power, which meant the president's decision trumped one made by an employee of the Justice Department. In a formal letter to Archibald Cox, Nixon lawyer Charles Alan Wright argued, "You are subject to the

---

* Richardson, in turn, did try. Without mentioning any ominous warning from the White House, he met with the special prosecutor and argued why the tapes or looking into eavesdropping should be outside his investigation's scope. Cox wouldn't have it and issued his own warning back to Richardson: "I think you are heading for trouble if you take that position, Elliot," he said. "Before you issue any instructions, you might want to carefully review your testimony before the Senate."

instructions of your superior, up to and including the president, and can have access to presidential papers only as and if the president sees fit to make them available to you." It was a powerful defense that undermined the very core of a legal challenge, positing that in reality there was no dispute between separate entities to be judged by an impartial court because the executive branch was a single and ultimate entity where the president's word trumped Cox's—this was just a routine workplace dispute, unreviewable by a court, in the same way that an assembly line worker can't sue the factory owner simply because he doesn't like his boss's decision.

Ervin and Cox, naturally, felt otherwise—Ervin viewed Congress as having an important role in overseeing the executive branch, and Cox believed, simply, that the president was beholden to the same law as anyone else. Separately, he and his team and Ervin and Dash on the Hill moved ahead to formalize responses.

In the end, Ervin's committee asked for five conversations between Dean and Nixon, plus about two-dozen other conversations; Cox's official demand added a ninth conversation to his original request for eight. By the end of the day, both had issued subpoenas. Cox spoke at a press conference at the Commerce Department, saying the tapes were necessary for "the impartial pursuit of justice according to law."

Signing the official subpoenas for the president, Ervin became emotional. With his wife, wearing a light brown polka-dot dress, sitting in the audience, her eyes closed as she listened to the hearing, Ervin explained how much his action pained him. "I love my country. I venerate the office of the President," he said, before continuing, "I deeply regret that this situation has arisen, because I think that the Watergate tragedy is the greatest tragedy this country has ever suffered. . . . I used to think that the Civil War was our country's greatest tragedy, but I do remember that there were some redeeming features in the Civil War in that there was some spirit of sacrifice and heroism displayed on both sides. I see no redeeming features in Watergate."

Now only one hurdle remained for the the investigative bodies: *How do you serve a subpoena on the President of the United States?* Normally, U.S. marshals handled the process, but when Cox's counsel Phil Lacovara spoke to them that afternoon, the marshals wanted nothing to do with it. Without another option, Lacovara and Peter Kreindler summoned a taxi and rode the half-dozen blocks over to the White House just after 6 p.m., where they were escorted to meet Buzhardt in Room 188½ in the Old Executive Office Building. Lacovara had never met nor seen the White House lawyer before, and they spent a few minutes engaging in small talk—partly, Lacovara explained later, so he could feel comfortable saying he had established that the man behind the large desk in the ornate room was indeed the president's lawyer if the White House ever argued the subpoena hadn't been properly served. After a digression into some of the stranger cases that Buzhardt had worked at the Pentagon, like a pregnant air force member whom the service had wanted to discharge, the moment of history arrived.

"What is there I can do for you?" Buzhardt said.

"I have something for you—a subpoena," Lacovara said.

"I expected you would," Buzhardt replied, solemnly, taking the document and signing it, per standard practice. A similar scene unfolded with the official—and equally historic—Senate subpoena.

Cox, in his office, watched the evening news about the historic day, and then dismissed his spokesman, Jim Doyle: "I guess all we can do is keep chopping wood."

As expected, Nixon rejected both orders, from the Ervin Committee and the special prosecutor, two days later. He had spent a year anticipating that the end of Watergate was right around the corner; Henry Petersen himself had said in May that the investigation was 90 percent done before Cox even started—yet almost every day seemed to spread the process in new directions. He'd endured months of embarrassing revelations, but so far no crime that had touched the presidency itself. "The subpoenas, as Nixon himself put it, were nothing more than last-ditch applications for a fishing license," Haig recalled.

Everyone involved knew that the case would be bound for the Supreme Court. Cox, in conversations with Lacovara and Kreindler, broke down the four paths forward, none of which sounded ideal: First, the court could establish for the first time an absolute presidential privilege, creating true immunity from prosecutor's prying eyes. Second, it could decide as a routine administrative matter that the special prosecutor, as an employee of the Justice Department, was subordinate to the president and thus could not pursue an action that contravened the chief executive's wishes, creating a de facto immunity from prosecution. Third, the court could validate the subpoena only to see the president resist or refuse to comply—which certainly, given Nixon's behavior thus far, seemed likely. It wasn't like Cox had an army to force White House compliance, nor could he envision a team of U.S. marshals bursting into the White House and ransacking the presidential quarters to seize the tapes. "For a man who had devoted his life to the law and whose assignment was to vindicate the rule of law, Cox was understandably uncomfortable about setting in motion a process that not only would generate a constitutional crisis but that might end with the President's defying the Supreme Court—and getting away with it," Lacovara recalled.

The fourth option seemed the least likely of all: The courts could (a) reject the president's authority over the special prosecutor as a subordinate employee of the executive branch, and also (b) recognize the validity of a presidential subpoena and dismiss any executive privilege claims, and then have the president (c) completely and voluntarily comply with the court's decision.

Cox was ready to move the moment word came of the president's rejection, and he summoned the grand jury to petition Judge Sirica to enforce the subpoena. In a regular ritual of the American justice system, made unique only by their target, the grand jury, one by one, asked the court to order the compliance of the president. It was the first time the country had glimpsed the men and women sitting in judgment on the case. Sirica's clerk struggled in the moment to pronounce each name, and so the foreman, Vladimir Pregelj, a Slovenian analyst at the Library of Congress who commuted to the court from his home on Capitol Hill, offered to help. Pregelj, the papers noted, had a large Van Dyke beard and impressed observers with his "muted but mod clothing."* The group moved ahead with a formal "show cause" order, directing the president's lawyers to appear

---

* Nixon's team would later claim that the makeup of the grand jury—full of Blacks and Democrats, as effectively all juries pulled from the District of Columbia were—biased it against Nixon, but as the special prosecutor's team noted, the antipathy toward the president's actions was largely universal. "In fact, the few white middle-class Republicans on the panels were often the best educated and most aggressive in questioning both the witnesses and the prosecutors," Doyle later recalled.

at an August 7 hearing to argue that the requested tapes and documents should not be turned over to the court.

After the subpoena drama unfolded, Richardson issued a halfhearted statement that managed to leave all three players in the drama unsatisfied, accepting the separation of powers argument blocking the Hill's access to the tapes, while praising both Nixon's decision to protect the confidentiality of presidential conversations and Cox's dedication to his work. At the next press conference, a reporter asked Cox about what he thought of his former Harvard Law student's statement: "Do you think you taught [Richardson] well?"

"I taught him labor law," Cox quipped.

*   *   *

On July 31, 1973, Massachusetts representative Robert Drinan—a Jesuit who had used an antiwar platform in 1970 to oust a three-decade incumbent and become the first-ever Roman Catholic priest in Congress—introduced a resolution calling for President Nixon's impeachment. Drinan's censure had nothing to do with Watergate, though, and instead focused on the "high crime or misdemeanor" of Nixon's decision to secretly bomb Cambodia without congressional notification or assent.

Tip O'Neill was furious with Drinan; O'Neill believed that Democrats needed to let Republicans come around to the need for action themselves. Worried that there was no broad support for impeachment at that point—especially if tied to the Cambodia question—the majority leader talked Drinan out of pushing his resolution further. "It would have been overwhelmingly defeated—by something like 400 to 20," O'Neill argued. And he knew that if representatives voted to oppose impeachment, it would be enormously difficult to get a second vote on Watergate down the road. ("Politically, he damn near blew it," O'Neill recalled.)

Even though Drinan agreed not to call for a vote, O'Neill feared another representative with a sense for mischief would; it seemed political catnip for the GOP. For weeks, O'Neill and his two main Democratic whips—John McFall and John Brademas—rotated turns watching the action on the House floor, ensuring one of them could table any quick call for a vote.

Eventually, O'Neill asked minority leader Gerald Ford if the GOP ever planned to bring up the resolution, only to learn that Nixon's party was just as eager to avoid the subject. "I took this up with the White House," Ford explained. "The feeling was that if we brought up this motion, people might think that where there was smoke, there was fire."

O'Neill couldn't help but think that Ford and Nixon had made a fatal miscalculation. "The Republicans could have turned impeachment into a party issue, which might have allowed Nixon to remain in office and blame the Democrats for harassing him," O'Neill recalled. "In the summer of 1973, the White House just couldn't imagine that Watergate would end in the downfall of the president. I, on the other hand, couldn't imagine anything else."

Chapter 35

Must-See TV

With the presidential subpoenas and congressional conflict, the Ervin Committee remained the nation's top story that summer; more than three dozen witnesses followed Butterfield and Dean into American living rooms. The major networks—ABC, CBS, and NBC—carried the hearings live daily, ultimately airing more than 237 hours of public testimony. Most days, hearings went from 10 a.m. to 5 or 6 p.m., with a two-hour lunch break.* Soon enough, Americans who had originally complained that the hearings replaced their regular midday soap operas embraced the one playing out daily in the Caucus Room. It was a dizzying array of accounts, counterclaims, half-truths, and quarter-lies. "The enormous and continually widening cast of characters, the complicated, often obscure and difficult plot made cross-reference obligatory for anyone who wanted to be 'in' on the fascinating event," wrote essayist Mary McCarthy that summer. "Did Mitchell, when told about the GEMSTONE file still in the CREEP offices, suggest that Jeb Magruder 'have a fire'? LaRue said yes; Mardian said no," she recalled, citing just one of the numerous witness conflicts. "What about the meeting when Magruder 'indicated'

---

* Each morning, Rufus Edmisten, Ervin's chief aide, would lean over to his boss mid-hearing, the day's Senate cafeteria shop menu concealed inside an open book, and Ervin would appear to studiously read the proffered page, until his finger stopped on the sandwich he wished to order for lunch.

that he was going to commit perjury—was Mardian present? LaRue said yes; Mardian said no." Altogether, the average American home watched around thirty hours of the hearing—nearly a full workweek's worth over about eleven weeks that summer.

Ulasewicz, LaRue, Mardian, Kalmbach, and Strachan all occupied the witness chair. All told, sixty-three witnesses would take the stand publicly across fifty-three days of hearings that would stretch into November. Thompson and other committee staff joked that after her testimony Sally Harmony, Liddy's secretary, surely would receive numerous job offers: She appeared to remember nothing she ever heard and nothing she ever typed. "If there's anything better than a good memory, it's a good forgettery," Ervin quipped behind closed doors.

Despite the amazingly poor memory of many involved, witness by witness, damaging testimony crept into view. When the Senate committee put Kleindienst, Petersen, and Gray on the stand, it asked about Nixon's April 30 statement in his national address that he'd taken personal control of the Watergate investigation on March 21, following Dean's "cancer on the presidency" warning, and ordered the full details of the case delivered forthwith. "Kleindienst, Petersen, and Gray declared that President Nixon never gave them any such order," Ervin later recalled.

Even Howard Baker, who had started out firmly in the camp of the president, began to worry about the massing evidence. "I believed that [the hearings were] a political ploy of the Democrats, that it would come to nothing," he said years later, "but a few weeks into that, it began to dawn on me that there was more to it than I thought, and more to it than I liked."

As it went on, the public support seemed to run about 90–10 in favor of the committee's probe. Beleaguered staff members shifted through nine thousand letters a day, pouring into its offices by the bagful and truckful. "The Watergate hearings became a spectacle unlike any other political event in the history of this or any other country," the *Post*'s Sussman wrote. In the evenings, PBS aired each day's hearings in prime time, drawing audiences five or six times larger than its normal ratings. The Ervin Committee, the *Los Angeles Times* TV critic quipped, was "the best thing that has happened to public television since *Sesame Street*."

Sam Ervin himself even became something of a cult hero; across the country, people began to sport "Uncle Sam" sweatshirts honoring the

North Carolina senator and the moral force and clarity he brought to the hearings. At one point, as Nixon financier Maurice Stans started to bluster about how previous campaigns had also been populated with dirty tricks—one of the Nixon team's favorite rejoinders—Ervin shot back, "You know there has been murder and larceny in every generation, but that hasn't made murder meritorious or larceny legal."*

While the attention was exciting, it could also be unsettling. Ervin and his wife had to switch to an unlisted home telephone number when their phone, which had been without incident listed for years in directories, began to ring at all hours. (One particularly persistent man from Kentucky called long-distance every night.) The chairman became used to various threats, bomb scares, and other similar life disruptions.†

Beyond Ervin himself, Thompson, Dash, and the committee's other senators all also suddenly found themselves celebrities. "At restaurants, *maitre d's* always had tables, and waiters gave superb service," Thompson recalled. One night, as he and his wife sat down for a dinner out, the tables around erupted in applause.‡ The Watergate Hotel itself became a regular stop on tourist circuits of the capital, and souvenir makers churned all manner of tchotchkes—including plastic and rubber spiders, beetles, and insects all labeled "The Watergate Bug."

The next main event was July 25: a week of testimony by Ehrlichman, followed by three days of testimony of Haldeman. Until late that spring, Ehrlichman had still been widely believed to be untainted by Watergate

---

* Stans, who would end up convicted of five campaign finance violations, long saw himself as unjustly caught up in the Watergate affair, and his outrage permeated both his Ervin Committee hearing and two later memoirs of the experience, one of which was called *The Terrors of Justice*. In the hearing, Stans was one of the few witnesses who availed himself of the chance to offer a final closing statement; looking directly at Ervin, Stans said, "You cannot feel the abuse to which I have been subjected because of the associations I fell into. All I ask, Mr. Chairman and Members of the Committee, is that when you write your report you give me back my good name."

† After a commencement address in Cincinnati, he found two police officers waiting at his hotel, assigned to protect him overnight after a telephoned assassination threat. As one officer quipped to him, "I don't know how much the chief is concerned about the possibility of your assassination, but I am absolutely convinced he doesn't want it to happen in Cincinnati."

‡ Another time, on his way through the Senate hallways, Thompson was flagged down by a woman begging for his autograph. As he walked away, he heard her exclaim as she examined her autograph book, "Just think—Senator Weicker!"

("More than once Baker expressed his pleasure that in Ehrlichman, at least, the White House had at least one top-level administrator who was untouched by scandal," Thompson recalled), but his role in the hearings had shifted after it became clear that he had had knowledge of—if not a direct role in—the Ellsberg burglary.

When he arrived at the July hearings, Ehrlichman came geared for battle—filibustering, pontificating, and deflecting. He sneered at senators, dismissed other players, from the burglars to Pat Gray, as fools, and generally evinced the sense that no one had consulted him on anything—but had anyone asked his opinion, he would have told them they were stupid. "In his own mind, there is not the faintest connection between him and the actions performed by other characters in the story," Mary McCarthy reported. "He lost no opportunity to patronize, bully, and affront the senators, as well as Majority Counsel Dash." No fight was too small and nothing was out of bounds; Ehrlichman argued every point and objected to the premise or assumptions of the committee's questions.

"Didn't you bug [Kalmbach's] telephone conversation with you?" Ervin asked, at one point.

"No, sir," Ehrlichman said.

"Didn't you record it, then?" Ervin tried again.

"Yes, sir," Ehrlichman replied.

It was a frustrating encounter for all; at one point, the whole Caucus Room heard Senator Inouye mutter, apparently believing his microphone was off, "What a liar."*

In a lengthy closing statement, Ehrlichman blasted the process one last time, defending the president's record, and appealing to Americans to reject the investigation. "I do not apologize for my loyalty to the President any more than I apologize for my love of this country," he

---

* The White House was particularly concerned that word of the Radford Affair, the 1971 spying scandal on Kissinger's National Security Council by the military's Joint Chiefs of Staff, would come out during the Haldeman-Ehrlichman testimony. A July 22 column by Jack Anderson about that still confusing Pakistan-India conflict in December 1971 had set investigators sniffing for more details, and the White House's Fred Buzhardt, wanting to prevent another Butterfield-style bombshell, sent Haldeman and Ehrlichman's lawyer a letter asserting executive privilege to enjoin them from speaking about a "1971 investigation" that "involve[s] most sensitive national security matters, the public disclosure of which would cause damage to the national security."

said. Later, he spoke directly to young Americans considering a role in government—"Be prepared to defend your sense of values when you come here"—looking pointedly at the committee members. "You'll encounter a local culture which scoffs at patriotism and family and morality just as it adulates the opposite."

When the hearing adjourned, a reporter came up to Dash. "That guy was tough as nails—you couldn't break him," he told the Senate counsel.

"Well, what do you think after hearing him?" Dash countered. "Was he involved in the cover-up?"

"Oh—up to here!" the reporter exclaimed, placing his hand at his forehead.

Dash shrugged: "Then what more do you want the committee to show?"

After James Wilson, the lawyer representing both Ehrlichman and Haldeman, had battled Ervin repeatedly on the finer points of courtroom procedure, hearsay, and constitutional rights, and watched the reception Ehrlichman received from the committee and the public, he switched tactics entirely for his second client.

H. R. Haldeman acted as a fully cooperative witness, who by mere coincidence could recall none of the needed facts, conversations, or details. Haldeman, the rock of Nixon's Berlin Wall, the man whose ever-vigilant "tickler" file of assigned deadlines had watched all-knowing and never-forgetting over the West Wing, came across on the witness stand as the world's most distracted and absentminded boss. It was, Dash recalled, Mitchell without the pipe. More than 150 times, Haldeman said some version of "I can't remember" or "I have no recollection." "I don't know who he thinks he's fooling," Weicker said later.

Haldeman, though, did appear to offer one important clarifying insight into Dean's report on the March 21 "cancer on the presidency" conversation. Reading off notes he made while listening to the recording of the meeting, the former chief of staff recounted that Nixon had probed the question of the Hunt hush money. Dean had explained the need to raise to $1 million, and commented, "but the problem is that it is hard to raise." Nixon, then, according to Haldeman had said, "There is no problem in raising $1 million—we can do that—but it would be wrong." It was a point both remarkable in the moment, as it seemed to downgrade the president's culpability in the cover-up, and also later: Unbeknownst to the committee at the time, Haldeman was lying, and the exchange would become the subject of a perjury charge against him. Haldeman's testimony that week was clearly predicated on the idea that no one but Nixon and Haldeman would ever hear the truth on the tapes.

On August 7, the Ervin Committee's must-see TV season came to an end with the start of the summer congressional recess, after thirty-seven days of hearings. While the hearings would reconvene in September and stretch into November, the public's attention moved on as later developments overtook Ervin's work. Uncovering the existence of the tapes had been a high-water mark, but the next stage of the national drama would focus on Cox and the battle for those tapes.

As August began, Roderick MacLeish wrote in the *Christian Science Monitor*, "The period immediately ahead holds little of bright promise for Mr. Nixon. The guns of August will be booming all around him as he embarks upon his high-risk strategy for survival."

Chapter 36

Spiro

On August 6, just when it seemed impossible for the White House to handle another scandal, the *Wall Street Journal* reported that a federal prosecutor in Baltimore was looking into bribery allegations against Vice President Spiro Agnew.

As FBI agents had pieced together, it was not a particularly complicated or innovative bribery and extortion plan: After being elected in 1962, Agnew had insisted on a 3 to 5 percent kickback on county contracts. The cash payments arrived regularly, usually in plain white envelopes, handed over in person. Agnew had participated in the scheme not only as a county executive in Baltimore, but also as Maryland governor and even—shockingly—as vice president, accepting payments in the White House complex itself, as well as in the hotel suite at the Sheraton Park where he lived. (When he became vice president, the key conduit simply called Agnew's secretary to set up handoffs, telling her he had "information" to deliver.) Prosecutors had based part of their case on the Secret Service visitor logs, which carefully—and unknowingly—recorded the precise dates and times of the meetings and payoffs. As far as they could tell, the vice president had used the money in similarly ordinary ways; there was no lavish lifestyle or dark secrets lurking in Agnew's day-to-day spending. He was just a run-of-the-mill crook who had ended up vice president.

"When all is said and done, Al, I suspect this will just turn out to be Maryland politics," Nixon had told Haig after Richardson first brought the matter to the Oval Office, though he knew it wasn't entirely true. In fact, the president had known about Agnew's behavior longer than either the attorney general or his chief of staff—and had already engaged in some light obstruction of justice to try to keep it under wraps.

Agnew had become aware of the investigation as early as February 1973, when word moved through Baltimore circles that federal prosecutors were digging into kickback schemes. In April, he'd sounded the alarm to the White House—not to raise the issue of political risk or to offer his resignation, but to ask for help in shutting down the probe. "The vice president called me over today and said he had a real problem," Haldeman recorded in his journal on April 10. Agnew had wanted Haldeman to put some pressure on Maryland's senator, Glenn Beall, whose brother, George, was the U.S. attorney investigating the case.

While Haldeman—just weeks from his own White House exit—declined to intervene, he relayed the conversation to Ehrlichman, who on April 13 warned Nixon about the situation. Ehrlichman recalled too an odd report from March 1970, from when Agnew had tried to seize control of federal government contracts being awarded in the mid-Atlantic; at the time, he and Haldeman had thought it was simply the vice president trying to carve out a larger profile for himself in the administration. Now they realized with horror that Agnew had been trying to set himself up to continue his bribery and kickback scheme on a national level.*

Richardson had first learned of the case in mid-June from George Beall, and brought it to Haig's attention. Agnew and Nixon discussed it directly on June 14. "I'm going to be indicted, it looks like," the vice president told the president during a meeting. "This thing they're calling a 'Little Watergate.' And this is the most ridiculous thing I've ever seen."

"Well, a 'Little Watergate' ought to be very small," Nixon replied, still seeming not to understand how dire the scandals for either of them would turn out to be. "You look at Watergate and all that was involved. What was it? A crappy little thing. A crappy little thing. There's nothing there—they didn't get anything. It hurt us in the election. We

---

* Ehrlichman says that Nixon told him in their final conversation in early May, "I'm going to have to get rid of him. They've got the evidence. Agnew has been on the take all the time he's been here."

would've got 3 or 4 percent more. What in the name of good God is this all about?!"

"It's just murder," Agnew continued, "but that's what's going on, and I think we ought to brace ourselves, 'cause this is going to get worse."

As the conversation continued, the president and vice president chewed over the ramifications of Agnew's criminality. "Let's talk about what we can do," Nixon said. "Let me say first, don't—as far as the line of concerned here, it's going to be hard-nosed. There isn't going to be anything to talk about. 'Well we better get a special prosecutor, and we've got to look into this.' Balls! We've gone down that road. We've made that mistake. No more."

Nixon then quizzed Agnew on the background of the prosecutor ("Is he a good boy? Why the hell did we appoint him?"), the collected evidence, and whether it would be possible to "destroy" the reputation of a key witness. The solution, the president decided, was for the prosecutor to charge a low-level figure in the case and move on. "Indict someone—just like we told that [Watergate] jury: Indict Magruder or whoever is guilty and get the hell out," Nixon said.

A few days later, on June 19—as Washington awaited John Dean's testimony—Nixon encouraged his chief of staff to subvert justice, telling Alexander Haig that he wanted to have Melvin Laird intercede with the Beall brothers. He cautioned, "I can't have it put out that I was trying to fix the case." Sorting out how to handle the case was a pressing priority; Agnew called Haig three times to discuss it, and Haig finally turned to the head of the Republican National Committee, George H. W. Bush, to contact the older Beall brother. "Senator Beall wasn't as responsive as he might have been, although he's damn upset about it," Haig reported back later.

Richardson never knew that Nixon had tried to interfere, and by late July, the attorney general passed word to Haig: "They say up in Baltimore that they have enough evidence to charge the vice president with 40 felony counts for violations of federal statutes on bribery, tax evasion, and corruption."

"There's no mistake on this?" asked Haig, who hadn't until then understood the scale of the issue and still made no mention of his earlier actions.

"There's no mistake," Richardson confirmed. "I've never seen such an open-and-shut case."

On August 1, Maryland U.S. Attorney George Beall officially notified the vice president that he was the target of the investigation. Chuck Colson helped line up a lawyer, and five days later, the allegations leaked in the *Wall Street Journal*: Agnew had received $1,000 a week in kickbacks for six years as Baltimore County executive and Maryland governor, and he'd taken some $50,000 in payments as vice president too. "Damned lies," he maintained in a press conference.

As Watergate deepened, the president had long joked that his number two's ferocity and unpleasantness was his best insurance policy against impeachment—not even the most rabid Democrat preferred Agnew over Nixon—but that's where the compliments stopped. In fact, he'd never much liked Agnew. They didn't get along personally, and Nixon, who had been vice president himself, thought the former governor had underperformed at every turn. If he'd behaved like Agnew, Nixon grumbled, "Ike would have fired my ass." Now they were facing the possibility of a double impeachment—a political disaster that if not properly managed and sequenced would deliver Democratic House Speaker Carl Albert to the White House to serve out the remainder of Nixon's term.

Nixon also spotted, though, in Agnew's troubles a potential opportunity. He had long hoped that Texas's John Connally would be his heir apparent and Republican successor as president; through that summer of '73, he had waited for the chance to nominate Connally if Agnew resigned. The problem was, Agnew didn't appear to be in any hurry to leave. "I have no intention to be skewered in this fashion," he said at an August 8 press conference, before retreating to Frank Sinatra's Palm Beach home to strategize.*

The gap between Agnew's outright denials of wrongdoing and the gathering evidence troubled the Nixon team. "I can't understand how he can make such flat denials in light of the facts that are bound to come out," Fred Buzhardt warned Nixon.

---

* Sinatra's friendship with Agnew would loom as one of the odd sideshows of the bribery scandal; the vice president made several trips west that summer and fall to relax, golf, and commiserate with his famous friend, and Agnew would later dedicate his scorched-earth memoir of his resignation, *Go Quietly . . . or Else*, to the Chairman of the Board.

"Everyone thinks he has to leave," Nixon, in turn, told Haig.

In August Nixon asked Henry Petersen for his own independent evaluation of Agnew's troubles, and the Justice Department official reported back on August 15 that the evidence was incontrovertible and damning. "[Nixon] had been reluctant earlier to invest what was left of his own credibility in the lost cause of Agnew's defense. Now he was determined not to get personally involved," Haig recalled in his memoirs.* As summer moved into fall, Haig, Buzhardt, and Nixon all faced the challenge of how best to push the vice president of the United States out of his own government.

*   *   *

On Monday, August 13, Senator Lowell Weicker went to the Danbury federal prison in his home state of Connecticut, to visit his newest constituents: Bernard Barker and the Cuban burglars. Barker's daughter had asked the Ervin Committee member to come, and in their meeting, he listened as the men explained their role in GEMSTONE and the Watergate break-in, complaining throughout about Hunt's betrayal— they had believed, because of his preexisting CIA relationship and how he'd represented his work at the White House, that they were working for a fully authorized and protected official U.S. government mission. Weicker asked when they realized otherwise. "I never fully realized," Barker replied, sadly.

He ultimately spent about six hours with the men and left angered by the unfairness of the justice system. "These were the little guys in Watergate, and they were being punished more severely than some of the big shots," he recalled.

That same day back in Washington, prosecutors were battling over the looming executive subpoenas. Cox, Lacovara, and Kreindler had spent the preceding two weeks researching, refining, and arguing among themselves

---

* Haig's memoirs, which mostly cover a period after the end of Nixon's White House recording system, are particularly suspect in certain exchanges. When his accounts are cross-referenced with the few conversations that overlap before Butterfield's July revelation of the tapes, Haig appears to deliver especially self-serving and personally sympathetic versions of conversations with the president.

about how to best position their case. In between organizing and hiring the office staff, investigating, and grading the last of his final exams for his spring course at Harvard, Cox had been brushing up on his presidential legal history—even spending a Sunday at the office reading an antique law book that traced the story of *United States v. Burr*, the only legal case in the entire history of the country prior to now in which a president had been subpoenaed.

The case during Thomas Jefferson's administration stemmed from when former vice president Aaron Burr had been accused of treason. After fleeing U.S. politics following his deadly 1804 duel with Alexander Hamilton, Burr had hatched a subsequent scheme—the exact contours of which today remain sketchy—to break away western portions of the Louisiana Territory, perhaps with the help of Britain or Spain, and stage a military uprising with a goal of installing himself as emperor. He was captured in Alabama and brought to trial in Richmond, Virginia, with Chief Justice Marshall presiding, and Burr's lawyers subpoenaed Thomas Jefferson to provide a series of letters relating to others involved in Burr's plan. Marshall's conclusion was clear: "That the president of the United States may be subpoenaed, and examined as a witness, and requested to produce any paper in his possession, is not controverted," he wrote. Jefferson half-complied, providing some of the requested material but excising what he deemed irrelevant, and the issue died with Burr's acquittal before anyone chose to push the president further.

Cox also examined the other landmark historical test of executive power, which came from the midst of the Korean War. A wage dispute with steel unions led to calls for a strike, and Harry Truman instead issued an executive order, citing vague emergency powers, seizing the steel mills and demanding production continue; lawyers for the mills appealed to federal court just twenty-seven minutes after the order was announced. The case, known as *Youngstown Sheet & Tube Co. v. Sawyer*, quickly found its way to the Supreme Court, where a deeply divided court ultimately ruled that the president lacked the inherent authority to seize the mills, since Congress hadn't explicitly provided such powers.

It was clear from such cases that the special prosecutor had a hard battle in front of him. The courts and Congress had traditionally given the president a great deal of leeway in deciding what was in the national

interest—particularly in the realm of foreign affairs and national security. "The broad framework of the case was simplicity itself, the clash of
two traditions of American law," Doyle later recalled. "Cox would point
to the early law books of Henry de Bracton, the Burr case in Jefferson's
time, and the steel seizure case during Truman's Presidency to show
that even a President must submit to the needs of the law. Charles Alan
Wright could point to the entire history of the American Presidency to
show that no President had ever been compelled to turn over his most
secret papers, that no court had gone so far as to interpose itself between
a President and his personal judgment of state secrets or of what must
remain confidential."

* * *

On August 15, Nixon delivered yet another national prime-time radio
and television address on Watergate—his third since April—repeating
his assertion that he had no prior knowledge of the break-in, that he
hadn't taken part in the subsequent cover-up, and that he had neither
"authorized nor encouraged" improper or illegal campaign tactics. "That
was and that is the simple truth," he said, continuing on to outline how
ill-served he'd been by Kleindienst, Gray, and Dean, all of whom he had
wrongly trusted. "Because I trusted the agencies conducting the investigations, because I believed the reports I was getting, I did not believe the
newspaper accounts that suggested a coverup. I was convinced there was
no coverup, because I was convinced that no one had anything to cover
up," he said. "Far from trying to hide the facts, my effort throughout has
been to discover the facts—and to lay those facts before the appropriate
law enforcement authorities so that justice could be done and the guilty
dealt with."

From there, he tried to reframe the public debate over his White
House tapes—the question, he argued, of presidential confidentiality
loomed larger than any legal questions about the Watergate cover-up.
"Each day, a President of the United States is required to make difficult
decisions on grave issues. It is absolutely necessary, if the President is
to be able to do his job as the country expects, that he be able to talk
openly and candidly with his advisers about issues and individuals. This

kind of frank discussion is only possible when those who take part in it know that what they say is in strictest confidence," he said. "That is why I shall continue to oppose efforts which would set a precedent that would cripple all future Presidents by inhibiting conversations between them and those they look to for advice."

He argued it was time after the summer's worth of hearings to move the country forward. "We have reached a point at which a continued, backward looking obsession with Watergate is causing this nation to neglect matters of far greater importance to all of the American people," he said. "We must not stay so mired in Watergate that we fail to respond to challenges of surpassing importance to America and the world. We cannot let an obsession with the past destroy our hopes for the future."

The next day, Jeb Stuart Magruder pleaded guilty to a single count of conspiracy; he would face a maximum of five years in prison. The special prosecutor's strategy was working. Next in their sights: John Dean.

*   *   *

Even as Nixon, desperate to change the subject, spoke to the nation, Cox and the FBI investigations proceeded apace. If anything, the probes were accelerating. The original grand jury had been meeting for more than a year, and, as Cox's spokesman James Doyle recalled, they "thought they had seen it all, and they would trust only themselves to do the job." As he wrote later, "[They] had been through two sets of prosecutors and tended to be wary, aggressive, and thorough in questioning witnesses. The leaders did not much care about the stature of either the witness or the prosecutor who appeared before them." In August, the special prosecutor empaneled a second grand jury to focus on the expanding threads of the investigation, from the break-in at Ellsberg's psychiatrist to the confusing circumstances of the ITT merger.

At the top of the agenda for the second grand jury was George Steinbrenner. The day after Nixon asked the country to untangle itself from Watergate, the FBI sent an "airtel" to its Cleveland Field Office with copies of seven subpoenas for employees of George Steinbrenner's shipbuilding company, who were suspected of illegally laundering corporate donations to the reelection campaign through fake "bonuses."

The probe had grown out of a civil lawsuit by the good-government group Common Cause, which had sued the Nixon campaign under the Federal Corrupt Practices Act to force disclosure of its donors—the very ones CREEP had hoped to hide by soliciting donations before the April 7, 1972, deadline of the new campaign finance law. As part of the lawsuit, Common Cause had uncovered that the campaign had kept a special record of two thousand top donors; Maurice Stans had destroyed his copy, but Common Cause found that Rose Mary Woods had held on to hers, and it obtained it through the lawsuit. It was an all but alphabetical list of potential financial crimes—so damning that the press had taken to calling the document "Rosemary's Baby," a name pulled from a bestselling 1960s horror novel and hit movie about a New York City woman who sires a son with Satan—and now the FBI was hot on the trail of those names too.

In the clipped language of the FBI, the August 16 message directed, "Cleveland insure that this case receives the same, immediate, and preferred handling as have other cases growing out of the Watergate affair." If the interviews elicited any admissions that the contributions were indeed phony, Archibald Cox should be notified immediately by teletype. "The Special Prosecutor has indicated extreme interest in this matter," the airtel said.

The subpoenas and interview requests came as investigators uncovered oddities throughout Steinbrenner's company—like one American Shipbuilding Company employee who earned $14,500 annually and had received steady annual bonuses of $1,200 until April 1972, when the new campaign finance law kicked in and he suddenly both received a $5,000 bonus and also made a $3,500 donation to a Nixon campaign committee so obscure he couldn't even remember its name.

When news of the probe broke publicly in the *Washington Star*, Steinbrenner disavowed any attempt to curry favor with Nixon for his shipbuilding company, saying his donations instead aimed to gain access for Cleveland civic projects. "I got taken," he complained. "I went in with my eyes open, but I got taken."

While there were numerous instances and cases involving Nixon's campaign finance irregularities unfolding across the country, Steinbrenner's situation stood out to prosecutors. "Steinbrenner had been the first such executive found to be resisting the investigation in an active, criminal manner, and [task force leader Tom] McBride meant to send a message to the business community that such conduct would not pay," Doyle recalled.

Soon, eight employees were granted immunity to testify about the gifts. The grand jurors sensed the employees' fear of implicating their boss as they gave vague answers and obfuscations—when one witness finally blurted out a sentence about participating in the scheme, the jurors applauded.

Steinbrenner's conspiracy was crumbling. Worse was coming for him.

*   *   *

The morning of August 22, 1972, began inauspiciously for Cox, as he prepared to face down Nixon defense lawyer Charles Alan Wright in Sirica's sixth-floor courtroom over the question of the presidential subpoena. As Sirica brought the courtroom to order at 10 a.m., sitting before a packed audience of three hundred living humans and four marble statues denoting the great legal minds of antiquity—Moses, Hammurabi, Solon, and Justinian—the special prosecutor nervously spilled his water across the table.

Wright was the first to have the floor, and he gave a detailed defense of the president's argument that he was exempt from any such subpoenas—deploying along the way one of the most famous lines of judicial scholarship, from Justice Benjamin Cardozo's 1921 lectures, "The Nature of the Judicial Process": "We must not throw to the winds the advantages of consistency and uniformity to do justice in the instance."

For his turn, Cox pointed to the decision in *U.S. v. Clark*, which allowed for the piercing of the secrecy of jury deliberations with the specific suspicion of wrongdoing. Judge Sirica, he argued, was being asked to apply the same rare exemption to presidential conversations. "There is not merely accusation but there is strong reason to believe that the integrity of the executive office has been corrupted—although the extent of the rot is not yet clear," Cox explained.

"Getting to the truth of Watergate is a goal of great worth," Wright agreed, when he regained the floor, "but there may well be times when there are other national interests that are more important than the fullest administration of criminal justice." The president's judgment of the national interest, he said, should be respected.

Cox had been anticipating this. With the specific page and paragraph reference in Wright's own *Federal Practice and Procedures* book, he refuted the defense, saying that Wright had argued that executive privilege was not an absolute authority and that the courts needed to draw its lines.

Wright was not going to have his own words thrown back at him. "I think this is a matter of much too grave moment for us to attempt to make debater's points by *ad hominem* argument against opposing counsel," he said, proceeding to explain the extreme sensitivity of the recordings involved. Though he possessed security clearance, he explained that Nixon had told him that "in one of the tapes that is the subject of the present subpoena there is national security material so highly sensitive that he does not feel free even to hint to me what the nature of it is. This is the kind of material that will necessarily be made public at least on demand of defendants, if these tapes were ordered produced." Now it was in the hands of the judge before them.

John Sirica had long understood that history would be made in his courtroom, but the idea of issuing an order targeting the President of the United States brought him pause. His actions in the Liddy case from January were still under review by the appeals court, and he worried about how further ones would be judged. Sirica believed Nixon deserved every benefit of the doubt, and as he weighed his ruling in the tapes subpoena, he found himself often taking walks around the D.C. courthouse to clear his head. The area adjacent, where he walked, was known as John Marshall Park, after the legendary chief justice with whom Sirica felt a distant historic communion. Marshall had held that there was nothing in U.S. law that would stop a president from being subpoenaed.

And if the president could be subpoenaed, Sirica reasoned, then that order must be enforceable.

*   *   *

As the two lawyers battled in court, Nixon hosted his first press conference in nearly half a year, appearing on the grounds of the Western White House to announce, among other items, that Secretary of State William

Rogers was resigning. He would be replaced with Henry Kissinger, who would add heading the State Department to his already heavy list of responsibilities, making the national security advisor one of the most powerful U.S. officials of the entire Cold War.

For more than fifty minutes, Nixon said he accepted blame for the climate in the White House that precipitated Watergate, but reemphasized his message from the August 15 national address that he was a man in the dark, betrayed by those around him. He held forth on the accused—saying that Haldeman and Ehrlichman were "two of the finest public servants" and that "they will be exonerated"—and stated that, if Mitchell was telling the truth that he'd withheld knowledge of the cover-up from the president simply because Nixon had never asked about it, "I would have expected Mr. Mitchell to tell me in the event that he was involved or that anybody else was." For further emphasis, Nixon added, "I regret that he did not, because he is exactly right—had he told me, I would have blown my stack."

As soon as the press had a chance to raise their hands, nearly all the questions dealt with Watergate.

James Deakin, of the *St. Louis Post-Dispatch*, pressed Nixon on whether he'd broken his oath of office by authorizing the Ellsberg burglary. Nixon dismissed the idea, saying the Supreme Court had said that the president had the inherent power to protect national security. "I should also point out to you that in the Kennedy years and the Johnson years through 1966, when burglarizing of this type did take place—when it was authorized on a very large scale—there was no talk of impeachment," Nixon said. "It was quite well known."

In Washington, the House Judiciary Committee chair Pete Rodino watched the press conference with growing fury and dread; the president was continuing to lie and obfuscate, throwing around the already dismissed notion that the Ellsberg burglary had any tie to national security concerns.* The president's tone-deaf stonewalling seemed unlikely to stave off worsening political trouble. The chairman wanted nothing more

---

* The references to the Ellsberg burglary's "national security" ties likely were actually less about the psychiatrist break-in and more about the Plumbers' work exposing the Moorer-Radford spying efforts on the National Security Council, a scandal the White House still seemed desperate to bury.

than to avoid impeachment, but he feared Nixon had chosen a path that all but guaranteed it.*

The climate only worsened when Helen Thomas filed another UPI column on August 26 full of dishy details from Martha Mitchell, who had been deeply angered by Nixon's remarks. When she'd tried to confront him by phone, White House operators had refused to let her speak to the president, so instead, she called Thomas in the middle of the night. Martha said she wished the Ervin Committee would call her as a witness, because she'd seen campaign documents outlining "Watergate-style operations," and knew that Nixon's denial about being informed of the operations was untrue.

"I saw the leather-bound campaign strategy book," she said. "It included the whole procedures of everything that has happened." She claimed that she was being kept from testifying by her husband, who hoped that if she kept silent Nixon would give him executive clemency. She explained the great toll the scandal had taken on their lives and marriage, decrying "what Watergate has done to our lives. We have been suffering."

Suffering indeed. One friend described their New York apartment in those final days of August and first days of September as "Tennessee Williams on Fifth Avenue, only worse." After another major row, during which Martha shattered a large mirror, John Mitchell gathered what he could while she slept and left Martha for good. He moved out of their apartment and into the Essex House hotel. Divorce proceedings began shortly thereafter. In the weeks ahead, Martha combed through their apartment, uncovering various campaign and White House documents that she turned over to reporters—all of which, she said, bolstered her claims that the whole Nixon enterprise was corrupt.

Martha and John never saw each other again.

---

* Rodino was hardly alone in his frustration with the Nixon press conference. The White House refused to offer any proof of Nixon's statement, and attorneys general for both Kennedy and Johnson rejected the assertion that presidents had behaved like that before. Hoover, yes, had carried out extensive eavesdropping, but never the presidents. The *New York Times* editorial page savaged the performance, saying, "It is hard to imagine any Presidential statement more calculated to undermine public confidence in the integrity of government than this blunderbuss intimation, unsupported by any evidence, that Mr. Nixon's predecessors issued orders wholesale for burglaries in the name of 'national security.'"

*   *   *

In late August, Judge Sirica's order on the executive privilege question came down, a surprising twist that broadly embraced the idea that the president was not above the law, but stopped short of insisting he turn the tapes over to prosecutors. "The court, however, cannot agree with [the president] that it is the executive that finally determines whether its privilege is properly invoked. The availability of evidence, including the validity and scope of privileges, is a judicial decision," he said in his argument. "The grand jury has a right to every man's evidence and that for purposes of gathering evidence, process may issue to anyone."

Instead of delegating the responsibility to the grand jury, Sirica ordered the tapes to be turned over to him. He would listen and determine what was privileged and what wasn't.

The judge's approach didn't sit well with either party—Cox saw an endless court battle over the standards and judgment Sirica would use in determining the relevance of various tapes, while Nixon's team maintained it cost the president the confidentiality he required to conduct the nation's business and secure its interests.

"It's a disaster," Kreindler complained to Cox, after retrieving a copy from the courthouse. "Sirica tried to walk a tightrope."

"—And he knocked both parties off," Lacovara interjected.

The president's team, in San Clemente, where Nixon was still on his summer escape from the capital, announced quickly, "The President . . . will not comply with this order." Nixon would appeal.

Both sides began to ready new legal briefs.

Chapter 37

"An Upheaval in Washington"

Washington had always been a city that lived on news, a city carved from the wilderness with no purpose other than to serve as the seat of government, its geographic location part George Washington's belief that the Potomac River ran as the grand gateway to the west and part delicate negotiation between the northern and southern states. Its growth had been shaped by three major events—the Civil War, the Great Depression, and World War II—but it had been decades since the city had been tested by a scandal of Watergate's longevity or magnitude. Not since the Teapot Dome debacle of the Harding years had the presidency been so enveloped by a cloud. "Watergate has been hard on the Washington nervous system," Elizabeth Drew observed in the fall of 1973, as the city wrestled, week by week, with the implosion of its carefully constructed sociopolitical fabric. When the fall's edition appeared of the capital's haughty, long-established, and anonymously compiled social register called the "Green Book," it was as if a hurricane had torn through the social ranks—gone were the Haldemans, the Ehrlichmans, the Deans, the Magruders, and even the Stanses, "an upheaval in Washington officialdom unprecedented without a change in administration."

After nearly two weeks away, Nixon had arrived back at the White House on September 1 amid that shift, struggling to balance the nation's agenda with the new realities of his own administration. His first meeting was a two-hour, closed-door session with his embattled vice president.

Nixon was torn over how to handle the situation; Agnew was his connection to the most rabid and hard-line GOP conservatives, what George Will had called the "constituency of the discontented," a population the president couldn't afford to lose or alienate himself from if he hoped to survive Watergate and serve out his term. Still, he was annoyed that the man hadn't offered to resign. Nixon, after all, had been in Agnew's same position in the 1952 presidential race, offering to step down when his secret fund controversy—the scandal that led to his defining and career-saving "Checkers" speech—threatened the Eisenhower administration. "[Agnew] has never said, 'I want to do what's best for the country,' " Nixon groused to Haig.

The next order of business was his first fall press conference, on September 5, which would likely be a circus in the wake of a new report that a California grand jury investigating the break-in at Ellsberg's psychiatrist's office had returned four sealed indictments; reporters were speculating that the targets were Ehrlichman, Krogh, Liddy, and Kissinger's aide David Young.

Despite the president's efforts to focus on other issues during the event—agriculture prices, the nation's pinched money supply, the federal budget, instability in the Middle East, and a coup in Chile—the inevitable first question came, from UPI's Helen Thomas, about Agnew. Over the next forty minutes the questions circled back to the president's finances and Watergate. "That's the fifth one," Nixon groused as yet another reporter asked about the tapes, ignoring his attempts to redirect to the minimum wage, oil and the Middle East, taxes, better schools, and better housing.

Despite the press attention, Haig and the president's team still didn't yet see a major shift in the polls. The president's message, that the nation needed to press forward and couldn't continue to "wallow in Watergate," actually seemed to be resonating; just 9 percent of the public said the scandal was their top concern, while more than two out of five—42 percent—instead pointed to inflation and the high cost of living. "Barring some new sensational revelations, it would appear that the tempest of publicity devoted to Watergate has passed its peak," pollster Thomas Benham wrote to Haig in an analysis. "Concern over the economy is much more fundamental to public attitudes and represents a more long-term threat to the president's standing with the public."

On Monday, September 10, Nixon sat down with the House leadership for breakfast, trying to appear confident that the worst of the scandal was now behind him. They ate sausages and eggs, talked golf, and passed around cheap cigars. *TIME* magazine reported that the morning seemed "the first faint stirrings of concerned men ready to sit down together and trying to make things work." (A photo of the breakfast ran in the *New York Times* alongside two separate stories with revelations about the administration's illegal bombing of Cambodia and the Kissinger wiretaps.) That day, the White House delivered a lengthy message to Congress that amounted effectively to a second State of the Union for the year, outlining its desired legislative agenda and top areas of policy concern. Nixon addressed the nation on the radio to ask again that "we get on with the business of government."

As he projected an image of calm control to the American people, Buzhardt and Haig set in place a plan that would deal yet another blow to the delicate balance of the capital. In a meeting with Spiro Agnew, they announced the White House's final position: *Resign, the sooner the better*. Agnew's lawyer interrupted them. The vice president, he said, didn't deserve to sit through such an insulting presentation.

Agnew stood up and left.

*   *   *

For Charles Alan Wright's forty-sixth birthday in September, his University of Texas colleagues gave him a gift: a brass plate that read "Buzhardt, Garment and Wright, Counselors at Law." It was a small plaque for a small defense team, one that increasingly seemed outmatched in the Watergate battle and lacked even the basic specialty required by the case. "There was, sad to say, not a single experienced criminal defense lawyer in the 'firm,'" Garment reflected later. They were an odd group of three men who never would have partnered together on the outside. As Garment recalled later, Buzhardt was "hunched over and skinny as a split rail, his face pinched by bad dentures and a consequently restricted diet" of soft foods. His forced monasticism contrasted sharply with Wright, who was "tall and slender, and [who] looked like a Texas sheriff who had happened to take a sabbatical at Cambridge," living for evenings of rich food and Scotch. "He was a superb lawyer and knew it," Garment recalled.

Wright was learning daily how different the law was when your client was the president; the team was being supervised by a non-lawyer, Al Haig, who they clashed with constantly—at least until they all commiserated about their shared Sisyphean struggle. ("The friction between us was constant, despite some synthetic middle-of-the-night Jack Daniel's warmth," Garment recalled.) And then there was the client himself: Wright's professional reputation was such that his clients often gave him free rein to make—and win—their case. Now he grimaced as every piece of paper "ground out of my typewriter" was carefully reviewed by Nixon. "If it is the President of the United States who is your client, on great state issues of this kind, lawyers don't have the freedom to drop a brief, send it to the printers and file it in court on their own authority," he explained to one interviewer.

It was also a very different court experience, with an unforeseeable amount of high-stakes wheeling, dealing, and negotiating with the other side—and nowhere was that becoming more apparent than in the complicated process of determining the necessity of the Nixon tapes in formal proceedings.

In mid-September, after hearing in-person arguments (Wright maintained that there was no scenario in which Nixon could be made to turn over the tapes), the appeals court made the unusual but unanimous decision to ask the parties to try to work out an agreement between themselves. They were given a week; if they couldn't agree, the appeals court would then step in and issue its ruling.

Over that seven days, Cox and Buzhardt traded a few options, each weighing for the public reaction and political benefits of a compromise. As the deadline approached, Buzhardt offered to submit written, third-person summaries of the tapes, with some direct quotations. Cox maintained the original material was preferred. Negotiations continued with little progress.

On Thursday the 20th, Cox arrived at the White House at 11 a.m. with a final offer in his pocket: partial transcripts double-checked by a respected third party who could testify that the remaining portions were irrelevant. Cox wanted William Rogers, the secretary of state who had just stepped down, or J. Lee Rankin, another former solicitor general, to take on the evaluation, but kept those names to himself when Nixon's team said they'd considered a similar concept. They mentioned retired chief justice Earl Warren or retired Kentucky senator John Sherman Cooper as options, both of whom Cox agreed could work. As the meeting ended at 1 p.m., he laid his six-page proposal on the table, saying it was open to negotiation and discussion.

An hour later, Buzhardt called Cox with an outright rejection. Nixon's team argued that the White House had already bent over backwards to accommodate the Watergate requests, "recognizing the unique character of Watergate," but that they would never delegate the president's "constitutional duties and prerogatives" to Cox and the courts. "That would move beyond accommodation to irresponsibility," they argued. The president, they said, "is accountable only to his country in his political character and to his own conscience." The strong response, the special prosecutor knew, would have been the same regardless of the details of his proposal. His presentation "had been complicated enough so that any person making a good faith effort to consider it would have needed more than 45 minutes," Doyle later recalled. "The abrupt rejection made it clear that Cox had never been even close to reaching an agreement with his White House counterparts."

With no agreement in sight, the appeals court would now have to weigh in. The details of the September negotiations and the proposed compromise never became public, setting Washington and the country up for a surprise October twist and a constitutional crisis of the president's own making. Behind the scenes, however, nearly everyone saw the confrontation looming. Richardson, after parrying the presidential complaints all summer, warned Cox, "I'm afraid that there is going to be an explosion. It will be bad for you, bad for the president, and bad for the country."

*　　*　　*

Still smarting from Haig and Buzhardt's suggestion that he step down, Agnew soon found that he and the Watergate burglars had something in common—they were, by and large, on their own. "Don't I get a presumption of innocence? I didn't suggest he ought to resign over Watergate," Agnew fumed.

The vice president, the Justice Department, and the White House continued to work hard, but unsuccessfully, on a plea bargain. Agnew explained that he would plead no contest to tax charges, but would refuse any deal that included bribery or extortion, but the attorney general and the prosecutors all believed Agnew's betrayal of the public trust was so egregious—the criminality so flagrant—that it demanded public accountability. Public pressure grew on Agnew and the White House—it was simply untenable for both the vice president and the president to be under simultaneous investigation.

There were intense disagreements behind the doors of the Justice Department about how one even plea-bargained with the sitting vice president. The department's in-house legal advisors, the Office of Legal Counsel, weighed in to decide whether it was even constitutional to indict the vice president, deciding that while the president could not be indicted, the number two had no such protections in office. During one marathon seven-hour strategy session at the Justice Department, Richardson had doodled as Henry Petersen and the other prosecutors talked through how to balance justice and the political imperatives of the case; Petersen, who had weathered now an intense year of political stress balancing the White House and the Justice Department, found himself repeatedly agitated by the Maryland assistant U.S. attorneys. In one meeting, he incredulously exclaimed, "The man is the goddamn vice president of the United States! What are you trying to do—get him to crawl on his belly?"

On September 25, Agnew went to the Hill and pleaded with House leaders to allow the Judiciary Committee to take over the federal investigation, claiming that he was the target of a vindictive and ambitious prosecutor. Agnew told the lawmakers he needed a fair and impartial congressional jury instead. Tip O'Neill resisted any effort to drag the House into the investigation, believing it would tie up Congress for months, distract from other matters, and—most of all—allow Agnew an undeserved lifeline to hold on to an office he seemed poised to lose. The next day, House Speaker Carl Albert invited reporters into his office and read a short statement: "The Vice President's letter relates to matters before the courts. In view of that fact, I, as Speaker, will not take any action on the letter at this time."

With options dwindling, Agnew's ferocity rose. In late September, he used a speech to the National Federation of Republican Women in Los Angeles to take the offensive. "Small and fearful men have been frightened into furnishing evidence against me," the vice president ranted to the two thousand sympathetic audience members. "I will not resign if indicted!" The audience roared with chants of "Fight Agnew fight!" and waved signs declaring, "Agnew for President." The speech worried both Nixon's circle, who feared their vice president's growing connection with the party's most rabid conservatives, and the Justice Department, who saw Agnew's speech as an assault on the rule of law. Nixon found himself squeezed—how could he not defend his own attorney general and Justice Department, but how could he attack his own vice president?

Haig continued unsuccessfully to push Agnew to resign. "The vice president was tough, cold, and aggressive in his demands," Haig recalled, "a large, smooth, bullet-headed man, impeccably groomed and tailored in the Washington style, and when he turned off his considerable charm he was capable of conveying a somewhat menacing impression." The situation got so tense that Haig joked to his wife that if he disappeared, she "might want to look inside any recently poured bridge pilings in Maryland."

Agnew and Watergate, although separate scandals with entirely unrelated players, had merged as a political problem, and Nixon knew he needed to relieve himself of Agnew before he could focus on his own challenge. As one late September meeting with the president on Agnew wrapped up, and as his attorney general headed to the door, Nixon changed the subject: *Once Agnew was gone, he intended to fire the special prosecutor.*

* * *

The tapes were never far from Nixon's mind that fall. According to the story that he would later tell, that final weekend of September, Nixon decided to review the contents of the recordings demanded by the special prosecutor, and ordered his personal aide Stephen Bull and his trusted, longtime secretary Rose Mary Woods to bring them to Camp David. Almost immediately, Bull reported back to Haig that he couldn't locate the tape for one of the subpoenaed conversations on June 20, 1972, a meeting between Nixon, Ehrlichman, and Haldeman. Buzhardt told him not to worry—the missing tape wasn't one of those requested by Cox, who Buzhardt believed, incorrectly, actually wanted another, different conversation from the same day.

In the end, the staffers brought the other eight relevant recordings, and cloistered from distractions and prying eyes, they worked diligently to transcribe them. Making sense of the scratchy, garbled, low-quality tapes was a nightmare—Nixon often had a habit of putting his feet on the desk and jangling coffee cups, which disrupted the recordings, as did the omnipresent background noise of the Oval Office. Woods alone spent some twenty-nine hours doing the work over just two days, completing only a single tape. Nixon himself swung by the Dogwood Cabin, where Woods and Bull were working—the Secret Service were stationed outside for security—and listened for a while Saturday afternoon. For seven minutes, he pushed buttons back and forth on the Sony recorder. When he was done, he told Woods that he empathized with her "terrible" task.

On Monday, Woods continued the work at the White House; following her complaints over the weekend about the slowness of the primitive recorder she was using, the Secret Service had procured her a fancier Uher 5000 recorder that came with a foot pedal to ease playback. Louis Sims, the head of the Secret Service's technical division, went downtown at lunchtime, purchased the machine at Fidelity Sound Co. for $528.80, tested it, and delivered it by 1:15 p.m.

Shortly before 2 p.m., as the president and his secretary would later recount, she became distracted from transcribing by a ringing telephone, and pressed the record button on the new, unfamiliar machine while she turned to answer the phone. Woods panicked when she realized she'd accidentally erased some of the tape and ran to the president in his hideaway office in the Executive Office Building. She interrupted his meeting with his White House physician at 2:08 p.m. to sheepishly admit that she'd damaged the tape. "There is no problem, because that is not a subpoenaed tape," the president reassured her, himself seemingly confused about which tapes were being ordered.

Through the rest of the week, Woods continued her diligent, painstaking transcription, working at the White House and later in Key Biscayne as the president headed south the following weekend. Bull personally carried the eight tapes south to Florida, where they were locked away in a villa safe under guard by the Secret Service. For security purposes, the typewriter ribbons Woods used were burned afterward. Finishing the transcriptions would ultimately take Woods until October 23—by which point the controversy around them would escalate into a constitutional crisis.

Chapter 38

Mud-Wrestling

October 1973 would prove to be perhaps the most historic single month in the history of the American presidency, as the man in the Oval Office confronted what would normally have ended up being three separate and mostly unrelated presidency-defining crises: one foreign, two domestic, one personal. It was a fall that on one level seemed awe-inspiring and momentous yet seemed more primal on another. White House lawyer Len Garment summed it up with two words: "mud wrestling."

Hardly a day would pass without one Watergate case or another playing out in some courtroom or on Capitol Hill; competing scandal storylines filled the front pages of the nation's newspapers. On October 1, Donald Segretti pleaded guilty to three misdemeanor counts of campaign law violations, for illegally distributing campaign literature, charges that stemmed from a Tampa case alleging he'd distributed cards during the Florida primary that read, "If you like Hitler, you'll love Wallace . . . vote for Muskie." Segretti's arrangement, in turn, helped Richard Davis's "dirty tricks" task force begin to form a perjury case against former White House appointments secretary Dwight Chapin. Two days later, Segretti testified before the Senate Watergate Committee that he'd reported regularly to his old USC classmate about his dirty tricks, considering him his "boss," a statement that contradicted Chapin's repeated assertions to the FBI that he'd barely had any contact with Segretti.

That same day, Ervin stood before the Senate and decried the unfolding legal showdown with the president. The tapes, the North Carolina senator said, were "highly important evidence tending to show what happened in connection with the Watergate affair, who participated in the ensuing coverup operations, and who was without legal or moral responsibility." He rattled off presidents who had cooperated with Congress and the courts before—Jefferson, Lincoln, Grant, and Teddy Roosevelt, among others—and denounced Nixon's autocratic view of presidential power, saying, "The president's position is, in reality, incompatible with the doctrine of separation of powers of government." In withholding the documents and recordings despite a proper, legal subpoena, the president was violating the constitutional oath of office he'd sworn, obstructing Congress, and "induc[ing] multitudes of people to believe that he is withholding the tapes and memorandums because their contents are adverse to him." It was one of a series of unprecedented moments that left citizens, politicians, and journalists unsure of where to look first, until the crisis involving their vice president became impossible to ignore.

On October 4, Haig cornered one of Agnew's top aides to tell him simply, "The clock is running." The vice president had neither support on Capitol Hill nor the unconditional backing of the president. When Haig added, "The president has a lot of power—don't forget that," the vice president knew it was the most direct warning he was likely to get that Nixon was done with him.

The prosecution and defense struggled to find an acceptable middle ground. The Justice Department wanted prison time, but Agnew saw that as a deal-breaker. "He would resign only if he could do so with no possibility of confinement and he could resign with dignity," his defense lawyer recalled years later. All nine of Maryland's federal judges had recused themselves from the case, so a judge from the neighboring district in Virginia was appointed. On October 8 the judge summoned the parties to the Old Colony Motel in Alexandria, Virginia, for a day of covert negotiations in Room 208—the government and defense lawyers perched on chairs and the sofa.* Private conferences were held in

---

* In a later interview with Rachel Maddow's team for her podcast on Agnew, *Bagman*, the prosecutors reported everyone was on twin beds, with the judge presiding from a desk chair in between.

the bathroom. They went through so many rounds of discussion that the various proposals were known by the drafter's initials and numbers; "HEP #3," Henry E. Petersen, Draft 3, became the outlines of a deal.

On October 9, Attorney General Richardson surprised Haig by calling to say that after much thought, he'd decided he could stomach allowing Agnew to avoid jail if he resigned, pleaded guilty to a minor charge, and allowed the evidence against him to become public. The change of heart, one of the prosecutors later explained, "had to do with the top-priority importance to the country of getting him out of the vice-presidency." Nixon's own battles were growing; the tension was too great for the government to hold. The attorney general felt the larger cause of justice was served by removing Agnew from office. "I am in a lonely spot over here," Richardson told Haig. "I am going to make clear to my own people that this is the result of my own prayerful consideration."

That night, prosecutors stayed up late preparing a detailed, forty-page recitation of the case against Agnew, summoning witnesses to the courthouse all through the evening and night to run through what amounted to an assembly line of evidence. (In an age before word processors, the prosecutors literally cut the transcribed statements apart with scissors and reassembled them with tape.) The attorney general and Petersen arrived around 2 a.m., bringing fresh doughnuts and coffee for a final push. They finished just ahead of their early-morning deadline, and U.S. marshals raced a copy by police escort—lights flashing and siren screaming—to Agnew's team in Washington, by 8:05 a.m. The whole process had unfolded in total secrecy.

*　　*　　*

The final hours of Agnew's vice presidency unfolded even as war broke open in the Middle East. Henry Kissinger had begun his shared role as national security advisor and the nation's fifty-fourth secretary of state on September 22—a Saturday, which had forced his parents, both Orthodox Jews careful to avoid travel on the Sabbath, to walk from their hotel to his swearing-in—and was just asleep in his suite at New York's Waldorf-Astoria on Saturday, October 6, when an aide awoke him with news that Egyptian air forces and armored vehicles had launched a massive, sustained attack on Israel in the Sinai Peninsula.

The fight, coming just as Israel began to mark Yom Kippur, quickly turned dire—officials were away, military units unready—as the country found itself under siege from a large Arab coalition led by Egypt and Syria. Hundreds of aircraft and thousands of tanks battled across the Sinai Peninsula and the Golan Heights, as Egypt seized the eastern bank of the Suez Canal to Israel's south and Syrian tanks advanced ten miles into the Golan Heights in the north. Nixon was back in Key Biscayne, and Kissinger rushed to Washington to chair a National Security Council crisis group meeting; he and Haig, who was down in Florida with the president, agreed that Nixon should not rush back to the White House also, a move that might appear to ratchet up the sense of geopolitical crisis. That first set of decisions set the tone for the rest of the conflict; over the days ahead, while Nixon and most of his inner circle found themselves consumed by Watergate and Agnew, Haig and Kissinger would all but independently navigate the war in the Middle East together.

Even as the judge, prosecutors, and Agnew's team met at the Old Colony Motel, an Israeli counterattack floundered in the Sinai on the other side of the world. In the initial hours and days of the conflict, the U.S. weighed how much support—and how openly—it could provide Israel; huge battlefield losses meant that the U.S. ally desperately needed assistance, supplies, and materiel. In the first twenty-four hours, Israel lost more than one thousand troops killed in action, more than it had lost in the entire Six Day War of 1967, and on the battlefield Israel found itself outnumbered two-to-one in tanks and aircraft. Kissinger, working with similarly newly appointed defense secretary James Schlesinger, who had only stepped into the role in July after Richardson had been moved to attorney general, initially agreed to restock Israel with missiles and ammunition, provided Israel could airlift it from the continental United States. Within days, though, it became clear that level of distance would doom Israel; it didn't have sufficient cargo planes to speed the weaponry six thousand miles to the battlefields. The Soviet Union, meanwhile, had no such compunction; on Wednesday, October 10, its cargo planes began feeding fuel and weapons to Syria.

That same morning in Washington, Nixon hosted a briefing for lawmakers on the unfolding Arab-Israeli war. They found him in an oddly jovial, almost manic mood, no matter the political and geopolitical storms engulfing his White House. He couldn't stop interrupting Kissinger's presentation to make fun of his aide's reputation as a lothario. "We had a lot of trouble finding Henry," Nixon teased. "He was in bed with a broad." The secretary of state and national security advisor appeared nonplussed and continued presenting, only to have Nixon interrupt again: "Which girl were you with? It's a terrible thing when you're with a girl and the Secret Service comes looking for you."

Scribbling in his notes at the meeting, Tip O'Neill wrote, *President is acting very strangely.* In their car ride back to Capitol Hill, the chair of the House Foreign Affairs Committee, Thomas "Doc" Morgan, also lamented to O'Neill the president's apparent distraction, but wrote it off as generalized stress: "He's in real trouble, but I guess if we had his problems, we'd be the same way."*

When O'Neill got back to the Hill, he went to the House floor. There a presidential messenger handed him a letter while he was mid-conversation with another congressman. O'Neill slipped it into his pocket absentmindedly as they spoke, and pulled it out later while he was smoking a cigar in the rear of the House chamber.

The letter, from Agnew, informed the House of his resignation.

*　　　*　　　*

At 2:01 on the afternoon of October 10, Spiro Agnew, wearing a light blue suit, walked into a Baltimore courtroom; in an adjacent room, an aide gave the signal by phone for a letter of resignation to be delivered to Kissinger in Washington. It was critical, everyone had agreed, that the resignation be sequenced first, so history wouldn't record a sitting vice president pleading out in court. Richardson and Petersen represented

---

* The bizarre encounter so worried O'Neill that he called his Senate counterpart, Mike Mansfield: "I'm worried about him. Is anybody over there watching to make sure he doesn't put his finger on the button?" Mansfield replied, "Don't you worry about it—we've got Haig and he's running the show right now."

the U.S. government at the prosecution's table alongside Maryland U.S. attorney George Beall, prepared to take on the full burden and public criticism of the lax plea arrangement. U.S. marshals then sealed the courtroom. Agnew pleaded "no contest" to a single count of tax evasion.

"You fully understand the charge?" the judge asked.

"I do, Your Honor," the now former vice president said, although later in the proceedings he denied all the other government's charges.

In a press conference after, Attorney General Richardson made clear that he believed leniency was in the interest of full justice. "I'm keenly aware first of the historic magnitude of the penalties inherent in the Vice President's resignation from his high office and his acceptance of a judgment of conviction for a felony," he said. "To propose that a man who has suffered these penalties should in addition be incarcerated in a penal institution, however briefly, is more than I as head of the Government prosecuting arm, can recommend or wish."

Under the terms of the plea agreement, Agnew avoided being fingerprinted or photographed; instead, he was quickly whisked out of court and taken, stricken, to a local funeral home. It had been a tragic twenty-four hours for the family; his half brother had died the day before. The Agnews, in grief and shock on multiple levels, dined on linguini with clam sauce that night in Baltimore's Little Italy.

Back in Washington, Agnew's staff was informed of the resignation; a weeping secretary confirmed the news when an AP reporter called moments later, leading to a surreal bulletin: *Vice President Spiro T. Agnew resigned today, his secretary said.* The law-and-order vice president had pleaded no contest to federal charges, just months after the law-and-order attorney general had himself been indicted. Everyone wondered: *Would the law-and-order president be next?**

It was a question Pete Rodino's House Judiciary Committee had been focusing on for some time in quiet. Now, though, was the time to move forward. The day after Agnew's resignation, Rodino's staff shipped a

---

* The irony of the case was such that after all of Nixon's jokes about Agnew being his insurance policy against impeachment or assassination, it was Nixon who served as Agnew's insurance policy: Thanks to the president's own scandal, Spiro Agnew got off easy. "[Agnew] was forgotten instantaneously by the public and the press, and I do not recall ever hearing his name mentioned in the White House again," Haig noted in his memoirs.

secret project off to government printers that provided the first concrete evidence of where Democrats suspected the Nixon inquiries would end. Without telling the Republicans, they had been working since August to gather historical documents, some of which had been out of print for a century or longer, about Congress's impeachment power. The resulting 718-page collection brought together everything from James Madison's summary of the original impeachment powers debate during the Constitutional Convention, to previous articles of impeachment that the House had voted on, to the transcript of the Senate trial of Andrew Johnson. Once printed, it would be available to the public for $4.40. (As O'Neill recalled, "I don't think anybody on Capitol Hill actually read the book, but it was the kind of concrete symbol that people were looking for.")

One morning, as the House of Representatives opened for business, there sat on each desk a copy of the book. On the front page, written in the same font as any other government report, was the word for the first time: "Impeachment."

Chapter 39

"He Is Essentially Alone"

As the week ended, Elliot Richardson—for once—was feeling good about his department. They had successfully navigated Agnew out of office, and morale rose in the wake of a concrete victory. After a press conference about the Agnew deal on Thursday, October 11, he took two top aides, Richard Darman and J. T. Smith, out for a celebratory lunch at a French restaurant. When they returned to the office, they found themselves back inside Watergate—while they lunched, Cox and his second grand jury had indicted Bud Krogh in relation to the Ellsberg psychiatrist break-in, on felony counts of "false declarations," a charge related to perjury but with a stiffer possible sentence. It was the first indictment to come out of the Special Prosecution Force and caught Richardson and the White House entirely by surprise.*

The charges, that day though, were the least of Nixon's concerns as the Arab-Israeli War worsened. Nixon had approved sending five F-4

---

* The Krogh indictment especially set off alarms at the White House, which believed Cox had clear instructions to stay away from "national security" cases. In their mind, Krogh's work with the Plumbers was tightly tied into fears about exposing the Moorer-Radford spying operation by the Joint Chiefs of Staff within the National Security Council. Cox and Richardson, though, never grasped how worried the White House was about that scandal and considered the charges against Krogh straightforward and unrelated to national security: Krogh had been asked if he knew of Hunt and Liddy's travels to Los Angeles, and replied, repeatedly, "No, I do not." Prosecutors, though, could show he did.

Phantom fighters to Israel, but he had still focused little on the crisis until that morning's papers indicated Israel feared for its very existence. U.S. aid was insufficient, it had declared, and too slow. The Pentagon remained resistant to an active role resupplying the U.S. ally by air, and Kissinger felt the pressure mounting. "As Israel began to fall apart, Henry began to fall apart," Defense Secretary Schlesinger recalled. It was a crisis that normally would have captured Nixon's attention, but instead his nation needed a new vice president—and he saw a moment to reset his own administration. After a long day weighing VP candidates, he helicoptered to Camp David, where he traded calls with Haig through the evening, talking about the critical choice he now had to make.

John Connally had remained at the top of the list until only just recently, when he found himself embroiled in the controversies over the donations from the milk producers—an open political liability that kept him from serious consideration. "Nixon had high respect for Connally and his ability, his political acumen, and so forth," Maurice Stans observed later. "He might have been president if that milk producers matter hadn't been raised."

The other possible options were not particularly creative or nuanced. In fact, when Nixon had polled the congressional leadership, he'd received blunt and unanimous advice: *Pick someone easy to confirm.* House Speaker Carl Albert offered only one name: Gerald Ford. "He would be the easiest man that I know of to confirm," Albert said, and O'Neill had echoed the sentiment: "If you want easy sledding, the guy you should have is Jerry Ford. He will get through for you without any problems." In the end, no other top candidate was seriously considered. Nixon sent word to his staff and the press that he would announce the new nominee Friday night at 9 p.m. in a speech from the White House.

For the time being, at Camp David, as he considered pressure on him in the Middle East and at home, Nixon began to drink. Mid-evening, the National Security Council contacted Kissinger to say that the UK prime minister wanted to speak to the president; Kissinger waved off the call. Nixon, he said, was "loaded."

On Friday, Nixon returned to the White House by 8:30 a.m., flying into a capital that was, the *New York Times* reported, "nearly apoplectic with speculation, suspense, and surmise." Never before had the nation had such a moment; the Twenty-Fifth Amendment, which had defined presidential succession in 1967, had never been invoked. Reporters besieged administration figures for speculation, tips, and gossip. "Virtually every conceivable name—and some inconceivable ones—had been run through Washington's high-powered rumor mill," the *Times* reported.

One theory emerged when a limousine carrying license plate number "126" was spotted outside the White House; gossiping Washingtonians noted that Judge Sirica himself had D.C. license plate 126. *Was this the ultimate new unity ticket?* Instead, it turned out that the limo, with U.S. government plate 126, belonged to the agriculture secretary. Another false rumor held that Virginia governor Linwood Holton had been snatched mid-speech in Lexington by Secret Service agents and raced to the White House, but the Secret Service had not been informed of the choice at all; they readied a detail of agents, but Nixon refused to tip his hand even to them.

That afternoon, as the rest of the capital buzzed, Elliot Richardson and Archibald Cox met to discuss the remaining elements of the Watergate case—Richardson, after hearing the alarm from the White House about Krogh, wanted to make sure he was more involved in future indictments. Cox noted that the attorney general was in an odd, introspective mood, talking about how he identified with the story of Sir Thomas More, who had refused to endorse Henry VIII's desire to divorce Catherine of Aragon when she failed to bear him a male heir. "We are heading into a difficult period," the attorney general told the special prosecutor. "There will be times when I will have to push you. I will never push you on matters of principle." Then he added, enigmatically, "It wouldn't seem to me that it would be good for the country if I were fired or if I had to fire you."

Back at the office around 6 p.m., Cox summoned Doyle and began to explain the encounter—"I just had the most Byzantine discussion with Elliot"—when Kreindler and Lacovara interrupted the conversation. The appeals court had reached a decision on the tapes.

*   *   *

Around 7 p.m. that Friday night, October 12, Nixon called Gerald Ford at home and asked his wife, Betty, to get on the phone too. "Jerry, I want you to be the vice president," he said simply. Betty Ford replied, "I didn't know whether to say thank you or not."

For Ford, the elevation to power marked a truly unexpected turn; just months earlier, he'd been weighing retiring from politics altogether, having seen his hope of becoming House speaker seemingly dashed in the '72 election—Nixon's massive national landslide had meant little lift for minority Republicans, and if the GOP couldn't win amid such a coast-to-coast victory, when would it ever? As a safeguard, Ford had been quietly trying to lobby O'Neill to raise the congressional pensions so that he could retire back to Michigan, practice law three days a week, and golf the other four. Politics wasn't quite Ford's game, the *New Yorker*'s Elizabeth Drew noted, explaining "Ford is a clubman, steady, courteous, and well-liked on Capitol Hill. There are no sharp edges on him—of brilliance or of meanness." This naturally (and perhaps ironically) made him the perfect man for Nixon—someone popular enough to win confirmation, but not so popular that Congress or the nation might begin to lust for him as president and hasten Nixon's own end. As one Hill aide would crack, "Jerry is popular because he is not a leader. If he were a leader, he would not be popular."

Nixon was willing to accept the marriage of convenience. The president and future vice president had long been friendly in Congress, part of a semi-secret society of Republican lawmakers known as the Chowder and Marching Club, and Ford, in turn, after talking it over with Betty, decided the vice presidency would be a nice way to finish out his political career. He accepted the president's offer.

At the White House reception following the announcement, as champagne was passed around the room, secretary of housing and urban development James Lynn good-naturedly marveled at the scene. "History is being made tonight," he told Tip O'Neill. "The 25th Amendment is being enacted for the first time—I bet we'll never see another night like this."

"Not for another eight months," O'Neill shot back.* Lynn blanched; as he headed home after, the cabinet secretary couldn't shake the ill feeling that O'Neill was better at reading the tea leaves ahead.

---

* As it turned out, O'Neill's estimate was off by only two months.

*　　*　　*

As the capital celebrated the new vice president, worrying reports continued to pour in from the Middle East; Israel relayed that it had just three days of ammunition remaining, and had lost one-third of its tank corps. Meanwhile, the Soviet cargo bridge was helping Syria replace its battlefield casualties. The possibility that Israel might be overrun, the country destroyed, seemed all-too possible. "The peace of the world was gravely threatened," Haig recalled.

After days of distraction, Nixon finally engaged and spurred the Pentagon to action. Early Saturday morning, defense secretary James Schlesinger ordered three C-5A cargo planes, the largest in the U.S. fleet, to start ferrying supplies east, but Nixon realized a larger effort was critical and ordered American cargo planes to begin a mammoth airlift, to be known as Operation Nickel Grass. "It's got to be the works," he said. "We are going to get blamed as much for three planes as for one hundred." It was one of the key lessons he had learned from the horror and quagmire of Vietnam—there should be no half-measures or hesitancy once military force was committed. Thirty transports took off on Saturday with U.S. Navy fighter escorts, flying a delicate, narrow route across the Mediterranean to avoid both European airspace to the north and hostile Arab airspace to the south; in Tel Aviv, Israelis cheered out their windows as the first planes arrived. "After a week spent dithering over whether it was possible to get five F-4 Phantoms to Israel, forty were delivered over the next ten days," Haig recalled.

By the middle of the week, the airlift was delivering a thousand tons of military supplies and weaponry a day, a pace larger than the Berlin Airlift of the Cold War. American pilots flew more than 130 F-4 Phantom and A-4 Skyhawk fighters directly to Israel, handing them off on the ground to Israeli flight crews, who rushed them into combat. The cargo was a literal lifesaver for the small nation tucked on the eastern shore of the Mediterranean; the battle turned quickly. By Monday, Israel was on the advance, and Nixon and Kissinger began to move from war leaders to peacemakers.

*　　*　　*

While Nixon and the Pentagon launched the airlift and Ford prepared for his unprecedented confirmation hearings, the special prosecutor, the White House counsels, and the press all were at work digesting the appeals court ruling over the president's tapes. Lamenting in a two-hundred-page opinion their "unavoidable" and "extraordinary" decision, the judges had voted 5–2 to force Nixon to turn over the recordings,* broadly rejecting the absolute privilege claims by the White House and saying the tapes were "peculiarly necessary" and any claims of executive privilege "must fail in the face of the uniquely powerful showing made by the special prosecutor in this case" of the relevance, suspicion, and importance of the subpoenaed tapes. They did note that there was some latitude to withhold "particular" statements, but said the White House would have to provide an analysis to the court and the special prosecutor about why; if there were debates as to the reasonableness of withholding the material, Judge Sirica would decide for himself by listening to the tapes *in camera*. "Though the President is elected by nationwide ballot and is often said to represent all the people, he does not embody the nation's sovereignty," the ruling concluded. "He is not above the law's commands."

The ball was in Nixon's court and Archibald Cox could only wait. That Sunday, he drove his Ford Falcon out to the Virginia mountains and spent much of the day hiking the Appalachian Trail by himself. Nixon had five days to decide—he could come to an agreement with the special prosecutor, choose to obey, or appeal to the Supreme Court. But as Sunday unfolded at the White House, it was clear a negotiated agreement wasn't what the president had in mind—he felt that his handling of the Yom Kippur War in the Middle East, Agnew's resignation, and Ford's nomination had earned him some political breathing room—perhaps he could still maneuver his way out of the situation without releasing the tapes. That morning, Nixon held one of his increasingly infrequent White House prayer sessions for the first time in six months—an event where the sole purpose seemed to be inviting Senator John Stennis. On the sidelines of the gathering, Nixon floated to the aging lawmaker the

---

* A single judge, George MacKinnon, fully dissented, arguing that the president did, in fact, possess absolute executive privilege.

possibility that he could help mediate the dispute. Or maybe, he wondered, he could even finally fire Archibald Cox altogether. As Garment would later recall, Nixon that weekend was "feeling presidential; he was feeling his oats."

*   *   *

Al Haig called Elliot Richardson on Sunday and asked him to come by the White House Monday morning. Richardson arrived in Haig's office at 9 a.m. to find the chief of staff and Buzhardt waiting—at first, nothing set off any alarms for the attorney general. They discussed the war in the Middle East, and Haig filled in the latest developments for Richardson. "Al, I'm ready to go—should I go home and tag my bags?" Richardson joked.

"No, Elliot, that's not really what I called you about," Haig said. The chief of staff abruptly pivoted, launching into a speech about how the White House believed Egypt had launched its war because Nixon appeared weak and distracted at home; there was no better time to destroy Israel than when its greatest ally was consumed by internal scandal. To preserve global peace, he explained, Nixon needed to be done with Watergate, and before Richardson could protest, Haig laid out an audacious plan: The president would prepare transcripts of the tapes, authenticate them, and deliver them to Judge Sirica, allowing the investigation to proceed. Then he would fire Cox to negate the appeals court case order to turn over the tapes themselves and end the controversy. "If you do that, Al, I'd have to resign," Richardson replied, already exhausted.

For more than two hours, the men debated the various paths. Haig maintained that the most important part was ending the fight now—this week, it seemed—and Buzhardt re-raised the suggestion of a third-party arbiter, citing Cox's proposal of the preceding month for someone like William Rogers to act as a neutral party in reviewing the tapes for release.

When he returned to the Justice Department after the ambush, Richardson summoned his deputy William Ruckelshaus, who had moved over to be deputy attorney general after serving briefly as the interim FBI director—now he was focused on Ford's confirmation and planned to spend the rest of that week in Michigan overseeing an unprecedented

488 Watergate

seventy-agent scramble as the bureau conducted an emergency background check of the vice presidential nominee. "We've got a problem that may be worse than Agnew," Richardson warned Ruckelshaus.

Over the next few hours, Richardson and Haig continued to trade phone calls. Haig now was floating the idea of using Senator Stennis as the third party—but, according to Nixon, Cox would have to agree that he'd ask for no further evidence from the president, and Richardson would have to promise that he'd fire Cox if the special prosecutor objected. Again Richardson balked; he took seriously the pledge he'd made when he'd hired Cox that the special prosecutor would only be fired for egregious violations.

By mid-afternoon, the "Stennis Proposal," as it would come to be known, had gathered momentum. John Stennis was one of the body's most powerful and longest-serving figures, a proud Mississippian who had battled desegregation and the Civil Rights Movement through his political career and been the "heart and soul" of the Dixiecrat movement in the 1940s.* Widely admired by his colleagues in the odd club that is the U.S. Senate, he was summed up by almost everyone in Washington as "courtly," and he had a strong reputation for integrity, having participated in two Senate investigations into its own members, Joseph McCarthy and Thomas Dodd. As the head of the armed services committee since 1969, Stennis had shepherded through all the Nixon budgets for the Vietnam War. In January of 1973, he had been mugged near his home in D.C. and shot twice; he'd undergone hours of surgery and lingered near death. His recovery had taken months, and he had only been back at work for five weeks when the White House enlisted him in the tapes battle.

That day, in a confusing meeting, Haig and Buzhardt sold the senator on a distorted version of Cox's September proposal. As Stennis understood it, the White House officials were asking him to be a third-party arbiter for the tapes with the Ervin Committee—there was no mention of the special prosecutor at all—and Buzhardt even volunteered to help decipher the tapes to assuage Stennis's concern about working solo. As the special prosecutor's spokesman James Doyle explained later, "Stennis

---

* He once told the chief of naval operations, "Blacks had come down from the trees a lot later than we did."

was left with the impression that he could work without publicity and that there would be no dispute over his performing this task."*

After, though they had no written agreement laying out the terms or scope, Haig and Buzhardt told Richardson that the senator was on board, and the attorney general—who believed from his conversation with the White House team that day that this was effectively the plan already proposed by Cox himself in September—summoned Cox to float it. At six that Monday night, the men met. Both understood, implicitly, the stakes of the conversation; their jobs likely hung in the balance. As they spoke and Cox lobbed increasingly confounding questions highlighting why the compromise was such a poor solution, Richardson at first doodled and then began to get dressed in his formal tuxedo for a White House dinner he was set to attend. The tension in the room rose as Richardson's answers kept falling short. Before long, Cox felt that the choice of Stennis was a trap—a figure who would provide a fig leaf of impartiality, with the strong support of the Senate, while actually bending entirely to the White House's whim. As the special prosecutor left Richardson's office that night, someone who spotted him in the hallway said he "look[ed] like he had just been told to clean out his desk."

The next morning, Richardson and Cox met again, the conversation a mix of negotiation and hostage diplomacy. The attorney general told Cox that they had until Friday to work out a deal. If not, he said, "the consequences will be very serious for both of us." He finally agreed to write out a formal proposal, and Cox left.

Tuesday night, October 16, NBC's John Chancellor announced on the evening news that negotiations were underway for a compromise between the White House and the special prosecutor—the first public word of a process that Nixon's team had hoped to keep secret.

Nixon, for his part, was fully entrenched in the Middle East crisis at Camp David (even watching that night the 1938 drama *Suez*, about the building of the canal that was now the focus of such geopolitical drama), but his first call Wednesday morning was to Buzhardt, and they talked for

---

* Haig's notes from the time make clear that the plan was basically to have Buzhardt summarize the tapes and have Stennis sign off. "Have Fred there. Fred will prepare report for him," Haig scribbled on October 15.

twenty minutes as the president ate breakfast. After helicoptering back to the White House, Nixon met with an assembled delegation of Arab foreign ministers, from Algeria, Kuwait, Morocco, and Saudi Arabia, to discuss how to advance peace in the Middle East.

Across town, Cox, clad in his signature bow tie, announced a trio of guilty pleas by major U.S. companies—American Airlines, Goodyear Tire and Rubber Company, and Minnesota Mining and Manufacturing Company—for making illegal contributions to Nixon's reelection campaign, the first convictions the campaign finance task force led by Tom McBride had won. Cox, in his remarks, also said he planned to charge personally the "responsible corporate officer" in each instance, and thus had secured guilty pleas from the board chairs of both Goodyear and Minnesota Mining. He explained that American's leadership was not being charged because the company and its chair, George Spater, had voluntarily come forward in July. "I believe that the example of American Airlines and Mr. Spater had a good deal to do with prompting others to come forward with voluntary disclosures of corporate contributions," he said.

It was a small victory for Cox in the face of another major development that Wednesday: Sirica had blocked the Ervin Committee's request to force Nixon to turn over the tapes to the Senate, arguing that since Congress hadn't explicitly authorized Ervin's lawsuit, the federal court had no jurisdiction. The ruling meant that Cox's lawsuit would stand alone before the appeals court, and the special prosecutor was on his own.*

Richardson, meanwhile, spent the day refining a written proposal for Stennis, going through multiple iterations with Buzhardt, who provided edits that appeared to the attorney general to have come directly from the president. They finalized a draft around 5 p.m. and sent it by messenger to Cox, written on a plain sheet of white paper and entitled only "A Proposal." Upon receipt, Cox called the attorney general. "I think I should respond in writing, Elliot," he said. "It would be more careful."

---

* Ervin, Baker, and the rest of the committee moved quickly to pass a special law specifically assigning jurisdiction of their legal case to the U.S. District Court and that the matter focused on vital legislative functions; the bill moved rapidly through the House and the Senate and would become law in December without the president's signature.

Right away, Cox listed the weighty pros and cons of the Stennis Proposal in a staff memo. The pros included "avoid the risk of a constitutional crisis," the "struggle over impeachment," and the "break-up of the Special Prosecution Force and dismissal of the Attorney General." The cons included the possibility that the evidence would be useless. "There is no reason to believe that an edited transcript would meet the needs of prosecution at the trial," one segment read. "It seemed to me that it would be hard to settle for any proposal where one man became the arbitrary instrument to replace the accepted systems of grand juries, judges, and petit juries," Doyle recalled telling Cox that day. "Part of our job was to convince the American people that the system operated, and operated with integrity."

That Wednesday night, Richardson had long planned to host a small party to celebrate William Ruckelshaus's Senate confirmation. As he drove home to prepare, he recalled, an offhand comment from earlier in the day weighed on him: He'd been eating a late lunch with Henry Kissinger at the State Department, when at 1:38 p.m., the secretary of state was interrupted by a telephone call update from Nixon about the progress of the Arab foreign ministers' talk at the White House. They spoke for just five minutes, but after hanging up, Kissinger had told Richardson how distracted Nixon seemed: "He must really want to get rid of Archie Cox badly. He started talking about it in the middle of our conversation about the Middle East."

Later that night, the twenty guests at Richardson's home witnessed an increasingly strange scene, as the attorney general seemed clearly in professional distress. He gave an odd philosophical toast, quoting a book called *McSorley's Wonderful Saloon*, and its line about "there are no little people," before moving into his study to speak about duty, obligation, and accountability. Driving home afterward around midnight, a puzzled *Washington Post* columnist David Broder asked his wife, "What the hell was going on back there?"

*   *   *

Across town, that night also found John Dean sitting in the Special Prosecutor's Office amid the final stages of negotiating a plea deal between

Jim Neal and Dean's lawyer, Charles Shaffer. Even though Dean had provided such vital early evidence about the cover-up, there was little debate among Cox's team that he needed to face his own felony guilty plea. "Archie Cox was particularly firm in his personal determination that Dean be prosecuted no matter what," Ben-Veniste and Frampton recalled. "Moral balancing aside, the realpolitik of the situation was that Dean would not be an effective witness at trial if he got a free ride."*

The single-felony-charge had become something of a go-to for the worst actors of the cover-up—a precedent first set with LaRue and Magruder, and James Neal had even put similar deals on the table for Haldeman and Mitchell, both of whom declined. They also had finally decided on the same approach for Bart Porter, the CRP scheduler who out of misguided loyalty had perjured himself to back up Magruder's cover story about the campaign money funneled to Liddy. None of the prosecutors had had much appetite for prosecuting such a little fish among the cabinet officials, White House leaders, and corporate titans who populated so many of the open cases, but Ben-Veniste also pushed: How could the Special Prosecution Force decline to prosecute such an open-and-shut case of lying to federal agents? "The chances are that Porter might never have been prosecuted at all if he had something the prosecutors needed, but he was not so lucky," Ben-Veniste and Frampton recalled. Porter too faced a single count, of making false statements to the FBI, and received a one-month prison sentence.

Now, even amid the showdown of the tapes, the case against Dean moved forward. Peter Reint, one of the investigators in the Special Prosecutor's Office, had been hard at work through the summer and fall trying to piece together a workable charge against Dean, whose conversations with Silbert's team about immunity early in the year had unfolded chaotically and tainted the chances of prosecuting many of the specific crimes he'd participated in. By comparing Dean's words, the prosecutors' work, and the available evidence, Reint zeroed in on two instances of obstruction that Dean had never volunteered—one, in the days after the burglary, when Dean had met with CIA's Vernon Walters and asked for money to pay off

---

* As Cox said one day, "If everything else goes down the drain, the one thing I can cling to is Dean's venality."

the burglars, and one in January 1973 when Dean enlisted John Caulfield to tell McCord that Nixon would grant him clemency if he kept quiet.

Late into that Wednesday evening, they discussed every facet of the deal and the specifics that Dean would mention in his guilty plea. Shaffer and Dean reviewed the letter that Cox would provide Dean in exchange for the plea, which contained a standard clause saying the former White House counsel could still be prosecuted for perjury if it was later proved he'd given false testimony. The moment that Shaffer signed off on the letter, Jim Neal had a sinking realization: Dean was staring down the possibility that the White House tapes that would corroborate or contradict his testimony would be released within hours, and he clearly was comfortable they would back his story. "When Charlie came back in that door and said, 'He says it's okay,' I knew John Dean's version of events was accurate, and I knew that Archie Cox was in serious trouble with the president," he recalled later.

By then, it was 2:30 a.m. Thursday morning. As Washington slept, overseas in the Middle East, a thousand Israeli and Egyptian tanks fought on the edge of the Suez, as the Yom Kippur War reached a potentially climactic stage. The Soviet Union launched calls for peace before its allies were overrun by the US-resupplied Israel, giving Richard Nixon a small victory.

*   *   *

Through the week, options for a friendly settlement narrowed between the White House and the Justice Department. Thursday, a *New York Times* column by renowned legal journalist Anthony Lewis traced the "warning signal from the White House of constitutional crises ahead" and how "over this long summer and fall, the tapes issue has taken on a life of its own. It has become a test of the principle that rulers in a democracy, like those ruled, are subject to the law." Day by day, congressional pressure on the White House to comply with the court order on the tapes grew, and the president's own allies and aides conceded that impeachment would be a foregone conclusion if he resisted.

Cox too was in an equally difficult position—"He is essentially alone in all this," Lewis wrote. "He has no institution behind him, no powerful colleagues, no party. The questions are not easy ones"—and he spent the day weighing those options, typing up and refining a two-page response to the proposal from Richardson and the White House. The pressure he felt was evident in a sentence he typed and then ultimately deleted from the final draft: "I can hardly be expected to negotiate these issues with the implicit threat of dismissal hanging over my head."

Elliot Richardson reviewed the counterproposal that night at the White House with Haig and all three of the president's Watergate lawyers: Buzhardt, Wright, and Garment. The team told Richardson, flatly, that Cox's rejection of the Stennis compromise required the attorney general to fire the special prosecutor. "I wondered whether I was the only sane man in the room or whether I was the one who was crazy," he said later. Richardson urged Wright to call Cox and talk directly.

The White House lawyer reached the special prosecutor that evening at his brother's house, where the family was eating dinner. Wright, who had been in Texas for most of the week and was coming into the Stennis Proposal conversation for the first time that day, enthusiastically pitched the idea to Cox and laid out "four stipulations" Cox had to agree to, including the previously mentioned prohibition on seeking any further presidential records.

"You catch me in a difficult position, Charlie," Cox said. "I'm sitting on the floor at my brother's house and we're in the middle of dinner. There are children running about. I don't think I ought to be put in a position of responding under these circumstances, do you?" He suggested that Wright draft a letter. He would respond the next day.

As Wright and Cox spoke, Richardson sat at home, pondering a question that had come up with increasing frequency: *Protect the country or protect his reputation and tenure?* He grabbed a yellow legal pad to answer it for himself. He started to write a list entitled, simply, "Why I Must Resign." He ended up with seven items, starting with "It was a consideration of my confirmation that I appoint a Special Prosecutor and I reserved the right to fire him only in the case of some egregiously unreasonable action." Rejecting the Stennis Proposal, in Richardson's mind, didn't qualify. He continued to write; the resulting list was a remarkably self-aware document—the type of which few leaders are ever honest enough to write privately about themselves, as Richardson argued that a special prosecutor was required precisely because he could never provide the requisite independence. "I am by temperament a team player," he wrote in number three. "I cannot now change spots completely enough to be perceived to be—or feel that I am—as independent as I should be." At the end of the day, Richardson felt that Nixon's position was simply wrong and increasingly indefensible. "Many problems and headaches could have been avoided by cooperation with [Cox] more and fighting him less."

His final sentence made clear what almost surely would come next: "I cannot stay if [Cox] goes."

Chapter 40

"The Mahogany Coffin"

Friday, October 19, 1973, was a perfect fall day in Washington—high in the mid-sixties, clear, with a gentle north breeze. It should have been marked with a great celebration—Henry Kissinger had received the Nobel Peace Prize that week, along with Le Duc Tho, for their work ending the American war in Vietnam—but no such enthusiasm could be found at the White House. The Middle East was in trouble, Nixon was in trouble, and now even his friends were in trouble: The *Miami Herald*'s front page that day had broken news that the special prosecutor was investigating the president's best friend Bebe Rebozo for possible tax violations stemming from a $100,000 payment he had managed from Howard Hughes, supposedly a campaign contribution. Rebozo had boarded a plane from Miami to D.C. that day to have dinner with Nixon; there's no record of their conversations, but it's hard to imagine they were joyful. Surely, part of it referenced all the trouble caused by Archibald Cox.

The special prosecutor had received Wright's letter around eight-thirty that morning and read it with a rising sense of dread. The White House lawyer had skipped over the four "stipulations" he'd established over the phone, and instead framed their conversation as Cox rejecting the "very reasonable proposal that the Attorney General put to you." Cox's counterproposals, Wright said, "depart[ed] so far from that proposal and the purpose for which it was made that we could not accede to them in any form." Cox realized what was happening: *He was being sandbagged, made to look like he was the unreasonable one.*

Cox set the letter down on the conference table before his top aides—Henry Ruth, Phil Lacovara, Peter Kreindler, and James Doyle—so they could read it too. "Very clever lies," he simply stated. The special prosecutor was due in Sirica's courtroom at 10 a.m. for Dean's guilty plea and quickly drafted his own response to Wright, writing in cursive pencil on a yellow legal pad. More for posterity than an actual need to respond, Cox wrote that the White House lawyer's summary of their conversation "require[d] a little fleshing out" and proceeded to enumerate the four "stipulations" given the night before. "These points should be borne in mind in considering whether the proposal put before me is very reasonable," he wrote. "I have a strong desire to avoid any form of confrontation but I could not conscientiously agree to your stipulations without unfaithfulness to the pledges which I gave the Senate prior to my appointment."

The special prosecutor's team understood the impasse and what it might mean for their investigation. At 9 a.m., one of the prosecutors, John Barker, went down to the bank on the building's first floor, opened a safe-deposit box, and placed copies of the correspondence with the White House inside. Other key files were spirited out to the dusty Virginia basement of George Frampton's grandmother.

At the Justice Department, Elliot Richardson had spent the morning reviewing his resignation list with his top advisors; no one argued against his conclusion. At 9:15 a.m., he called Haig at the White House, who related the phone call between Cox and Wright the night before. "If you reach an impasse, I would like to see the president as soon as possible," Richardson told him. Haig knew that the attorney general intended to submit his resignation.

By 10 a.m., as the press, prosecutors, and Dean's team were arriving at the courthouse downtown, the White House had received Cox's message. Haig called Richardson to tell him the president would see him immediately. Richardson carefully shook hands with each of his aides as he left, expecting that he might never return to the building.

At the courthouse, Jim Neal met Shaffer and Dean in the basement garage and began to head upstairs to Sirica's courtroom. On the way, Neal pulled Shaffer aside: "Charlie, I'm not supposed to talk about this, but you ought to know before we go up there. We are heading for a horrendous confrontation with the White House over these tapes. I just thought you ought to know."

"What do you think is going to happen, Jim?" Shaffer asked.

"To tell you the truth, I don't think we are going to be around much longer, Charlie," the prosecutor replied. "If you don't want to go through with this today, that's okay."

For a moment, Shaffer weighed his client's options. "No—shit, Jim, we've done it," the defense attorney said. "He wants to do it."

Upstairs, the press had been notified that a court proceeding would take place, but no other details had been provided. As soon as Shaffer and Dean entered, however, reporters sprinted for the telephone, leaving even before the session got underway. At first Dean placed the wrong hand on the Bible as he was sworn in; after correcting, he was ready to submit his plea. Judge Sirica, looking at the president's former counsel, thought he looked even younger than he did on TV.*

*　　*　　*

At the White House, Haig stopped Richardson before he made it to the Oval Office, and offered a final option. There was no need, he said, to fire Cox—they should just move ahead with the Stennis Proposal over his objections if they got the approval of Ervin's committee. Richardson didn't see a reason to reject the idea outright, so he holed up with Ruckelshaus and his top aides in the attorney general's private dining room, trying to find their way through to a compromise and solution.

The rest of the day was a confusing and confounding jumble of meetings, telephone calls, and letter-drafting, almost impossible to disentangle or reconstruct, particularly when it comes to Haig. While his own accounts of this period portray him as a loyal sherpa, shuttling

---

* Dean's guilty plea marked the end of Jim Neal's tenure at the Special Prosecutor's Office; he had only ever intended to stay two weeks and his law practice back in Nashville had been devastated by his prolonged absence. "A prosecutor has to be a guy who doesn't give a damn about anything," Neal told Doyle. "I'm half in and half out. I've got a family in Nashville that needs attention, and a law practice that needs me. I've got to cut out. With Dean brought in it's easier to go."

dutifully between an intransigent president and a hardheaded attorney general, it seems just as likely he spent the day acting as a desperate plate-spinner—never quite fully leveling with anyone about the other side's position while trying to keep everything in motion, hoping wildly that an acceptable accommodation would prevent everything crashing down.*

There is similar confusion about how well the White House understood Richardson's position and his threat to quit; throughout the backroom negotiations, its goal was to maneuver the attorney general to a point where Cox could be fired but Richardson would stay, preserving the veneer of integrity and minimizing political damage. Throughout the week, Richardson had seemed to leave his own position ambiguous with the White House staff; by the time they realized they'd lost him, Nixon's position was firmly set. "The need to believe a solution existed overwhelmed the necessity for determining whether the ingredients were in hand," Garment recalled later.

Buzhardt tracked down Senators Ervin in New Orleans and Baker in Chicago, and all but ordered them to the capital. Mid-afternoon, they met with Nixon's team and then the president himself, who explained how eager he was to find a reasonable accommodation with the unreasonable special prosecutor. He outlined the Stennis Proposal, hoping it would satisfy the leaders of the Watergate select committee. Ervin and Baker hedged their support, saying they'd have to discuss it with their colleagues, but they left the meeting with the sense from Nixon's team that the special prosecutor and the attorney general supported the proposal. Like Stennis, "I had no inkling at the time that President Nixon was not acting in good faith," Ervin lamented later. "I gave him the benefit of all doubts."

On Friday, Cox was surprised by the hours of silence from the White House and Justice Department—the phone hadn't rung at all since he returned from court and the Dean plea—and he finally announced to his colleagues around one-thirty that he was heading to the local bookstore to find some weekend reading.

---

* Though in much Watergate literature Haig is portrayed as a brilliant combination of Machiavelli and Rasputin, the true conniving power behind the Nixon throne, there's an equally strong—if not stronger—narrative that he was in far over his head, desperate to be liked by all, ill-serving a difficult and mercurial boss, and consistently given to saying whatever was necessary to get out of the conversation of the moment.

About a half hour later, Richardson's office finally called; the attorney general's secretary appeared confounded that the special prosecutor wasn't at his desk. A half-dozen staff, including Ruth, Kreindler, Doyle, and Barker, rushed the ten blocks toward the bookstore at 11th and Pennsylvania, splitting up to cover every conceivable route Cox might have taken. Ruth and Kreindler found him on the street and brought him back to the office.

Both Cox and the attorney general were guarded on the phone, each evincing a forced casualness and collegiality that neither felt in the moment. Richardson presented a potential new crisis—he said he had heard that Cox was about to name Nixon as an unindicted co-conspirator related to the dairy price fixing case; Cox quickly—and truthfully—dismissed the rumor. The day's legal surprises, he promised, began and ended with Dean's plea.

Afterward, Richardson called the White House to tell Haig he objected to what he called the "linked proposal," and that he felt the White House could proceed with the Stennis Proposal without worrying about placing stipulations on Cox at the same time—the two fights could play out independently, while the White House celebrated the apparent victory. Richardson, based on his conversations with Buzhardt and Haig that afternoon, considered the matter settled and breathed a momentary sigh of relief. Perhaps the crisis had been averted.

Friday night, as Israeli troops encircled Egypt's Third Army in the Sinai Peninsula, Brezhnev sent an "urgent" message to Kissinger summoning the U.S. secretary of state to Moscow for peace talks. Haig updated Richardson on the reversal of fortunes in the Middle East. "The Soviets have sent us a desperate message. The Arabs are unraveling," he said. "It's not good." All the attorney general could muster was "Jesus!"

"This puts Cuba to shame," Haig said, referencing the 1962 Cuban Missile Crisis. In retaliation for the U.S. ferrying supplies to Israel, the oil-producing cartel of Arab nations had announced a cut in global production and launched an oil embargo aimed at the U.S. and other Israeli allies.

At 5 p.m. in Washington, the Supreme Court closed its doors with no sign of a *certiorari* petition from the White House asking to review the decision mandating that the president turn over the subpoenaed tapes.

There was no appeal, no legal drama left. The showdown was now solely a contest of wills between Nixon, Cox, and Richardson.

At 5:23, a White House messenger arrived at the Special Prosecutor's Office with a final letter for Cox from Wright, written, as the president's lawyer said, "only in the interest of historical accuracy in the unhappy event that our correspondence should see the light of day."

The four-paragraph letter marked an end to the negotiations, Wright explained. "As I read your comments of the 18th and your letter of the 19th, the differences between us remain so great that no purpose would be served by further discussion of what I continue to think was a 'very reasonable'—indeed an unprecedently generous—proposal that the Attorney General put to you in an effort, in the national interest, to resolve our disputes by mutual agreement." With nothing left to say, Wright warned, "We will be forced to take the actions that the President deems appropriate in these circumstances."

The special prosecutor's team digested the letter. "Within ninety minutes, you'll be fired on live television from the East Room," Doyle solemnly predicted—and yet, the minutes ticked by with no further word. Kreindler and Carl Feldbaum walked through the office, visiting each task force, pointing out key files and reports and suggesting, "It might be a good idea if you took these home over the holiday weekend to review."*

At 6:30 p.m., everybody went home to begin a three-day weekend. At home, Cox was near tears. "I can't fight with the President of the United States," he told his wife. "I was brought up to honor and respect the President of the United States."

At 7 p.m., Haig telephoned Richardson to say a letter from the president was on its way; just two paragraphs long, it effectively confirmed to Richardson that the president was adopting the Stennis Proposal, a move Nixon considered to be a magnanimous compromise. "I have reluctantly agreed to a limited breach of Presidential confidentiality in order that our country may be spared the agony of further indecision and litigation about those tapes at a time when we are confronted with other issues of much greater moment to the country and the world," he wrote.

---

* That weekend in 1973 marked the third year of what turned out to be a brief, seven-year period when the U.S. celebrated Veterans Day in October.

The second paragraph, though, blindsided Richardson: "As a part of these actions I am instructing you to direct Special Prosecutor Archibald Cox of the Watergate Special Prosecution Force that he is to make no further attempts by judicial process to obtain tapes, notes, or memoranda of Presidential conversations. I regret the necessity of intruding to this very limited extent on the independence that I promised you with regard to Watergate when I announced your appointment. This would not have been necessary if the Special Prosecutor agreed to the very reasonable proposal you made to him this week."

Richardson was furious with Haig, and called him to tell him as much; he didn't understand how such a consequential instruction could come without notice or consultation. After hanging up, his anger still boiling, he called Cox and read the White House letter over the phone. "You can tell the press I read it to you for your information only," he counseled, making clear that he was not executing the presidential order.

In a rush, Cox hurriedly tried to reassemble his team at the offices, able to reach Kreindler, Lacovara, Doyle, and Ruth, but only a single secretary, Suzanne Westfall, whom he sent over to the *Los Angeles Times* bureau to find a copy of the lengthy, thousand-word statement released by Ron Ziegler—the only copy of the president's words that the special prosecutor and the attorney general received.

To explain his reasoning, Nixon had cited the need for stability in the Middle East, saying he could not allow foreign adversaries to doubt America's resolve or focus in the wake of the "strain imposed on the American people by the aftermath of Watergate." The announcement outlined the Stennis Proposal, an idea that would comply "with the spirit of the decision of the Court of Appeals," and which—in Nixon's telling—had been the brainchild of Richardson himself and endorsed by Ervin and Baker. Digesting it at their own homes, both Baker and Ervin were puzzled and troubled—they knew they'd endorsed no such thing. Nor, actually, had Stennis.

In the final paragraphs of the statement, Nixon repeated the message he'd surprised Richardson with earlier in the evening—turning over the Stennis-approved summaries would mark the end of the search. Richardson and Cox were instructed to cease any further requests. "I believe that by these actions I have taken today America will be spared the anguish of further indecision and litigation about tapes," Nixon said.

The White House announcement caught the press off-guard—on CBS, Fred Graham reported the news still dressed in a tuxedo, as he'd been pulled out of a gala dinner and rushed on air to cover the breaking story. Cox dictated a statement of his own to Doyle, making clear, "In my judgment, the president is refusing to comply with the court's decree" and that following the president's orders "would violate my solemn pledge to the Senate and the country to invoke judicial process to challenge exaggerated claims of executive privilege." Doyle then raced upstairs to the special prosecutor's law library, where reporters had gathered and were using the library's two phones to read the statements back to their newsrooms. The words clattered over teletype machines coast-to-coast via the wires while Cox read the statement aloud for the TV cameras. Doyle announced that there would be a follow-up press conference at 1 p.m. Saturday.

That evening, Richardson talked to Nixon aide Bryce Harlow, complaining about how the chief of staff had treated him throughout the ordeal—"Bryce, I have been treated shabbily by Haig"—but later that night, when Haig called Richardson, he recalled the attorney general's mood as almost sanguine: "Well, I'm home now. I've had a drink. Things look a little better, and we'll see where we go from here." Richardson had a pretty good idea. In their house, Richardson's wife referred to going out in style as being buried in a mahogany coffin; that night, as he drank, Richardson jotted down notes about what to do next.

He titled his list, "The Mahogany Coffin."

Chapter 41

The Massacre

Saturday morning began inauspiciously for the special prosecutor: Cox left for downtown around 8:50 a.m. and arrived at the K Street office to find that he'd forgotten or misplaced his normal green staff ID badge. Instead, the guard helpfully fitted him with a numbered yellow badge that read, ominously, "Temporary Employee."

Everyone inside the office understood the impact of Nixon's announcement; emotions were high and theories and advice for Cox plentiful, much of it conflicting or strained. Many of the Special Prosecution Force hadn't realized the drama unfolding around the tapes, and the previous twenty-four hours had come as an unpleasant shock. "It was the first time in my memory that I saw confusion in that room," Doyle recalled. Phones rang, and the Western Union machine clattered away. Staff compiled lists of evidence that had not yet been turned over, and Cox himself sat in his office, writing on a yellow legal pad what he thought he should say at the afternoon press conference. A sign on his door discouraged visitors: "Please Don't Enter. Archie Is Busy."

At 11 a.m., the staff convened in the tenth-floor library; it was the first time they'd all been brought together since the welcome gathering at the start of the investigations months before. Just like on the day of his swearing-in, Cox had forsaken his normal bow tie for a regular maroon-and-white striped necktie. Now he began to outline to the staff the developments thus far, adding that he didn't know what was to come, but that he was grateful for their dedication and hard work. He and a small group of the office leadership then left for his event at the National Press Club, which the networks planned to carry live, coast-to-coast.

The group walked the six blocks across town, distracted and silent, and when they arrived at the club, Ruth pulled aside the task force leaders. "We should try to reach some consensus on what we will do if Archie is fired," he told them. "We'll need to show complete unity." It was a smart and prescient comment—moments before Cox went out into the ballroom to meet the nation's assembled press corps, Richardson reached the special prosecutor in the private holding room. The attorney general relayed that he'd sent a new letter to the White House rejecting the new conditions on the Stennis compromise and standing by Cox's investigation. To Cox, it was a critical endorsement at a critical moment. He was ready.

The special prosecutor walked to the front of the room holding hands with his wife, parting only as he settled in to speak. "I read in one of the newspapers this morning the headline 'Cox Defiant,'" he began. "I don't feel defiant." He continued on, laying out the dispute with the administration, the failed efforts to bring resolution, and his realization that he had to speak up. "I'm not looking for a confrontation," Cox said. "I've worried a good deal through my life about problems of imposing too much strain upon our constitutional institutions, and I'm certainly not out to get the President of the United States." As he finished his lengthy summary—his edited remarks would fill half-a-page in many newspapers the following day—reporters asked repeatedly whether he expected to be fired. Cox, after explaining what he saw as the procedures around his dismissal and who might possess the right authority, simply replied: "Eventually, a president can always work his will."

At a time when the presidency was still viewed with awe and reverence in Washington, despite the events of the last year, Cox's lonely confidence to stand against Nixon seemed to humble the normally voracious press corps—watching the scene unfold, the *New Yorker*'s Elizabeth Drew noted Cox's "folksy, tentative, Jimmy Stewart–like character."

"Sir, you are rather unique in our history because you personally rebuffed the President of the United States. And you come in here today hand-holding with your wife, and it took a lot of moral courage," reporter Sarah McClendon said after Cox had finished. "My question is, how could you expect to succeed in this job? How could you expect to succeed?"

"I thought it was worth a try. I thought it was important," Cox answered. "If it could be done, I thought it would help the country; and if I lost, what the hell?"

Later, as he walked back to the office with his wife and a handful of staff, Cox sighed. "I know there is a regulation against spiritous beverages on federal reservations, but I could do with a drink," he said. John Barker stopped at a liquor store for beer and a bottle of Old Fitzgerald whiskey. At the office, Cox sipped a beer as he analyzed the press conference with aides; everyone felt it had gone well. Then, the special prosecutor decided it was time to head home. He wanted to go for a hike as the rest of Washington contemplated his fate.

*   *   *

Across town, the White House was in crisis mode. Haig and Nixon's team had only imagined three possible paths for Cox—accept the president's order to stand down, ask the court on Tuesday to find the president in noncompliance, or resign in protest—and hadn't counted on such a public, sympathetic, and principled stand.

At 2:07, Leonard Garment called Richardson, asking if the attorney general would consider firing Cox and then resigning in protest. He refused. Garment passed along the message to Nixon. "What the hell can I do?" the president asked. "Can I back down?" His aides said no.

Just thirteen minutes later, Haig called Richardson back to inform him that the president was ordering the attorney general to fire the special prosecutor. Richardson replied sadly: "I can't do that. I guess I better come over and resign."

Immediately, Richardson summoned his deputy, Ruckelshaus, who confirmed he would stand by the attorney general's refusal. Next, they summoned the Justice Department's third-ranking official, solicitor general Robert Bork. Bork, a rising star in the conservative legal world, had only been in office for four months, and his responsibilities had kept him far from Watergate; representing the government before the Supreme

Court meant his portfolio focused primarily on a philosophical approach to the law, not an operational one.

As Richardson filled him in and explained that he might have to decide whether to execute the president's order, Bork grew angry and started pacing. He loved his job—just weeks earlier he'd told a group of antitrust lawyers it was the best one he'd ever had—but this wasn't what he'd signed up for.* Now he was being pushed into an awful position at the center of the most contentious moment in the entire scandal—and moreover, he would be left responsible for the unpopular opinion. Despite whatever personal moral discomfort he felt, Bork's view of executive power held that Nixon had the right to fire Cox and so, as an employee of the executive branch, he felt it would be his duty to do so. If Bork quit in protest too, it wasn't clear who could lead the department—the Justice Department at the time had no clear order of succession beyond the attorney general, deputy attorney general, and solicitor general. Above all, however, one reason to leave stood out above the rest: He had a bright future in Republican politics, and becoming Nixon's hatchetman could sink his career. "I don't want to appear to be an apparatchik," he sheepishly protested.

"Elliot and I will say publicly that we urged you to stay," Ruckelshaus encouraged.

Later, at the White House, Haig met alone with Richardson, pressuring him with every argument he could deploy to protect the presidency and change the attorney general's mind. Perhaps, if Richardson felt it necessary to resign, Haig suggested, he could release his resignation letter in a week, once the Middle East crisis had passed. "C'mon, Al," Richardson replied, dismissively.

Finally, out of arguments, he took Richardson down to the Oval Office, where the attorney general sensed Nixon's anger as soon as he walked in. The men haggled; Nixon wanted Cox gone, and Richardson

---

* In fact, Bork had actively tried to steer clear of the controversy: he'd refused an offer from Haig that summer to head the president's defense, in part because Haig had refused to allow him to listen to the tapes if he took the job. "[Haig] was great at waving the flag and telling you the republic depended on you," Bork recalled of the job pitch. At that time, in July, Haig had promised, "If [Nixon] is ever forced to turn over those tapes, he will burn them first and then resign."

to remain until the Middle East imbroglio was over. He couldn't afford America—or the presidency—to look weak in the face of such a crisis. "Brezhnev would never understand if I let Cox defy my instructions," he said, citing the Soviet leader he'd faced down all month as the Yom Kippur War unfolded. "I wish you could see it not in terms of your personal commitments but rather in terms of the national interest," Nixon argued.

"Mr. President, we may not see this in exactly the same terms, but I would like at least to be understood as acting in the light of what I believe is the national interest," the attorney general replied. They talked for sixteen minutes, from 4:42 to 4:58 p.m., and the impasse held. "I feel I have no choice but to go forward with this," Richardson told the president.

When Richardson arrived back at the Justice Department, his staff saw immediately from his face how the meeting had gone. Ruckelshaus knew history was about to bear down upon him. Minutes later, his secretary found him in Richardson's suite and told him the White House was on the phone. Ruckelshaus headed off to take the call, and Richardson turned to Bork: "Bob, you've got about five minutes to make up your mind. Somebody has got to do it. He is going to be fired. You should do it. You've got the nerve and the brains."*

Downstairs, Ruckelshaus received the same talking points Richardson had been fed in the Oval Office: The Middle East was in crisis, and American power hung in the balance. "Your commander-in-chief is giving you an order, Bill," Haig said. "You don't have any alternative under your oath of office." The chief of staff's voice sounded so normal, Ruckelshaus thought, it was almost easy to forget how remarkable the order truly was.

"Al, this isn't the first time I've given this any thought," the now acting attorney general responded, before outlining another path through the crisis. "I've had a week to think about it, and I cannot do it. If it's that crucial, why don't you wait a week to fire Cox? There is no magic in the court of appeals deadline. If you want me to stay around a week, I'll be happy to do it, but I won't fire Cox before I go."

---

* Later—much later, when the true cost of the looming professional decision became clear to Bork—he'd note that Richardson's advice was both more ambiguous and less complimentary than it might have appeared to him in that moment.

As he listened, Ruckelshaus tried to imagine the scene at the White House. He'd been a lifelong Republican, but having led the FBI earlier that summer he'd come to know the Watergate case intimately. "My assessment, having spent three months running the investigation, was that the president was involved," he recalled later. He sensed that Nixon's orders weren't truly altruistic, a means to protect the separation of powers and the power of the presidency for future occupants. This was a corrupt order from a corrupt man. Haig was speaking so grandiosely, he wondered whether Nixon himself was listening—perhaps even present in the room. "Your commander-in-chief has given you an order," Haig repeated. Ruckelshaus tendered his resignation, but Haig refused to accept it. Instead, he fired him outright.

As expected, Bork was next summoned to the White House personally, picked up in a limo with Garment and Buzhardt inside. Bork, seeing Garment in the passenger seat and Buzhardt in the rear of the car, joked darkly about whether he was being taken for a ride, Mafia-style. Nobody laughed.

At the White House, Haig got right to the point: "Bob, the stability of the executive branch is in doubt, and the situation in the Middle East right now is one of grave jeopardy. We cannot have the President weakened tonight."

"I've already decided to fire Cox," the solicitor general replied. "The only question is whether I resign after I do it." Haig's office began drafting a letter removing the special prosecutor and ordered the Justice Department to send over stationery; the sheets of letterhead were driven up Pennsylvania Avenue by the same man who had twice already made the trip to deliver resignation letters. Bork read over the brusque and businesslike dismissal. "Dear Mr. Cox: As provided by Title 28, section 508 (b) of the United States Code and Title 28, section 0.132(a) of the Code of Federal Regulations, I have today assumed the duties of Acting Attorney General. In that capacity I am, as instructed by the President, discharging you, effective at once, from your position as Special Prosecutor, Watergate Special Prosecution Force. Very Truly Yours."

Bork signed.

At 5:59 p.m., just one hour and one minute after Richardson had left, Bork entered the Oval Office as the new acting attorney general.

It was only the third time Nixon and Bork had ever met. During their nine-minute meeting, Bork sized up the president; the man had won, but looked defeated. "Well, you've got guts," the president told Bork. "Do you want to be attorney general?"

"That would be inappropriate, Mr. President," Bork replied.

"All I want is a prosecution, not a persecution," Nixon pleaded.

As the drama continued, Richardson called Cox to warn him, feeling broken himself. Ever since he and Nixon had met at Camp David at the end of April, he had believed the president truly wanted to find compromise. Now it was clear that the entire process had been a sham; he had never intended to get to the bottom of Watergate, never intended to allow a fulsome investigation, never intended to shake himself free of his aides' cover-up. And on top of all of that, he had tried to enlist Richardson—and Richardson's integrity—as an accomplice in his conspiracy.

He closed his call to the special prosecutor by quoting a verse of *The Iliad* that had been a favorite of Judge Learned Hand, whom they had both clerked for early in their careers: "Now, though numberless fates of death beset us which no mortal can escape or avoid, let us go forward together, and either we shall give honor to one another, or another to us."

Chapter 42

"We Have No Functional President"

I n the wake of the Justice Department debacle, the president retreated to the White House residence, with Bebe Rebozo. After calling Haig seemingly every few minutes for updates, he settled into the White House movie theater around 8:25 p.m. to watch *The Searching Wind*, a 1946 film about the mistakes of an American diplomat in Europe.

At almost the same time, Ron Ziegler announced the day's dramatic developments to the world: "The office of the Watergate Special Prosecution Force has been abolished." The news rocked Washington. "The country tonight is in the midst of what may be the most serious constitutional crisis in its history," John Chancellor declared on NBC News. Reports from the capital sounded as breathless and anxious as any from the front lines of Vietnam—and as the very practice of democracy appeared under threat, the country still lacked a vice president and the opposition stood next in line to the presidency.*

---

* Haig, for his part, continued to juggle the Middle East and the special prosecutor firestorm. In the midst of the resignation showdown, Kissinger called from Moscow to complain about his marching orders from the administration. "Will you get off my back?" Haig shot back. "I have troubles of my own." Kissinger sounded incredulous: "What troubles can you possibly have in Washington on a Saturday night?"

What was instantly dubbed the "Saturday Night Massacre" inter-rupted long-weekend getaways and dinner parties, one of which was being held for columnist Art Buchwald's birthday; the backyard steadily emptied as news spread. All across town, members of the Special Pros-ecution Force began to rush back to their offices. That evening, as the investigation's FBI case agent, Angelo Lano, pulled into his driveway—his kids were asleep in the backseat of the car—he and his wife could hear the phone ringing from outside as they opened the car doors. The head of the bureau's Washington Field Office was frantic; Lano had to rush to the Special Prosecution Force's Office and secure the premises. "Nothing in or out," the special agent in charge told Lano; the orders evidently came direct from Haig himself. "The people can come and go, but no outsiders."

Lano arrived at the K Street offices at 9:05 p.m., and quickly found himself in a standoff by the elevators with prosecutors. "Please, just don't take anything out of here," Lano begged. Henry Ruth, Cox's deputy who suddenly found himself pushed into the top job, arrived soon after and began negotiating with the agent; together, they called Henry Petersen at the Justice Department for guidance. Prosecutors began slipping key documents out of the office even as the agents debated their correct course of action.

Next, Ruth and Phil Lacovara, the office's in-house counsel, telephoned Bork. As best as anyone could determine, Nixon had abolished the Spe-cial Prosecution Force, but he hadn't fired the attorneys—they remained employed by the Justice Department, able to pursue the investigation under new supervision. "The president's failure once again to do his dirty work artfully would come back to haunt him," Ben-Veniste and Frampton recalled. "It was the same pattern we had seen over and over again in the White House containment of Watergate—equal measures of corrupt intent on the one hand and incompetence on the other."

One of the last to know what had happened, officially at least, was Cox. Around 8 p.m., a White House aide had called to ask his address; the aide didn't say why, but Cox guessed. He called Jim Doyle, talked briefly, and dictated a statement for the press: "Whether ours shall con-tinue to be a government of laws and not of men is now for Congress and ultimately the American people."

At the Special Prosecutor's Office, Ruth held an impromptu press conference in the library. "Everything has happened so suddenly that I can't think through what it all means for the country," he said. Tension was high, uncertainty defined the evening. Late in the evening, the staff gathered; no one was sure who was in charge, or even whether any of them had jobs. "Welcome to Moscow," Ruth told them, darkly. "I assume all of you will be here Tuesday morning so we can try to continue. We will have to take things one day at a time for awhile."

Finally, out in Virginia, the White House messenger arrived, after crisscrossing the Blue Ridge Mountains in search of Cox's house. Cox looked at the man on the doorstep, carrying a sheaf of papers, wearing an open-necked shirt. It was official: He was fired. After signing for the message, Cox turned to his wife: "Couldn't they have sent a chap with a proper necktie?"

*   *   *

Watching the press coverage that Sunday at the Justice Department, now acting attorney general Robert Bork lamented just how ill-executed the whole operation had been. The Nixon White House's general approach to governing had long been "studied ambiguity," but the lack of follow-through planning had proved fatal. The media's use of the word "massacre" seemed more deliberate than any of the main actors felt the decision-making had actually been—"I suppose 'Saturday Night Involuntary Manslaughter' didn't have the same ring," Bork rued. Bork himself was traumatized by the events; his deputy solicitor general, a woman named Jewel Lafontant, had called to congratulate him on becoming acting attorney general, only to hear Bork all but wail, "Catastrophes don't call for congratulations."

His first telephone call after firing Cox had been to Henry Petersen—White House operators had managed, somehow, to locate him on his boat on the Chesapeake Bay and get him ashore to a phone. Bork had explained that Cox had been fired, and both Richardson and Ruckelshaus had resigned. "[Petersen] was flabbergasted," Bork recalled later.

As Sunday unfolded, the "ferocious intensity" of the public response startled Nixon as well; he recalled later in his memoirs that while he'd been prepared for a "major and adverse reaction," the tidal wave of opprobrium made the White House instantly reconsider its position. Condemnation of the president's actions flowed from political allies and foes alike, and even from church pulpits across the country. Oregon Republican senator Mark O. Hatfield told the *Washington Post* over the phone, "It seems to me the President is almost intent on committing political hara-kiri." Telegraph offices found themselves overwhelmed; telephone switchboards were swamped; Congress was deluged with mail. Nearly a half-million mailgrams and telegrams flooded Washington, quadruple the previous record. Cox had come across in Saturday's press conference as the ultimate sympathetic figure, and America responded en masse to his firing. The TV correspondents reporting from the White House lawn on the crisis were all but drowned out by passing cars honking on Pennsylvania Avenue, as protesters along the street there held signs urging "Honk to Impeach Nixon."

The Nixon team reeled, even as they maintained they'd acted correctly. "Every action that the president took was completely within his legal right and prerogative," White House communications director Ken Clawson told the *New Yorker*'s Elizabeth Drew. "What crime or misdemeanor did he commit this weekend?"

That afternoon, James Doyle hosted a press briefing, forcing the reporters camped outside the Special Prosecutor's Office in past the FBI agents standing watch. In no uncertain terms, Doyle explained that the office planned to keep working. "We have reason to believe that some very serious crimes have been committed and we are a criminal prosecution force," he said. "Most of the people who work here are part of the civil service system. There are rules that apply before you can abolish an agency," he continued. "The White House announced we were abolished, but you know if they announce the sky is green and you look up and see the sky is blue . . ." He let his words hang in the air. Watching Doyle's remarks, his colleagues appreciated his projected confidence, but few felt it would help.

Monday morning, worried that their offices had been bugged, the senior staff of the Watergate Special Prosecution Force convened for a meeting in the conference room of a nearby law firm. They were dejected and unsure what sanctions they could push against the president, if any. Someone suggested asking New York and California to disbar Nixon, but the idea was dismissed as a fool's errand. As the day progressed, however, the prosecutors began to feel buoyed by the building public outrage; the head of the American Bar Association, an organization not known for its quick reactions or for its backbone amid public controversy, accused Nixon of attempting to "abort the established processes of law." Oregon Republican senator Bob Packwood made a public statement that "the office of President does not carry with it a license to destroy justice," and Virginia representative William Whitehurst, a loyal Republican, complained, "I've carried Nixon's flag faithfully for five years, and it's getting pretty heavy." Fresh polling showed the president's approval rating, which over the summer had already been lower than the worst numbers Lyndon Johnson ever saw at the height of the Vietnam War, down to just 24 percent.

Hank Ruth made a case to the staff that they should remain and work as diligently as before; a united front was key. ("Why waste our resignations?" Ben-Veniste agreed.) Doyle added a warning about making any demands of the administration. "Our job is to rub their noses in it every day and force them to stop us," he explained. "We should carry on and let them make the next move." And so they did.

That evening, Bork met with the leaders of the Special Prosecution Force at the Justice Department. When he said, "I hope you guys have strong cases. If you lose them, I'm going to be accused of bagging them," the sense of relief in the air was obvious. Some combination of Bork's commitment to the rule of law and political self-preservation had clearly kicked in; he didn't want them going anywhere. They began to discuss how exactly to proceed, and the conversation turned tense. Petersen was agitated, angrily stalking up to Lacovara and calling him "you little squirt" amid a profanity-laced tirade that left Hank Ruth worried the assistant attorney general was going to strike the prosecutor. Bork was equally terrified. The last thing he needed was more resignations rippling through Cox's deputies. Any further departures might unravel the entire department.

In an equally testy follow-up meeting the next day with the larger staff, Bork continued to try to reassure investigators and project stability and unity, despite Petersen's continued aggravations. "I'll back you up," Bork told the Special Prosecution Force. "Go to court for any tapes and documents you need, and resign if the White House gives you any trouble."

*   *   *

Almost hour by hour Tuesday, the Nixon team found themselves backed further into a corner. When Bryce Harlow and another aide went to meet with GOP leaders on Capitol Hill, the leader of the House Republican conference, Representative John Anderson, was blunt in his message to Nixon's team: "If you want Republican members to support you, tell the president he has to turn over the tapes."

That day, House majority leader Tip O'Neill rose on the House floor to speak on Watergate for the first time. "No other President in the history of this nation has brought the highest office in the land into such low repute," he declared. "His conduct must bring shame to us all."

The mood of the body was clear; in just a few days' time, eighty-four representatives introduced impeachment resolutions and ninety-eight brought forward bills calling for the appointment of a special prosecutor; across the Capitol, in the Senate, fifty-seven senators—nearly three out of five—did the same. West Virginia representative Ken Hechler joined Maryland's Parren Mitchell with the simplest impeachment motion: "Resolved, that Richard M. Nixon, President of the United States, is impeached of high crimes and misdemeanors." Amid the tumult, Tennessee Republican Dan Kuykendall warned colleagues in his own floor speech "to go slow and not be part of a legislative lynch mob." To emphasize his point, he raised a noose over his head. Away from the Capitol, consumer advocate Ralph Nader filed a lawsuit asking federal courts to declare Nixon's firing of Cox illegal and to reinstate him as special prosecutor.

As he concluded his remarks, O'Neill explained that only Nixon could determine what happened next. The president "has left the people no recourse. They have had enough double-dealing. In their anger and exasperation, the people have turned to the House of Representatives. It is the responsibility of the House to examine its constitutional responsibilities in this matter."

*   *   *

Judge John Sirica, like much of the rest of the country, had watched the Saturday press conference on television, away from D.C. on a college visit with his daughter in Connecticut. As the events unfolded, he seethed. "I was just plain damned angry," he recalled. "As far as I was concerned, the president was breaking the law." Any other defendant who defied a court order like Nixon appeared to be doing would be inviting a jail term for contempt. Sirica and his clerk worked through the rest of the weekend to figure out the proper response. On the Monday holiday, Charles Alan Wright delivered the formal Stennis compromise the president planned to implement, a solution Sirica found woefully inadequate. He weighed instead whether he could appoint his own special prosecutor to step into the case, but ultimately rejected that approach.

On Tuesday morning, the prosecutors were shocked to find that Sirica had assembled the two grand juries working on Watergate matters to hear a prepared statement. "The grand juries on which you serve remain operative and intact," he said. There was nothing Nixon could do to their work, Sirica explained, and so they should continue.* He then adjourned until the 2 p.m. hearing on the status of the tapes, but had his clerk ask Henry Ruth to join him in his chambers. When the special prosecutor arrived, the judge praised the office for its stance over the weekend and promised that the law would resolve the matter. Even as Sirica spoke the words, he wasn't sure they were true.

At the White House, Nixon assessed the damage with Buzhardt, Garment, Wright, and Haig by phone and in person. They quickly came to a shared conclusion: They had almost no choice but to obey.

When Sirica's courtroom convened again at 2 p.m., nearly a dozen members of the leaderless Special Prosecution Force crowded around the prosecutor's table; as they settled in, elbow-to-elbow, they noted the awkwardness of sitting at the table reserved for "the government" as they faced a table filled with the president's lawyers. "Which government?" they asked themselves.

---

* That weekend, after his firing, Cox wrote a private letter to the judge—unreleased until 2018—that offered his services to the court if needed, perhaps to be appointed as counsel to the grand jury, a rarely used mechanism that provides legal advice directly to jurors outside of the prosecutor. "I am genuinely doubtful concerning my professional duty," Cox wrote. "It seems quite possible that my dismissal does not terminate my duties to the court in these capacities [with the grand jury]; and although I am reluctant to intrude myself; I wish not to shrink from any obligations." Sirica found the proposal "an interesting idea," but worried that it would be too controversial.

The tension was palpable. Sirica was so nervous he stumbled over the afternoon's agenda, reading aloud his order on the tapes before realizing he'd already done so. Anticipating the president would defy the court order, the judge had prepared a nine-page list of questions to run through with Wright, excavating each tape in turn, before issuing an order for the president to appear the following day or face a possible contempt of court charge.* He'd already gone so far as to type out the draft contempt order.

Yet when it came time for the president's lawyer to speak, he surprised the room. Wright, who had walked out of the Oval Office just twenty-two minutes before, rose to say that Richard Nixon intended to turn over the tapes and would "comply in all respects." He explained that it would take some time to gather and index the requisite files, but that the president fully acknowledged the authority of the court. "The president does not defy the law," he said as a final point.

As they left the room, the special prosecutor's Watergate task force leader Richard Ben-Veniste thought about the words Wright had used—not a blanket future promise, but an assertion that the president wasn't going to defy the law on *this* occasion because he now believed that the American people wouldn't let him get away with it.

*   *   *

In the midst of national outrage and turmoil, Henry Kissinger continued to work to bring peace to the Middle East. On Sunday the 21st, as outraged telegrams deluged Washington the morning after the massacre, he and the Soviet government had hammered out the outlines of a plan to bring the Yom Kippur War to a close (a plan he had actually tried to delay for a few hours to give the advancing Israeli forces more time to gain territory), for the approval of which he'd then flown to Israel, before arriving back in Washington.

Unfortunately, what had seemed largely settled over the weekend appeared far more precarious by Wednesday. Egypt's leader, Anwar Sadat,

---

* He knew he couldn't really order the president to jail, but he could levy a massive daily fine between $25,000 and $50,000 a day until he turned over the tapes. "I knew the president loved money," Sirica reflected later.

was requesting both U.S. and Soviet troops—potentially under a mandate from the United Nations—to help enforce and police the cease-fire lines. The Soviet Union, which had withdrawn its last forces from the Middle East just a year earlier, now promised to send troops to protect Sadat's lines regardless of U.S. participation. Intelligence reports suggested a massive Soviet force was on the move, perhaps fifty thousand troops and an armada of eighty-five naval ships. Kissinger, who viewed the earlier Soviet withdrawal from the region as one of his (many) triumphs, recalled later that he was "determined to resist by force if necessary the introduction of Soviet troops in the Middle East regardless of the pretext."

For much of that night, Kissinger found himself operating alone with Haig, without presidential counsel. Normally the most important commodity of an administration is the president's time, but Nixon's daily schedules had gotten lighter and lighter as Watergate enveloped him; he retreated for longer periods, and entire afternoons would go by with him alone in his executive hideaway, seeing only a tiny handful of staff—aides like Ron Ziegler, Pat Buchanan, Stephen Bull, Buzhardt, and Haig. Entire hours would pass where Nixon sat entirely alone, presumably reading, writing on his yellow legal pads, listening to classical music, or simply stewing. When Kissinger finally spoke to Nixon around 7 p.m., it was clear how the stress of the Saturday Night Massacre fallout had overwhelmed him. The president seemed to have been drinking and was despondent.

Realizing he was effectively on his own, Kissinger forged ahead without the president, assembling a crisis meeting in the White House Situation Room that included Defense Secretary Schlesinger, CIA Director William Colby, and Joint Chiefs Chairman Moorer.* Moorer's contemporaneous notes, declassified decades later, depicted Kissinger saying the

---

* Haig's version of the night, recounted in his 1992 memoirs, holds that he and the president had communicated clearly hours earlier about the president's desires and that he knew how to act on the president's wishes. He wrote that "after leaving Nixon in the Oval Office, I joined [the meeting in the Situation Room]," which is technically true only in that he had an Oval Office meeting earlier in the day with Nixon that ended at 12:30 p.m. and ten hours "after" that, the Situation Room meeting convened at 10:30 p.m. White House records show that as the evening unfolded, Haig only spoke once to Nixon after 8 p.m., by telephone at 10:20 p.m., and then not again until 7:55 the following morning.

Soviet moves were coming "since we have no functional president, in their eyes, and consequently we must prevent them from getting away with this."

The group decided to put the U.S. military and its nuclear force on a global alert, a signal the Soviets couldn't miss. For one of the only times in the entire Cold War, U.S. forces moved midway between DEFCON 5 peacetime status and DEFCON 1, signifying an active global thermonuclear war, to DEFCON 3. Nixon was never consulted. By the time Kissinger briefed him at 8 a.m. the next day, the scare was over. At an extraordinary meeting of the Politburo early that morning in Moscow, Soviet leaders, worried by the U.S. move, chose not to escalate. According to an account published only in 1991, Prime Minister Alexei Kosygin said, "The United States will not start a war, and we have no reason to start it." Egypt withdrew its request for troops, and the Soviet Union moved ahead, suggesting a force of nonmilitary observers to police the cease-fire.

"Do you think we overreacted?" Kissinger later asked the CIA director.

"I don't think you had any choice," Colby replied. "The Soviets may not have had the intention of going much further, but they sure sounded like it."

On Thursday, October 25, lawmakers arrived at the White House for an early-morning briefing. Kissinger started, only to be quickly interrupted by the president. "[Nixon] started talking to us about the history of communism in the Soviet Union. He rambled on for almost half an hour about the czars and the revolution, about Marx and Lenin, and even the assassination of Trotsky in Mexico," Tip O'Neill recalled. "Nobody could understand what, if anything, all of this had to do with the Middle East War." Nixon finally lost steam and handed back the floor to Kissinger, only to again interrupt minutes later and continue on until the meeting ended without lawmakers ever hearing Kissinger's update.

Thursday night, Nixon retreated again to Camp David. Around 7 p.m., he called Kissinger with an idea: The White House should invite in major TV and newspaper correspondents and walk through how resolute and inspiring Nixon's leadership had been through the Yom Kippur War and the Wednesday-night crisis. Kissinger was baffled by the suggestion; the president hadn't even been there.

Friday night, the president went ahead and hosted a news conference where he trumpeted his strength amid the chaos of the week. "The tougher it gets, the cooler I get," he said. Kissinger refused to talk in depth about the events of that night—it would be years before the full story was ever told.

Chapter 43

The Patriotic Monkey

The next—and perhaps heaviest—shoe in the investigation of the President of the United States dropped on October 30, 1973, when Judge Sirica gathered the president's legal team and the Special Prosecutor's Office together to discuss the process for the White House to turn over the subpoenaed tapes. In that meeting, Fred Buzhardt confessed that two of the nine requested tapes didn't appear to exist—the White House could find no recording of a June 20, 1972, telephone call between Mitchell and Nixon, or of a Nixon-Dean meeting on April 15, 1973.

Sirica, stern and obviously troubled, announced the conversation would have to continue the next day, on the record, in public view. "Incredible," he thought. "Every time I thought this case was on track, something happened to derail it."

Two days of testimony followed, from Secret Service agents and aides, that bordered on farce. After Buzhardt blamed the missing tape on a malfunction, an expert technician explained that he'd never heard of such a thing. Witnesses produced brown paper wrapping, scratched with pencil notations that were evidently the White House custody records of the sensitive tape recordings; testimony and records showed tapes had been signed out without ever being signed back in, and the story changed frequently when someone was asked whether the recording machines had malfunctioned during the critical conversations or just run out of tape.

Then, there were the troubling inferences: One April 15 tape reel had been labeled "Part I"—seeming to imply that a "Part II" had existed too—and was revealed to have been one of the recordings made available for Haldeman to take home and listen to that July as he prepared for his Ervin Committee testimony. Richard Ben-Veniste, a former New York prosecutor who had taken over as the task force leader with the departure of Jim Neal, was eager to show his courtroom skills, and as Doyle recalled, "Ben-Veniste and his colleagues delivered body blows to the Nixon administration." Buzhardt seemed so haggard from the experience that Sirica started to feel sorry for the president's lawyer.

As the courtroom antics, public outrage, and congressional pressure continued, it became clear within days that Nixon and Bork would have to appoint a new special prosecutor; it wouldn't do politically for Bork and Petersen to supervise the investigation themselves, and while the staff seemed perfectly capable and willing to carry on, symbolically the office needed a leader.

At the White House, Al Haig had come to the same conclusion and begun frantically calling around the country. One name quickly came up: Leon Jaworski, a former president of the American Bar Association and a former war crimes prosecutor from the Nuremberg trials. Jaworski excited both Bork and the White House; for whatever reason, Haig seemed to think that Jaworski would be more malleable on issues of national security than Cox had been, and according to the quick research the chief of staff had done, the man appeared to be a political ally of John Connally, which seemed to augur well of him. "Just get the man," Nixon ordered. "If he's a decent fellow, get him."*

Haig reached a dubious Jaworski in Texas and dispatched an air force jet to deliver him to Washington. "I'm putting the patriotic monkey on your back, Leon. The situation in this country is almost revolutionary," he said when they met at the White House. He tried to invite Jaworski in to meet the president—Jaworski passed, rightly understanding that

---

* The entire controversy frustrated Nixon no end—he felt his lawyers and the press had misconstrued the whole problem. He jotted himself four notes on the side of a briefing paper: "There were no missing tapes / There were never any / The conversations in question were not taped. / Why couldn't we get that across to people?"

if he took the job, it was better to have never spoken to Nixon—and Haig dangled too the possibility of a Supreme Court seat someday, which Jaworski brushed aside. "My serving on the Supreme Court was discussed in the Lyndon Johnson administration. I had no interest in it then and I have none now," he said. The Texas lawyer explained that after what had happened with Cox, he didn't see how he could take the job without an assurance of independence; Haig explained the president's new offer—complete independence, with removal only following the assent of six of the eight leaders of Congress, both House and Senate. A number of White House officials passed through Haig's office to add their own pressure: Bork and Senator William Saxbe, who would soon be named Nixon's new attorney general nominee, then Buzhardt and Garment, then Melvin Laird and Bryce Harlow. Finally, Jaworski assented—in part, he said later, because if he said no, he'd always wonder whether it was because he lacked the courage to take on such a fraught assignment.

Haig exhaled. "Remember the key words in any news conference are that you've got the right to take the president to court," he said.

"I'll remember," Jaworski replied.

*   *   *

As much as Ford was well liked by his Democratic colleagues, it wasn't entirely clear to all of them that they should rush through a new vice presidential nomination. With Agnew gone, their own speaker, Carl Albert, would ascend to the presidency if Watergate ended up felling Nixon. Albert had made clear he would entertain neither the idea nor the talk of his ascendance beyond his current role, not least of all because he hated the Secret Service who now attended to him wherever he went. Ford's confirmation, he ordered, must move ahead as quickly as possible to enable serious consideration of an impeachment inquiry. One representative, Maryland's Clarence Long, joked, "While Ford voted wrong most of the time, at least he was decently wrong."*

* Ted Sorensen, the Kennedy speechwriter, went so far as to offer a twenty-page "contingency plan" for Albert's presidency, including thoughts on his inaugural address and recommendations for Albert's own vice presidential pick.

Despite the overwhelming support, the House leadership was still unsure how or even who should take up the impeachment question. Many on Capitol Hill seemed to want Congress to appoint its own special prosecutor, but there were real doubts among colleagues whether Pete Rodino, who had taken over the Judiciary Committee after the surprising primary election defeat of its chair, Manny Celler, had the stomach for the politics of it all. He was cautious by nature—as O'Neill would say later, "He doesn't like to move until he knows where he's going"—and his fellow members worried he lacked the will to take on the executive branch. As an alternative, Representative John Moss petitioned for the House to set up its own select committee, as the Senate had with the Ervin Committee, and various members recommended themselves or others to lead it.*

Albert and O'Neill's decree came down: Rodino would be in charge. At the end of October, on a strictly party-line vote, 21–17, the House Judiciary Committee granted its chair subpoena power to pursue the president—the same subpoena power that thirteen months earlier Wright Patman had been denied. Similarly, the Democrats voted down awarding the GOP's ranking member joint subpoena authority. This would be a Democratic show alone, run by Rodino and O'Neill.

The chairman brought together the Democrats of the Judiciary Committee to outline a plan for the months ahead, which included confirming Ford as rapidly as possible. His committee counsel, Jerome Zeifman, immediately started trying to recruit investigators from Congress's Government Accounting Office. Rodino told the press, "I have initiated a broad scale investigation to be conducted by an expanded staff that will be assembled immediately."

The president now faced an even more empowered and independent prosecutor, an impeachment inquiry on Capitol Hill, and perhaps, worst of all, back on his heels, he was facing his integrity under ongoing assault in court. The *Washington Post*'s Senate writer, Spencer Rich, captured

---

* Behind the scenes, the White House encouraged friendly oil industry voices from Oklahoma, the home state of the House speaker, to lobby Albert and engineer a special committee that might have enough conservative Democratic voices to save Nixon. "Carl Albert didn't appreciate being pressured, and when the calls started coming, he realized he didn't want any part of a special committee," O'Neill recalled.

the "gloomy" mood of the president's own GOP on Capitol Hill as the confirmation hearings for Gerald Ford began in the Senate, saying that Nixon faced "a massive hemorrhaging of support."

On November 1, attempting to minimize the ongoing damage, Nixon announced the nomination of Senator William Saxbe as the new attorney general, and Bork, still serving in the acting capacity, announced the selection of Jaworski.*

Sixteen months after the burglary, after Earl Silbert, Wright Patman, Ted Kennedy, John Sirica, Sam Ervin, and Archibald Cox had all trod the ground, Leon Jaworski and Pete Rodino picked up the baton for the final lap.

---

* Saxbe, Nixon's outspoken fourth attorney general, would serve in the role for just over a year. He would find himself largely a spectator to the events of 1974. While his desk at the Justice Department contained a direct line to the president, he found Nixon all but unreachable. "I never could get through to Nixon, so that became a dust-collector," he wrote in his memoirs.

Chapter 44

"I am Not a Crook"

When one looks back on the Watergate era, there are a number of key moments that alter its entire trajectory, the roots of diverging trails that, if they had been traveled any differently, might have changed the course of our future. One of those moments began on Friday, November 2, not in a courtroom, an executive office, or a closed-door meeting, but in a newspaper editorial calling for the president's resignation. Its author, Joe Alsop, was one of the capital's social fixtures and stalwart traditionalists, who had all but browbeat Kay Graham at parties for a year about his belief in Nixon's innocence. "The time has come for President Nixon to offer his resignation," he wrote, saying he'd "reached the foregoing conclusions with extreme reluctance." That such a figure had undergone such a distinct change of heart demonstrated how far Nixon's credibility had fallen—so quickly—and signaled a broader opening of the floodgates. The *New York Times'* James Reston echoed the same demand, and Massachusetts's Edward Brooke became the first Republican senator to support the idea publicly. Within twenty-four hours, the editorial pages of papers as varied as the *New York Times*, the *Denver Post*, and the *Detroit News* were all in agreement: the President of the United States was no longer fit to serve in his post. *TIME* even broke a fifty-year streak of avoiding editorials, adding its call for his removal from office. "Richard Nixon and the nation have passed a tragic point of no return," the magazine's editors wrote. "He has irredeemably lost his moral authority, the confidence of most of the country, and therefore his ability to govern effectively."

Nixon had tried to escape the outrage in Florida, boating in Key Biscayne with Bebe Rebozo and Bob Abplanalp, but Watergate followed him south. On Saturday the 3rd, after carefully weighing their options all week as one bad story tumbled into another, Buzhardt and Garment finally took an Eastern Airlines flight to Miami to urge the president to consider resigning. Over the past few days, Garment had tried to put things in perspective by cataloging nearly two-dozen different scandals dogging the president—all sketched out on a yellow legal pad, from ITT to the milk producers and more. "The totality spelled a vast and, I thought, fatal erosion of presidential authority," he recalled.

Aside from the practical details of so many investigations, the two lawyers had grown increasingly concerned about the president's behavior in the preceding days. He continued to drink, derail meetings, and suggest troubling "solutions" to his current predicament: In one conversation with Buzhardt, Nixon casually noted that rather than report one recording "missing," he could just re-create the conversation from existing notes. The lawyer was stunned. "We knew Nixon's suggestion was talk from a desperate man about a collateral issue, but we were also weary from months of legal tightrope walking," Garment recalled.

Saturday night, Buzhardt and Garment met with Haig and Ziegler in one of the staff villas. The mood was dark, and the message to Haig was clear: We're getting dragged into this cover-up ourselves, the arc of Nixon's presidency seems clear—he wouldn't survive the full second term—and it didn't seem impossible that everyone in the villa might face an obstruction of justice charge. The focus needed to be on how to gracefully move the president out, and when—after all, Gerald Ford still hadn't been confirmed as vice president. "Everything after this is a damage-limiting operation," Garment warned.

Ziegler and Haig rejected the resignation recommendation out of hand. Haig argued the groundwork wasn't right: "Nixon wasn't ready. The country wasn't ready. There were too many crises in the world. Ford was not yet up to the job," Garment recalled. "All true, we conceded, but Nixon had to prepare for what was coming." They asked for a chance to present their argument to the president directly; Haig objected, but agreed to bring it up himself with the president. The next day, he met with Nixon and after returned to the villa with a clear message: "The president doesn't want to see you." (Nixon recalled in his memoirs only getting a "diluted report" of Haig's meeting, so it's not clear how much he understood what his lawyers hoped to accomplish.) For Garment the meeting marked the end of his wholehearted commitment to the president; he would "gradually phase out of Watergate" in the weeks ahead, unable and unwilling to continue the fight. "I had outlived my usefulness," he explained later.

As Nixon recalled, "That weekend in Florida was a new low point for me personally." But he would fight on, with a plan for a new phase. "We will take some desperate, strong measure, and this time there is no margin for error," he told Ziegler. That week, they would launch what the press quickly dubbed "Operation Candor," a public relations campaign par excellence that would convince the nation of Nixon's innocence.

*　　*　　*

Monday morning, November 5, Leon Jaworski arrived in Washington to start his new job, landing at Dulles International Airport and telling the reporters who met him that he was confident in his ability to be independent. His wife had shared her own thoughts when the *Washington Post* reached her by phone after his appointment: "It's a terrible job. I just feel sorry for him."

The sixty-eight-year-old Jaworski came from the opposite end of the American establishment. He'd grown up on the frontier, the son of a buckboard-riding preacher and missionary in Texas, and entered law school at just sixteen, soon becoming the youngest person ever admitted to the Texas bar. He had started his career defending bootleggers amid Prohibition in the 1920s, and by the time Haig called him, Jaworski was the force behind one of the nation's top law firms—Fulbright and Jaworski. He commanded great respect at home in Houston and in legal circles around the country, and his respect for the primacy of the law was unquestioned.

Despite the reputation for integrity, the remaining members of the Watergate Special Prosecution Force wondered how a Texan "good ole boy" might mesh with the Ivy Leaguers Cox had built around him. They all assumed that Nixon's team was shoving Jaworski on them to wrap up the case with minimum fuss or complication. Jaworski's sterling credentials were actually a source of suspicion, not reassurance. "It was a bad omen that the President was able to snag such a prestigious person to play the role of fixer," Ben-Veniste and Frampton later recalled thinking.

At the first staff meeting, Jaworski assured his new team that he saw no reason to make any immediate changes. "I have accepted an awesome task, a gigantic one, and I have no full answer why I did," he explained. "I have not been precluded from taking any action against the president that I consider necessary. I have the right to move immediately if I choose." He closed with a half-compliment, half-admonition: "I begin by believing in you, and I hope that will be a two-way street." He looked out at the crowd, taken aback at how young the faces were staring at him. He realized with a start that the feeling was likely not mutual—there is a generation chasm here, not just a gap, he thought, a feeling that would only grow as he tried to maintain control. It would fall to deputy Hank Ruth to bridge the divide.*

Right away, Ruth propelled Jaworski through back-to-back briefings on seemingly every corner of the many cases, task forces, and prosecutions underway. On his second day, Jaworski met for an off-the-record chat with CBS's Dan Rather, whom he'd known back in Texas. "Dan, I'm impressed by two things: One is the professionalism of this staff; the other is the evidence," he said. To the team's amazement, Jaworski stuck by his promise of consistency. As Doyle recalled, "They had waited for his reinforcements [from Texas] to arrive and soon began to realize that Jaworski was indeed the lone stranger who rode into town at high noon."

As one of his first new investigative steps, the prosecutor sent four fresh requests for additional tapes and documents on behalf of the ITT investigation, the Plumbers team, and the burglary task force, totaling together more than twelve pages. His aggressiveness quickly signaled to

---

* Part of the staff's dubiousness about Jaworski stemmed from confusion over whether he wanted the staff to call him "Colonel," an honorific dating back to his time as army prosecutor that had been carried on by his friends and colleagues in Houston. "Well, if he opens up a fried chicken joint in the basement, I'll call him Colonel. Until then, he's Mr. Jaworski to me," Doyle grumbled to Ruth.

the team a willingness to go toe-to-toe with the president—if anything, he acted even more aggressively than Cox and won their admiration.

When weeks passed without a response to the new demands, he pressed Buzhardt in a follow-up letter. "Your failure to respond is delaying and in some instances impeding our investigations," he wrote. "In light of past experience, I believe it entirely appropriate to ask you to acknowledge each of these requests and explain your current position." Still no response came, so Jaworski called a friend who had been brought in to work on Nixon's defense. The two men walked the White House grounds, while Jaworski petitioned him for answers and action. "Somebody better get word to the president that he's about to end up in more difficulty," explained the new special prosecutor. He then warned that he would file suit against Nixon in two days unless the materials appeared.*

In less than twenty-four hours, Buzhardt was on the phone laying out a timeline. "How did he sound?" Doyle asked, after the conversation was over.

"He was as friendly as a French pervert," Jaworski said.

* * *

Across town, as Rodino's committee buckled down, nearly everyone agreed: Impeachment was a terrible remedy, fraught with peril for the politicians pushing it, hard for the country, distracting for the president, and potentially damaging to the nation's survival—and yet, still, it seemed to be a necessary step.

In the Senate on November 7, Vermont Republican George Aiken— one of the body's most respected voices—spoke out about the scandal, warning of the "politics of righteous indignation" creeping in and that

---

* The other major issue at the top of Jaworski's docket as he took over was Egil "Bud" Krogh's case. Jaworski and prosecutor Bill Merrill leaned hard on Krogh. "I tried to make it clear that I saw him as a decent person who was caught in this vise," Merrill recalled later. Then, Jaworski closed in, recounting his experiences as a war crimes prosecutor at Nuremberg, where he'd help try the villains behind the Dachau concentration camp. "Those who came out of that experience whole were the ones who admitted responsibility for their actions," he said. "It is not enough to say, 'I followed orders.'" Krogh pleaded guilty to conspiracy to violate the civil rights of Ellsberg's psychiatrist, Lewis Fielding. In exchange, Jaworski dropped the perjury charge he faced.

the effort to hold Nixon accountable would be a long road by design. The process was not meant to be easy or quick; the Founders had designed a system of laws to guard against waves of reactionism. Congress shouldn't count on the courts to relieve it of the difficult decision, nor on any mythic special prosecutor "with the virtues of Caesar's wife and the unfettered authority of her husband," Aiken said. Nor did Nixon owe the country his resignation; he had been elected to govern and his responsibility was to do just that. Surely the White House had screwed up, he agreed, and "handled its domestic troubles with such relentless incompetence that those of us who would like to help have been like swimmers searching for a way out of the water only to run into one smooth and slippery rock after another," he said. "The President's public explanations of the Watergate mess have been astonishingly inept," but ineptitude was not impeachable. Congress needed to make up its mind to act—or not. There should be no languishing. It was time, he said, to follow the advice given to him by a fellow Vermonter: "Either impeach him or get off his back."

Over the course of the next week, Congress plunged forward. The same day that Aiken spoke, both bodies of Congress overrode Nixon's veto on the War Powers Act, which set important limits on a president's ability to commit the nation's armed forces to combat overseas. It was the first in nine veto override attempts that year to succeed.

The House also appropriated itself $1 million for the Judiciary Committee's impeachment inquiry in a 361–51 vote. When Republicans protested that it was far too much money, Tip O'Neill replied, "If it were not for the scandalous action on the part of this administration, it would not cost anything." Reporters and lawmakers could hardly miss the symbolism that the vote came on the one-year anniversary of Nixon's 520-vote electoral college landslide. O'Neill had a saying as he'd navigated political life: "Power is when people think you have power." And people were beginning to see that Nixon's power was flowing away.

*   *   *

In the late fall of 1973, Lowell Weicker bumped into his neighbor John Dean outside their townhouses in Alexandria, just after Dean had pleaded guilty to obstruction. Curious for the former White House counsel's perspective, Weicker asked about the current impeachment drama and the state of his Ervin Committee's work. "Is there something else?" Weicker said. "Something we missed?"

Dean shook his head. Probably not, he said, before speaking up again. "Except for the tax fraud."

Weicker took the bait. After the Chennault Affair, the Huston Plan, the Kissinger wiretaps, and the illegal bombing of Cambodia, the Pentagon Papers and the Ellsberg burglary, ITT and the Dita Beard memo, the Vesco donation, the milk price fixing, the Watergate burglary and cover-up, the campaign "rat-fucking," and Spiro Agnew's bribery case, there was still *more*?

As Weicker's staff and other investigators began to uncover, Nixon appeared to have been concocting a self-serving scheme to bolster his legacy while minimizing his own taxes. He had followed the example of Lyndon Johnson by donating his pre-presidential papers to the National Archives when he took office—a donation intended to someday become part of his presidential library. Johnson's move in the 1960s, though, hardly seemed one to emulate: It had spawned outrage after he had claimed a massive tax deduction for the donation, and Congress, angered, had promptly passed a 1969 law banning the practice. Yet Nixon had rushed that year to follow LBJ's lead before that law took effect, turning over his vice presidential papers to the National Archives, estimating their worth at $576,000 (about $3.6 million in 2021 dollars) and planning to spread the equivalent tax deduction over his years as president.

The resulting tax bills for 1968 through 1972 seemed outrageous: $789 in federal income tax in 1970 and $878 in 1971, meaning that he had earned $525,000 over 1970 and 1971 but paid less in income taxes than someone who had earned just $9,800. In 1972, he still only paid $4,298.*

As Weicker and Senate investigators looked further into the matter, the fishier and less altruistic the president's "donation" seemed. For one thing, there was no original official deed of gift at the National Archives,

---

* The totals were so low that when Lowell Weicker first heard them, he'd not been particularly concerned because he'd assumed the tax bills referred to Nixon's weekly income tax payments—not his annual tax bill.

or a record of the papers being turned over. A deed had been delivered to the National Archives in April 1970, with signatures from a White House lawyer and a lawyer from Kalmbach's firm, both dated April 21, 1969, an apparent attempt to illegally backdate before the new law took effect. The transfer of the papers appeared to come with the stipulation that archivists couldn't fully access the records, which also would have negated the effect of a "gift" under the tax law. As far as Weicker's team could determine, the arrangement with the National Archives was less a tax-deductible gift to benefit Americans and more a taxpayer-financed storage facility.

This inevitably led to other questions about Nixon's personal finances. Reporters and investigators had been trying all year to piece together the financial transactions behind his vacation homes in San Clemente and Key Biscayne; Nixon had originally bought the whole twenty-six-acre Casa Pacifica estate with a loan from Abplanalp, and later sold most of the adjoining land to Abplanalp and Rebozo, who then sold his share back to Abplanalp. Thanks to deft legal work by Kalmbach, the transactions had all flown under the radar.

That fall, amid everything else, allegations swirled that Howard Hughes had helped finance the purchase of the Casa Pacifica; ABC reported that Nixon held a million-dollar "secret investment portfolio" of old campaign funds, and Jack Anderson hinted at Swiss bank accounts. At one point, Pat Nixon even faced her own allegations that she'd kept for personal use jewels given to her as first lady. "What more can they possibly want us to do?" Pat asked Richard, in despair.

All those allegations proved false, but the public fixated on the true controversy that as much as $10 million had been spent on "improvements" to the Nixon getaways in San Clemente and Key Biscayne, a huge figure compiled by Congress and the General Services Administration that primarily captured the routine communications and security infrastructure installed for presidents away from Washington, much of which would be removed at the conclusion of Nixon's term.* However, plenty

---

* Those security requirements had exploded only since the Kennedy assassination, and Nixon felt again held to a double standard as Lyndon Johnson had seen similar—and even some more outrageous—government-funded construction work on his Texas ranch without criticism.

of the "improvements" seemed to be about Nixon's comfort than security and eyebrows went up across Washington as Congress and reporters dug deeper. Pat Nixon was horrified at the scandal. "She came to believe that nothing hastened the turning of public opinion against the Nixon presidency more than the suggestion of profiting at the taxpayers' expense," Julie Nixon wrote later.

Needless to say, the fresh questions began to undermine the administration's Operation Candor campaign. Over the course of a week, Nixon had hosted nine separate sessions with lawmakers, each stretching across two hours and allowing for a meaty conversation about Watergate and Nixon's plans for the path ahead; all told, he met with 241 Republican lawmakers and 46 Democrats, hoping that the transparency push would make clear he was leveling with the American people. However, at every turn, the sessions seemed instead to highlight how many questions he wasn't willing to answer directly. Nixon grew increasingly frustrated, unsure how he could ever move past it all. ("I know in the history books 25 years from now, what will really matter is the fact that the President of the United States in the period from 1969 to 1976 changed the world," he lamented in one conversation.)

On November 17, he made a quick trip from Key Biscayne to Orlando to speak at the annual meeting of Associated Press newspaper editors as part of his transparency tour. During a sometimes tense but nonetheless expansive hour-long question-and-answer session, he fielded inquiries on all manner of the scandals he found himself embroiled in. When one questioner asked about his taxes and personal finances, Nixon launched into a lengthy soliloquy that harkened back to his famous "Checkers speech." When he'd left Washington in 1960, the president explained, his net worth after fourteen years of government work had been just $47,000 and a 1958 Oldsmobile. Over his eight years in the private sector, though, he'd prospered (left unsaid was that his newfound wealth came in no small part thanks to John Mitchell's law firm and guidance), and eventually, upon entering the White House, he converted those assets into real estate, which to him had seemed more appropriate than holding stocks as president.

Continuing, Nixon told the four hundred assembled newspaper editors, "Let me just say this, and I want to say this to the television audience:

I made my mistakes, but in all of my years of public life, I have never profited, never profited from public service—I have earned every cent. And in all of my years of public life, I have never obstructed justice."

As he put it, "I welcome this kind of examination, because people have got to know whether or not their President is a crook. Well, I am not a crook. I have earned everything I have got."

Later, amid the questions and answers, Nixon did elicit one round of good-natured laughter when asked about the nation's still unfolding energy crisis and need for conservation. In response, he alluded to the fact that he'd canceled the standard practice of having a backup presidential jet shadow Air Force One: "If this [plane] goes down, they don't have to impeach."

A few days later, Nixon faced the nation's Republican governors and issued similar reassurances. Oregon's governor, Tom McCall, asked Nixon point-blank, "Are we going to be blindsided by any more Watergate bombs?"

"If there are any more bombs, I'm not aware of them," Nixon said confidently.

Within twenty-four hours, McCall and the rest of the country would learn that it was a lie.

*   *   *

The day before Thanksgiving, Wednesday, November 21, Fred Buzhardt called Leon Jaworski at 9:30 with an urgent message: The White House lawyer needed to "discuss a serious problem . . . in the strictest confidence." That afternoon, he visited the Special Prosecutor's Office for the first time and explained, haltingly, that they'd identified a problem with one of the subpoenaed tapes—the conversation on June 20, 1972, between Haldeman and Nixon had a gap in the middle stretching across more than eighteen minutes. The words between the president and his chief of staff, whatever they had been, were gone. It was almost certainly a critical conversation, understood to be the first the two men had had at the White House following the burglary, after a morning of meetings and intelligence gathering by Haldeman around the West Wing.

The issue had consumed the White House's top echelon over the preceding days, as Buzhardt had been cataloging the tapes to hand over to the court—listening hours on end, chain-smoking unfiltered Camels and trying to decipher what was being said on the scratchy recordings piped through what his colleagues called his Mickey Mouse earphones. He had stumbled upon the gap on November 14 and quickly realized it was far more than just the accidental five-minute erasure Rose Mary Woods had supposedly reported to the president in October.*

Now Buzhardt was direct with Jaworski. "I see no way that this could have been done accidentally," he said, before firmly pointing the finger at Rose Mary Woods.† The lawyer relayed that they'd spoken with her, a conversation in which she maintained she had no explanation for the erased tape. They planned to tell her to get her own criminal defense attorney.

"Well, I guess we better go see the judge," Jaworski sighed. Buzhardt recoiled. He had hoped to wait until after Thanksgiving. Jaworski wouldn't have it; he didn't want to be accused by anyone, friend or foe, of being party to another stage of a White House cover-up.

That afternoon, Buzhardt, Garment, and Jaworski arrived in Sirica's chambers. As soon as the trio entered, Sirica noted that Buzhardt, who rarely looked well, now looked pale as a ghost. The judge was horrified by their admission too—Buzhardt referred to it oddly as an "obliteration of the intelligence"—and he only got angrier as the president's counsel explained that the missing portion of the tape came about three minutes into Nixon and Haldeman's conversation. Buzhardt explained that they had located Haldeman's handwritten notes about the meeting and confirmed that the erased portion—eighteen minutes, fifteen seconds long—dealt with Watergate. The tape picked back up as Haldeman and Nixon were speaking about an unrelated topic. The erasure seemed almost surely purposeful. "[Sirica] was almost impassive," Jaworski recalled.

---

* No one had been happy to hear the news; Haig exploded to Buzhardt, "Dammit Fred, this is a pretty late date to be telling me something like that," and Nixon, in turn, exploded at Haig when told, saying, "What the hell do you expect me to do about it?"

† Buzhardt would long maintain Woods as his prime suspect, in part, he said much later, because Nixon was such a transparent liar he didn't imagine the president could have done it without somehow telegraphing that in conversation—or confessing outright.

"With his shock of black hair and strong brown features, he looked on that afternoon like an Apache chieftain."

Finally, the judge spoke. "This calls for another hearing." He wanted the problem and the explanation on the record and in public as quickly as possible. Buzhardt protested, saying he needed time to organize the White House's response, and Sirica granted him an hour, though he thought even that was generous.

Sirica ordered the tapes delivered to him by Monday and set a schedule for additional hearings to understand how exactly a critical piece of evidence, supposedly under tight guard in one of the most tightly guarded compounds in the world, had been erased.

Speaking to reporters after, Richard Ben-Veniste was quick to answer what subsequent hearings might uncover. "Obstruction of justice," he said.

So much for Operation Candor.

Chapter 45

The Rose Mary Stretch

C oming on the eve of a long national holiday, the timing of the revelations of the eighteen-minute gap couldn't have been worse. Across
the country, members of Congress flowed home to their districts only to
receive an earful from their constituents about the president's behavior
and ongoing obfuscations. The Monday after Thanksgiving, there was a
long line of Democratic congressmen waiting to share those frustrations
with Tip O'Neill and pressure him to move forward on impeachment.
"When are we going to get moving?" Ohio representative Jim Stanton
asked. "My constituents aren't just disgusted with Nixon, they're starting to get on me, too. They don't think we're doing anything about it."

O'Neill's patience was wearing thin, as was his remaining caution. The
House majority leader knew that the impeachment question wasn't about
the law anymore; it was political. He pushed judiciary chair Rodino to
move faster in launching a real impeachment inquiry. Exasperated with
Rodino's foot-dragging, O'Neill delivered an order: *Pick a main lawyer
for impeachment before Christmas.*

That same Monday, seven reels of tape—all covering the conversations of June 20, 1972—arrived at the D.C. courthouse from the White
House. To protect them, Judge Sirica had contacted the National Security
Agency, who installed a special secure safe in his chambers; he and his
clerk memorized the combination—his wife's birthday, December 27,
1923, reversed as 23-27-12—and told no one else. U.S. marshals took

up a twenty-four-hour guard outside, and soon a security camera watched over the door as well.

The judge also immediately convened a hearing to get to the bottom of the eighteen-minute gap. It would be the starring moment for Jill Volner, the only female prosecutor on the Watergate task force. In an era with few high-profile female lawyers and when federal rules actually then barred women from wearing pants to court, the young, fashionable Volner captivated the courtroom and nation beyond; nearly every mention of her would contain a description like "the miniskirted lawyer," a phrase like "blonde bombshell," or a reference to her "peaches-and-cream complexion." (Her boss, Jaworski, described her in his memoir as "an attractive, perceptive woman of thirty.") A photo of her wearing a flouncy fur coat as she walked into the courthouse became one of the scandal's most famous photos. She was a tough interrogator.*

Over three days of questioning, Rose Mary Woods and Volner sparred back and forth as Nixon's longtime secretary sought to explain the erasure without risking any damage to her boss.

Woods had been the president's confidante, closest associate, and ultimate gatekeeper throughout his entire public life. Though her role was labeled as "secretary," Woods was far more than that—at the White House, she'd actually had three secretaries of her own—and she'd long been the president's political memory, remembering friendships and holding grudges as long as necessary. Never married and roughly the age of Richard and Pat, she was known as "Aunt Rose" to the two Nixon daughters, and referred to by outsiders as the "Fifth Nixon." She even traded clothes with the first lady, since both wore a size 10. While she'd mostly be remembered as a punchline in the Watergate story, she had commanded widespread respect before the scandal. In 1962, the *Los Angeles Times* had named her "Woman of the Year," and early in Nixon's presidency, *Ladies' Home Journal* had named her one of the nation's "75 most

---

* Volner, who after her divorce and remarriage would go by Jill Wine-Banks, became the first female general counsel of the Army and first female head of the American Bar Association, and would be a frequent television commentator during the Trump years.

important women," alongside Joan Baez, Coretta Scott King, and even Katharine Graham herself.

The hostility between Woods and Volner seemed almost palpable in the courtroom—"Volner got her story from her with the calm tenacity of a plowman striving for a straight furrow," Jaworski recalled—a tension that had likely carried over from the last time Volner had questioned her about the missing tapes, asking what had been done to protect their integrity. ("I used my head—it is the only one I had to use," Woods had shot back.)

Now, just three weeks later, Woods was telling an entirely different story—in this version, she maintained that she'd carelessly and distractedly damaged the key conversation by accident. Sirica was galled realizing that she'd sat in his courtroom weeks earlier and said nothing, despite knowing that one of the tapes was damaged in her transcription efforts.

After being advised on the record by Volner of her Fifth Amendment right to avoid self-incrimination, Woods recounted her experience attempting to transcribe the tapes at the end of September and beginning of October at Camp David, the White House, and Key Biscayne. While working on the unfamiliar Uher 5000 recorder, she explained, she must've accidentally pressed the record button while reaching to answer a nearby phone and then kept her foot on the pedal during the telephone call; she'd immediately realized her mistake, informed the president, and then been assured that the mistaken erasure wasn't part of the subpoenaed tapes. It was only in November, the White House said, that it realized the affected tape was part of the batch demanded by Archibald Cox.

To test the theory, Volner gave Woods a similar tape recorder and asked her to demonstrate her stretch as she reached for the telephone—as soon as she did, her foot came off the pedal. (A photo later released by the White House of Woods, at her desk, awkwardly re-creating her stretch to answer the phone while keeping her foot on the pedal was almost laughable in her contortions; it ran on the cover of *Newsweek* with the headline "Rose Mary's Boo Boo.")

Even if Woods's story was believable, it still only accounted for five or six minutes of the eighteen-minute gap, and over the course of the three days, she never tried to offer an explanation for the full loss. Moreover, the timelines she'd listed didn't add up. Woods said she'd spent more than two hours transcribing the tape on October 1, but the Uher 5000 machine was only delivered to her sometime after 1:15 p.m., and she said she reported the problem to Nixon at 2:08 p.m., a time stamp backed up by White House records.

Later, on the witness stand, Al Haig, who had made it through most of his testimony with crisp, no-nonsense answers, stumbled when asked how the other thirteen minutes of the tape were erased. "Perhaps some sinister force had come in and applied the other energy source and taken care of the information on that tape," Haig posited.

Sirica all but guffawed. "Has anyone ever suggested who that sinister force might be?" the judge asked.

Haig, trying to catch himself, said that only Woods and Bull had access to the tapes, but outside the courtroom, he brushed aside the thirteen-minute discrepancy as nothing more than the normal confusion of the fair sex: "I've known women that think they've talked for five minutes and have talked an hour."

Volner's own theory, ultimately, was that Woods and Nixon did it together; she reasoned that Nixon was almost certainly too technically inept to manage to erase the tape himself, and Woods was blindly committed to the president. The June 20 tape, she noted and theorized, was the first one listed in the subpoena, so it likely would have been the first Nixon himself listened to. Horrified by what he realized it documented, he'd then attempted to erase the most damaging bit—but then moved onto the second tape and the third and realized, collectively, that others were just as problematic. As she suggested in a later memoir, "He realized that he couldn't keep erasing subpoenaed material, so he adopted the total stonewall approach. The only solution he saw was to prevent the tapes from ever becoming public."

Once the FBI and prosecutors had exhausted every investigative avenue they could consider in who might have erased the tape, Jaworski met with the staff, reviewed the available evidence, and concluded, "Three people could have erased the tape, but for a successful prosecution that's two too many." Everyone concurred. Besides, as their work continued, it was clear that the eighteen-minute erasure hardly removed the only incriminating material on the tapes. "[The erasure's] importance was more symbolic than substantive," Sirica later said. "There turned out to be plenty of evidence left."

On December 12, the first batch of seven reels arrived at the Special Prosecutor's Office—all that evidently existed of the nine originally requested conversations. A half-dozen investigators crammed in Ben-Veniste's office to begin listening to the critical March 21 conversation, the one in which John Dean had testified he'd confronted Nixon about the "cancer close to the presidency." It was the first time that anyone outside the White House, other than Sirica himself, had had the chance to cross-check the most explosive aspect of Dean's June testimony to the Ervin Committee.

Listening on a single Sony 800B tape recorder, they strained to hear the twists and turns of the conversation, playing it over and over to catch the nuances. "At first we kept playing short segments and rewinding and playing, looking for phrases like 'It would be wrong,' and the key testimony about raising a million dollars," one of the prosecutors later recalled. Then the prosecutors realized that Nixon was taking the obstruction conspiracy for granted. They listened all the way through. The listener recalled: "It sent a chill through you. You wondered what would happen next. It was as if this conversation was taking place at the time, perhaps in the next room, and you were eavesdropping. It enveloped you. We just stood there and stared at each other, incredulous."

They played the tape over and over; it was far more damaging to Nixon than the investigators had ever imagined. The most astounding realization was that Hunt's hush money hadn't yet been paid at the time of Dean's conversation with the president—until that moment, everyone had assumed Fred LaRue had delivered the $75,000 on March 19 or March 20, but they listened as Dean recounted the demand and Nixon all but directed it to be paid. The prosecutors had heard enough. They turned off the machine and sat in silence for a few moments, exhausted. "We knew that we had turned the corner on Watergate," Ben-Veniste recalled later.

It soon became clear to nearly everyone else in the office that something big was happening behind Ben-Veniste's closed door. The prosecutors summoned Hank Ruth and then, in turn, Jaworski, to listen for themselves. As he did, Jaworski's face reddened; he couldn't fathom the idea of the president, sitting in the Oval Office, suborning perjury from his own staff. Walking out of his office, Ben-Veniste muttered, "The guy got hit with his own bat."

One of the prosecutors wondered aloud, "I don't understand why they gave us this tape?"

"Can you imagine what was on the one they erased?" another replied.

Feldbaum, astounded, was even more direct: "We've got a case against the president."

*   *   *

The arrival of the tapes was hardly the only troubling development; Haig had recently allowed a member of the prosecution team supervised access at the White House to certain sets of files, to search for needed evidence, and the investigator, Chuck Breyer, had noticed immediately as he flipped through the papers that certain documents had been retyped to remove or rewrite certain paragraphs—there was no telling what documents might have been removed entirely. "I'm certain that everybody who had a chance to get at those files has done so and removed what they could," Jaworski explained at a meeting on December 13. The Special Prosecutor's Office was going to have to plan to compel testimony from the aides and assistants themselves to reconstruct what might have gone missing.

Jaworski's aggressiveness in those final weeks of 1973 indicated Nixon's supreme miscalculation; as annoyed as the president had been by Cox, the original special prosecutor had been cautious and deferential to the White House, trying to work in harmony with the president and the Justice Department. He was not a courtroom litigator, or a politician, and his background as a mediator and legal scholar had shown through in his approach to the job. Jaworski was the opposite. "For the greatest gut fight of his career, President Nixon made the mistake of choosing as an opponent a first-class gut-fighter," Ben-Veniste and Frampton wrote later.

As the year drew to a close, Jaworski wondered, since the White House legal team had listened to the tapes too and clearly knew at least—if not more—than he did about the president's potential crimes, at what point would Nixon's team tell the president he wouldn't survive the scandal ahead?

The special prosecutor made one last attempt to raise the issue with Haig directly. Just before Christmas, with the White House decorated festively for the holiday, the two men met privately in the Map Room, where FDR had once monitored World War II. It was December 21, the first day of winter, and Jaworski was headed home to Texas. The pressure on the White House was coming from all sides; that day, as part of the investigation into the president's abuse of executive power, Congress had disclosed that, in September 1972, John Dean had urged the IRS to investigate 575 of the president's enemies; on the economic front, the government had calculated that consumer prices had risen nearly 8.5 percent in the previous year, the highest peacetime increase ever. Americans could feel that pinch every day; across D.C. and the rest of the country, as gasoline shortages continued, some states were even asking citizens not to put up Christmas lights, as a way to meet the ongoing energy crisis. It was a rude and unwelcome comeuppance for a nation that had gorged itself for twenty years on cheap gas and cheap energy as the suburbs expanded.

Sitting in the Map Room, talking bluntly, the chief of staff and the special prosecutor bargained over tapes and documents, and Jaworski raised the March 21 tape. Haig dismissed it, saying the White House lawyers had said it didn't rise to a crime. "Al, I think you should get the finest criminal lawyer you can find and let him listen to the tape," Jaworski said. The president was in a bad position, he emphasized, and there was other evidence to back that up.

After, the men walked to the South Portico; a rare D.C. snowfall had blanketed the city, and Mrs. Nixon's staff had built a snowman on the lawn before them to greet the many officials tromping through the building for holiday receptions. Jaworski understood the immense stress the chief of staff faced. "It's important, Al—get that lawyer, the best you can find," Jaworski advised.

As he got into his car, Jaworski saw tears in Haig's eyes.

Chapter 46

"Do I Fight?"

Gerald Ford was confirmed as Nixon's new vice president in early December, having passed the FBI, IRS, press, and congressional inquiries with flying colors. Investigators had gone over every government contract totaling more than $50,000 directed to his district since his first election and found none that indicated any untoward favor or personal gain.* The FBI's background report had taken 1,700 single-spaced pages to conclude what everyone had suspected from the beginning: He was even-tempered, honest, and modest in personality, ambition, and lifestyle. He didn't even carry a mortgage.

As a man who had dedicated so much of his life to the swirls and traditions of Capitol Hill, the approval of both the House and Senate meant a great deal to him; he was the first American in history to be chosen for the nation's second-highest office in such a bipartisan, bicameral manner, and his swearing-in brought Washington a collective sigh of relief. The nation had a fully functioning, uncompromised vice president for the first time in months; whatever came next would not

---

* After auditing seven years of taxes and double-checking every check and expense Ford had paid during that period, the IRS had found only one quibble, disallowing two suits he'd deducted as a business expense during the '72 Republican convention, an issue he'd settled with a payment of $435.77.

be seen as a political coup to install Democratic speaker Carl Albert as leader of the free world.*

Nixon's troubles surely didn't let up as Ford arrived. His tax scandal continued to unfurl throughout December, and in response, the president released what he claimed was a fulsome accounting of his personal finances. He also argued that some of the papers at the National Archives still belonged to him—which, if true, would undermine his massive earlier tax deductions. Weicker's office turned over to the IRS midmonth his calculation that Nixon owed $235,000 in back taxes. The investigation grew, and forensic examiners from California secretary of state Jerry Brown's office determined that the National Archives deed had indeed been illegally backdated, matching the letter to a typewriter at Kalmbach's firm that had only been purchased after the expiration of the tax loophole.

It was also revealed, shockingly, that Nixon had paid no local or state taxes in either D.C. or California. "In terms of public opinion, the extravagant, improper tax deduction was the straw that broke Nixon's back," Weicker recalled later. "For a president to pay no more in taxes than an indigent was more than people could bear." Many parts of Watergate were complex, opaque, confusing, and contradictory. But a $700 tax bill? That was something Americans could understand.

In mid-December, Barry Goldwater—long one of Nixon's strongest backers—worried aloud to the *Christian Science Monitor* about how the president's scandals compounded and reinforced the doubt that Nixon could be trusted. "I don't think it's Watergate, frankly, as much as it's just a question in people's mind of just how honest is this man," the Arizona senator said. "I hate to think of the old adage 'Would you buy a used car from Dick Nixon?' but, that's what people are asking around the country."

---

* The new role changed Ford's life minimally in some ways: He continued to live in his regular home in Virginia, since Congress had only recently designated for the first time an official vice presidential residence and it was still under renovation. Instead, the Secret Service expanded his driveway in Alexandria, to accommodate the vice presidential limo, and bricked up and soundproofed his garage to serve as their new command post, and the White House Communications Agency electrified his attic to accommodate the new telephone systems it had to install.

*   *   *

As the headlines churned with troubling questions about Nixon, Pete Rodino's Judiciary Committee followed through on O'Neill's order to select a chief counsel by Christmas. The pool of lawyers who met the intellectual test necessary for such an intense, high-profile job, as well as possessed the nonpartisan respect and stature required, was minimal. Rodino considered a handful of former prosecutors, as well as the name partner of the prominent law firm Jenner & Block, Albert Jenner, Jr., who had served on the Warren Commission, investigating the Kennedy assassination. One name, though, continued to be mentioned, "a guy who worked at Justice in the sixties." Rodino and his team struggled to track down a résumé or bio for this supposed legal unicorn, but finally found him on November 20, at the Bedford-Stuyvesant Restoration Corporation.

John Doar was in his office when he received a call from the dean of Yale Law School. Now fifty-two years old, Doar had spent most of the prior decade as a Justice Department lawyer. He'd ended up on the literal front lines of the Civil Rights Movement—prosecuting Klan killers, protecting the Freedom Riders, the march at Selma, and James Meredith as he enrolled at Ole Miss—serving day after day as the physical manifestation of the immense but often tenuous power of the federal government on the ground across the segregated South. In '67, he had left for private practice, joining the nation's first community development corporation in New York City.

Now Abraham Goldsmith, the Yale dean, had a simple query: "Would you be interested in being the special counsel to the chairman of the House Judiciary Committee?"

"Yes, I would," Doar said.

"Well, that's all I have to ask you," the Yale dean replied. The men hung up.

When Rodino and Doar met a few nights later, the chairman's first question was simple: "Have you made up your mind yet on whether there should be an impeachment?" Doar said he hadn't. By the end of the chat, Rodino sensed Doar was the right man—respected and respectful, hardened and thoughtful. They spoke again and again over the weeks ahead, as Rodino's main committee counsel Jerry Zeifman built the initial team that would assist Doar if he accepted. One of the first was Wisconsin lawyer–turned-farmer Richard Cates, who had earned a solid reputation as a county prosecutor and trial attorney. Cates spent days reviewing the available evidence and parsing the draft impeachment resolutions already introduced in the House. Before long, he had pieced together what he thought was a convincing theory that the president had obstructed justice. "My god—if this wasn't the president of the United States and I couldn't secure a conviction, they could take my license," he had told Zeifman. "It is horrendously solid." (It would take the rest of the nation another nine months to prove him right.)

As he reviewed the evidence from the summer Senate hearings, Cates also grew suspicious of the $75,000 payout to Howard Hunt; after all, Liddy had been the White House tie to the Watergate burglary. *So why was the money going to Hunt?* The only conclusion Cates could see seemed clear: Hunt had something on the White House aside from Watergate. Cates had gotten so far along that Rodino invited him and Zeifman to dinner at the Monocle Restaurant, just off Capitol Hill, at the end of November and cautioned him to slow down—they needed to wait for a special counsel, then for the evidence to marinate with investigators and committee members. This wasn't about convincing 12 jurors in a Wisconsin courtroom; this was about convincing the equivalent of 435 grand jurors and then 100 actual jurors to gamble their careers, party, and branch of government on a rare and extreme constitutional remedy unused for a century. The potential jury was hardly a collection of pure, angelic innocents when it came to matters of questionable campaign contributions, deals with major supporters, or dirty elections. The investigation could move only at the pace of politics, the ever-cautious Rodino explained. What was nominally a process about law and order and guilt versus innocence truly boiled down to the simple, self-interested question that drove almost every decision by a congressman or senator: *Was it good for me politically?*

By mid-December, Rodino had settled on Doar, though by then everyone had come to the shared assumption he was the choice—including Doar, who found out that the committee's hotel reservation for him at the Carroll Arms was open-ended. His two main staff counterparts were Jerome Zeifman, the counsel for the full Judiciary Committee, and Albert Jenner, who would serve as the minority counsel for the inquiry committee. Zeifman and Doar quickly became antagonists, wrestling each other for control of the committee's overall strategy, but Doar found a close partner in the Republican Jenner. At sixty-six, Jenner had served as the senior counsel to the Warren Commission's investigation into the Kennedy assassination, dressed religiously in a rotating number of some three hundred bow ties, and became convinced quickly that Nixon's behavior warranted removal. He and Doar would almost end up working together as co-leaders of the inquiry.*

The staffing efforts in the final weeks of 1973 marked the early formation of what would end up being a team of more than one hundred. The Judiciary Committee commandeered the second floor of what was then known as the Congressional Hotel, an eight-floor, postwar hotel across from the Cannon House Office Building that for twenty years had served as the in-town home for numerous members of Congress. The House had recently taken it over fully and converted it into House Annex #1, a much-needed answer to the crush of additional Hill staff. As they began their work, the space and amenities still very much retained the look and feel of a converted hotel; staffers grew used to storing piles of papers in the abundant bathtubs.

The initial step for Doar, whose first day was December 20, was ensuring that no one without approved access had entry to the floor—the windows were barred, the doors reinforced by steel and secured with special locks, motion detectors installed, and guards posted throughout.

On December 21, an inquiry staffer named Larry Kieves typed up a single, seven-ply index card, recording and summarizing a White House press release about Nixon's personal finances. At the bottom, he typed "**PF-1-IG," short for "personal finances, number one, inquiry general file." Then he separated the cards—yellow on top, then pink, then four green, and finally a blue one, all interspersed with carbons—and began filing them away in the "library," the large, long room that would become the center of the inquiry's workspace, gradually filling with filing cabinets and safes.

---

* Jenner's "defection" understandably bothered Nixon's defense lawyer, James St. Clair, who grumbled, "We will have to become counsel to the minority, in effect. Someone has to defend the cause and obviously he isn't."

The so-called "chron cards" were a labor-intensive system that Doar, wary of the newfangled computers then expanding into the workplace, had developed and sworn by during his civil rights work; he maintained that the tactile cards as they were arranged and rearranged could tell stories invisible to the human eye. "I don't want anything done by machine that can be done by a human being," he had told his team, and indeed in the months ahead the committee would end up retaining nearly thirty typists just to generate cards, briefs, and letters.* The attorneys and investigators kept the pink cards for themselves, then filed the yellow cards into a shared chronological file, the green ones into person files, and the blue copies by subject matter. Together, you could cross-reference any nugget of information you needed. Ultimately, the inquiry would amass more than five hundred thousand cross-referenced index cards; by March, engineers had been called to reinforce the library floor.

Days after Kieves created that first card, another equally momentous single piece of paper arrived in Rodino's office, typed out on official stationery. It was from the House speaker, confirming that pursuant to the passage of H. Res. 702, $1 million had been deposited into the clerk of the House's account to be allocated to the impeachment inquiry. The House investigation was officially underway.

* * *

As Richard Nixon's loneliness deepened toward the end of the year, his staff were restless and eyeing the exits, having finally had the chance to grasp the peril that lay within the magnetic reels. Pat Buchanan had listened; Haig had read. Haig had invited Republican senator Hugh Scott to read some transcripts too, mostly to encourage the minority leader to cease talking publicly encouraging their release. Even loyalists like Bryce Harlow and Ray Price were trying to leave the administration, worn down by scandal. A final, humbling insult from 1973 came in the form of *TIME* magazine declaring Judge John Sirica "Man of the Year," on the cover of an issue that dramatically outsold the one celebrating Nixon only a year before.

---

* Doar liked to recruit the typists from Catholic high schools; he felt that the nuns inculcated a sense of mission and purpose that jibed with his quest for justice and democracy.

The president spent the weekend before Christmas at Camp David, having driven to the rustic Maryland retreat rather than helicoptering, in order to save gas. Outside of Watergate, the oil embargo following the war in the Middle East had tipped the nation over into an energy crisis—the stock market wobbled and prices were rising. A year earlier, just after his landslide victory, he'd written in his diary, "1973 will be a better year," but now the end of the year felt more ominous; on December 23, at the presidential retreat, he scrawled across the top of a page: "Last Christmas here?"

After Christmas, frantic to show he understood the hardship, Nixon, his family, and thirteen Secret Service agents flew to California unannounced aboard a commercial United Airlines DC-10, the first and only time a president flew on a commercial airliner, known then by the callsign Executive One. The presidential Irish setter, King Timahoe, came too, for a pet fee of $24.

Once Nixon was sequestered in the Western White House, entire days would pass with no notations on his official schedule. Haig had remained concerned about the president's drinking and sleeping; the former seeming to start earlier and the latter lasting longer into the morning. On Saturday the 29th Nixon spoke on the phone just three times, for a total of twenty-one minutes; another day during the trip the sum total of his official duties was a single, six-minute phone conversation with Henry Kissinger.

Instead, his final meetings of the year were all about his troubles. Overlooking a gray Pacific, Nixon sat with his friend Bebe Rebozo, who had been hounded through the year over the $100,000 Hughes donation. Rebozo had promised earlier that year that he'd returned the money untouched—his lawyers said the serial numbers of the original donation had matched the bills returned to Hughes—but investigators were still wondering whether it had actually been used to finance illegal activity. The Ervin Committee had grilled Rebozo at least four times, and the IRS spent fourteen weeks auditing him.* ("As we in the family watched

---

* It wasn't until January 1975 that the special prosecutor finally cleared Rebozo, after a $2 million government investigation that included more than two hundred subpoenas and the questioning of more than 120 people, 28 of them before the grand jury; no charges were ever brought against him or Abplanalp.

Bebe endure the harassment, the attack on him was like attacking one of us," Julie wrote later.) Despite the difficulties, Rebozo pushed Nixon to stay and fight.

On New Year's Eve, the president sat alone after midnight, scribbling his woes on a yellow legal pad. "The basic question is: Do I fight it all out or do I now begin the long process to prepare for a change, meaning, in effect, resignation." The topic had begun to come up, privately, in the president's conversations with aides, but he wouldn't seriously entertain it yet. "The answer—fight," Nixon concluded that night, echoing their advice in the first minutes of 1974.

The idea seemed to enliven him, his pen scratched out line after line: "Fight because if I am forced to resign, the press will become too much of a dominant force in the nation, not only in this administration but for years to come. Fight because resignation would set a precedent and result in a permanent and very destructive change in our whole constitutional system. Fight because resignation could lead to a collapse of our foreign policy initiatives."

To lead that fight forward, the president knew he needed help. At his boss's instruction, Al Haig had recruited James St. Clair, one of the most experienced and respected trial lawyers in the country. It was, in some respects, St. Clair's third pass at the Watergate scandal; Archibald Cox had tried, unsuccessfully, as special prosecutor to recruit him to be his deputy, and more recently he'd been retained briefly by Charles Colson. Now he signed up to take on all three of the president's own legal fronts: the Senate Ervin Committee, the House Judiciary impeachment inquiry, and the special prosecutor's investigation. In his pitch, Haig avoided mention of the trouble buried in the transcripts, or the fact that Garment and Buzhardt—St. Clair's purported predecessors in the role—were removing themselves in part because they considered the political wounds already fatal and resignation the only foreseeable outcome.

St. Clair had been on vacation with his wife when the chief of staff called, and he met with the White House team in San Clemente just after New Year's. He started in the Executive Office Building on January 4, his new world encompassing a suite in that building and a room at the luxurious Fairfax Hotel. He assembled his own team of seven lawyers;

Garment would be eased off the case, and Buzhardt's role would focus solely on the custody of tapes and records.

There would be no further cooperation, no further candor. Nixon sat down on January 5, at 5 a.m., and added to his New Year's note. "Above all else: Dignity, command, head high, no fear, building a new spirt, drive, act like a President, act like a winner. Opponents are destroyers, haters. Time to use the full power of the President to fight overwhelming forces arrayed against us."

PART V

Inferno

1974

Chapter 47

Flutter and Wow

The tapes were just half-a-millimeter wide, a thin strip of magnetic coating atop plastic film. To avoid having to frequently change the reels on the Secret Service's Sony 800B recorders, locked away in the White House basement, technicians had set the recording speed to an unusually slow 15/16th inches per second. That speed compromised sound quality, muddling and muffling the sounds of history, a trade-off that would forever haunt investigators and scholars.

As the White House, John Doar, and Judge Sirica turned their attention to the tapes, they convened an illustrious group of outside experts—half-a-dozen men with years of industry experience in magnetic tape—to analyze whether the recordings had been tampered with. They met with the panel late one Sunday evening over the winter to discuss their process, gathering at a conference room in a corner of the Executive Office Building so obscure they required guides to direct them. The conversation turned technical fairly quickly, which frustrated and bored the lawyers. "The discussion became more and more arcane—analysis of flutter and wow, spectrographic examination, the capacity for analyzing high- and low-frequency hum," prosecutor Richard Ben-Veniste recalled later. "The scientists became increasingly animated and, absorbed in their own intellectual world, discontinued the simultaneous translation they had been providing for the lawyers."

As the discussion turned to the finer points of what the scientists referred to as "hum analysis," both Ben-Veniste and Len Garment, who had remained on the case until James St. Clair could get up to speed, excused themselves from the conference room. Outside in the hallway, they both broke out laughing, their emotions cresting after the month's overwhelming tension and absurdity. "The American presidency hung in the balance, and we bleary-eyed attorneys were locked away in a chambering of the castle of Dr. Frankenstein, trying to monitor the excited scientists' audio-gibberish," Garment recalled.

A few moments later, prosecutor Carl Feldbaum and the White House's Douglas Parker joined them in the stairwell, their own laughter spreading and building until tears ran down their faces. Doubled-over, Garment jokingly suggested to the prosecutors that rather than spend the weeks ahead learning the finer points of audio analysis, they settle the case right then: Suppose he could deliver a guilty plea from Ron Ziegler and a nolo contendere from Kissinger?

Absolutely not—they wouldn't settle for less than a future draft pick for vice president, Ben-Veniste and Feldbaum retorted.

Finally, calmed down, everyone returned inside to the industry minutiae; the scientists, still debating, hadn't seemed to notice their absence. "It was like that with Watergate: Some days were more Buster Keaton than Al Capone," Garment recalled.

In the following weeks, different reels of tape traveled the country, moving from one expert laboratory to another, each under guard of a team of U.S. marshals and ferried in special antimagnetic containers to ensure no further damage. A member of the special prosecutor's team, Jim Boczar, and a rotating representative of the White House lawyers also accompanied the tapes and were present for all tests. Most of the testing happened during long overnight shifts, when the needed computers were available for extended sessions, giving rise to Boczar's team nickname: Dracula.

Analyzing the tapes for tampering, though, was just the first step; the next was deciphering what was on them. One member of the outside expert panel, Mark Weiss, the vice president of acoustics research at the Federal Scientific Corporation, had invented a sophisticated machine that worked to remove distortion and enhance quality, known as a "coherent spectrum shaper"—at the time the world's most cutting-edge sound

analysis tool. The only one belonged to the CIA, and the Special Prosecution Force was stunned when Sirica convinced the agency to lend it
out. "Such was the power of the federal judge that the CIA delivered it to
the courthouse with no more fanfare than if it had been a borrowed cup
of sugar," Ben-Veniste and Frampton recalled. The oversized machine—
which took twelve hours just to warm up—was reconstructed in the jury
room, and there Weiss and his assistant carefully tuned it, adjusting
circuits and tubes. When he came in to review the setup, Sirica treated
it as if he were approaching the Dead Sea Scrolls. As the machine got
to work, enhancing and copying the tapes, Boczar and a White House
counterpart settled in for another overnight shift. When the work was
done, the CIA covertly ushered the contraption out of the building under
a gray tarp to avoid prying eyes.

Given the abysmal quality of the underlying tapes, simply hearing
them was not enough; like the White House staff before them, investigators would have to transcribe each recording, a fraught, challenging,
and intense process that turned into countless hours of work—archivists
would later estimate it took about one hundred hours to transcribe just
a single hour of conversation.

Listening to the tapes jarred everyone. The president's casual and
repeated use of profanity stunned Sirica and his clerk. "I came up the hard
way, and the language was far from unfamiliar to me. But the shock, for
me at least, was the contrast between the coarse, private Nixon speech and
the utterly correct public speech I had heard so often," the judge recalled
in his memoir. More shocking, however, was the impression that became
clear as they listened to more and more reels: Nixon had never intended
to clean up Watergate. They listened in vain for outrage or any remorse at
his aides' actions. "I found the whole thing disgusting," Sirica concluded.
"From that moment on, there was no longer any doubt in my mind that
there had been a conspiracy to obstruct justice inside the White House."

Sirica couldn't help but wonder how Jaworski would respond—and
even more so, how the grand jury would respond when they began to
hear the tapes too.

On January 15, 1974, the expert panel released their report, a damning and unanimous conclusion that the eighteen-minute gap on the June
20 tape had been caused by an erasure—or, more accurately, at least five

distinct segments of erasure. "The amount of information the experts were able to glean from the June 20 tape was nothing short of astonishing," Ben-Veniste recalled. Together, they had seemingly excavated every nugget, scrape, or tidbit of information imprinted on the magnetic tape—everything, that is, except what had actually been said during the gap. Explaining their work to Sirica's court, acoustic expert Richard Bolt said that the panel had put the equivalent of three hundred workdays into examining the tapes in just two months, moving between various labs and settings in Manhattan, Cambridge, Salt Lake City, New Haven, Murray Hill, New Jersey, and Los Gatos, California. The expert examination had been supplemented by an FBI investigation led by agent Angelo Lano, who had gone to Camp David to study the typewriters there and compare them to the IBM Model D Executive used at the White House by Rose Mary Woods. That intel helped confirm precisely how far she'd gotten in her transcription efforts at the presidential retreat. ("It turned out that Rose had told the truth about one thing," Volner noted later.) Efforts to polygraph three likely erasure suspects—Woods, Haig, and personal aide Stephen Bull—went nowhere.

The panel concluded that the White House's Uher 5000 machine was the one likely used in the erasures. The acoustic experts had also studied the different "signatures" from the foot pedal and the hand keyboard imprinted on the magnetic tape and were able to determine that the erasures came via the hand keys, not the foot pedal that Woods had testified she'd used. The electromagnetic heads of the Uher 5000 were spaced exactly 28.6 millimeters apart, allowing the experts to match up the corresponding marks on the tape. That alone was significant because October 1, the day Rose Mary Woods was working to transcribe the tapes at the White House, had been the first time any tape had been played on a Uher machine. All previous playbacks, for Nixon and Haldeman, had occurred on Sony machines.

To see the exact moments of erasures, the experts had coated the tapes in magnetic fluid, allowing them to study the minute markings and identify a "quartet signature" of four tiny lines, each less than a millimeter high, that the Uher 5000 tape recorder made each time the erasing function stopped. Across the eighteen minutes of wiped tape, they found signatures of five "stops" and nine "starts," indicating that four of the erasure attempts were, in turn, erased by later attempts to wipe the tape. While the experts stopped short of saying that the erasures were "deliberate," since they couldn't discern the motives of the person doing the erasing, the expert panel told Sirica, "It would have to be an accident that was repeated at least five separate times."

The conclusion was clear: Either Rose Mary Woods was lying—or someone else had tampered with the tapes without her knowledge or any record in White House files. There was no doubt that Woods's story of an accidental erasure was simply wrong.

The president's own remaining allies immediately realized the severity of the report's implications and consequences; Representative John Anderson, the head of the House Republican Conference, believed Watergate was in its final stages, saying, "This is the most serious single bit of evidence to date. The theory that there has been a conscious effort to conceal evidence is no longer a theory." Conservative columnist George F. Will compared the Nixon team's mental gymnastics to preserve his innocence to the White Queen in *Alice in Wonderland*, who was capable of believing "six impossible things before breakfast."

In response to the report, Sirica referred the matter to the FBI for further investigation and possible criminal prosecution. In its next issue, *TIME* ticked off the possible charges: "obstruction of justice, suppression of evidence, contempt of court for failing to produce evidence, and perjury," but none would come to fruition. Volner, for her part, couldn't bring herself to recommend perjury charges against Woods, despite the clear and convincing evidence that she'd lied in at least some—if not much—of her testimony. "The White House treated her so shabbily," Volner recalled. "It was hard not to see her as a victim whose chief crime had been her loyalty to Nixon."

*　　*　　*

The deeper the investigators got into the tapes and transcripts, the more they grew concerned; two other dictation tapes the president turned over, both aimed to mitigate the original missing conversation recordings, appeared to have possible deletions of their own, cutting off mid-sentence. One of the suspicious cutoffs came in Nixon's own dictation and summary of the March 21 conversation with John Dean; the tape fell silent for fifty-nine seconds just as the president recounted how he told Dean to "hunker down" and avoid any statement about the cover-up, since it would be "too dangerous as far . . ." The White House aides brushed the concerns aside, saying the cause of the gap was likely due to the uncoordinated Nixon stopping recording while still speaking.

"Other tapes contained audible blips that lasted a few seconds and that as a result obliterated key words," Doyle recalled. "Listening to them was like watching the Johnny Carson show during its raunchier moments. One understood what the speaker was saying, but the blips kept the incriminating words from being heard."*

On January 16, the morning after the expert panel brought their report forward, Leon Jaworski appeared before the grand jury and explained that they were about to be given a "new line" of evidence "more sensitive than any they had heard before." Until then, the prosecutors had not mentioned the existence of the tapes at all, and as Ben-Veniste and Frampton recalled, "We were eager to see their reactions: Whether twenty ordinary people well versed in the facts of the case but lacking a lawyer's perspective would find the tapes as startling and as damaging to the president as we found them."

To make sure the process remained as controlled as possible, Frampton and Carl Feldbaum spent hours wiring the jury room with twenty-three sets of earphones. As the jurors listened, they passed among themselves a large bag of potato chips. At first, the prosecutors wondered if anyone would hear the tapes over the crunching chips, but as the minutes passed, they got their answer. The facial expressions changed. The jurors were listening—and they were horrified.

*　　*　　*

On January 30, Richard Nixon arrived at the Capitol to deliver his State of the Union address, a night that he noted marked the twenty-seventh

---

* After the huge study of the June 20 tape, Sirica decided that the court couldn't endlessly fund additional studies of additional gaps and deletions, and thus the deliberateness of the subsequent gaps was never examined.

anniversary of the night he and another freshman congressman named John F. Kennedy had listened to their first address from Harry Truman.

For a year, the implicit question in the Watergate scandal had been whether the good of Richard Nixon outweighed—or was at least worth— the bad, a delicate issue of balance that was evident to anyone listening to that evening's speech. Outside of Watergate and its associated investiga- tion, the president had managed to draw Vietnam to a close, reopen China, bring détente with the Soviet Union, and remake America's monetary policy—surely all accomplishments that counted against a shambolic, third-rate burglary carried out by some overeager aides? And yet was it really "just" a question of CREEP, some loose money, and—perhaps at its worst—a few well-meaning aides like Ehrlichman and Haldeman?

The current state of geopolitics and the economy didn't help bolster the situation. The Arab embargo had led to the price of oil quadrupling from $2.90 a barrel to $11.65 a barrel between October and January, and countries across the West were feeling the pinch. In Paris, the French began to turn off the lights of the Eiffel Tower overnight. Nixon had called for the heating in federal buildings to be turned down to between sixty-five and sixty-eight degrees and asked for a lower, more efficient fifty-mile-per-hour national speed limit. In the U.S., long lines at gas stations became a regular sight; rationing became common; that winter, half of the respondents to a government economic survey reported being unable to buy all the gasoline they needed. Inflation grew at an uncom- fortable speed. The government calculated that prices were rising at a 14 percent annual clip, a psychologically devastating rate for families and workers. Industry was hard hit; food prices soared. As households felt pain, Nixon's consumer affairs advisor Virginia Knauer advised people to eat more "liver, kidney, brains, and heart," to minimize the doubling of meat prices.

Now, as Nixon spoke to both legislative houses and the American pub- lic, he forcefully and eloquently laid out an ambitious ten-point agenda for the country—signaling both his commitment to confronting hard challenges ahead and, more subtly, the reason why his presidency contin- ued to be good for the nation. He noted his administration's "overriding aim to establish a new structure of peace in the world that can free future generations of the scourge of war," and the need to "break the back of the energy crisis," specifically mentioning efforts to boost transportation spending and increase cash assistance to struggling Americans.

In the last moments of the speech, he finally turned to Watergate, pleading with the nation that the country's progress required the cessation of the ongoing inquiries. "I believe the time has come to bring that investigation and the other investigations of this matter to an end. One year of Watergate is enough," he said. "I have no intention whatever of ever walking away from the job that the people elected me to do for the people of the United States."

The president's words, defense, and promises met a mixed reaction in the Capitol. "One minute of Watergate was too much," Ervin responded, explaining to reporters that it was the president's ongoing obfuscations and stalling that were dragging out the investigation. Others, like Tip O'Neill, sat in frustration. That week, in the wake of the erasure revelations, he had said he'd sponsor legislation offering immunity from prosecution if Nixon resigned, but to no avail. As fiercely partisan as he was, O'Neill knew his role as majority leader was to lead his caucus to get the maximum support from the American people. Reading the political landscape remained challenging; as low as Nixon's approval ratings were—just 27 percent in Gallup's poll—the country was equally split, 46–46, on whether he should resign.

Two days after the address, Jaworski and Haig met again. Whatever warmth or spirit of cooperation had existed between them in the special prosecutor's first two months had evaporated thanks to James St. Clair's new strategy of fighting every step of the way. The White House now protested or delayed even routine exchanges, complaining about FBI interviews of staffers and once even forcing Jaworski to be escorted by security on White House grounds. Haig explained that the White House strategically couldn't cooperate with the special prosecutor without giving oxygen to the burgeoning House impeachment inquiry too, but Jaworski said he was sick of the new blockages. "Every time you get a little bit ahead of the game, you make some decision that plunges you behind again," Jaworski cautioned. "I'm going to have to go to the Hill and tell them about this, and then I'm going to litigate the piss out of you."

It was a serious but necessary threat. The pressure on Jaworski throughout the winter had been crushing; isolated and alone, he felt at odds with the White House, his own staff, and even the Watergate grand jurors. The deeper he got into the case, the worse his view of this specific president and politics became, particularly after hearing a non–Watergate related tape containing a "disgusting display of uncontrolled backbiting by the President and Colson regarding other White House aides of the highest rank." The whole experience had disillusioned him to Washington. He was living in a suite at the Jefferson Hotel on 16th Street NW, and the stakes of his work seemed omnipresent—nearly the first thing he saw in the morning walking to work and the last thing he saw in the evening returning from it was the White House down the street.

His Spartan office telegraphed a sense of temporariness and dislocation. He hadn't hung anything on the walls since taking over from Cox, and rumors circulated regularly through the capital that he would be removed imminently by the president—an unlikely event, due to the need for concurrence of congressional leaders, but hardly a helpful mental backdrop for decision-making. At one point, St. Clair met with him and assured the special prosecutor, "I want you to know that you are in no danger of being fired."

"That would be the biggest favor you could do me," Jaworski replied.

On February 12, the special prosecutor attended a small, off-the-record dinner at the *TIME* Washington bureau, with the magazine's leaders and top reporters, part of the get-to-know-you gatherings that James Doyle often organized for major news outlets. As the dinner unfolded, Jaworski asked, abstractly, "Suppose I heard a tape that makes it very clear that the President is guilty of criminal conduct? Suppose the President knows I've seen this incriminating material. What would the President do?"

"Resign!" Ed Magnuson, who had been feverishly writing the magazine's cover stories about the scandal for the past year, said. Everybody at the table laughed.

Except Jaworski.

It was the first clue the magazine's staff had of the trouble ahead. "I believe it was always his intention to get Nixon to resign rather than go through the impeachment procedure," correspondent John Stacks later reflected. "I felt he was trying to send a message to the press and squeeze Nixon out of office."

*   *   *

As winter and investigations pressed on, figuring out where to draw the line between "inescapable inferences" and grounds for criminal charges or impeachment consumed the president's defense team, Jaworski's prosecutors, and the House Judiciary Committee staff. "The information in 1973 had moved faster than the processes, the information flow had been so immense that the expectancy it created for immediate action was tremendous," observed David Halberstam. "Now the legal and political processes were working, but they were working more slowly, in older rhythms." Throughout the process, each group found themselves drawing narrow distinctions and stymied by their own constraints.

In January and February, Jaworski had had the evidence and the capability to compel cooperation from the president, but not the mission to take him on. During the same period, Doar had the mission, but not the evidence or the capability. Even figuring how to define their own framework had been difficult; the Judiciary Committee had sharp debates over whether Nixon's lawyers would be allowed to participate, with Doar arguing that the House inquiry was similar to a grand jury, which excluded defense lawyers, even as committee Democrats felt that the unique circumstances of a presidential impeachment process meant they needed to make room for James St. Clair.

Two days after the *TIME* dinner, St. Clair and Doar met to debate the standards for an impeachment. The White House lawyer argued that the committee should narrowly interpret its mission as charging only identifiable felonies, while Doar and Jenner both argued that the president could face impeachment for serious misconduct or abuses of power that were not strictly criminal in nature. As Congress saw it, "Impeachment is a Constitutional remedy addressed to serious offenses against a system of government." The House Judiciary Committee believed that violations of the presidential duties under the Constitution, which required the officeholder to "preserve, protect, and defend the Constitution" and "take care that the laws be faithfully executed," could spark an impeachment. As a whole, Doar was focused on proving a pattern of behavior—he felt that removing a president should be focused on multiple incidents, not just a single crime, almost regardless of severity. "There had to be something of a persistent problem that went over time, that didn't show an error that was transitory, but something that went on," impeachment staffer Evan Davis recalled.

To find that pattern, if it existed, Rodino, Doar, and the House Judiciary Committee assembled a formidable team. In response to one memo on hiring, Doar scrawled across the top what mattered to him: "Are they careful? Do they pay meticulous attention to detail? Do they take nothing for granted? Do they organize their work? And are they neat? Are they stubborn?"

He underlined "stubborn."

In addition to the squads of typists, fourteen investigators, fourteen clerks, and other consultants and specialists, the committee recruited forty-three lawyers, some of whom would become the brightest of their generation, including one future secretary of state (Hillary Rodham), one future governor (William Weld), and one future CEO of the Boston Red Sox (Larry Lucchino).* Maureen Barden was just twenty-five, having finished a stint working on the Attica Commission investigating the riot and state police massacre that had unfolded in the prison there in '71. Rodham, just out of law school, had joined the team after Doar tried to hire her boyfriend; when Bill Clinton told Doar he was unavailable because he planned to return to Arkansas to run for governor, he suggested, "How about hiring my girlfriend?"

Doar also recruited David Robert "Bob" Owen, a former Justice Department colleague who at age thirty-one had prosecuted the first voting-rights case ever brought to trial by the U.S. government and had risked his life leading the indictments for the murder of three civil rights workers in Mississippi in 1964.

Altogether, the team was a "whirlpool of sparkling legal talent" that far "outmatched" Rodino himself, columnist Holmes Alexander noted. It

---

* There were at least five marriages that grew out of the inquiry staff, mostly pairings between the male attorneys and the female research staff.

was left unnoted that nearly all the members of the team were white men; just four were Black, and Rodham became a point of media fascination as one of just four women on the team. "How does it feel to be the Jill Wine Volner of the impeachment committee?" ABC's Sam Donaldson asked her at one point. They were collectively sworn to secrecy, liable to be fired immediately if they spoke to the press.

Doar also made clear he wanted tight lines around the investigation, and he purposefully didn't want to retread old ground, believing that if the House committee was seen to be repeating hearings or investigations already covered by others, it would poison the public perception of their work. He focused the inquiry staff on six distinct areas, careful to emphasize that just because the inquiry was investigating something didn't mean a crime had occurred: (1) "Domestic surveillance activities conducted by or at the direction of the White House"; (2) "allegations concerning intelligence activities conducted by or at the direction of the White House for the purposes of the presidential election of 1972," aka the campaign dirty tricks; (3) the Watergate burglary itself and the resulting cover-up; (4) the president's personal finances and expenses; (5) misuse of government agencies for political purposes and illegal campaign contributions; (6) a general catch-all category that included all other allegations, including the secret bombing of Cambodia. A seventh inquiry task force was in charge of sorting through the complex constitutional and legal questions stemming from prosecuting a case in Congress against the head of a co-equal branch of government.

Bob Owen found the first chink in the president's defenses relatively quickly; sitting at a table in the main library room, he had been arranging and rearranging the index cards pertaining to the day of the burglary itself and the day after, June 17 and 18, when something stuck out to him: "McCord," he said, wondering out loud. "McCord is fired from his job at the reelection committee—fine. But now where is Liddy on the 18th?" Confused, he brought the question to Maureen Barden.

"He is still listed as working for the committee," she replied.

"When did he leave the committee?"

"Not until the 28th," Barden explained. "He refused to talk to the FBI and they fired him."

"Not till the 28th? And only when they had to get rid of him?"

The two investigators reexamined the timeline; McCord had been fired right away, but the committee had kept on Liddy for more than a week, despite the knowledge that the whole operation had been his to begin with. No one fired Liddy until they had to. Owen, in a flash, realized Doar's thesis was right: Nixon had been in on it from the beginning.

Chapter 48

Le Grand Fromage

The Special Prosecutor's Office was a hive of activity at all hours as the prosecutors, secretaries, lawyers, and FBI special agents assembled cases—all amid a stream of witnesses, cooperating defendants, and defense attorneys. One Saturday morning, at work as usual, James Doyle found a note on the office vending machine: "This machine owes me 20¢—John Dean."

During a brief and ultimately unsuccessful attempt to confront John Ehrlichman with the evidence investigators had marshaled about his role in the cover-up, Leon Jaworski and Henry Ruth met with the former aide and his lawyers in hopes of spurring a plea negotiation. Ehrlichman listened impassively, fiddling with a pencil as Jaworski recited thirteen distinct charges that they believed they could make stick. The thirteenth charge involved Ehrlichman appearing to have cut up a specific memo to remove incriminating information, likely using scissors. Jaworski began "The last possible charge is mutilation of a government document—" only to be interrupted by Ehrlichman twisting up his face and throwing the pencil to the floor.

"*That* I did not do," he said, forcefully.

Ehrlichman's lawyers sat in stunned silence.

There would be no plea, it became clear, and instead the prosecutors would have to move forward with an indictment. In many ways, the cases against Ehrlichman and the other White House personnel were the easy ones—the real thorny challenge was the the potential defendant Ben-Veniste nicknamed "Le Grand Fromage," Nixon himself. The nickname, "GF" for short, was delivered first in jest, but soon became the unofficial but universal code name to avoid even speaking the potential defendant's name aloud. Unbeknownst to nearly everyone, Leon Jaworski's staff was working on two parallel tracks to study the unique challenges and culpability of the president—both efforts hidden to others in the office and even, in some cases, from each other.

As a first step, lawyer Richard Weinberg was tasked with researching the basic question: *Can you indict a sitting president?* The short answer, after wading through a lot of obscure legal questions, constitutional precedents, judicial opinions, and American history, appeared to be: "Yes, but you shouldn't." There was no specific prohibition in the Constitution or elsewhere, but there were real questions about the institutional "propriety" of the Justice Department bringing charges against the head of the executive branch.* Weinberg composed a memo with Phil Lacovara that focused on two different approaches they could take—relying either on the "alternative mechanisms" designed to hold the president accountable in office, e.g., impeachment, or on resolving the case with a "disposition or settlement in the public interest," e.g., how prosecutors had negotiated a plea deal with Agnew in exchange for his resignation. Their conclusion was that their highest service had to be to what was best for the nation, not just what was best for justice.

Seperately, Lacovara had been working with George Frampton to draft a document collecting evidence, and analyzing and outlining the crimes the prosecutors believed the president had committed—by the time they finished, months later, the memo would stretch to 128 pages. As Jaworski, Ruth, and Lacovara read the assembled information, the evidence was compelling and hardly subtle. In the matter of the hush money payments, for instance, prosecutors found at least fifteen different instances where Nixon had either advanced the conspiracy or confirmed his awareness of

---

* Weinberg's findings were consistent with the work done by the department's Office of Legal Counsel—its own in-house law firm—during the Agnew scandal as it weighed whether it could bring charges against the sitting vice president. There it had concluded yes, but the presidency itself was different.

it in conversation; ten episodes backed up his participation in the conspiracy to offer presidential clemency in exchange for witness's silence, and a dozen others highlighted what Jaworski called his "counseling, facilitating, assisting, and giving of false statements testimony." Charges were even clearer: 18 USC §3 (accessory after the fact) and 18 USC §4 (misprision of a felony); 18 USC §201(d) (bribery); 18 U.S. Code §371 (conspiracy to obstruct justice); and 18 USC §1510 (obstruction of a criminal investigation through bribery to prevent communication to the prosecutors).

The memo, as it was fleshed out and drafted, became the most sensitive document in the entire prosecution; just eight copies were made. Though many members of his team advocated for an immediate indictment, Jaworski felt the law was too unsettled; the nation couldn't face the turmoil, distraction, and trauma that would unfold during months—if not years—of uncertainty about how a presidential trial would play out. Moreover, while the memo outlined damning evidence, most of it was still only known to the special prosecutors. They needed to tread lightly to avoid getting ahead of public opinion.

As he made that clear, "a ferocious battle of wills ensued," Volner recalled. "He saw us as a band of renegades who were too young and too zealous for our own—and our nation's good."

One morning, Ruth found on a secretary's desk a draft presidential indictment drawn up by Peter Rient as an experiment, a three-page document laying out the charges against Nixon himself entitled *The United States of America vs. Richard M. Nixon.* "Ruth was apoplectic," Ben-Veniste and Frampton recalled. "The last thing he needed now was for Special Prosecutor Jaworski to come upon a document like this." Another memo pushing for a presidential indictment, written by four of the prosecutors—Carl Feldbaum, George Frampton, Jerry Goldman, and Rient—led to an explosive dispute between Jaworski and Richard Ben-Veniste.

As the disagreements and stress mounted, so did suspicions. The staff noticed that once or twice a week, Jaworski would hurriedly don his coat around 5 p.m., with no meeting on his calendar, and leave with his briefcase, returning fifteen to twenty minutes later. Staff wondered if he was delivering sensitive papers to someone covertly, and Ruth and others began mapping the odd departures. *Did they always happen on the same day? Or were they consistently a certain number of days apart?* No one ever figured out the truth, which was much less sinister: On nights when he realized he would be working late, Jaworski simply went for a short walk, aimlessly rounding the block, before settling back in. As he explained much later, "Why carry the attaché case? Often I would be recognized as I walked and it was much easier for me to explain that I was hurrying to an appointment than to engage in conversation with strangers."

Finally, over a dinner with Jaworski at Volner's house, the team began to edge toward a compromise on the president's case: The grand jury might not be able to indict the president, but it could name Nixon an unindicted co-conspirator and then attempt to hold that information back from the public as long as possible. The prosecutors knew that they needed to work Nixon into the indictment somehow, not just to demonstrate culpability, but because it would allow a jury to hear the full tapes and recordings of conversations in the Oval Office. If the president was not included, then his portion of the conversations would have to be excised, leaving prosecutors to play only snippets and undermining the entire case by robbing the conversations of vital context and nuance.

They agreed that they could keep the names of unindicted co-conspirators sealed until much closer to trial, thereby keeping Nixon's role a secret for some period after the cover-up indictment and giving the "alternative mechanisms" time to play out on Capitol Hill without prejudice. Ben-Veniste offered an unprecedented suggestion to maximize secrecy and flexibility: The grand jury could stop short of formally naming Nixon an unindicted co-conspirator and vote instead to authorize Jaworski to name the president later, if needed. The move would be codified in the official, secret minutes of the grand jury, which would preserve the prosecution's trial strategy without necessarily forcing a disclosure timeline.

The solution was elegant, but prompted another thorny question: If they weren't going to indict the president, how could they transmit the evidence they had gathered to the House Judiciary Committee for impeachment purposes? Normally there were strict rules against the publication of evidence gathered under the cloak of secrecy in a grand jury, but there appeared to be some constitutional exceptions. Staff found an 1811 precedent of a county grand jury in the Mississippi Territory passing along a report to the House for the impeachment of a federal judge early in the nation's history, which established that they could transmit information to the House, but not the prosecutors.

With an agreed-upon plan, the special prosecutors settled on building what they called a "road map," an almost clinical collection and organization of indexed evidence that contrasted the president's public statements denying knowledge of the cover-up with the evidence to the contrary; it would not be written in the form of an indictment or "presentment," and stop short of drawing any specific conclusions.

On February 25, Jaworski himself, along with other prosecutors, presented their arguments to the grand jury. For two hours, they laid out their approach, recommendations, and request that the jury vote to allow them to name Nixon himself a co-conspirator.

There was little doubt in the grand jury's mind about the president's guilt, and patience had grown thin among the citizen body. The main Watergate grand jury, composed of twenty-three civilians pulled from their daily lives, had met more than one hundred times by the beginning of February, so often that two jurors had lost their jobs due to missing so much work. "They were in a militant mood," Ben-Veniste and Frampton recalled. Frustrated by the president's ongoing non-cooperation, the foreman of the grand jury had written a secret three-page letter in late January on behalf of the panel, pleading directly for Nixon to testify. "Evidence presented to the Grand Jury in the form of testimony and tangible evidence—including tape recordings and documents—indicates you have information that is highly relevant to the Grand Jury's inquiry," the foreman, Vladimir Pregelj, wrote. "I am hereby requesting you on behalf of the Grand Jury to appear before it—at the White House or such other place as would be appropriate—to testify as other witnesses on matters that are subject of our investigation." Pregelj concluded by writing, "Inasmuch as we are in the closing stages of our investigation, we would appreciate an early response to this request." Nixon continued to refuse cooperation.

Now Pregelj argued briefly with Jaworski that the grand jury should take the presidential indictment question to the Supreme Court, but as the back-and-forth continued, it was clear the special prosecutor's proposal would be accepted. One juror stood up and thanked the special prosecutor, "Mr. Jaworski, we appreciate what you are doing. I have to admit that I had reservations about you when you first came."

"You were not the only one," Jaworski replied.

The resulting vote was 19–0, with a single abstention, to authorize the naming of the co-conspirators. As the stenographer took down the official alphabetical list, her eyes bulged when they got to N: "Richard M. Nixon."*

*   *   *

Hoping to prevent any confusion or court battles about the legal boundaries of its inquiry, the House authorized Rodino's Judiciary Committee to investigate the need for impeachment "fully and completely" and to subpoena any person or information "it deems necessary." The Ervin Committee, for its part, ceased public activity to avoid "interfer[ing] unduly with the ongoing impeachment process"; its final report would be written in private.

On February 25, Doar's team met with Pete Rodino and the GOP ranking member, Edward Hutchinson, to present a draft five-page letter for the White House that requested access to "all tapes, dictabelts or other electronic recordings, transcripts, memoranda, notes or other writings or things relating to" a specific list of particular meetings and conversations between President Nixon, Haldeman, Ehrlichman, Dean, Kleindienst, and Petersen in February, March, and April 1973. The letter outlined the days, topics, and even in many cases the times of the meetings, pulled from White House records, but focused around the crucial March 1973 time period that John Dean had already testified to. That, House investigators felt, was the most noncontroversial place to start. After both

---

* With the approach to the president settled, the grand jury and Jaworski's team moved to wrap up the other charges in the case. Among those, Herb Kalmbach pleaded guilty in late February both to gathering illegal campaign donations as well as promising a donor an ambassadorship in exchange for a $100,000 contribution. The special prosecutor had come to believe that Nixon's lawyer actually was as naive as he appeared to be; the fancy title, Jaworski decided, was nothing more than "window-dressing" for a middling gofer. ("Jaworski had spent his life with sharp lawyers, and he judged that Kalmbach was not one of them," Doyle recalled.) As hard as it was for them to believe initially, they became convinced that he really had begun raising the money used for the hush money payments without ever bothering to understand why.

Rodino and Hutchinson approved the request, the impeachment staff's sergeant-at-arms hand-delivered it to James St. Clair at the White House.

Over the next two weeks, Washington publicly debated the merits of the House request, even though no one other than the senior leaders of the inquiry knew precisely what it contained; when Representative Elizabeth Holtzman went over to the inquiry offices at the Congressional Hotel to try to read the letter, she was blocked by Doar's staff. Republican representatives privately and publicly urged the White House's voluntary cooperation. The letter was purposefully not a subpoena, but it was understood that the next message from the House might be.

Speaking at a March 13 press conference, Rodino and Hutchinson made a combined plea to the White House to cooperate. "What we have asked for is very reasonable and very relevant," the Republican ranking member said. "It is necessary to the inquiry. There would be no inquiry if there were no suspicion about the President's actions in connection with the so-called Watergate cover-up." As they spoke, reporters noted the calendar: It was the 106th anniversary of the day that the House voted to impeach Andrew Johnson.

$$* \quad * \quad *$$

The handing down of the final indictment for the Watergate cover-up was carefully timed to avoid interfering with the Vesco trial of John Mitchell and Maurice Stans in New York. As soon as it was clear that that jury would be chosen and sequestered by Thursday, February 28, the Special Prosecution Force rushed to roll out their magnum opus.

As part of their cover-up investigation, the prosecutors had agreed not to focus on the Watergate bugging operation itself; under legal principles, the break-in planning and burglary seemed to represent a "separate conspiracy," which would muddle the ability to present evidence admissible only against some of the defendants in the cover-up. There was a big difference between the burglary, which was really a campaign operation, and the cover-up, which was a White House operation involving the highest officials of government. Most of all, though, the evidence on the burglary was just inconclusive; while they had a sense that some of the cover-up defendants had foreknowledge of the burglary, the only direct testimony they had was Magruder's against Mitchell, and it seemed weak.

Instead, the indictment picked up with the events of June 17 itself, walking hour by hour through the cover-up efforts and the flailing efforts by Nixon's inner circle to hush up the White House's links to the crime. "The Watergate cover-up resembled an ordinary organized-crime case," Ben-Veniste and Frampton recalled. "Serious offenses had been committed: obstruction of justice, tampering with witnesses, payoffs, misuse of investigative information, perjury. All of the defendants had some knowledge of what was going on. They met and discussed the problems that the federal criminal investigation posed for them." The only thing that was remarkable was that the defendants were meeting in the Oval Office.

When Jaworski's office photocopier broke down while they prepared four hundred copies of the fifty-page indictment, Doar's team retreated to the neighboring office of the National Endowment for the Arts to finish. U.S. marshals escorted them to the courthouse; when an elevator arrived on the ninth floor of the offices at 1425 K Street NW with other passengers already on board, the marshals barked, "This elevator is impounded—everybody off," and then, once the elevator was empty, they wheeled aboard the cart of indictments.

On March 1, the twenty-one grand jurors filed into Sirica's courtroom—two were absent that day—all dressed to the nines; many of the women wore their favored church hats. Foreman Vladimir Pregelj handed an indictment and other supporting materials over to the judge; Ben-Veniste stepped forward with the locked briefcase that held the sealed Impeachment Roadmap. The whole thing took just fifteen minutes.

John Mitchell, H. R. Haldeman, John Ehrlichman, Chuck Colson, Gordon Strachan, Robert Mardian, and Kenneth Parkinson—a one-time CREEP lawyer—all faced conspiracy charges; six faced additional obstruction of justice charges, as well as sundry charges against several for perjury and/or giving false statement to the FBI or grand jury. (It also noted, without naming any, eighteen unindicted co-conspirators.) There were almost not enough columns across a front page for the nation's newspapers to run headshots of all those charged.

In the wake of the indictments, the *Washington Post*'s Richard Cohen calculated that twenty-eight people around the White House or the president's reelection campaign had now been charged, as well as ten corporations or their officers charged with illegal campaign contributions to Nixon. And there was still more to come. Just days later, a grand jury on the other side of the country indicted John Ehrlichman and Chuck Colson in the ham-handed burglary at the office of Daniel Ellsberg's psychiatrist, charging the two former White House aides with conspiring to violate the civil rights of Dr. Lewis Fielding, as well as indicting Liddy, Barker, and Martinez, who had also been charged in the Watergate burglary. The threads of the Watergate scandal were beginning to connect, as Americans and the news media began to understand clearly how the DNC break-in represented not the "only" criminal act, but just one of a broader, longer series of troublesome actions by presidential aides that had begun at least a year earlier and continued—at least according to some—right up until the present moment.

The arraignment for the new "Watergate Seven" occurred the following Saturday—an unusual weekend appearance scheduled around John Mitchell, who was still on trial in New York. A large crowd of gawkers waited outside the courthouse on the blustery gray day, some holding signs with slogans like "Jail to the Chief" and mocking Mitchell's reputation as "Mr. Law and Order"; one demonstrator even wore a giant papier-mâché head of Nixon. Inside, the prosecutors tried not to gawk as they watched the rogue's gallery of the nation's most powerful men file into the courtroom and, awkwardly, greet one another; Kenneth Parkinson had never even met Haldeman and Ehrlichman before finding himself alongside them at the defendants' table. "Thrown together now in a manner not of their own choosing, these were proud, arrogant, and unforgiving men whose mutual dislike and distrust were manifest," Ben-Veniste and Frampton recalled. For years before the burglary they had jockeyed for position and power around Nixon, and then for ten months afterward, they'd worked to lay the blame on one another. Now they were all bound together, for better or worse.

Jaworski walked over to greet Mitchell, who had been attorney general when he headed the American Bar Association. He looked, Jaworski observed, like a fraction of his former self—pallid and shrunken. "You must be very busy these days," Mitchell said, rising to greet the special prosecutor.

"More so than I wish, John," Jaworski replied.

Almost immediately, defense lawyers asked Sirica to allow the men to skip the normal mugshots and fingerprintings, but the judge ordered that they be treated as any other defendants. The men were then trooped down Pennsylvania Avenue to the FBI's offices in the Old Post Office building, their fall from grace complete.

Hours after the court appearances, Carl Bernstein called to double-check a tip that the grand jury had taken a straw vote to indict Nixon himself. Not having heard anything of the sort, Jaworski's office panicked, denied the story, and even called Katharine Graham herself. "It's not true," the office's deputy spokesman, John Barker, told her. "You have to kill the story." Barker emphasized how damaging it would be to public confidence if the *Post* reported an informal poll—a move that would be seen as foreshadowing a real, live presidential indictment. Unable to find a second source, the *Post* never ran the story, but in the days ahead the paper and other outlets reported that the grand jury would have willingly indicted the president if asked. Finally, on March 5, CBS's Daniel Schorr reported that the grand jury had taken a straw poll in support of indicting Nixon.

It wasn't until eight years later, during an ABC News special, that the special prosecutor's team discovered how accurate the Bernstein tip had been. In the interview, it was revealed that during a session when the jurors were evaluating evidence without the prosecutors present, they had indeed taken a straw poll. "There were 19 people in the grand-jury room that particular day," juror Elayne Edlund told ABC's *20/20*, "and we all raised our hands about wanting an indictment—all of us. And some of us raised both hands."

*   *   *

In the days after the indictment, the Special Prosecution Force had hoped that Judge Sirica would immediately give the Impeachment Roadmap, which Ben-Veniste had delivered to court along with the public indictment, to John Doar's team on the House Judiciary Committee. They feared that any delay would allow the president's lawyers to bottle it up forever, but while Judge Sirica initially hesitated, "to our surprise the

President did not object to the transmission of the report," Ben-Veniste and Frampton recalled.*

On March 26, Doar, Albert Jenner, and a Capitol Police officer went to the courthouse to pick up the material from Sirica's chambers, opening the locked files and cross-checking the contents against the grand jury's index before taking it into their possession. Later, back at the Congressional Hotel, they began reading through the remarkable evidence accumulated by Jaworski and the grand jury—a fifty-five-page outline of presidential criminality, all delineated in dry, factual prose supported by tape recordings, restaurant and hotel bills, airline tickets, and all manner of other documentary evidence that established the precise whereabouts, timelines, and participants of the conversations in question.

For four hours, Rodino and Hutchinson listened carefully to the scratchy, hard-to-decipher private words of the president and his aides as the tapes played in the inquiry's offices. Though Hutchinson told reporters afterward that he heard nothing on the tapes that implicated the president in a crime, behind closed doors, he was less sure: As the committee's battle over its initial document and tapes request stretched to a month, he increasingly felt Nixon's stonewalling could only be because the tapes were incriminating. Nixon, he felt sure, had something worth hiding.

Pete Rodino too was conflicted. A Judiciary Committee member for much of his political career, he had been elected to Congress in 1948 and, like many of his Watergate investigation peers, had been a leader on civil rights—he'd stood next to Martin Luther King, Jr., at the signing of the landmark 1964 Civil Rights Act and been the floor manager for the follow-up legislation, the 1966 Civil Rights Act—but in 1973 he was still little known nationally, and his best-known legislative achievement was ushering Columbus Day in as a national holiday.

Now he faced a challenge unlike anything since Reconstruction. He was committed to avoiding even the slightest appearance of prejudice

* As the special prosecutors carefully packaged up the Impeachment Roadmap at their K Street offices, George Frampton attached an orange anti-Nixon bumper sticker to the outside of one of the briefcases: "Say Good-Bye, Dick." Everyone laughed, and then—following a glare from Henry Ruth—Frampton carefully removed it and threw it away before delivering the files to court.

or bias in the impeachment inquiry—a framed photograph of Richard Nixon signing one of Rodino's bills remained in his office throughout the inquiry to avoid any eagle-eyed reporter noticing its absence. (He wouldn't remove it until Nixon resigned in August 1974.)

Everyone he met seemed to have a different theory about what he was doing wrong, even as he worked sixteen- and eighteen-hour days. He had given up his paddleball exercise routine in the House gym, so he'd quit eating lunch during the week to compensate weight-wise. At one point that winter, after a day of juggling difficult questions—including how the inquiry would keep information confidential and what role the president's defense attorney should have in the proceedings—Rodino felt a growing pain in his chest, sending him to the Capitol physician and then to Bethesda Naval Hospital. The doctors' diagnosis: severe exhaustion. Rodino stayed in the hospital for four days, resting.

The chair was hardly the only member burdened that winter. Even the Republicans on the committee felt as the winter progressed that their work would end up historic. Representative Tom Railsback told the *New Yorker*'s Elizabeth Drew, "We don't think we're on a fishing expedition." The congressman from Illinois—known as "Rails" to colleagues—was genial and well plugged in; he used the House gym frequently and was, as Nixon and Ford had been when they were in Congress, a member of the Chowder and Marching Club, an informal club of conservatives that served as something like a multigeneration backbone for the party. The fact that he continued to have such respect and belief in the process ahead was a bad sign for Nixon, Drew thought. "If we don't get the material in one fashion or another, I think he's in trouble. I think it would offend many members of Congress. I think it would offend the American people," he continued. "I'll be glad when this thing is over—it's a real headache."

Chapter 49

"Don't Miss Page 503"

Nationally, by spring 1974, the major players of Watergate had become celebrities—a copy of the *Incredible Hulk* comic book featured the superhero duo of June Volper and Ben Vincent tackling a White House overrun by monsters set on destroying the country. Then, on April 6, the capital celebrated the ribald white-tie Gridiron Club's Dinner, where members of the elite press club mix with invited officials over a grand banquet dinner at the Statler-Hilton Hotel, to roast newsmakers in costume. Judge Sirica, Gerald Ford, George McGovern, and 450 other formally dressed guests listened and roared through the club's chorus skits, including a parody of "'S Wonderful" remade into "Nixon's Wonderland." The journalists sang, "'s *Wonderful, marvelous. / We're the G.O.P. / Nixon's great, Watergate / 's ancient history.*"

Across town, to protest the all-male club's ongoing refusal to admit women, some eight hundred media and boldface names partied at a raucous "Counter-Gridiron" protest, dancing and circulating among concession booths raising money for charity. At one, Martha Mitchell sold phone calls, offering to call anyone.* Nearby, Jill Volner and Dan

---

* The *Arkansas Gazette*'s Washington correspondent had Martha prank call his own newspaper, telling the confused night news desk, "Arkansas doesn't seem to be doing very well with its senators, and I am thinking I might run."

Rather teamed up to sell kisses. Len Garment played the clarinet in one of the event's two dance bands, while Fred Buzhardt watched from the crowd.

Late in the evening, Volner made her way to another booth, where Elliot Richardson was selling his famous doodles. She purchased one, and as Richardson autographed it, he looked at her with recognition: "I know you," he said, laughing. "I lost my job because of you."

Of course, Watergate was anything but ancient history. Just the day before, George Steinbrenner had become the first corporate executive to face felony charges from the Special Prosecutor's Office, when he was hit with a fifteen-count indictment, outlining not just the scheme to launder donations through shipbuilding employees, but also that Steinbrenner had instituted a company-wide bonus system "to camouflage the bonuses that had already been given." Nine other executives of his American Shipbuilding Company were charged as well.* Steinbrenner was arraigned on the 19th, pleading not guilty, but it seemed far more a negotiating position than a real defense. Already, fellow company executives were pleading guilty.

Cases stemming from Watergate continued to unfold across the country; the lieutenant governor of California, Edwin Reinecke, was also indicted in early April, on three counts of lying to the Senate when he testified as part of its ITT investigation. Jaworski's office continued forward with its own tax investigation, as an IRS and congressional report found that the president owed some $476,000 in back taxes and interest covering his years in the White House. The payment, aides said, "almost virtually wiped out" the president's life savings.

The sum total of the weight of the scandals proved exhausting. "We're all very weary," one Democratic senator told the *New Yorker*'s Elizabeth Drew over dinner early that month. "This thing is a strain on all of us. We're all on trial. We all want to get it over with. We Democrats are counting on the Republicans' great desire to get Ford in by November."

---

* The indictments landed the day before the opening of the baseball season, infuriating Steinbrenner, who in 1973 had purchased the New York Yankees. Rather than celebrating the Yankees-Indians opening game, he found himself announcing he was removing himself from day-to-day management of the team to contend with his case.

Ford was all too clear where the scandal was headed, and he wanted to stay as far removed from the fray as he could. On a trip that April to Sunnylands, Walter Annenberg's lush estate, he ended up having a casual chat with *Newsweek*'s Tom DeFrank, in which they pondered the attitude of the onetime Nixon loyalists who seemed to be turning on the president. "They're angry and they're bitter because they know Nixon is finished," DeFrank observed. "It's over. He can't survive, and you're going to be president."

"You're right," Ford shot back, in an exchange that would remain off the record until 2007. "But when the pages of history are written, nobody can say I contributed to it."

* * *

Rodino began every morning at the Congressional Hotel offices, drinking coffee at 8:15 with Doar and Jenner, and ended nearly every evening with Doar, and Rodino's top aide, Frank O'Brien, meeting to talk through the thorny constitutional, political, and procedural questions before the inquiry. Despite the long hours and thoughtful discussions, Rodino increasingly worried about what he had to show for all the time and effort. He had originally set an April 30 deadline for impeachment, but it was clear not only that that was not possible, but that he'd actually made little apparent progress at all. The president had continued to stonewall, and the committee had burned through its entire initial million-dollar budget and needed to return to the House for another appropriation. The White House still refused to hand over requested documents and tapes, even as St. Clair continued to advocate for his own role in the impeachment proceedings—perhaps even the ability to call his own witnesses.

The two issues—one carrot, one stick—came to a head on the morning of April 11, as the Judiciary Committee gathered for a hearing. Minutes before, St. Clair had called Doar in Rodino's office to promise that a first set of tapes would be turned over in the next day or two. Doar, realizing the president was now on the defensive, pulled St. Clair's letter from his briefcase and read aloud the portion about "complet[ing] the inquiry promptly." Over the phone, he informed St. Clair that the February 25 request was just the *start* of the committee's work; the committee was now ready with further requests relevant to the ITT matter and the dairy price fixing issue. St. Clair would be allowed to participate, Rodino said, but the committee would proceed on its own timetable.

The hearing that followed was unusually tense; the committee's early camaraderie had melted away and partisan politics were more nakedly apparent. (In a rare burst of public irritation, Rodino admonished Maryland Republican Larry Hogan, saying, "The chair recognized the gentleman for a parliamentary inquiry and not for one of his harangues.") That afternoon, after extensive debate and a GOP amendment to make the committee's request more specific, the Judiciary Committee voted 33–3 to issue a subpoena to "summon Richard M. Nixon, President of the United States, or any subordinate officer, official or employee with custody or control of the things described in the attached schedule" to appear before the committee with the requested materials "on or before April 25, 1974, at the hour of 10 a.m."

Meanwhile, Leon Jaworski's office continued to press forward with its own investigations, even as its work increasingly seemed a sideshow to the House. In mid-April, he subpoenaed an additional sixty-four tape recordings, including the conversations between H. R. Haldeman and Richard Nixon on June 23, 1972. Jaworski's subpoena required a response by May 2.

The clock on a constitutional crisis was now ticking.

* * *

Under two separate deadlines, the president spent much of the last week of April listening to tapes, editing transcripts, and simply stewing.* On Monday, April 22, the official record of his day noted just two telephone calls, each one minute long—a total of two minutes of "presidential" work in an entire twenty-four-hour day. The next day, between the hours of 9 a.m. and 4 p.m., his schedule recorded only a single four-minute call with Kissinger.

---

* "Nixon spent hours listening to them, over and over and over again," his attorney general William Saxbe recalled. "He didn't have time for me or any other member of his cabinet, for that matter, except for Secretary of State Henry Kissinger."

Friday Nixon had just five telephone calls, totaling twelve minutes between 9 a.m. and 3:30 p.m., before leaving for Camp David, where he spent Saturday and Sunday immersed in the final transcript editing. It was surely, in its sheer emptiness and solitude, one of the oddest weeks in all of modern presidential history.

As he listened, he knew he was in trouble. "It is not possible to describe what it is like to see long-forgotten conversations reappear as lengthy transcripts," he recounted later in his memoirs. "When the words of an ordinary conversation are put on paper they acquire a rigidity that despite a literal accuracy in terms of what was said, may completely fail to capture or reflect the nature of the meeting or conversation as it actually took place."

Ultimately, however, the president saw the tapes as his to handle as he wanted, clinging to the belief that the discussions didn't matter, only his resulting actions. This put his lawyers in a challenging position; their client clearly wanted to conceal as much as possible, and yet as officers of the court, they couldn't knowingly withhold relevant information.

"We've got to be consistent," Buzhardt warned, but creating the transcripts had proved to be an exercise in chaos; typists withheld words, seemingly choosing what was "unpresidential" speech, and Nixon himself had excised entire passages, radically changing the context and conclusion of a meeting through the cuts, and leaving large blank spaces that could not be ignored—"Why so many deletions?" secretary Linde Zier asked her colleague Pamela Dallas one night as they finished the day's work. The documents were sure to raise more questions with investigators, exposing new risks and undermining the very defenses they were meant to bolster. To combat those potential problems, Nixon worked on a speech with Pat Buchanan, Ray Price, and Ron Ziegler to provide context and a framework for the transcripts, while St. Clair worked up a forty-page cover brief attacking Dean's credibility.

Their efforts were briefly interrupted on Sunday afternoon, when the Vesco jury found John Mitchell and Maurice Stans not guilty—a stunning verdict that cleared them of all eighteen charges. Upon hearing the words, the former commerce secretary embraced his lawyers and collapsed on the defense table, near tears—"My heart stopped for 30 seconds, I feel reborn," Stans later told reporters. Mitchell, relieved and grateful, did cry. "If there is one place I'm fairly convinced you can get justice," he said, "that is from the American people. That's why I had great faith in Americans, and why I love this country." At Camp David, Nixon rejoiced, feeling personal vindication.* It was time to move ahead with his own transcript release, he told Haig, before throwing away a few pages he'd been struggling to edit.

In the wake of the verdict, something approaching enthusiasm and euphoria—even perhaps confidence—appeared in the White House for the first time in months. "Watergate is going to go away tomorrow," communications director Ken Clawson promised, as the team readied the final release of the tape transcripts. St. Clair, in another conversation, concurred: "We're definitely out of the woods."

On April 29, after a month of frantic work and a five-day reprieve from the House, Nixon sat before a tall pile of blue notebooks and announced he was publicly releasing more than 1,300 pages of conversation transcripts that covered forty-six tapes, most of which had been requested by the Judiciary Committee. "These transcripts will show that what I have stated from the beginning to be the truth has been the truth: that I personally had no knowledge of the break-in before it occurred, that I had no knowledge of the coverup until I was informed of it by John Dean on March 21," he told the American people.

The next day—the one-year anniversary of Dean, Ehrlichman, Haldeman, and Kleindienst's firings—a station wagon pulled up in the curved Congressional Hotel driveway, where a half-dozen White House aides unloaded thirty-eight copies of the transcripts, one for each committee member. In his cover note, St. Clair had written, "The attached transcripts represent the best efforts accurately to transcribe the material contained on the recording tapes. Expletives have been omitted in the interest of good taste, except where necessary to depict accurately the context of the conversation. Characterization of third persons, in fairness to them, and other material not relating to the President's conduct has been omitted, except where inclusion is relevant and material as bearing on the President's conduct."

---

* Woodward and Bernstein's book, *The Final Days*, says Nixon called Stans and Mitchell to congratulate them, although there's no record of any such phone call in the president's daily diaries for April or early May.

They had beaten the subpoena deadline by one hour, but the committee soon found that the White House hadn't included any of the additional documents or tapes they had requested—in fact, only thirty-one of the forty-two requested conversations had been transcribed, and seven others that were included had not been requested at all. From the special prosecutor's perspective, Nixon's release covered just twenty of the sixty-four conversations under official subpoena. As they began poring over the transcripts and the American people began to read for themselves, it quickly became clear that St. Clair's statement was a lie.

*   *   *

The impact was brutal and swift. *Newsweek* published a special seventy-five-page section; *TIME* ran twenty pages; the usually pro-Nixon *Chicago Tribune* ran the entirety of the transcripts. Both the *Washington Post* and the *New York Times* rushed out paperback books encompassing all 1,308 pages, which quickly turned into bestsellers. Three million copies were printed. The Government Printing Office published its own copy, bound with a light blue cover, and it soon came to be known as the "blue book" in the capital.* As people began to actually absorb the content, things got worse. Congress was furious, Nixon defenders dumbstruck, and the general public was repulsed.

Page after page, there was just no sense from the president or his aides that they were disgusted by the burglary or wanted to get to the bottom of it or the subsequent cover-up; instead, they radiated cynicism and callous indifference to nearly everyone and everything, including the rule of law. Their only interest was their own survival. "Not that these conversations seemed diabolical: to the contrary, they revealed incompetent bumbling and an utter failure to comprehend what was happening in the real world," Ben-Veniste and Frampton recalled. "The level of discourse was appalling." Others agreed. "Sheer flesh-crawling repulsion," Joe Alsop wrote, describing his reaction to reading the conversations.

---

* A copy was dispatched to Henry Kissinger, then in the Middle East, where he skipped his trip's planned pleasure reading—including a chess manual and a pornographic novel—to read something arguably even more tawdry: the commander in chief's private conversations.

The transcripts, Alsop wrote, didn't read like they were worthy of the White House, they read like "the back room of a second-rate advertising agency in a suburb of hell." The language—and sheer pettiness—of the tapes surprised even some senior aides, who had never been fully exposed to the darkest version of the president.

There also were indications that the president's version of events had been altered. The Special Prosecutor's Office already possessed tapes of eight conversations now released by the White House, and the staff quickly began comparing. "The president's transcripts of these recordings were so replete with obvious errors that we had no confidence in the remainder," Jaworski recalled. In fact, the special prosecutor's staff was stunned at how wrong the transcripts managed to be in nearly every direction. "Some statements were transcribed in such a manner that the substance and tone of the actual conversation were completely misrepresented," Jaworski said. "Statements on the recordings were omitted in the transcripts. Statements not on the recordings appeared in the transcripts. Statements were attributed to one speaker when they actually were made by another. Statements were marked 'unintelligible' in the transcripts when they were clear on the tapes."

The House committee ran through the same exercise. "Before the end of the day, the word had been passed among most of the committee members that the White House versions were the worst of the lot," UPI's Howard Fields reported. Even Judiciary Committee Republicans like Railsback, Cohen, and Fish said they weren't happy. Hugh Scott, the Senate minority leader, worriedly read through the newly released version of the March 21 conversation and recalled the transcript he'd read in December at Haig's invitation; much of what he remembered was missing. The transcript ploy seemed impossible to defend. His public statement called the tapes "deplorable, disgusting, shabby, immoral."

The controversy prompted the House committee to leak the full unexpurgated sentence to the press, the first of what would turn out to be a whole series of releases highlighting how Nixon's transcripts distorted or minimized key conversations—each simultaneously adding evidence of the president's misconduct and undermining his ongoing credibility. As Len Garment later recalled, "Nixon released a thousand pages of mumbled plotting, twisting, turning, and double-dealing, all the numbing sleaziness of political men in desperate trouble, the whole mess compounded by countless transcription mistakes, arbitrary omissions, and perhaps worst of all, innumerable references throughout to 'expletive deleted.' "*

For days, Washingtonians shared their favorite quotes. ("Don't miss page 503—the president tells Ehrlichman to tell Magruder that he has his 'personal affection,' " one diner stopped to tell Elizabeth Drew during lunch.) Americans immediately filled in "(expletive deleted)" with their own vile curses, often far worse than Nixon's generally pedestrian "damns," "Chrissakes," and "goddamns."

The cumulative effect was devastating. "What was in the President's transcripts would overwhelm any strategy that could be devised to hide or distort it. Richard Nixon, it seemed to us, had just committed political suicide," Ben-Veniste and Frampton recalled. A Harris poll for the first time showed that a majority of the American people favored presidential impeachment.

✳　　✳　　✳

As publicly damaging as the transcripts were, there was the even bigger legal problem they presented: They still weren't what either Jaworski or the House had asked for. "The subpoena was for tapes and we got no tapes," Rodino said.† Prosecutors speculated that Nixon's aggressive misdirection with the transcripts likely stemmed from mistaken hubris—given that the president's name didn't appear in the March 1 indictments, the White House seemed to calculate that Jaworski had decided to take no direct action against him.

"We did not subpoena an edited White House version of partial transcripts of portions of presidential conversations. We did not subpoena a

---

* Visiting the Special Prosecutor's Office one day, to listen to some of the tapes to be used against him at trial, Haldeman joked to Henry Ruth, "Do you know how a Polish President would have handled Watergate?" Pausing for the punchline, Haldeman added: "The way that Nixon did."

† Behind closed doors, Rodino was even more blunt. "Rodino said that's like if a cop pulls you over and he asks you for your driver's license and you hand him your credit card," Republican representative William Cohen recalled later.

presidential interpretation of what is necessary or relevant for our inquiry. And we did not subpoena a lawyer's argument presented before we have heard any of the evidence," Rodino told the committee in a rare speech on May 1.

Stopping short of an article of impeachment, the committee ultimately approved a new letter to the president explaining it felt he was in noncompliance. Maine's William Cohen was the only Republican to support it. The letter, signed by Rodino and delivered to the White House, read in its entirety: "Dear Mr. President: The Committee on the Judiciary has directed me to advise you that it finds that as of 10:00 a.m., April 30, you have failed to comply with the Committee's subpoena of April 11, 1974."

Friday night, Nixon led a delegation of party leaders, including his friend Barry Goldwater, to Arizona for a rally. There, he told the crowd, "The time has come to get Watergate behind us and to get on with the business of America," a call more desperate than hopeful as his options dwindled.

In early May, James St. Clair tried to block Jaworski's latest subpoena for more tapes by seizing on what he believed was an important technicality: The requested tapes represented "inadmissible heresay," since Nixon himself wasn't a member of the Watergate conspiracy. The argument was a clear Hail Mary pass, and Jaworski found himself in a position to respond with equal intensity.

On Sunday, May 5, Jaworski, Lacovara, and Ben-Veniste went to the White House, settling again into the Map Room. The special prosecutor broke the news to Al Haig and James St. Clair that the grand jury had authorized the naming of the president as a co-conspirator. "About fifteen members of my staff have known about this and have kept it quiet out of fairness to the president," Jaworski said. "Now you are forcing me to come out with it in a hearing."

He then showed the brief he planned to file, as well as the minutes of the grand jury meeting that had confirmed all believed Nixon to be involved. He offered a compromise: He would drop the subpoena, and thus delay any announcement, if the White House released just eighteen specific conversations from the full list of sixty-four originally requested. All but sputtering, St. Clair asked for a few days to consider the proposal.

"This is an attempt to embarrass the president," he replied, and then implied the compromise seemed like blackmail. The conversation took less than thirty minutes; the lines had been drawn.

Haig too was clearly worried. "I'm not trying to save the president, Leon," he had said as they left the room. "I'm trying to save the presidency."

"You may be *destroying* the presidency," Jaworski countered. Later, logs would show that within minutes of the special prosecutor's departure, the eighteen tapes in question were retrieved from their secure storage area.

That very night, Stephen Bull set up a tape recorder for the president; minute by minute, Richard Nixon listened to his June 23, 1972, conversation with Haldeman. It's unknown whether he had precisely remembered the conversation until then, but in that moment, sentence by sentence, the worst of the cover-up unfolded. The plot was unmistakable, the abuse of power unconscionable. It took only until Tuesday for St. Clair to call Jaworski and declare, definitively, that there would be no further tapes. "The president does not wish to make any agreement," he said.

In his office, Jaworski hung up the phone and contemplated the message, the timing and subtext of which was crystal clear yet deeply troubling. Nixon had listened to the tapes, and thought they were so incriminating that there could be no further compromise. Jaworski shuddered to think what that must mean they contained, but then realized that Nixon must not have shared that incriminating evidence with his own aides; Haig and St. Clair would never have engaged in an active cover-up, especially at this stage.*

Nixon had been backed into his final corner; he would go forward alone. "The mistake may be to assume that there is such a thing as a White House strategy. In the matter of impeachment, there is no White House—there is only the President," the *New Yorker*'s Elizabeth Drew wrote that spring. "The President may not have a strategy other than taking it day by day, getting through each dangerous passage as best he can, and hoping for the best. No one really knows."

---

* Jaworski's hunch was correct—amazingly, no White House aide had followed Nixon's lead and listened to the requested conversations. Whatever Nixon had left to hide, it was clear they hadn't wanted to know.

The next morning, Nixon spent less than an hour in meetings—half of which was the ceremonial swearing-in of the new treasury secretary—and then cloistered himself for six hours alone in his hideaway office. He had dinner, alone, on the presidential yacht, the *Sequoia*.

That night, he sent his steak back—it had too much fat.

*   *   *

On May 9—the day that the pro-Nixon *Chicago Tribune* broke with the president and called for his resignation—committee members gathered for the first actual impeachment hearings. Walking up to Room 2141, the hearing room for the House Judiciary Committee that spring, the *New Yorker*'s Elizabeth Drew noticed familiar stanchions and yellow rope greeting her. "One could almost follow the story of Watergate and the impeachment by tracing the route of the yellow ropes," she observed. They had first appeared the previous summer outside the Ervin Committee. In the fall, they'd been outside the Senate Judiciary Committee, as it investigated the firing of Archibald Cox. Next, they'd been outside the hearings of the Senate Rules and Administration Committee as it conducted confirmation hearings for Gerald Ford. And now they were outside the beginnings of the impeachment hearings.

The hearings began in a very different environment than even just a few weeks before; the miscalculation of releasing the tape transcripts had undermined the president's already precarious position on Capitol Hill, and even Nixon's closest allies were eyeing him differently. Rogers Morton, the interior secretary, said in a speech, "We have seen a breakdown in our ethics government which I deplore and which I am having a very difficult time living with."

Impeachment by design is always a political process, not a criminal one—with no fixed milestones, no formal definable criminal code, and a burden of proof that shifts as power waxes and wanes. As then Republican minority leader Gerald Ford had himself said in 1970, as he'd advocated for impeachment of Supreme Court Justice William O. Douglas, "An impeachable offense is whatever a majority of the House of Representatives considers it to be at a given moment in history." Guilt versus innocence was calculated not independently, but among a group of jurors—both in the House and the Senate—who faced pressure and possible career repercussions on multiple fronts, at home from their voters and constituents, as well as from their colleagues in Congress.

As Pete Rodino weighed the inquiry's complex politics, success came down to three conservative Southern Democrats: James Mann of South Carolina, Walter Flowers of Alabama, and Ray Thornton of Arkansas. Impeachment, Thornton explained, was a "safety valve to eliminate any forces which would tend to overthrow or destroy the structure of government itself." Crimes, whether simple misdemeanors or serious felonies, were not the sine qua non for removing an officeholder; the crimes had to be directly tied to the structure and work of government itself.

Flowers, for his part, was overwhelmed with the idea that he might vote to remove a president—*the* president!—from office. As he told Elizabeth Drew that spring, "I think of this as a once-in-a-lifetime proposition. I don't mean to be melodramatic. I feel I just happened to be in the breech when the gun got loaded with this particular shell." (By late spring, the stress, the sleepless nights, the political uncertainty, all had combined to bring back an ulcer.)

The staff and the committee had to navigate that distinction. "When I was able to hold Mann, Thornton, and Flowers, then I knew it could be done," Rodino told reporter Jimmy Breslin. "I had to have them. Once I had them I could start to put it together." Beyond the conservative Democrats, Rodino studiously and artfully courted other moderates, like Maine Republican William Cohen. Impeachment, when and if it came, could not be a party-line vote. It was political, absolutely, but it couldn't be partisan.

The public who made it past the yellow ropes didn't get to watch for long. After opening statements from Rodino and Hutchinson, the committee voted to close the remainder of the hearing so it could deliberate and hear evidence in private. The TV lights went dark, the rows of press and public emptied, and at 1:40 p.m., police locked the committee room doors. All thirty-eight committee members were in their seats inside, each now staring at the headphones that had been installed at their desks. St. Clair sat nearby at the defense counsel's table. Everyone seemed nervous; when Rodino noted to the president's defense attorney that he should be bound by the same confidentiality rules as the committee members, St. Clair stumbled: "I do, Your Honor—Mr. Chairman, excuse me."

"We begin at the beginning," John Doar began, a statement both figurative and literal. "On January 20, 1969, Richard Nixon was inaugurated as the 37th President of the United States." He proceeded, in a flat almost monotone voice. "President Nixon is a very disciplined President. He likes order and his system of management of the White House clearly reflects that. That will be apparent, members of the committee, as you go through these hearings."

That first day was a big success, and to celebrate, Doar took committee staffers Maureen Barden and Barbara Campbell out to dinner at Trader Vic's. Driving through town in the evening, Barden—a New Yorker—realized how little of the capital she'd seen in her months on the inquiry staff. "Oh my gosh. Look at that. That's beautiful. What is that?" she said, pointing to a garden and fountain outside the window. When he turned to look, Doar was astonished; Barden was pointing out the lawn of the White House, which she had yet to lay eyes on.

*   *   *

On Friday, May 10, in a private session inside Sirica's chambers, crowded with prosecutors, White House attorneys, and attorneys for the cover-up defendants, Jaworski handed out a thirty-nine-page legal brief announcing that the grand jury did believe Richard Nixon had been part of a conspiracy and that he would be naming him an unindicted co-conspirator.

Except among the president's lawyers, there was total surprise. Sirica, shocked that this development had been kept a secret this long already, argued that the discussion should take place in public. Jaworski pushed for discretion a bit longer, backed by various defense attorneys. In the end, Sirica agreed, and ordered that the special prosecutor's subpoena for the sixty-four tapes be enforced. The damaging news he'd learned, for now, would remain a secret. The situation, he figured, could not get worse: "I figured the president was doomed."

Chapter 50

The United States
v. Richard M. Nixon

With the Supreme Court's traditional summer recess fast approaching, Leon Jaworski knew that he could not wait for the normal appeals process to unfold. Time was of the essence, and with that in mind, the special prosecutor asked the Supreme Court to review the legality of the subpoena immediately—hoping to avoid an appeal that drifted into October and pushed a trial for the "Watergate Seven" into 1975 or beyond. It was a rare move—the last time the Supreme Court had agreed to such a maneuver was in the midst of the Korean War—and a risky one.

Jaworski knew that a rejection from the Supreme Court might also come with a verbal slap and delay the scandal for the better part of a year (St. Clair indeed objected to bypassing the regular appeals process, saying it undermined the required "careful reflection and deliberation"), but the Special Prosecutor's Office raced to file its so-called "writ of *certiorari*," with Lacovara delivering it to the Supreme Court clerk just as the doors closed at 6 p.m. The justices took only a day to approve their direct review. "[It was] a truly extraordinary mechanism that the Supreme Court entertains only once every twenty years or so," Lacovara explained.

The move by Jaworski's team allowed them to reorient the nation's viewing of the case and the stakes in a subtle but important way, reducing the president from an "office" to a "man." When the president argued with Sirica in the lower-level district court, the dispute had been captioned simply and routinely. Now, at the Supreme Court, the special prosecutor renamed the case. "Our goal was to strengthen our constitutional arguments by assuming the mantle of 'counsel for the sovereign people of the United States' seeking to enforce the obligation of every citizen," Lacovara later explained.

And so *Nixon v. Sirica* became *The United States v. Richard M. Nixon.*

*   *   *

Through May, the capital remained tense, watching the impeachment hearings begin on Capitol Hill and trying to discern the worried looks of people heading in and out of private meetings. In the case around the Ellsberg burglary, Judge Gerhard Gesell had recently ruled against Ehrlichman and Colson that there was no Fourth Amendment exception for national security—they couldn't argue that their breaking-and-entering operation in California had been justified under some hazy hand wave of protecting the country. Rumors of a presidential resignation abounded. During a trip to Buffalo, Gerald Ford's team were forced to specifically deny a report that the vice president had emerged from a morning meeting with the president and declared that his staff should be on "red alert."

As much as the administration tried to downplay the resignation rumors, it was in obvious peril. On Tuesday the 14th, Ford—in his ceremonial role as the president of the Senate—met with Mike Mansfield, the majority leader, and Hugh Scott, the minority leader. The two legislative leaders explained that a Senate impeachment trial looked near certain. "Jerry, there's a better than 50-50 chance that you will be president before long," Scott said, a statement that worried him as the minority leader almost as much as it worried Ford himself.

Meanwhile the House's two top Republicans, minority leader John Rhodes—who had taken over the role when Ford ascended to the vice presidency—and conference chair John Anderson, fretted about the party's electoral prospects and its future. Rhodes, who had suggested resignation might be a possibility following the bungled release of the transcripts, had been pushed hard since by party loyalists to rally to Nixon's aid, and he feared the utter collapse of the party in the fall's '74 midterm elections if they broke with the president. Anderson, however, saw the move as perhaps the only chance for survival amid an angry and disillusioned national electorate.

Behind the scenes, the White House staff began to subtly prepare contingency plans. That spring, Philip Buchen—a former law partner of Ford's who now worked on his staff—had dinner with Clay White-head, the head of the White House's telecommunications policy team. As they ate and digested the latest scandal developments, Buchen told his colleague, "We have to do some planning for Jerry. We have to face the fact the president may resign." In the days ahead, they gathered three others—a former Elliot Richardson aide, Jonathan Moore, as well as an assistant interior secretary, Laurence Lynn, and one of Whitehead's White House assistants, Brian Lamb—and the secret team of five began to plan for the transition none of them hoped for, but that all of them assumed was only a matter of time. They knew that their work needed to remain a tightly held secret—especially from the vice president, who continued to dance around the president's troubles, trying to be supportive without necessarily lashing himself to a sinking ship. "Time will tell," he said at one point, when asked if the president had committed impeachable offenses. Time, indeed.

* * *

"If John Doar fit any stereotype, it was that of a meticulous, compulsive librarian," UPI's Howard Fields wrote, in an excellent categorization of the impeachment counsel's personality. As the hearings began, his inquiry staff were spending their nights organizing more than forty identical binders, with all the evidence and material backup for the questioning; they did the process a total of thirty-six times, each time gathering a different "Statement of Information" that outlined a different set of evidence around a different question. Binder after binder, night after night. They were all modeled after the grand jury's original roadmap—each factual assertion tied to the supporting evidence. Everything was collated and cross-referenced, to both official documents or sometimes even news reporting.

"We truly did nothing but work. And we worked. We worked," Maureen Barden recalled. Once, when her sister came to visit and the two went out to dinner, Barden fell asleep right at the table. A woman who dated inquiry staffer Larry Kieves was quoted in the newspaper saying, "He's the most boring person in the world. All he does is work and he can't talk about that and he can't talk about anything else."*

Fortunately, the work was not for nothing. Over nineteen hours in the first four days of hearings, Doar, colleague Evan Davis, and other staff read through page after page of background, established facts, summarized and direct testimony, and documentary evidence. By the end of the first week, committee members had begun to hear—and understand—precisely the presidential patterns of conduct that added up in their minds to impeachment. They listened intently to the tapes, as scratchy and hard-to-discern as they were, but gradually came to be convinced of the thoroughness of the inquiry's transcripts. "It made the conversations come alive. We got the emphasis, the voice inflections, and the tone of the conversation," Representative Tom Railsback told a reporter at the time.

All told, for ten weeks, Tuesday through Thursday, the lawmakers heard some 7,200 pages of evidence. For the first time, "Watergate" was being told as a single story, from the burglary and the cover-up to the other scandals that had, until then, technically been unrelated—ITT, campaign finance illegalities, dirty tricks, the milk producers bribery case, and others that converged into a broad, sweeping indictment of Richard Nixon's abuse of the presidency. There was no particular rhyme nor reason to the House committee's presentation, other than what evidence was first ready, but the scope of the misconduct could not be missed or

---

* Staff got used to seeing Jenner in the evening in the lobby of their office building, nattily dressed with a gaudy handkerchief, carrying his loafers in his hand. He had a habit of taking off his shoes at his desk, then working such a long day that his swollen feet at the end wouldn't fit back into his shoes. Owen, for his part, was smoking so much—first three packs, then four—that some days his teeth hurt.

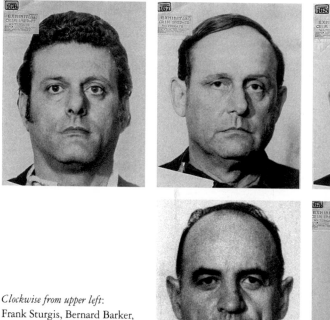

Security guard Frank Wills's log for the night of June 17, 1972, reports the infamous burglary.

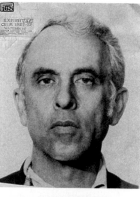

Clockwise from upper left:
Frank Sturgis, Bernard Barker,
Eugenio Martinez, Virgilio
Gonzalez, and James McCord
didn't exactly look like a
run-of-the-mill burglary gang.

Washington Post publisher Katharine Graham, reporters Carl Bernstein and Bob Woodward, managing editor Howard Simons, and executive editor Ben Bradlee helped drive the early Watergate coverage, along with city editor Barry Sussman (*not pictured*). (*Photo by Mark Godfrey*)

8

No. 131138

First Bank and Trust Company of Boca Raton, N.A.

BOCA RATON, FLORIDA April 10, 1972

63-623
670

PAY →

PAY 25,000 00 CTS

TO THE
ORDER OF   Kenneth H. Dahlberg ✳✳✳✳✳✳✳✳✳✳✳✳✳✳✳✳✳✳✳✳✳✳✳ $ 25,000.00

CASHIER'S CHECK

Kenneth H. Dahlberg
REMITTER

Thomas P. Monahan

AUTHORIZED SIGNATURE

⑆0670⑈0623⑈ ⑈00⑈101⑈5⑈ ⑈000 2500000⑈

Bernstein's reporting of the Kenneth Dahlberg check, laundered through the president's reelection campaign, was the first major public scoop of the case.

Bernard Barker's address book showed a mysterious entry for "HH" at the "WH."

9

10

11

13

12

Clockwise from upper left: Richard Kleindienst, Henry Petersen, E. Howard Hunt, and Judge John Sirica.
(Sirica portrait by David Hume Kennerly)

14

Senate Watergate Committee Chairman Sam Ervin, right, confers with, from left, Republican senators Howard Baker and Lowell Weicker, as well as committee staffers Terry Lenzner and Rufus Edmisten.

15

The public testimony of John Dean, with his wife, Maureen, looking on, electrified the nation in the summer of 1973. *(Photo by JP Laffont)*

16

Through the summer and fall of 1973, the parade of witnesses, like Howard Hunt, before the Ervin Committee kept Watergate front and center. *(Photo by David Hume Kennerly)*

17

GRAND JURY
Subpoena Duces Tecum SUBPOENA DUCES TECUM

United States District Court
For the District of Columbia

Misc. #47-73

THE UNITED STATES
vs.

JOHN DOE

To: Richard M. Nixon, The White House, Washington, D. C., or any subordinate officer, official, or employee with custody or control of the documents or objects hereinafter described on the attached schedule.

REPORT TO UNITED STATES DISTRICT COURT HOUSE
Between 3d Street and John Marshall Place and on Constitution Avenue NW.
XXXXXXXXX Grand Jury Room 3
Washington, D.C.

FILED ✓
JUL 24 1973
JAMES F. DAVEY, Clerk

You are hereby commanded to attend before the Grand Jury of said Court on **Thursday** the **26th** day of **July**, 19 **73**, at **10** o'clock **A. M.**, to testify on behalf of the United States, and not depart the Court without leave of the Court or District Attorney, and to bring with you the documents or objects listed on the attached sched- *WITNESS: The Honorable* **John J. Sirica** *Chief Judge of said Court, this* ule.

23rd day of **July**, 19 **73**.
JAMES F. DAVEY, *Clerk.*

Archibald Cox
ARCHIBALD COX
Attorney for **the United States**

By *Robert L. Line*
Deputy Clerk.

Form No. USA-9x-184 (Rev. 7-1-71)

34

The presidential subpoena.

18

Archibald Cox's press conference on the weekend of the Saturday Night Massacre.
(*Photo by David Hume Kennerly*)

19

The night of the Saturday Night Massacre, prosecutors and press descended on the offices of the Special Prosecution Force, trying to discern the future of the investigation.
(*Photo by David Hume Kennerly*)

The "Rose Mary Stretch" was widely mocked after she demonstrated how she possibly erased the eighteen-and-a-half-minute gap.

Prosecutors Richard Ben-Veniste and Jill Volner would play a key role in the investigation.

Nixon's public gambit in April 1974 to release his own edited transcripts backfired.

Leon Jaworski stepped
in after Cox's firing.

Representative Pete Rodino
found himself the center
of the Watergate firestorm in
the spring of 1974.

House Judiciary Committee
counsel John Doar assembled
an all-star team to help
him, including a young
Hillary Rodham.
*(All photos this page by
David Hume Kennerly)*

Nixon's goodbye from the White House.

THE WHITE HOUSE
WASHINGTON

August 9, 1974

Dear Mr. Secretary:

I hereby resign the Office of President of the
United States.

Sincerely,

Richard Nixon

11.35 AM

HK

The Honorable Henry A. Kissinger
The Secretary of State
Washington, D.C. 20520

The letter of resignation.

Minutes after Nixon left the White House, Gerald Ford took the oath of office.

explained away. "You go into a grocery store and see a whole section of nice-looking tomatoes. You pick one up, and it's rotten, on the bottom. You figure, all right, it's possible to have one rotten tomato. You pick up another tomato and it's rotten," Maryland Democratic representative Paul Sarbanes said. "After eight or 10 rotten tomatoes you wonder about the whole grocery store."

To the committee members, two elements of the investigation's narrative seemed particularly troubling: First, there was Nixon's misuse of "national security," the area where the presidency is typically afforded the most leeway and flexibility. "You would use national security as a cover for things that didn't have anything to do with national security," impeachment staffer Evan Davis said. "To use falsely national security as a cover seemed to me a compounding problem to find subversion of the Constitution."

They were also confounded by the president's indifference to the legality of his actions and those of his aides. It wasn't that Nixon had carefully threaded through a gray area in the law; he had charged ahead without caring what was right or wrong. "It's a compounding fact for finding a constitutional high crime or misdemeanor because it relates directly to the duty to take care that the law has been faithfully executed," Davis recalled. "Indifference to legality is a particular problem for a President in terms of his role under the Constitution."

*   *   *

James St. Clair found himself by early June in an absolutely impossible position—caught amid a weakening public case, a peeved judiciary tired of his delays, and an intransigent and isolated client, leading a restless defense team that wondered how much their client cared about their work to begin with. Most of his junior lawyers had never even met the president. Many days it felt like there were just too many cases involving the president, too many aides in too much trouble.

On Monday, June 3, the White House counsel was in the courtroom of Judge Gerhard Gesell, the D.C. federal judge who would lead the trial of the second "Watergate Seven" and who had ordered

White House files be turned over to aid the defense of Colson and Ehrlichman. Nixon had declined, and St. Clair was worried that day whether Gesell might actually find the president in contempt. Instead, he was as surprised as anyone when Chuck Colson said, "I plead guilty, Your Honor."

The unexpected change resulted from an odd bargaining session over the previous week between Jaworski's office and Colson, who had gone through what he called a religious awakening amid the case. He now felt weighed down by a guilty conscience, but not for the crime he'd been charged with—he insisted he was not guilty of the existing conspiracy indictment, but he agreed to plead guilty to attempting to obstruct justice by interfering with the Ellsberg trial. "I regret what I attempted to do to Dr. Ellsberg," Colson said. "All of us who have been involved in this unhappy chapter of history, along with all of those who occupy public office today, have an overriding obligation to do everything in our power to help restore the confidence of the American people in this Government."

Inside the courtroom, St. Clair handed his assistant a dime and dispatched him to call the White House with the surprise update. Later, when he returned to the White House, he took the fourteen lawyers and staff, all men, who had been working feverishly to hold back the onrushing trouble, for a ten-minute audience in the Oval Office. They chatted awkwardly and then took a group picture. After they were ushered out, Nixon spent an hour meeting with St. Clair before spending another three hours sitting alone.

The next day, news cameras followed Jeb Stuart Magruder as he reported to prison on his perjury plea for what would ultimately be a seven-month sentence. Soon, Herbert Kalmbach followed, beginning a minimum six-month prison term. As Gesell said, "The court recognizes that men of ambition, affected by blind, impulsive loyalty, react to the atmosphere in which they work and which they helped create. But this does not change the individual responsibility of each public servant. Morality is a higher force than expediency."

* * *

On Wednesday, June 5, the *Los Angeles Times'* Robert Jackson and Ron Ostrow confirmed and reported the contents of the mysterious briefcase handed to Judge Sirica back in March. The story that Nixon had been named an unindicted co-conspirator ran on front pages coast-to-coast. The members of the House Judiciary Committee were taken by surprise. (Doar's staff had known about the vote, but hadn't told the committee.) Within a day, St. Clair conceded the report was indeed true. "It is going to have a hell of an impact on the Hill," an anonymous defense attorney for one of the Watergate Seven defendants told the *New York Times.* "It makes the White House position far weaker in resisting tapes requests."

Nixon held strong. Sunday afternoon, he addressed a crowd of fourteen hundred at the Shoreham Hotel, a group called the "National Citizens Committee for Fairness to the Presidency," founded by a Ukrainian-born rabbi named Baruch Korff. Korff and Nixon had met in 1967, and the rabbi had grown an increasingly strong connection to the president, largely in gratitude for his deep, loyal support of Israel. That spring, as Nixon came under increasing threat, Korff had rallied the new citizens committee to boost the president politically and help raise money for his legal defense. In May, as he spent longer and longer stretches alone, Nixon had met with Korff in the Oval Office, speaking for ninety minutes as part of what Korff hoped would be a book project to save the presidency. "I am not the press's favorite pin-up boy," Nixon told the rabbi. "If it hadn't been Watergate, there would probably have been something else. So now they have this. But I will survive it and I just hope they will survive it with, shall we say, as much serenity as I have." Now the Shoreham Hotel crowd was about as warm a reception as Nixon would see that year, a chance to take a victory lap. The speakers stressed that the best of Nixon's presidency remained ahead—there was so much still to do with the final 965 days in the White House.

As the president himself told the crowd, "The cause you have worked for, my friends, is not simply for a man, but the cause you have worked for and are working for is much bigger than one man or one President. The cause you are working for is for this office, which is so important—actually which is indispensable—to what we want to build, we as Americans:

a peaceful world for our children and our grandchildren and for those of others who have been our friends, and even those who have been our adversaries and our enemies."

The brave statements of fortitude and resilience increasingly belied the lonely paralysis that gripped the White House. Inside, the president's work had all but stopped; more and more, Al Haig had come to serve as something like a prime minister or "deputy president," ensuring that the multitudes of paper required to run the U.S. government continued to churn, even if the man in charge had all but ceased participating in his own administration. "Nixon was a haunted man," an aide told journalist Teddy White. "[He was] able to focus only on foreign affairs, which both intrigued and distracted him."

On June 10, the president left on a whirlwind, fifteen-thousand-mile trip, spanning five Middle East nations: Egypt, Saudi Arabia, Syria, Jordan, and Israel. At a first stop in Austria, he complained of an inflamed leg, and his personal physician, Major General Walter Tkach, diagnosed a blood clot. The physician recommended immediate cancellation of remainder of the trip and that the president be hospitalized overseas; continuing the trip might very well kill him. When he was stable, Tkach offered, he could return directly to the United States. Nixon rejected the idea out of hand. "The purpose of this trip is more important than my life," he said. At home in Washington, he was a defendant and co-conspirator, but overseas, he was still clearly the president—the commander in chief of a great nation, campaigning for peace as vigorously as he'd ever campaigned for election. A quick honorable death overseas, in service of world peace, looked better than a slow political death at home.

Day after day, Tkach and another physician watched, worried, as Nixon gritted his way through obvious pain. At every stop, he seemed to ignore advice, standing for long stretches and walking at length, including touring the Giza pyramids with Anwar Sadat while in Egypt. "The president has a death wish," Tkach told fellow staff. He returned from the Middle East only to leave three days later for more diplomatic maneuvers, this time in Brussels and the Soviet Union, for a major summit with Brezhnev—what the White House would call "Summit III," to discuss nuclear weapon limitations and other subjects. He flew back across the Atlantic on June 25, his leg still elevated for its crushing pain aboard the plane.*

*   *   *

While Nixon was overseas, Bob Woodward and Carl Bernstein's first-person account of their hunt for the truth about Watergate arrived in bookstores, in time for the second anniversary of the break-in. Instantly, *All the President's Men* became a national sensation, selling out its entire 75,000-copy initial printing—Simon & Schuster was quick to reprint another 135,000 copies—and it spent fifteen weeks on the bestseller lists. The reporters' simple retelling of the saga, one that focused on their own roles at the expense of all other players and investigators—the name of FBI case agent Angelo Lano, for example, is never even mentioned—set records for sales, resales, and subsidiary rights. The proceeds—the $1 million paperback sale, the $30,000 magazine excerpts to *Playboy*, the myriad foreign translations, $100,000 from the Book of the Month Club, and the $450,000 movie sale to Robert Redford—suddenly made Woodward and Bernstein wealthy in a way that was all but unimaginable for two reporters whose combined annual salary in June 1972 had been about $30,000. The book also served as a crib sheet for Americans just as the scandal reached its pinnacle; a *Wall Street Journal* reviewer praised it as "a great guide for people like me who still have trouble figuring out where Ehrlichman begins and Haldeman ends."†

The publication—and specifically, the excerpt in *Playboy*, which was the first word on the subject—revealed that the *Post* reporters had an apparently high-level inside source they called Deep Throat, a fact that astounded and fascinated readers and kicked off immediate, fevered speculation about the anonymous source's identity.

---

* Nixon was hardly the only one suffering as the pressures of Watergate seemed to manifest in physical stress too: While the president was at Egypt's Qubba Palace in Cairo, back in Washington Fred Buzhardt suffered a serious heart attack and was rushed to the hospital.

† The movie version would prove even more popular when it was released in 1976, becoming the second-biggest movie of the year after *Rocky*. Warner Bros. touted it as how two young reporters "solved the greatest detective story in American history."

Woodward had actually hoped to identify Felt in the book, but the former FBI deputy angrily rejected the proposition when Woodward called. "He exploded. 'Absolutely not,'" Woodward recounted later. "'Was I mad to even make such a request?'" Felt hung up, telling Woodward never to contact him again, so the reporter instead used the paper's internal nickname. The literary device began a parlor game that would continue for decades and yield not just articles but entire books, college classes, and more investigations that parsed the finest details of the book, Woodward's background, and the Watergate bread crumbs to figure out who "he" could be. Key suspects included Al Haig, Pat Buchanan, John Dean, and Patrick Gray, although a pantheon of less well-known players were also "outed" by sometimes even authoritative researchers: David Gergen, Fred Fielding, John Sears, and Diane Sawyer, among others.

While the "mystery" of Deep Throat's identity would persist until 2005—and it wouldn't be clear for decades that Nixon himself had long suspected Felt of leaking—the FBI official made the short-list quickly too, only to be overlooked and discounted by many for forty years. Writing in the June issue of the *Washingtonian*, within days of the book's publication, editor Jack Limpert asked, "Who did have motive and opportunity and method? Who hated what Nixon was doing to him? Who had access to all the material? Who had the resources to set up a system to leak it? The FBI, that's who."

In the next paragraph, Limpert continued, "Read the February 28 and March 13 Presidential transcripts and then try someone like Mark Felt on for size. A Hoover loyalist and number-two man to Pat Gray, he had every reason and resource for leaking the Watergate story and destroying Nixon. Why would someone like Felt pick Woodward and Bernstein? Why not? Why pick someone like Jeremiah O'Leary of the *Star-News* who has been getting FBI leaks for years? Why not pick the last two reporters who would ever be suspected of being FBI conduits?"

While the book became an instant entry in the canon of Watergate—and journalistic—writing, it also set off long-running questions about how accurate a retelling the book really was. One focus, for example, was how Woodward claimed to have used a small cloth flag in a flowerpot on his apartment balcony at 1718 P Street NW to request meetings with Deep Throat—moving it to the front of the balcony to indicate that the two should meet that evening at 2 a.m. on the bottom level of the parking garage underneath 1401 Wilson Boulevard. If Deep Throat needed to meet Woodward, the source would intercept the reporter's home-delivered copy of the *New York Times*—it's still a mystery how—circle page 20, and draw a clock on the page indicating the meeting time.

Critics noted that the flowerpot system seemed uniquely complex and challenging to execute; Woodward had an enclosed courtyard, meaning that someone would have had to go out of their way to inspect it every day, passing down through a back alley, despite what Woodward seems to identify as meetings that took place only every six to eight weeks.*

Beyond questions about plot or character were comments about the writing process itself. The book draft had gone through many iterations and failed starts as the reporters tried to write it alongside their day jobs and all-consuming reporting and only really gained momentum when Robert Redford expressed interest in it as a movie; as a result, many scenes seem tinged with more than a little cinematic drama. In reviewing the account for his 1993 biography of Woodward and Bernstein, Adrian

---

* One theory is that Felt relied on others to scout the apartment—perhaps an FBI agent elsewhere in the building or one attached to a surveillance post nearby—but even repeated in-person scouting seems likely to have raised suspicions among Woodward's neighbors. "Those mundane tasks were probably entrusted to reliable agents, possibly one or more of Felt's aides," concluded Watergate historian Max Holland. Gray, for his part, always suspected that Deep Throat was a compilation of sources, rather than a single person, which was long believed too by some of Woodward and Bernstein's competitors on the beat: As the *Los Angeles Times*' Ronald Ostrow said, "When we got some of the same stories, we know they did not all come from the same person." Years later, after Felt's identity became public, a former senior FBI agent named Paul Daly explained that Felt had indeed headed "a clandestine group of high-ranking agents who agreed to leak information about the Watergate break-in" for a "noble purpose" and protect the bureau's public integrity. The group included not just Felt but its assistant director of the criminal division, Charles Bates, and the head of the Washington Field Office, Robert Kunkel.

Havill cross-checked local weather reports and found that many didn't line up with the dramatic tableaus the men wrote.[*]

There was also the odd tale of how Bernstein had tried to avoid a subpoena from the DNC's civil suit against CREEP by hiding out in a movie theater for the afternoon of February 26, 1973, at Bradlee's urging. "Get out of the building," Bradlee is said to have told Bernstein, on page 260. "Go see a movie and call me at five o'clock." As the authors write, "Bernstein went to see *Deep Throat*—the movie version." It's a playful aside, almost an inside joke to the reader—and it almost certainly didn't happen. The hard-core porn movie had been playing in D.C. in the summer and fall of 1972—its pop culture notoriety at the time was what inspired Howard Simons's moniker—but an FBI crackdown that fall saw agents raid D.C.'s dozen or so pornographic movie houses, confiscate films, and charge the proprietors with "interstate transportation of obscene materials for the purpose of distribution." Accordingly, the hard-core movies were gone from theaters by February. "There were no ads in the *Post* or the newly named *Star-News* that day or week for anything resembling the film," Havill's book notes.

Years later, in an interview for his own memoir with a young journalist, Barbara Feinman, Ben Bradlee said, "You know I have a little problem with Deep Throat. I know who they identify as—Bob identifies

---

[*] For example, a scene where Woodward and Bernstein, after their humiliating lunch with their literary agent and editor on October 25, 1972, following their messed-up scoop about Hugh Sloan and Haldeman's control of Nixon's secret fund, raced back in the rain to the newsroom, holding copies of the newspaper above their head and arrived "soaked and shivering." A great dramatic scene for a movie, except that according to the National Weather Service records that I double-checked as well, it didn't rain at all that day in D.C., and the temperature at the end of lunch was nearly 60 degrees. Could their meeting with an agent have happened another day when it did rain? Maybe—it appears to have rained, gently, after lunch on October 19, but then their meeting with their book editor wouldn't have occurred in the shadow of their biggest screwup. Similarly, when Bernstein journeyed on September 18, 1972, to try to speak with Hugh Sloan, his trip to Northern Virginia took far longer than expected "in the rain," he got "soaked" searching for Sloan's house, and when he finally returned "a few hours later" to speak with Sloan after he arrived home, the campaign treasurer "let Bernstein step out of the rain and into the hallway." Except, again, it was hardly pouring rain that day. The total precipitation recorded that evening by the National Weather Service was 2/100ths of an inch in the 4 p.m. hour and 4/100ths of an inch in the 5 p.m. hour. Unless there was a Linus-like rainstorm hovering over Sloan's house alone, those totals would have been barely a few passing drops of rain, hardly the punishing, multi-hour downpour Bernstein relates. Other examples of dramatic detail fail to line up to recorded weather reports too.

as Deep Throat. Did that potted palm incident ever happen? [Apparently Bradlee is referring to the flowerpot on the balcony.] That seems like a dumb [inaudible] to me. And meeting in some garage? One meeting in a garage? Fifty meetings in a garage? I don't know how many meetings in the garage." Continuing a few moments later, Bradlee added, "There's a residual fear in my soul that that isn't quite straight."

The quote—and any underlying concerns Bradlee had about the full veracity of Deep Throat's story arc—never made it into his memoir, *A Good Life*, and the quote lay buried until biographer Jeff Himmelman uncovered the interview transcript in Bradlee's files in 2010.* Himmelman, who had been a researcher for Woodward before he began the Bradlee project, confronted Woodward with the quote, and over days of conversation, he, Bradlee, and Woodward all chewed it over. Woodward, Himmelman wrote, seemed "frantic" and "shaken" over Bradlee's doubts, even though it's clear from the broader context that Bradlee was only concerned about the veracity of Woodward's tradecraft, not the information or existence of Deep Throat.

The star reporter pleaded with Himmelman not to publish the quote from his former editor. As Woodward said, "Don't give fodder to the fuckers."

*   *   *

While it may have been the most popular, *All the President's Men* was hardly the only damaging report on the president's activities that month. In late June, the Ervin Committee finished and released its 1,094-page report, which outlined all manner of White House scheming in exhaustive detail but stopped short of assigning responsibility directly to the president. As Ervin said, "You can draw the picture of a horse in two ways. You can draw a very good likeness of a horse, and say nothing, or you can draw a picture of a horse and write under it: 'This is a horse.' We just drew the picture."

---

* In an appropriately mysterious Watergatian twist, the original tape of Bradlee's 1990 interview with Feinman is the only one of a dozen such lengthy interviews for his memoir that Himmelman found was missing.

The literature of Watergate was piling up fast, thousands of pages of hearings, testimony, evidence, books, and transcripts. "It is no time for slow readers," the *New Yorker*'s Elizabeth Drew noted. The consensus, however, remained largely the same; as the *Washington Star*'s Jack Germond wrote, "The smoking pistol has yet to be found in President Nixon's hand."

On June 21, Tip O'Neill plopped down in a seat on the House floor next to Pete Rodino. It was time to act, the majority leader told the judiciary chair.

"Get off my back," Rodino shot back.

"Get off your back? I got 240 guys on *my* back. When are you going to move?" O'Neill snapped.

That night, dining at the D.C. institution Duke Ziebert's, O'Neill retold the story and added how much respect he'd gained for Rodino: "When the rest of us are all forgotten, [Peter] is the one who will be in the history books." The next day, Rodino came to the majority leader and handed over a timeline. The countdown clock had started.

On June 24, the committee wrapped its grueling hearings, spending its last hours fighting over whether to call witnesses of its own or whether St. Clair should be allowed to call defense witnesses like Colson, Haldeman, Ehrlichman, and Dean. Rodino, though, sensed now the committee would vote for impeachment and didn't want to upset the delicate momentum for Nixon's removal. The committee also voted to release its evidence publicly ahead of the final impeachment vote, giving the American people a complete understanding of what had been seen behind the locked door of Room 2141.

As St. Clair began two days of counterarguments on June 27, Rodino almost upset that delicate balance himself, when, speaking off the cuff to reporters in his House office during a lunch break, he speculated that all the committee Democrats would vote to impeach and that they would win five Republican votes. Jack Nelson ran the remarks the next day in the *Los Angeles Times*, causing an instant furor. Republican members of Congress decried Rodino's "bias," and the White House even said he should be "discharged" from overseeing the inquiry. Chagrined, Rodino quickly disavowed the story, but Nelson's report was backed up by other reporters who had heard the same thing. Rodino instead offered to appease his Republican colleagues by subpoenaing the witnesses St. Clair wanted to present. That defense, though, wouldn't amount to much: In a party-line vote, the committee decided to take the witness testimony behind closed doors. One anonymous Republican member of the committee told the *New York Times*' James Naughton, "Things have gotten out of hand, but I'm afraid they're going to get worse."

*   *   *

All spring, the Nixon team had been digging for dirt on Rodino, hoping that it could smear the inquiry chair and show he'd engaged in improprieties similar to those charged against Nixon. In June, they seized a unique opportunity: At the Allenwood prison where Jeb Magruder was being held, the former campaign staffer sought out a onetime representative, Neil Gallagher, an old Rodino ally who himself had started a two-year prison sentence in June 1973 stemming from tax evasion charges. Allenwood was as close to a federal country club as prisons got—just four buildings in the Pennsylvania hills, with no walls or guard towers—and in June, Magruder cornered Gallagher while the two men played tennis, to ask if he had scandals to share. "If you could do anything to help, the President would be able to do something for you," Magruder promised. "When we come up with something on Rodino, the public will be so revolted that the president could make it through. You'd be out of here clean—with a pardon."

The ploy, like every other trick Nixon's circle had tried, failed.

Chapter 51

Impeachment

Richard Nixon arrived back in the United States from his Soviet Union summit at the beginning of July, timing his return to the minute, just as he had for his China trip, so his triumphant landing in Maine would make the evening newscasts. He told the crowd, "It's always good to come home to America," but the sentiment seemed empty. The House committee had finished its draft articles of impeachment just as Nixon returned from the summit. As the month began, though, a bipartisan impeachment looked unlikely. Republican members had begun to talk of perhaps just censuring Nixon and moving along, though the approach was publicly dismissed by the House minority leader. "What we are trying to do is to strengthen the Presidency one way or another, not weaken it," Representative John Rhodes said. "To censure the President and leave him in office would be doing the country a grave disservice. It would completely cripple the man and would be giving him the worst of two worlds."

On Tuesday, July 2, the House committee heard its first witness in its impeachment hearings. For ten hours, presidential aide Alexander Butterfield answered questions from John Doar, Albert Jenner, and James St. Clair, as well as assorted committee members, his testimony reinforcing the notion that Nixon was too much of a control freak to not know what was swirling around the Watergate actions.

Doar had always promised that at the right moment after he'd presented the cold, hard evidence objectively, he would adopt a more advocacy-oriented approach and put his own thumb—and opinions—on the scales. That moment finally arrived following Congress's traditional Fourth of July recess, when he and the inquiry's senior staff—Richard Cates, Bernard Nussbaum, Evan Davis, and Richard Gill—began presenting to the committee what they called "seminars," detailed sessions connecting the evidence and what it collectively might mean. By day, the committee heard from witnesses, and after, the staff ran such evening "night schools" that proved equally critical to developing the case.

Cates had believed since late November that the case for impeachment was there, and the subsequent months of new evidence and facts had only strengthened his resolve. He spent every breakfast, dinner, and evening of that first week in July sequestered with groups from two to a dozen members, walking through the robust and clear case for presidential misconduct. He excelled at connecting puzzle pieces, explaining the logic of evidence, and helping members fill in the motives and thoughts of the conspiracy participants based on known reactions and evidence. He laid out what was known—and, perhaps most helpfully, what didn't need to be known to understand events. He dissected the cover-up in detail, walking members through what would have been exposed at each stage of the burglary investigation had it been allowed to proceed unimpeded.

Had Nixon's team not stonewalled that first week, Cates explained, it all might have unraveled much quicker. "There would be an immediate realization that there was a relationship between CREEP and the burglaries that would no longer be hidden," he said.

*   *   *

The Supreme Court oral argument over the special prosecutor's subpoena for the sixty-four tapes had been set for 10 a.m. on Monday, July 8. The public had been allocated 136 seats in the court's grand chamber, as well as 27 seats that would rotate in and out every five minutes, and the crowd began forming on Saturday, stretching out onto the Capitol lawn across the street.

In readying for their big day, Lacovara had suggested to Jaworski that they wear the traditional morning coat with tails worn by the solicitor general before the court, to emphasize their role as the government's advocates, but Jaworski resisted. It was his fourth time before the court, and he felt that the formal outfit relegated him to a penguin. "If you keep it up, I'll show up in cowboy boots and jeans," Jaworski chided. He and Lacovara ultimately arrived at the court in conservative navy suits. It was a brutally hot D.C. summer day, humid and sticky already as the day's participants arrived, and the most popular man outside the court building ran the Popsicle cart.

As he arrived, Jaworski seemed confident in the case ahead. "Our brief is one of the strongest I've ever seen," he said. Over the past weeks, St. Clair had seemingly gathered up all manner of relevant and irrelevant arguments on behalf of the president and even floated the possibility that Nixon wouldn't abide by the court's ruling if it went against him. It was a shocking statement, but surely one that the court would weigh as it considered the case. Some of the arguments put forth by the president's attorney—including one that the request for twenty of the sixty-four tapes was irrelevant because Nixon had already released transcripts—seemed downright shabby. St. Clair had also included the argument that as an employee in the executive branch, Jaworski couldn't sue the president—an argument the special prosecutor saw as betraying the explicit agreement he'd made with Al Haig before taking the job.

Now the courtroom pulsed with the electricity that had accumulated over the last month—the justices were sharp and interrupted often. During Jaworski's opening hour of oral arguments, he was stopped 115 times and all told the justices asked 350 questions. It was clear the question of whether Jaworski could sue would be ignored in favor of the case's underlying merits. Jaworski framed the legal question simply, saying it went to the "heart of our basic constitutional system"—the justices, in short, needed to decide who could interpret the Constitution.

"We all know the President has embraced the Constitution as offering him support for his refusal to supply the subpoenaed tapes," the special prosecutor explained. "Now, the President may be right in how he reads the Constitution. But he may also be wrong. And if he is wrong who is there to tell him so? And if there is no one, then the President, of course, is free to pursue his course of erroneous interpretations. What then becomes of our constitutional form of government?"

Continuing on, he argued, "In our view this nation's constitutional form of government is in serious jeopardy if the President—any President—is to say that the Constitution means what he says it does, and that there is no one, not even the Supreme Court, to tell him otherwise."

St. Clair, his hands stately folded on the lectern, replied at his turn that the president's argument was narrower than Jaworski led the justices to believe: "The President is not above the law. Nor does he contend that he is. What he does contend is that as President the law can be applied to him in only one way, and that is by impeachment."

The justices were clearly dubious. If executive privilege was as powerful as Nixon argued and the only remedy was a formal impeachment process, Justice Marshall queried, how would anyone ever learn of or investigate presidential transgressions that deserved impeachment? "You lose me someplace along there," he said.

"Very few things forever are hidden," St. Clair replied.

Leaving court, Jaworski expressed confidence that he would prevail. At the White House, after, St. Clair expressed similar confidence to the president: Nixon, he said, would win.

Even as Jaworski, St. Clair, and Lacovara argued before the justices, a few blocks down the road, John Ehrlichman was on the stand in Courtroom 6 facing trial for the Ellsberg burglary, looking out at the other defense tables containing Liddy, Barker, and Martinez. In Alabama that day, Chuck Colson reported to prison—the first member of the White House staff to be incarcerated was given a new title: Prisoner #23226. He faced a one- to three-year sentence—the stiffest sentence yet.

The day after the Supreme Court showdown, Pete Rodino's committee released its 131-page line-by-line comparison between the tapes and Nixon's transcripts. The document revealed a mountain of important discrepancies, among them the March 22, 1973, conversation between Nixon, Mitchell, Haldeman, Ehrlichman, and Dean that left out entirely what investigators like Jaworski thought had been one of the president's most troubling statements of the entire scandal. "I don't give a shit what happens," the president had said on the recordings. "I want you all to stonewall it, let them plead the Fifth Amendment, cover up, or anything else, if it'll save it—save the plan. That's the whole point." The accumulation of a hundred omissions and damning edits was unmistakable:

Nixon was still trying to hide the truth—and the truth was worse than Nixon said.

As the week continued, Doar's staff began publicly releasing its "Statements of Information," laying out the evidence of the cover-up and the president's culpability. The first installment contained eight thick volumes, totaling 4,133 pages. While the analysis-free reports tried to avoid biasing readers, the actual effect was to make the scandal seem endless and exhausting. "The Rodino Committee released millions of words of information, but not a single sentence explaining the significance of the findings," the *Post*'s Barry Sussman recalled. A committee staffer complained, anonymously, to the AP that the volumes were like "a giant erector set. You have all the pieces but you don't have the instructions on how to put it together."*

On Thursday, John Dean took the stand in the impeachment hearings, to face James St. Clair. Nixon's defense team had long sought just such a public forum, thinking that they could dismantle and crush the former aide's self-serving cover stories, but cross-examination failed spectacularly. St. Clair tried repeatedly to undermine Dean's memory, only to have Dean keep correcting him on timelines and facts. When his time was up, the White House counsel sat almost stunned; slumped in his chair, staring at the ceiling, his eyes taking long blinks, he knew he'd wasted the big moment. California Democrat representative George Danielson told reporters after listening to Dean, "I think I have a clear, constitutional duty to vote for a bill of impeachment."

After Dean's testimony, Representative Hutchinson—the committee's senior Republican ranking member, whose stodgy style of address made him appear a relic—tried to strong-arm his GOP colleagues. "Republicans cannot vote for impeachment," he told them, instructing his colleagues to raise their hands if they intended to join the Democrats in pushing forward impeachment. The conversation quickly devolved in anger, as other members, like Tom Railsback, said they weren't sure what they might do and that any such effort was surely going to backfire.

---

* Nixon was more blunt—and angry—in his summation of the judiciary reports in his memoirs: "The quantity of the evidence was overwhelming, but its quality was weak; most of it had little or no direct bearing on my own actions."

Later, over lunch at the Capitol Hill Club, Railsback, William Cohen, Hamilton Fish, and Caldwell Butler began to talk openly among themselves about supporting impeachment. As a first step, they decided they wanted to sit through their own "night schools" with the committee staff, like those Cates had been holding to walk the Democrats through the available evidence. They too wanted to hear the best theory for impeachment firsthand.

* * *

That Thursday night, Nixon, his family, and a set of his daughter's friends took a sail on the *Sequoia*. Julie Nixon Eisenhower watched in dread as the president picked, distractedly, at his dinner. "Daddy, eat your steak," she said. Later, when the steward came by for dessert, she suggested to her father, "Have some apple pie."

The president shook his head.

"Have some ice cream," she tried, again.

The president declined.

She went ahead and ordered him ice cream and chocolate sauce anyway.

The next day, July 12, Nixon headed west to begin what was supposed to be a two-week working vacation in San Clemente. About an hour after he left the capital, a Washington jury announced that after just three hours of deliberations, it had found John Ehrlichman guilty of four of the five charges stemming from the Ellsberg break-in, including both conspiring to violate the civil rights of Dr. Lewis Fielding, as well as various false statements he'd made to investigators. Liddy, Barker, and Martinez were all found guilty too.

Hearing the news aboard Air Force One, Nixon groused. How could it be that Ellsberg, the leaker of top-secret information, had gone free while Ehrlichman, who had been trying to stop such national security threats, faced prison?

* * *

In the middle of July, just days before the final House Judiciary Committee presentation, Doar's colleague Bob Owen was still hard at work on the summation. The only problem was he just couldn't shake the sense that there was something he was missing. He dug out the colored chron cards again, looking at June 17, 18, 19, and 20, the week of the burglary. Finally, he spotted the hole—a dog, so to speak, that didn't bark. "Now this is awfully peculiar," he said.

The Presidential Daily Diary for Tuesday, June 20, the first day back at the White House from Key Biscayne, post-burglary, had noted breakfast at 8:40 a.m, then movement to the Oval at 9. One minute later: "The President met with his Deputy Assistant, Alexander P. Butterfield." It was just a three-minute conversation, with Butterfield exiting at 9:04 a.m. And then . . . nothing. The President of the United States had sat by himself for seventy-six more minutes, no one in or out, no phone calls placed or received.

Owen called in Doar and others. They looked again at the Tuesday cards, all laid out, and finally the pieces clicked together. During the hour that Nixon sat alone in his office, H. R. Haldeman, John Ehrlichman, and John Mitchell had gathered upstairs to chat, joined in short order by John Dean and Richard Kleindienst.

Then, according to the diary, as soon as the staff meeting broke up, Nixon had walked across to his hideaway in the Old Executive Office Building, where he met alone with Ehrlichman from 10:25 a.m. to 11:20 a.m. Six minutes later, he met alone with Haldeman, a meeting that had lasted until 12:45—the same meeting that, mysteriously, had seen eighteen-and-a-half minutes erased by a sinister force. None of it added up; Nixon and Ehrlichman both had said they never spoke about Watergate, and yet Ehrlichman had come right out of a meeting with all the senior staff the first day back after the burglary and walked right into the president's office. How could it not have come up? To Doar and Owen, it was the clearest sign they'd seen yet that Nixon was in on the cover-up from those first moments.

On July 19, in a 306-page "Summary of Information," Doar's team organized the misconduct they saw into four distinct articles of impeachment. There was the Watergate burglary cover-up; a "massive and persistent" presidential abuse of power involving the dirty tricks, eavesdropping, and burglaries; contempt of Congress for Nixon's stonewalling of subpoenas and withholding of critical evidence; and, lastly, Nixon's "willful" tax evasion and his failure to uphold the nation's laws.

Rodino understood that he needed to motivate the mild-tempered Doar before the July 19 hearing, and so he pulled the special counsel into his office to criticize him, saying the work thus far wasn't good enough, and that the committee was sick of hearing bland summaries of the evidence—*did they have a case for impeachment or not?* Then Rodino walked out, leaving a red-faced Doar stewing. As soon as the hearing started, committee members realized something was different; one Republican noted that Doar's jaw was firmly set as he went about outlining what he told the committee was the president's "central part in the planning and executing of this terrible deed of subverting the Constitution."

"My judgment is that the facts are overwhelming in this case that the President of the United States authorized a broad general plan of illegal electronic surveillance and that that plan was put into operation by his subordinates," he began.

No, the evidence wasn't perfect—they didn't have all the answers they might want, or every smoking gun about every corner of the scheme—but that, Doar argued over the course of ninety minutes, was precisely the challenge and brilliance of the Watergate scheme. "You find yourself down in the labyrinth of the White House, in that Byzantine empire where yes meant no and go was stop and maybe meant certainly, and it is confusing, perplexing and puzzling and difficult for any group of people to sort out," he said, the passion in his voice finally breaking out of months of passive presentation. "But that is just the very nature of the crime—that in executing the means, everything will be done to confuse and to fool, to misconstrue, so that the purpose of the decision is concealed."

He continued to lay out, among other damning moments, the odd inaction Owen had noticed in the chron cards of June 20, 1972, the morning that the cover-up appeared to unfold all around Nixon without his participation. "This is the first day that the president has come back faced with a possibility of certainly a very serious scandal within his administration. What does the President do while his people, his key advisors are discussing the matter? The president is alone in his office," Doar explained. "He does not participate, he does not inquire, does not question, does not search out for facts." In some ways, Nixon's instinct to launch a cover-up was reflexively human, Doar allowed, but his office and his responsibility and his power went far beyond what was acceptable for an ordinary American.

"I realize that most people would understand an effort to conceal a mistake, but this was not done by a private citizen and the people who are working for President Nixon are not private citizens," Doar said, by way of a conclusion. "This was the president of the United States. What he decided should be done following the Watergate break-in caused action not only by his own servants, but by the agencies of the United States, including the Department of Justice, the FBI, the CIA, and the Secret Service. It required perjury, destruction of evidence, obstruction of justice, all crimes. But, most important, it required deliberate, contrived, continued, and continuing deception of the American people." It was simple: "Reasonable men acting reasonably would find the president guilty." The committee was captivated and some were even convinced.

That night, driving home from Capitol Hill, Republican Representative Lawrence Hogan churned the testimony and evidence over in his mind. He was a solid Republican, running for governor in Maryland, but hearing the tapes and reading the transcripts had been a body blow for him, black-and-white evidence that the president had not been an innocent bystander. He realized he needed to vote to impeach. Arriving home, he told his wife. Her only response was a simple "Good." It was, however, Hogan recalled later, "the first direct political advice she'd ever offered."

The next morning, Sunday, July 21, Representative Tom Railsback went back through Doar's report, underlining page after page of the president's involvement, assembling for himself a damning portrait of a leader who had abused his power. He represented a largely rural district in north-central Illinois, spread along the Mississippi River, and knew that voting for impeachment might well mean the end of his congressional career, but the evidence he saw now was overwhelming.

Hamilton Fish too felt the weight of history upon him. The New York Republican had beaten G. Gordon Liddy in their district's primary in 1968 to represent the Hudson Valley, becoming a fourth-generation representative of a great New York dynasty.* He spent the weekend talking

---

* Hamilton, his father, grandfather, and great-grandfather were all named after Alexander, the friend of their ancestor Nicholas, who had fought in the Revolution alongside the Founder.

over the matter with his family—what, they pondered, did impeachment mean to the country and the presidency? Saturday, he listened again to the tapes at the Congressional Hotel, an exercise that left him confident he could vote for impeachment if it came to it.

Within days of Doar's summation, Texas's Jack Brooks, a longstanding Nixon critic who had kept a cigar firmly chomped in his mouth through the long hearings that spring, began to circulate his own draft articles of impeachment—condemnations of the president that were sweeping in scope and damning in tone. For many members, it was the first time that they'd considered in writing what the final charges against Nixon might look like—what, someday, perhaps soon, they might be asked to vote upon and link themselves forever in history for or against. The ferocity of Brooks's draft helped spur others to action, each trying to strike a more moderate and thoughtful tone. As one staff leader later explained, "That got the members thinking. They also began to wake up to the fact that they shouldn't leave it to Doar and the staff." Many turned to the committee's regular counsel, Jerome Zeifman, for help. Thornton holed up in a room at the Coronet Hotel and drafted a full list of the offenses that seemed to him to be impeachable.

That Monday, July 22, conservative Alabama Democrat Walter Flowers crossed paths in the Rayburn Building with Railsback, just a day after he'd underlined the Doar report. Both of them understood the delicate political calculus ahead—and the momentous global stakes of their own personal decisions. "I have a couple of guys," Flowers said. "Why don't you get your guys and we'll get together and talk about it." Railsback started calling his colleagues, asking if they were interested in joining the conversation; he told them, frankly, he had no idea who would show up.

The next morning, at 8:30, seven members gathered in Railsback's office: the three conservative southern Democrats long identified as the key for Rodino—Flowers, Thornton, and South Carolina's James Mann—as well as Railsback and three of his colleagues: Fish, Maine's William Cohen, and Virginia's Caldwell Butler. Everyone looked around and took stock, surprised by who was present and who wasn't. ("Butler [was] a very strong conservative from Virginia whom I never expected to see at that meeting," Cohen recalled.)

"Well, we know what we're here for—what are we thinking? Where are we?" Railsback began. Spread among a long black leather couch and chairs arranged around Railsback's office coffee table, the seven "maybes" talked as they ate pastries and nursed coffees. "Toss me a danish," Cohen said; Railsback threw one the length of the room.

Their conversation, as it turned out, was searching and distressing, but ultimately conclusive: Nixon had abused the office of the presidency and deserved impeachment. "We can all agree on those things. And if we hang together, we can make sure this passes on a bipartisan basis," Cohen recalled. "It wasn't really until that moment that I decided without any reservation I was going to vote for impeachment."

Railsback said he'd draft an article of impeachment alleging obstruction; Mann volunteered to tackle one about abuse of power. "It was a terrible butterfly-in-the-stomach day," Fish said.

It didn't take Nixon long to hear of the private meeting's outcome. Understanding the stakes, he called George Wallace to ask if he would lean on Flowers. Wallace offered only to pray for Nixon; he couldn't intercede. As he hung up the phone, Nixon turned to Haig: "Well, Al, there goes the presidency."

*   *   *

On that same Tuesday, July 23, Maryland's Hogan held a surprising fifteen-minute press conference, in which he announced that he would be the first member of the president's party to support impeachment. "The evidence convinces me that my President has lied repeatedly, deceiving public officials and the American people. Instead of cooperating with prosecutors and investigators, as he said publicly, he concealed and covered up evidence, and coached witnesses so that their testimony would show things that really were not true," Hogan said. "He praised and rewarded those who he knew had committed perjury. He actively participated in an extended and extensive conspiracy to obstruct justice."

Hogan argued that impeachment was the only right move—one necessary to protect the nation and the presidency itself. "Those who oppose impeachment say it would weaken the Presidency," he said. "In my view, if we do not impeach the President after all that he has done, we would be weakening the Presidency even more."

The last defenses were crumbling. Exhausted and emotionally drained, Rodino fell asleep that night on his office couch, while on the other side of the country, Nixon brooded. He had been prepared to lose one, perhaps two, but never all three of the Judiciary Committee's southern Democrats. He distractedly sketched notes for a major economic address, sitting in his study underneath a nearly century-old portrait of his mother, aged twelve. *What would she—born just three days into the presidency of Grover Cleveland in 1885—have made of her son, this moment, this America?* Nixon wrote, "12:01 A.M. Lowest point in my presidency, and Supreme Court to come."

Hours later, the court's decision would arrive before he even awoke.

*　　*　　*

In a job that had been lonely from the start, Leon Jaworski had never felt more alone than when he was awaiting the Supreme Court's ruling; he had gone up against the President of the United States, in the ultimate forum, and all he could do now was wait. His family had returned to Texas, and he was living alone at the Jefferson Hotel, no longer going consistently to the office. One particularly dark day, he told Jill Volner he was considering resigning. The staff, which had been won over gradually by their boss, tried to keep up his spirits by delivering supportive letters and telegrams twice a day to the hotel.

Jaworski's mood stemmed, in part, from the fact that he understood that either outcome from the Supreme Court posed risks to him, his investigation, and the nation at large. What if the Supreme Court ordered the tapes turned over and Nixon still resisted—or ignored the court entirely? What if the tapes were turned over and they were as damning as he feared—how could the nation navigate the unprecedented damage? He might not be able to indict a sitting president, but what if Nixon was about to be a former president? Could he plea bargain with the president for a resignation, as Elliot Richardson had done with Spiro Agnew the fall before?

He need not have worried. On July 24, Jaworski sat in the well of the Supreme Court chamber with Phil Lacovara and Jim Neal, who had been lured back from his Nashville law office to head the prep work for the looming September trial. They felt humbled before the high bench of the court as the chief justice and his colleagues filed out from behind the drapes and took their places across the bench. Justice itself seemed to hang in the air amid the pregnant silence.

Technically, there were two petitions before the court: *Case No. 73-1766, United States vs. Richard Nixon*, and the president's counter, *Case No. 73-1834, Richard Nixon vs. United States*, and the chief justice—understanding the importance of the case—had written the decision himself.

Point by point, Chief Justice Burger affirmed aloud the special prosecutor's case, beginning with his ability to sue the president. Then, he answered affirmatively that it was the Supreme Court's role to tell the president what was and was not constitutional. As he read, Jaworski watched the other justices. William O. Douglas, who had served on the court since the Great Depression, looked to be quite bored; Byron White, a Kennedy appointee, watched intently, drumming his fingers on the bench.

Everyone in the courtroom noticed Burger pause as he got to the key section, weighing for a fraction of a second the sense of history as he—the leader of one co-equal branch of government—sat in judgment of the head of another. Finally, he spoke: "Accordingly, we affirm the order of the District Court that subpoenaed materials be transmitted to that court," he said.

The order was unanimous. Jaworski had won, powerfully and without question.

The courtroom erupted. The steps outside were, as press reports said, "near pandemonium." Neal, a onetime college football player, had to steadily maneuver the special prosecutor to the car through the crowd.

It wasn't until he was ensconced in the backseat of the car, leaving the court, that Jaworski realized the magnitude of the victory. "The unanimous holding, I was convinced, had saved the country from an even more terrible trauma than it was experiencing," he recalled later. He celebrated by going to lunch and ordering a midday carafe of white wine. His dining companion, the journalist Teddy White, joined him, later writing, "He was an old man, today weary, tufts of white hair about the face of a friendly goblin, the voice firm, not precise, then again grandfatherly." There was, White noted, no elation in Jaworski's voice about the victory, but he clearly understood the momentousness of the occasion. As he sipped the wine, Jaworski told White, "What happened this morning proved what we teach in schools, it proved what we teach in colleges, it proved everything we've been trying to get across—that no man is above the law."*

* At the same time, lost amid the history of Nixon's undoing, was another point that would have profound impacts on future presidencies. "He won on a major constitutional issue," Lacovara later explained. "The Court ruled that executive privilege does exist. And it is not simply some judicially fashioned common-law evidentiary privilege, but a full-fledged constitutional privilege rooted in the separation of powers, albeit a qualified rather than absolute privilege."

Chapter 52

The Smoking Pistol

Out in California, the news of the Supreme Court's decision arrived before 8:30 a.m. local time and utterly stunned the president's circle. St. Clair had been confident he'd won the most important case of his career, for his most important client, in the most important venue in the country. Instead, he'd lost—resoundingly. The decision text, as he read, left no doubt: The tapes would have to be turned over if the president was to avoid a full constitutional breach.

Al Haig telephoned the president, still in his bedroom, to report, "Unanimous. There's no air in it at all." Nixon was furious, feeling completely betrayed by Burger, Blackmun, and Powell, three men he had put on the court himself. As he saw it, they had hurt not only him, but the presidency. He quickly called for a caucus with Haig and St. Clair in his study, and when Haig called Buzhardt a few minutes later, Nixon physically took the phone from his chief of staff. It was the first time he and his counsel had spoken in a long time. "There might be a problem with the June 23 tape, Fred," the president said. "Get right on it and get back to Al."

It took about an hour for the tape to be delivered to Buzhardt's office, where he took the reel from its cardboard box and began to listen. The conversation between Bob Haldeman and the president, the first on the tape, began immediately. Buzhardt's body filled with dread as the minutes passed. When the recording ended, he rewound and listened a second time.

"Now, on the investigation," Haldeman began, "you know, the Democratic break-in thing, we're back to the-in the, the problem area because the FBI is not under control, because Gray doesn't exactly know how to control them, and they have, their investigation is now leading into some productive areas, because they've been able to trace the money, not through the money itself, but through the bank, you know, sources—the banker himself. And, and it goes in some directions we don't want it to go. Ah, also there have been some things, like an informant came in off the street to the FBI in Miami, who was a photographer or has a friend who is a photographer who developed some films through this guy, Barker, and the films had pictures of Democratic National Committee letter head documents and things. So I guess, so it's things like that that are gonna, that are filtering in. Mitchell came up with yesterday, and John Dean analyzed very carefully last night and concludes, concurs now with Mitchell's recommendation that the only way to solve this, and we're set up beautifully to do it, ah, in that and that . . . the only network that paid any attention to it last night was NBC . . . they did a massive story on the Cuban . . ."

"That's right," Nixon agreed.

"—thing," Haldeman finished.

"Right," Nixon repeated.

"That the way to handle this now is for us to have Walters call Pat Gray and just say, 'Stay the hell out of this . . . this is ah, business here we don't want you to go any further on it.' That's not an unusual development . . ."

"Um huh," Nixon grunted.

". . . and, uh, that would take care of it."

"What about Pat Gray, ah, you mean he doesn't want to?" Nixon asked.

"Pat does want to. He doesn't know how to, and he doesn't have, he doesn't have any basis for doing it. Given this, he will then have the basis. He'll call Mark Felt in, and the two of them . . . and Mark Felt wants to cooperate because he's ambitious."

"Yeah," Nixon agreed.

"Ah, he'll call him in and say, 'We've got the signal from across the river to, to put the hold on this.' And that will fit rather well because the FBI agents who are working the case, at this point, feel that's what it is. This is CIA," Haldeman opined.

The conversation continued for some time—none of it any better for the president. Quite the opposite, in fact—toward the end, Nixon himself had weighed in on strategy, suggesting to his chief of staff, "When you get in these people when you . . . get these people in, say: 'Look, the problem is that this will open the whole, the whole Bay of Pigs thing, and the President just feels that'—ah, without going into the details . . . don't, don't lie to them to the extent to say there is no involvement, but just say this is sort of a comedy of errors, bizarre, without getting into it, 'The President believes that it is going to open the whole Bay of Pigs thing up again. And, ah because these people are playing for, for keeps and that they should call the FBI in and say that we wish for the country, don't go any further into this case,' period!"

There was no mistaking the conversation's intent, nor its potential for damage. The White House had intended to stonewall the FBI investigation from the start, and Nixon was in on it. Just the week before, James St. Clair had argued the opposite to the House Judiciary Committee.

Buzhardt put down the headphones and sat there for a minute. *School's out*, he thought, before calling Haig. "Well, we've found the smoking pistol," he said, unequivocally.

"Are you sure?" Haig asked.

"Yes, it's the ball game," Buzhardt replied. "The president ought to think about his options."

The president spent the entire day churning over the court and its implications, talking with Haig and St. Clair for hours. There was no path forward, he finally understood, but full compliance. At this point, the options had seemingly narrowed to three very bad ones: be impeached for refusing to hand over the tapes, be impeached after turning over the tapes, or resign preemptively. After eight hours of public silence, St. Clair and the Western White House addressed an eager, expectant press corps, pledging the president would abide by the court's decision: "The President has always been a firm believer in the rule of law."

*　　*　　*

That evening, across the country, in Washington, the House Judiciary Committee members began to unify around two articles of impeachment—obstruction of justice and abuse of power—and left open the possibility of a third, obstruction of Congress, focusing on the president ignoring the congressional subpoenas. Railsback and others had convinced their colleagues that ancillary issues like the bombing of Cambodia and tax fraud didn't warrant a place in the debate. The three conservative Democrats and the seven Republicans, a group that had dubbed themselves "the Unholy Alliance," had come together around those first two articles of impeachment. "A lot of the real nuts and bolts were put together by [South Carolina's James] Mann," one participant said later, but the Unholy Alliance's draft was publicly introduced by Massachusetts representative Harold Donahue, the committee's second most senior Democrat, who had known the president since they served together in the navy in World War II. The final paragraph of each article had been written by Jerry Zeifman: "Wherefore, Richard M. Nixon, by such conduct, warrants impeachment and trial and removal from office."

Through the day, America waited for the proceedings to begin. Fifi Clay, a Nixon supporter from Covington, Kentucky, had secured the first spot in line after spending the preceding night on the ground outside the Rayburn House Office Building; she and twenty-two other members of the public were ushered into Room 2141 to see the debate. Committee staff, press, members of Congress, and others filled the room's blue chairs. Everything about the event seemed historic. Press received special green passes, while Walter Flowers wore jaunty red, white, and blue saddle shoes. Many members wore blue shirts for the occasion, which would show up better on television.

At 7:44 p.m., Rodino gaveled the committee into session. Then, for the benefit of the crush of photographers, he hit the gavel twice more.

In a rare move, he spoke first, laying out the history that had brought Congress and the country to this moment. "Make no mistake about it. This is a turning point, whatever we decided. Our judgment is not concerned with an individual but with a system of constitutional government," he said. "Let us leave the Constitution as unimpaired for our children as our predecessors left it for us."

Freshman representative Elizabeth Holtzman was next to speak, calling the resulting evidence "a seamless web of misconduct so serious that it leaves me shaken."

"I am overwhelmed by the stark contrast [the Constitution] present to the president's words and actions," Holtzman said. "Nowhere in the thousands of pages of evidence presented to this committee does the president ask, 'What does the Constitution say? What are the limits of my power? What does my oath of office require of me? What is the right thing to do?' In fact, those thousands of pages bring to light things that I never even dreamed of."

California representative Jerome Waldie for his turn concluded, "Common sense tells you that a President of the United States does not condemn the payment of over $400,000 to seven people occupying a D.C. jail because they have committed a burglary unless he wants something from them," and Virginia Republican Caldwell Butler spoke, sadly, about the state of the presidency and the nation, saying that he would vote to impeach, "but there will be no joy in it for me." The gangly, good-natured Butler had been a strong Nixonite—supporting the candidate throughout his campaigns and earning his own congressional seat on the president's coattails in the '72 landslide. "For years we Republicans have campaigned against corruption and misconduct," he had told the committee, "but Watergate is our shame." Syndicated columnist Mary McGrory, who would win a Pulitzer for her columns covering the impeachment, called Butler's words "the single most fiery and liberating sentence spoken" throughout the Watergate investigations, as Butler became "the first Republican to slash the comforting myth that somebody else, of unknown party origin, was to blame."

Drafting and revising the specific articles continued through Thursday and Friday, the hearings seeming to alternate between historic solemnity and a grand circus. Bomb threats interrupted debate regularly, and police bodyguards had taken to following Rodino wherever he went.

Amid member after member's dire and dark statements, New York's Charlie Rangel tried to reframe the evening's discussion as a sign of national strength. "Some say this is a sad day in America's history," he said. "I think it could perhaps be one of our brightest days. It could be really a test of the strength of our Constitution, because what I think it means to most Americans is that when this or any other President violates his sacred oath of office, the people are not left helpless."

*   *   *

Despite two years of burgeoning controversy and spreading scandal, there had always remained at the core of Nixon's world a certain confidence—the idea that both because he was Richard Nixon, the politician whose phoenixlike ability to rise from the ashes always surprised his critics, and because he was the president, bathed in the office's unique mystique, he would manage to power his way through the worst. He'd always imagined, in Garment's words, that the dog would talk. The White House stood still in shock as it realized that that confidence no longer held true.

And there was still the matter of the tapes. St. Clair faced the difficult task of negotiating a schedule to hand over the tapes to Sirica's court—on their way to the courthouse Friday, his assistant, Jack McCahill, thought he'd never seen his boss so worried and upset, clearly concerned that Nixon might still not comply.

Jaworski asked for an aggressive schedule to receive the tapes: twenty conversations in two days, twenty-one more within six days, and the final twenty-three within ten days, arguing he needed them quickly to prepare for the scheduled September trial of the Watergate Seven. Over seventy-five minutes, he and St. Clair hashed out a compromise, setting the special prosecutor up to receive most of the tapes within eight days—provided, that is, Nixon agreed, but as they prepared to wrap up, Sirica himself added a condition. The judge insisted that St. Clair himself listen to the tapes; he knew that the White House lawyer had been industriously avoiding the liability and responsibility that would come from hearing the tapes himself, but doing so would bind him ethically and morally as an officer of the court to ensure their accuracy and the president's full compliance. He tried to protest the judge's order, saying he was "a poor listener." Sirica held firm until St. Clair agreed.

"Now I think we're getting somewhere," Sirica said, closing the meeting.

*   *   *

The House vote came down on Saturday night, July 27. Doar's presentations and evidence proved, in the end, to be enough. Amid the many voices on the Judiciary Committee, just ten of the votes really mattered: The so-called Unholy Alliance, of the three conservative Democrats targeted from the start by Rodino and the seven Republicans. Alabama representative Walter Flowers was the last to speak. "There are many people in my district who will disagree with my vote here. Some will say that it hurts them deeply for me to vote for impeachment. I can assure them that I probably have enough pain for them and me," he said.

In a final attempt to stall or disrupt the debate, New Jersey representative Charles Sandman, a lit cigar before him on the dais, offered a series of amendments to strike each paragraph of the impeachment article one by one—but then backed down after he realized he lacked the necessary support. Rodino called for the vote; in the Byzantine language of House proceedings, his actual words gave little sense of their historical importance. "The question occurs on the substitute offered by the gentleman from Maryland, as amended," he instructed the committee, turning to clerk Jim Cline for the roll call vote.

As it began, reporters noted that three members appeared close to tears. One by one, every member of the committee stood before history. A ripple of murmurs coursed through the crowd of three hundred in the hearing room as Wisconsin Republican Harold Froehlich cast a yes, and the first no, from Republican Edward Hutchison, seemed to observers to be almost "buoyant," as opposed to the more "mournful" assents. The seven Republican members of the Unholy Alliance, whose cooperation and negotiation had brought the country to this moment, each voted in turn.

"Mr. McClory?"

"Aye."

"Mr. Railsback?"

"Aye."

"Mr. Fish?"

"Aye."

"Mr. Hogan?"

"Aye."

"Mr. Butler?"

"Aye."

"Mr. Cohen?"

"Aye."

"Mr. Froehlich?"

"Aye."

A few minutes after 7 p.m.—reporters differed whether it was precisely 7:05 or 7:07—the House Judiciary Committee adopted an article of impeachment against the President of the United States; the vote was a resounding 27–11.

The spell that had settled over the room was broken when the House sergeant at arms slipped up to Rodino to report that a plane had just left National Airport on a kamikaze mission to crash into the Rayburn Building. Rodino ordered the room evacuated, and he and Doar retreated together into the chairman's office. Word then came that there was no kamikaze plane. Rodino—the cautious, conservative congressman who had once wanted to write songs and poems—finally stood from his chair and left the office, to be alone as he was overwhelmed by tears.

Nixon had just finished a swim in California when he received word of the committee's vote. The man set to become the first president impeached in 106 years got the news barefoot, standing in a trailer, wearing old pants and a blue windbreaker with the presidential seal. As he walked back to the compound with his daughter, Tricia noted what a wonderful woman her mother was. Nixon agreed and thought about how much she'd been through in the last twenty-five years, in and out of politics: "God, how she could have gone through what she does, I simply don't know."

*   *   *

On July 29, Vice President Ford, Tip O'Neill, and other golf aficionados in the congressional leadership flew to Worcester, Massachusetts, to play in the Pleasant Valley Classic. O'Neill teased Ford as he was late to the plane, having been caught up reviewing drapes for the new vice president's mansion at the Naval Observatory: "What are you bothering with that for? You're never going to live in that house—you're going to be living on Pennsylvania Avenue."

Ford's response was quick: "Don't talk like that."

Once in the air, the House Republican whip, Les Arends—an Illinois farmer who had first arrived in Congress in 1935—went off with Ford to the private compartment at the back of the plane. "Jesus, Jerry, do you have any idea how serious this thing is?" he asked. "You could be the new president very soon." Arends was hardly expressing a secret or a controversial opinion—the president's departure was an open topic of conversation across town. Mississippi representative Trent Lott, whose district had recorded the nation's most pro-Nixon vote in the '72 election, told reporters, "Secretly, maybe all of us are hoping for resignation, and maybe I care enough for my colleagues to think that's the best course."

That same evening at 11 p.m. the Judiciary Committee approved a second article of impeachment, charging the president with abuse of power. The next day, July 30, it approved a third, charging obstruction of Congress, and voted down two others—one focused on the bombing of Cambodia was rejected in part, as Cohen said, because Nixon's actions were partially driven by "sloth and default on the part of the Congress," while the fifth article under consideration, on tax fraud and the president's personal finances, was rejected 12–26. The committee's debate had stretched for nearly thirty-five hours.

On Monday, as the House debated, John Connally, Nixon's friend and the man he'd hoped to choose as his vice president and eventual successor in '76, was indicted, as part of the milk price fixing scandal, on five charges, including accepting a bribe, obstruction of justice, and perjury, the last of the Nixon dominos to fall.

Nixon, furious over what he saw as the railroading of a friend and ally, called the Justice Department to demand that Henry Petersen had to go. The deputy attorney general, after consulting with Attorney General Saxbe, explained that it was too late. Power is ephemeral, and cities like Washington that live and die on its use develop a finely tuned ability to sense the subtle shifts, murmurs that become stampedes, ripples that become tsunamis. And so it was a capital that had not even heard the "smoking pistol" tape—was not, even, largely aware of the existence of the "smoking pistol"—that sensed the impending end of Richard Nixon. Nixon might still be president, but he had lost the moral authority to make such moves. "Tell him to go piss up a rope," Saxbe said, colorfully.

The next afternoon, around three-thirty, James St. Clair took the first batch of twenty tapes and went to John Sirica's courtroom. At 3:48, he handed the tapes over, as subpoenaed by the special prosecutor, ordered by the U.S. District, and affirmed by the U.S. Supreme Court. At the same time, from 3:25 to 4:26, Nixon met with treasury secretary William Simon and his economic advisor, to discuss Simon's recent trip through the Middle East and Europe. Later, Simon would tell reporters he had never seen the president as calm, confident, and strong as that afternoon. In the moment, as they gathered in the Oval Office and the White House photographer snapped a picture, no one knew the significance of the gathering. It was the last "presidential" meeting that ever appeared on Richard Nixon's official calendar.

*   *   *

Everyone in Washington seemed physically and emotionally shattered as July ended—the press, Congress, the White House, the investigators. On Capitol Hill, the committee staff began to prepare for the coming debate on the House floor. They expected to have just three weeks to prepare a final report outlining the charges and evidence for impeachment with the floor debate scheduled to start August 19.

Day by day, the president's core of support in the House and Senate lessened; the White House had originally counted upon thirty-five to forty hard-core Nixon supporters who would vote to acquit in the Senate—he needed at least thirty-four—but the jurors who would sit in judgment were considerably less sure of the president's prospects at trial. Wednesday, Tennessee senator William Brock estimated the president's floor was closer to twenty to twenty-six votes. Barry Goldwater too lamented that there didn't appear to be a way to avoid calamity: "If the president wanted to listen, he would have listened already." Across the board, among aides and family, Nixon's ultimate culpability had set in. "He's guilty as hell," Haig told aide David Gergen.

Both Haig and St. Clair had finally been convinced of the existential peril of the June 23 tape. For St. Clair, it had taken three listens before he seemed to grasp the context, the players, and the timeline enough to see the damage to the president and the defense he'd mounted to the House committee earlier that month. Haig had still only read Buzhardt's transcript, but for him, it was sufficient: "He had given the order that legitimized, in the minds of his underlings, everything that they subsequently did to cover up the Watergate crimes." St. Clair and Buzhardt now explained to Haig their professional obligations: They were in possession of knowledge that the president had misled the court, and if the president didn't come forward himself, they had to do so independently.*

The doubts and the end-of-the-line feeling had finally reached the president too. Nixon wrote in his diary, "We have to try to work out what we can do to live out whatever life I have left as president and thereafter in a decent way." If he was impeached and removed from office, there were not just political considerations to address, but personal ones as well—he would lose his presidential pension and the federal allowances for staff support, including the government money due his widow when he died. There was also the question of his own legal liability; at what point after leaving office would he face criminal charges, and what might those be? Perhaps, Haig had reasoned, a resignation—an unprecedented, humiliating announcement of guilt—would serve to mollify the crowd crowing for a pound of flesh. "By resigning, he might preserve his health, some fragment of his reputation, and the possibility of winning back the good opinion of his fellow citizens," Haig recalled thinking.

Thursday morning, Nixon told Haig he had decided. "Al, it's over," the president said. "We've done our best. We haven't got the votes." The president's plan, he explained, was to escape to Camp David for the weekend with his family, explain his decision to them, announce his resignation Monday night to the nation, and then spend perhaps two weeks wrapping up his presidency before departing Washington. Haig

---

* It's worth noting that in this final full week of Nixon's presidency, accounts and recollections get muddy; across the half-dozen central memoirs, including Nixon's and Haig's, and the books that record this moment, like Woodward and Bernstein's *The Final Days*, there are conflicting accounts of who said what in which meeting, who read or listened to the June 23 tape on which day, and so forth. There are even contradictions about Haig's actions between his own memoir and *The Final Days*, where he was clearly an integral source. The arc of all the stories, though, is the same: The foundation of Nixon's presidency unraveled steadily as the week progressed, meeting by meeting, conversation by conversation.

cautioned against such a long glide path, recommending that perhaps Nixon would be better served to leave before the "smoking pistol" tape became public.

"No, it will be Monday," Nixon said, his voice almost gentle. "Get Ray Price working on a resignation speech."

Chapter 53

The Final Days

The American presidency always exists on two levels, one flesh and blood, one spiritual—there's the president, a human who embodies the title temporarily, subject to election or other life event, and the presidency, a perpetual office and constellation of powers and responsibilities that continues ever onward, guided by the Constitution's Twenty-Fifth Amendment, which ensures it is never vacant.

It was on August 1, 1974, arguably, that the two roles—the man and the office—began to fully separate, the presidency departing Nixon and floating, nebulously, for a few days as Haig and others maneuvered Nixon's politically impotent and fatally wounded presidency to Gerald Ford. "The clock had stopped in Richard Nixon's White House," Haig recalled in his memoirs. According to those memoirs, Nixon gave only the loosest of instructions to his chief of staff; in what Haig says was the only conversation they ever had about the transfer of the presidency, Nixon told him, "Al, you've got to tell Ford to be ready. Tell him I want absolute secrecy. Tell him what's coming. Explain the reasoning. But don't tell him when."

On that Thursday, over a series of conversations, Haig explained the situation to a reeling vice president. The June 23 tape, he said, would be the end. ("You should prepare yourself for changes in your life," Haig said.) They spoke, briefly, about the pardon powers of the presidency, and Haig seemed to dangle a request for a deal, to which Ford, wary, wondered aloud abstractly what might be the options available to what he referred to as "a president." Haig presented a typed-up rundown of possible options for Nixon, ranging from fighting through a trial to resigning in exchange for a pardon, and asked which course of action Ford would recommend. The vice president, thinking quickly, refused to engage. "Al, I don't think it would be proper for me to make any recommendations at all. I am an interested party," he said.

After Haig left, Ford slumped, angry and disappointed, in a chair; the president had lied to him. "The hurt was very deep," he recalled later. An aide who walked in on him moments later recalled that he looked like a man thunderstruck.

Down Pennsylvania Avenue, the president's staff understood that they needed Nixon's most ardent supporters to declare a cease-fire. The first to be told was California Republican Charles Wiggins, who had cheerleaded the president's defense on the Judiciary Committee. St. Clair summoned him to the White House and urged him to read the transcript—then read it again and again and again. Each time, Wiggins's dread spread. "That's extremely damaging information to the president," the congressman finally said. "It's a bombshell. It established a count of obstruction of justice. You ought to be considering the possible resignation of the president." Upon returning to the Hill, Wiggins surveyed the work he'd been doing when St. Clair summoned him—spread across his office were all the materials to prepare a vigorous defense of the president. Wiggins instead told his staff he was heading home. The tape, it seemed, would come out on Monday.

Friday night, Ford called Haig unexpectedly at the urging of his aides and read, stiffly, a prepared statement: "I want you to understand that I have no intention of recommending what the President should do about resigning or not resigning, and nothing we talked about yesterday afternoon should be given any consideration in whatever decision the President may wish to make."

Haig understood the awkwardly worded message: Ford was establishing, for the future record, that there was no deal in place nor negotiation underway about trading Nixon's presidency for a pardon. The phone call was, in its own way, Gerald Ford's declaration of independence. His political loyalty had ended; he now had to be concerned about his own ability to govern as president.

Meanwhile, Nixon told Bebe Rebozo of his decision as they sailed together on the *Sequoia*, before he told his own family. Rebozo, the ultimate confidant, one who had stayed loyal even as his own life and privacy had been upended by the investigations around the president, protested when his friend said the end had come. Nixon, Rebozo argued, still maintained the support of millions of Americans; the president countered with the political reality: "Millions" no longer mattered. His presidency hinged on the support of just thirty-four men, the votes needed to acquit him in the Senate. After dinner, Rebozo drifted away to talk with the yacht's crew, as he often did, and Nixon sat, alone, watching the Potomac and the capital drift by.*

*   *   *

In a country that had seen a few seemingly accidental presidents, men plucked from obscurity in the vice presidency and thrust into office by illness (Millard Fillmore) or an assassin's bullet (Chester A. Arthur), Gerald Ford stood alone as the only man ever to ascend to the presidency without ever being elected by the American people—neither as vice president nor as president—and there was probably no one more unhappy about his impending elevation than he was himself.

Born Leslie L. King, Jr., the son and namesake of an awful, abusive father whom his mother had fled just sixteen days after their son's birth in 1913, Ford had eventually taken the name of his mother's hardworking and far more amiable second husband. Always affable and well liked, "Junie Ford" first glimpsed Washington, D.C., after winning a high school contest as the most popular senior in Grand Rapids, Michigan, and the experience of watching the House at work from the visitor's gallery was part of what inspired him to become a lawyer. He was a Hall of Fame football player at the University of Michigan, whose college yearbook

---

* That day, John Mitchell lamented to *Newsweek*'s Hal Bruno, "The president does understand the dimension of the problem. They miscounted the Supreme Court. They miscounted the Judiciary Committee. Now, for the first time, they are counting accurately and it is too late in the game." The former attorney general explained he expected a resignation within a week or ten days, but there was no guarantee: "The only thing that could stand in the way is the President being neurotic or crazy enough to let everything fall in on him."

finished a string of compliments by recording, "We can't find anything really nasty to say about him."

He had been just a few months out of Yale Law School when Pearl Harbor was attacked, and he enlisted in the navy the next day, bravely serving aboard an aircraft carrier in the Pacific Theater during the war, before returning to Grand Rapids to practice law again at the city's top firm. "People believed in him," his biographer later wrote. "Whether it was his earnestness, seriousness of purpose, readiness to listen, genial nature, or other qualities, there was something about him as a boy and a young man that brought people to see promise and possibilities." Soon, he was headed to Congress, having defeated a decade-long incumbent in the Republican primary; he was married that fall to his wife, Betty, in shoes still muddy from campaigning earlier in the day. He loved being in the House of Representatives, the arm of the federal government that by structure and culture bore the closest relationship with the people it governed.

There his unwavering support throughout the president's scandals had stemmed from more than just friendship; at a basic level, he trusted the president and all the denials. "You have to believe the president, and I did believe him," Ford said later. "He had never lied to me."

Now, in the nine months that he'd been vice president, he'd come to love the job; it was the first time in his political career that his schedule was his own—not operating on a calendar developed by the opposition party—and given how much he loved the mechanics of the federal government, the role had opened up a new, powerful, and fun world. He'd devoured the briefings on world affairs from Henry Kissinger, Brent Scowcroft, and others, and kept up a grueling domestic travel schedule that to others would have seemed a form of punishment, crisscrossing the country on a stubby, noisy, twin-propeller Convair VC-131H. ("He deliberately fled Washington, very deliberately," his aide Bob Hartmann explained later.) It had been an appealing position, but it was all about to change.

He had broken the news to Betty over a bourbon and water at home: "Either we will go to the White House next week, or we'll be dangling for six months while the impeachment process takes place." Together, the two Fords prayed. They held hands and said, "God, give us strength, give us wisdom, give us guidance as the possibility of a new life confronts us." The decision was made.

Ford's first congressional victory in 1948 had been a rare Republican win in a cycle that saw Truman reelected and Democrats sweep the House and Senate. He had always remembered seeing on Truman's desk, during his first visit to the Oval Office, the little plaque saying, "The Buck Stops Here." It was, Ford would recall, "a good description of a President's job." Soon, it seemed, that weight would be his.

*   *   *

After long, halting, and dispirited conversations with his family in the White House residence, Richard Nixon decided in a stunning display of denial and stubbornness to forge ahead. Sitting before a crackling fire in the residence even as the air-conditioning ran around them, his family and Rebozo—who was as much as family, if not more—reviewed the transcript for themselves and then told him that they believed there was enough ambiguity in the words on June 23 that he shouldn't resign prematurely. Richard Nixon, his feet up on an ottoman, still wearing his suit and tie as he debated his future, was a survivor.

"Let them impeach me," Nixon later told Haig over the phone. "We'll fight it out to the end." Nixon would grit it out and hope for an acquittal at trial in the Senate. He had been saved before from apparent political death—the memory of his Checkers speech loomed large for him that weekend, a moment when he had turned peril and ruin into one of the defining and proudest victories of his career. Perhaps he could do it again. Perhaps he was one brilliant speech away from turning the tide. *Perhaps the dog will talk.* The family sat quietly for a few moments, and Nixon finally asked the room: "Was it worth it?" After, they left him, alone, smoking his pipe, staring into the fire.*

Haig, the press team, and the legal team leaned together against the oar, knowing the fight was futile. "There is nothing so tiring as

---

* Even the most stalwart staff were beginning to give up. Buchanan, the most loyal of loyal, had even refused to take a midnight phone call from Julie Eisenhower Friday night; he told his wife to explain he was asleep.

unproductive work, and Saturday was a long, hard frustrating day," Haig recalled later. After the president and his family left for Camp David, Haig and his wife went to the Kennedy Center to watch Eugene O'Neill's *Desire Under the Elms*, they and the Kissingers sitting in the presidential box, perhaps weighing whether their remaining access to such perks was measured in hours or days. Haig realized later that he had no memory of watching the play at all.

On Sunday, the final volunteers left on Nixon's barricade begrudgingly journeyed to Camp David, including Haig, Ziegler, St. Clair, Price, and Buchanan. As the week ended, all of them had concluded that resignation was inevitable, but beyond that issue, St. Clair was increasingly concerned that the ongoing efforts to fight might expose him and the other aides to obstruction of justice charges. It became clear that the staff could no longer voice the full-throated and uncompromising defense the president wanted, and their work reflected it.

"Damn it, Al, this is not what I asked for," Nixon said after reading over a statement draft. He pushed on the chief of staff his own hand-written notes, sketched on one of his ubiquitous yellow legal pads, about the message he wanted delivered Monday alongside the tape's release.

"It's no use, Mr. President. We've been at it hammer and tongs all afternoon and this is the best we can do," Haig said he replied. "The lawyers will jump ship if I ask them to change it."

Nixon, Haig recalled, glowered. "The hell with it. It doesn't really matter. They can put out whatever they want."

As he left, Haig reflected on the sadness of the moment. The president, he thought, had lost the power to demand the words he wanted on a White House statement. His own words were no longer his. The presidency was gone.

Sunday afternoon, Haig called the House minority leader, John Rhodes, who had scheduled a press conference for Monday to announce his ongoing support of the president. He told Rhodes that the White House was preparing to release new information and encouraged Rhodes to remain on the sidelines.

The press corps was told that, unfortunately, Rhodes had a cold and had to postpone the press conference. He would have to stay home and silent all day, as Washington roiled.

*   *   *

The president decided that he would take his family out on the *Sequoia* as the tape of his June 23 conversation with Haldeman was released; he wanted to ensure that none of his family had to watch the evening newscast. America wouldn't actually hear the tape itself for more than two years, but the written transcript released Monday afternoon was bad enough. "Well here it is," Tip O'Neill said, as he began reading the paper copy aloud to colleagues on the House floor. "Confession is good for the soul, but it doesn't save the body."

St. Clair spent the day circulating among congressional meetings, handing over and explaining the transcript as best as he could, while Haig met with an auditorium full of White House staff, explaining that he hoped everyone would remain in their roles in the days ahead, "if not out of loyalty to the President, then out of loyalty to the nation." As Nixon left the White House for the yacht and the isolation available on the Potomac River, staffers lined up to respectfully cheer their president. He walked among them awkwardly, summoning his deepest reserves for human emotion, shaking hands, thanking them, unsure who was supposed to be cheering whom.

Aboard the yacht as they cruised, his family noticed that their husband, their father, their president, was now referring to his tenure in the past tense, saying, "It has been fun having use of the yacht."

On the six o'clock news, Representative Charles Wiggins finally announced publicly that he felt the president should resign or else the "magnificent career of public service of Richard Nixon must be terminated involuntarily." The remaining no votes on the Judiciary Committee in turn announced their switch. Pete Rodino would be able to say when the full House took up impeachment that the committee was united against the president's abuse of power. Vice President Ford, for his part, issued a purposefully obtuse statement, explaining "the public interest is no longer served" by repeating his statement that "the president is not guilty of an impeachable offense."

The *New Yorker*'s Elizabeth Drew expressed the reaction of many when she wrote, "There is an inexplicable difference between the experiences of suspecting a lie and being whacked in the face with the evidence of one."

America, Drew noted, had come over the previous two years to sense its president was a liar, that Nixon's relationship with the truth was fungible and situational, but that the June 23 transcript proved that he had known all along—even participated from the very start of the cover-up. "I wonder whether the enormity of his lying has sunk in yet—whether we have, or can, come to terms with the thought that so much of what he said to us was just noise, words, and that we can no longer begin by accepting any of it as truth," she wrote that night.

Chapter 54

"A Day for Tears"

Though Nixon's presidency had days left, the spreading realization that his power had all but evaporated became apparent to him the morning after the tape's release. At a desultory cabinet meeting on Tuesday, Nixon's hand-chosen men seized control of the gathering from the president, who had hoped to focus on economic policy—perhaps, he suggested, he could even host a national domestic summit to combat inflation. "Mr. President, I don't think we ought to have a summit conference. We ought to be sure you have the ability to govern," Attorney General William Saxbe interjected. Even more remarkable was a secondary interruption by George H. W. Bush, the head of the Republican National Committee, who had been seated on the edge of the room as a courtesy: It was time, Bush told the party's leader, to resign.*

After the cabinet meeting, Haig phoned Barry Goldwater for the senator's assessment of the president's remaining support on Capitol Hill. "Al, the President has only 12 votes in the Senate," the Arizona senator replied, suspecting that Nixon himself was listening. "He has lied to me for the last time and lied to my colleagues for the last time." Goldwater's sentiment was widely shared; during their weekly policy

---

* Reflecting on the meeting, Kissinger would say, "It was cruel. And it was necessary. For Nixon's own appointees to turn on him was not the best way to end a presidency. Yet he had left them no other choice."

luncheon that day, the Senate Republicans, one by one, had voiced their frustration with how Nixon had misled them. Even as some pleaded with their colleagues to keep an open mind—in theory they might soon be jurors in Nixon's impeachment trial—there was a strong consensus that a delegation of party leaders needed to go to the White House to confront the president and push him to leave office. "If he doesn't resign now, serious harm will come to the country and the party," Massachusetts's Edward Brooke said. The assessment of the White House by the afternoon was that Nixon could count on just seven Senate votes—four Republicans and three Democrats.*

Even as attention focused on the White House, Watergate headlines continued to emit from the nation's courtrooms, new developments rushed out by the wire services: A key figure in the milk pricing scandal, Jake Jacobsen, was pleading guilty and would testify against John Connally; James St. Clair had also admitted, with all the necessary sheepishness, to Judge Sirica that nine of the sixty-four conversations demanded by the special prosecutor—and ordered to be produced by the White House in the Supreme Court's 8–0 opinion—were nowhere to be found. Either they had never been recorded or the tapes had been lost. It was hardly news that helped the president's case before Congress. Goldwater, frustrated by false new reports and rumors through the day, stormed into the Senate chamber, asked for the floor to speak, and then indignantly shook his fist at the press gallery above: "You are a rotten bunch!" He left the floor to applause from the visitor's gallery.

Seeing the sea change, Nixon continued to vacillate between defiance and reality; he talked with Haig for two hours, "chewing cud" as his advisors said, turning over the problem again and again, examining every option and every path. "I can resign and save everyone a lot of time and trouble," Nixon said, according to Haig's memoirs. "That's a temptation. On the other hand Al, I may just run it out, go through the Senate trial, put my defense on the record, accept conviction if that's what's in the cards, go on trial, go to prison, lose everything—but go

---

* Haig, when he heard of the pending move to send a congressional delegation to the White House, was horrified; he didn't believe that the legislative branch should be trying to dictate to the leader of the executive branch.

out with my head held high." The entire exercise, Haig recalled, was simply Nixon "struggling against the obvious." Even as the president spoke, the scenarios outlined clearly fell short of anything that would allow him to preserve his dignity.

After much internal debate, the president told Haig for a second time that he would resign, announcing it in a speech to the nation on Thursday. From there, he would depart the White House Friday morning and leave behind a resignation effective at noon. "That will put me over Chicago as Jerry Ford takes the oath," he determined.

At 5:15 p.m. that Tuesday evening, Nixon met with Haig and Ron Ziegler in his hideaway office. He passed along page after page of notes to guide a resignation address, words he had written alone. "I will do this without rancor and with dignity," he stressed. "I'll go out gracefully."

As Nixon's mind had churned that afternoon, he had made a comment that chilled his chief of staff: "You know, Al, you soldiers have the best way of dealing with a situation like this: You just leave a man alone in a room with a loaded pistol." As Haig recalled the allusion to suicide later, he said there was no doubt in his mind that it was the president speaking figuratively. He didn't imagine that the president was truly suicidal, but not all of the president's advisors were as sanguine about the president's rationality.

Members of Congress and defense secretary James Schlesinger also recalled a worrisome remark from December, when during one of the group meetings in the White House dining room with senators and representatives as part of the "Operation Candor" push, Nixon had blurted out a bizarre answer to a question about fighting Communism. "I can go in my office and pick up a telephone, and in 25 minutes, millions of people will be dead," the president had said.

The comment had "alarmed the congressmen because they were just afraid that under these tremendous tensions, this president might in effect 'flip' and that nuclear war might be the consequence," Democratic California senator Alan Cranston remembered, and afterward Cranston had called the defense secretary to warn about "the need for keeping a berserk president from plunging us into a holocaust."

Now Schlesinger again feared that a berserk president, who in comments like the one to Haig seemed depressed and perhaps even destructive, might order Armageddon. The truth was that there were no formal systems in place to prevent the president from unilaterally taking action and launching nuclear weapons. Moreover, Schlesinger and the chairman of the Joint Chiefs, General George Brown, both kept in mind the controversy over the October 1973 military alert amid the Yom Kippur War and the Saturday Night Massacre. They worried about a genuine emergency arising, as well as the possibility that the military might be used as cover or a distraction from Nixon's political troubles.

Quietly, the Pentagon chief implemented his own instructions, sending word to the nation's military leaders: *If the president gave any nuclear launch order, military commanders should check with either him or Secretary of State Henry Kissinger before executing.* It was not a legally or constitutionally correct order—Kissinger had no place in the chain of command, nor even did a military unit have to double-check with the civilian defense secretary a direct order from the president—but Schlesinger felt the nation's unprecedented situation, and survival, required it.

For decades, the propriety and very existence of such an order from Schlesinger remained a matter of debate. For years, there was no proof such an order even existed beyond Schlesinger's own word, but in 2020 I located the first possible proof: a front-line officer, posted in Cold War Germany to a unit with nuclear weapons on immediate, two-hour alert, who had been on duty the night of Thursday, August 8, and recalled clearly receiving just such an order. "The message was blunt," the officer recalled, requesting anonymity to speak about classified orders even almost a half century later. He paraphrased the order he saw that night in Bavaria: "'No troops shall be deployed unless co-signed by Dr. Henry Kissinger, Secretary of State. Please inform Command. Sent: James R Schlesinger, Secretary of Defense.'" The warning sparked a brief flurry of activity, as the unit debated its legality and constitutionality. In the end, the officer recalled, "my impression was that all agreed that this arrangement was not in accordance with the established chain, but since it came from the Pentagon, we were duty-bound to follow orders."

In the end, no alert came. No trouble arose. The final hours of Nixon's presidency would remain quiet across the globe.

*   *   *

In Washington, as the president weighed his future, political opponents and onetime allies alike assessed their next steps too. Gerald Ford, who hadn't yet spoken with Nixon about the president's decision, felt what was coming and directed his aide Bob Hartmann to begin writing an inaugural address. That night, over dinner at their Alexandria home, the vice president and his wife watched the evening news with Ford's friend and onetime law partner, Philip Buchen. The *CBS Evening News* announced, "The GOP gave up today on Richard Nixon." Ford told Buchen, "I think this will all be over in 72 hours or less."

In response, much to Ford's surprise, Buchen began to lay out the covert transition planning he and others had been working on for months. As suddenly appreciative as the vice president was of the work, he immediately realized he needed even more help than the handful of junior aides Buchen had recruited in secret. Betty Ford fetched her address book to gather phone numbers as Ford rattled off administration leaders and national political figures he wanted to enlist in a smooth transition. In his mind, the unprecedented change in leadership provided a key moment for the country, a chance to emphasize not the crimes of Richard Nixon but the resilience of American democracy.

By Wednesday, the press was frantic for answers, heaving heard rumors for days about the impending resignation. Ron Ziegler's team was besieged by questions in the White House press office, and on Capitol Hill, when Bob Dole was asked by a reporter if something big was in the offing, the senator replied, "It sure feels like it. There are too many people walking back and forth for something not to be going on."

Across Washington, the administration, and the White House the rush to wrap up the Nixon presidency and begin the Ford presidency had sped up in earnest. Behind the scenes, Haldeman and Ehrlichman lobbied for a blanket presidential pardon before Nixon left office for those associated with Watergate, channeling their requests through Haig, Julie Nixon Eisenhower, and Rose Mary Woods. While some loyalists felt the idea of executive clemency for the president's co-conspirators was a small price to pay if it eased and sped up Nixon's own departure, Len Garment and Fred Buzhardt expressed their concern that the move would so anger Americans that it would all but guarantee a criminal trial for the president after he left office.

That afternoon, Barry Goldwater, House minority leader John Rhodes, and Senate minority leader Hugh Scott went to the Oval Office to explain to the president that Nixon's support on Capitol Hill was all but gone. At Haig's urging, the House and Senate leaders stopped short of ever mentioning resignation, instead just emphasizing that the president could not count on more than a dozen votes to acquit in the Senate—perhaps even as few as four. "Mr. President, this isn't pleasant, but you want to know the situation and it isn't good," Goldwater said.

The president's mood shifted through the conversation, his initial calm facade giving way to something more approaching anger. "It's grim," said Scott, who kept an unlit pipe clenched in his teeth through the emotional conversation. Nixon later recalled that he winced "involuntarily" as the party leaders listed off the defectors, men Nixon had considered not just allies but friends. Upon leaving the White House, Goldwater told reporters, "Whatever decision he makes, it will be in the best interest of our country."

The Nixon staff began to talk openly about Ford's swearing-in, telling the vice president it would have to be small since it should be in the Oval Office. "The hell with what they want—it's what do you want? You are going to be president," Hartmann protested to Ford.

That evening, the Nixon family met in the White House solarium. "Your father has decided to resign," Pat told their daughters.

"We're going back to California," Nixon added.

Later that night, he summoned Henry Kissinger to the White House. ("It was the only time I ever saw HAK run," Kissinger's assistant later recalled.) When the secretary of state arrived, the president was alone in the Lincoln Sitting Room.* It was time for him to go, Nixon said. Through the night, he kept calling Ron Ziegler and Ray Price with edits to the proposed resignation speech. Tricia Nixon, writing in her diary, reported, "A day for tears. I could not control their flow. I did not even try."

* * *

---

* Kissinger's memoir says this meeting took place in the Oval Office, but *The Final Days* says it was in the Sitting Room.

On Thursday morning, Nixon met with Gerald Ford and informed him that he would ascend to the presidency the next day. "I know you'll do a good job," he said, seeming finally to relax. "It was like a burden had been lifted from him," Ford recalled later. Nixon rolled his chair away from the oversized desk, leaned back, kicked his feet up, and began to expound at length on what he thought his successor should know—observations on policy issues, strategies for geopolitics, and even tips for dealing with advisors like Kissinger. As incredible and historic as the transition would be, Ford found himself relieved. "For the previous nine months, I had been sitting on a time bomb," he recalled later. The national crisis had now come to a final resolution.

As the two men spoke, warmly, almost as friends, the White House shut down the presidential autopen, marking the end of "Richard Nixon" as president in routine business; there would be no more looping Rs and slanted Ns headed out on letters, proclamations, birthday wishes, anniversary celebrations, executive orders, nominations, and other correspondence. "To hell with it—let Ford do it," aide Stephen Bull had said, dismissively, when presented with the afternoon's pile of paperwork for the president's signature. In Alexandria, Virginia, police and Secret Service moved to block off the quiet residential street where the Fords lived. Nixon felt his power ebb. "A president's power begins to slip away the moment it is known he is going to leave," he recalled, thinking back to the three transitions he'd lived through in public life, Truman in '52, Ike in '60, and LBJ in '68. He knew that "my role was already a symbolic one, and that Gerald Ford's was now the constructive one."

Ford moved quickly, tracking down Chief Justice Warren Burger on summer travel in the Netherlands and dispatching an air force jet to fetch him to Washington in time for the next day's swearing-in. Then he began calling members of Congress to ask them to attend. "Are wives invited?" Tip O'Neill said. "I've already told Millie to pack her things and get down here."

"Actually, wives were not invited," Ford said, "but they are now!"

As the call wrapped up, the majority leader offered his former Capitol Hill colleague a wry observation: "Jerry, isn't this a wonderful country? Here we can talk like this and we can be friends, and eighteen months from now I'll be going around the country kicking your ass in!"

Nixon spent the remainder of his final day as president in his hideaway—sitting a final time in the brown chair in Room 175 of the Executive Office Building that had served as his getaway for so long—sorting through the legal questions surrounding his future, weighing and ultimately rejecting any final pardons while wondering whether he might face jail time himself. Haig, meanwhile, had met clandestinely with Jaworski at the chief of staff's home. Jaworski was careful to not tip his hand, and he stayed well short of anything that appeared to be a deal, but Haig left the meeting with the impression that Jaworski would probably not prosecute the president after he left office.

A few minutes after noon, Ron Ziegler went into the press briefing room and announced the day's milestones. "The President of the United States will meet various members of the bipartisan leadership of Congress here at the White House early this evening," he said. "Tonight, at nine o'clock Eastern Daylight Time, the President of the United States will address the nation on radio and television from his Oval Office." CBS's Robert Pierpoint sheepishly inquired after: "When Ron said 'the President of the United States,' did he mean President Ford or President Nixon?" Ziegler, who had been struggling emotionally with the unraveling of the administration and whose voice had cracked as he'd started speaking in the press room moments earlier, laughed and clarified: Nixon.

Chapter 55

"I Shall Resign"

For his final address as president, Richard Nixon picked out the same slate-blue suit he'd worn in Moscow in 1972; it was lightweight and would stay cool. After meeting with a solemn congressional delegation to tell them of his official decision, he settled into the desk in the Oval Office, under the hot television lights, and, one minute after 9 p.m., began his address. "This is the 37th time I have spoken to you from this office, where so many decisions have been made that shaped the history of this Nation," he told the television audience. "In all the decisions I have made in my public life, I have always tried to do what was best for the Nation. Throughout the long and difficult period of Watergate, I have felt it was my duty to persevere, to make every possible effort to complete the term of office to which you elected me. In the past few days, however, it has become evident to me that I no longer have a strong enough political base in the Congress to justify continuing that effort."

In a speech that mixed sadness and defiance, national duty and family, the thirty-seventh president of the United States explained that while he would have preferred to see through the impeachment process, he now believed it would be too difficult for the country given his weakness politically. "Therefore," he announced, "I shall resign the Presidency effective at noon tomorrow. Vice President Ford will be sworn in as President at that hour in this office." He then spent the remainder (and majority) of the sixteen-minute speech recounting his administration's five-and-a-half years of accomplishments, from the opening to China to the drawdown in Vietnam to peace in the Middle East. When the lights and camera turned off, he handed out the remaining engraved presidential souvenirs in his desk to the CBS crew who had filmed the address.

Gerald Ford watched the speech from his cozy living room in Alexandria, surrounded by his family. After, he spoke amid a drizzle to reporters on his front lawn: "This is one of the most difficult and very saddest periods, and one of the saddest incidents I've ever witnessed."

At 12:20 a.m., Len Garment's phone rang. He'd dined earlier that evening with Fred Buzhardt and former Nixon aide William Safire at D.C.'s tony Sans Souci, then watched the speech with them back at the White House. Now, to his surprise, Nixon himself was calling. "He was phoning old friends, making his disciplined rounds, saying good-bye, thanks for the help, sorry I let you down," Garment recalled. And indeed, it came: "I'm sorry I let you down, Len," Nixon said. All together, the president spent nearly two hours, until nearly 2 a.m., placing more than a dozen calls to supporters and friends. He slept little, continuing to work on his farewell speech, flipping through a nearby pile of presidential memoirs for inspiration.

The next morning, August 9, 1973, he deviated from his usual breakfast routine and asked for corned beef hash and poached eggs. Then, fortified, he signed the official resignation. David Gergen had drafted three different versions of the letter, each just one sentence long, before the speechwriters had settled on a final draft: "Dear Mr. Secretary: I hereby resign the office of President of the United States. Sincerely, Richard Nixon."

It was an act that Nixon hoped would spare him from further punishment, but Leon Jaworski made a point to publicly state such clemency was not guaranteed. "There has been no agreement or understanding of any sort between the President or his representatives and the Special Prosecutor relating in any way to the President's resignation," he announced. Nixon tried to joke about the threat, saying, "Lenin and Gandhi did some of their best writing in jail."

With his wife by his side, he said goodbye to the assembled staff of the residence and professional White House, then went to the East Room, which was filled with the cabinet and White House political staff. A military aide announced for the last time before his entrance, "Ladies and gentlemen, the President of the United States," and the Marine Band launched into a final rendition of "Hail to the Chief." People wept as the president thanked those who had served his administration and the nation at his side. It was a tortured, emotional speech, the president's eyes clearly moist as he drank in a final three-minute standing ovation, his hands gripping a lectern adorned by the presidential seal that would be taken from him just moments later. He spoke of the wonder of public service and the American presidency—and, holding back sobs, his admiration for his mother and her struggle to raise his family. He joked about his need to pay his taxes, and he told his staff to be strong. "Never get discouraged. Never be petty. Always remember, others may hate you—but those who hate you don't win unless you hate them, and then you destroy yourself," he cautioned, observations that seemed to come five-and-a-half years too late in his presidency.

Washington, the nation, and the world beyond watched the dramatic events unfold on television. At the *Post* newsroom, Bob Woodward ate a sandwich, his eyes fixed on the television screen, as Bradlee walked through the newsroom telling reporters not to gloat. John Dean watched filled with painkillers, recovering from the four wisdom teeth he'd had removed as part of the medical work he was getting out of the way before reporting to prison. Jaworski himself noted the president's apparent lack of remorse; the farewell remarks seemed better tailored to a president unexpectedly leaving office under far more favorable circumstances. "It was not the speech of a President who had violated his constitutional oath and duty by obstructing justice, by abusing the power of his office, by transforming the Oval Office into a mean den where perjury and low scheming became a way of life," he recalled later.

On Capitol Hill, Tip O'Neill marveled at how straightforward such a monumental political event turned out to be—in the end, the first resignation of an American president, driven from office by scandal, crime, and corruption had occurred with the same pomp and circumstance as any other presidential transition. "The whole world was watching, and other nations couldn't help but be impressed," the majority leader proudly realized. "Our transition was orderly and by the book."

At the White House, Gerald Ford bid the president goodbye from the South Portico. "Drop us a line if you get the chance. Let us know how you are doing," he said, stiffly, as if he were saying goodbye to a child headed to summer camp. Then, after a long walk across the lawn, Richard Nixon boarded the steps of Army One, the helicopter that would fly him away from the White House. At the top, he paused, turned, and surveyed the crowded lawn before him, filled with supporters who had sacrificed so much to help him. He flashed a triumphant, defiant victory sign, and departed, the helicopter rotors speeding up and the engine straining as it lifted off and away. At 11:35 a.m., with Air Force One winging toward the Pacific, already somewhere over the Midwest, came Al Haig's final act as Nixon's chief of staff: delivering Richard Milhous Nixon's resignation letter to Henry Kissinger, as decreed by law. Aboard Air Force One, Nixon ordered a martini.

Below him, the nation moved on. Looking down from the White House balcony, Defense Secretary James Schlesinger puffed on his pipe, standing with a White House chef and an NSC aide named David Michael Ransom. "I'm going to prepare lunch for the president," the chef said by way of a goodbye. The comment's sheer normalcy struck Ransom; one president had left, but the presidency moved onward. By lunchtime, there would be a new commander in chief.

The Fords, hand in hand, walked back into the White House, where they entered the East Room, now remade for his swearing-in as the nation's thirty-eighth president. Warren Burger, fresh from Europe, administered the oath of office, as Betty held the Bible, open to Proverbs 3:5–6, his favorite prayer: "Trust in the Lord with all thine heart; / and lean not unto thine own understanding. / In all thy ways acknowledge him, / and he shall direct thy paths."

After listening by radio to Ford's swearing-in, Ralph Albertazzie, the pilot of the iconic blue-and-white Boeing 707 carrying Richard Nixon to San Clemente, keyed his own radio: "Kansas City, this is Air Force One. Will you change our call sign to SAM 27000?" There was no president aboard any longer; the flight was now, according to the military, a simple Special Air Mission. Nixon finished the flight a private citizen, sitting alone in the padded swivel chair of his onboard office; his wife, similarly alone, sat in her own private cabin next door.

*　　*　　*

In a room packed with Nixon's cabinet, members of Congress, and representatives from the diplomatic corps, Ford addressed the nation at 12:05 p.m. "I assume the Presidency under extraordinary circumstances never before experienced by Americans. This is an hour of history that troubles our minds and hurts our hearts," he said. "I am acutely aware that you have not elected me as your President by your ballots, and so I ask you to confirm me as your President with your prayers. And I hope that such prayers will also be the first of many."

In an eight-minute speech, one he carefully explained was neither an inaugural address nor a fireside chat nor a stump speech but instead "a little straight talk among friends," Ford promised the nation and its elected and appointed leaders assembled before him his integrity and candor, asked for cooperation and help from Congress, and pledged to the world beyond "an uninterrupted and sincere search for peace," saying, "America will remain strong and united, but its strength will remain dedicated to the safety and sanity of the entire family of man, as well as to our own precious freedom."

Then, obliquely, he addressed the incredible story that had delivered him—and the nation—to this moment. "I believe that truth is the glue that holds government together, not only our government but civilization itself. That bond, though strained, is unbroken at home and abroad," Ford said. "My fellow Americans, our long national nightmare is over."

When Ford finished, the Marine Band played "America the Beautiful."

Nixon's Curse

At 7 a.m. on August 10, the new president appeared on his Alexandria doorstep in baby-blue pajamas, picked up the morning paper, and went inside for orange juice and an English muffin before beginning his first day as the leader of the free world. Though he had promised the American people closure from one of its darkest chapters, Watergate would not quite yet fade into history.

TIME's resignation special, filled with three times its normal number of pages, sold 527,000 copies on the newsstand—the most of any newsweekly ever, even more than the issue announcing the end of World War II—and the nation would remain fascinated by the story for a half century.

Weeks after Nixon left office, the House Judiciary Committee published its final report, 528 pages of detailed allegations documenting what it concluded were thirty-six instances of obstruction of justice. With the impeachment question moot now that the former president was out of office, the world waited anxiously to see if Jaworski would pursue a case. "Do you think people want to pick the carcass?" Nixon asked a confidant one day that summer, a question that was actually quite common (and complicated) among reasonable citizens. Had the political price of being forced from office served sufficient justice? The head of the American Bar Association lectured, "No man is above the law," but many—especially Republicans—were eager to move past the scandal. The idea of a former president spending years on trial and appeals, perhaps even heading to prison, seemed like an unnecessary national distraction.

At the Special Prosecutor's Office, Jaworski and his team wrestled with the question themselves—it became known as the "monkey problem," Richard Ben-Veniste and George Frampton recalled. "On whose back was the monkey going to end up: the prosecutors, Congress, the White House, the grand jury, the court?" Who would settle Nixon's fate? Posters went up in the office from the movie *King Kong*. Frampton and other prosecutors prepared a lengthy—and persuasive—memo arguing that prosecuting the president was necessary for the country and the rule of law. The public sentiment that Nixon had already suffered was not adequate when balanced against the judgment of history and the frameworks of the rule of law, the memo explained. "I do not think that the political system can 'walk away' from this one," deputy special prosecutor Henry Ruth agreed.

No one wrestled harder with the monkey than Gerald Ford, as press inquiries hectored the administration on whether he would offer a pardon. Behind the scenes, Al Haig—whom Ford had asked to stay on at the White House for a smooth transition—pushed for clemency. Ford was inclined to do so to halt the story and give his own presidency as much a chance as possible of moving beyond Watergate. "If eventually, why not now?" he asked in an Oval Office meeting on August 30. "Is there ever a right time?" The silence in the room as Ford refilled his pipe was so deafening that his chief of staff, Robert Hartmann, thought that the ticking antique clock in the Oval Office sounded like machine-gun fire.

On September 8, Ford announced his pardon, calling Nixon's actions "an American tragedy." Speaking solemnly from the Oval Office, he said, "Someone must write the end to it. I have concluded that only I can do that, and if I can, I must." The move was met with widespread national indignation; Ford's own press secretary resigned in protest and a cascade of telegrams and letters condemned the act of clemency.

When he first heard of the clemency during a telephone call with Ford, Tip O'Neill sputtered. "You're crazy," O'Neill protested. "This will cost you the election. I hope it's not part of any deal?"

"No, there's no deal," Ford said, adding that Nixon seemed emotionally fatigued and in a dark place mentally, broken by the impeachment ordeal. Plus, America didn't need a president in jail. "I don't think the American people are vindictive," he said. "Nixon has suffered enough. Besides, I can't run this office while this business drags on day after day."

Amid the public's outrage, many repeated O'Neill's question about whether there was a deal to deliver a pardon in exchange for Nixon's resignation, and indeed subsequent years would piece together something far murkier; Nixon may not have been explicitly promised a pardon, but such hints "greased Nixon's departure," his biographer Jay Farrell concluded.* Even the staff of the special prosecutor wondered what precisely Leon Jaworski and Al Haig had discussed during their "courtesy" meeting at Haig's house, just hours before Nixon announced he was leaving.

The former president offered what was supposed to be a conciliatory statement in response to the pardon, telling the American people, "That the way I tried to deal with Watergate was the wrong way is a burden I shall bear for every day of the life that is left to me." That burden did seem almost physically tangible that fall—he suffered a serious flare-up of his phlebitis and ended up hospitalized, lingering in grave condition for a few days before recovering enough to continue grumbling about his treatment.

That fall, the next of the major trials began. For thirteen weeks, the nation gawked as the most powerful men in Nixon's White House sat in the D.C. courthouse, at the defendant's table like common street crooks; on the first day of jury selection, a passerby spat on John Ehrlichman. "[They were] the flotsam of politics, now left behind on the beach by the wave that had carried them so high," Teddy White observed from inside the courtroom. "They fought hopelessly against the sound of their own voices played back on tapes." U.S. marshals assembled the trial's already imprisoned witnesses—Magruder, Kalmbach, Colson, and Dean—at a small facility near Baltimore, known as Fort Holabird, which usually was used to isolate at-risk mafia turncoats. "Welcome to the club, John," Magruder had said as Dean arrived at the small twenty-one-person prison. "This place almost looks like the White House."

* "I told him he would be pardoned if he resigned," Mel Laird said later.

In the end, John Mitchell, Bob Haldeman, and John Ehrlichman were all found guilty, as was Robert Mardian.* The verdicts and lengthy sentences from Sirica hit those involved hard. Ehrlichman was bitter. "If I had known Nixon was taping my conversations, I would have acted differently," he lamented, his sarcasm dripping. ("John takes things too personally," Nixon said, in response.) The court cases spooled onward for years. Beyond the trials of the core Nixon team, nearly thirty corporate executives pleaded guilty or were convicted of charges stemming from illegal campaign donations related to Watergate; three went to jail.

Even though he hadn't been on trial, the guilty verdicts crushed Nixon; he hid in his den, alone, for days and had trouble eating and sleeping. The men most loyal to him had all now either betrayed him or faced the consequences. Nixon bore his own literal cost too. The scandals had all but ruined him financially; he faced nearly a million dollars in legal bills, plus medical bills, his back taxes, and the pricey upkeep on the Casa Pacifica. At one point in 1975, Nixon was down to just $500 in his bank account.

Thus, the disgraced leader effectively dedicated the latter half of the 1970s to two large-scale legacy-making enterprises, designed to shore up his finances and begin rewriting the nation's memory of his presidency. The British talk show host David Frost offered $600,000, plus a chunk of any profits, to the former president for a series of lengthy recorded interview sessions that he would edit into a blockbuster television special. Nixon agreed.

The Frost/Nixon interviews were a national sensation, the most watched in television history with some 50 million Americans tuning in to soak up the president's words. Frost was a weak interviewer and Nixon a powerful filibusterer, but the series sparked headlines and controversy nonetheless as a largely unrepentant former president mostly batted away the idea that he'd done wrong. In one of his most elegiac soliloquies, Nixon lamented how distracted John Mitchell had been through the spring of 1972; his wife, who had died in 1976 of blood disease, had simply been too much for the attorney general. "I am convinced that if

---

* The final defendant, Kenneth Parkinson, was acquitted; Mardian's conviction was later overturned on appeal.

it hadn't been for Martha—and God rest her soul, because she in her heart was a good person, she just had a mental and emotional problem nobody knew about—if it hadn't been for Martha, there'd have been no Watergate. Because John wasn't minding that store. He was out of his mind about Martha in the spring of 1972! He was letting Magruder and all these boys—these kids, these nuts—run this thing."

He also argued he'd always had the nation's best interests at heart—trying to protect national security amid a time of turmoil and revolution—and that he'd always had the executive authority to do what he and his men did. "When the president does it, that means that it is not illegal," Nixon said at one point, to the shock of not only his interviewer, but the world beyond.

Next came the memoirs, sold for an eye-popping $2.5 million and drawing on ten thousand pages of White House diaries and thousands more pages of notes and re-creations put together by a team that included a young Diane Sawyer. The thousand-page volume raced to the top of the nation's bestseller list when it was finally published in 1978. He'd engaged with Watergate in the book only with great reluctance, fearful as always that the bad would overshadow all of the world-changing good he believed he'd done. ("For chrissakes, I don't even know Donald Segretti," he complained to his aides during the drafting.) To celebrate the book's completion, Nixon toasted from a bottle of brandy he'd only touched twice—once, with Kissinger, to mark the secret negotiations for the opening to China and a second time on his final night in the White House. "To the book and to the future," he said.

*   *   *

Richard Nixon, first in victory and then in defeat, remade the nation's politics for a half century. The electoral playbook he and John Mitchell developed in '68 and '72 has become the bible for decades of Republican wins since, but in the immediate aftermath of the scandal, the fall midterms ushered in a wave of Democratic lawmakers—dozens of new representatives and senators surged into Washington, many of them young enough that the class of 1974 was nicknamed the "Watergate babies." All told, there were ninety-two new members of Congress that season, including seventy-five Democrats. Their energy transformed the House and Senate, beginning a sea change that would upend the staid institutions, democratize power beyond the committee chairs, and usher in an age of transparency and watchdog journalism that would sharply limit the clubby days and comfortable, southern plantation–like atmosphere that had long permeated the building built by enslaved African-Americans atop Jenkins Hill in 1793. By the time Tip O'Neill became speaker himself in 1980, only 15 of the 289 Democrats predated his own arrival, and 3 in 5 had arrived in the 1970s.

Some of the most significant changes came when Congress began to reform the nation's privacy, surveillance, and intelligence laws to ensure that future administrations and agencies could never hark back to similar abuses of power. Senator Sam Ervin worked over the course of the year following Nixon's resignation to push through Congress three major bills that would rein in future presidents and block any further shenanigans: One sharply limited a president's ability to "impound" funds appropriated by Congress; a second stopped Nixon himself from gaining access to the recordings of his White House taping system and destroying them if he so desired. The third, the so-called Federal Election Campaign Act of 1974, followed through on reforming campaign financing and reporting requirements.

Beyond the presidency, the Watergate investigations also tore away the protective cloak of secrecy that had long kept politicians from delving too deeply into the work of the country's law enforcement and intelligence agencies. Nixon's protests through the scandal had been right in some respects: What he'd been accused of doing was part and parcel in many ways of what predecessor presidents had done. The difference had only been that Nixon had brought the work into the White House itself, removing the arm's-length deniability that had protected his predecessors. "The whole mess fell on Nixon," Bryce Harlow said later. "The White House had proven too big, too powerful, too irresponsible, too independent, too self-satisfied and arrogant." Neither the White House, the FBI, nor the CIA would ever be the same.

Idaho senator Frank Church led a new select committee to investigate what other illegal and reprehensible acts U.S. intelligence agencies had undertaken without congressional knowledge; a representative Otis

Pike took up a similar probe in the House. Both found plenty of areas of concern. The revelations from the Church and Pike committees that the CIA had spied on domestic political opponents, undertaken assassinations overseas, and even experimented with LSD on unwitting Americans further rocked the nation's already shaken trust in government post-Watergate; a series of reform efforts blossomed, and new, strict regimes of surveillance and intelligence powers came into force. "Watergate did what the Bay of Pigs had not: It undermined the consensus of trust in Washington which was a truer source of the Agency's strength than its legal charter," observed Thomas Powers, CIA director Richard Helms's biographer. "Watergate made the CIA fair game."

The abuses appeared equally systemic and rampant on the FBI's side, as Americans recoiled at learning the bureau had kept files on five hundred thousand Americans whose political beliefs it considered suspect. Altogether, it had run more than two thousand so-called Counter Intelligence Program (COINTELPRO) operations against not just Communist and hate groups but also civil rights organizers, women's rights advocates, and other civic reform groups. The fault for these abuses of the FBI fell, the Church Committee wrote, to "the long line of Attorneys General, Presidents, and Congresses who have given power and responsibility to the FBI, but have failed to give it adequate guidance, direction, and control." The first reforms, the Privacy Act of 1974, rewrote the government's compact with its citizens; others, like the Foreign Intelligence Surveillance Act of 1978, laid out tight controls about wiretaps and other investigative methods, a multi-branch system of checks and balances that would ensure no one would ever amass the power once solely held by J. Edgar Hoover.

Much of the reform effort unfolded under Gerald Ford's attorney general, Edward Levi, who found himself tasked with rebuilding and securing the nation's trust in the Justice Department and the FBI, which had been whiplashed by six attorneys general in less than six years (counting Bork's interregnum as the acting), two of whom had faced criminal charges and a third, Richardson, who had resigned amid the turmoil of Watergate. The new attorney general established what came to be known as the "Levi guidelines," which set clear, strict standards and boundaries around how and when the FBI could pursue domestic security and intelligence investigations and aimed to better balance the free speech protections of the First Amendment. Even the U.S. Postal Service issued a series of reforms, meant to limit the long-standing practice of "mail covers" that allowed the FBI and others to surveil the mail of targets and suspects.

One of the biggest cultural changes, though, came in the press. After a generation of journalists that had probably trusted government too much came a generation of journalists who seemed to believe that Watergates existed inside every government office and corporate headquarters. "This post-Watergate fervor left the feeling that the only government reporting worth doing was government screw-ups and venality," one media history explained.

Nixon left all his worst enemies emboldened. As journalist Teddy White wrote in his 1975 history of the era, *Breach of Faith*, the news media in the capital would never look at the White House the same again: "If Nixon has bequeathed to his presidential successors a permanently hostile news system, he has cursed them all."

White's worst fears indeed came to pass—and more.

*   *   *

The Watergate-related cases continued to play out in courts for years; a civil lawsuit by Morton Halperin against Nixon, Kissinger, Haldeman, and Mitchell for their illegal wiretapping of his conversations continued into the 1980s. Halperin, at one point, was awarded a symbolic $5 in damages for the violations of his Fourth Amendment right to avoid unlawful searches and seizures.

The national outrage over the government's abuse of Americans' civil liberties culminated in the indictment in 1978 of a trio of FBI leaders from the Nixon administration: Pat Gray, Mark Felt, and Edward Miller, who had headed the bureau's Domestic Intelligence Division. Prosecutors argued that the bureau officials had okayed a total of nine "surreptitious entries," what were known in the Hoover years as "black bag jobs," targeting members of the Weather Underground in 1972 and 1973, long after Hoover had put an end to the practice.

On November 1, 1980, Nixon himself took the stand; he had avoided testifying in all of the core Watergate trials, but volunteered to appear in the FBI trial, ironically to help defend two men—Gray and Felt—who had served him so poorly. Flush now with publishing monies, he even contributed to their defense fund.

"How are you employed?" the prosecutor asked.

"I'm retired," Nixon said.

"Were you once the President of the United States?"

"Yes," he said, smiling.

Over the course of his testimony, Nixon lectured the courtroom about the tension and drama of the early 1970s. "We were at war," he said. The operations okayed by Felt and Miller were part and parcel of Nixon's approach to governing and protecting the nation, and he didn't shy away from them at all. The FBI leaders had inherent authority, from him, to pursue investigations and protect the nation's security, he argued. The FBI was backed with the full power of the presidency. "It was the office, not the man," he said, drawing the same distinction he'd used in the Frost interviews: When the president does it, it's not illegal.

The jury didn't buy it. Both Felt and Miller were found guilty. Felt, speaking to reporters after on the steps outside, said, disheartened, "I spent my entire adult life working for the government and I always tried to do what I thought was right and what was in the best interest of this country and what would protect the safety of this country. Obviously the jury didn't agree with me."

President Reagan ultimately issued both men full presidential pardons. Following the pardons, Nixon sent Felt and Miller a bottle of champagne. The accompanying note from the president read, "Justice ultimately prevails."*

*   *   *

The mythology of Watergate—and specifically the mythology of the press in Watergate—began quickly. The movie version of *All the President's Men*

---

* Gray was deeply bitter over the charges, feeling betrayed—again—by his country and also betrayed by Felt and Miller, who he long argued had kept knowledge of the black bag jobs from him in the first place. Prosecutors ultimately dropped the charges against Gray, feeling that they couldn't prove he'd actually approved the alleged break-ins, and since he was never charged in the Watergate cases himself, he and his family would wage a decades-long fight against how Gray was usually lumped in with the villains of Watergate, including on the cover of *All the President's Men*.

debuted in 1976, with Robert Redford portraying Woodward, Dustin Hoffman as Bernstein, and Watergate security guard Frank Wills playing himself. Hal Holbrook, who played the shadowy unknown figure of Deep Throat, stole the movie and launched the quest to identify the real-life counterpart into a decades-long obsession. The film introduced the maxim "Follow the money," a line that no one ever said during the scandal but that would become one of its most associated lines. The film met huge critical success, opening at number one at the box office; when its premiere happened in D.C., at the Kennedy Center, Gerald Ford sent the *Post*'s Katharine Graham the tickets for his presidential box and had its refrigerator stocked with champagne.

The Nixon pardon effectively cost Gerald Ford the '76 election, just as Tip O'Neill had known it would. Seven percent of voters reported voting against him explicitly because of the pardon. "The spirit of this country has been damaged by Richard Nixon and Gerald Ford," the victorious Jimmy Carter proclaimed. The only time Gerald Ford ever appeared on a national ballot was when the nation's voters returned the incumbent president to Michigan. Asked, after losing, if he would have pardoned Nixon knowing the full cost, Ford pensively replied, "I think I still would have."

Smaller, but no less consequential details of Watergate continued to trickle out for years, thanks to the booming tell-all industry fueled by its key players. Haldeman sold a two-hour TV interview for $100,000 and wrote his memoir in prison while working maintenance in the sewage plant, a job suggested by Ehrlichman because of its copious free time. Dozens of the key players would pen their own versions of the truth in the years ahead, some, like Richard Kleindienst's *Justice* and Bud Krogh's *Integrity*, laying claim to virtues and character traits that were often in short supply during their actual tenures.

Almost alone among the defendants of Watergate, Mitchell never asked for quarter. He never gave evidence on co-conspirators, or wrote a book later. He took his sentence in stride. "It could have been worse," Mitchell said. "They could have sentenced me to spend the rest of my life with Martha Mitchell." The man now known as Federal Prisoner No. 24171-157 tried to make clear he was still in a joking mood as he became the highest-ranking U.S. government official ever to report to prison. "It's nice to be back in Alabama," John Mitchell told reporters as he arrived at the federal prison camp on the grounds of Maxwell Air Force Base outside Montgomery.

With time, many of the witting and unwitting star figures of Watergate faded from public view. Jeb Stuart Magruder and Chuck Colson both found faith amid their time in political purgatory, emerging as inspirational religious leaders—Magruder became a Presbyterian minister in Ohio, while his former colleague founded a prison Christian evangelical ministry fellowship.

Sam Ervin retired from the Senate after the '74 election, heading out on the lecture circuit. America, in the years ahead, would see him again in American Express ads; the joke of the ad was that now that he wasn't in the Senate anymore, the exclusive credit card helped him ensure he was treated like someone important.

Pete Rodino, who would come to be seen as such a hero that strangers would offer to buy his coffee, crossed paths with Richard Nixon only once in the quarter century following Watergate. While commuting to Washington from his hometown in Newark, Rodino was told by the airline that his usual first-class seat, 2B, was already taken. Upon boarding, he noticed Nixon sitting quietly there. Rodino simply walked past. "I didn't say a word to him, but I figured it was fair," Rodino said, telling the story years later. "I had taken his seat, so he took mine."

Congressman Tom Railsback, on whose conscience so much of the House Judiciary Committee debate hung, died in January 2020, just as the U.S. Congress was wrapping up what would turn out to be the first set of impeachment charges against the forty-fifth President of the United States, Donald J. Trump, an era that seemed to harken a brief resurgence of Nixon's men, as dirty trickster Roger Stone became a key player and pundits like John Dean, David Gergen, Bob Woodward, and Carl Bernstein filled the nation's TV screens again to pontificate and argue over impeachment and presidential malfeasance.

In the final weeks of writing this book, G. Gordon Liddy, the last of the burglars, Eugenio Martinez, and Hal Holbrook, the actor who played Deep Throat in *All the President's Men*, all died. Their deaths were widely reported, but others had faded into obscurity long before. By the time James McCord died, aged ninety-three, he had so disappeared from the national radar that his death went unremarked by the media for two years.

Other personalities chose to disappear from the public eye in their own way. Tony Ulasewicz left New York City for upstate, where he took up raising chickens. He named the smartest one "Sirica."

* * *

Though the American people seemed generally satisfied by the outcome of the Watergate investigation, some figures—namely Gordon Liddy and John Dean—would continue to excavate its depths for decades, even clashing directly during a decade-long libel lawsuit over Dean's precise role in and motivations around the burglary.

Recently, the conversation found new life as more Nixon tapes were released, more documents were uncovered, and long-buried records were unsealed. After a decades-long guessing game, Mark Felt outed himself as Deep Throat in a 2005 essay in *Vanity Fair*; hobbled by age and memory, he never meaningfully spoke about his decision to cooperate with Woodward.

Today, we'll never really know the full truth of Watergate. The remaining mysteries are spread among too many people, many of whom are now dead, their secrets buried alongside them. There remain big, unanswered—and perhaps now forever unknowable—questions even about the central Watergate break-in itself: Who ultimately ordered it? What was the actual purpose and target of the burglars? Were its central players, Hunt and McCord, cooperating with the CIA even as they carried out the operation at the DNC's offices? Were the burglars really after political intelligence or were they hunting for blackmail material?

Haldeman, speaking decades later, said, "No one here today, nor anybody else I can identify, knows who ordered the break-in at the Watergate or why it was ordered." Ehrlichman, for his part said, "The break-in itself made no sense to me; it never has."

* * *

In the early 1980s, as the final chapter of the Felt/Gray/FBI saga played out, the Nixons moved back east, with the thirty-seventh president returning to the New York stomping grounds where he'd spent his wilderness years two decades earlier. He was ready, again, for a fresh start. "A man is not finished when he is defeated. He is finished when he quits," Nixon had said in a pre-move visit to the Big Apple, when a columnist visited him in the Waldorf Towers. "The greatest test is not when you are standing, but when you are down on that floor. You've got to get up and start banging again."

The man who had done so much for so long to confound those who wrote his political obituaries, only to be brought low by his own demons, threw a mock punch and said again, with enthusiasm, "Get up and start banging again!"

Acknowledgments and Methodology

I t was impossible to write this book without feeling the symbolic weight of the story of Watergate in American history and in the history of publishing too. The idea for the book grew out of a single offhand comment made by Jonathan Karp: "I've always thought Watergate's a really complicated story, and there's not really a good one-volume that tells it." Three years later, it seems fitting that the book should emerge from a Simon & Schuster now helmed by Jon Karp himself—the publishing house that more than any other has told the story of Watergate since its original landmark volume in 1974, *All the President's Men*. Over the last half century, Simon & Schuster has published multiple drafts of that history, including memoirs by key Watergate players John Dean, Maureen Dean, and John Ehrlichman; prosecutors Richard Ben-Veniste and George Frampton, Jr.; CIA director William Colby; Julie Nixon Eisenhower; and Richard Nixon himself. It has published seminal journalism and history texts including Woodward and Bernstein's *The Final Days*, Richard Reeves's *President Nixon: Alone in the White House*, Robert Sam Anson's *Exile*, Stephen Ambrose's three-volume Nixon biography, and Walter Isaacson's *Kissinger*, among many others.

Every time I sat down to research, write, and revise, I waded into that deep, long stream of history; many reporters reported, researchers researched, writers wrote, and publishers published to make this book possible. They've all remained interested for so long because Watergate remains one of the biggest, most fascinating stories in American politics, and its fingerprints on our capital, politics, and nation are evident in ways big and small.

Throughout the twenty years that I've worked in and around politics, Watergate's shadow has been ever-present, and I've had the chance to cross paths with many of the story's key players. In the late 1990s, as a Senate page for one of the original "Watergate Babies," Pat Leahy, I served scandal figures like Daniel Inouye, Ted Kennedy, and Fred Thompson, and one of my first jobs in Washington was in the Watergate itself. One of the first big stories I covered as a media blogger (remember blogs?!) for FishbowlDC was the revelation of Mark Felt as Deep Throat; later, Jack Limpert, who first guessed Deep Throat, was my first editor in D.C., at the *Washingtonian*, where Spiro Agnew's long-ago press secretary Vic Gold was also a colleague. I remember distinctly covering one Nixon-related event at which Daniel Schorr spoke up from the audience and began, "Well, as someone who was on Nixon's enemy list . . ."

As a magazine editor myself, I've had the chance to publish Watergate snippets and reporters and researchers who have sliced off their own bit of this vast story—Max Holland, one of the great independent researchers on Watergate, Craig Shirley, Tom DeFrank, and others.

In 2012, when I wrote a history of the FBI, I found myself in a studio across from G. Gordon Liddy on his radio show, the former agent still fascinated by the bureau, and when I was at *Politico*, photographer extraordinaire David Hume Kennerly first told me the wild story of Martha Mitchell over breakfast at a Marriott in New York, sparking a fascination that would only grow in the years ahead. During the Trump years, I often found myself a guest on CNN alongside John Dean. And, of course, Bob Woodward today still drives the national political agenda— his latest book, with Robert Costa, topping the bestseller lists as I write this—and the type of journalism he and Bernstein pioneered has set the tone for today's confrontational press. It was hard to escape the feeling that all of them—and many others—were peering over my shoulder.

My goal was not to re-investigate; not to re-plow every furrow of Watergate. I believed from the start that there was no single Rosebud moment to come—grasping the full story of this scandal didn't lie in the umpteenth interview, fifty years after the fact, with a key player who had already spent decades telling, refining, and positioning his story. Personal accounts by now are inescapably colored and affected by the years of passing revelations, claims, counterclaims, disputes, and feuds that mark so much of the Watergate landscape. It's also become increasingly hard to distinguish the interviews people give from the myths and legends that have agglomerated as the story has grown more complex and competitive. As such, I purposefully chose not to conduct fresh interviews. Instead, my approach was to rely on the voluminous existing primary and secondary sources and to tell the story based on the documentary archival record. In the process, I cross-checked sources and sifted through the story both as it was contemporaneously recorded and as it's been revised by later releases of information and documentation.

I'm deeply indebted to the hundreds of historians, journalists, and archivists who have come before me. I want to note and acknowledge in particular a small canon of Nixon and Watergate books that helped guide and shape my research in ways far beyond what my endnotes might otherwise indicate.

Nixon is a well-documented and almost insanely thoroughly biographized president. Beyond the aforementioned texts by Richard Reeves and Stephen Ambrose, four others in particular stand above the rest: Tom Wicker's *One of Us: Richard Nixon and the American Dream*, Tim Weiner's *One Man Against the World: The Tragedy of Richard Nixon*, Evan Thomas's *Being Nixon: A Man Divided*, and John Aloysius Farrell's magisterial *Richard Nixon: The Life.* They are simply the best of a crowded class.

Similarly, there are four canonical books on the scandal itself: Barry Sussman's engaging and insightful *The Great Cover-Up: Nixon and the Scandal of Watergate*, from 1974; J. Anthony Lukas's 1976 classic *Nightmare: The Underside of the Nixon Years*, which managed to capture so much so early; Stanley Kutler's 1992 classic *The Wars of Watergate: The Last Crisis of Richard Nixon*, which still stands as the preeminent exegesis of the scandal; and Fred Emery's 1994 *Watergate: The Corruption of American Politics and the Fall of Richard Nixon.*

Ken Hughes was the first to piece together the definitive story of Nixon's trickery amid the 1968 presidential campaign with his *Chasing*

Shadows: The Nixon Tapes, the Chennault Affair, and the Origins of Watergate.
The story of Mark Felt would be impossible to write without the man-
ifold contributions of Max Holland, whose *Leak: Why Mark Felt Became
Deep Throat* provided such rich new understanding of that era. Amid the
gazillions of words written about Watergate, Melissa Graves, a professor
at The Citadel, is about the only one to dive deeply into the work of the
FBI investigators, and I found her *Nixon's FBI* invaluable. James Doyle's
Not Above the Law is an engaging and informative inside tale of the Watergate Special Prosecution Force; Richard Cohen and Jules Witcover's *A
Heartbeat Away* tells the Spiro Agnew story in rich detail; Howard Fields's
High Crimes and Misdemeanors is a useful and often overlooked volume on
the House Judiciary Committee's work in the spring of 1974. I would
be remiss not to mention that Elizabeth Drew's *Washington Journal* was
probably the most fun book I read in my research.

Rick Perlstein's tetralogy on modern conservatism, including espe-
cially the middle two volumes, *Nixonland: The Rise of a President and the
Fracturing of America* and *The Invisible Bridge: The Fall of Nixon and the
Rise of Reagan,* are particularly useful for understanding this moment in
American politics, as is—always—Teddy White's *Making of the President*
series.

Stanley Kutler dedicated years of his life to fighting for a more robust
record of Watergate—initiating an important lawsuit with Public Citizen that forced the release of hundreds of hours of the Nixon tapes—as
has Tim Naftali, who in his previous role with the Nixon Library did
an enormous amount to push to tell the full story of Watergate and to
capture, in his numerous and invaluable oral histories, the accounts of
key participants. There are three published volumes of tape transcripts
painstakingly assembled by Kutler, Douglas Brinkley, and Luke Nichter
that stand as a gift to history. Ben Wittes, Jack Goldsmith, and Stephen
Bates fought for the release of the "Impeachment Road Map," what they
called the "last great still-secret Watergate document," in 2018.

*   *   *

Researching a book heavy on archival materials in the midst of the
Covid-19 pandemic was no small challenge, and yet I had some amazing

luck along the way. Barely an hour after my emailed request, Lee Cloninger at Duke University's Goodson Law Library was able to provide me with incredible primary source materials from Howard Fields's unparalleled research into the Rodino committee. I've long believed that America's presidential libraries are some of the greatest national treasures we have, and the Richard Nixon Presidential Library and Museum, in Yorba Linda, California, offers great online resources. Their digitized collection of Presidential Daily Diaries spent months open on my computer as I paged through Nixon's presidency day by day, meeting by meeting, hour by hour. Joel Westphal, at the Gerald R. Ford Presidential Library and Museum, has become a friend over the course of my trips to Grand Rapids and Ann Arbor, and he was instrumental in helping me understand the man who followed Nixon into the White House.

It was hard too not to think about publishing and history as Simon & Schuster lost two of its North Stars: Carolyn Reidy, who had always been a kind and generous supporter of my work, and the legendary Alice Mayhew, who edited so many of the best writers and books of the last half century. She almost single-handedly birthed the idea of the popular political narrative with her work on *All the President's Men* in 1974, and helped train and mentor my own editor a generation later. This work owes a deep psychic debt to both of them in ways big and small.

This is my third book with publishing's next-generation dynamic duo of Jofie Ferrari-Adler and Julianna Haubner. In our near-decade of working together, Julianna and Jofie have together grown into the most important intellectual relationship of my life—the type of full day-to-day friendship and partnership that I've ever only previously read about in biographies of Max Perkins and Robert Gottlieb's memoir. They and Ben Loehnen, Lauren Wein, and the rest of the crew at Avid Reader Press have built what I think is the most interesting and dynamic stable of writers in the industry. I have loved working with Meredith Vilarello, Jordan Rodman, Alison Forner, Carolyn Kelly, and Morgan Hoit, who will always be part of the family.

Jofie is a brilliant and ambitious thinker who understands publishing deep in his soul and has done much to steer and shape my career and help me write the books I've published; and he's steered me away from a dozen other topics along the way. Julianna and I have now been through nearly one million words together, and she combines the patience of Job, the persistence of Sisyphus, the obsession of Carrie Mathison, and the relentless cutting prowess of the world's sharpest diamond blade. I've come to trust her implicitly to find anything amiss.

I'm lucky too to have ended up with Howard Yoon and the team at Ross Yoon—Gail, Dara, Jennifer, and Shannon—who have helped me navigate publishing; my agents at UTA, Andrew Lear and Geoff Morley; and my lawyer, Jaime Wolf.

Jonathan Evans and Rick Willett did yeoman's work helping to scrub the manuscript in copyediting, and I'm grateful to them for saving me from numerous embarrassing mistakes. Ultimately, of course, all the editorial decisions (and remaining mistakes) are mine alone. Simon & Schuster's audio team—Chris Lynch, Elisa Shokoff, Tom Spain, and Scott Sherratt, among others—have been wonderful colleagues, set a high bar for excellence, and also happen to be among the last people I saw in real life before the world shut down in March 2020.

✳   ✳   ✳

Emily Piche, Erin Delmore, and Mary Lim helped with initial research and getting me organized at the start. The book never would have been finished without the incredible, diligent work of Gillian Brassil, a best-in-class researcher who somehow crossed my path and whom I now hope to convince to keep working with me on future projects forever.

Tim Naftali, James Rosen, and Rick Perlstein, among others—including a few who asked to remain nameless but who know my gratitude to them—helped me work through some of the trickier questions of historiography and were generous in sharing their vast knowledge of Nixon generally and Watergate in particular. Few people have excavated Watergate as Rosen has, and his ability to quote chapter, verse, date, and minutiae is astounding. Adam Higginbotham magnanimously shared some of his own unpublished research, and David Friend helped me parse the story of *Vanity Fair*'s scoop of the century in 2006: the reveal of Mark Felt.

In my Aspen Institute life, I'm grateful to Vivian Schiller, the world's greatest boss, for giving me the freedom to tackle "hobbies" like writing a six-hundred-page book, and my colleagues David Forscey, Beth Semel, Ryan Merkley and the rest of the Aspen Digital team for their collegiality. I have missed Savilla Pitt every day since January 16, 2021.

More broadly, there's a long list of people who have been critical to my being who and where I am today. Among them: Charlotte Stocek, Mary Creeden, Mike Baginski, Rome Aja, Kerrin McCadden, and Charlie Phillips; John Rosenberg, Richard Mederos, Brian DeLay, Peter J. Gomes, Stephen Shoemaker, and Jennifer Axsom; Kit Seelye, Pat Leahy, Rusty Greiff, Tim Seldes, Jesseca Salky, Paul Elie, Tom Friedman, Jack Limpert, Geoff Shandler, Susan Glasser, and, not least of all, Cousin Connie, to whom I owe a debt that I strive to repay each day. My parents, Chris and Nancy Price Graff, encouraged me to write from an early age, instilling in me a love of history and research and an intellectual curiosity that benefit me daily, and my sister Lindsay has always been my biggest fan—and I hers.

I wrote my first two books in a D.C. coffee shop, but now that I live in Vermont and write at home, morning coffee and fuel remain an important part of the process. I'm lucky to live in a city with incredible coffee and world-class food, and the spiritual lift from Speeder & Earl's coffee in the morning and Abby and Emily Portman's lunchtime sandwiches at Poppy Café deserve special recognition; I challenge anyone to find better sandwiches than the ones Poppy Café cranks out.

Overall, I do not recommend trying to write a book during a global pandemic, a contested presidential election, and a low-grade American insurrection—and especially not with one daughter and a second son born along the way. I am enormously privileged to have a support structure at home that allows me the time and space to write: the calm presence and help of our nanny, Renèe Hallowell, and my wonderful in-laws, Donna and Paul Birrow, who ended up effectively moving in with us for the pandemic. My wife, Katherine, suffered graciously even more than usual through this book, and I recognize the burden I added to the family with this project. Thank you, as always, KB.

—Garrett M. Graff
Burlington, VT
September 2021

Notes

Introduction

xv *Tears welled up*: W. Mark Felt, *The FBI Pyramid from the Inside* (New York: Putnam, 1979), 338.

xv *"did unlawfully, willfully and knowingly combine"*: Anthony Marro, "Gray and 2 Ex-F.B.I. Aides Deny Guilt as 700 at Court Applaud Them," *New York Times*, April 21, 1978, https://timesmachine.nytimes.com/timesmachine/1978/04/21/110838543.html?page Number=18.

xv *Seventy other FBI agents*: Charles R. Babcock, "Gray, 2 High-Ranking Aides Are Indicted in FBI Break-Ins," *Washington Post*, April 11, 1978, https://www.washingtonpost.com /archive/politics/1978/04/11/gray-2-high-ranking-aides-are-indicted-in-fbi-break-ins /ed0c09a0-f8bd-4192-b090–38fe9147efbc/.

xv *"When these men acted"*: Associated Press, "F.B.I. Indictments Anger Group of Former Agents," *New York Times*, April 13, 1978, https://www.nytimes.com/1978/04/13/archives /new-jersey-pages-fbi-indictments-anger-group-of-former-agents.html?searchResult Position=3.

xvi *"God bless you all"*: Felt, *The FBI Pyramid*, 338.

xvii *"The Nixon presidency was an intense one"*: Kenneth W. Thompson, ed., *The Nixon Presidency: Twenty-Two Intimate Perspectives of Richard M. Nixon* (Lanham, MD: University Press of America, 1987), 35.

xvii *Nixon filled the cover of TIME*: "The 55 Times Richard Nixon Was on the Cover of TIME," *Time*, August 5, 2014, https://time.com/3080127/nixons-time-magazine-covers/.

xviii *"To view Watergate in perspective"*: Donald G. Sanders, "Watergate Reminiscences," *Journal of American History* 75, no. 4 (1989): 1228, https://doi.org/10.1093/jahist/75.4.1228.

xix *"Watergate," wrote Tad Szulc*: Tad Szulc, *Compulsive Spy: The Strange Career of E. Howard Hunt* (New York: Viking, 1974), 3.

xxii *"It tells you an awful lot"*: Jack Limpert, "Deep Throat: If It Isn't Tricia It Must Be . . . ," *Washingtonian*, June 1974, https://www.washingtonian.com/2008/12/22/deep-throat-if-it -isnt-tricia-it-must-be/.

xxii *"Power is Washington's main marketable product"*: Jack Anderson, *The Anderson Papers* (London: Millington, 1973), 3.

xxii   *"I had thrown down a gauntlet"*: Richard Nixon, *RN: The Memoirs of Richard Nixon* (New York: Grosset & Dunlap, 1978), 850.

xxiii *Woodward and Bernstein's classic*: Carl Bernstein and Bob Woodward, *All the President's Men* (New York: Simon & Schuster, 1974), 1.

xxiii *Sam Dash, the chief counsel*: Samuel Dash, *Chief Counsel: Inside the Ervin Committee—The Untold Story of Watergate* (New York: Random House, 1976), 167.

xxiii *in profiling the security guard who busted the burglars*: Simeon Booker, "Untold Story of Black Hero of Watergate!," *JET*, May 17, 1973, http://www.itsabouttimebpp.com/underground_news/pdf/Untold_Story_Frank_Willis.pdf.

xxiii *H. R. Haldeman mis-assigns*: H. R. Haldeman, *The Ends of Power* (New York: Times Books, 1978), 104.

xxiv   *in written testimony to Congress*: *Nomination of Earl J. Silbert to be United States Attorney: Hearings Before the Committee on the Judiciary*, 93rd Congr. 68 (1974), https://books.google.com/books?id=WkMPGEEWUfQC.

xxiv   *Egil Krogh, in his memoir*: Egil Krogh, *Integrity: Good People, Bad Choices, and Life Lessons from the White House* (New York: Public Affairs, 2007), 22.

xxiv   *Howard Hunt incorrectly dates*: E. Howard Hunt, *Undercover: Memoirs of an American Secret Agent* (New York: Berkley, 1974), 153.

xxiv   *"He would turn the same rock"*: Thompson, *The Nixon Presidency*, 128.

xxv   *"nervous tension"*: Henry Kissinger, *Years of Upheaval* (Boston: Little, Brown, 1982), 96.

xxvi   *"I don't think the dust"*: Helen Thomas, *Front Row at the White House* (New York: Scribner, 1999), 204.

Prologue The Pentagon Papers

xxvii   *The doctor who had delivered*: John A. Farrell, *Richard Nixon: The Life* (New York: Doubleday, 2017), 43.

xxviii *"I would like to study"*: Ibid., 57.

xxviii *"Pat and I were happier"*: Jonathan Aitken, *Nixon: A Life* (Washington, D.C.: Regnery, 1993), 154.

xxix   *"To be with Bebe Rebozo"*: John Ehrlichman, *Witness to Power: The Nixon Years* (New York: Simon & Schuster, 1982), 6.

xxix   *He never learned to spell*: Ibid., 77.

xxix   *"To this day, he doesn't know"*: Haldeman, *The Ends of Power*, 70–72.

xxix   *By his second term*: Farrell, *Richard Nixon*, 353.

xxix   *"Richard Nixon went up the walls"*: Ibid., 48.

xxix   *He ate the same lunch*: Ibid., 355.

xxx   *"there existed, within the angry man"*: Ibid., 70.

xxx   *"No matter how terrible"*: Evan Thomas, *Being Nixon: A Man Divided* (New York: Random House, 2015), xi.

xxx   *While running for vice president*: Farrell, *Richard Nixon*, 203.

xxx   *"Mike, we don't have to get those votes"*: Ibid., 407.

xxx   *"I don't know, Chuck"*: Gerald S. Strober and Deborah Hart Strober, *Nixon: An Oral History of His Presidency* (New York: HarperCollins, 1994), 51.

xxx   *In the closing days of the 1960 presidential election*: "Nixon Will Stump Alaska Today, but Kennedy Is Favorite There," *New York Times*, November 6, 1960, https://timesmachine.nytimes.com/timesmachine/1960/11/06/100888163.html?pageNumber=76.

xxx   *"compassionate, humane, fatherly"*: Stanley I. Kutler, *The Wars of Watergate: The Last Crisis of Richard Nixon* (New York: Knopf, 1990), 1.

xxxi   *"Some of his most devious methods"*: Henry Kissinger, *Years of Upheaval* (Boston: Little, Brown, 1982), 1183.

xxxi   *It was that mixing of idealistic light*: Robert Dallek, *Nixon and Kissinger: Partners in Power* (New York: HarperCollins, 2007), 3.

xxxi   *"His rise to the presidency"*: Richard Reeves, *President Nixon: Alone in the White House* (New York: Simon & Schuster, 2001), 11.

xxxi   *"He was too suspicious"*: Ibid., 13.

xxxi   *"He liked rolling in the dust"*: Farrell, *Richard Nixon*, 159.

xxxii   *"It was a day that all of us will always remember"*: Nixon, *RN*, 508.

xxxii   *"diminutive, ethereal, blond daughter"*: Nan Robertson, "Tricia Nixon Takes Vows in Garden at White House," *New York Times*, June 13, 1971, https://timesmachine.nytimes.com/times machine/1971/06/13/170503892.html?pageNumber=1.

xxxii   *"If it were the Kennedys"*: Farrell, *Richard Nixon*, 417.

xxxii   *"I just don't like that paper"*: Katharine Graham, Personal History (New York: Knopf, 1997), 440–42.

xxxii   *"Let's go face the enemy"*: Farrell, *Richard Nixon*, 205.

xxxiii   *He and Pat knew they lived*: Ibid.

xxxiii   *"Was Nixon paranoid?"*: Ibid., 398.

xxxiii   *"He had strong opinions"*: Strober and Strober, *Nixon*, 46.

xxxiii   *"It was eating at him"*: Patrick J. Buchanan, *Nixon's White House Wars: The Battles That Made and Broke a President and Divided America Forever* (New York: Crown, 2017), 19, 53.

xxxiii   *"I just don't understand how the hell"*: Ibid.

Chapter 1   All the President's Men

3   *"It would be god damn easy"*: H. R. Haldeman, *The Haldeman Diaries: Inside the Nixon White House* (New York: Putnam's, 1994), 289.

4   *"The confidence of the early sixties"*: Richard N. Goodwin, *Remembering America: A Voice from the Sixties* (Boston: Little, Brown, 1988), 470.

4   *"welfare mess"*: Dan Rather and Gary Paul Gates, *The Palace Guard* (New York: Harper & Row, 1974), 5.

5   *"The enemy was liberalism"*: Ibid., 224.

5   *Despite a job larger and more powerful than ever*: Rowland Evans, Jr., and Robert D. Novak, *Nixon in the White House: The Frustration of Power* (New York: Random House, 1971), 105.

5   *"Just one dinky little phone"*: Rather and Gates, *The Palace Guard*, 30.

6   *"That's a real time-saver!"*: Farrell, *Richard Nixon*, 355.

6   *Reporters who covered the administration*: See, e.g., Lloyd Shearer, "What's Your Origin?," *Sunday Press* (Binghamton, NY), September 12, 1971, https://www.newspapers.com /image/255484710/.

6   *"Never before had so much authority"*: Rather and Gates, *The Palace Guard*, 21.

6   *Haldeman had long idolized*: Ibid., 121.

6   *"What appealed to me first"*: Ibid., 113.

6   *"vot{ing} straight down the line"*: Dallek, *Nixon and Kissinger*, 14.

7   *"How he loved that case!"*: Haldeman, *The Ends of Power*, 49.

7   *"Pink Lady"*: Dallek, *Nixon and Kissinger*, 19.

7 *"most notorious, controversial campaign"*: Ibid., 21.

7 *one of his greatest product launches*: Rather and Gates, *The Palace Guard*, 130–31.

8 *Once in the White House*: Thompson, *The Nixon Presidency*, 76–77.

8 *The chief of staff, one of just a handful*: Haldeman, *The Ends of Power*, 51.

8 *"Spiky and glaring"*: Ibid., 55.

8 *"Harry Robbins Haldeman is"*: Ibid., 54.

9 *He said he doubted*: Ibid., xx.

9 *"I have been accused"*: Ibid., xiii.

9 *"Nixon was an aggressive campaigner"*: Ibid., 50.

9 *"He dealt with most people"*: Jeb Stuart Magruder, *An American Life: One Man's Road to Watergate* (New York: Atheneum, 1974), 58.

9 *"There were to be results"*: Haldeman, *The Ends of Power*, 53.

10 *He had been elected with a campaign trail reprise*: See, e.g., Rather and Gates, *The Palace Guard*, 67–110.

10 *"Domestic policy under Ehrlichman's reign"*: Ibid., 231.

11 *Some plugged-in Washingtonians*: Ibid., 25.

11 *"a figure of real distinction and glamour"*: Ibid., 24.

11 *"I have never met such a gang"*: Dallek, *Nixon and Kissinger*, 81.

11 *"I can't explain how difficult"*: Ibid., 93.

12 *"Kissinger and Nixon both had degrees"*: Ibid., 92.

12 *"I've always thought that this country could run"*: Theodore H. White, *The Making of the President 1968* (New York: Atheneum, 1969), 147.

13 *"{Nixon and Kissinger} both had a penchant"*: Walter Isaacson, *Kissinger: A Biography* (New York: Simon & Schuster, 2013), 141.

13 *"the brutal truth"*: Dallek, *Nixon and Kissinger*, 102.

13 *"a listing of the Kissinger staff"*: Evans and Novak, *Nixon in the White House*, 96.

13 New York Times *reporter*: William Beecher, "Raids in Cambodia by U.S. Unprotested," *New York Times*, May 9, 1969, https://timesmachine.nytimes.com/timesmachine/1969/05/09/88992642.html?pageNumber=1.

13 *while President Nixon lounged*: President Richard Nixon's Daily Diary, May 1–15, 1969, Richard Nixon Presidential Library and Museum, https://www.nixonlibrary.gov/sites/default/files/virtuallibrary/documents/PDD/1969/008%20May%201–15%201969.pdf.

13 *All through that first spring*: Nixon, *RN*, 386.

14 *"What is this cock-sucking story?"*: Isaacson, *Kissinger: A Biography*, 217.

14 *"Dr. Kissinger said they wondered"*: David C. Humphrey, ed., *Foreign Relations of the United States, 1969–1976*, Vol. 2 (Washington: Government Printing Office, 2006), Document 39, https://history.state.gov/historicaldocuments/frus1969–76v02/d39.

14 *One of the oddities*: Ken Hughes, *Chasing Shadows: The Nixon Tapes, the Chennault Affair, and the Origins of Watergate* (Charlottesville: University of Virginia Press, 2014), 93.

14 *"Simply . . . no one remembered"*: Felt, *The FBI Pyramid*, 143.

14 *"the highest authority"*: William C. Sullivan, *The Bureau: My Thirty Years in Hoover's FBI* (New York: Norton, 1979), 219.

14 *"The FBI would place"*: Haldeman, *The Ends of Power*, 103.

15 *Sullivan sent some thirty-seven*: J. Anthony Lukas, *Nightmare: The Underside of the Nixon Years* (New York: Viking, 1976), 63.

15 *Even more, fifty-two*: Ibid., 65.

15 *"A dry hole"*: Haldeman, *The Ends of Power*, 103.

15 *Ragan had been one of the Bureau's*: John Caulfield, *Caulfield, Shield #911-NYPD* (Bloomington, IN: iUniverse, 2012), 65.

15 *He and another man surreptitiously*: Statement of Information: Hearings Before the Committee on the Judiciary Pursuant to H. Res. 803, 93rd Congr. 7:315 (1974), https://books.google.com /books?id=MBkQgXo1KsYC.

15 *Finally, the frustrated order*: Sullivan, *The Bureau*, 221.

Chapter 2 "Ellsberg? I've Never Heard of Him"

17 *"You know, they could hang"*: Brian VanDeMark, *Road to Disaster: A New History of America's Descent into Vietnam* (New York: Custom House, 2018), 383.

18 *"this goddamn New York Times"*: Douglas Brinkley and Luke Nichter, *The Nixon Tapes: 1971–1972* (Boston: Houghton Mifflin Harcourt, 2014), 171.

18 *"Had some process removed"*: Ehrlichman, *Witness to Power*, 301.

18 *Journalist Fred Emery*: Fred Emery, *Watergate: The Corruption of American Politics and the Fall of Richard Nixon* (New York: Times Books, 1994), 39.

18 *"It shows you're a weakling"*: Haldeman, *The Ends of Power*, 110.

19 *"Ellsberg? I've never heard"*: James Rosen, *The Strong Man: John Mitchell and the Secrets of Watergate* (New York: Doubleday, 2008), 157.

19 *"Henry had a problem"*: Emery, *Watergate*, 44.

19 *"shared Nixon's views"*: Kissinger, *Years of Upheaval*, 116.

19 *"The two of them are in a frenzy"*: Reeves, *President Nixon*, 333.

19 *"These leaks are slowly"*: Charles W. Colson, *Born Again* (Old Tappan, NJ: Chosen Books, 1976), 57.

20 *"Once this thing gets going"*: Dallek, *Nixon and Kissinger*, 289.

20 *In a conversation with Kissinger*: Ken Hughes, ed., "Richard Nixon, Henry A. Kissinger, and John N. Mitchell on 14 June 1971," Conversation 005–070, *Presidential Recordings Digital Edition*, http://prde.upress.virginia.edu/conversations/4002139.

21 *"Let's go. Let's publish"*: Marilyn Berger, "Katharine Graham, Former Publisher of Washington Post, Dies at 84," *New York Times*, July 17, 2001, https://www.nytimes.com/2001/07/17 /obituaries/katharine-graham-former-publisher-of-washington-post-dies-at-84.html.

21 *"The security of the Nation is not at the ramparts"*: "Judge Gurfein's First Case," *New York Times*, December 18, 1979, https://timesmachine.nytimes.com/timesmachine/1979 /12/18/111213202.html?pageNumber=18.

22 *"I hope that the truth"*: Daniel Ellsberg, interview by Walter Cronkite, June 23, 1971, transcript, http://law2.umkc.edu/faculty/projects/ftrials/ellsberg/cronkiteinterview .html.

22 *"We've got a counter-government"*: Seymour M. Hersh, "Colson Asserts Kissinger Wanted Ellsberg Stopped," *New York Times*, April 30, 1974, https://timesmachine.nytimes.com /timesmachine/1974/04/30/99167389.html?pageNumber=33. More detailed versions of this conversation came out in the Nixon tapes.

23 *"was one of the meanest people"*: Strober and Strober, *Nixon*, 273.

23 *"He always had about sixteen balls"*: Jonathan Aitken, *Charles W. Colson: A Life Redeemed* (New York: WaterBrook, 2005), 132.

23 *"Within a short time"*: Ibid., 126.

23 *"the president's liaison with the outside world"*: Ibid., 122.

23 *He relished planting stories*: Strober and Strober, *Nixon*, 277.

24 *"Chuck sat and listened"*: Ibid., 274.

24 *"Who is Colson's constituency?"*: Ibid., 280.

24 *each project he kept organized*: Ibid., 276.

24 *"We had a very good staff system"*: Ibid., 277

24 *In fact, Nixon seemed to relish*: Thompson, *The Nixon Presidency*, 78.

24 *"I was the man for the straight"*: Haldeman, *The Ends of Power*, 61.

24 *His speechwriting team existed*: Thompson, *The Nixon Presidency*, 78.

25 *"Most of us operated"*: Ehrlichman, *Witness to Power*, 342.

25 *"The relation of the various Nixon aides"*: Kissinger, *Years of Upheaval*, 77.

Chapter 3 **The Chennault Affair**

27 *"He just could not leave"*: Thompson, *The Nixon Presidency*, 137.

27 *"Set up budget"*: Farrell, *Richard Nixon*, 17.

27 *"It was easy to get combative"*: Farrell, *Richard Nixon*, 306.

28 *"risk for peace"*: R. W. Apple, Jr., "Humphrey Vows Halt in Bombing if Hanoi Reacts," *New York Times*, October 1, 1968, https://timesmachine.nytimes.com/timesmachine/1968 /10/01/76885700.html?pageNumber=1.

29 *"Look, I've hated Nixon"*: Isaacson, *Kissinger*, 133.

29 *Kissinger at that point had established*: Seymour M. Hersh, *The Price of Power: Kissinger in the Nixon White House* (New York: Summit, 1983), 14.

30 *"I've got one this morning"*: Hughes, *Chasing Shadows*, 5.

31 *"Anna Chennault was an ideal intermediary"*: William Bundy, *A Tangled Web: The Making of Foreign Policy in the Nixon Presidency* (New York: Hill & Wang, 1998), 38.

31 *"Many Republican friends"*: Bui Diem, *In the Jaws of History* (Boston: Houghton Mifflin, 1987), 244.

31 *"If it became known"*: *Foreign Intelligence Surveillance Act of 1978: Hearings Before the Subcommittee on Intelligence and the Rights of Americans of the Select Committee on Intelligence*, 95000 Congr. 291 (1978), https://books.google.com/books?id=Vts1AAAAIAAJ.

32 *"Anna, I'm speaking on behalf"*: Bundy, *A Tangled Web*, 41.

33 *"contacted Vietnamese ambassador"*: Shane O'Sullivan, *Dirty Tricks: Nixon, Watergate, and the CIA* (New York: Hot Books, 2018), 32–33.

34 *"a sensational dispatch from Saigon"*: Hughes, *Chasing Shadows*, 52.

34 *"I do not believe that any president can make any use"*: Ibid., 54.

35 *"good for the country"*: Ibid., 63.

35 *"either one of the noblest in American political history"*: Bundy, *A Tangled Web*, 43.

35 *"No visiting head of state"*: Hughes, *Chasing Shadows*, 63.

35 *"Keep Anna Chennault working"*: Farrell, *Richard Nixon*, 638.

36 *"If I had only known what a beautiful woman"*: Joseph Rodota, *The Watergate: Inside America's Most Infamous Address* (New York: William Morrow, 2018), 86.

36 *"They got away with it"*: John A. Farrell, "When a Candidate Conspired with a Foreign Power to Win an Election," *Politico*, August 6, 2017, https://www.politico.com/magazine /story/2017/08/06/nixon-vietnam-candidate-conspired-with-foreign-power-win-election -215461/.

36 *"The evidence in the case"*: Hughes, *Chasing Shadows*, 70.

36 *"Clearly Mitchell was directly"*: Tom Charles Huston, interview by Timothy Naftali,

June 27, 2008, transcript, Richard Nixon Presidential Library and Museum, https://www.nixonlibrary.gov/sites/default/files/virtuallibrary/documents/histories/huston-2008-06-27.pdf.

37 *"All these documents are top secret"*: Hughes, *Chasing Shadows*, 70.

37 *"I need it"*: Ken Hughes, ed., "Richard Nixon, John D. Ehrlichman, H. R. 'Bob' Haldeman, Henry A. Kissinger, and Ronald L. Ziegler on 17 June 1971," Conversation 525–001 (*PRDE* Excerpt A), *Presidential Recordings Digital Edition*, https://prde.upress.virginia.edu/conversations/4006738.

Chapter 4 The Huston Plan

39 *"a fomentation of hippies"*: Melissa Graves, *Nixon's FBI: Hoover, Watergate, and a Bureau in Crisis* (Boulder, CO: Lynne Rienner, 2020), 11.

39 *"If you didn't experience it"*: Buchanan, *Nixon's White House Wars*, 166.

40 *"In the '68 campaign"*: Rosen, *The Strong Man*, 70.

40 *"The evolutionary circle of violent dissent"*: Nixon, *RN*, 469.

40 *"You're really working a crisis center"*: Strober and Strober, *Nixon*, 72.

40 *"The result was a highly-charged atmosphere"*: Lukas, *Nightmare*, 12.

40 *One Saturday staffers*: Caulfield, *Caulfield*, 73.

41 *"though lucrative hardly teaches"*: White, *The Making of the President 1972*, 291.

41 *He had a habit*: Ibid.

41 *"Pragmatism"*: Rosen, *The Strong Man*, 28.

41 *The two men had forged*: Ibid., 31.

41 *Mitchell sometimes referred*: Ibid., 35.

41 *"the more Negroes"*: James Boyd, "Nixon's Southern Strategy: 'It's All in the Charts,'" *New York Times Magazine*, May 17, 1970, https://timesmachine.nytimes.com/timesmachine/1970/05/17/354962432.html?pageNumber=25.

41 *remarkably effective*: Rather and Gates, *The Palace Guard*, 209.

42 *"Of all the public officials"*: Rosen, *The Strong Man*, 65.

42 *"Oh, I've heard of you"*: Ibid., 35.

42 *"It was less fraternal"*: Lukas, *Nightmare*, 5.

42 *he turned down the job*: Rosen, *The Strong Man*, 66.

42 *agreeing to serve only*: Richard Kleindienst, *Justice: The Memoirs of Attorney General Richard Kleindienst* (Ottawa, IL: Jameson, 1985), 61.

42 *"He was, and is, an unusually"*: Ibid., 41.

42 *"He had a superior intellect"*: Ibid., 46.

42 *"to interpret in unequivocal language"*: Ibid.

42 *"the prime advocate of no-knock laws"*: Lukas, *Nightmare*, 5.

43 *In a surprisingly short timeframe*: Rosen, *The Strong Man*, 72–74.

43 *"We screamed 'Fuck you'"*: Ibid., 93.

43 *"We're going to enforce the law"*: Nancy Zaroulis and Gerald Sullivan, *Who Spoke Up?: American Protest Against the War in Vietnam 1963–1975* (New York: Holt, Rinehart and Winston, 1984), 249.

44 *"10 percent lawman"*: Jack Anderson, *Peace, War, and Politics: An Eyewitness Account* (New York: Forge, 1999), 157.

44 *Later, Hoover always brushed*: Megan Gambino, "Document Deep Dive: Richard Nixon's

Application to Join the FBI," *Smithsonian*, April 1, 2014, https://www.smithsonianmag
.com/history/document-deep-dive-richard-nixons-application-join-fbi-180950329/.

44 *"lacking in aggression"*: Sullivan, *The Bureau*, 196.

44 *"Dick, you will come to depend"*: Thomas, *Being Nixon*, 286.

45 *"In general, the FBI investigative work"*: Ehrlichman, *Witness to Power*, 158.

45 *Whereas the CIA's authority*: Graves, *Nixon's FBI*, 6–7.

45 *Asked at one point*: Ibid., 93; Felt, *The FBI Pyramid*, 102.

46 *"Hoover wanted the FBI to be"*: Graves, *Nixon's FBI*, 4.

46 *"History abundantly documents"*: "Excerpts from Ruling on Wiretapping," *New York Times*,
June 20, 1972, https://timesmachine.nytimes.com/timesmachine/1972/06/20/80793239
.html?pageNumber=23.

46 *"When that support was lacking"*: Ibid., 32.

46 *Hoover that year asked*: Felt, *The FBI Pyramid*, 105.

46–47 *Even the CIA, which was supposed*: Rosen, *The Strong Man*, 78–83.

47 *Amid growing frustration*: Ehrlichman, *Witness to Power*, 162.

47 *"Hoover seemed to me like an old boxer"*: Ibid., 166.

48 *"Most of what he was saying"*: Reeves, *President Nixon*, 223.

48 *Late that May, the Weathermen*: John Kifner, "A Radical 'Declaration' Warns of an Attack
by Weathermen," *New York Times*, May 25, 1970, https://timesmachine.nytimes.com
/timesmachine/1970/05/25/76761126.html?pageNumber=27.

48 *"over 40,000 bombings"*: Nixon, *RN*, 470.

48 *"Nixon became convinced"*: Kissinger, *Years of Upheaval*, 88.

49 *he'd led the national group*: Christopher Saunders, "How We Got Here: The Education of
Tom Charles Huston," *Avocado*, June 8, 2019, https://the-avocado.org/2019/06/08/how
-we-got-here-the-education-of-tom-charles-huston/.

49 *An early backer of Nixon*: Tom Charles Huston, interview by Timothy Naftali, April 30,
2008, transcript, Richard Nixon Presidential Library and Museum, https://www.nixon
library.gov/sites/default/files/virtuallibrary/documents/histories/huston-2008-04-30.pdf

49 *"the most logical target"*: Reeves, *President Nixon*, 175.

49 *"intense, cadaverous"*: Raymond K. Price, *With Nixon* (New York: Viking, 1977), 227.

49 *He had already shown*: Lukas, *Nightmare*, 24–26, and Stanley Kutler, *The Wars of Watergate:
The Last Crisis of Richard Nixon* (New York: Alfred A. Knopf, 1990), 105.

50 *"It was as if he had said two plus two"*: Sullivan, *The Bureau*, 207.

50 *"We are now confronted with a new and grave crisis"*: *Supplementary Detailed Staff Reports
on Intelligence Activities and the Rights of Americans: Final Report of the Select Committee to
Study Governmental Operations*, 94th Congr. 936–37 (1976), https://books.google.com
/books?id=gFovAAAAIAAJ.

51 *"Present procedures should be changed"*: *Impeachment of Richard M. Nixon, President of the United
States: Report of the Committee on the Judiciary*, 93rd Congr. 454 (1974), https://books.google
.com/books?id=sAUqAQAAMAAJ.

51 *"He saw the president as above the law"*: Graves, *Nixon's FBI*, 29.

51 *"The hippie did this"*: Sullivan, *The Bureau*, 211.

52 *"At some point Hoover has to be told"*: Curt Gentry, *J. Edgar Hoover: The Man and the Secrets*
(New York: Norton, 1991), 658.

52 *"Even though the Huston plan was dead"*: *Intelligence Activities, Senate Resolution 21: Hearings
Before the Select Committee to Study Governmental Operations with Respect to Intelligence Activities*,
94th Congr. 2:71 (1976), https://books.google.com/books?id=IxrSnLa-C98C.

52 *"doing whatever you goddamn lawyers do"*: John W. Dean, *Blind Ambition: The White House Years* (New York: Simon & Schuster, 1976), 17.

52 *"In an almost fatherly way"*: Ibid., 12–13.

53 *"It was just too good"*: Strober and Strober, *Nixon*, 61.

53 *"Bob hasn't decided"*: Dean, *Blind Ambition*, 30.

53 *For his first assignment*: Ibid., 33.

53 *"He was extremely ambitious"*: Strober and Strober, *Nixon*, 281.

54 *"He was a snake"*: Ibid., 282–83.

54 *"He lived a little fancier"*: Len Colodny and Robert Gettlin, *Silent Coup: The Removal of a President* (New York: St. Martin's, 1991), 97.

54 *"lived beyond his salary"*: Ibid., 97.

54 *"Word soon got around"*: Dean, *Blind Ambition*, 39.

54 *"Richard M. Dixon"*: Ibid., 40.

54 *One day, in the White House bunker*: Ibid., 29.

55 *Early on, Caulfield recruited*: Tony Ulasewicz with Stuart A. McKeever, *The President's Private Eye: The Journey of Detective Tony U. from N.Y.P.D. to the Nixon White House* (Westport, CT: Macsam, 1990), 177.

55–56 *"the most mysterious figure"*: Everett R. Holles, "Next Watergate Witness: Herbert Warren Kalmbach," *New York Times*, July 16, 1973, https://timesmachine.nytimes.com/timesmachine/1973/07/16/90452811.html?pageNumber=22.

56 *"If you have business with Washington"*: Lukas, *Nightmare*, 120.

56 *"He handled Mr. Nixon's 1969 acquisition"*: Holles, "Next Watergate Witness."

56 *When the Nixon administration took office*: Lukas, *Nightmare*, 119–21.

57 *In 1970, the cash had been used*: William Claiborne, "Wallace Primary Foe's Aides Admit Getting GOP Funds," *Washington Post*, October 8, 1973, http://jfk.hood.edu/Collection/White%20%20Files/Watergate/Watergate%20Items%2006858%20to%2007095/Watergate%2007050.pdf.

57 *Ulasewicz promptly created*: Ulasewicz, *The President's Private Eye*, 183.

57 *One day in July 1969*: Caulfield, *Caulfield*, 72.

57 *"It doesn't matter who you were"*: Lukas, *Nightmare*, 12.

58 *Alexander P. Butterfield was one of the nation's*: Bob Woodward, *The Last of the President's Men* (New York: Simon & Schuster, 2015), 1–17.

58 *"Alex is the perfect buffer"*: Ibid., 64.

58 *One December evening in 1969*: Ibid., 56.

58 *Butterfield studiously learned*: Ibid., 61.

59 *The room had been decorated*: Michael Dobbs, *King Richard: Nixon and Watergate—An American Tragedy* (New York: Knopf, 2021), 21.

60 *The Washington establishment*: Ehrlichman, *Witness to Power*, 311.

60 *"We knew Henry as the 'hawk of hawks'"*: Haldeman, *The Ends of Power*, 94.

60 *"Anytime that anything gets used"*: Woodward, *The Last of the President's Men*, 78–81.

60 *From February 16, 1971*: Hughes, *Chasing Shadows*, ix.

61 *Inside John Mitchell's Justice Department*: G. Gordon Liddy, *Will: The Autobiography of G. Gordon Liddy* (New York: St. Martin's, 1980), 144.

61 *The court cases stemming*: Aryeh Neier, "How the ACLU Won the Largest Mass Acquittal in American History," *ACLU*, January 17, 2020, https://www.aclu.org/issues/free-speech/rights-protesters/how-aclu-won-largest-mass-acquittal-american-history.

61 *"Live bomb found suspended"*: Reeves, *President Nixon*, 320.

61 *"I'll do it," Colson said*: Dean, *Blind Ambition*, 43.

61 *"Best of luck"*: Reeves, *President Nixon*, 321, https://www.google.com/books/edition/The_War_Within/F_ldCwAAQBAJ?hl=en&gbpv=1&bsq=oranges.

61 *"Damn Colson thing"*: "Excerpts from White House Tape of a Nixon-Haldeman Talk in May 1971," *New York Times*, September 24, 1981, https://timesmachine.nytimes.com/timesmachine/1981/09/24/024537.html?pageNumber=108.s

Chapter 5 **Burglarizing Brookings**

63 *"I want a look at any sensitive areas"*: Ken Hughes, ed., "Richard Nixon and H. R. 'Bob' Haldeman on 3 July 1971," Conversation 536–016 (PRDE Excerpt A), Presidential Recordings Digital Edition, https://prde.upress.virginia.edu/conversations/4006745.

63 *"Don't worry about his trial"*: Stanley I. Kutler, *Abuse of Power: The New Nixon Tapes* (New York: Free Press, 1997), 6.

63 *"They have a lot of material"*: Ibid.

64 *"Helms says he's ruthless"*: Reeves, *President Nixon*, 339.

64 *"I have no such recollection"*: Christopher Matthews, " 'Break In and Take It Out! You Understand?,'" *Chicago Tribune*, November 22, 1996, https://www.chicagotribune.com/news/ct-xpm-1996–11–22–9611220111-story.html.

64 *"Did they get the Brookings Institute raided"*: Kutler, *Abuse of Power*, 8.

64 *"I think you need a team"*: " 'You Need a Team,'" Tape 534–012 A, Miller Center, https://millercenter.org/the-presidency/secret-white-house-tapes/you-need-team.

65 *"The FBI won't get into this"*: " 'I Really Need a Son of a Bitch,'" Tape 534–002 C, Miller Center, https://millercenter.org/the-presidency/secret-white-house-tapes/son-of-a-bitch.

65 *"Nixon did have reason to believe"*: Hughes, *Chasing Shadows*, 3.

67 *Overall, Hunt was not well liked*: Szulc, *Compulsive Spy*, 74.

67 *In fact, lost in the later shorthand biographies*: Ibid., 47–51.

68 *His family, by tradition*: Ibid., 104.

68 *He immersed himself in Washington*: Hunt, *Undercover*, 138.

68 *during the May Day Tribe protests*: Ibid., 143.

68 *"Ellsberg's deed seemed the culmination"*: Ibid., 155.

69 *"Colson's phones were constantly"*: Ibid., 150.

69 *"The way Hunt went about"*: Szulc, *Compulsive Spy*, 41.

69 *As a New Yorker unfamiliar*: Ulasewicz, *The President's Private Eye*, 232.

69 *"The security on that vault"*: Dean, *Blind Ambition*, 45.

70 *"Chuck, that Brookings thing"*: Ibid., 47.

70 *"I flew to California"*: "Transcript of a Recording of a Meeting Among the President, John Dean, and H. R. Haldeman in the Oval Office, on March 21, 1973, from 10:12 to 11:55 AM," Richard Nixon Presidential Library and Museum, https://www.nixonlibrary.gov/sites/default/files/forresearchers/find/tapes/watergate/trial/exhibit_12.pdf.

70 *On his way west*: Dean, *Blind Ambition*, 46.

71 *"You talk about wearing flags"*: Sally Quinn, "Patriotic Mardian Placed Loyalty to Others First," *Enquirer and News* (Battle Creek, MI), July 29, 1973, https://www.newspapers.com/image/204656344/.

71 *"Mardian," Sullivan later reported*: Sullivan, *The Bureau*, 223.

72 *"{The FBI} is the nearest"*: Graves, *Nixon's FBI*, 88

72 *Adding to the embarrassment*: Felt, *The FBI Pyramid*, 88.

72 *"We emperors have our problems"*: Christopher Lydon, "J. Edgar Hoover Made the F.B.I. Formidable with Politics, Publicity and Results," *New York Times*, May 3, 1972, https://timesmachine.nytimes.com/timesmachine/1972/05/03/82222873.html?pageNumber=52.

73 *Tolson, who was ailing himself:* Jack Anderson, "Inflation-Boom Debate Sizzles," *Bismarck (ND) Tribune*, July 1, 1971, https://www.newspapers.com/image/345463050/.

74 *"Re: grand jury—dont worry"*: Emery, *Watergate*, 46.

74 *"He was very upset"*: Strober and Strober, *Nixon*, 209.

74 *White House records don't show*: President Richard Nixon's Daily Diary, July 1–15, 1971, Richard Nixon Presidential Library and Museum, https://www.nixonlibrary.gov/sites/default/files/virtuallibrary/documents/PDD/1971/055%20July%201–15%201971.pdf.

75 *Once back in Washington*: "William Safire Part 06 of 06," FBI Records: The Vault, 50, https://vault.fbi.gov/William%20Safire/William%20Safire%20Part%2006%20of%2006/view.

75 *Nixon had Ehrlichman take custody*: Timothy S. Robinson, "Nixon Ordered Tap Files Safeguarded, Aide Says," *Washington Post*, December 2, 1975, http://jfk.hood.edu/Collection/Weisberg%20Subject%20Index%20Files/H%20Disk/Helperin%20Milton%20H%20Dr/Item%2012.pdf.

Chapter 6 **The Plumbers**

78 *"We seek friendly relations"*: "Richard Nixon Announces He Will Visit China, July 15, 1971," USC US-China Institute, transcript, https://china.usc.edu/richard-nixon-announces-he-will-visit-china-july-15-1971.

78 *Young was Kissinger's boy wonder*: Ehrlichman, *Witness to Power*, 303.

78 *"bureaucratic genius"*: Thomas, *Being Nixon*, 339.

79 *After, Ehrlichman, a longtime family friend*: Krogh, *Integrity*, 17.

79 *"He serves as my Bob Cratchit"*: Ibid., 20.

79 *As a starting point, Ehrlichman said*: Ibid., 22.

79 *"{This case} involved the security"*: Ibid., 24.

80 *"Hunt was presented to me"*: Thomas, *Being Nixon*, 344.

80 *They kept track of their assignments*: Lukas, *Nightmare*, 81.

80 *"an exceptionally articulate man"*: Emery, *Watergate*, 55.

80 *When they first met*: Krogh, *Integrity*, 36.

81 *In recalling his childhood*: Liddy, *Will*, 2.

81 *he later found his dreams*: Ibid., 52.

81 *according to family lore*: Ibid., 5.

81 *Upon starting as a political appointee*: Ibid., 131.

81 *he tried for numerous senior*: Ibid., 144.

81 *"He projected a warrior-type charisma"*: Krogh, *Integrity*, 36.

82 *He liked to boast*: Thomas, *Being Nixon*, 343; Liddy, *Will*, 60.

82 *"He seemed decisive"*: Hunt, *Undercover*, 156.

82 *They lunched together*: Lukas, *Nightmare*, 95; Lukas misidentifies the City Tavern Club as the Tavern Inn.

82 *"They were narcissists"*: Jim Hougan, *Secret Agenda: Watergate, Deep Throat, and the CIA* (New York: Random House, 1984), 44.

82 *Hunt especially loved*: Szulc, *Compulsive Spy*, 135.

82 *"Our organization had been directed"*: Liddy, *Will*, 147.

82 *"I am helping the president stop some leaks"*: John W. Dean, *The Nixon Defense: What He Knew and When He Knew It* (New York: Viking, 2014), 662.

82 *"A mood of manic resolve"*: Krogh, *Integrity*, 41.

83 *Krogh and Young, meanwhile*: Statement of Information, 7:52.

83 *When they showed Nixon*: Krogh, *Integrity*, 46.

83 *"The SIU was now operating"*: Ibid., 54.

84 *"We felt a covert operation"*: Ibid., 67.

85 *Sunday night, in a surprise*: Roger Lowenstein, "The Nixon Shock," *Bloomberg*, August 4, 2011, https://www.bloomberg.com/news/articles/2011–08–04/the-nixon-shock.

85 *"We unhesitatingly applaud"*: "Call to Economic Revival," *New York Times*, August 16, 1971, https://timesmachine.nytimes.com/timesmachine/1971/08/16/79403542.html.

Chapter 7 **The Enemies List**

87 *"I'm sure he must have forgotten"*: Thompson, *The Nixon Presidency*, 81.

87 *The efforts had begun at the White House*: Ehrlichman, *Witness to Power*, 274.

88 *"Am I wrong to assume"*: Reeves, *President Nixon*, 298.

88 *"Attached is a list of opponents"*: Impeachment Inquiry: Hearings Before the Committee on the Judiciary Pursuant to H. Res. 803, 93rd Congr. 2:1260 (1974), https://books.google.com/books?id=reKw3tMcnkgC.

88 *"how we can maximize the fact"*: The Final Report of the Select Committee on Presidential Campaign Activities Pursuant to S. Res. 60, 93rd Congr. 7 (1974), https://books.google.com/books?id=IvCbAAAAMAAJ.

89 *The very next day, CBS reporter*: Freedom of the Press: Hearing Before the Committee on Constitutional Rights of the Committee on the Judiciary, 92nd Congr. 989 (1972), https://books.google.com/books?id=9lUf41OsnqcC.

89 *"We just ran a name check"*: "Transcript Prepared by the Impeachment Inquiry Staff for the House Judiciary Committee of a Recording of the President's Work-Day, June 4, 1973," Richard Nixon Presidential Library and Museum, https://www.nixonlibrary.gov/sites/default/files/forresearchers/find/tapes/watergate/wspf/442–001–069.pdf.

89 *These Nixon folks seemed far too comfortable*: Felt, *The FBI Pyramid*, 135.

000 *Liddy penned a long update*: Liddy, *Will*, 160.

90 *"pretty much carte blanche"*: Summary of Information: Hearings Before the Committee on the Judiciary Pursuant to H. Res. 803, 93rd Congr. 36 (1974), https://books.google.com/books?id=g6AnAAAAMAAJ.

90 *"I've been charged with quite a highly sensitive mission"*: Szulc, *Compulsive Spy*, 123.

91 *"{Hunt} was different"*: Eugenio Martinez, "Mission Impossible: The Watergate Bunglers," *Harper's*, October 1974, https://harpers.org/archive/1974/10/heroes-and-fools-3/.

92 *"We did not think he had come to Miami"*: Ibid.

92 *"To me this was a great honor"*: Ibid.

92 *he'd "restrain" Hunt*: "Excerpts from Testimony Before the Senate Watergate Committee," *New York Times*, August 4, 1973, https://timesmachine.nytimes.com/timesmachine/1973/08/04/106108385.html?pageNumber=11.

92 *"On the assumption that the proposed undertaking"*: United States v. Ehrlichman, 546 F.2d 910 (D.C. Cir. 1976), https://casetext.com/case/united-states-v-ehrlichman-2.

93 *"For God's sake, don't get caught!"*: Liddy, *Will*, 165.

93 *"Get clothes for two or three days"*: Martinez, "Mission Impossible."

93 *"There was nothing of Ellsberg's"*: Ibid.

94 *"was so relieved that nothing"*: Liddy, *Will*, 168.

94 *"looked as if it had been fingered"*: *Statement of Information*, 7:1294, https://books.google.com /books?id=bvyYJ-aNWOEC.

94 *Fielding's filing cabinet today*: Owen Edwards, "The World's Most Famous Filing Cabinet," *Smithsonian*, October 2012, https://www.smithsonianmag.com/history/the-worlds-most -famous-filing-cabinet-36568830/.

94 *The next morning as the Cubans*: Magruder, *An American Life*, 173.

94 *"To prove we had not spent"*: Strober and Strober, *Nixon*, 223.

95 *"Hang onto those tools"*: Liddy, *Will*, 169.

95 *"Too expensive"*: Ibid., 172.

96 *"The appointment of W. Mark Felt has prompted"*: Robert M. Smith, "F.B.I. Man's Promotion Raises Question of Hoover Successor," *New York Times*, August 21, 1971, https://times machine.nytimes.com/timesmachine/1971/08/21/79148573.html?pageNumber=8.

96 *"Some had dubbed him"*: Max Holland, *Leak: Why Mark Felt Became Deep Throat* (Lawrence: University Press of Kansas, 2012), 21.

97 *Days later, a column by Evans*: Rowland Evans, Jr., and Robert Novak, "Hoover's Bailiwick Is in Sad Disrepair," *Philadelphia Inquirer*, October 11, 1971, https://www.newspapers .com/image/180042882/.

97 *"It did not cross my mind"*: Felt, *The FBI Pyramid*, 178.

97 *"No go"*: Haldeman, *The Haldeman Diaries*, 357.

97 *"It was a little bit like killing"*: Thompson, *The Nixon Presidency*, 139.

97 *"He oughta resign"*: Graves, *Nixon's FBI*, 117.

97 *Krogh, in turn, tasked Liddy*: Liddy, *Will*, 172–80.

98 *"Sullivan was the man who executed"*: Robert L. Jackson and Ronald J. Ostrow, "Nixon Discussed Use of 'Thugs,' New Tapes Show," *Los Angeles Times*, June 5, 1991, https:// www.latimes.com/archives/la-xpm-1991-06-05-mn-216-story.html.

98 *"How can we get J. Edgar Hoover"*: Cartha DeLoach, *Hoover's FBI: The Inside Story by Hoover's Trusted Lieutenant* (Washington, D.C.: Regnery, 1995), 412.

98 *"We may have on our hands"*: "Transcript of a Recording of a Meeting in the Oval Office Between President Nixon and John Ehrlichman, October 25, 1971, from 12:35 to 2:05 p.m.," Richard Nixon Presidential Library and Museum, https://www.nixonlibrary.gov /sites/default/files/forresearchers/find/tapes/watergate/wspf/601–033.pdf.

98 *"That's a very good fellow"*: Ibid.

Chapter 8 **Sandwedge**

99 *a storied dark-arts investigative firm*: Frank J. Prial, "Concern Fights Crime in Business, *New York Times*, July 26, 1970, https://timesmachine.nytimes.com/timesmachine /1970/07/26/90613166.html?pageNumber=103.

99 *"Should this Kennedy mafia"*: *Presidential Campaign Activities of 1972, Senate Resolution 60: Executive Session Hearings Before the Select Committee on Presidential Campaign Activities*, 93rd Congr. 21:9990 (1974), https://books.google.com/books?id=32iki2YW9egC.

99 *SANDWEDGE would help*: Colodny and Gettlin, *Silent Coup*, 104–5.

100 *Caulfield received $50,000*: "Evidence: Texts of 3 Memos on 'Political Matters' from Strachan to Haldeman," *New York Times*, July 12, 1974, https://timesmachine.nytimes.com /timesmachine/1974/07/12/79582680.html?pageNumber=21.

100 *"intelligence shouldn't receive a greater allocation"*: Statement of Information, App. 3, 9, https://books.google.com/books?id=HJrVn5X-T80C.

100 *"I sensed that an Irish cop"*: Dean, Blind Ambition, 74.

101 *"I want a hold on it"*: Ibid.

101 *"How about Gordon Liddy?"*: Ibid., 76.

101 *"He bristled with energy"*: Ibid.

101 *"Dean tells me there's plenty"*: Hunt, Undercover, 186. Exactly how Liddy's conversation with Dean unfolded is a point of departure between Liddy and Dean. However, both Liddy and Hunt's recollection come the closest to overlapping.

101 *In December, journalist Jack Anderson*: "Jack Anderson of United Features Syndicate," Pulitzer Prizes, https://www.pulitzer.org/winners/jack-anderson.

102 *"I even stopped reading newspapers"*: Colodny and Gettlin, Silent Coup, 5.

102 *While the Plumbers hadn't been able*: Ibid., 40.

103 *Nixon quickly decided it would be better*: Ibid., 51.

103 *"I tell you, Mr. President"*: Ehrlichman, Witness to Power, 307.

103 *"I'd never seen fingernails"*: Ibid., 307.

103 *"Damn, you know, I created"*: Mark Feldstein, Poisoning the Press: Richard Nixon, Jack Anderson, and the Rise of Washington's Scandal Culture (New York: Farrar, Straus and Giroux, 2010), 197.

104 *"I would just like to get a hold of this Anderson"*: Ibid., 202.

104 *"it would have taken"*: Rosen, The Strong Man, 176.

104 *"the first irreversible step"*: Krogh, Integrity, 77.

104 *"It was like a culture"*: Jonathan Aitken, Nixon: A Life, 419.

105 *"SANDWEDGE has been scrapped"*: "03. Book I: Events prior to the Watergate break-in, December 2, 1971-June 17, 1972," Santa Clara Law Digital Commons, https://digital commons.law.scu.edu/cgi/viewcontent.cgi?article=1002&context=watergate.

105 *In the final days of 1971*: Caulfield, Caulfield, 78.

Chapter 9 The Committee to Re-Elect

109 *"planting of our operatives"*: Liddy, Will, 190.

109 *"My sense of purpose"*: Ibid., 193, 196.

110 *Magruder, in his telling of the story*: Magruder, An American Life, 173.

110 *"The poll results suggested"*: Ibid., 154.

110 *As Nixon geared up for the reelection*: Reeves, President Nixon, 423.

110 *The team had agreed to largely forgo*: Lukas, Nightmare, 7.

111 *"He was the white-collar hustler"*: Theodore H. White, Breach of Faith: The Fall of Richard Nixon (New York: Atheneum, 1975), 144.

111 *"The committee was afloat"*: White, The Making of the President 1972, 301.

111 *The vast resources were necessary*: Lukas, Nightmare, 2–3.

112 *"The victory over Humphrey had been far too close"*: Nixon, RN, 357.

112 *"I vowed that I would never again"*: Ibid., 226.

112 *Jeb Stuart Magruder had come into White House orbit*: Magruder, An American Life, 1–53.

113 *"The possible threat"*: The Antitrust Improvements Act of 1975: Hearings Before the Subcommittee on Antitrust and Monopoly of the Committee on the Judiciary, 94th Congr. 442 (1975), https://books.google.com/books?id=mcs2gJlNfpUC.

113 *"a tiny, enclosed fraternity"*: Spiro T. Agnew, "Television News Coverage, Des Moines, IA,"

November 13, 1969, American Rhetoric, https://www.americanrhetoric.com/speeches /spiroagnewtvnewscoverage.htm.

113 *"Nixon found Agnew a shallow malcontent"*: Tom Wicker, *One of Us: Richard Nixon and the American Dream* (New York: Random House, 1991), 636.

114 *"Gangbusters!"*: Buchanan, *Nixon's White House Wars*, 74.

114 *A native of Pine Bluff, Arkansas*: Winzola McLendon, *Martha: The Life of Martha Mitchell* (New York: Random House, 1979), 45.

115 *She and John had fallen deeply*: Ibid., 53.

115 *One oft-told story*: Ibid., 57.

115 *Scotch became such a regular part*: Ibid., 60

115 *"being a Cabinet wife"*: Ibid., 66

116 *Her national profile had begun to rise*: Ibid., 157

116 *"She suddenly became this folk hero"*: Ibid., 109

116 *"No woman in public life"*: Ibid., 108

117 *"It was not that she drank too much"*: Anna Chennault, *The Education of Anna* (New York: Times Books, 1980), 182.

117 *"My heart went out to her"*: Magruder, *An American Life*, 164.

117 *"The Vietnam War stinks"*: Associated Press, "Martha Mitchell Raps Viet War, Fulbright," *San Francisco Chronicle*, September 7, 1970, http://jfk.hood.edu/Collection/White%20 Materials/Nixon%20Administration/Nixon%200291.pdf.

117 *"She's the best thing"*: McLendon, *Martha*, 100.

117 *"John and I have the perfect arrangement"*: Ibid., 171.

118 *"{potential recruits} must believe"*: Liddy, *Will*, 190.

118 *At dinner in California*: Ibid.

118 *Between them, Hunt bragged*: Ibid., 192.

118 *At the end of their conversation*: Ibid., 196.

118 *"I knew exactly what had to be done"*: Ibid., 193.

118 *Once passing a Vietnam War protester*: Ibid., 137.

119 *"an* Einsatzgruppe*"*: Ibid., 196–200.

120 *"I frequently found it necessary"*: Kleindienst, *Justice*, 46.

121 *"Excuse me for saying this"*: Dean, *Blind Ambition*, 87.

121 *"Bob, this stuff is incredible"*: Ibid.

122 *"Liddy's a romantic"*: Ibid., 79.

122 *"I wanted the leading Democrats"*: Nixon, *RN*, 774.

123 *After Hunt started working with Liddy*: The Final Report, 189.

123 *"Mitchell's attitude struck me"*: Magruder, *An American Life*, 166.

123 *The RUBY operation*: Ibid., 150, 165.

123 *"political hobgoblin"*: Tom Hamburger, "Dick Tuck, Democratic Prankster Who Targeted Nixon, Dies at 94," *Washington Post*, May 30, 2018, https://www.washingtonpost.com/local /obituaries/dick-tuck-democratic-prankster-who-targeted-nixon-dies-at-94/2018/05 /29/0cd03c2e-63b1–11e8–99d2–0d678ec08c2f_story.html.

123 *"Dick Tuck, you've done your last advance"*: Ibid.

123 *"glorious improvisations"*: William F. Buckley, Jr., "Subpoena Dick Tuck in Watergate Caper Probe," *Beaver County (PA) Times*, December 14, 1972, https://news.google.com /newspapers?id=ErIiAAAAIBAJ&sjid=RbMFAAAAIBAJ&pg=782,3638007.

123 *arranging for garbage trucks*: Hamburger, "Dick Tuck, Democratic Prankster"; Dylan Smith, "Nixon's Nemesis: Political Prankster Dick Tuck Dead at 94," *Tucson Sentinel*, May 29,

2018, http://www.tucsonsentinel.com/local/report/052818_dick_tuck/nixons-nemesis
-political-prankster-dick-tuck-dead-94/.

124 *They also recruited a man named Roger Greaves*: The Final Report, 190.

124 *recruited some hostile picketers*: John M. Crewdson, "Sabotaging the G.O.P.'s Rivals: Story
of a $100,000 Operation," *New York Times*, July 9, 1973, https://timesmachine.nytimes
.com/timesmachine/1973/07/09/99155189.html.

124 *Herb Porter enlisted Stone*: The Final Report, 192–94.

126 *"Whether it's a peccadillo"*: Anderson, *The Anderson Papers*, 17.

126 *At one point, he'd gotten into a high-profile flap*: Mark Feldstein, "The Last Muckraker," *Washington Post*, July 28, 2004, https://www.washingtonpost.com/wp-dyn/articles/A19730–2004
Jul27.html.

126 *The CIA that month*: Timothy S. Robinson, "CIA Elaborately Tracked Columnist," *Washington Post*, May 4, 1977, https://www.washingtonpost.com/archive/politics/1977/05/04
/cia-elaborately-tracked-columnist/46eef9eb-c74d-44a9-b3ee-671bb5820c48/.

Chapter 10 **The Dita Beard Memo**

128 *He had been learning on the job*: Kleindienst, *Justice*, 63.

128 *"When the attorney general"*: Anderson, *The Anderson Papers*, 26.

128 *Some of the department's early moves*: Ibid., 27.

128 *Mitchell and Kleindienst additionally seemed*: Strober and Strober, *Nixon*, 246.

129 *"Mitchell knew that it was his manifest destiny"*: Ibid., 252.

129 *"He's been running it"*: McLendon, *Martha*, 166.

129 *"the greatest attorney general"*: Fred P. Graham, "Mitchell Quits; Nomination Goes to
Kleindienst," *New York Times*, February 16, 1972, https://timesmachine.nytimes.com
/timesmachine/1972/02/16/79421286.html?pageNumber=1.

129 *"We encountered the curious phenomenon"*: Dallek, *Nixon and Kissinger*, 368.

130 *That public warning*: E. W. Kenworthy, "What's Good for a Corporate Giant May Not Be
Good for Everybody Else," *New York Times*, December 16, 1973, https://timesmachine
.nytimes.com/timesmachine/1973/12/16/91056098.html?pageNumber=233.

130 *CEO Howard "Hal" Geneen's vision*: "Business: In the Dough," *TIME*, May 31, 1968, http://
content.time.com/time/subscriber/article/0,33009,844559,00.html

130 *Growth largely came*: Anderson, *The Anderson Papers*, 32.

131 *"If {the} Antitrust {Division}"*: Robert M. Smith, "McLaren Memo on I.T.T. Merger
Revealed," *New York Times*, May 2, 1972, https://timesmachine.nytimes.com/times
machine/1972/05/02/79467315.html?pageNumber=29.

131 *He asked for permission to seek*: Gene Smith, "I.T.T.-Hartford Deal Is Voted," *New
York Times*, November 11, 1969, https://timesmachine.nytimes.com/timesmachine
/1969/11/11/79435836.html?pageNumber=61.

131 *For the better part of two years*: Anderson, *The Anderson Papers*, 32; Kenworthy, "What's
Good for a Corporate Giant."

131 *"I immediately smelled a rat"*: Edward M. Kennedy, *True Compass: A Memoir* (New York:
Twelve, 2009), 324.

132 *"aura of scandal"*: Jack Anderson, "Presidential Hopefuls Seek Tainted Funds," *Daily Journal*
(Vineland, NJ), December 9, 1971, https://www.newspapers.com/image/281342665/.

132 *"Our noble commitment"*: Anderson, *The Anderson Papers*, 43–44.

132 *"{Kleindienst} insisted that he had never talked"*: Kennedy, *True Compass*, 325.

133 *Robert Mardian called Mark Felt*: Anderson, *The Anderson Papers*, 81.

133 *"I did not like the assignment"*: Felt, *The FBI Pyramid*, 137.

133 *"Falstaffian"*: Michael Kernan and Dorothy McCardle, "Dita Beard," *Washington Post*, November 26, 1971, http://jfk.hood.edu/Collection/Weisberg%20Subject%20Index%20 Files/K%20Disk/Kleindienst%20Richard%20G/Item%20071.pdf.

133 *"But that would be a lie"*: Anderson, *The Anderson Papers*, 55.

134 *When Beard finally resurfaced*: Ibid., 98.

134 *Colson dispatched Hunt*: Hunt, *Undercover*, 202.

135 *"forgery, a fraud, and a hoax"*: Anderson, *The Anderson Papers*, 102.

135 *"Don't we have some spurious stuff"*: Feldstein, *Poisoning the Press*, 281.

135 *"Do we have anything on Hume?"*: Ibid., 236.

135 *"I assumed, as I usually do with Colson"*: "After the Coup: Hunt, Barker & Phillips," http:// the-puzzle-palace.com/files/nodule20.htm.

136 *Hunt immediately teamed up*: Liddy, *Will*, 210.

137 *"I know it violates the sensibilities"*: G. Barry Golson, ed., *The Playboy Interview: Volume II* (New York: Perigee Books, 1983), 353.

137 *"He was a strong and vigorous-looking man"*: Felt, *The FBI Pyramid*, 167.

137 *Gray handed the FBI executive an envelope*: Ibid., 167–72.

139 *"{Beard} was a crusty, fast-talking woman"*: Kennedy, *True Compass*, 326.

139 *Two Denver doctors later said*: Anderson, *The Anderson Papers*, 106.

139 *Back at the White House, a worried Colson*: "Text of Memo from Colson to Haldeman on Kleindienst Nomination," *New York Times*, August 2, 1973, https://timesmachine.nytimes .com/timesmachine/1973/08/02/90460600.html?pageNumber=18.

139 *"I want something clearly understood"*: "Transcript Prepared by the Impeachment Inquiry Staff for the House Judiciary Committee of a Recording of a Telephone Conversation Between the President and Richard Kleindienst on April 19, 1971, from 3:04 to 3:09 P.M.," Richard Nixon Presidential Library and Museum, https://www.nixonlibrary.gov /sites/default/files/forresearchers/find/tapes/watergate/wspf/002–001_002–002.pdf.

140 *"the only people who were falling"*: Anderson, *The Anderson Papers*, 106.

140 *"{ITT} was the true beginning"*: Kennedy, *True Compass*, 328.

140 *"He wrote that a private investigator"*: Anderson, *The Anderson Papers*, 129.

Chapter 11 "He's Our Hitler"

142 *"He had been serving in the administration"*: Dean, *Blind Ambition*, 105.

142 *"I don't know why they have to be here"*: Magruder, *An American Life*, 195.

142 *"Why don't you guys get off the stick"*: Lukas, *Nightmare*, 186.

142 *"pipsqueak"*: Liddy, *Will*, 213.

142 *"bantam rooster"*: Magruder, *An American Life*, 174.

143 *"Well, you'd better watch"*: Ibid., 175.

143 *A final falling-out*: Ibid., 191; Liddy, *Will*, 212.

143 *"He did a good job"*: Strober and Strober, *Nixon*, 253.

143 *"Liddy's a Hitler"*: Magruder, *An American Life*, 193.

144 *"There was no question"*: McLendon, *Martha*, 167.

144 *"How do we know that these guys"*: Magruder, *An American Life*, 195.

144 *"It was another of what I called {Mitchell's} throwaway decisions"*: Ibid.

144 *It was, in some ways, the ultimate example*: Ibid., 196.

144 *"Once you accept the premise"*: Ibid., 175.

144 *"It was agreed that Liddy"*: Ibid., 195.

144 *It seems just as likely*: Colodny and Gettlin, *Silent Coup*, 125.

144 *"Magruder reports that 1701"*: Rosen, *The Strong Man*, 278.

145 *"Basically, the guy that's lying"*: Ibid., 273.

145 *"more loophole than law"*: Lyndon B. Johnson, "Statement by the President Upon Signing the Foreign Investors Tax Act and the Presidential Election Fund Act," November 13, 1966, American Presidency Project, https://www.presidency.ucsb.edu/documents/state ment-the-president-upon-signing-the-foreign-investors-tax-act-and-the-presidential.

145 *In early 1972, Congress finally passed*: R. Sam Garrett, "The State of Campaign Finance Policy: Recent Developments and Issues for Congress," Congressional Research Service, June 23, 2016, https://s3.documentcloud.org/documents/4163270/Congressional -Research-Service-Campaign-Finance.pdf.

146 *By that point, the president's Newport Beach lawyer*: Lukas, *Nightmare*, 122.

146 *By the time all was said and done*: Warren Weaver, Jr., "'72 Election Set Spending Record," *New York Times*, April 25, 1976, https://timesmachine.nytimes.com/times machine/1976/04/25/79752740.html?pageNumber=35.

146 *Nixon's top ten contributors*: Fred Wertheimer, "Citizens United: Watergate Redux," *Politico*, June 14, 2012, https://www.politico.com/story/2012/06/citizens-united-watergate-redux -077436.

146 *On November 18, 1970*: President Nixon's Daily Diary, November 16–30, 1970, Richard Nixon Presidential Library and Museum, https://www.nixonlibrary.gov/sites/default/files /virtuallibrary/documents/PDD/1970/040%20November%2016–30%201970.pdf.

146 *his airline was in the midst of a merger*: Christopher Lydon, "Cabinet Units Split on Plan to Merge 2 Major Airlines," *New York Times*, September 1, 1971, https://timesmachine .nytimes.com/timesmachine/1971/09/01/79150785.html?pageNumber=1.

147 *"Anybody who wants to be an ambassador"*: George Lardner, Jr., and Walter Pincus, "Nixon Set Minimum Contribution for Choice Diplomatic Posts," *Washington Post*, October 30, 1997, https://www.washingtonpost.com/wp-srv/national/longterm/nixon/103097envoy.htm

147 *Sometimes—illegally—the trade was specific*: Lukas, *Nightmare*, 150.

149 *The payoff was fast*: *Statement of Information*, 6:768, https://books.google.com/books?id=zyAp J5AQQSoC.

150 *"We couldn't even pick up"*: Lukas, *Nightmare*, 152.

150 *All told, they collected*: Ben A. Franklin, "5-Million Given for Nixon in 2 Days Predating Law," *New York Times*, September 30, 1973, https://timesmachine.nytimes.com/times machine/1973/09/30/90985116.html?pageNumber=61.

151 *As Sloan would later recall*: Rosen, *The Strong Man*, 233.

151 *In his role as the campaign finance committee's counsel*: Liddy, *Will*, 215.

151 *At the White House on April 6*: Testimony of Witnesses: *Hearings Before the Committee on the Judiciary Pursuant to H. Res. 803*, 93rd Congr. 52–55 (1974), https://books.google.com /books?id=3vu3Ugfa3dMC.

152 *"When you work in the White House"*: Barry Sussman, *The Great Cover-Up: Nixon and the Scandal of Watergate* (New York: Signet, 1974), 252.

152 *"George McGovern was the perfect"*: Ehrlichman, *Witness to Power*, 317.

153 *Roger Stone urged McMinoway*: *The Final Report*, 195.

153 *"Get in there as soon as you can"*: Liddy, *Will*, 221.

154 *"Al Baldwin is probably the most gauche"*: Charlotte Curtis, "Mrs. Nixon's Aide Disputes

Mrs. Mitchell," *New York Times*, May 5, 1973, https://timesmachine.nytimes.com/times machine/1973/05/05/90938817.html?pageNumber=16.

154 *Mark Felt was at his desk*: Felt, *The FBI Pyramid*, 177.

154 *The body was readied immediately*: Nan Robertson, "Hoover Lies in State in Capitol," *New York Times*, May 4, 1972, https://timesmachine.nytimes.com/timesmachine /1972/05/04/91328106.html?pageNumber=18.

154 *Mr. Hoover almost singlehandedly transformed*: Memorial Tributes to J. Edgar Hoover in the Congress of the United States, 93rd Congr. 30 (1974), https://books.google.com/books?id=vXZN AQAAMAAJ.

154–55 *"If there is such a thing as a cumulative total"*: Christopher Lydon, "J. Edgar Hoover Made the F.B.I. Formidable with Politics, Publicity and Results," *New York Times*, May 3, 1972, https://timesmachine.nytimes.com/timesmachine/1972/05/03/82222873.html ?pageNumber=52.

155 *Unbeknownst to Felt*: DeLoach, *Hoover's FBI*, 415.

155 *"name a man in whom he has implicit"*: Robert M. Smith, "Nixon Names Aide as Chief of F.B.I. Until Elections," *New York Times*, May 4, 1972, https://timesmachine.nytimes.com /timesmachine/1972/05/04/91328042.html?pageNumber=1.

156 *"That's our next job"*: Hunt, *Undercover*, 213.

Chapter 12 **Third-Rate Burglars**

157 *Under different circumstances*: L. Patrick Gray III, *In Nixon's Web: A Year in the Crosshairs of Watergate* (New York: Henry Holt, 2008), xx.

158 *"The plain truth of the matter"*: Ibid., 23.

158 *From the start, Gray, mistakenly*: Ibid., 51.

158 *Gray drowned in the volume*: Sanford J. Unger, *FBI: An Uncensored Look Behind the Walls* (Boston: Little, Brown, 1976), 514.

159 *Felt leaked details about the thoroughness*: Kevin Leonard, "The Laurel Roots of Watergate's 'Deep Throat,'" *Baltimore Sun*, September 4, 2018, https://www.baltimoresun.com/mary land/laurel/ph-ll-deep-throat-connection-0830-story.html.

160 *When the DNC had moved*: Tip O'Neill with William Novak, *Man of the House: The Life and Political Memoirs of Speaker Tip O'Neill* (New York: Random House, 1987), 241.

160 *"If it only had a tennis court"*: "Problems of Watergate, 'In' Place of the Capital, Anger Many Residents," *New York Times*, March 12, 1972, https://timesmachine.nytimes.com /timesmachine/1972/03/12/91322005.html?pageNumber=34.

160 *The ambitious, grand complex*: Rodota, *The Watergate*, 38.

160 *The design, its Italian backers explained*: Ibid., 52.

160 *Prices ranged from $17,500*: Drew Lindsay, "The Watergate: The Building That Changed Washington," *Washingtonian*, October 1, 2005, https://www.washingtonian .com/2005/10/01/the-watergate-the-building-that-changed-washington/.

160 *"a strip dancer performing"*: Ibid.

160 *After the '68 election, the residential complex*: Rodota, *The Watergate*, 91.

160 *joined over time by the postmaster general*: Ibid., 93.

161 *"Republican Bastille"*: Lindsay, "The Watergate."

161 *"this place was built like low-income housing"*: Ibid.

161 *"Intruders will have difficulty"*: Rodota, *The Watergate*, 56.

161 *"It's really tragic"*: Ibid., 95.

161 *"The youth was becoming a bundle of nerves"*: Hunt, *Undercover*, 215.

162 *"dismissed him as a slick operator"*: Ulasewicz, *The President's Private Eye*, 242.

162 *Their scouting determined*: Richard Ben-Veniste and George Frampton, Jr., *Stonewall: The Real Story of the Watergate Prosecution* (New York: Simon & Schuster, 1977), 49.

162 *On May 26, the team checked in*: Liddy, *Will*, 231.

163 *On Monday morning, May 29*: Ulasewicz, *The President's Private Eye*, 247.

164 *"Not to my surprise"*: Liddy, *Will*, 236.

164 *"palpable, damnable lie"*: "The Watergate Testimony So Far: Questions Remain on Eight Major Issues," *New York Times*, August 12, 1973, https://timesmachine.nytimes.com /timesmachine/1973/08/12/90463876.html?pageNumber=46.

164 *"Looks like high risk"*: Liddy, *Will*, 238.

164 *"The Big Man wants the operation"*: Hunt, *Undercover*, 233.

164 *"Take all the men"*: Liddy, *Will*, 237.

165 *Nixon had a full nineteen-point lead*: Dallek, *Nixon and Kissinger*, 400.

165 *At the beginning of June*: President Richard Nixon's Daily Diary, June 1–15, 1972, Richard Nixon Presidential Library and Museum, https://www.nixonlibrary.gov/sites/default/files /virtuallibrary/documents/PDD/1972/077%20June%201–15%201972.pdf.

165 *The entire reelection apparatus*: Associated Press, "GOP War Chest Bulging: Big Givers for Nixon," *San Francisco Examiner*, June 13, 1972, http://jfk.hood.edu/Collection/White%20 Materials/Watergate/Watergate%20Items%2000001%20to%2000180/Watergate%20 00004.pdf.

165 *On June 14 she predicted*: United Press, "Martha Says It's Teddy," *San Francisco Examiner*, June 15, 1972, http://jfk.hood.edu/Collection/White%20Materials/Watergate/Water gate%20Items%2000001%20to%2000180/Watergate%2000006.pdf.

165 *"They were a collection"*: Anderson, *The Anderson Papers*, 129.

166 *"Private business"*: Ibid.

166 *"This is getting too deep"*: Hunt, *Undercover*, 237.

167 *Frank Wills, a Savannah, Georgia, native*: Booker, "Untold Story of Black Hero of Watergate!"

167 *The truth, however, uncovered in 2012*: Craig Shirley, "The Bartender's Tale: How the Watergate Burglars Got Caught," *Washingtonian*, June 20, 2012, https://www.washingtonian .com/2012/06/20/the-bartenders-tale-how-the-watergate-burglars-got-caught/.

168 *"I must admit that when I saw"*: Fred Blumenthal, "What Happened to the Cop Who Arrested the Watergate 5?," *Parade* (*Washington Post*), June 16, 1974, http://jfk.hood.edu /Collection/White%20Materials/Watergate/Watergate%20Items%2015448%20to%20 15717/Watergate%2015492.pdf.

169 *"I'll be in touch tomorrow"*: Hunt, *Undercover*, 3.

169 *As a reward for his vigilance*: Booker, "Untold Story."

169 *"I hate to wake you up"*: Hunt, *Undercover*, 244–46.

170 *"Anything wrong?"*: Liddy, *Will*, 246.

170 *"Why did you fellows"*: Ehrlichman, *Witness to Power*, 341.

170 *No one was ever charged*: Strober and Strober, *Nixon*, 323.

171 *Jeb Magruder and John Dean have both explained*: John Dean, *Blind Ambition: Updated Edition: The End of the Story*, (Palm Springs, CA: Polimedia Publishers, 2009), 512–26.

172 *Indeed, in later testimony, Hunt says*: Dean, *Blind Ambition: Updated Edition*, 522.

172 *During a January 3, 1973, conversation*: Kutler, *Abuse of Power*, 196.

172 *"The purpose of the second Watergate break-in"*: Liddy, *Will*, 237.

173 *"We wouldn't be sitting around"*: O'Sullivan, *Dirty Tricks*, 388.

173 *John Dean argues the Oliver bugging*: Dean, *Blind Ambition: Updated Edition*, 524.

173 *"the implication of Colodny and Gettlin's narrative"*: G. Gordon Liddy, *When I Was a Kid, This Was a Free Country* (Washington, D.C.: Regnery, 2002), 182.

174 *When Silent Coup was published*: Howard Kurtz, "Watergate Book Opens to Tough Audience," *Washington Post*, May 21, 1991: https://www.washingtonpost.com/archive /lifestyle/1991/05/21/watergate-book-opens-to-tough-audience/af81c5e7-a6d6-41d2 -86b5-13a7185f0074/

174 *The* Washington Post *at various times*: George Lardner, Jr., "Watergate Libel Suit Set-tled," *Washington Post*, July 23, 1997. https://www.washingtonpost.com/archive/life style/1997/07/23/watergate-libel-suit-settled/baa27e24-a13f-4ed6-b357–6426381e772c/.

174 *Another lawsuit*: ABC News, "Liddy Defamation Case Dismissed," January 6, 2006. https:// abcnews.go.com/Politics/story?id=121924&page=1.

175 *Greek journalist Elias Demetracopoulos*: James Barron, *The Greek Connection: The Life of Elias Dematracopoulos and the Untold Story of Watergate* (Brooklyn: Melville House, 2020).

175 *Christopher Hitchens, in his book*: Christopher Hitchens, *The Trial of Henry Kissinger* (New York: Verso, 2001), 167–86.

175 *One of the top officials at the Greek embassy*: Barron, *The Greek Connection*, 361–62, 366; Kissinger's role in discouraging the inquiry was reported in 1975 by writer Nick Thim-mesch, "Birth of a Salesman," *New York Times Magazine*, October 26, 1975, and then later also reported in Hersh, *Price of Power*, 648.

176 *"McCord did not come"*: Martinez, "Mission Impossible."

177 *"This secret CIA operation"*: Anthony Marro, "Deep Throat, Phone Home," *Washington Post*, November 25, 1984, https://www.washingtonpost.com/archive/entertainment /books/1984/11/25/deep-throat-phone-home/db691af1-8ed7-42d1-85f6-53634cf0b59d/.

177 *"Nixon and {CIA Director Richard} Helms"*: Kutler, *The Wars of Watergate*, 201.

Chapter 13 "A Crime That Could Destroy Us All"

179 *As investigators and prosecutors rushed*: Liddy, *Will*, 248–49.

180 *"This was a crime"*: Magruder, *An American Life*, 220.

180 *"This thing has all kinds"*: Felt, *The FBI Pyramid*, 196.

181 *In* Silent Coup, *Len Colodny*: Colodny and Gettlin, *Silent Coup*, 172.

181 *Watergate historians have already supposed*: Haldeman, *The Ends of Power*, 4.

181 *Nixon, on the other hand*: Woodward, *The Last of the President's Men*, 105.

183 *"I'm sure it was Dean"*: Colodny and Gettlin, *Silent Coup*, 148.

183 *"I know—there's no way"*: Liddy, *Will*, 252.

183 *"Henry, I don't know what"*: Kleindienst, *Justice*, 145–46.

183 *While Kleindienst says he recalls*: John M. Crewdson, "Kleindienst Talk with Liddy Cited," *New York Times*, March 29, 1974, https://timesmachine.nytimes.com/times machine/1974/03/29/91437164.html?pageNumber=17.

184 *"I never solved any of them"*: Angelo Lano, "Watergate: Forty Years Later," *Grapevine*, June /July 2014, https://fbistudies.com/wp-content/uploads/2014/09/Watergate_Angelo _Lano.pdf.

184 *"They clearly didn't look like ordinary knuckleheads"*: Ibid.

184 *"That's the $64,000 question"*: O'Sullivan, *Dirty Tricks*, 218.

185 *Interviewed by another Spanish-speaking agent*: Graves, *Nixon's FBI*, 166.

185 *"Neither Stan nor I knew"*: Lawrence F. O'Brien, *No Final Victories: A Life in Politics from John F. Kennedy to Watergate* (Garden City, NY: Doubleday, 1974), 297.

185 *"One of the men had $814"*: Bernstein and Woodward, *All the President's Men*, 18.

186 *"Though I had failed the tryout"*: Bob Woodward, *The Secret Man: The Story of Watergate's Deep Throat* (New York: Simon & Schuster, 2005), 31.

186 *"Bernstein also had an unnerving habit"*: Leonard Downie, Jr., *The New Muckrakers: An Inside Look at America's Investigative Reporters* (Washington, D.C.: New Republic, 1976), 5.

187 *"As we read it over"*: Sussman, *The Great Cover-Up*, 17.

187 *"Nothing was more un-chic"*: Harrison E. Salisbury, *Without Fear or Favor: The* New York Times *and Its Times* (New York: Times Books, 1980), 419.

187 *Instead, one of the paper's young minority interns*: Philip Nobile, "Extra!," *Esquire*, May 1, 1975, https://classic.esquire.com/article/1975/5/1/extra.

188 *"That Watergate thing is a hell of a thing"*: Gray, *In Nixon's Web*, 61.

188 *"Those were the last decent words"*: McLendon, *Martha*, 7.

188 *"They had me at a brunch"*: Vivian Cadden, "Martha Mitchell: The Day the Laughing Stopped," *McCall's*, July 1973, http://jfk.hood.edu/Collection/White%20Materials/Watergate/Watergate%20Items%2004357%20to%2004655/Watergate%204358.pdf.

188 *"The person involved is the proprietor"*: *Testimony of Witnesses*, 212.

189 *On the other side of the country*: Associated Press, "White House Reaction: Nixon 'Ignoring' Demo Incident," *San Francisco Chronicle*, June 20, 1972, http://jfk.hood.edu/Collection/White%20Materials/Watergate/Watergate%20Items%2000001%20to%2000180/Watergate%2000017.pdf.

189 *According to Pat Gray's 2008 memoir*: Gray, *In Nixon's Web*, 69.

189 *"We had one hundred and some days"*: Thompson, *The Nixon Presidency*, 136.

189 *Back at the* Post: Downie, *The New Muckrakers*, 15.

190 *Bernstein's colleagues knew him*: Sussman, *The Great Cover-Up*, 54.

190 *"I didn't really think a lot"*: Alicia C. Shepard, *Woodward and Bernstein: Life in the Shadow of Watergate* (Hoboken, NJ: Wiley, 2007), 16.

190 *Bernstein by comparison*: Sussman, *The Great Cover-Up*, 54.

190 *That night, Woodward drove out*: Bernstein and Woodward, *All the President's Men*, 20–22.

191 *Early Monday morning*: Sussman, *The Great Cover-Up*, 18.

191 *With that, Hunt left the White House*: Hunt, *Undercover*, 255.

191 *"Good God!"*: Bernstein and Woodward, *All the President's Men*, 24.

191 *Confoundingly, Hunt in his memoir*: Hunt, *Undercover*, 249.

192 *"command presence"*: Woodward, *The Secret Man*, 17.

192 *"like two passengers sitting"*: Ibid., 19.

192 *"I peppered him"*: Ibid., 21.

193 *"original back-room boys"*: Robert B. Semple, Jr., "Seldom-Seen Aides Protect Nixon's Political Flank," *New York Times*, June 22, 1970, https://timesmachine.nytimes.com/timesmachine/1970/06/22/98370993.html?pageNumber=33.

Chapter 14 "Boys Will Be Boys"

195 *"Gordon, let's face it"*: Magruder, *An American Life*, 223–24.

195 *"Chuck sounded like he hardly knew"*: Dean, *Blind Ambition*, 93.

196 *"Am I correct in assuming"*: Liddy, *Will*, 255.

196 *"That goes without saying"*: Ibid., 256–60.

197 *Afterward, Liddy called Hunt*: Hunt, *Undercover*, 257.

197 *Within forty minutes, Dean called*: Liddy, *Will*, 255–61.

198 *"Mickey Mouse operation"*: Washington Post Service, "Bugging Called Bungled Job," *San Francisco Chronicle*, June 19, 1972, http://jfk.hood.edu/Collection/White%20Materials /Watergate/Watergate%20Items%2000001%20to%2000180/Watergate%2000012.pdf.

198 *One* New York Times *journalist*: Tad Szulc, "Democratic Raid Tied to Realtor," *New York Times*, June 19, 1972, http://jfk.hood.edu/Collection/White%20Materials/Watergate /Watergate%20Items%2000001%20to%2000180/Watergate%2000009.pdf.

198 *"the ugliest questions"*: United Press and Associated Press, "Demo HQ 'Bugging' Try— Nixon Aide Is a Suspect," *San Francisco Chronicle*, June 19, 1972, http://jfk.hood.edu /Collection/White%20Materials/Watergate/Watergate%20Items%2000001%20to%20 00180/Watergate%2000010.pdf.

198 *He swiftly filed a million-dollar civil suit*: "Demos Sue Nixon Unit on Break-In," *San Francisco Examiner*, June 20, 1972, http://jfk.hood.edu/Collection/White%20Materials/Watergate /Watergate%20Items%2000001%20to%2000180/Watergate%2000020.pdf.

198 *"I foresee no difficulty"*: Ed Montgomery, "Acting FBI Head Plays Tough Role in Press Parley," *San Francisco Examiner*, June 20, 1972, https://sfexaminer.newspapers.com /image/460675335/.

198 *Ron Ziegler continued to dismiss*: Associated Press, "White House Reaction."

199 *"McCord, Hunt, Liddy—none of these names"*: Strober and Strober, *Nixon*, 215.

199 *When they brought in Colson*: Dean, *Blind Ambition*, 103.

199 *At the end of the day, Ehrlichman finally*: Haldeman, *The Ends of Power*, 23.

200 *That scheme, though, quickly grew*: Ibid., 23–27.

200 *Later, when Haldeman passed along*: Ibid., 28–29.

201 *"Burglary is bad enough"*: Patricia Sullivan, "Robert Mardian: Attorney Caught Up in Watergate Scandal," *Washington Post*, July 21, 2006, https://www.washingtonpost.com /politics/robert-mardian-attorney-caught-up-in-watergate-scandal/2012/05/31/gJQARJ 6vFV_story.html.

201 *"I was learning what the job really meant"*: Dean, *Blind Ambition*, 107.

201 *Mitchell's wife, still in California*: Rosen, *The Strong Man*, 304.

201 *As the deputy campaign director later recalled*: Ibid., 309.

Chapter 15 **"Stay the Hell Out of This"**

203 *"Bob Dole and I were talking"*: Bernstein and Woodward, *All the President's Men*, 29.

203 *"To this day, I believe that I was right"*: Rosen, *The Strong Man*, 312.

204 *Far from Washington, in Brooklyn*: "Elizabeth Holtzman," *New York Times*, June 22, 1972, https://timesmachine.nytimes.com/timesmachine/1972/06/22/90716963.html?page Number=46.

204 *"The primary election between Holtzman and Celler"*: Jimmy Breslin, *How the Good Guys Finally Won: Notes from an Impeachment Summer* (New York, Viking, 1975), 93.

204 *Liddy, meanwhile, scoured his life*: Liddy, *Will*, 262.

205 *James McCord's wife: Jack* Anderson, "Watergate Forces Retirement at CIA," *Washington Post*, April 2, 1974, https://www.cia.gov/readingroom/docs/CIA-RDP84-004 99R000200010002-2.pdf.

205 *Around two-thirty that afternoon*: "Transcript of a Meeting Between the President and Charles Colson on June 20, 1972, from 2:20 to 3:30 P.M.," Richard Nixon Presidential

Library and Museum, https://www.nixonlibrary.gov/sites/default/files/forresearchers/find/tapes/watergate/wspf/342–027.pdf.

206 *Liddy promised that everyone*: Hunt, *Undercover*, 264.

207 *"His was the one name"*: Shepard, *Woodward and Bernstein*, 34.

207 *"As it happened, what often seemed"*: Sussman, *The Great Cover-Up*, 55.

207 *"He was well ahead of me"*: Graham, *Personal History*, 463.

208 *"John Dean is going to be handling"*: Gray, *In Nixon's Web*, 63.

208 *"None of us in the FBI"*: Ibid., 65.

208 *For his part, Henry Petersen*: Dean, *Blind Ambition*, 121.

209 *"We just could not see"*: "04. Book II, Vol. 1: Events following the Watergate break-in, June 17, 1972-February 9, 1973," Santa Clara Law Digital Commons, https://digital commons.law.scu.edu/cgi/viewcontent.cgi?article=1003&context=watergate.

209 *"{The head of the FBI Washington Field Office}"*: Lano, "Watergate: Forty Years Later."

210 *"The way to handle this"*: "The 'Smoking Gun' Transcript," *Los Angeles Times*, July 21, 1990, https://www.latimes.com/archives/la-xpm-1990–07–21-mn-345-story.html.

210 *"The scheme … relied on Nixon's cherished powers"*: Wicker, *One of Us*, 685.

211 *"most violent attack"*: Robert T. Hartmann, "Ordeal in Venezuela," *Los Angeles Times*, May 26, 1958.

211 *"Haldeman said that the 'bugging' affair"*: *Statement of Information*, 2:380, https://books.google.com/books?id=GNlFYAKTRNMC.

211 *"I'm just following my instructions"*: Haldeman, *The Ends of Power*, 37–39.

211 *"I had been in Washington"*: Vernon A. Walters, *Silent Missions* (Garden City, NY: Doubleday, 1978), 588–89.

212 *"I was totally aware"*: Dean, *Blind Ambition*, 202.

213 *"Holy shit"*: Lukas, *Nightmare*, 247–48.

213 *"I distinctly recall"*: "Excerpts from Testimony."

213 *Gray seemed to understand he was doing something wrong*: Sanford J. Ungar, *FBI: An Uncensored Look Behind the Walls* (Boston: Little, Brown, 1976), 532.

Chapter 16 **"Keep My Mouth Shut"**

215 *"I would have understood it"*: McLendon, *Martha*, 11.

216 *The United Press article*: United Press, "What Martha Said She Told John," *San Francisco Chronicle*, June 23, 1972, http://jfk.hood.edu/Collection/White%20Materials/Watergate/Watergate%20Items%2000001%20to%2000180/Watergate%2000031.pdf.

216 *Steve King*: Quoted in "Steve King's non-denial denial," Xoff Files, August 5, 2006, archived at: https://web.archive.org/web/20160819063954/http://thexofffiles.blogspot.com/2006/08/steve-kings-non-denial-denial.html

216 *"They pulled down my pants"*: McLendon, *Martha*, 15.

217 *"If you could see me"*: Ibid., 18.

217 *The next day's Daily News*: Cadden, "Martha Mitchell."

218 SOMEONE IN THE FBI: Gray, *In Nixon's Web*, 74.

218 *Decades after the fact*: Holland, *Leak*, 35.

218 *"warning to Gray"*: W. Mark Felt and John D. O'Connor, *A G-Man's Life: The FBI, Being 'Deep Throat,' and the Struggle for Honor in Washington* (New York: PublicAffairs, 2007), 198.

219 *"The facts set forth"*: Lano, "Watergate: Forty Years Later."

220 *"Keep my mouth shut"*: Liddy, *Will*, 268.

220 *"The longer you wait"*: *Summary of Information*, 42.

221 *"A hell of a lot of people"*: Ibid.

221 *"Investigation today turned up no evidence"*: Robert B. Semple, Jr., "Mitchell Quits Post, Putting Family First," *New York Times*, July 2, 1972, https://timesmachine.nytimes.com /timesmachine/1972/07/02/170545052.html.

221 *"If my own investigation had turned up"*: Robert B. Semple, Jr., "Mitchell Relaxes in New Office Only 50 Paces from His Old," *New York Times*, July 8, 1972, http://jfk.hood.edu /Collection/White%20Materials/Watergate/Watergate%20Items%2000001%20to%20 00180/Watergate%2000057.pdf.

221 *"She spent a million dollars"*: Rosen, *The Strong Man*, 326.

222 *Dean promptly called Felt*: *Inquiry Into the Alleged Involvement of the Central Intelligence Agency in the Watergate and Ellsberg Matters: Hearings Before the Special Subcommittee on Intelligence of the Committee on Armed Services*, 94th Congr. 221 (1975), https://books.google.com /books?id=bgPSAAAAMAAJ.

222 *The article on Hunt's safe*: Holland, *Leak*, 39.

Chapter 17 The Arrival of Mr. Rivers

223 *"I was rumored to be"*: Hunt, *Undercover*, 262.

224 *"a story of deceit"*: Szulc, *Compulsive Spy*, 159.

225 *"Kalmbach gulped"*: Dean, *Blind Ambition*, 123.

225 *Bittman received an anonymous phone call*: Hunt, *Undercover*, 269.

225 *"Dean thinks you're the man"*: Ulasewicz, *The President's Private Eye*, 251.

225 *"Kalmbach was still the President's attorney"*: Ibid.

225 *"I didn't trust Dean"*: Ibid.

226 *Dorothy Hunt provided*: Hunt, *Undercover*, 271.

226 *Liddy received his own coded call*: Liddy, *Will*, 270.

226 *The private eye found himself*: Ulasewicz, *The President's Private Eye*, 258.

226 *Columnist Joseph Kraft reminded*: Joseph Kraft, "Wherein Dirty Work Is Encouraged," *Boston Globe*, June 26, 1972, newspapers.com/image/435492927/.

227 *"The story died like a fourth of July skyrocket"*: Salisbury, *Without Fear or Favor*, 422.

227 *"I would've gone in a song"*: Jeff Himmelman, *Yours in Truth: A Personal Portrait of Ben Bradlee* (New York: Random House, 2012), 151.

227 *With his family, Woodward tried*: Adrian Havill, *Deep Truth: The Lives of Bob Woodward and Carl Bernstein* (Secaucus, NJ: Carol Publishing, 1993), 75.

227 *"I had a long association with the President"*: *Inquiry Into the Alleged Involvement*, 158.

228 *"Dick Walters and I feel"*: *Presidential Campaign Activities of 1972, Senate Resolution 60: Hearings Before the Select Committee on Presidential Campaign Activities*. Vols. 7–9. 93rd Congr. 9:3462 (1973), https://books.google.com/books?id=2hf15pdgu78C.

228 *Even as Gray and Nixon spoke*: Magruder, *An American Life*, 240.

229 *"was in regard to a man talking"*: "Watergate: Part 19 of 101," FBI Records: The Vault, https://vault.fbi.gov/watergate/watergate-part-19–20-of, 17–31.

229 *"He gave us some very valuable evidence"*: Earl J. Silbert, interview by William F. Causey, February 29 and March 7, 1992, Oral History Project, The Historical Society of the District of Columbia Circuit, https://dcchs.org/sb_pdf/complete-oral-history-silbert/.

230 *"In our view, {Liddy} and Hunt"*: Ibid.

230 *"I need some time to think about that"*: Magruder, *An American Life*, 236.

231 *"I was beginning to sense"*: Ibid., 244.

231 *"soldier of fortune"*: "Watergate: Part 19 of 101," 237–38.

231 *"My own feeling was that Henry"*: Sussman, *The Great Cover-Up*, 81.

231 *Gray at one point even brought Felt*: Felt, *The FBI Pyramid*, 212.

231 *"silent obstruction"*: Ibid., 202.

Chapter 18 **The Dahlberg Check**

233 *"From the moment McCord was identified"*: Salisbury, *Without Fear or Favor*, 421.

233 *"just dreadful"*: Ibid., 416.

234 *Early in July, he flew*: Robert H. Phelps, *God and the Editor: My Search for Meaning at the New York Times* (Syracuse, NY: Syracuse University Press, 2009), 170.

234 *On July 25, the* New York Times *published*: Walter Rugaber, "Calls to C.O.P. Unit Linked to Raid on the Democrats," *New York Times*, July 25, 1972, https://timesmachine.nytimes.com/timesmachine/1972/07/25/83449290.html.

234 *"Why didn't we have that?"*: David Halberstam, *The Powers That Be* (New York: Knopf, 1979), 618.

234 *"{Simons was} the day-to-day agitator"*: Carol Felsenthal, "Ben Bradlee's Secret Weapon," *Politico*, October 28, 2014, https://www.politico.com/magazine/story/2014/10/howard-simons-ben-bradlees-secret-weapon-112291/.

234 *"I don't have anything good to say"*: Shepard, *Woodward and Bernstein*, 84.

235 *Rugaber's latest scoop*: Walter Rugaber, "Cash in Capital Raid Traced to Mexico," *New York Times*, July 31, 1972, https://timesmachine.nytimes.com/timesmachine/1972/07/31/90718114.html?pageNumber=1.

235 *"arguably the most important decision"*: Himmelman, *Yours in Truth*, 161.

235 *"Whatever you said about Bernstein"*: Ibid., 152.

236 *"I don't have the vaguest idea"*: Bernstein and Woodward, *All the President's Men*, 44.

236 *"It was, as Rugaber said, the smoking pistol"*: Salisbury, *Without Fear or Favor*, 425.

236 *Based on the reports*: Sussman, *The Great Cover-Up*, 86; Robert M. Smith, "Elections Agency and F.B.I. Examine G.O.P. Unit Funds," *New York Times*, August 2, 1972, http://jfk.hood.edu/Collection/White%20Materials/Watergate/Watergate%20Items%2000001%20to%2000180/Watergate%2000074.pdf.

237 *"The President's view"*: "Nixon Gives OK to Probe," *San Francisco Examiner*, August 2, 1972, http://jfk.hood.edu/Collection/White%20Materials/Watergate/Watergate%20Items%2000001%20to%2000180/Watergate%2000075.pdf.

237 *"I'm not that worried about it"*: " 'If It Blows, It Blows,'" Tape 758–011 A, Miller Center, https://millercenter.org/the-presidency/secret-white-house-tapes/if-it-blows-it-blows.

238 *He had escaped*: Magruder, *An American Life*, 251.

000 *Nixon fared just as well*: Sussman, *The Great Cover-Up*, 20.

238 *"As the cover-up progressed"*: Dean, *Blind Ambition*, 127.

238 *"buried even on the* Post*'s front page"*: James M. Perry, "Watergate Case Study," Columbia School of Journalism, http://www.columbia.edu/itc/journalism/j6075/edit/readings/watergate.html.

238 *That August, Democratic candidate*: O'Brien, *No Final Victories*, 319–21.

238 *"Until you made your argument"*: Evan Thomas, *The Man to See: Edward Bennett Williams: Ultimate Insider, Legendary Trial Lawyer* (New York, Simon & Schuster, 1991), 270.

239   *In the next morning's newspaper*: Walter Rugaber, "Stans Asserts He Doesn't Know How Suspect Got G.O.P. Funds," *New York Times*, August 25, 1972, https://timesmachine .nytimes.com/timesmachine/1972/08/25/93418168.html?pageNumber=1.

239   *Adding insult to injury, the GAO*: Bernard Gwertzman, "G.A.O. Report Asks Justice Inquiry into G.O.P. Funds," *New York Times*, August 27, 1972, https://timesmachine.nytimes .com/timesmachine/1972/08/27/91341857.html?pageNumber=1.

240   *"a rat's nest"*: Graves, *Nixon's FBI*, 167–68.

240   *"Anything less can only destroy"*: "Nixon Gifts Case Sent to Justice Department," *St. Louis Post Dispatch*, August 27, 1972, https://www.newspapers.com/image/140691296/.

240   *"Our efforts to make Watergate"*: O'Brien, *No Final Victories*, 333.

240   *"an honest man and one who is very meticulous"*: Richard Nixon, "The President's News Conference," August 29, 1972, American Presidency Project, https://www.presidency.ucsb .edu/documents/the-presidents-news-conference-90.

241   *"damn near fell off the bed"*: Dean, *Blind Ambition*, 129.

Chapter 19   **The Patman Probe**

243   *Speaker of the House Carl Albert*: Carl Albert, *Little Giant: The Life and Times of Speaker Carl Albert* (Norman: University of Oklahoma Press, 1990), 358.

243   *"To Wright Patman," the* New York Times *explained*: Eileen Shanahan, "Wright Patman, 82, Dean of House, Dies," *New York Times*, March 8, 1976, https://timesmachine.nytimes .com/timesmachine/1976/03/08/96992398.html?pageNumber=1.

244   *"He's something of a crank"*: Ibid.

244   *From the start, Patman saw the markers*: Sussman, *The Great Cover-Up*, 88.

244   *Accusing the labor union CIO's political action committee*: "National Affairs: New Faces in the House," *TIME*, November 18, 1946, https://web.archive.org/web/20130721150928 /http://www.time.com/time/magazine/article/0,9171,777278,00.html.

244   *"As soon as we asked the question"*: Leon Neyfakh, "The Defeat of Wright Patman," *Slow Burn*, December 6, 2017, https://slate.com/news-and-politics/2019/09/slow-burn-season -1-episode-2-transcript.html.

245   *"The case had begun to resemble"*: "Republicans: Watergate, Contd.," *TIME*, August 14, 1972, http://content.time.com/time/subscriber/article/0,33009,906203,00.html.

245   *"The 'revelations' in newspaper and magazine stories"*: Gray, *In Nixon's Web*, 197.

246   *"The answer is, I don't know"*: Holland, *Leak*, 54.

246   *Baldwin's role in the burglary*: Ibid., 77.

246   *"It did not occur to them"*: Ibid.

246–47   *"The article which appeared in the* Washington Post": Ibid.

247   *"wanderings of Republican campaign funds"*: United Press, "GOP Complaints to Bring House Committee Probe of Dem Headquarters Break-In," *Sandusky (OH) Register*, September 7, 1972, https://newspaperarchive.com/sandusky-register-sep-07–1972-p-6/.

Chapter 20   **"A Hell of a Story"**

249   *John J. Sirica, a scrappy and streetwise*: John J. Sirica, *To Set the Record Straight: The Break-In, the Tapes, the Conspirators, the Pardon* (New York: Norton, 1979), 32.

250   *"regarded near the bottom"*: Sussman, *The Great Cover-Up*, 140.

251   *"Well, you had quite a day today"*: "Transcript of a Recording of a Meeting Among the

President, H. R. Haldeman, and John Dean, on September 15, 1972, at 5:27 to 6:17 P.M. (First Installment)," Gerald R. Ford Presidential Library and Museum, https://www .fordlibrarymuseum.gov/museum/exhibits/watergate_files/document_transcript_4_2.pdf.

253 *"lonely, frustrating, tedious"*: Downie, *The New Muckrakers*, 10.

253 *Sussman grew used to the sight*: Shepard, *Woodward and Bernstein*, 65.

253 *"Don't you guys work together?"*: Bernstein and Woodward, *All the President's Men*, 50.

254 *"Reporters didn't do that then"*: Shepard, *Woodward and Bernstein*, 46.

254 *"It was like selling magazine subscriptions"*: Havill, *Deep Truth*, 77.

254 *"Well how did they harass them?"*: Bernstein and Woodward, *All the President's Men*, 63.

254 *"It can safely be said"*: Ibid., 70.

255 *"No one employed by this committee"*: Bob Woodward and Carl Bernstein, "Spy Funds Linked to GOP Aides," *Washington Post*, September 17, 1972, https://www.pulitzer.org/winners /washington-post.

255 *"I went down in good faith"*: Bernstein and Woodward, *All the President's Men*, 75.

256 *"Oh my god"*: Holland, *Leak*, 82.

256 *"wanted no part"*: Bob Woodward and Carl Bernstein, "2 Linked to Secret GOP Fund," *Washington Post*, September 18, 1972, https://www.pulitzer.org/winners/washington-post.

256 *"I haven't talked to the press"*: Bernstein and Woodward, *All the President's Men*, 81.

256 *"a massive 'house-cleaning'"*: Bob Woodward and Carl Bernstein, "Watergate Data Destruction Charged," *Washington Post*, September 20, 1972, https://www.pulitzer.org/winners /washington-post.

256 *"The sources of the* Washington Post*"*: Bernstein and Woodward, *All the President's Men*, 90.

256 *"the biggest lot of crap"*: Ibid., 91.

257 *"Sir, I'm sorry to bother you"*: Ibid., 105.

257 *"Leave everything in"*: Ibid., 106.

258 *"We thought, 'If this is such a hell of a story'"*: Carol Felsenthal, *Power, Privilege, and the Post: The Katharine Graham Story* (New York: Putnam's, 1993), 315.

258 *"What they didn't realize is that you can't ruin"*: Elaine Woo, "Jack Nelson Dies at 80," *Los Angeles Times*, October 21, 2009, https://www.latimes.com/archives/la-xpm-2009-oct -21-la-me-jack-nelson22–2009oct22-story.html.

258 *Nelson had worked the Watergate beat*: Halberstam, *The Powers That Be*, 634.

258 *Even coming from the normally conservative paper*: Ibid., 636.

259 *the paper didn't endorse*: "L.A. Times Gives First Presidential Endorsements Since Nixon," *East Bay Times*, February 2, 2008, https://www.eastbaytimes.com/2008/02/02/l-a-times -gives-first-presidential-endorsements-since-nixon/.

259 *seemed accurate*: Felsenthal, *Power, Privilege, and the Post*, 315.

259 *"Nobody is paying any attention"*: Bernstein and Woodward, *All the President's Men*, 79.

259 *"Everyone wants to talk to Al"*: Ibid., 109.

260 *As their meeting wound down*: Halberstam, *The Powers That Be*, 639.

260 *Around noon, Judge Sirica*: Robert L. Jackson and Ronald J. Ostrow, "Congressmen Attack Watergate 'Gag'; Support by U.S. Hinted," *Los Angeles Times*, October 6, 1972, https:// www.newspapers.com/image/386000087/.

260 *His order enjoined the Justice Department*: Sirica, *To Set the Record Straight*, 50; *Nomination of Earl J. Silbert*, 11.

260 *"Across the street in the Democratic National Committee"*: Alfred C. Baldwin III, "An Insider's Account of the Watergate Bugging," *Los Angeles Times*, October 5, 1972, https://www .newspapers.com/image/385989532/.

261 *The story rocked Washington*: Sussman, *The Great Cover-Up*, 141.

261 *"perhaps the most important Watergate story"*: Halberstam, *The Powers That Be*, 640.

261 *Hunt's lawyers subpoenaed*: Walter Rugaber, "Los Angeles Times Is Ordered to Give Court Tape of Interview," *New York Times*, December 15, 1972, https://timesmachine.nytimes .com/timesmachine/1972/12/15/83452217.html?pageNumber=35.

261 *When the* Times *refused to turn over the tapes*: Walter Rugaber, "Newsman Jailed in Refusal to Yield Watergate Tapes," *New York Times*, December 20, 1972, https://timesmachine .nytimes.com/timesmachine/1972/12/20/79484694.html?pageNumber=29.

261 *"This was supremely cynical"*: Dean, *Blind Ambition*, 143.

262 *"This is a serious case"*: Summary of Information: Hearings Before the Committee on the Judiciary Pursuant to H. Res. 803, 93rd Congr. 118 (1974), https://books.google.com/books?id=g6A nAAAAMAAJ.

262 *"Politics should stay out"*: "House Panel Bars Pre-Nov. 7 Inquiry into Bugging Case," *New York Times*, October 4, 1972, https://timesmachine.nytimes.com/timesmachine /1972/10/04/90720543.html?pageNumber=1.

262 *Patman lost his bid*: Ibid.

262 *"I predict that the facts will come out"*: Ibid.

263 *"It would be absolutely crazy"*: "Patman Bids 4 Nixon Aides Testify on Watergate Case," *New York Times*, October 11, 1972, https://timesmachine.nytimes.com/timesmachine /1972/10/11/79431617.html?pageNumber=27.

263 *"This is a sad spectacle"*: "Nixon Aides Balk on Watergate Hearing," *New York Times*, October 12, 1972, https://timesmachine.nytimes.com/timesmachine/1972/10/12/91352321 .html?pageNumber=40.

Chapter 21 "I Can't Talk About Segretti"

265 *Subsequent evidence has indicated*: Holland, *Leak*, 89.

265 *"You guys are causing big trouble"*: Bernstein and Woodward, *All the President's Men*, 175–76.

266 *Bernstein also used a confidential source*: Ibid., 112–22.

267 *"This is ridiculous"*: Ibid., 124.

267 *"This is material for a good novel"*: Sussman, *The Great Cover-Up*, 112.

267 *"I can't talk about {Segretti}"*: Bernstein and Woodward, *All the President's Men*, 126.

267 *"I was shocked when I learned"*: Ibid., 129.

268 *"Why don't we put it on paper"*: Sussman, *The Great Cover-Up*, 113.

268 *The identity of Woodward's source*: Ibid., 111.

268 *"Remember, you don't do those 1,500 {FBI} interviews"*: Bernstein and Woodward, *All the President's Men*, 135.

269 *"Our understanding of Watergate"*: Sussman, *The Great Cover-Up*, 113.

269 *"FBI agents have established"*: Carl Bernstein and Bob Woodward, "FBI Finds Nixon Aides Sabotaged Democrats," *Washington Post*, October 10, 1972, https://www.washingtonpost .com/wp-srv/national/longterm/watergate/articles/101072-1.htm.

270 *Woodward, even in the heat of Watergate*: Shepard, *Woodward and Bernstein*, 42.

270 *"absolutely false"*: Gray, *In Nixon's Web*, 128.

270 *for months, Simons would bug*: Phelps, *God and the Editor*, 173.

270 *As it came out later, they both*: John M. Crewdson, "Sabotaging the G.O.P.'s Rivals: Story of a $100,000 Operation," *New York Times*, July 9, 1973, https://timesmachine.nytimes .com/timesmachine/1973/07/09/99155189.html?pageNumber=1.

270 *After the article ran*: Gray, *In Nixon's Web*, 129.

270 *"You know, materials are leaked"*: Richard A. Moss, ed., Conversation 370–9, Segment 1, National Security Archive, https://nsarchive2.gwu.edu//NSAEBB/NSAEBB156/370 -09.pdf.

271 *It's not clear from the conversation*: Holland, *Leak*, 235 (note 26); Kutler, *Abuse of Power*, 173; Woodward, *The Secret Man*, 87.

272 *"We found the FBI leak"*: H. R. Haldeman, "Diaries Collection, January 18, 1969-April 30, 1973," National Archives and Records Administration, https://www.nixonlibrary .gov/sites/default/files/virtuallibrary/documents/haldeman-diaries/37-hrhd-audio cassette-ac26a-19721020-pa.pdf

272 *"He's leaking, Pat"*: Gray, *In Nixon's Web*, 129.

272 *"There are leaks in the FBI"*: Ibid., 131.

272 *"While the White House has tried"*: "The FBI: Political Orders," *TIME*, November 6, 1972, http://content.time.com/time/subscriber/article/0,33009,942582,00.html.

273 *Playing both arsonist and firefighter*: Gray, *In Nixon's Web*, 132.

273 *"{Woodward and Bernstein's} stories"*: W. Mark Felt to Robert Gebhardt, memorandum, February 21, 1973, National Security Archives, https://nsarchive2.gwu.edu/NSAEBB /NSAEBB156/1935.pdf.

273 *An October Gallup poll*: Alicia C. Shepard, "If Walter Cronkite Said It Was a Story, It Was," NPR, July 20, 2009, https://www.npr.org/templates/story/story.php?storyId=106806208.

273 *"It was from Baldwin that I first got a sense"*: Daniel Schorr, *Clearing the Air* (Boston: Houghton Mifflin, 1977), 25.

273 *"How is Larry O'Brien's press corps?"*: Ibid., 22.

274 *"authorized to approve payments"*: Carl Bernstein and Bob Woodward, "Testimony Ties Top Nixon Aide to Secret Fund," *Washington Post*, October 25, 1972, http://jfk.hood.edu /Collection/Weisberg%20Subject%20Index%20Files/B%20Disk/Bugging%201971 /Item%2018.pdf.

274 *"We categorically deny"*: Peter Osnos, "White House, GOP Flay 'Fund' Story," *Akron (OH) Beacon Journal*, October 26, 1972, https://www.newspapers.com/image/152470500/.

274 *"my lowest moment in Watergate"*: Schorr, *Clearing the Air*, 29.

274 *In a later, lengthy statement to the FBI*: "Cable, Washington Field Office to Acting Director, 'James Walter McCord, Jr., etal; Burglary, Democratic National Committee Headquarters, Washington, D.C. June Seventeen Seventy Two,'" National Security Archive, https:// nsarchive2.gwu.edu/NSAEBB/NSAEBB156/1414.pdf.

274 *"The numbers {are} getting"*: Bernstein and Woodward, *All the President's Men*, 179.

274 *"Your inquiry is based on misinformation"*: Ibid., 181.

275 *"shabby journalism"*: Ibid., 184.

275 *"Your story is wrong"*: Ibid.

275 *"This is no fucking joke"*: Ibid., 189.

275 *"one of the agent's superiors"*: Ibid., 190.

276 *"You're getting no answers"*: Ibid., 190–91.

276 *"You don't know where you are"*: Ibid., 192.

276 *"I never said it before"*: Ibid., 193.

276 *"Well, Haldeman slipped away"*: Ibid., 195.

276 *"Bernstein and Woodward have obviously gotten themselves"*: "Cable, Washington Field Office."

277 *Across town at the* New York Times: Phelps, *God and the Editor*, 186.

277 *"They were writing stuff"*: Salisbury, *Without Fear or Favor*, 429.

277 *He was the embodiment of journalistic gravitas*: Shepard, "If Walter Cronkite."

278 *"a kind of extra-legal shadow government"*: Schorr, *Clearing the Air*, 32.

278 *"You saved us"*: Halberstam, *The Powers That Be*, 662.

278 *"There are still no definitive, conclusive answers"*: Walter Rugaber, "The Watergate Mystery," *New York Times*, November 1, 1972, https://timesmachine.nytimes.com/timesmachine /1972/11/01/110096820.html?pageNumber=28.

Chapter 22 Landslide

279 *Thirty thousand people or more*: White, *The Making of the President 1972*, 1.

279 *"I believe that we have the chance"*: Richard Nixon, "Remarks at Ontario, California," November 4, 1972, American Presidency Project, https://www.presidency.ucsb.edu/documents /remarks-ontario-california.

279 *"The only sour note"*: Nixon, *RN*, 714.

280 *"like coming home from an easy win"*: White, *The Making of the President 1972*, 7.

280 *Ziegler joked that the next day*: Ibid.

280 *At home in the White House*: President Richard Nixon's Daily Diary, November 1–15, 1972, Richard Nixon Presidential Library and Museum, https://www.nixonlibrary.gov /sites/default/files/virtuallibrary/documents/PDD/1972/087%20November%201–15%20 1972.pdf.

280 *"There was no air of triumph"*: Colson, *Born Again*, 1.

280 *"He could show no charity"*: Ibid., 5.

280 *"Richard Milhous Nixon yesterday"*: David S. Broder, "Nixon Wins Landslide Victory; Democrats Hold Senate, House," *Washington Post*, November 8, 1972, https://www .washingtonpost.com/wp-srv/national/longterm/watergate/articles/110872–1.htm.

281 *"Nixon believed that second terms"*: Strober and Strober, *Nixon*, 272.

281 *"It was cruel"*: Ibid.

281 *"There's one guy we can't afford"*: Dean, *Blind Ambition*, 149.

281 *"This is the time to face up"*: Strober and Strober, *Nixon*, 270.

281 *"every goddamn Cabinet officer"*: Thomas Powers, *The Man Who Kept the Secrets: Richard Helms & the CIA* (New York: Knopf, 1979), 241.

281 *"During the first term, we stopped"*: Rather and Gates, *The Palace Guard*, 8.

282 *"I think I'm going to switch"*: Dean, *Blind Ambition*, 162

282 *"Colson can be more valuable"*: Sussman, *The Great Cover-Up*, 151.

282 *"{Dean} said the important thing"*: Kutler, *Abuse of Power*, 178.

282 *"I took a sweaty tour"*: Dean, *Blind Ambition*, 168.

284 *"I left the telephone"*: Hunt, *Undercover*, 277.

284 *On November 11, just a week*: Bernstein and Woodward, *All the President's Men*, 201.

284 *"Everybody dried up"*: Shepard, *Woodward and Bernstein*, 63.

285 *"No beating anyone over the head"*: Bernstein and Woodward, *All the President's Men*, 207.

286 *When the paper promised*: Ibid., 224.

286–87 *"returned to more conventional sources"*: Ibid., 212.

287 *"checked w. grand jury list number"*: Himmelman, *Yours in Truth*, 206.

287 *In a five-hundred-word statement*: Joel Achenbach, "Woodward and Bernstein Respond to Himmelman," *Washington Post*, April 30, 2012, https://www.washingtonpost.com /blogs/achenblog/post/woodward-and-bernstein-respond-to-himmelman/2012/04/30 /gIQAt9irrT_blog.html.

288 *Thirty pages after the Z mention*: Bernstein and Woodward, *All the President's Men*, 248.

288 *"Maybe the moral of the story"*: Himmelman, *Yours in Truth*, 209.

288 *"There ain't going to be"*: Kutler, *Abuse of Power*, 174.

288 *"Tying it to us"*: Ibid., 175.

288 *"Please check for me"*: Felsenthal, *Power, Privilege, and the Post*, 315.

288 *Another plot, uncovered later*: Graham, *Personal History*, 477.

289 *"Ben, the kids have got to be right"*: Thomas, *The Man to See*, 275.

289 *"I was feeling beleaguered"*: Graham, *Personal History*, 468.

289 *"What appears in the* Post*"*: Ibid., 473.

289 *Graham actually ran into Bob Dole*: Ibid., 475.

289 *"She had bet the paper"*: Himmelman, *Yours in Truth*, 147.

290 *"I just want everyone in this room"*: Liddy, *Will*, TK.

290 *"Papa, in the car"*: Hunt, *Undercover*, 279.

290 *"We all know who should have handled this"*: Kutler, *Abuse of Power*, 183–84.

291 *"If Helms goes"*: Dash, *Chief Counsel*, 33. The exact text of this letter has varied in various printings, but the gist of the letter and the key phrases have always been constant.

292 *"The clear implication of the substance and tone"*: "Excerpts from Testimony."

292 *"They told me something interesting"*: Salisbury, *Without Fear or Favor*, 434.

Chapter 23 **"Something Was Rotten"**

295 *"With the full blood of Cork City"*: Breslin, *How the Good Guys Finally Won*, 50.

295 *Then, just three weeks before the November election*: Robin Barefield, "The Mysterious Disappearance of Cessna N1812H," July 14, 2018, https://medium.com/@robinbarefield76 /the-mysterious-disappearance-of-cessna-n1812h-8e19dd5cb3ee.

296 *The House itself was also in flux*: Albert, *Little Giant*, 315.

296 *He had witnessed plenty of hardball politics*: O'Neill, *Man of the House*, 241.

296 *"I'm a Democrat, but I'll give you"*: Breslin, *How the Good Guys Finally Won*, 22.

297 *"They had practically blackjacked"*: O'Neill, *Man of the House*, 339.

297 *"Tom didn't reveal any dirty secret"*: Ibid., 239.

297 *"I was convinced that something was rotten"*: Ibid., 235.

297 *"The time is going to come"*: Breslin, *How the Good Guys Finally Won*, 12.

298 *The Republican House minority leader*: Gerald R. Ford, "House Floor Speech: Impeach Justice Douglas," April 15, 1970, Gerald R. Ford Presidential Library and Museum, https://www .fordlibrarymuseum.gov/library/document/0054/4526271.pdf; Marjorie Hunter, "Ford Asks Douglas's Ouster," *New York Times*, April 16, 1970, https://timesmachine.nytimes .com/timesmachine/1970/04/16/78113887.html?pageNumber=1.

298 *"By 1973, the history books"*: Howard Fields, *High Crimes and Misdemeanors* (New York: Norton, 1978), xi.

298 *"You're not a lawyer"*: O'Neill, *Man of the House*, 242.

298 *Richard Nixon turned sixty on January 9*: Associated Press, "Nixon, at 60, Gives Formula for Living: 'Never Slow Down,'" *New York Times*, January 9, 1973, https://timesmachine .nytimes.com/timesmachine/1973/01/09/issue.html.

299 *"the most anonymous Cabinet"*: John Herbers, "Nixon's Presidency: Centralized Control," *New York Times*, March 6, 1973, https://timesmachine.nytimes.com/timesmachine /1973/03/06/90919819.html?pageNumber=1.

299 *Gallup showed him with a national favorable rating*: James Doyle, *Not Above the Law: The Battles of Watergate Prosecutors Cox and Jaworski: A Behind-the-Scenes Account* (New York: Morrow, 1977), 33.

299 *"My instincts told me"*: Sirica, *To Set the Record Straight*, 62.

299 *"The indictment they had prepared"*: Ibid., 57.

300 *"Earl the Pearl" Silbert*: "The Prosecutors: Good Guy, Bad Guy, Chief," *New York Times*, May 3, 1973, https://timesmachine.nytimes.com/timesmachine/1973/05/03/90937873 .html?pageNumber=32.

300 *The forty-six-year-old Seymour Glanzer*: Ibid.

300 *Donald Campbell, whose bald head*: Ibid.

300 *"That really strengthened our case"*: Silbert, interview.

300 *"I mean, are we ever going to know"*: Halberstam, *The Powers That Be*, 677.

Chapter 24 Guilty Pleas

301 *Every seat in D.C.'s largest ceremonial courtroom*: Walter Rugaber, "Jury Is Completed for Trial of 7 in the Watergate Case," *New York Times*, January 10, 1973, https://timesmachine .nytimes.com/timesmachine/1973/01/10/90911931.html?pageNumber=20.

301 *Everyone was in position*: Sussman, *The Great Cover-Up*, 143.

302 *"{It} signaled to me that Earl Silbert"*: Sirica, *To Set the Record Straight*, 64.

302 *"He was a pathetic figure"*: Ibid., 68.

302 *"Anything I may have done"*: Hunt, *Undercover*, 291.

302 *The story had formed after Hersh*: Seymour M. Hersh, *Reporter: A Memoir* (New York: Knopf, 2018), 177.

303 *"One of the defendants, Frank A. Sturgis"*: Seymour M. Hersh, "4 Watergate Defendants Reported Still Being Paid," *New York Times*, January 14, 1973, https://timesmachine .nytimes.com/timesmachine/1973/01/14/91429205.html?pageNumber=1.

303 *"{It was} a newspaper that hated"*: Hersh, *Reporter*, 178.

303 *As part of its recognition*: David Folkenflik, "Veteran Watergate Reporters Looking for Respect," NPR, June 3, 2005, https://www.npr.org/templates/story/story.php?story Id=4679745; Phelps, *God and the Editor*, 186.

303 *"great pressure"*: Seymour M. Hersh, "Pressures to Plead Guilty Alleged in Watergate Case," *New York Times*, January 15, 1973, https://timesmachine.nytimes.com/timesmachine /1973/01/15/99110049.html?pageNumber=13.

303 *That Monday morning, Hersh was surprised*: Seymour M. Hersh, "If Watergate Happened Now, It Would Stay a Secret," *Literary Hub*, July 13, 2018, https://lithub.com/if-water gate-happened-now-it-would-stay-a-secret/.

303 *"I'm sorry"*: Sirica, *To Set the Record Straight*, 71.

304 *the cover-up was actually both still strong*: Liddy, *Will*, 283.

304 *"Gordon, I think you'll recognize"*: Ibid., 278.

304 *Dean's version of this phone call*: Dean, *Blind Ambition*, 181.

305 *"We'll build that son of a bitch up"*: "The Nation: Wagons Around the President," *TIME*, December 2, 1974, http://content.time.com/time/subscriber/article/0,33009,945287,00 .html.

305 *"Jimmy was not prepared"*: Strober and Strober, *Nixon*, 291.

305 *"I have always followed the rule"*: Caulfield, *Caulfield*, 91.

306 *"highest level of the White House"*: Ibid.

307 *The reaction stemmed from a lunch*: Charles Morgan, Jr., *One Man, One Voice* (New York: Holt, Rinehart and Winston, 1979), 199–230.

307 the Washington Post*'s twenty-two-page special section*: Sussman, *The Great Cover-Up*, 147.

308 *The trial produced almost nothing of drama*: Ibid., 148.

308 *"{Silbert} swallowed the perjury"*: Liddy, *Will*, 284.

308 *Unsatisfied by Silbert's prosecutorial efforts*: Sussman, *The Great Cover-Up*, 142.

309 *"Watergate was kept alive"*: O'Brien, *No Final Victories*, 339.

309 *"Take it easy, kid"*: Liddy, *Will*, 285.

309 *"I am still not satisfied"*: Sirica, *To Set the Record Straight*, 88.

309 *"I would frankly hope"*: Dash, *Chief Counsel*, 5.

309–10 *"Destroying the notebooks"*: Dean, *Blind Ambition*, 182.

310 *The Hermès notebook episode*: Ibid.; Geoff Shepard, *The Secret Plot to Make Ted Kennedy President: Inside the Real Watergate Conspiracy* (New York: Sentinel, 2008), 237.

310 *"There is something rancid"*: John Ehrlichman to H. R. Haldeman, memorandum, January 25, 1973, Richard Nixon Presidential Library and Museum, https://www.nixonlibrary .gov/sites/default/files/virtuallibrary/documents/jan10/075.pdf.

Chapter 25 The "Country Lawyer" Enters

311 *"when Watergate jokes were going around"*: Don Oberdorfer, *Senator Mansfield: The Extraordinary Life of a Great Statesman and Diplomat* (Washington, D.C.: Smithsonian), 431.

312 *A former state associate supreme court justice*: Karl E. Campbell, *Senator Sam Ervin, Last of the Founding Fathers* (Chapel Hill: University of North Carolina Press, 2007), 279.

312 *"I knew he'd be fair-minded"*: Oberdorfer, *Senator Mansfield*, 432.

312 *"Ervin works harder than most"*: "Edited Transcripts of Conversations Taped in the White House," *New York Times*, May 1, 1974, https://timesmachine.nytimes.com/timesmachine /1974/05/01/101021413.html?pageNumber=27.

312 *"I suspected the committee might discover"*: Sam J. Ervin, Jr., *The Whole Truth: The Watergate Conspiracy* (New York: Random House, 1980), xi.

313 *"This Watergate investigation"*: Dash, *Chief Counsel*, 6.

313 *"The only names I could recall without prompting"*: Fred Thompson, *At That Point in Time: The Inside Story of the Senate Watergate Committee* (New York: Quadrangle/The New York Times Book Co., 1975), 5.

314 *"Physically, he seemed to dominate"*: Dash, *Chief Counsel*, 15.

314 *"We're not going to need a year"*: Ibid., 16.

314 *"Bellino appeared easygoing"*: Thompson, *At That Point in Time*, 34.

314 *Despite the scope of the investigations ahead*: Lowell P. Weicker, *Maverick: A Life in Politics* (Boston: Little, Brown, 1995), 59.

314 *"I don't believe any senator"*: Terry F. Lenzner, *The Investigator: Fifty Years of Uncovering the Truth* (New York: Blue Rider Press, 2013), 105.

315 *"Mind you, he wasn't even accusing"*: David Thelen, "Remembering the Discovery of the Watergate Tapes," *Journal of American History* 75, no. 4 (March 1989), https://www.jstor .org/stable/1908637.

315 *To start, Lenzner had asked the staff*: Thompson, *At That Point in Time*, 26.

315 *"Bob agreed to help"*: Dash, *Chief Counsel*, 24.

316   *With time, they refined a strategy*: *Presidential Campaign Activities of 1972*, Vols. 1–4, 3:982–83, https://books.google.com/books?id=4stFAQAAMAAJ.

316   *"The coverup had become a way of life"*: Ibid., 983.

317   *Ehrlichman, who had long tried to avoid*: Ervin, *The Whole Truth*, 26.

317   *"I heard enough to trouble me"*: Ehrlichman, *Witness to Power*, page 367.

317   *"When I'm speaking of Watergate"*: James M. Naughton and Anthony Marro, "New Tapes Link Nixon to Watergate Scheme 3 Days After Break-In," *New York Times*, May 1, 1977, https://timesmachine.nytimes.com/timesmachine/1977/05/01/140460952.html?pageNumber=1.

317   *"Jim, I have worked with these people"*: *Presidential Campaign Activities of 1972*, 1:260.

Chapter 26   **"Twist Slowly, Slowly in the Wind"**

319   *The catastrophic miscalculations*: Holland, *Leak*, 108.

319   *"It is a true story"*: Nixon, *RN*, 778.

319   *"{Gray} is a guy we can tell to do things"*: Douglas Brinkley and Luke Nichter, *The Nixon Tapes: 1973* (Boston: Houghton Mifflin Harcourt, 2015), 65.

320   *"This country, this bureaucracy"*: Gray, *In Nixon's Web*, 173.

320   *"The point you ought to make"*: "Transcript of a Recording of a Conversation of February 16, 1973, between President Nixon, John Ehrlichman and L. Patrick Gray from approximately 9:08 to 9:39 a.m. in the Oval Office," Richard Nixon Presidential Library and Museum, https://www.nixonlibrary.gov/sites/default/files/forresearchers/find/tapes/watergate/wspf/858–003.pdf.

320   *"For thirty minutes, he lectured me"*: Gray, *In Nixon's Web*, 176.

320   *"You did what?!"*: Graves, *Nixon's FBI*, 191.

321   *"What's the matter with him?"*: Thomas, *Being Nixon*, 433.

321   *Back at FBI headquarters*: Felt to Gebhardt, memorandum.

321   *"Until February 28, 1973"*: Sussman, *The Great Cover-Up*, 166.

322   *Though Gray kept citing the "presumption of regularity"*: Graves, *Nixon's FBI*, 148.

322   *"Everything is accepted at face value"*: *Louis Patrick Gray III: Hearings Before the Committee on the Judiciary*, 93rd Congr. 669 (1974), https://books.google.com/books?id=lgYcApPO6CcC.

322   *"stand awful tight in the saddle"*: Sussman, *The Great Cover-Up*, 169.

322   *"It makes me gag"*: Gray, *In Nixon's Web*, 213.

322   *"After going through the hell"*: Ibid., 220.

323   *"Ron, since both Mr. Kalmbach"*: Sussman, *The Great Cover-Up*, 173.

323   *through February, March, and April*: Ehrlichman, *Witness to Power*, 343.

323   *Dean too moved further*: Sussman, *The Great Cover-Up*, 152.

323   *"This could stretch into the White House"*: Stephen E. Ambrose, *Nixon: Ruin and Recovery, 1973–1990* (New York: Simon & Schuster, 1991), 48.

323   *"One of the things that stands out"*: Ibid., 81.

324   *"This was Watergate: an endless clash"*: Rosen, *The Strong Man*, 298.

324   *At one point, they discussed calling in*: Statement of Information, 3:1179, https://books.google.com/books?id=sH1qDFYOIG8C.

324   *"It's your view the vulnerabilities"*: Dean, *Blind Ambition*, 189.

325   *"If they send you to prison"*: Ibid., 191.

325   *"After nine months, the hot torch"*: Ibid., 194.

325   *"I wanted to talk with you"*: "Edited Transcripts of Conversations Taped in the White House."

326 *"There is no business that could be run"*: Archibald Cox, "Executive Privilege," *University of Pennsylvania Law Review* 122, no. 6 (June 1974), https://scholarship.law.upenn.edu/cgi/viewcontent.cgi?article=5725&context=penn_law_review.

326 *In March, he explained publicly*: Kenneth Bredemeier, "Tapes Show Nixon Role in Firing of Ernest Fitzgerald," *Washington Post*, March 7, 1979, https://www.washingtonpost.com/archive/politics/1979/03/07/tapes-show-nixon-role-in-firing-of-ernest-fitzgerald/048cd88e-60e5-498d-a8e2-e3b39461356b/.

326 *"In the performance of their duties"*: Richard Nixon, "Statement About Executive Privilege," March 12, 1973, American Presidency Project, https://www.presidency.ucsb.edu/documents/statement-about-executive-privilege.

326 *"executive privilege will not be used"*: Ibid.

328 *"sort of one of the unknown"*: "Excerpts from New Transcripts of 201 Hours of Secret Nixon Tapes," *New York Times*, October 31, 1997, https://timesmachine.nytimes.com/timesmachine/1997/10/31/890731.html?pageNumber=18.

328 *"No problem"*: Ibid.

328 *"I want you to know that. . . I'm aware"*: George Lardner, Jr., and Walter Pincus, "Nixon's Fateful Reversal," *Washington Post*, October 30, 1997, https://www.washingtonpost.com/archive/politics/1997/10/30/nixons-fateful-reversal/91e1ce61-e7e4-4c66-a76a-af2c55f1327e/.

328 *"a few pipsqueaks down the line"*: Kutler, *Abuse of Power*, 226.

328 *"Can I report"*: Dean, *Blind Ambition*, 197.

328 *"We could probably do it"*: Ibid., 200.

329 *"The reason I thought we ought to talk"*: Brinkley and Nichter, *The Nixon Tapes: 1973*, 277–310.

332 *As Nixon stood up from his desk*: *President Richard Nixon Standing in the Oval Office with Members of the Russian Soviet Women's Gymnastics Team*, 1973, photograph, Richard Nixon Presidential Library and Museum, https://catalog.archives.gov/id/7268206.

332 *"I watched the Olympics on television"*: Memorandum of Conversation: March 21, 1973, Nixon, Soviet Women's Gymnastics Team," Gerald R. Ford Presidential Library and Museum, https://www.fordlibrarymuseum.gov/library/document/0314/1552571.pdf.

332 *"What the hell is he going to disclose"*: "The 'Cancer on the Presidency' Conversation," Conversation 886–8, Watergate CLE II, http://www.watergatecle.com/wp-content/uploads/2012/06/March-211973-Cancer-on-the-presidency-transcript.pdf.

333 *"We may have a need for substantial"*: Kutler, *Abuse of Power*, 287–88.

333 *"I could count on no further assistance"*: Hunt, *Undercover*, 297.

333 *"He lied to the agents"*: *Statement of Information*, 2:336.

333 *"Gray is dead"*: Gray, *In Nixon's Web*, 229.

334 *"What words of wisdom"*: Brinkley and Nichter, *The Nixon Tapes*, 341.

334 *"I don't give a shit what happens"*: *Summary of Information, 87.*

334 *"You think we want to go this route"*: Dean, *Blind Ambition*, 212; *Transcripts of Eight Recorded Presidential Conversations: Hearings Before the Committee on the Judiciary Pursuant to H. Res. 803,* 93rd Congr. 179 (1974), https://books.google.com/books?id=r2RFAQAAMAAJ.

Chapter 27 **"Perjury Occurred"**

337 *"I think you should be present"*: Dash, *Chief Counsel*, 27.

337 *"Prior to the beginning"*: Ibid., 28.

337 *"Be that as it may"*: Ibid., 29.

338 *"For the first time really"*: Himmelman, *Yours in Truth*, 236.

339 *"I was too embarrassed to let McCord"*: Dash, *Chief Counsel*, 31.

339 *"For the time being, I thought it best"*: Ibid., 32.

339 *"I, in addition to my own sworn testimony"*: Ibid., 34.

340 *"The whole cover-up depended"*: Ibid., 36.

341 *"The truth might persuade him"*: Dean, *Blind Ambition*, 218.

341 *"News leaks of massive proportions"*: Sussman, *The Great Cover-Up*, 189.

342 *"We've been protecting Mitchell"*: Dean, *Blind Ambition*, 221.

342 *"What is Mitchell's option?"*: "Transcript of a Recording of a Meeting Among the President, H. R. Haldeman, John Ehrlichman, and Ronald Ziegler on March 27, 1973, from 11:10 A.M. to 1:30 P.M.," Richard Nixon Presidential Library and Museum, https://www.nixonlibrary.gov/sites/default/files/forresearchers/find/tapes/watergate/wspf/423-003.pdf.

343 *"They were sitting on the hottest committee"*: Dash, *Chief Counsel*, 45.

343 *"It was the first solid indication"*: Thompson, *At That Point in Time*, 19.

343 *"His testimony was damaging"*: Ibid., 23.

344 *"People's lives and futures"*: Dash, *Chief Counsel*, 59.

344 *"The chronology of the affair"*: Magruder, *An American Life*, 288.

345 *"a sense of stoic dignity"*: Dash, *Chief Counsel*, 59.

345 *"Never!"*: Ibid., 60.

345 *"Frankly, under the regular rules"*: Ibid., 67.

345 *"Nonsense"*: Ibid., 70.

345 *"If the members of the committee"*: Thompson, *At That Point in Time*, 28.

346 *"What do you think?"*: Dean, *Blind Ambition*, 227–28.

346 *"I think Shaffer can help us"*: Ibid., 230.

347 *In fact, Liddy in some ways seemed*: Liddy, *Will*, 309.

347 *"Remember that once the toothpaste"*: Dean, *Blind Ambition*, 235.

347 *"The thrust of what he was saying"*: Silbert, interview.

348 *"The hell with Dean"*: Kutler, *Abuse of Power*, 292.

349 *"The whole thing had become ridiculous"*: Magruder, *An American Life*, 292.

350 *"Dean was as involved {in Watergate}"*: Rosen, *The Strong Man*, 295.

350 *"It was too much"*: Silbert, interview.

351 *"Would {his new testimony} be inconsistent"*: Kleindienst, *Justice*, 159.

351 *"When we arrived at his home"*: Ibid., 161.

351 *The next day, Kleindienst went directly*: Impeachment of Richard M. Nixon, 415.

351 *"Absolutely not"*: Kleindienst, *Justice*, 163.

352 *"I was the last senior White House staffer"*: Leonard Garment, *Crazy Rhythm: My Journey from Brooklyn, Jazz, and Wall Street to Nixon's White House, Watergate, and Beyond* (New York: Times Books, 1997), 256.

352 *"Whoever was the culprit"*: Kissinger, *Years of Upheaval*, 75.

352 *"It's just a question of putting together"*: Statement of Information, 4:684, https://books.google.com/books?id=xcVPOY-i-9YC.

353 *"We had already heard a lot of shocking disclosures"*: Silbert, interview.

353 *"I hope someday you'll know"*: Dean, *Blind Ambition*, 261.

Chapter 28 **"What Meat Do They Eat?"**

355 *Joseph Montoya, for one, never seemed*: Lenzner, *The Investigator*, 108.

355 *"Except you, Danny"*: Ibid.

355 *The committee's two rank-and-file Republicans*: Weicker, *Maverick*, 46.

356 *"I don't think he's afraid"*: Thompson, *At That Point in Time*, 14.

356 *The Ervin Committee staff inherited*: John A. Farrell, *Tip O'Neill and the Democratic Century* (Boston: Little, Brown, 2001), 337.

356 *"{We} had more jurisdiction"*: Lenzner, *The Investigator*, 136.

356 *"The Nixon White House probably put down"*: Dash, *Chief Counsel*, 135–36.

357 *Ervin called a rare press conference*: Ervin, *The Whole Truth*, 66; Walter Rugaber, "Ervin in a Clash with White House Over Watergate," *New York Times*, April 3, 1973, https://timesmachine.nytimes.com/timesmachine/1973/04/03/99138454.html?pageNumber=1.

357 *"What meat do they eat"*: Rugaber, "Ervin in a Clash."

358 *"You don't have to tell me why you called"*: Woodward, *The Secret Man*, 95.

358 *On March 21, as a result*: "Text of Nixon's Statement," *New York Times*, April 18, 1973, https://timesmachine.nytimes.com/timesmachine/1973/04/18/79852630.html?pageNumber=97.

358 *that he'd worked on frantically*: "Transcript of a Recording of a Meeting Among the President, John Ehrlichman, Ronald Ziegler, and H. R. Haldeman, in the Oval Office on April 17, 1973, from 3:50 to 4:35 P.M.," Richard Nixon Presidential Library and Museum, https://www.nixonlibrary.gov/sites/default/files/forresearchers/find/tapes/watergate/wspf/898-023_899-001.pdf.

358 *On Capitol Hill, Dash immediately wondered*: Dash, *Chief Counsel*, 71.

359 *"We're cognizant Dean's going to make"*: "Transcript of a Recording, April 17, 1973."

359 *"the fear of God"*: Kissinger, *Years of Upheaval*, 90.

359 *"Some may hope or think"*: Dean, *Blind Ambition*, 270.

359 *"inoperative"*: R. W. Apple, Jr., "Nixon Reports 'Major' Findings in Watergate Inquiry He Made," *New York Times*, April 18, 1973, https://timesmachine.nytimes.com/timesmachine/1973/04/18/79852136.html?pageNumber=1.

359 *"They had not thought of their conduct"*: Kissinger, *Years of Upheaval*, 99.

359 *"Goddamn, I think of these good men"*: "Excerpts from New Transcripts."

360 *"How can you possibly expect"*: Dash, *Chief Counsel*, 73.

361 *"The only thing Liddy appeared"*: Ibid., 75.

361 *"Kalmbach's tale sounded like a combination"*: Ibid., 78.

361 *"John, I'm looking"*: *Statement of Information*, 1:269, https://books.google.com/books?id=GN1FYAKTRNMC.

362 *"The focus is on the president"*: Thompson, *At That Point in Time*, 38.

362 *"Don't know what the son of a bitch"*: "The Nation: Wagons."

362 *"Good morning, John"*: Dean, *Blind Ambition*, 272.

Chapter 29 **"Voice of Doom"**

365 *"If Mitchell really planned Watergate"*: Curtis Prendergast, *The World of Time Inc.: The Intimate History of a Changing Enterprise, 1960–1980* (New York: Atheneum, 1986), 355.

365–66 *"Only in his disgrace"*: Halberstam, *The Powers That Be*, 688.

366 *"offended a sense of justice"*: Martin Arnold, "New Trial Barred," *New York Times*, May 12,

1973, https://timesmachine.nytimes.com/timesmachine/1973/05/12/79855703.html
?pageNumber=1.

366 *"Let me tell you something, Pete"*: Fields, *High Crimes and Misdemeanors*, 28.

366 *Gray wanted to make sure he ended up*: Gray, *In Nixon's Web*, 239.

366 *"I could not accept the fact"*: Ibid., 240.

366 *"A director of the FBI destroying"*: Bernstein and Woodward, *All the President's Men*, 307.

367 *"the intensifying Watergate crisis"*: Walter Rugaber, "A Sudden Decision," *New York Times*,
April 28, 1973, https://timesmachine.nytimes.com/timesmachine/1973/04/28/79854621
.html?pageNumber=14.

367 *"No matter who is involved"*: Ibid.

367 *"faith in Dean began to waver"*: Jack Anderson, "Watergate Scandal Burst Like Bubble," *Daily
Reporter* (Dover, OH), April 26, 1973, https://www.newspapers.com/image/19831009/.

368 *"I think it's entirely conceivable"*: Brinkley and Nichter, *The Nixon Tapes: 1973*, 604–5.

368 *"You, Ehrlichman, and I"*: White, *Breach of Faith*, 217.

368 *"one jump ahead of the fucking sheriff"*: Tom Mathews and Nicholas Horrock, " 'One Jump
Ahead of the Sheriff,'" *Newsweek*, May 9, 1977, http://jfk.hood.edu/Collection/White%20
Materials/Watergate/Watergate%20Items%2022753%20to%2023027/Watergate%20
22876.pdf.

368 *"Now if he's going to have this pissing contest"*: "Transcript of a Recording of a Telephone
Conversation Between the President and H. R. Haldeman on April 25, 1973, from 7:46
to 7:53 P.M.," Richard Nixon Presidential Library and Museum, https://www.nixonlibrary
.gov/sites/default/files/forresearchers/find/tapes/watergate/wspf/038–156_038–157.pdf.

368 *"Do you think the people"*: Mathews and Horrock, " 'One Jump Ahead of the Sheriff.'"

368 *"My god—what the hell"*: Kutler, *The Wars of Watergate*, 315.

368 *"The press has got to realize"*: "Excerpts from New Transcripts."

369 *"Voice of doom"*: Haldeman, *The Ends of Power*, 291.

369 *"Just explain all this"*: Ehrlichman, *Witness to Power*, 390.

369 *"the toughest thing I've ever done"*: Elliot L. Richardson, *The Creative Balance: Government,
Politics, and the Individual in America's Third Century* (New York: Holt, Rinehart and
Winston, 1976), 4.

369 *Richardson, the fifty-two-year-old defense secretary*: Bart Barnes, "Elliot Richardson Dies
at 79," *Washington Post*, January 1, 2000, https://www.washingtonpost.com/archive
/local/2000/01/01/elliot-richardson-dies-at-79/ff53334e-07a2-4f79-9d97-399ab74f7821/.

370 *"It had come to be the cliché"*: Elizabeth Drew, *Washington Journal: Reporting Watergate and
Richard Nixon's Downfall* (New York: Overlook Duckworth, 2014), 64.

370 *"I had no knowledge of any of this"*: Ken Gormley, *Archibald Cox: Conscience of a Nation*
(Reading, MA: Perseus, 1997), 248.

370 *"I wish somehow deep inside"*: Thompson, *The Nixon Presidency*, 54; Richardson related a
slightly different version of this quotation in *The Creative Balance*, 5.

371 *James Polk, a reporter for the* Washington Star-News: Matt Schudel, "James Polk, Pulitzer
Winner for Watergate Reporting, Dies at 83," *Washington Post*, July 24, 2021, https://www
.washingtonpost.com/local/obituaries/james-polk-dead/2021/07/24/a62f2b5c-ec14–11eb
-8950-d73b3e93ff7f_story.html; Peter Kihss, "Pulitzers Given for Reporting on Vesco
and Nixon Tax; No Play or Novel Cited," *New York Times*, May 7, 1974, https://archive
.nytimes.com/www.nytimes.com/books/98/09/06/specials/boorstin-pulitzer.html.

371 *"How do you like them apples?"*: James McCartney, "The Washington 'Post' and Watergate:
How Two Davids Slew Goliath," *Columbia Journalism Review* 12, no. 2 (July 1973), https://

search.proquest.com/openview/38d52575720f0f009f30d44e09ef748e/1?pq-origsite=g
scholar&cbl=1817229.

371 *"I want to talk to you tonight from my heart"*: Richard Nixon, "Address to the Nation About
the Watergate Investigations," April 30, 1973, Miller Center, https://millercenter.org
/the-presidency/presidential-speeches/april-30–1973-address-nation-about-watergate
-investigations.

372 *"It's a tough thing, Bob"*: Tom Curry, "Angry Nixon: New Tapes Reveal an Overwrought
President in Grips of Watergate," NBC News, August 21, 2013, https://www.nbcnews
.com/politics/politics-news/angry-nixon-new-tapes-reveal-overwrought-president-grips
-watergate-flna6C10972359.

Chapter 30   The End of Mark Felt

373 *The agents, armed*: Unger, *FBI*, 549.

374 *"It's bad enough I have to see"*: Bill O'Reilly, unpublished interview by Adam Higginbotham,
2014.

374 *"You're wrong about me"*: Kleindienst, *Justice*, 170.

375 *"The paper had its cock"*: Shepard, *Woodward and Bernstein*, 73.

375 *After months of tentativeness*: Ervin, *The Whole Truth*, 62.

375 *"an unimaginable explosion"*: Hersh, *Reporter*, 180.

375 *On May 2, he published*: Ibid., 180–81.

376 *"Tell him I'm writing a story"*: Doyle, *Not Above the Law*, 72.

376 *"Tell Strachan to watch"*: Downie, *The New Muckrakers*, 86

376 *"became particularly fascinated"*: Ibid., 85.

376 *The competitors met with Bernstein*: Ibid., 85–86.

376 *"This was a turning point"*: Shepard, *Woodward and Bernstein*, 70.

377 *"There has been an obscene affection"*: Ibid., 85.

377 *"It's a little hard to just come off"*: Thompson, *At That Point in Time*, 42.

377 *"All right, Ron"*: Ibid., 43.

378 *"Jim, I have the feeling"*: Dash, *Chief Counsel*, 92.

378 *"He's told me a fantastic story"*: Thompson, *At That Point in Time*, 26; Doug Walker, "Weicker
Gets Wickens: Watergate Probe Helps Taft Ease Aide Off Staff," *Dayton (OH) Daily News*,
April 1, 1973, https://www.newspapers.com/image/405338375/.

378 *"Just think Sam"*: Dash, *Chief Counsel*, 93.

378 *"That's the damndest conversation"*: Dean, *Blind Ambition*, 279.

379 *"I'll be goddamned if I'm going to sit down"*: Ibid., 291.

379 *"I couldn't break his story"*: Dash, *Chief Counsel*, 116.

379 *As his mid-May deadline to start*: Ibid., 87.

380 *"It was my plan"*: Ibid., 88.

380 *Haig had been a below-average student*: Dallek, *Nixon and Kissinger*, 101.

380 *His time on Kissinger's staff*: Marjorie Hunter, "4-Star Diplomat in the White House,"
New York Times, May 5, 1973, https://timesmachine.nytimes.com/timesmachine
/1973/05/05/90938809.html?pageNumber=14.

381 *"a phenomenal individual"*: Alexander M. Haig, Jr., *Inner Circles: How America Changed the
World: A Memoir* (New York: Warner, 1992), 271.

381 *"the most outstanding flag officer"*: Ibid., 272.

381 *Haig's calculating nature*: John Herbers, "Haig to Quit Army to Hold Haldeman Post as

Civilian," *New York Times*, June 7, 1973, https://timesmachine.nytimes.com/timesmachine /1973/06/07/90443204.html?pageNumber=1.

381 *"The original crime was stupid"*: Haig, *Inner Circles*, 338.

381 *"We were in for a long and bloody struggle"*: Nixon, *RN*, 857.

381 *"The changes were fundamentally"*: Colodny and Gettlin, *Silent Coup*, 293.

382 *"My God,"* Haig replied: Kutler, *Abuse of Power*, 407–8.

382 *"He's a hell of a competent guy"*: Ray Locker, *Haig's Coup: How Richard Nixon's Closest Aide Forced Him from Office* (Lincoln, NE: Potomac Books, 2019), 31.

382 *Buzhardt, known behind his back as "Buzzard"*: Peter Kihss, "Fred Buzhardt Jr., Nixon's Counsel in Watergate, Dies," *New York Times*, December 17, 1978, https://timesmachine .nytimes.com/timesmachine/1978/12/17/112826381.html?pageNumber=44.

383 *"If you need a job done with no traces"*: Doyle, *Not Above the Law*, 141.

383 *"She thought President Nixon was lying"*: Dale Van Atta, *With Honor: Melvin Laird in War, Peace, and Politics* (Madison: University of Wisconsin Press, 2008), 441.

383 *"{He's} somebody to go out"*: Ibid., 442.

383 *"Nixon was too shattered"*: Kissinger, *Years of Upheaval*, 106.

383 *On May 10, John Mitchell was indicted*: Arnold H. Lubasch, "$200,000 Donation: Charge Said to Involve Effort to Obstruct S.E.C. Inquiry," *New York Times*, May 10, 1973, https:// timesmachine.nytimes.com/timesmachine/1973/05/10/90950137.html?pageNumber=1.

383 *"They couldn't wait"*: McLendon, *Martha*, 237.

383 *"All this crap"*: Kutler, *Abuse of Power*, 448.

384 *A few days later, John Crewdson published*: John M. Crewdson, "'69 Phone Taps Reported on Newsmen at 3 Papers," *New York Times*, May 11, 1973, https://timesmachine.nytimes .com/timesmachine/1973/05/11/79855277.html?pageNumber=18.

384 *came directly from the most knowledgeable anonymous source*: Holland, *Leak*, 8.

385 *He had drafted and assembled*: Calvin Woodward, " 'Deep Throat' Touted to Lead FBI," *Telegram & Gazette* (Worcester, MA), November 29, 2007, https://www.telegram.com /article/20071129/NEWS/711290424.

385 *"Yes, the president mentioned it"*: Holland, *Leak*, 141.

385 *"just very concerned about the situation"*: Ibid., 7.

385 *"Bad guy. Now last night"*: Ibid., 146–48.

386 *It wouldn't be long before Nixon announced*: John Herbers, "Nixon Names Kelley for F.B.I.," *New York Times*, June 8, 1973, https://timesmachine.nytimes.com/timesmachine /1973/06/08/79860798.html?pageNumber=1.

387 *"Don't it seem like"*: Kutler, *Abuse of Power*, 507.

388 *"Everyone's life is in danger"*: Woodward, *The Secret Man*, 98–99.

388 *Seymour Hersh had been finishing*: Seymour M. Hersh, "Kissinger Said to Have Asked F.B.I. to Wiretap a Number of His Aides," *New York Times*, May 17, 1973, https://timesmachine .nytimes.com/timesmachine/1973/05/17/99144829.html?pageNumber=1.

388 *"You're Jewish, aren't you"*: Hersh, *Reporter*, 190. A shorter, less colorful version of this same exchange was reported in Hersh, *The Price of Power*, 400.

389 *"It was a bombshell"*: Gray, *In Nixon's Web*, 248.

389 *"Helms hoped to keep"*: Thomas Powers, *The Man Who Kept the Secrets: Richard Helms and the CIA* (New York: Pocket Books, 1981), 342.

Chapter 31 "A No-Win Job"

391 *"It had the appearance of a grand old downtown railroad terminal"*: Sussman, *The Great Cover-Up*, 233.

392 *"If the many allegations to this date"*: Dash, *Chief Counsel*, 128.

392 *"The gut question for the committee"*: *Presidential Campaign Activities of 1972*, 1:8.

392 *"If you like to watch grass grow"*: Jules Witcover, "The First Day of Watergate: Not Exactly High Drama," *Washington Post*, May 18, 1973, https://www.washingtonpost.com/politics /the-first-day-of-watergate-not-exactly-high-drama/2012/06/04/gJQAsqjDJV_story.html.

393 *The committee agreed to recall*: Dash, *Chief Counsel*, 132.

393 *"Presidential involvement in Watergate"*: Ibid., 133.

393 *"He's our biggest asset"*: Locker, *Haig's Coup*, 78.

393 *"If he ever retired, I think he'd go dig"*: Linda Charlton, " 'Perfectionist' Watergate Counsel: Samuel Dash," *New York Times*, May 18, 1973, https://timesmachine.nytimes.com /timesmachine/1973/05/18/90959270.html?pageNumber=19.

394 *"Did you ever hear of the Watergate affair?"*: *Nomination of Elliot L. Richardson to Be Attorney General: Hearings Before the Committee on the Judiciary*, 93rd Congr. 3–4 (1974), https:// books.google.com/books?id=uYqWBfd9uSIC.

394 *"arbitrary or capricious or irrational"*: Ibid., 99.

394 *The White House suggested two former Democratic governors*: "NBC Evening News for 1973-05-14," transcript, Vanderbilt Television News Archive, https://tvnews.vanderbilt.edu /programs/470222.

394 *Meanwhile, his own first four choices*: George Lardner, Jr., "Richardson Narrows Field for Prosecutor," *Washington Post*, May 15, 1973, https://osupublicationarchives.osu.edu/?a= d&d=LTN19730515–01.2.16.

394 *"scorecard on refusals"*: David E. Rosenbaum, "Tyler Turns Down Job as Prosecutor in Watergate Case," *New York Times*, May 16, 1973, https://timesmachine.nytimes.com /timesmachine/1973/05/16/93289446.html?pageNumber=27.

394–95 *"The smart ones knew"*: Gormley, *Archibald Cox*, 235.

395 *The former US solicitor general*: Ibid., 234.

395 *"unfailing fairness and firmness"*: Richardson, *The Creative Balance*, 37.

395 *"This is probably a no-win job"*: Gormley, *Archibald Cox*, 241.

395 *"This is a task of tremendous importance"*: George Lardner, Jr., "Cox Is Chosen as Special Prosecutor," *Washington Post*, May 19, 1973, https://www.washingtonpost.com/wp-srv /national/longterm/watergate/articles/051973–1.htm.

396 *The next day, Leonard Garment appeared*: Garment, *Crazy Rhythm*, 273.

396 *The statement had grown out of days of labor*: Ibid., 271.

396 *Nixon again argued*: Richard Nixon, "Statements About the Watergate Investigations," May 22, 1973, American Presidency Project, https://www.presidency.ucsb.edu/documents /statements-about-the-watergate-investigations.

397 *"The assumption was that I would get to see"*: Gormley, *Archibald Cox*, 244.

397 *"A kind of sleaziness"*: John W. Finney, "Richardson Determined to Get 'Sleaziness' Out," *New York Times*, May 25, 1973, https://timesmachine.nytimes.com/timesmachine /1973/05/25/79857311.html?pageNumber=17.

397 *"The attorney general would be happy"*: Doyle, *Not Above the Law*, 47.

397 *the Richard M. Nixon Foundation announced*: Everett R. Holless, "Watergate Halts Nixon

Library Plan," *New York Times*, May 23, 1973, https://timesmachine.nytimes.com/times machine/1973/05/23/90441300.html?pageNumber=1.

398 *"Wouldn't it really be better"*: Locker, *Haig's Coup*, 90.

398 *"Do you think I should resign?"*: Julie Nixon Eisenhower, *Pat Nixon: The Untold Story* (New York: Simon & Schuster, 1986), 372–75.

398 *Next to it was another headline*: Ben A. Franklin, "A House Member Apparent Suicide," *New York Times*, May 25, 1973, https://timesmachine.nytimes.com/timesmachine /1973/05/25/79857215.html?pageNumber=1.

Chapter 32 **"A Russian Novel"**

401 *"I fed them and watched them"*: Gormley, *Archibald Cox*, 249.

401 *In D.C., Cox started to build*: Doyle, *Not Above the Law*, 49.

402 *"Prosecutors are supposed to have the instincts"*: Ibid., 48.

402 *"being asked to play god"*: Ibid., 49.

402 *Cox also met with Earl Silbert*: Seymour M. Hersh, "3 Prosecutors Nearly Quit," *New York Times*, May 23, 1973, https://timesmachine.nytimes.com/timesmachine/1973/05/23/90441298 .html?pageNumber=1.

403 *"I have had {it} with the case"*: Gormley, *Archibald Cox*, 257.

403 *"It doesn't seem to make any sense"*: Dash, *Chief Counsel*, 141.

404 *Cox doubted Buzhardt's version*: Doyle, *Not Above the Law*, 83.

404 *During their first days organizing*: Samantha Raphelson, "Glen E. Pommerening, Justice Dept. Lawyer," *Washington Post*, October 7, 2013, https://www.washingtonpost.com /local/obituaries/glen-e-pommerening-justice-dept-lawyer/2013/10/07/8164cf9c-2f8a-11 e3-8906-3daa2bcde110_story.html.

404 *the operation would eventually be larger*: Doyle, *Not Above the Law*, 59.

404 *"This is the first case I've worked"*: Ibid., 54.

405 *"You S.O.B., you started this!"*: Lukas, *Nightmare*, 159.

405 *"it began to take on the characteristics"*: Drew, *Washington Journal*, 15.

405 *"Who thought you up?"*: *Presidential Campaign Activities of 1972*, Vols. 4–6, 6:2263, https:// books.google.com/books?id=TfCTLSY21i0C.

405 *"It was like going to church"*: Magruder, *An American Life*, 304.

405 *"He appeared totally insensitive"*: Dash, *Chief Counsel*, 147.

406 *"No witness in my experience"*: Jill Wine-Banks, *The Watergate Girl: My Fight for Truth and Justice Against a Criminal President* (New York: Henry Holt, 2020), 30.

406 *"This won't do"*: Dash, *Chief Counsel*, 148.

406 *"You've got to tell"*: Ibid., 149.

406 *"Dean, I felt, was re-creating"*: Nixon, *RN*, 890.

407 *"Counsel will call the first witness"*: *Presidential Campaign Activities of 1972*, 3:911–15.

407 *"The effeminate Pretty-Boy image"*: Mary McCarthy, *Mask of State: Watergate Portraits* (New York: Harcourt Brace Jovanovich, 1974), 40.

407 *"I do not know how well I carried off"*: Schorr, *Clearing the Air*, 89.

408 *"The worst fears of most Americans"*: Sussman, *The Great Cover-Up*, 243.

408 *but now to the Senate, he had given*: *Presidential Campaign Activities of 1972*, 3:915.

408 *"He left us no explanation"*: Hughes, *Chasing Shadows*, 162.

408 *As he emerged at the public center*: Breslin, *How the Good Guys Finally Won*, 31.

408 *"I know damn well that if Dean"*: Fields, *High Crimes and Misdemeanors*, 33.

409 *"Conspiracy to obstruct justice"*: "Excerpts from Dean's Testimony Before Senate Panel Investigating Watergate," *New York Times*, June 29, 1973, https://timesmachine.nytimes.com /timesmachine/1973/06/29/101020890.html?pageNumber=23.

409 *"I say before you and before the American people"*: David E. Rosenbaum, "G.O.P. Senator Charges Effort to Intimidate Him," *New York Times*, June 29, 1973, https://timesmachine .nytimes.com/timesmachine/1973/06/29/101020780.html?pageNumber=1.

409 *"How could you be proud"*: Weicker, *Maverick*, 77.

409 *"Tip realized he was going to have to act"*: Farrell, *Tip O'Neill*, 341.

409 *The rest would just be process*: Breslin, *How the Good Guys Finally Won*, 43.

410 *"the fullest cooperation possible"*: Dash, *Chief Counsel*, 167.

410 *That said, Dash reminded them*: Fields, *High Crimes and Misdemeanors*, 34.

410 *With Dean's testimony still rippling*: Ben-Veniste and Frampton, *Stonewall*, 62.

411 *"The president was involved"*: Van Atta, *With Honor*, 444–45.

411 *"the morning after"*: Ibid., 445.

411 *However, as historian Ray Locker traced*: Locker, *Haig's Coup*, 111.

Chapter 33 **"We Need You Today"**

415 *Finally, they settled on Hank Ruth*: Matt Schudel, "Henry S. Ruth, Special Prosecutor During Watergate Probe, Dies at 80," *Washington Post*, March 24, 2012, https://www .washingtonpost.com/politics/whitehouse/henry-s-ruth-special-prosecutor-during-water gate-probe-dies-at-80/2012/03/23/gIQADKQuYS_story.html.

415 *"Cox tends to be"*: Doyle, *Not Above the Law*, 65.

415 *Beyond the deputy, the rest of the team*: Anthony Ripley, "Cox Names Former Hogan Aide to Watergate Staff," *New York Times*, June 1, 1973, https://timesmachine.nytimes.com /timesmachine/1973/06/01/99147751.html?pageNumber=17.

416 *"I'll take mine black"*: Wine-Banks, *The Watergate Girl*, 27.

416 *"We need you today"*: Ibid., 12.

416 *"He was one of those people who finished"*: Doyle, *Not Above the Law*, 63.

417 *"He had a short attention span"*: Ben-Veniste and Frampton, *Stonewall*, 38.

417 *Enduring Neal's work sessions*: Wine-Banks, *The Watergate Girl*, 17.

418 *"{Cox} seemed like a scholarly, calm, objective professional"*: Garment, *Crazy Rhythm*, 261–62.

418 *"I disagree," Cox said*: Doyle, *Not Above the Law*, 76.

419 *"malicious, ill-founded"*: John Herbers, "Ziegler Scores Articles in Press on Nixon Estate as 'Malicious,'" *New York Times*, July 4, 1973, https://timesmachine.nytimes.com/times machine/1973/07/04/99152296.html?pageNumber=22.

419 *In Washington, Sam Dash announced*: Seymour M. Hersh, "Senators Will Recall Dean on Nixon Estate Purchase," *New York Times*, July 4, 1973, https://timesmachine.nytimes .com/timesmachine/1973/07/04/99152078.html?&pageNumber=1.

419 *"the struggle to preserve my independence"*: Richardson, *The Creative Balance*, 36.

419 *"The President, it seemed, could not or would not"*: Ibid., 16.

420 *"I never did know much about Watergate"*: Gormley, *Archibald Cox*, 294.

420 *Each day, as the Watergate Special Prosecution Force*: Ibid., 264; NSA Security Education Program, *Loose Talk Is Explosive . . . Anytime* (1972), poster, https://www.wrc.noaa.gov /wrso/posters/Security_Awareness_Posters-i0151.htm.

420 *Their defense lawyers promptly protested the leak*: Gormley, *Archibald Cox*, 263.

420 *"Archie Cox is a bit of a softie"*: Doyle, *Not Above the Law*, 73.
420 *"He's too quiet"*: Gormley, *Archibald Cox*, 263.
420 *"diligence and judgment"*: Ibid., 330.
420 *"Cox's predominant characteristic"*: Ben-Veniste and Frampton, *Stonewall*, 22.
421 *"Lincoln's Rule"*: Gormley, *Archibald Cox*, 330.
421 *"Each of the three 'witnesses'"*: Ben-Veniste and Frampton, *Stonewall*, 81.
421 *"Guilt or innocence in the political-corruption case"*: Ibid., 57.
422 *"More frustrating than the lack of hard evidence"*: Ibid., 90.
422 *"I'm afraid I didn't sleep"*: Doyle, *Not Above the Law*, 82.
422 *In July, Seymour Hersh began reporting*: Hersh, *Reporter*, 193.
423 *Crewdson struck more journalistic gold*: Phelps, *God and the Editor*, 192.
423 *"the Republican party's effort to sabotage"*: Crewdson, "Sabotaging the G.O.P.'s Rivals."
423 *Around the same time, Archibald Cox announced*: Seymour M. Hersh, "Airline Discloses Illegal Donation to Nixon Drive," *New York Times*, July 7, 1973, https://timesmachine.nytimes.com/timesmachine/1973/07/07/90449942.html?pageNumber=1.
424 *"It is fair to say"*: *Statement of Information*, 9:334, https://books.google.com/books?id=gVjc_wCPt5gC.
424 *"Somebody has tried to make"*: United Press, "Mitchell Rejects Role of 'Fall Guy,'" *New York Times*, May 20, 1973, https://timesmachine.nytimes.com/timesmachine/1973/05/20/90439103.html?pageNumber=1.
424 *"You are part of the Communists"*: McLendon, *Martha*, 240–41.
424 *"Young man, that was very kind"*: Rufus Edmisten, *That's Rufus: A Memoir of Tar Heel Politics, Watergate, and Public Life* (Jefferson, NC: McFarland & Co., 2019), 91.
424 *"Throughout his long testimony"*: Dash, *Chief Counsel*, 194.
424 *"He gave the impression"*: Thompson, *At That Point in Time*, 71.
424 *"Did you at any time tell the President"*: *Presidential Campaign Activities of 1972*, 5:1865.
425 *"You tell Howard to get John so mad"*: Thompson, *At That Point in Time*, 75.
425 *"No attempt was made"*: McCarthy, *Mask of State*, 57.
425 *"The way I see it"*: Dash, *Chief Counsel*, 169–70.
426 *"I'm sorry we can't work this out,"* Edmisten, *That's Rufus*, 102.
426 *"I'm glad I was so tough on him"*: "949," audio, July 12, 1973, Richard Nixon Presidential Library and Museum, https://www.nixonlibrary.gov/white-house-tapes/949.
427 *"The hell with {Ervin's committee}"*: Kutler, *Abuse of Power*, 628–36.

Chapter 34 Butterfield's Bombshell

429 *Alexander Butterfield had spent nearly all*: Woodward, *The Last of the President's Men*, 147.
430 *"I think the best thing for me to do"*: Ibid., 151.
430 *The man had abused him*: Ibid.
430 *"I have to agree"*: Haldeman, *The Ends of Power*, 203.
430 *Butterfield's interview in Room G-334*: Thelen, "Remembering the Discovery."
432 *On Sunday, while Nixon was still in the hospital*: Thompson, *At That Point in Time*, 87.
432 *"Just between us, I have a record of everything"*: Locker, *Haig's Coup*, 44.
432 *"This is going to be quite a blow"*: Dash, *Chief Counsel*, 182.
432 *"We've got a bombshell for you"*: McCarthy, *Mask of State*, 72.
433 *"There was no doubt in my mind"*: "Excerpts from Testimony."
433 *"I was no longer the sole accuser"*: Dean, *Blind Ambition*, 334.

433 *"Suddenly, a debate that appeared"*: Philip Allen Lacovara, "United States v. Nixon: The Prelude," *Minnesota Law Review* 83 (1999), https://scholarship.law.umn.edu/cgi/viewcontent.cgi?article=3093&context=mlr.

434 *"Let's get started"*: Doyle, *Not Above the Law*, 91–93.

434 *"The immediate problem was to pinpoint"*: Ibid., 96.

435 *"Once you convinced the courts"*: Ibid.

435 *"We could not even make up our minds"*: Ben-Veniste and Frampton, *Stonewall*, 116.

435 *"I had believed that the existence"*: Nixon, *RN*, 900.

435 *"Destroy the tapes"*: Haig, *Inner Circles*, 378.

435 *Spiro Agnew, in another meeting*: Strober and Strober, *Nixon*, 395.

436 *Garment cautioned that anyone who destroyed*: Garment, *Crazy Rhythm*, 278.

436 *"We know that Dean lied"*: Haig, *Inner Circles*, 379.

436 *"{Nixon} didn't believe he could survive"*: Dash, *Chief Counsel*, 190.

437 *"{Nixon} relied in the end"*: Garment, *Crazy Rhythm*, 282.

437 *"just plain poppy cock"*: R. W. Apple, Jr., "Nixon Denounces Resignation Talk; Taping Is Halted," *New York Times*, July 21, 1973, https://timesmachine.nytimes.com/timesmachine/1973/07/21/90454975.html?pageNumber=1.

437 *"The president is uptight about Cox"*: Doyle, *Not Above the Law*, 101.

437 *"I think you are heading for trouble"*: Ibid.

437–38 *"You are subject to the instructions"*: Ibid., 102; Lacovara, "United States v. Nixon."

438 *"the impartial pursuit"*: "A Sense of the Inevitable," *New York Times*, July 29, 1973, https://timesmachine.nytimes.com/timesmachine/1973/07/29/404911781.html?pageNumber=18.

438 *"I love my country"*: *Presidential Campaign Activities of 1972*, 5:2480.

439 *"I guess all we can do is keep"*: Gormley, *Archibald Cox*, 289.

439 *"The subpoenas, as Nixon himself put it"*: Haig, *Inner Circles*, 383.

439 *Everyone involved knew that the case*: Lacovara, "United States v. Nixon."

440 *"For a man who had devoted"*: Ibid.

440 *It was the first time the country*: Associated Press, "Public Gets Look at Grand Jurors," *New York Times*, July 28, 1973, https://timesmachine.nytimes.com/timesmachine/1973/07/28/90459043.html?pageNumber=10.

440 *"muted but mod clothing"*: Ibid.

440 *"In fact, the few white middle-class Republicans"*: Doyle, *Not Above the Law*, 126.

441 *"Do you think you taught"*: Ibid., 107.

441 *"It would have been overwhelmingly defeated"*: O'Neill, *Man of the House*, 247.

441 *"Politically, he damn near blew it"*: Ibid.

442 *"I took this up with the White House"*: Ibid., 248.

442 *"The Republicans could have turned"*: Ibid., 248–49.

Chapter 35 **Must-See TV**

443 *Each morning, Rufus Edmisten*: Edmisten, *That's Rufus*, 97.

443 *"The enormous and continually widening cast"*: McCarthy, *Mask of State*, 6–7.

444 *Altogether, the average American home*: Sirica, *To Set the Record Straight*, 134.

444 *All told, sixty-three witnesses would take*: Ervin, *The Whole Truth*, 128.

444 *"If there's anything better than a good memory"*: Thompson, *At That Point in Time*, 53.

444 *"Kleindienst, Petersen, and Gray declared"*: Ervin, *The Whole Truth*, 171.

444 *"I believed that {the hearings were} a political ploy"*: Victoria Bassetti, "The Curious History of 'What Did the President Know, and When Did He Know It?,'" March 12, 2018, Brennan Center, https://www.brennancenter.org/our-work/analysis-opinion/curious-history-what -did-president-know-and-when-did-he-know-it.

444 *As it went on, the public support*: Dash, *Chief Counsel*, 190.

444 *"The Watergate hearings became a spectacle"*: Sussman, *The Great Cover-Up*, 235.

444 *"the best thing that has happened to public television"*: Lauren Raab, "Video: Sen. Howard Baker Asked: What Did Nixon Know and When Did He Know It?," *Los Angeles Times*, June 26, 2014, https://www.latimes.com/nation/politics/politicsnow/la-na-pn-howard-baker -watergate-20140626-htmlstory.html.

445 *"You know there has been murder"*: Sussman, *The Great Cover-Up*, 235.

445 *"You cannot feel the abuse"*: J. Anthony Lukas, "No Crook Either," *New York Times Book Review*, January 14, 1979, https://timesmachine.nytimes.com/timesmachine /1979/01/14/111000191.html?pageNumber=332.

445 *One particularly persistent man*: Ervin, *The Whole Truth*, 122.

445 *"I don't know how much the chief"*: Ibid., 215.

445 *"At restaurants, maitre d's always had tables"*: Thompson, *At That Point in Time*, 57.

446 *"More than once Baker expressed"*: Ibid., 93.

446 *"In his own mind, there is not the faintest"*: McCarthy, *Mask of State*, 96.

446 *"Didn't you bug {Kalmbach's} telephone conversation"*: Presidential Campaign Activities of 1972, 6:2572.

446 *"involve{s} most sensitive national security matters"*: Colodny and Gettlin, *Silent Coup*, 313.

446 *"I do not apologize for my loyalty"*: Presidential Campaign Activities of 1972, 7:2864.

447 *"That guy was tough as nails"*: Dash, *Chief Counsel*, 195.

447 *More than 150 times, Haldeman said*: Sussman, *The Great Cover-Up*, 256.

447 *"I don't know who he thinks he's fooling"*: Weicker, *Maverick*, 81.

448 *On August 7, the Ervin Committee's must-see TV*: Sussman, *The Great Cover-Up*, 255.

448 *"The period immediately ahead"*: Gormley, *Archibald Cox*, 294.

Chapter 36 **Spiro**

449 *"When all is said and done"*: Haig, *Inner Circles*, 351.

450 *"The vice president called me over"*: Haldeman, *The Haldeman Diaries*, 629.

450 *"I'm going to have to get rid of him"*: Ehrlichman, *Witness to Power*, 142–44.

450 *"I'm going to be indicted"*: Nicole Hemmer, ed., "Richard Nixon, Spiro T. Agnew, and Alexander Haig Jr. on 14 June 1973," Conversation 940–002 (PRDE Excerpt A), Presidential Recordings Digital Edition, https://prde.upress.virginia.edu/conversations/4004312.

451 *"I can't have it put out"*: Rachel Maddow and Michael Yarvitz, *Bag Man: The Wild Crimes, Audacious Cover-Up & Spectacular Downfall of a Brazen Crook in the White House* (New York: Crown, 2020), 125.

451 *"Senator Beall wasn't as responsive"*: Ibid., 127.

451 *"They say up in Baltimore"*: Haig, *Inner Circles*, 352.

452 *"Damned lies"*: Christopher Lydon, "Agnew Says 'Damned Lies' to Report of Kickbacks," *New York Times*, August 9, 1973, https://timesmachine.nytimes.com/timesmachine /1973/08/09/90462798.html?pageNumber=1.

453 *"Everyone thinks he has to leave"*: Haig, *Inner Circles*, 354–57.

453 *"I never fully realized"*: Weicker, *Maverick*, 83–85.

453 *"These were the little guys in Watergate"*: Ibid., 85.

453 *That same day back in Washington*: Doyle, *Not Above the Law*, 100.

454 *"That the president of the United States"*: *United States v. Burr*, 25 F. Cas. 187 (1807), https://cite.case.law/f-cas/25/187/.

455 *"The broad framework of the case"*: Doyle, *Not Above the Law*, 110.

455 *"authorized nor encouraged"*: Richard Nixon, "Address to the Nation About the Watergate Investigations," August 15, 1973, American Presidency Project, https://www.presidency.ucsb.edu/documents/address-the-nation-about-the-watergate-investigations.

456 *"thought they had seen it all"*: Doyle, *Not Above the Law*, 126.

457 *"Cleveland insure that this case"*: "George Steinbrenner: Part 02 of 12," FBI Records: The Vault, 1, https://vault.fbi.gov/george-steinbrenner/george-steinbrenner-part-02-of-12.

457 *The subpoenas and interview requests came*: Ibid.

457 *"I got taken"*: James R. Polk, "Secret Nixon Donation by Shipbuilder Probed," *Washington Star-News*, September 6, 1973, https://vault.fbi.gov/george-steinbrenner/george-steinbrenner-part-07-of-12.

457 *"Steinbrenner had been the first"*: Doyle, *Not Above the Law*, 130.

458 *Soon, eight employees were granted immunity*: Ibid., 127. Doyle recounts this story anonymously, in keeping with the secrecy of grand jury proceedings; however, the timeline, questions, and circumstances strongly suggest it focused on Steinbrenner.

458 *"We must not throw to the winds"*: Doyle, *Not Above the Law*, 111.

458 *"There is not merely accusation"*: Maddow and Yarvitz, *Bag Man*, 142.

458 *"Getting to the truth"*: Ibid.

459 *"I think this is a matter"*: Doyle, *Not Above the Law*, 112–13.

459 *John Sirica had long understood*: Sirica, *To Set the Record Straight*, 158–59.

460 *Over fifty minutes, Nixon said he accepted*: Richard Nixon, "The President's News Conference," August 22, 1973, American Presidency Project, https://www.presidency.ucsb.edu/documents/the-presidents-news-conference-87.

461 *"It is hard to imagine any Presidential statement"*: " 'Everybody Does It,'" *New York Times*, August 25, 1973, https://timesmachine.nytimes.com/timesmachine/1973/08/25/90470586.html?pageNumber=22.

461 *"Watergate-style operations"*: United Press, "Martha Mitchell Says President Lied, *Washington Post*, August 26, 1973, http://jfk.hood.edu/Collection/Weisberg%20Subject%20Index%20Files/N%20Disk/Nixon%20Richard%20M%20President%20Watergate%20Files/73-08-22%20Press%20Conference%20San%20Clemente/Item%2013.pdf.

461 *"Tennessee Williams on Fifth Avenue"*: McLendon, *Martha*, 251.

462 *"The court, however, cannot agree"*: "Text of Chief Judge Sirica's Opinion in Ordering the President to Submit Tapes," *New York Times*, August 30, 1973, https://timesmachine.nytimes.com/timesmachine/1973/08/30/106108857.html?pageNumber=20.

462 *"It's a disaster"*: Doyle, *Not Above the Law*, 113.

Chapter 37 **"An Upheaval in Washington"**

463 *"Watergate has been hard"*: Drew, *Washington Journal*, 22.

463 *"an upheaval in Washington officialdom"*: Ibid., 35.

464 *"{Agnew} has never said, 'I want to do'"*: Haig, *Inner Circles*, 360.

464 *a new report that a California grand jury*: "Grand Jury Acts in Coast Break-In," *New*

York Times, September 5, 1973, https://timesmachine.nytimes.com/timesmachine /1973/09/05/90475682.html?pageNumber=1.

464 *Despite the president's efforts to focus*: Richard Nixon, "The President's News Conference," September 5, 1973, https://www.presidency.ucsb.edu/documents/the-presidents-news -conference-89.

464 *"Barring some new sensational revelations"*: O'Neill, *Man of the House*, 345.

465 *On Monday, September 10, Nixon sat*: President Richard Nixon's Daily Diary, September 1–15, 1973, Richard Nixon Presidential Library and Museum, https://www.nixon library.gov/sites/default/files/virtuallibrary/documents/PDD/1973/107%20September%20 1-15%201973.pdf.

465 *"the first faint stirrings"*: Hugh Sidey, "Of Reconciliation and Detachment," *TIME*, September 24, 1973, http://content.time.com/time/subscriber/article/0,33009,907925,00 .html.

465 *A photo of the breakfast*: New York Times, September 11, 1973, https://timesmachine.nytimes .com/timesmachine/1973/09/11/issue.html.

465 *"we get on with the business"*: Richard Nixon, "Radio Address About a Special Message to the Congress on National Legislative Goals," September 9, 1973, American Presidency Project, https://www.presidency.ucsb.edu/documents/radio-address-about-special-message -the-congress-national-legislative-goals.

465 *In a meeting with Spiro Agnew, they announced*: Spiro T. Agnew, *Go Quietly . . . Or Else* (New York: Morrow, 1980), 142.

465 *For Charles Alan Wright's forty-sixth birthday*: Warren Weaver, Jr., "Charles Alan Wright: Special Case, Special Client, Special Lawyer," *New York Times*, September 9, 1973, https:// timesmachine.nytimes.com/timesmachine/1973/09/09/90478495.html?pageNum ber=204.

465 *"There was, sad to say, not a single"*: Garment, *Crazy Rhythm*, 264.

465 *"hunched over and skinny"*: Ibid.

465 *"tall and slender, and {who} looked like a Texas sheriff"*: Ibid., 265.

466 *"ground out of my typewriter"*: Weaver, "Charles Alan Wright."

467 *"recognizing the unique character"*: Weekly Compilation of Presidential Documents: Monday, July 2, 1973, Vol. 9, No. 26, 1162, https://books.google.com/books?id=yTNSe9rk6hUC.

467 *"had been complicated enough"*: Doyle, *Not Above the Law*, 122.

467 *"I'm afraid that there is going to be an explosion"*: Ibid., 125.

467–68 *"Don't I get a presumption"*: Jules Witcover, *Very Strange Bedfellows: The Short and Unhappy Marriage of Richard Nixon and Spiro Agnew* (New York: PublicAffairs, 2007), 326.

468 *"The man is the goddamn vice president"*: Richard M. Cohen and Jules Witcover, *A Heartbeat Away: The Investigation and Resignation of Vice President Spiro T. Agnew* (New York: Viking, 1974), 234.

468 *On September 25, Agnew went to the Hill*: O'Neill, *Man of the House*, 258.

468 *Tip O'Neill resisted any effort*: Ibid., 349.

468 *"The Vice President's letter"*: Richard L. Madden, "Albert Bars House Inquiry on Agnew Now Because of 'Matters Before the Courts': A Speedy Decision," *New York Times*, September 27, 1973, https://timesmachine.nytimes.com/timesmachine/1973/09/27/issue .html.

469 *"Small and fearful men"*: Cohen and Witcover, *A Heartbeat Away*, 266.

469 *"The vice president was tough"*: Haig, *Inner Circles*, 365.

469 *"might want to look"*: Ibid., 366.

469 Once Agnew was gone, he intended: "Richardson Affidavit on Nixon's Concern Over Cox," *New York Times*, July 2, 1974, https://timesmachine.nytimes.com/timesmachine /1974/07/21/93278029.html?pageNumber=37.

470 *On Monday, Woods continued the work*: "The Crisis: A Telltale Tape Deepens Nixon's Dilemma," *TIME*, January 28, 1974, http://content.time.com/time/subscriber/article /0,33009,911049,00.html.

471 *Through the rest of the week, Woods continued*: "Tape Hearings Before Sirica—November 8, 1973: Summary," 9/25 Exhibits folder, 2 of 3, National Archives and Records Administration, https://nara-media-001.s3.amazonaws.com/arcmedia/research/nixon-grand -jury/9–25/9–25-Exhibits-2of3-Part1.pdf.

Chapter 38 Mud-Wrestling

473 *"mud-wrestling"*: Garment, *Crazy Rhythm*, 266.

473 *Donald Segretti pleaded guilty*: Anthony Ripley, "Segretti Agrees to Plead Guilty," *New York Times*, September 18, 1973, https://timesmachine.nytimes.com/timesmachine /1973/09/18/90969525.html?pageNumber=1.

473 *"If you like Hitler, you'll love Wallace"*: David E. Rosenbaum, "Segretti Describes Chapin as Boss of 'Dirty Tricks,'" *New York Times*, October 4, 1973, https://timesmachine.nytimes .com/timesmachine/1973/10/04/90994652.html?pageNumber=1.

473 *Two days later, Segretti testified*: Ibid.

474 *"highly important evidence tending to show"*: Ervin, *The Whole Truth*, 217–19.

474 *It was one of a series of unprecedented moments*: Ben Bradlee, *A Good Life: Newspapering and Other Adventures* (New York: Simon & Schuster, 1995), 370.

474 *"The clock is running"*: Agnew, *Go Quietly*, 159.

474 *"He would resign only if he could do so"*: Maddow and Yarvitz, *Bag Man*, 158.

474 *On October 8 the judge summoned*: Cohen and Witcover, *A Heartbeat Away*, 304.

474 *In a later interview with Rachel Maddow's team*: Maddow and Yarvitz, *Bag Man*, 200.

475 *"had to do with the top-priority importance"*: Ibid.

475 *"I am in a lonely spot"*: Haig, *Inner Circles*, 366.

475 *That night, prosecutors stayed up*: Cohen and Witcover, *A Heartbeat Away*, 336.

475 *Henry Kissinger had begun his shared role*: Isaacson, *Kissinger*, 505.

477 *"We had a lot of trouble finding Henry"*: O'Neill, *Man of the House*, 254.

477 *Scribbling in his notes*: Breslin, *How the Good Guys Finally Won*, 67.

477 *"He's in real trouble"*: O'Neill, *Man of the House*, 255; Farrell, *Tip O'Neill*, 357. O'Neill dates this to a later October 25 White House briefing, whereas Farrell dates it to this October 10 briefing. A review of the Presidential Daily Diary shows that Morgan only attended the October 10 briefing.

477 *"I'm worried about him"*: O'Neill, *Man of the House*, 254–55.

477 *At 2:01 p.m. on the afternoon of October 10*: Cohen and Witcover, *A Heartbeat Away*, 342.

478 *US marshals then sealed*: Loye Miller, Jr., "Shocked, Packed Courtroom Watches Agnew's Demise," *Detroit Free Press*, October 11, 1973, https://www.newspapers.com/image /98296171/.

478 *"You fully understand"*: Maddow and Yarvitz, *Bag Man*, 211.

478 *"I'm keenly aware first of the historic magnitude"*: "Transcript of the Attorney General's News

Conference on Agnew Resignation," *New York Times*, October 12, 1973, https://times machine.nytimes.com/timesmachine/1973/10/12/91007819.html?pageNumber=26.

478 *"{Agnew} was forgotten instantaneously"*: Haig, *Inner Circles*, 367.

479 *The resulting 718-page collection*: Associated Press, "Book Explaining Impeachment Published by House Committee," *New York Times*, October 21, 1973, https://timesmachine .nytimes.com/timesmachine/1973/10/21/91014964.html?pageNumber=52.

479 *"I don't think anybody on Capitol Hill"*: O'Neill, *Man of the House*, 253.

Chapter 39 "He Is Essentially Alone"

481 *As the week ended, Elliot Richardson*: Doyle, *Not Above the Law*, 133; "Transcript of the Attorney General's News Conference."

481 *Cox and his second grand jury had indicted*: William Robbins, "Krogh Is Indicted for Lies to Panel on Ellsberg Case," *New York Times*, October 12, 1973, https://timesmachine .nytimes.com/timesmachine/1973/10/12/91007691.html?pageNumber=1.

481 *It was the first indictment to come out*: Ibid.; Doyle, *Not Above the Law*, 133.

481 *Krogh had been asked if he knew of Hunt and Liddy's travels*: Robbins, "Krogh Is Indicted."

482 *"As Israel began to fall apart"*: Isaacson, *Kissinger*, 521.

482 *"Nixon had high respect for Connally"*: Thompson, *The Nixon Presidency*, 45.

482 *"He would be the easiest man"*: O'Neill, *Man of the House*, 352.

482 *"If you want easy sledding"*: Ibid.

482 *Nixon began to drink*: Locker, *Haig's Coup*, 178.

483 *"Virtually every conceivable name"*: Philip Shabecoff, "A Setting for Speculation and Suspense," *New York Times*, October 14, 1973, https://timesmachine.nytimes.com/times machine/1973/10/14/119455243.html?pageNumber=46.

483 *"I just had the most Byzantine discussion"*: Doyle, *Not Above the Law*, 135.

483–84 *"Jerry, I want you to be the vice president"*: James Cannon, *Time and Chance: Gerald Ford's Appointment with History* (New York: HarperCollins, 1994), 212.

484 *"Ford is a clubman"*: Drew, *Washington Journal*, 41.

484 *"History is being made tonight"*: O'Neill, *Man of the House*, 261.

485 *"The peace of the world was gravely threatened"*: Haig, *Inner Circles*, 409.

485 *"It's got to be the works"*: Nina Howland and Craig Daigle, eds., *Foreign Relations of the United States, 1969–1976*, Vol. 25 (Washington: Government Printing Office, 2011), Document 180, https://history.state.gov/historicaldocuments/frus1969–76v25/d180.

485 *"After a week spent dithering"*: Haig, *Inner Circles*, 522.

486 *"Though the President is elected by nationwide ballot"*: Lesley Oelsner, "Judges Rule 5–2: Historic Decision Finds President Not Above Law's Commands," *New York Times*, October 13, 1973, https://timesmachine.nytimes.com/timesmachine/1973/10/13/91009388 .html?pageNumber=1.

487 *"feeling presidential; he was feeling his oats"*: Gormley, *Archibald Cox*, 325.

487 *"Al, I'm ready to go"*: Ibid., 323.

488 *"We've got a problem"*: Doyle, *Not Above the Law*, 143.

488 *John Stennis was one of the body's most powerful*: Reuben Keith Green, "The Case for Renaming the USS John C. Stennis," *Proceedings* (US Naval Institute) 146, no. 6 (June 2020), https:// www.usni.org/magazines/proceedings/2020/june/case-renaming-uss-john-c-stennis.

488 *"Blacks had come down from the trees"*: Ibid.

488 *In January of 1973, Stennis had been mugged*: James T. Wooten, "Stennis Is Shot in Robbery in Front of Home in Capital," *New York Times*, January 31, 1973, https://timesmachine .nytimes.com/timesmachine/1973/01/31/79837188.html?pageNumber=1.

488–89 *"Stennis was left with the impression"*: Doyle, *Not Above the Law*, 145.

489 *"Have Fred there"*: Gormley, *Archibald Cox*, 375.

489 *a White House dinner he was set to attend*: President Richard Nixon's Daily Diary, October 1–15, 1973, Richard Nixon Presidential Library and Museum, https://www.nixon library.gov/sites/default/files/virtuallibrary/documents/PDD/1973/109%20October%20 1–15%201973.pdf.

489 *"look{ed} like he had just been told"*: Doyle, *Not Above the Law*, 148.

490 *Across town, Cox, clad in his signature bow tie*: Lesley Oelsner, "3 Concerns Plead Guilty on Gifts to '72 Nixon Drive," *New York Times*, October 18, 1973, https://timesmachine .nytimes.com/timesmachine/1973/10/18/91013071.html?pageNumber=1.

490 *Ervin, Baker, and the rest of the committee*: Ervin, *The Whole Truth*, 221.

490 *entitled only "A Proposal"*: Statement of Information, 9:778–85.

491 *"There is no reason to believe that an edited transcript"*: Gormley, *Archibald Cox*, 329.

491 *"It seemed to me that it would be hard"*: Doyle, *Not Above the Law*, 151.

491 *"He must really want to get rid"*: Ibid., 152; President Richard Nixon's Daily Diary, October 16–31, 1973, Richard Nixon Presidential Library and Museum, https://www.nixon library.gov/sites/default/files/virtuallibrary/documents/PDD/1973/110%20October%20 16–31%201973.pdf.

491 *"What the hell was going on"*: Doyle, *Not Above the Law*, 153.

492 *"Archie Cox was particularly firm"*: Ben-Veniste and Frampton, *Stonewall*, 107.

492 *"If everything else goes down the drain"*: Ibid.

492 *"The chances are that Porter"*: Ibid., 66.

492 *Now, even amid the showdown*: Doyle, *Not Above the Law*, 128.

493 *"When Charlie came back in"*: Ibid., 153.

493 *"warning signal from the White House"*: Anthony Lewis, "The Pressure on Cox," *New York Times*, October 18, 1973, https://timesmachine.nytimes.com/timesmachine/1973/10/18 /issue.html.

493 *"He is essentially alone"*: Doyle, *Not Above the Law*, 155.

494 *"I can hardly be expected"*: Ibid., 156.

494 *"I wondered whether I was"*: Sussman, *The Great Cover-Up*, 268.

494 *"You catch me in a difficult"*: Doyle, *Not Above the Law*, 158.

494 *Richardson sat at home*: Ibid., 143.

494 *"Why I Must Resign"*: Statement of Information, 9:785.

Chapter 40 **The Mahogany Coffin**

497 *"stipulations"*: Kleindienst, *Justice*, 182.

498 *"Very clever lies"*: Doyle, *Not Above the Law*, 161.

498 *"These points should be borne in mind"*: Statement of Information, 9:791.

498 *At 9 a.m., one of the prosecutors*: Doyle, *Not Above the Law*, 161.

498 *Other key files were spirited*: Ben-Veniste and Frampton, *Stonewall*, 141.

498 *"If you reach an impasse"*: Doyle, *Not Above the Law*, 160.

498 *"Charlie, I'm not supposed to talk"*: Ibid., 162.

499 *Judge Sirica, looking at the president's former counsel*: Sirica, *To Set the Record Straight*, 15.

499 *"A prosecutor has to be a guy"*: Doyle, *Not Above the Law*, 162.

500 *"The need to believe a solution existed"*: Garment, *Crazy Rhythm*, 285.

500 *"I had no inkling"*: Ervin, *The Whole Truth*, 235.

500 *On Friday, Cox was surprised*: Doyle, *Not Above the Law*, 168.

501 *"This puts Cuba to shame"*: Haig, *Inner Circles*, 414.

502 *"only in the interest of historical accuracy"*: *Statement of Information*, 9:795.

502 *"Within ninety minutes"*: Doyle, *Not Above the Law*, 171.

502 *"It might be a good idea"*: Ibid.

502 *"I can't fight with the President of the United States"*: Gormley, *Archibald Cox*, 346.

502 *"I have reluctantly"*: Ibid., 342.

503 *"You can tell the press"*: Doyle, *Not Above the Law*, 174.

503 *"strain imposed on the American people"*: Richard Nixon, "Statement Announcing Procedures for Providing Information from Presidential Tape Recordings," October 19, 1973, American Presidency Project, https://www.presidency.ucsb.edu/documents/statement-announcing-procedures-for-providing-information-from-presidential-tape.

504 *"In my judgment"*: Doyle, *Not Above the Law*, 176.

504 *"Bryce, I have been treated shabbily"*: Ibid., 175.

504 *"The Mahogany Coffin"*: Richardson, *The Creative Balance*, 43.

Chapter 41 **The Massacre**

505 *"Temporary Employee"*: Doyle, *Not Above the Law*, 176.

505 *"It was the first time in my memory"*: Ibid., 177.

506 *"We should try to reach"*: Ibid., 180.

506 *"I read in one of the newspapers"*: Gormley, *Archibald Cox*, 351.

506 *"Eventually, a president"*: Doyle, *Not Above the Law*, 182.

506 *"folksy, tentative, Jimmy Stewart-like character"*: Drew, *Washington Journal*, 49.

506 *"Sir, you are rather unique"*: Doyle, *Not Above the Law*, 184–85.

507 *"I know there is a regulation"*: Ibid., 189.

507 *"What the hell can I do?"*: Ibid., 187.

508 *As Richardson filled him in*: Robert H. Bork, *Saving Justice: Watergate, the Sunday Night Massacre and Other Adventures of a Solicitor General* (New York: Encounter Books, 2013), 3.

508 *"{Haig} was great at waving the flag"*: Ibid., 40.

508 *I don't want to appear to be an apparatchik*: Ibid., 82.

508 *"C'mon, Al"*: Gormley, *Archibald Cox*, 355.

509 *"Brezhnev would never"*: Doyle, *Not Above the Law*, 190.

509 *"Your commander-in-chief"*: Ibid., 191–92.

510 *"My assessment, having spent three months"*: Gormley, *Archibald Cox*, 365.

510 *As expected, Bork was next summoned*: Bork, *Saving Justice*, 83.

510 *"Bob, the stability"*: Doyle, *Not Above the Law*, 192.

510 *"Dear Mr. Cox"*: Ibid., 192–93.

511 *"Well, you've got guts"*: Ibid., 193.

511 *"Now, though numberless fates"*: Thomas, *Being Nixon*, 472.

Chapter 42 "We Have No Functional President"

513 *"Will you get off my back?"*: Isaacson, *Kissinger*, 525.

514 *one of which was being held for columnist Art Buchwald's birthday*: Graham, *Personal History*, 491.

514 *"Nothing in or out"*: Doyle, *Not Above the Law*, 194.

514 *"Please, just don't take"*: Ibid., 196.

514 *"The president's failure once again"*: Ben-Veniste and Frampton, *Stonewall*, 142.

514 *"Whether ours shall continue to be a government"*: Doyle, *Not Above the Law*, 198.

515 *"Everything has happened so suddenly"*: Ibid.

515 *"I suppose 'Saturday Night Involuntary Manslaughter'"*: Bork, *Saving Justice*, 84.

515 *"Catastrophes don't call"*: Ibid., 89.

515 *"{Petersen} was flabbergasted"*: Ibid., 87.

515 *"ferocious intensity"*: Nixon, *RN*, 935.

516 *"It seems to me the President is almost intent"*: Jules Witcover, "Pressure for Impeachment Mounting," *Washington Post*, October 21, 1973, https://www.washingtonpost.com/wp-srv /national/longterm/watergate/articles/102173–1.htm.

516 *Nearly a half-million mailgrams*: Gormley, *Archibald Cox*, 362.

516 *"Every action that the president took"*: Drew, *Washington Journal*, 58.

516 *"We have reason to believe that some very serious crimes"*: Ben-Veniste and Frampton, *Stonewall*, 146.

516 *Monday morning, worried that their offices*: Ibid., 147.

517 *"abort the established processes"*: Ibid., 150.

517 *"I've carried Nixon's flag"*: Sussman, *The Great Cover-Up*, 275.

517 *"Why waste our resignations?"*: Ben-Veniste and Frampton, *Stonewall*, 150.

517 *"Our job is to rub their noses"*: Doyle, *Not Above the Law*, 212.

517 *"I hope you guys have strong cases"*: Ibid., 214.

518 *"If you want Republican members"*: Ibid., 219.

518 *"No other President"*: Price, *With Nixon*, 263.

518 *The mood of the body*: Ervin, *The Whole Truth*, 243–44.

518 *"Resolved, that Richard M. Nixon, President"*: Fields, *High Crimes and Misdemeanors*, 50.

518 *"to go slow"*: Marjorie Hunter, "House Pressing Its Drive for Impeachment Inquiry," *New York Times*, October 24, 1973, https://timesmachine.nytimes.com/timesmachine /1973/10/24/80809839.html?pageNumber=34.

519 *"I was just plain"*: Sirica, *To Set the Record Straight*, 168.

519 *"Which government?"*: Ben-Veniste and Frampton, *Stonewall*, 152.

520 *Sirica was so nervous*: Sirica, *To Set the Record Straight*, 177.

520 *"I knew the president loved money"*: Ibid., 179.

520 *"comply in all respects"*: Ibid., 178.

520 *Richard Ben-Veniste thought about the words*: Ben-Veniste and Frampton, *Stonewall*, 155; Fields, *High Crimes and Misdemeanors*, 50.

521 *Intelligence reports suggested*: Nixon, *RN*, 937.

521 *"determined to resist"*: Kissinger, *Years of Upheaval*, 580.

521 *Haig's version of the night*: Haig, *Inner Circles*, 416.

522 *"since we have no functional president"*: Locker, *Haig's Coup*, 193.

522 *"The United States will not start a war"*: Victor Israelian, "Nuclear Showdown as Nixon Slept," *Christian Science Monitor*, November 3, 1993, https://www.csmonitor .com/1993/1103/03191.html.

522 *"Do you think we overreacted?"*: Isaacson, *Kissinger*, 533.

522 *On Thursday, October 25, lawmakers arrived*: Nixon's Daily Diary, October 16–31, 1973.

522 *"{Nixon} started talking to us"*: Ambrose, *Nixon: Ruin and Recovery*, 255.

522 *Thursday night, Nixon retreated again*: Isaacson, *Kissinger*, 534.

523 *"The tougher it gets, the cooler I get"*: Richard Nixon, "The President's News Conference," October 26, 1973, American Presidency Project, https://www.presidency.ucsb.edu/doc uments/the-presidents-news-conference-84.

Chapter 43 The Patriotic Monkey

525 *"Incredible," he thought*: Sirica, *To Set the Record Straight*, 182.

526 *One April 15th tape reel*: Ben-Veniste and Frampton, *Stonewall*, 161.

526 *"Ben-Veniste and his colleagues delivered"*: Doyle, *Not Above the Law*, 232.

526 *As the courtroom antics, public outrage*: Gormley, *Archibald Cox*, 371.

526 *Jaworski excited both Bork*: Bork, *Saving Justice*, 102.

526 *"Just get the man"*: Haig, *Inner Circles*, 437.

526 *"There were no missing tapes"*: Nixon, *RN*, 945.

526 *"I'm putting the patriotic monkey"*: Leon Jaworski, *The Right and the Power: The Prosecution of Watergate* (New York: Reader's Digest Press, 1976), 6.

527 *"While Ford voted wrong"*: O'Neill, *Man of the House*, 260.

527 *Albert had made clear he would entertain*: Fields, *High Crimes and Misdemeanors*, 47–48.

528 *"Carl Albert didn't appreciate"*: O'Neill, *Man of the House*, 250.

528 *"I have initiated a broad scale investigation"*: Fields, *High Crimes and Misdemeanors*, 53.

529 *"a massive hemorrhaging"*: Drew, *Washington Journal*, 91.

529 *"I never could get through"*: William B. Saxbe, *I've Seen the Elephant: An Autobiography* (Kent, OH: Kent State University Press, 2000), 153.

Chapter 44 "I Am Not a Crook"

531 *"The time has come"*: Joseph Alsop, "An Impaired Ability to Function," *Asheville Citizen-Times*, November 6, 1973, p. 4, https://www.newspapers.com/image/200358587/.

531 *TIME even broke a fifty-year streak*: "To Our Readers: An Editorial: The President Should Resign," *TIME*, November 12, 1973, http://content.time.com/time/subscriber/article /0,33009,944643,00.html; Prendergast, *The World of Time Inc.*, 354.

532 *"The totality spelled a vast"*: Garment, *Crazy Rhythm*, 290.

532 *"Nixon wasn't ready"*: Ibid., 291.

533 *"The president doesn't want to see you"*: Bob Woodward and Carl Bernstein, *The Final Days* (New York: Simon & Schuster, 1976), 30.

533 *"gradually phase out of Watergate"*: Garment, *Crazy Rhythm*, 291.

533 *"That weekend in Florida"*: Nixon, *RN*, 946.

533 *"It's a terrible job"*: Jaworski, *The Right and the Power*, 7.

534 *"It was a bad omen"*: Ben-Veniste and Frampton, *Stonewall*, 189.

534 *"I have accepted an awesome task"*: Doyle, *Not Above the Law*, 246.

534 *He looked out at the crowd*: Jaworski, *The Right and the Power*, 8.

534 *"Well, if he opens up a fried chicken joint"*: Doyle, *Not Above the Law*, 246.

534 *"Dan, I'm impressed by two things"*: Ibid., 249.

534 *"They had waited for his reinforcements"*: Ibid., 252.

535 *"Your failure to respond"*: Ibid., 250.

535 *"Somebody better get"*: Ibid.

535 *"I tried to make it clear"*: Ibid., 252.

535 *"Those who came out of that"*: Ibid., 252–53.

535 *"How did he sound?"*: Ibid., 251.

535 *"politics of righteous indignation"*: "Excerpts from the Statement by Aiken," *New York Times*, November 8, 1973, https://timesmachine.nytimes.com/timesmachine/1973/11/08/80812209.html?pageNumber=35.

536 *Over the course of the next week, Congress plunged*: Richard L. Madden, "House and Senate Override Veto by Nixon on Curb of War Powers," *New York Times*, November 8, 1973, https://timesmachine.nytimes.com/timesmachine/1973/11/08/80812045.html?pageNumber=1.

537 *"Is there something else?"*: Weicker, *Maverick*, 89.

537 *The totals were so low*: Ibid., 93.

538 *"What more can they possibly want"*: Nixon, *RN*, 963.

539 *"She came to believe that nothing hastened"*: Eisenhower, *Pat Nixon*, 387.

539 *Over the course of a week, Nixon had hosted*: Nixon, *RN*, 947.

539 *"I know in the history books"*: Ibid., 948.

539 *"I made my mistakes"*: Carroll Kilpatrick, "Nixon Tells Editors, 'I'm Not a Crook,'" *Washington Post*, November 18, 1973, https://www.washingtonpost.com/wp-srv/national/longterm/watergate/articles/111873–1.htm.

540 *A few days later, Nixon faced*: Christopher Lydon, "Nixon Assures Governors He Will Allay Public Doubt," *New York Times*, November 21, 1973, https://timesmachine.nytimes.com/timesmachine/1973/11/21/issue.html.

541 *"Dammit Fred, this is a pretty late date"*: Woodward and Bernstein, *The Final Days*, 82, 84.

541 *"Well, I guess we better go see"*: Doyle, *Not Above the Law*, 254.

541 *Sirica noted that Buzhardt*: Sirica, *To Set the Record Straight*, 189.

541 *"{Sirica} was almost impassive"*: Jaworski, *The Right and the Power*, 27.

542 *"Obstruction of justice"*: Doyle, *Not Above the Law*, 255.

Chapter 45 **The Rose Mary Stretch**

543 *"When are we going to get moving?"*: O'Neill, *Man of the House*, 255.

543 *O'Neill's patience was wearing thin*: Ibid., 256.

543 *Exasperated with Rodino's foot-dragging*: Breslin, *How the Good Guys Finally Won*, 82.

544 *"the miniskirted lawyer"*: Ben-Veniste and Frampton, *Stonewall*, 167.

544 *"an attractive, perceptive woman"*: Jaworski, *The Right and the Power*, 28.

544 *"Because you have more"*: Wine-Banks, *The Watergate Girl*, 13.

545 *"Volner got her story"*: Jaworski, *The Right and the Power*, 28.

545 *"I used my head"*: Statement of Information, 9:689.

546 *"Perhaps some sinister force"*: Ben-Veniste and Frampton, *Stonewall*, 182.

546 *"He realized that he couldn't keep erasing"*: Wine-Banks, *The Watergate Girl*, 138.

546 *"Three people could have erased"*: Jaworski, *The Right and the Power*, 69.

546–67 *"{The erasure's} importance was more symbolic"*: Sirica, *To Set the Record Straight*, 201.

547 *"At first we kept playing short segments"*: Doyle, *Not Above the Law*, 263.

547 *They played the tape over and over*: Ben-Veniste and Frampton, *Stonewall*, 205.

547   *"We knew that we had turned the corner"*: Ibid.

548   *"The guy got hit with his own bat"*: Doyle, *Not Above the Law*, 264.

548   *"I'm certain that everybody who had a chance"*: Ibid., 267.

548   *"For the greatest gut fight"*: Ben-Veniste and Frampton, *Stonewall*, 197.

549   *The pressure on the White House was coming*: Drew, *Washington Journal*, 153.

549   *Mrs. Nixon's staff had built a snowman*: Oliver F. Atkins, *President and Mrs. Nixon Pose with a Snowman* (1973), photograph, White House Historical Association, https://library.white househistory.org/fotoweb/archives/5017-Digital-Library/Main%20Index/Events/1127926 .jpg.info; Carl Sferrazza Anthony, "The Nixon White House Christmas Seasons," December 21, 2018, https://medium.com/@nixonfoundation/the-nixon-white-house-christmas -seasons-1e5870693db8.

549   *"It's important, Al"*: Jaworski, *The Right and the Power*, 54.

549   *As he got into his car, Jaworski saw*: Doyle, *Not Above the Law*, 269.

Chapter 46   "Do I Fight?"

551   *Gerald Ford was confirmed*: Cannon, *Time and Chance*, 231

551   *As a man who had dedicated*: Ibid., 258.

552   *He continued to live in his regular home*: "National Register of Historic Places Nomination Form: President Gerald R. Ford, Jr., House," National Park Service, https://npgallery .nps.gov/NRHP/GetAsset/NHLS/85003048_text.

552   *Weicker's office turned over to the IRS*: Weicker, *Maverick*, 95–96.

552   *"In terms of public opinion"*: Ibid., 96.

552   *"I don't think it's Watergate, frankly"*: "Goldwater Says Doubt Lingers Over 'How Honest' President Is," *New York Times*, December 18, 1973, https://timesmachine.nytimes.com /timesmachine/1973/12/18/91059429.html?pageNumber=31.

553   *"Would you be interested"*: Breslin, *How the Good Guys Finally Won*, 95.

553   *"Have you made up"*: Ibid., 97.

554   *"My god, if this wasn't the president"*: Fields, *High Crimes and Misdemeanors*, 74.

554   *By mid-December, Rodino had settled*: Ibid., 73.

555   *"We will have to become counsel"*: Ibid., 118.

555   *The staffing efforts in the final weeks*: "Whereas: Stories from the People's House," July 30, 2019, U.S. House of Representatives History, Art & Archives, https://history.house.gov /Blog/2019/July/7-30-hotel_congressional/.

555   *On December 21, an inquiry staffer*: Breslin, *How the Good Guys Finally Won*, 110–11.

556   *"I don't want anything done by machine"*: Ibid., 111.

556   *The attorneys and investigators kept the pink cards*: Maureen Barden, interview by Timothy Naftali, September 28, 2011, transcript, Richard Nixon Presidential Library and Museum, https://www.nixonlibrary.gov/sites/default/files/forresearchers/find/histories /barden-2011–09–28.pdf.

556   *Ultimately, the inquiry would amass*: Benjamin Jonas Koch, "Watchmen in the Night: The House Judiciary Committee's Impeachment Inquiry of Richard Nixon" (PhD diss., University of Texas at Austin, 2011), https://repositories.lib.utexas.edu/bitstream /handle/2152/ETD-UT-2011–05–2696/KOCH-DISSERTATION.pdf.

556   *Days after Kieves created that first card*: Breslin, *How the Good Guys Finally Won*, 104–05.

556   *A final, humbling insult from 1973*: Halberstam, *The Powers That Be*, 692.

557   *After Christmas, frantic to show*: "The Administration: Cutting Back on Candor," *TIME*,

January 7, 1974, http://content.time.com/time/subscriber/article/0,33009,910952,00 .html.

557 *Once Nixon was sequestered*: Woodward and Bernstein, *The Final Days*, 104.

557 *"As we in the family"*: Eisenhower, *Pat Nixon*, 397.

Chapter 47 Flutter and Wow

563 *The tapes were just half-a-millimeter wide*: "White House Tapes: Taping System History: Technology of the White House Tapes," Richard Nixon Presidential Library and Museum, https://www.nixonlibrary.gov/white-house-tapes.

564 *"The American presidency hung in the balance"*: Garment, *Crazy Rhythm*, 289.

564 *A few moments later, prosecutor Carl Feldbaum*: Ben-Veniste and Frampton, *Stonewall*, 172–73.

564 *"It was like that with Watergate"*: Garment, *Crazy Rhythm*, 289.

564 *Most of the testing happened*: Ben-Veniste and Frampton, *Stonewall*, 180.

565 *"Such was the power of the federal judge"*: Ibid., 173, 183.

565 *"I came up the hard way"*: Sirica, *To Set the Record Straight*, 204.

565 *"I found the whole thing disgusting"*: Ibid., 205.

566 *"The amount of information the experts were able to glean"*: Ben-Veniste and Frampton, *Stonewall*, 183.

566 *Together, they had seemingly excavated*: Lesley Oelsner, "Sirica Court Told Erasures on Tape Came After Oct. 1," *New York Times*, January 17, 1974, https://timesmachine.nytimes .com/timesmachine/1974/01/17/79637466.html?pageNumber=1.

566 *Explaining their work to Sirica's court*: Doyle, *Not Above the Law*, 275.

566 *The electromagnetic heads*: Advisory Panel on White House Tapes, "The EOB Tape of June 20, 1972: Report on a Technical Investigation Conducted for the U.S. District Court for the District of Columbia," May 31, 1974, https://www.aes.org/aeshc/docs/forensic.audio /watergate.tapes.technotes1–2.pdf.

567 *"It would have to be an accident"*: Sirica, *To Set the Record Straight*, 199.

567 *"six impossible things"*: George F. Will, "End of the Nixon Administration?," *Washington Post*, January 18, 1974, http://jfk.hood.edu/Collection/White%20Materials/Watergate/Water gate%20Items%2010290%20to%2010597/Watergate%2010434.pdf.

567 *"obstruction of justice, suppression of evidence"*: "The Crisis: A Telltale Tape."

567 *"The White House treated her so shabbily"*: Wine-Banks, *The Watergate Girl*, 138.

567 *The deeper the investigators got*: Jaworski, *The Right and the Power*, 123.

568 *"Other tapes contained audible blips"*: Doyle, *Not Above the Law*, 313.

568 *After the huge study of the June 20 tape*: Ibid., 315.

568 *"We were eager to see their reactions"*: Ben-Veniste and Frampton, *Stonewall*, 216.

568 *On January 30, Richard Nixon arrived*: Richard Nixon, "Address on the State of the Union Delivered Before a Joint Session of the Congress," January 30, 1974, American Presidency Project, https://www.presidency.ucsb.edu/documents/address-the-state-the-union-delivered -before-joint-session-the-congress.

569 *The Arab embargo had led*: David Bird, "The Energy Crisis, an Upheaval No Nation Can Escape," *New York Times*, January 27, 1974, https://timesmachine.nytimes.com/times machine/1974/01/27/148763902.html?pageNumber=157.

569 *that winter, half of the respondents*: James R. Murray et al., "The Impact of the 1973–1974 Oil Embargo on the American Household," NORC Report No. 126 (1974), https://www .norc.org/PDFs/publications/NORCRpt_126.pdf.

569 *The government calculated that prices*: Drew, *Washington Journal*, 24.

569 *"liver, kidney, brains"*: Rick Perlstein, *The Invisible Bridge: The Fall of Nixon and the Rise of Reagan* (New York: Simon & Schuster, 2014), 57.

569 *"overriding aim"*: Nixon, "Address on the State of the Union."

570 *"One minute of Watergate"*: Ervin, *The Whole Truth*, 261.

570 *"Every time you get a little bit ahead"*: Doyle, *Not Above the Law*, 316.

571 *"a disgusting display of uncontrolled backbiting"*: Ben-Veniste and Frampton, *Stonewall*, 196.

571 *"I want you to know that you are in no danger"*: Doyle, *Not Above the Law*, 301.

571 *On February 12, the special prosecutor attended*: Prendergast, *The World of Time Inc.*, 363.

571 *"I believe it was always his intention"*: Ibid., 364.

572 *"The information in 1973 had moved faster"*: Halberstam, *The Powers That Be*, 692.

572 *The White House lawyer argued*: Bill Kovach, "White House Moves to Narrow Grounds for an Impeachment," *New York Times*, March 1, 1974, https://timesmachine.nytimes.com/timesmachine/1974/03/01/356972062.html?pageNumber=1.

572 *Doar and Jenner both argued*: "How a Fragile Centrist Bloc Emerged as House Panel Weighed Impeachment," *New York Times*, August 5, 1974, https://timesmachine.nytimes.com/timesmachine/1974/08/05/79632795.html?pageNumber=14.

572 *"Impeachment is a Constitutional remedy"*: Drew, *Washington Journal*, 162.

573 *"There had to be something of a persistent problem,"* Evan Davis, interview, September 29, 2011, C-SPAN, https://www.c-span.org/video/?306747–1/evan-davis-oral-history-inverview.

573 *"Are they careful?"*: Barden, interview.

573 *In addition to the squads of typists*: Koch, "Watchmen in the Night."

573 *"How about hiring my girlfriend?"*: Barden, interview.

573 *Doar also recruited David Robert "Bob" Owen*: Breslin, *How the Good Guys Finally Won*, 118; Peter Kihss, "David Robert Owen, Prosecuted Significant Rights Cases in South," *New York Times*, January 5, 1981, https://timesmachine.nytimes.com/timesmachine/1981/01/05/210548.html?pageNumber=28; Maureen Joyce, "David R. Owen Dies," *Washington Post*, January 5, 1981, https://www.washingtonpost.com/archive/local/1981/01/05/david-r-owen-dies/0e18dd3e-d13d-4707–9f70–8b09112a5d49/.

573 *"whirlpool of sparkling legal talent"*: Holmes Alexander, "The President Fights Back, Staggers Chairman Rodino," *Reading (PA) Eagle*, May 10, 1974, https://news.google.com/newspapers?nid=1955&dat=19740510&id=JcotAAAAIBAJ&sjid=cpoFAAAAIBAJ&pg=6386,6205220.

574 *one of just four women*: Barden, interview.

574 *"How does it feel to be the Jill Wine Volner"*: Donnie Radcliffe, *Hillary Rodham Clinton: The Evolution of a First Lady* (New York: Warner, 1999), 124.

574 *"Domestic surveillance activities"*: Fields, *High Crimes and Misdemeanors*, 112.

574 *"McCord," he said, wondering out loud*: Breslin, *How the Good Guys Finally Won*, 120.

Chapter 48 Le Grand Fromage

577 *"This machine owes"*: Doyle, *Not Above the Law*, 299.

577 *"The last possible charge is mutilation"*: Jaworski, *The Right and the Power*, 38.

578 *"Le Grand Fromage"*: Ben-Veniste and Frampton, *Stonewall*, 226.

578 *Separately, Lacovara had been working*: Doyle, *Not Above the Law*, 265.

578 *In the matter of the hush money payments*: Jaworski, *The Right and the Power*, 178.

579 *The memo, as it was fleshed out*: Ben-Veniste and Frampton, *Stonewall*, 232.

579 *"a ferocious battle of wills ensued"*: Wine-Banks, *The Watergate Girl*, 140.

579 *"Ruth was apopleptic"*: Ben-Veniste and Frampton, *Stonewall*, 234.

580 *"Why carry the attaché case?"*: Doyle, *Not Above the Law*, 296.

580 *The solution was elegant*: Ben-Veniste and Frampton, *Stonewall*, 241.

581 *"They were in a militant mood"*: Ibid., 236.

582 *"Mr. Jaworski, we appreciate"*: Doyle, *Not Above the Law*, 309.

582 *The resulting vote was 19–0*: Ibid.

582 *Herb Kalmbach pleaded guilty*: Anthony Ripley, "Kalmbach Pleads Guilty to 2 Campaign Charges; May Be Jaworski Witness," *New York Times*, February 26, 1974, https://times machine.nytimes.com/timesmachine/1974/02/26/87596967.html?pageNumber=1.

582 *"window-dressing"*: Jaworski, *The Right and the Power*, 78.

582 *"Jaworski had spent his life"*: Doyle, *Not Above the Law*, 297.

582 *"interfer{ing} unduly with the ongoing impeachment process"*: Ervin, *The Whole Truth*, 262.

583 *when representative Elizabeth Holtzman went over*: Fields, *High Crimes and Misdemeanors*, 125.

583 *"What we have asked for is very reasonable"*: Bill Kovach, "Rodino Unit Firm on Tapes but Bars Early Showdown," *New York Times*, March 14, 1974, https://timesmachine.nytimes .com/timesmachine/1974/03/14/99163157.html?pageNumber=1.

584 *"The Watergate cover-up resembled"*: Ben-Veniste and Frampton, *Stonewall*, 261.

584 *"This elevator is impounded"*: Doyle, *Not Above the Law*, 309–10.

584 *There were almost not enough columns*: *New York Times*, March 2, 1974, https://timesmachine .nytimes.com/timesmachine/1974/03/02/79865448.html?pageNumber=1.

585 *"Thrown together now"*: Ben-Veniste and Frampton, *Stonewall*, 266.

585 *"You must be very busy"*: Jaworski, *The Right and the Power*, 109.

586 *"It's not true"*: Wine-Banks, *The Watergate Girl*, 146.

586 *"There were 19 people in the grand-jury room"*: United Press, "Watergate Grand Jury Tried to Indict President Richard Nixon," June 17, 1982, https://www.upi.com/Archives /1982/06/17/Watergate-grand-jury-tried-to-indict-President-Richard-Nixon/67843 93134400/.

586–87 *"to our surprise the President did not object"*: Ben-Veniste and Frampton, *Stonewall*, 264.

587 *As the special prosecutors carefully packaged*: Wine-Banks, *The Watergate Girl*, 149.

587 *A Judiciary Committee member for much of his political career*: Adam Bernstein, "Rep. Peter Rodino, 95," *Washington Post*, May 8, 2005, https://www.washingtonpost.com/archive /local/2005/05/08/rep-peter-rodino-95/358b2281–94df-48cf-9056-a01372409978/; Michael T. Kaufman, "Former Rep. Peter W. Rodino Jr. Is Dead at 95; Led House Watergate Hearings," *New York Times*, May 9, 2005, https://www.nytimes.com/2005/05/09 /nyregion/former-rep-peter-w-rodino-jr-is-dead-at-95-led-house-watergate.html.

588 *a framed photograph of Richard Nixon*: Fields, *High Crimes and Misdemeanors*, 9.

588 *Everyone he met seemed to have a different theory*: Ibid., 105.

588 *"If we don't get the material"*: Drew, *Washington Journal*, 206.

Chapter 49 **"Don't Miss Page 503"**

589 *"Nixon's Wonderland"*: Anthony Ripley, "A Fortress Is Dented by Women," *New York Times*, April 8, 1974, https://timesmachine.nytimes.com/timesmachine/1974/04/08/79621764 .html?pageNumber=21.

589 *"Arkansas doesn't seem"*: Ibid.

590 *"I know you," he said, laughing*: Wine-Banks, *The Watergate Girl*, 165.

590 *"to camouflage the bonuses"*: Anthony Ripley, "An Owner of Yankees Indicted in Ship Concern's Election Gifts," *New York Times*, April 6, 1974, https://timesmachine.nytimes.com /timesmachine/1974/04/06/79906844.html?pageNumber=14.

590 *Nine other executives*: Ibid.

590 *The indictments landed the day before the opening*: United Press, "No Baseball Now for Steinbrenner," *Cleveland (OH) Press*, April 9, 1974, https://vault.fbi.gov/george-steinbrenner /george-steinbrenner-part-03-of-12.

590 *Steinbrenner was arraigned on the 19th*: Christine J. Jindra, "Steinbrenner Pleads Innocent, Is Confident Jury Will Clear Him," *Cleveland (OH) Plain Dealer*, April 20, 1974, https:// vault.fbi.gov/george-steinbrenner/george-steinbrenner-part-03-of-12.

590 *an IRS and congressional report found*: Joseph J. Thorndike, "JCT Investigation of Nixon's Tax Returns," February 2016, United States Capitol Historical Society, https://uschs.org /wp-content/uploads/2016/02/USCHS-History-Role-Joint-Committee-Taxation-Thorn dike.pdf.

590 *"We're all very weary"*: Drew, *Washington Journal*, 229.

591 *"They're angry and they're bitter"*: Thomas M. DeFrank, *Write It When I'm Gone: Remarkable Off-the-Record Conversations with Gerald R. Ford* (New York: Putnam's, 2007), 12.

592 *Meanwhile, Leon Jaworski's office*: Ben-Veniste and Frampton, *Stonewall*, 269.

592 *"Nixon spent hours listening to them"*: Saxbe, *I've Seen the Elephant*, 165.

593 *Friday Nixon had just five telephone calls*: President Richard Nixon's Daily Diary, April 16–30, 1974, Richard Nixon Presidential Library and Museum, https://www.nixonlibrary .gov/sites/default/files/virtuallibrary/documents/PDD/1974/122%20April%2016–30%20 1974.pdf.

593 *"It is not possible to describe"*: Nixon, *RN*, 995.

593 *"We've got to be consistent"*: Woodward and Bernstein, *The Final Days*, 126.

593 *"Why so many deletions?"*: Ibid., 135.

593 *"My heart stopped for 30 seconds"*: Martin Arnold, "Mitchell and Stans Are Acquitted on All Counts After 48-Day Trial," *New York Times*, April 29, 1974, https://timesmachine .nytimes.com/timesmachine/1974/04/29/91438953.html?pageNumber=1.

594 *Woodward and Bernstein's book,* The Final Days: Woodward and Bernstein, *The Final Days*, 138.

594 *"Watergate is going to go away"*: Ibid., 139.

594 *"These transcripts will show"*: Richard Nixon, "Address to the Nation Announcing Answer to the House Judiciary Committee Subpoena for Additional Presidential Tape Recordings," April 29, 1974, American Presidency Project, https://www.presidency.ucsb.edu /documents/address-the-nation-announcing-answer-the-house-judiciary-committee-sub poena-for-additional.

595 *They had beaten the subpoena deadline*: Jaworski, *The Right and the Power*, 131.

595 *"Not that these conversations seemed"*: Ben-Veniste and Frampton, *Stonewall*, 271–72.

595 *"Sheer flesh-crawling repulsion"*: Joseph Alsop, "The 'Repellent Tapes': Will They Help Mr. Nixon?," *Washington Post*, May 3, 1974, http://jfk.hood.edu/Collection/White%20 Materials/Watergate/Watergate%20Items%2013573%20to%2013797/Watergate%20 13752.pdf.

596 *"The president's transcripts of these recordings"*: Jaworski, *The Right and the Power*, 132.

596 *"Before the end of the day, the word had been passed"*: Fields, *High Crimes and Misdemeanors*, 153.

596 *"Nixon released a thousand pages"*: Garment, *Crazy Rhythm*, 293.

597 *"Don't miss page 503"*: Drew, *Washington Journal*, 261.

597 *"What was in the President's transcripts would overwhelm"*: Ben-Veniste and Frampton, *Stonewall*, 271.

597 *"Rodino said that's like if a cop"*: Spencer Bokat-Lindell, " 'Nixon at His Worst Wouldn't Do That,'" *New York Times*, December 19, 2019, https://www.nytimes.com/2019/12/19/opinion/trump-impeachment-nixon.html.

587 *"We did not subpoena an edited White House version"*: Drew, *Washington Journal*, 261.

598 *"Dear Mr. President"*: Doyle, *Not Above the Law*, 319.

598 *In early May, James St. Clair tried to block*: Ibid., 321.

598 *"About fifteen members of my staff have known"*: Woodward and Bernstein, *The Final Days*, 150.

599 *"This is an attempt to embarrass"*: Ibid., 152.

599 *"I'm not trying to save"*: Emery, *Watergate*, 432.

599 *"The president does not wish to make"*: Woodward and Bernstein, *The Final Days*, 157.

599 *In his office, Jaworski hung up*: Jaworski, *The Right and the Power*, 136.

599 *"The mistake may be to assume"*: Drew, *Washington Journal*, 185.

600 *The next morning, Nixon spent less than an hour*: President Richard Nixon's Daily Diary, May 1–15, 1974, Richard Nixon Presidential Library and Museum, https://www.nixonlibrary.gov/sites/default/files/virtuallibrary/documents/PDD/1974/123%20May%201–15%20 1974.pdf; Woodward and Bernstein, *The Final Days*, 159.

600 *"One could almost follow the story of Watergate"*: Drew, *Washington Journal*, 226.

600 *The hearings began in a very different environment*: Woodward and Bernstein, *The Final Days*, 160.

600 *"We have seen a breakdown"*: Christopher Lydon, "Rhodes Urges That Nixon Again Consider Resigning," *New York Times*, May 10, 1974, https://timesmachine.nytimes.com/timesmachine/1974/05/10/issue.html.

601 *"safety valve to eliminate"*: Fields, *High Crimes and Misdemeanors*, 121.

601 *After opening statements from Rodino*: Ibid., 158.

601 *"I do, Your Honor"*: *Impeachment Inquiry*, 1:552, https://books.google.com/books?id=knJFA QAAMAAJ.

602 *"We begin at the beginning"*: "How a Fragile Centrist Bloc."

602 *"On January 20, 1969"*: *Impeachment Inquiry*, 1:554–55.

602 *That first day was a big success*: Barden, interview.

602 *Except among the president's lawyers*: Sirica, *To Set the Record Straight*, 223.

Chapter 50 *The United States v. Richard M. Nixon*

603 *Jaworski knew that a rejection*: Jaworski, *The Right and the Power*, 163.

603 *"{It was} a truly extraordinary mechanism"*: Lacovara, "United States v. Nixon."

604 *"Our goal was to strengthen"*: Ibid.

604 *Rumors of a presidential resignation*: James M. Naughton, "White House Moves to End Rumors Nixon Will Resign; His Support in G.O.P. Ebbs," *New York Times*, May 11, 1974, https://timesmachine.nytimes.com/timesmachine/1974/05/11/99168496.html ?pageNumber=1.

604 *"Jerry, there's a better than 50–50 chance"*: Woodward and Bernstein, *The Final Days*, 175.

604 *Meanwhile the House's two top Republicans*: Ibid., 176.

605 *"We have to do some planning"*: Richard Reeves, *A Ford, Not a Lincoln* (New York: Harcourt Brace Jovanovich, 1975), 52.

605 *"Time will tell"*: Drew, *Washington Journal*, 219.

605 *"We truly did nothing but work"*: Barden, interview.

606 *"He's the most boring person"*: Ibid.

606 *All told, for ten weeks*: Drew, *Washington Journal*, 281.

606 *"You go into a grocery store"*: "How a Fragile Centrist Bloc."

607 *"You would use national security as a cover"*: Evan Davis, interview by Timothy Naftali, September 29, 2011, transcript, Richard Nixon Presidential Library and Museum, https://www
.nixonlibrary.gov/sites/default/files/forresearchers/find/histories/davis-2011–09–29.pdf.

607 *"It's a compounding fact"*: Ibid.

608 *"I regret what I attempted to do"*: "Text of Colson Statement After Guilty Plea on Obstruction
of Justice," *New York Times*, June 4, 1974, https://timesmachine.nytimes.com/timesmachine
/1974/06/04/79626486.html?pageNumber=24.

608 *Inside the courtroom, St. Clair handed*: Woodward and Bernstein, *The Final Days*, 205.

608 *After they were ushered out*: President Richard Nixon's Daily Diary, June 1–15, 1974, Richard
Nixon Presidential Library and Museum, https://www.nixonlibrary.gov/sites/default/files
/virtuallibrary/documents/PDD/1974/125%20June%201–15%201974.pdf.

608 *"The court recognizes that men of ambition"*: Drew, *Washington Journal*, 294.

608 *On Wednesday, June 5, the* Los Angeles Times' *Robert Jackson*: Ronald J. Ostrow and Robert
L. Jackson, "Nixon Named Conspirator by Jury, L.A. Times Says," *The Charlotte (NC)
Observer*, June 6, 1974, https://www.newspapers.com/image/622407383/.

608 *Within a day, St. Clair conceded*: Anthony Ripley, "Grand Jury Named Nixon Watergate
Co-Conspirator but Didn't Indict," *New York Times*, June 7, 1974, https://timesmachine
.nytimes.com/timesmachine/1974/06/07/issue.html.

608 *"It is going to have a hell of an impact"*: Ibid.

609 *a group called the "National Citizens Committee"*: "Baruch Korff, 'Nixon's Rabbi,' Dies
at Age 81," *Washington Post*, July 27, 1995, https://www.washingtonpost.com/archive
/local/1995/07/27/baruch-korff-nixons-rabbi-dies-at-age-81/3ef20d47–9220–461d-a47b
-28ce70b103cf/.

609 *"I am not the press's favorite pin-up boy"*: Woodward and Bernstein, *The Final Days*, 173.

609 *"The cause you have worked for"*: Richard Nixon, "Remarks at a Luncheon of the National
Citizens' Committee for Fairness to the Presidency," June 9, 1974, American Presidency
Project, https://www.presidency.ucsb.edu/documents/remarks-luncheon-the-national
-citizens-committee-for-fairness-the-presidency.

609 *"Nixon was a haunted man"*: Theodore H. White, *Breach of Faith: The Fall of Richard Nixon*
(New York: Atheneum, 1975), 9.

610 *"The purpose of this trip is more important"*: Woodward and Bernstein, *The Final Days*, 213.

610 *"The president has a death wish"*: Ibid., 214.

000 *back in Washington Fred Buzhardt*: Philip Shabecoff, "Buzhardt in Hospital with Pains in
Chest; Condition 'Serious,'" *New York Times*, June 14, 1974, https://timesmachine.nytimes
.com/timesmachine/1974/06/14/93295358.html?pageNumber=1.

611 *"a great guide"*: W. Joseph Campbell, *Getting It Wrong: Debunking the Greatest Myths in
American Journalism*, 2nd ed. (Berkeley: University of California Press, 2017), 153.

611 *"solved the greatest detective story"*: Ibid., 154.

611 *"He exploded"*: Woodward, *The Secret Man*, 110.

612 *"Who did have motive and opportunity"*: Limpert, "Deep Throat."

613 *"Those mundane tasks"*: Holland, *Leak*, 40.

613 *"When we got some of the same stories"*: Campbell, *Getting It Wrong*, 162.

613 *"a clandestine group"*: Holland, *Leak*, 41.

613 *For example, a scene where Woodward and Bernstein, after their humiliating lunch*: Bernstein and Woodward, *All the President's Men*, 187.

613 *according to the National Weather Service records*: "Arlington County, VA Weather History: October 25, 1972," Weather Underground, https://www.wunderground.com/history /daily/KDCA/date/1972-10-25.

614 *"interstate transportation of obscene materials"*: Tom Shales, "Scaring Off the Sex Films," *Washington Post*, November 27, 1972.

614 *"There were no ads in the* Post": Havill, *Deep Truth*, 87.

614 *"You know I have a little problem"*: Himmelman, *Yours in Truth*, 214.

614–15 *Woodward, Himmelman wrote, seemed "frantic"*: Ibid., 212–31.

615 *"You can draw the picture of a horse"*: Ervin, *The Whole Truth*, 272.

615 *"It is no time for slow readers"*: Drew, *Washington Journal*, 253.

615 *"When the rest of us are all forgotten"*: O'Neill, *Man of the House*, 375.

616 *Republican members of Congress decried*: David E. Rosenbaum, "Some in G.O.P. Say Rodino Is Biased on Impeachment," *New York Times*, June 29, 1974, https://timesmachine.nytimes .com/timesmachine/1974/06/29/119732798.html?pageNumber=12.

616 *"Things have gotten out of hand"*: James M. Naughton, "Impeachment Panel Rift May Spread in Congress," *New York Times*, June 30, 1974, https://timesmachine.nytimes.com /timesmachine/1974/06/30/148834262.html?pageNumber=1.

617 *"If you could do anything to help"*: Breslin, *How the Good Guys Finally Won*, 146–48.

Chapter 51 Impeachment

619 *"What we are trying to do is to strengthen"*: Naughton, "Impeachment Panel Rift."

620 *Cates had believed since late November*: Fields, *High Crimes and Misdemeanors*, 192.

620 *In readying for their big day, Lacovara had suggested*: Lacovara, "United States v. Nixon."

621 *"If you keep it up, I'll show up"*: Doyle, *Not Above the Law*, 331.

621 *"Our brief is one of the strongest"*: Ibid., 330.

621 *"heart of our basic constitutional system"*: *Special Report of the Joint Committee on Congressional Operations Pursuant to Section 402(a)(2) of the Legislative Reorganization Act of 1970*, 93rd Congr. 480 (1974), https://books.google.com/books?id=guxFLsg9IPkC.

622 *"The President is not above the law"*: "The United States v. Richard M. Nixon, President, et al.," *TIME*, July 22, 1974, http://content.time.com/time/subscriber/printout /0,8816,942924,00.html.

622 *"You lose me someplace"*: *Special Report of the Joint Committee*, 519.

622 *"I don't give a shit"*: Brinkley and Nichter, *The Nixon Tapes: 1973*, 368.

623 *"The Rodino Committee released millions of words"*: Sussman, *The Great Cover-Up*, 297.

623 *"a giant erector set"*: Donald M. Rothberg, "No Clue in Judiciary Releases as to Final Impeachment Verdict," *Greely (CO) Daily Tribune*, July 11, 1974, https://www.newspapers .com/image/27293817/.

623 *"The quantity of the evidence"*: Nixon, *RN*, 1019.

623 *On Thursday, John Dean took the stand*: Woodward and Bernstein, *The Final Days*, 241.

623 *"I think I have a clear"*: United Press, "Both Sides Claim Dean Strengthens Their Cases," *Bennington (VT) Banner*, July 12, 1974, https://www.newspapers.com/image/630 37502/.

623 *"Republicans cannot vote"*: "How a Fragile Centrist Bloc."

624 *"Daddy, eat your steak"*: Woodward and Bernstein, *The Final Days*, 246.

624 *Hearing the news aboard Air Force One*: Nixon, *RN*, 1045.

625 *"Now this is awfully peculiar"*: Breslin, *How the Good Guys Finally Won*, 166.

625 *"The President met with his Deputy Assistant"*: President Richard Nixon's Daily Diary, June 16–30, 1972, Richard Nixon Presidential Library and Museum, https://www.nixonlibrary .gov/sites/default/files/virtuallibrary/documents/PDD/1972/078%20June%2016–30%20 1972.pdf.

626 *"central part in the planning and executing"*: Impeachment Inquiry, 3:1926–36, https://books .google.com/books?id=W6QnAAAAMAAJ.

627 *"the first direct political advice"*: "The Fateful Vote to Impeach," *TIME*, August 5, 1974, https://web.archive.org/web/20071001005014/http://www.time.com/time/printout /0,8816,879405,00.html.

627 *The next morning, Sunday July 21*: "How a Fragile Centrist Bloc."

627 *Hamilton Fish too felt the weight*: Ibid.

628 *Within days of Doar's summation*: Fields, *High Crimes and Misdemeanors*, 12.

628 *For many members, it was the first time*: "The Fateful Vote to Impeach."

628 *"That got the members thinking"*: "How a Fragile Centrist Bloc."

628 *"Butler {was} a very strong conservative"*: Bokat-Lindell, " 'Nixon at His Worst."

629 *"Well, we know what we're here for"*: Fields, *High Crimes and Misdemeanors*, 219.

629 *"Toss me a danish"*: "How a Fragile Centrist Bloc."

629 *"We can all agree"*: Ibid.

629 *"It was a terrible butterfly-in-the-stomach day"*: Ibid.

629 *On that same Tuesday, July 23, Maryland's Hogan*: "Hogan Gives Reasons for His Decision," *New York Times*, July 24, 1974, https://timesmachine.nytimes.com/timesmachine /1974/07/24/79336668.html?pageNumber=29.

630 *"12:01 A.M. Lowest point"*: Nixon, *RN*, 1051.

630 *One particularly dark day, he told Jill Volner*: Wine-Banks, *The Watergate Girl*, 170.

631 *Point by point, Chief Justice Burger affirmed*: White, *Breach of Faith*, 4.

631 *The order was unanimous*: Lacovara, "United States v. Nixon."

631 *"The unanimous holding, I was convinced"*: Jaworski, *The Right and the Power*, 204.

631 *"He was an old man"*: White, *Breach of Faith*, 5.

632 *"He won on a major constitutional issue"*: Lacovara, "United States v. Nixon."

Chapter 52 The Smoking Pistol

633 *Nixon was furious, completely betrayed*: Woodward and Bernstein, *The Final Days*, 263.

635 *"Well, we've found the smoking pistol"*: Ibid., 272.

635 *"The President has always been a firm believer"*: Ibid., 279.

636 *"A lot of the real nuts and bolts"*: "The Fateful Vote to Impeach."

636 *"Wherefore, Richard M. Nixon"*: Fields, *High Crimes and Misdemeanors*, 222.

636 *Fifi Clay, a Nixon supporter*: Ibid., 224.

636 *Press received special green passes*: Drew, *Washington Journal*, 334.

637 *"I am overwhelmed by the stark contrast"*: Fields, *High Crimes and Misdemeanors*, 245.

637 *"For years we Republicans have campaigned"*: Douglas Martin, "M. Caldwell Butler, a Key Vote Against Nixon, Dies at 89," *New York Times*, July 29, 2014, https://www.nytimes .com/2014/07/30/us/politics/m-caldwell-butler-89-key-vote-to-impeach-dies.html.

638 *Despite two years of burgeoning controversy*: John Herbers, "White House Aides Upset and

Concerned by Events," *New York Times*, July 26, 1974, https://timesmachine.nytimes
.com/timesmachine/1974/07/26/79631893.html?pageNumber=1.

638 *"Now I think we're getting somewhere"*: Woodward and Bernstein, *The Final Days*, 287.

639 *"There are many people in my district"*: *Debate on Articles of Impeachment: Hearings of the Committee on the Judiciary*, 93rd Congr. 326 (1974), https://books.google.com/books?id=1E9x
94gKnnYC.

639 *"The question occurs"*: Ibid., 327.

640 *The spell that had settled*: "How a Fragile Centrist Bloc."

640 *"God, how she could have gone through"*: Nixon, *RN*, 1053.

640 *"What are you bothering"*: O'Neill, *Man of the House*, 263–64.

641 *"Jesus, Jerry"*: Ibid., 264.

641 *"Secretly, maybe all of us are hoping"*: Drew, *Washington Journal*, 366.

641 *"sloth and default"*: *Debate on Articles of Impeachment*, 495.

641 *"Tell him to go piss up a rope"*: Saxbe, *I've Seen the Elephant*, 170.

642 *The next afternoon, around three-thirty*: Woodward and Bernstein, *The Final Days*, 307.

642 *Later, Simon would tell reporters*: Ibid., 306.

642 *Day by day, the president's core of support*: Ibid., 316.

642 *"He's guilty as hell"*: Ibid., 300.

642 *Both Haig and St. Clair had finally been convinced*: Ibid., 308.

643 *"He had given the order"*: Haig, *Inner Circles*, 476.

643 *"We have to try to work out"*: Nixon, *RN*, 1054.

643 *"By resigning, he might preserve"*: Haig, *Inner Circles*, 478.

643 *"Al, it's over"*: Ibid.

Chapter 53 The Final Days

645 *"The clock had stopped"*: Ibid., 476.

645 *"Al, you've got to tell Ford"*: Ibid., 480.

646 *"Al, I don't think it would be proper"*: Cannon, *Time and Chance*, 293.

646 *"The hurt was very deep"*: Ibid., 295.

646 *"That's extremely damaging information"*: Fields, *High Crimes and Misdemeanors*, 285.

647 *"The president does understand the dimension"*: Cannon, *Time and Chance*, 308.

647 *Born Leslie L. King, Jr., the son and namesake*: Ibid., 1–17.

648 *"People believed in him"*: Ibid., 41.

648 *"You have to believe the president"*: Ibid.,152.

648 *Now, in the nine months that he'd been vice president*: Ibid., 259.

648 *crisscrossing the country*: Thomas DeFrank, "The Things It Carried," *Air & Space*, July 2008, https://www.airspacemag.com/history-of-flight/the-things-it-carried-45246668/.

648 *"He deliberately fled Washington"*: Cannon, *Time and Chance*, 273.

648 *"Either we will go to the White House"*: Ibid., 299.

649 *"a good description of a President's job"*: Ibid., 54.

649 *After long, halting, and dispirited conversations*: Woodward and Bernstein, *The Final Days*, 343.

649 *"There is nothing so tiring"*: Haig, *Inner Circles*, 489.

650 *"Damn it, Al, this is not what I asked for"*: Ibid., 491.

651 *"Well here it is"*: O'Neill, *Man of the House*, 379.

651 *"if not out of loyalty"*: Woodward and Bernstein, *The Final Days*, 376.

651 *"It has been fun having use of the yacht"*: Ibid., 380.

651 *"magnificent career"*: Ibid., 379.

651 *"the public interest is no longer served"*: Thomas J. Foley, "Vice President Will Halt His Public Defense of President," *Los Angeles Times*, August 6, 1974, https://www.newspapers.com /clip/37033012/the-los-angeles-times/.

651 *"There is an inexplicable difference"*: Drew, *Washington Journal*, 392.

652 *"I wonder whether the enormity"*: Ibid.

Chapter 54 "A Day for Tears"

653 *"Mr. President, I don't think we ought to have"*: Cannon, *Time and Chance*, 317.

653 *"It was cruel"*: Kissinger, *Years of Upheaval*, 1204.

653 *"Al, the President has only 12 votes"*: Woodward and Bernstein, *The Final Days*, 391.

654 *"If he doesn't resign now"*: Ibid., 392.

654 *"You are a rotten bunch!"*: Ibid., 398.

654 *"I can resign"*: Haig, *Inner Circles*, 495–96.

655 *"I will do this without rancor"*: Ibid., 496.

655 *"You know, Al, you soldiers"*: Ibid.

655 *"I can go in my office"*: Associated Press, "Congressman Says Nixon Threat of Atomic War Wasn't Serious," *San Bernardino (CA) Sun*, February 10, 1976, https://cdnc.ucr.edu /?a=d&d=SBS19760210.1.2.

656 *Moreover, Schlesinger and the chairman*: Bernard Gwertzman, "Pentagon Kept a Tight Rein in Last Days of Nixon Rule," *New York Times*, August 25, 1974, https://timesmachine .nytimes.com/timesmachine/1974/08/25/93280856.html?pageNumber=1.

657 *"It sure feels like it"*: David E. Rosenbaum, "Senators Unable to Agree on Any Move Over Nixon," *New York Times*, August 8, 1974, https://timesmachine.nytimes.com/timesmachine /1974/08/08/79584296.html?pageNumber=1.

658 *"Mr. President, this isn't pleasant"*: Nixon, *RN*, 1073.

658 *"Whatever decision he makes"*: Associated Press, "GOP Leaders Say Nixon Hasn't Reached Decision," *Jacksonville (IL) Daily Journal*, August 8, 1974, https://www.newspapers.com /image/32293218/.

658 *"The hell with what they want"*: Cannon, *Time and Chance*, 325.

658 *"Your father has decided to resign"*: Woodward and Bernstein, *The Final Days*, 421.

658 *"It was the only time I ever saw HAK run"*: Cannon, *Time and Chance*, 330.

658 *"A day for tears"*: Nixon, *RN*, 1068.

659 *"I know you'll do a good job"*: Cannon, *Time and Chance*, 333.

659 *"For the previous nine months"*: Ibid., 421.

659 *"To hell with it—let Ford do it"*: Woodward and Bernstein, *The Final Days*, 437.

659 *"A president's power begins to slip away"*: Nixon, *RN*, 1077.

659 *"Are wives invited?"*: O'Neill, *Man of the House*, 267.

660 *"The President of the United States will meet various members"*: Woodward and Bernstein, *The Final Days*, 432.

Chapter 55 "I Shall Resign"

661 *"This is the 37th time"*: Richard Nixon, "Address to the Nation Announcing Decision to Resign the Office of President of the United States," August 8, 1974, American Presidency

Project, https://www.presidency.ucsb.edu/documents/address-the-nation-announcing
-decision-resign-the-office-president-the-united-states.

662 *When the lights and camera*: Woodward and Bernstein, *The Final Days*, 447.

662 *"This is one of the most difficult"*: Anthony Ripley, "Nixon Resigns; Ford Will Take the Oath Today," *New York Times*, August 9, 1974, https://timesmachine.nytimes.com/timesmachine /1974/08/09/79585848.html?pageNumber=4.

662 *"He was phoning old friends"*: Garment, *Crazy Rhythm*, 296.

662 *"Dear Mr. Secretary"*: Richard Nixon to Henry Kissinger, letter, August 9, 1974, National Archives and Records Administration, https://www.archives.gov/historical-docs/todays -doc/?dod-date=809.

662 *"There has been no agreement"*: Richard D. Lyons, "Jaworski Asserts No Deal Was Made," *New York times*, August 9, 1974, https://timesmachine.nytimes.com/timesmachine /1974/08/09/79585870.html?pageNumber=2.

662 *"Lenin and Gandhi"*: Haig, *Inner Circles*, 502.

663 *"Never get discouraged"*: Richard Nixon, "Remarks on Departure from the White House," August 9, 1974, American Presidency Project, https://www.presidency.ucsb.edu/documents /remarks-departure-from-the-white-house.

663 *"It was not the speech of a President"*: Jaworski, *The Right and the Power*, 220.

663 *"The whole world was watching"*: O'Neill, *Man of the House*, 271.

663 *"Drop us a line"*: Robert Sam Anson, *Exile: The Unquiet Oblivion of Richard M. Nixon* (New York: Simon & Schuster, 1984), 20.

664 *"I'm going to prepare lunch"*: Tim Weiner, *One Man Against the World: The Tragedy of Richard Nixon* (New York: Henry Holt, 2015), 314.

664 *"Trust in the Lord"*: "Swearing In Bible," Gerald R. Ford Presidential Library and Museum, https://www.fordlibrarymuseum.gov/swearinginbible.asp.

664 *"Kansas City, this is Air Force One"*: Anson, *Exile*, 19.

665 *"I assume the Presidency"*: Gerald R. Ford, "Remarks on Taking the Oath of Office," August 9, 1974, American Presidency Project, https://www.presidency.ucsb.edu/documents /remarks-taking-the-oath-office/.

Epilogue Nixon's Curse

667 *"Do you think people want to pick the carcass?"*: Anson, Exile, 37.

668 *"monkey problem"*: Ben-Veniste and Frampton, *Stonewall*, 299.

668 *"I do not think that the political system"*: Jaworski, *The Right and the Power*, 229.

668 *"If eventually, why not now?"*: Cannon, *Time and Chance*, 373.

668 *"You're crazy"*: O'Neill, *Man of the House*, 268.

669 *"greased Nixon's departure"*: Farrell, *Richard Nixon*, 536.

669 *Even the staff of the special prosecutor wondered*: Doyle, *Not Above the Law*, 347.

669 *"{They were} the flotsam"*: White, *Breach of Faith*, 341.

669 *"Welcome to the club, John"*: Dean, *Blind Ambition*, 367.

670 *"If I had known Nixon"*: Anson, *Exile*, 85.

670 *"John takes things too personally"*: Ibid., 206.

670 *"I am convinced"*: Rosen, *The Strong Man*, 470.

671 *"When the president does it"*: Anson, *Exile*, 159.

671 *Next came the memoirs*: Craig Fehrman, "All the President's Memories," *New York Times*, November 4, 2010, https://www.nytimes.com/2010/11/07/books/review/Fehrman-t.html.

671 *"For chrissakes, I don't even know"*: Anson, *Exile*, 180.

671 *"To the book and to the future"*: Aitken, *Nixon: A Life*, 520.

672 *By the time Tip O'Neill became speaker*: O'Neill, *Man of the House*, 419.

672 *Senator Sam Ervin worked over the course of the year*: Campbell, *Senator Sam Ervin*, 295.

672 *"The whole mess fell on Nixon"*: Farrell, *Richard Nixon*, 542.

673 *"Watergate did what the Bay of Pigs had not"*: Powers, *The Man Who Kept the Secrets*, 259.

674 *"This post-Watergate fervor"*: Prendergast, *The World of Time Inc.*, 367.

674 *"If Nixon has bequeathed"*: White, *Breach of Faith*, 337.

675 *"I spent my entire adult life"*: Laura A. Kiernan, "Ex-FBI Officials Felt, Miller Guilty in 'Black Bag' Cases," *Washington Post*, November 7, 1980, https://www.washingtonpost.com/archive/politics/1980/11/07/ex-fbi-officials-felt-miller-guilty-in-black-bag-cases/ebf7eb2d-e94d-4478-896f-2d36af7ab760/.

675 *President Reagan ultimately issued*: Robert Pear, "President Reagan Pardons 2 Ex-F.B.I. Officials in 1970's Break-Ins," *New York Times*, April 16, 1981, https://timesmachine.nytimes.com/timesmachine/1981/04/16/086213.html?pageNumber=1.

675 *Gray was deeply bitter*: Gray, *In Nixon's Web*, 270–71.

676 *when its premiere happened in D.C.*: Graham, *Personal History*, 503.

676 *"The spirit of this country"*: Anson, *Exile*, 150.

676 *"I think I still would have"*: Ibid.

676 *wrote his memoir in prison*: Ibid., 205.

676 *"It could have been worse"*: Rosen, *The Strong Man*, 442.

676 *"It's nice to be back in Alabama"*: Ibid., xi.

677 *"I didn't say a word to him"*: Clifford D. May, "After 40 Years Making the Law, Rodino Now Teaches It," *New York Times*, January 27, 1989, https://timesmachine.nytimes.com/timesmachine/1989/01/27/591389.html?pageNumber=33.

678 *"No one here today, nor anybody else"*: Thompson, *The Nixon Presidency*, 95.

678 *"The break-in itself made no sense"*: Ibid., 137.

679 *"A man is not finished"*: Nick Thimmesch, "Nixon Not Finished Yet," *Daily Oklahoman* (Oklahoma City), December 10, 1978, https://www.newspapers.com/image/452042203/.

Index

Image Credits

Insert 1

1 White House Photo, Richard Nixon Library WHPO-6570-18A
2 Photo by Jean-Pierre (JP) Laffont
3 Official White House photo, Nixon Library
4 Photo by David Hume Kennerly, Courtesy of Center for Creative Photography, The University of Arizona: David Hume Kennerly, and © Center for Creative Photography, Arizona Board of Regents
5 Official White House portrait by Oliver Atkins, Nixon Library NLRN-WHPO-C5500-02
6 Official White House portrait by Oliver Atkins, Nixon Library NLRN-WHPO-1040-22A
7 Official White House portrait by Oliver Atkins, Nixon Library NLRN-WHPO-E0398-20A
8 Official White House portrait by Oliver Atkins, Nixon Library NLRN-WHPO-1040-22A
9 Official White House photo, Nixon Library NLRN-WHPO-1175-18
10 Official White House photo by Robert L. Knudson
11 Official White House photo by Robert L. Knudson, Nixon Library NLRN-WHPO-7935-30A
12 Official White House photo by Oliver Atkins, Nixon Library NLRN-WHPO-C5487-04
13 Official White House photo, Nixon Library WHPO-5465-34

14 Official White House photo by Karl Schumacher, Nixon Library NLRN-WHPO-2286-01
15 Official White House photo by Oliver Atkins, Nixon Library NLRN-WHPO-C0868
16 Official White House photo by Oliver Atkins, Nixon Library
17 Photo by David Hume Kennerly
18 Official US Government Portrait, FBI
19 Official White House photo
20 Official US Government photo, FBI collection, National Archives
21 Official White House portrait by Robert L. Knudson, Nixon Library NLRN-WHPO-2865-15A
22 Official White House photo, Nixon Library WHPO-5606-21
23 Official White House portrait by Karl Schumacher
24 Photo courtesy of Bettman Archives, Getty Images
25 Official White House portrait by Oliver Atkins, Nixon Library

Insert 2

1 Files of the Watergate Special Prosecution Force, National Archives 304970
2 Files of the Watergate Special Prosecution Force, National Archives
3 Files of the Watergate Special Prosecution Force, National Archives
4 Files of the Watergate Special Prosecution Force, National Archives
5 Files of the Watergate Special Prosecution Force, National Archives
6 Files of the Watergate Special Prosecution Force, National Archives
7 Photo by Mark Godfrey
8 Files of the Watergate Special Prosecution Force, National Archives
9 Files of the Watergate Special Prosecution Force, National Archives 304966
10 Official Department of Justice portrait
11 Official Department of Justice portrait
12 Official FBI portrait
13 Photo by David Hume Kennerly, Courtesy of Center for Creative Photography, The University of Arizona: David Hume Kennerly, and © Center for Creative Photography, Arizona Board of Regents
14 Photo courtesy of Bettman Archive, Getty Images

15 Photo by JP Laffont
16 Photo by David Hume Kennerly, Courtesy of Center for Creative Photography, The University of Arizona: David Hume Kennerly, and © Center for Creative Photography, Arizona Board of Regents
17 Files of the Watergate Special Prosecution Force, National Archives
18 Photo by David Hume Kennerly, Courtesy of Center for Creative Photography, The University of Arizona: David Hume Kennerly, and © Center for Creative Photography, Arizona Board of Regents
19 Exhibit 73, Files of the Watergate Special Prosecution Force, National Archives 7582819
20 Photo by David Hume Kennerly, Courtesy of Center for Creative Photography, The University of Arizona: David Hume Kennerly, and © Center for Creative Photography, Arizona Board of Regents
21 Photo by Charles Tasnadi/AP/Shutterstock
22 Official White House photo by Jack E. Kightlinger, Nixon Library WHPO-E2678-14
23 Photo by David Hume Kennerly, Courtesy of Center for Creative Photography, The University of Arizona: David Hume Kennerly, and © Center for Creative Photography, Arizona Board of Regents
24 Photo by David Hume Kennerly, Courtesy of Center for Creative Photography, The University of Arizona: David Hume Kennerly, and © Center for Creative Photography, Arizona Board of Regents
25 Photo by David Hume Kennerly, Courtesy of Center for Creative Photography, The University of Arizona: David Hume Kennerly, and © Center for Creative Photography, Arizona Board of Regents
26 Official White House photo, Nixon Library WHPO-E3398-09
27 National Archives 302035
28 Official White House photo, Gerald Ford Library A0004-10

Endpapers

Front Endpaper: Watergate exhibit photos, US Government, National Archives 304965
Rear Endpaper: Nixon departure sequence by David Hume Kennerly

About the Author

Garrett M. Graff, a distinguished journalist and bestselling historian, has spent nearly two decades covering politics, technology, and national security. He serves as the director of cyber initiatives for The Aspen Institute and is a contributor to *WIRED* and CNN. He's written for publications from *Esquire* to *Rolling Stone* to the *New York Times*, and served as editor of two of Washington's most prestigious magazines, *Washingtonian* and *POLITICO Magazine.*

Graff, who lives in Vermont, is the author of multiple books, including *The Threat Matrix: Inside Robert Mueller's FBI and the War on Global Terror* and the national bestseller *Raven Rock*, about the government's Cold War Doomsday plans. His most recent book, an instant *New York Times* bestseller and #1 national bestseller *The Only Plane in the Sky: An Oral History of 9/11*, was called a "a priceless civic gift" by the *Wall Street Journal* and won the 2020 Audiobook of the Year at the Audie Awards. A regular voice and analyst on NPR, *PBS NewsHour*, the History Channel, and other outlets, he is also the host of *Long Shadow*, an eight-episode podcast series about the lingering questions of 9/11, and executive producer of *While the Rest of Us Die*, a VICE TV series based on his book *Raven Rock*, among other multimedia projects.